CATIA V5-6R2017
Basics

Tutorial Books

Download Resource Files from:
www.tutorialbook.info

For Technical Support, send us an email to:
online.books999@gmail.com

Contents

Introduction

Welcome to the *CATIA V5-6R2017 for Beginners* book. This book is written to help students, designers, and engineering professionals. It covers the important features and functionalities of CATIA V5 using relevant examples and exercises.

This book is written for new users, who can use it as a self-study resource to learn CATIA V5. In addition, it can also be used as a reference for experienced users. The focus of this book is part modeling, assembly modeling, drawings, sheet metal, and surface design.

Topics covered in this Book

Chapter 1, "Getting Started with CATIA V5-6R2017", introduces CATIA V5. The user interface and terminology are discussed in this chapter.

Chapter 2, "Sketcher Workbench", explores the sketching commands in CATIA V5. You will learn to create parametric sketches.

Chapter 3, "Basic Sketch-Based features", teaches you to create basic 3D geometry using the Pad and Shaft commands. You will also learn to create reference elements, which will act as supporting geometry.

Chapter 4, "Holes and Dress-up Features", covers the features, which can be created without using sketches.

Chapter 5, "Patterned Geometry", explores the commands to create patterned and mirrored geometry.

Chapter 6, "Rib Features", teaches you to create basic and complex features by sweeping a profile along a path.

Chapter 7, "Multi-Sections Solid", teaches you to create features by using different cross-sections.

Chapter 8, "Additional Features and Multibody Parts", covers additional commands to create complex geometry. In addition, the multibody parts are also covered.

Chapter 9, "Modifying Parts", explores the commands and techniques to modify the part geometry.

Chapter 10, "Assemblies", explains you to create assemblies using the bottom-up and top-down design approaches.

Chapter 11, "Drawings", covers how to create 2D drawings from 3D parts and assemblies.

Chapter 12, "Sheet Metal Design", covers how to create sheet metal parts and flat patterns.

Chapter 13, "Surface Design", covers how to create complex shapes using surface design commands.

Chapter 1: Getting Started with CATIA V5-6R2017

Introduction to CATIA V5-6R2017

CATIA V5-6R2017 is a parametric and feature-based system that allows you to create 3D parts, assemblies, and 2D drawings. The design process in CATIA V5 is shown below.

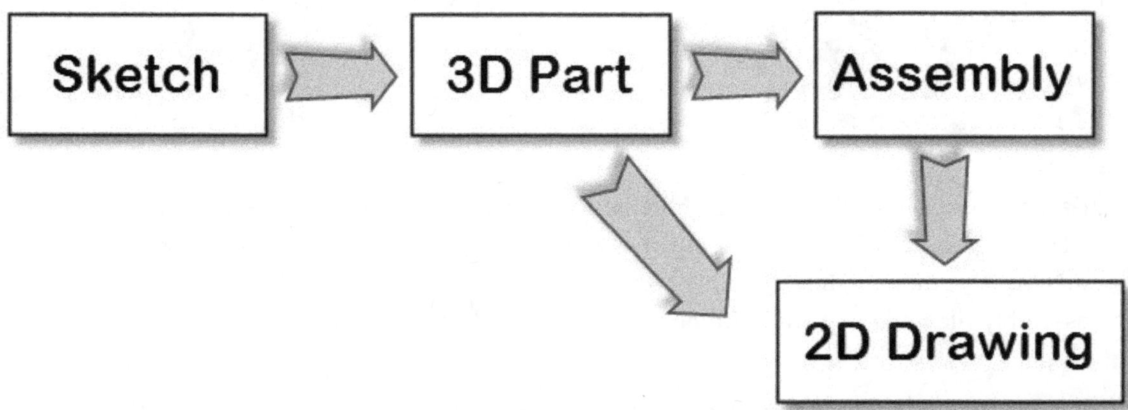

Workbenches in CATIA V5-6R2017

CATIA V5 offers many workbenches to carry out a different type of processes. For example, CATIA V5 provides you with the **Generative Sheetmetal Design** workbench to design a sheet metal part. Likewise, there are many workbenches to perform advanced operations such are static analysis, mold design, automotive design, and so on. However, in this book we cover the basic workbenches such as **Sketcher**, **Part Design**, **Assembly Design**, **Drafting**, **Generative Sheetmetal Design**, and **Generative Shape Design**. A brief introduction to these workbenches is given next.

Part Design

The **Part Design** workbench provides you with commands to create parametric solid models. You can activate this workbench by clicking **Start > Mechanical Design > Part Design** on the Menu bar. To create solid models, you must draw parametric sketches in the **Sketcher** workbench, and then convert them into solids. However, you can add some additional features to the solid models, which do not require sketches.

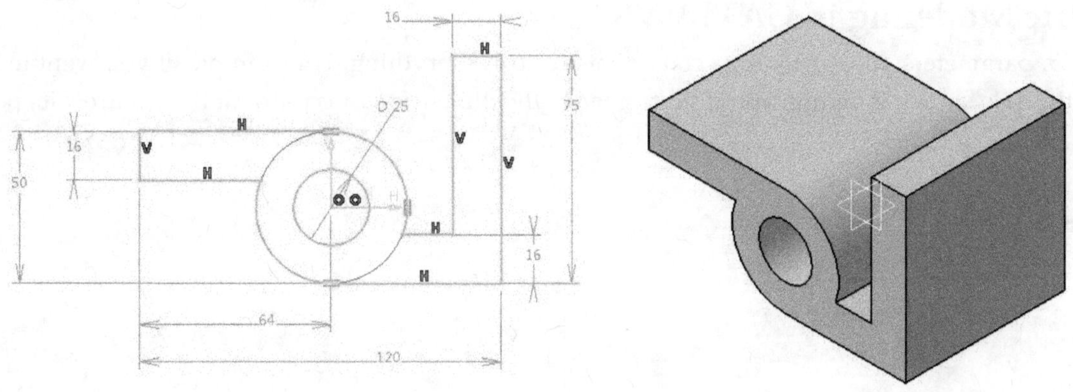

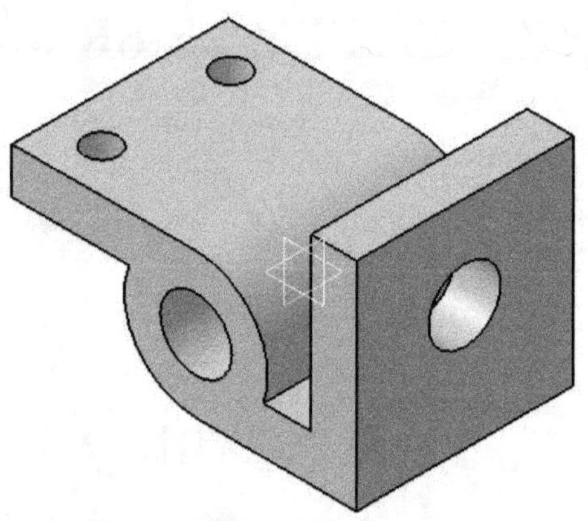
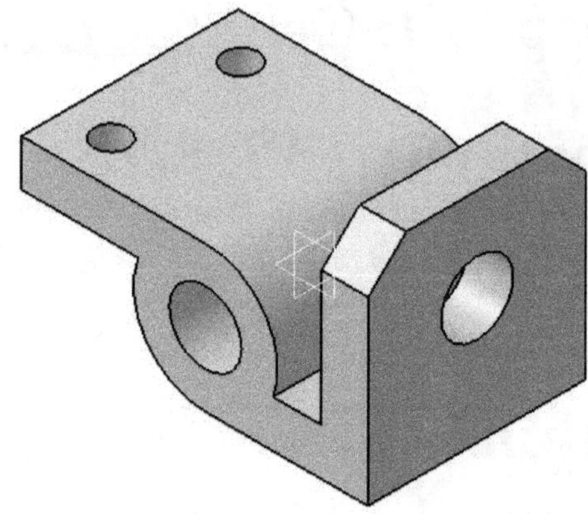

Assembly Design

The **Assembly Design** workbench (click **Start > Mechanical Design > Assembly Design**) has commands to combine individual parts in an assembly. There are two ways to create an assembly. The first way is to create individual parts and assemble them in the **Assembly Design** Workbench (Bottom-up assembly design). The second way is to start an assembly file and create individual parts in it (Top-down assembly design).

Drafting

The **Drafting** workbench (click **Start > Mechanical Design > Drafting**) has commands to create 2D drawings, which can be used for the manufacturing process. There are two ways to create drawings. The first way is to generate the standard views of a 3D component or assembly. The second way is to sketch the drawings, manually.

Generative Sheetmetal Design

The **Generative Sheetmetal Design** workbench (click **Start > Mechanical Design > Generative Sheetmetal Design**) has commands to create sheet metal geometry. You can create a sheet metal model either by building features in a systematic manner or by converting a part geometry into a sheet metal.

Generative Shape Design

The **Generative Shape Design** workbench (click **Start > Shape > Generative Shape Design**) has commands to create complex geometries, which cannot be created by using the commands in the **Part Design** workbench. You can create a surface geometry, and then convert it in a solid geometry. A surface is an infinitely thin feature, which acts as reference. Whereas, a solid geometry has properties such as weight, center of gravity, and so on.

Parametric Modeling in CATIA V5

In CATIA V5, parameters, dimensions, or constraints control everything. For example, if you want to change the position of the hole shown in figure, you need to change the dimension or constraint that controls its position.

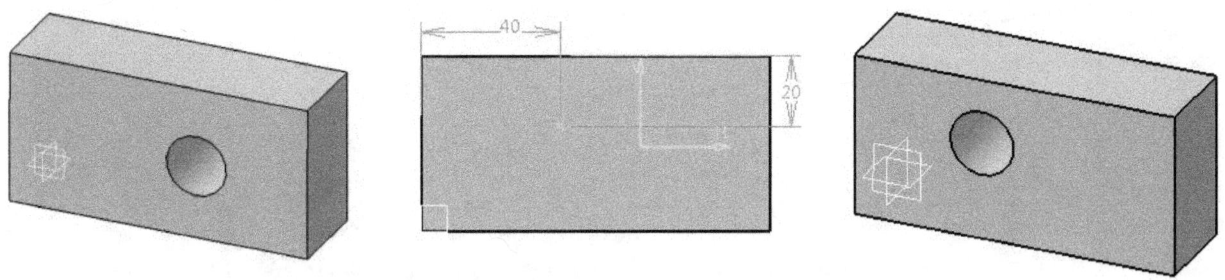

The parameters and constraints that you set up allow you to have control over the design intent. The design intent describes the way your 3D model will behave when you apply dimensions and constraints to it. For example, if you want to position the hole at the center of the block, one way is to add dimensions between the hole and the adjacent edges. However, when you change the size of the block, the hole will not be at the center.

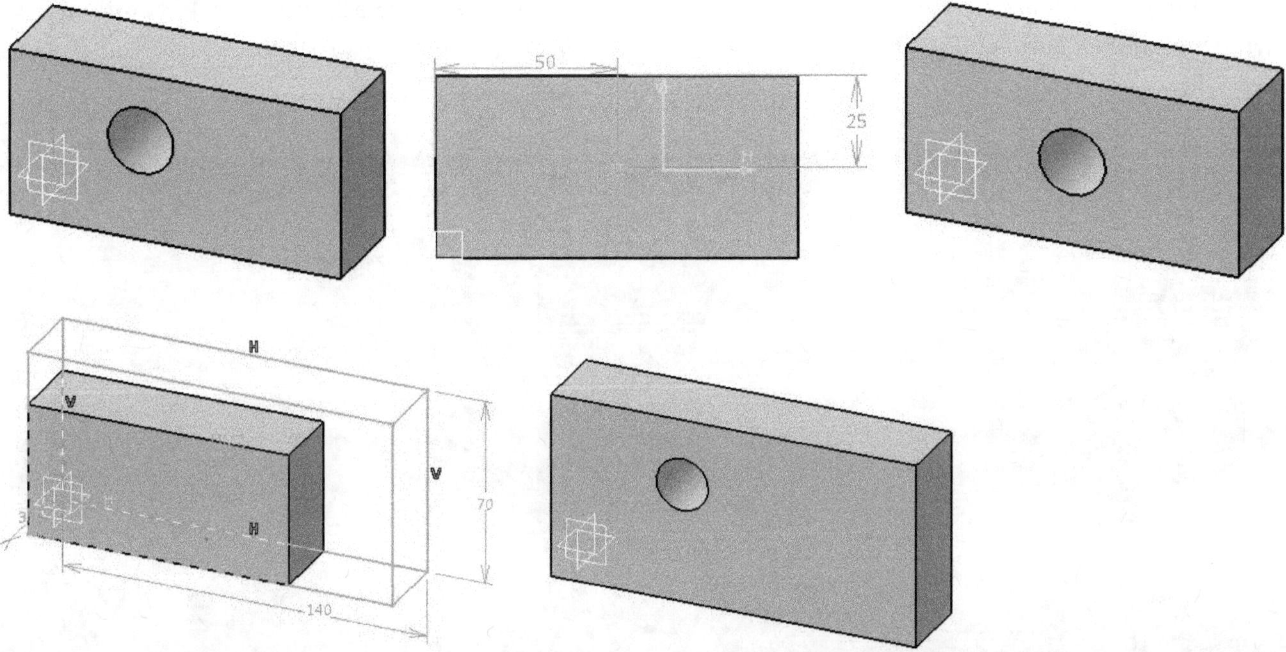

You can make the hole to be at the center, even if the size of the block changes. To do this, you need to delete the dimensions and create a diagonal line. Next, apply the **Midpoint** constraint between the hole point and the diagonal line. Now, even if you change the size of the block, the hole will always remain at the center.

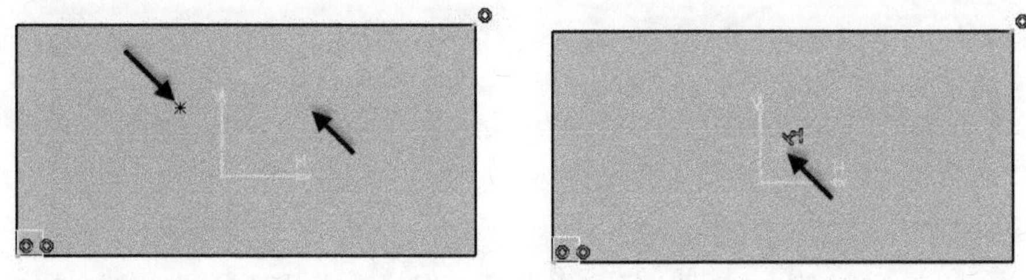

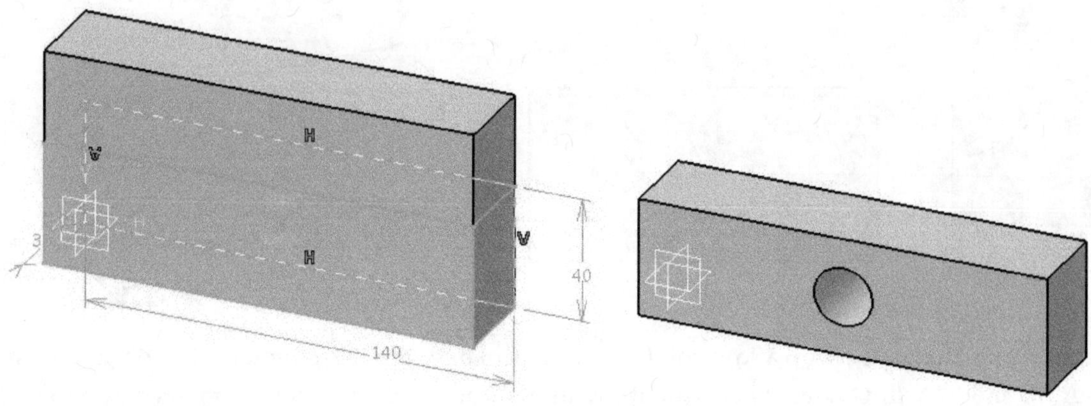

Associativity

The other big advantage of CATIA V5 is the associativity between parts, assemblies and drawings. When you make changes to the design of a part, the changes will take place in the corresponding assembly file. In addition, the 2D drawing will update automatically.

File Types in CATIA V5

CATIA V5 offers three main file types:

CATPart: This type of file has geometry of individual part. The files created in **Sketcher**, **Part Design**, **Generative Sheetmetal Design**, and **Wireframe and Surface Design**, and so on will have this extension.

CATProduct: This type of file is an assembly of one or more parts. In fact, it is a link of one or more parts.

CATDrawing: The files created in the Drafting workbench have this extension.

Starting CATIA V5-6R2017

To start **CATIA V5-6R2017**, click the **CATIA V5-6R2017** icon on your computer screen (or) click **Start > All Programs > CATIA > CATIA V5-6R2017**.

User Interface

The following image shows the **CATIA V5-6R2017** application window.

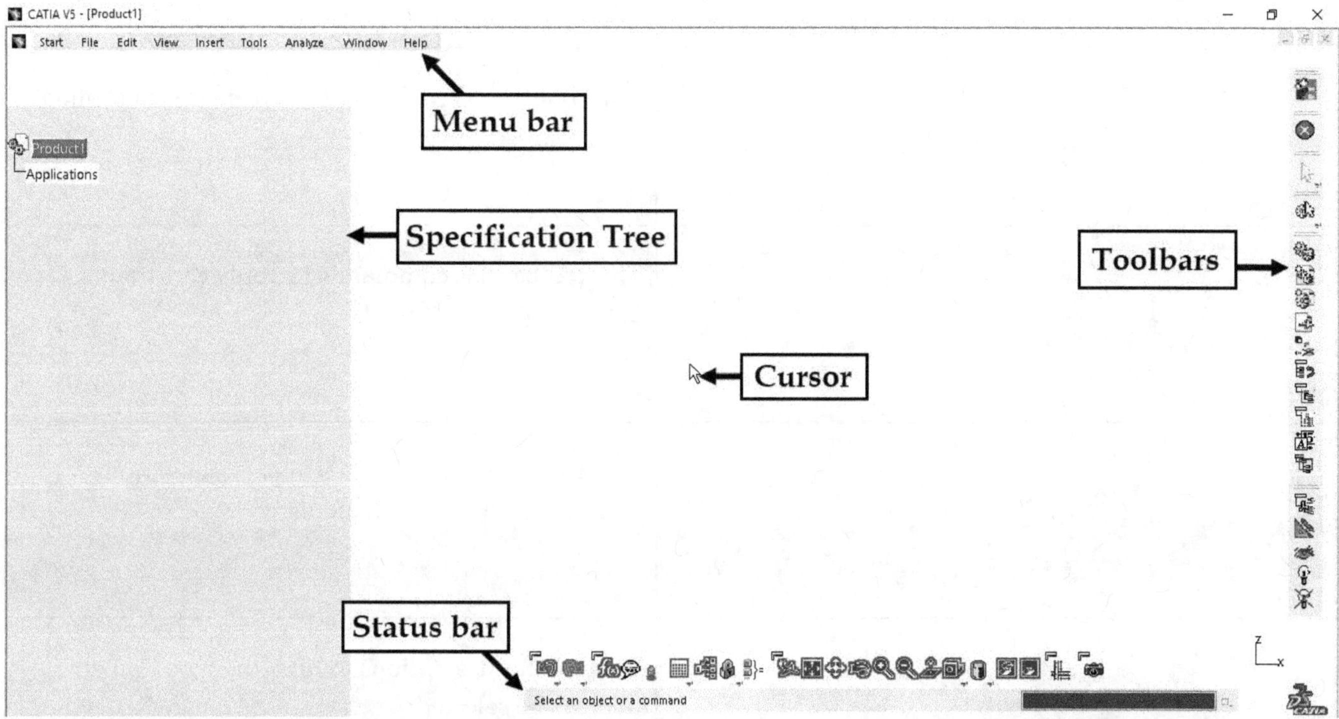

Various components of the user interface are:

Start Menu

The **Start Menu** appears when you click on the **Start** button located at the top left corner of the window. The **Start Menu** has a list of workbenches. You can switch between different workbenches using this menu.

Menu bar

Menu bar is located at the top of the window. It has various options (menu titles). When you click on a menu title, a drop-down appears. Select any option from this drop-down.

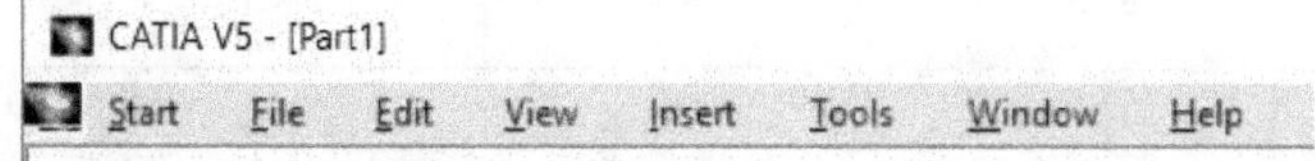

Toolbar

A toolbar is a set of commands, which help you to perform various operations. Various toolbars available in different workbenches are given next.

Part Design Toolbars	
S...	Starts the **Sketcher** workbench
Profile	This toolbar has commands to create sketch elements
Constraint	This toolbar has commands to apply constraints between sketch elements.
Operation	This toolbar has commands to perform various operations on sketch elements.
User Selection Filter	This toolbar has options to filter the type element that can be selected.
Sketch tools	This toolbar has options that help you to create sketch elements.
Workb...	Exits the workbench.

Sketch-Based Features	This toolbar has commands to create solid features based on the sketch geometry.
Transformation Feat...	This toolbar has commands to replicate solid features.
Dress-Up Features	This toolbar has commands to add features, which do not require any sketch.
Measure	This toolbar has commands to measure physical properties of the geometry.
D..	Sections the geometry to view its inside portion.
A..	Applies material to a solid geometry.
Surface-Based Fea...	This toolbar has commands to convert a surface model in to solid.
View	This toolbar has commands to zoom, pan, rotate, or change the view of a 3D model.
Assembly Design Toolbars	
Product Structure Tools	This toolbar has commands to create components or insert existing components into an assembly.

<table>
<tr><td>Constraints</td><td>This toolbar has commands to apply constraints between components.</td></tr>
<tr><td>Move</td><td>This toolbar has commands to manipulate the position of a component.</td></tr>
<tr><td colspan="2">Generative Shape design Toolbars</td></tr>
<tr><td>ShapeDesignToolBarWireFrame</td><td>This toolbar has commands to create three dimensional curves and wireframe geometry.</td></tr>
<tr><td>ShapeDesignToolBarSurf</td><td>This toolbar has commands to create surfaces.</td></tr>
<tr><td>ShapeDesignToolBarModif</td><td>The commands on this toolbar help you to modify or transform surfaces.</td></tr>
<tr><td colspan="2">Generative Sheetmetal Design Toolbars</td></tr>
<tr><td>Walls</td><td>The commands on this toolbar help you to create walls of a sheet metal part.</td></tr>
<tr><td>Bending</td><td>The commands on this toolbar help you to apply bends to a sheet metal wall.</td></tr>
<tr><td>Cutting/Stamping</td><td>This toolbar has commands to add cuts and stamps to a sheet metal part.</td></tr>
</table>

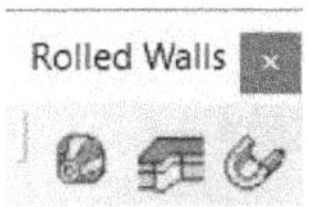 Rolled Walls	This toolbar has commands to create rolled sheets and funnels.
 Views	This toolbar has commands to switch between folded and unfolded views of a sheet metal part.
Drafting Toolbars	
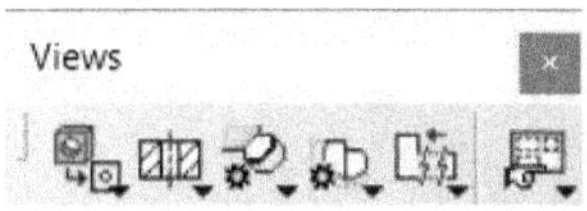 Views	This toolbar has commands to generate standard views of a 3D geometry.
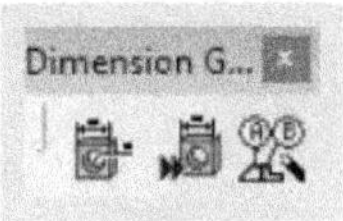 Dimension G...	This toolbar has commands to generate dimensions and balloons.
 Drawing	The commands on this toolbar will help you to add a new sheet, drawing view etc.
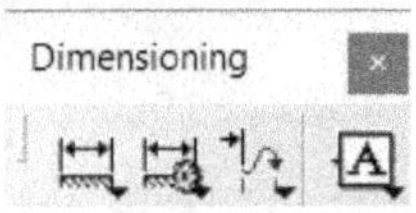 Dimensioning	The commands on this toolbar help you to add driven dimensions to the drawing views.
 Dress-up	This toolbar has commands to add centerlines, hatches, and arrows the drawing view.

Some toolbars are not visible by default. To display a particular toolbar, right-click on any toolbar, and then select the toolbar name from the list displayed.

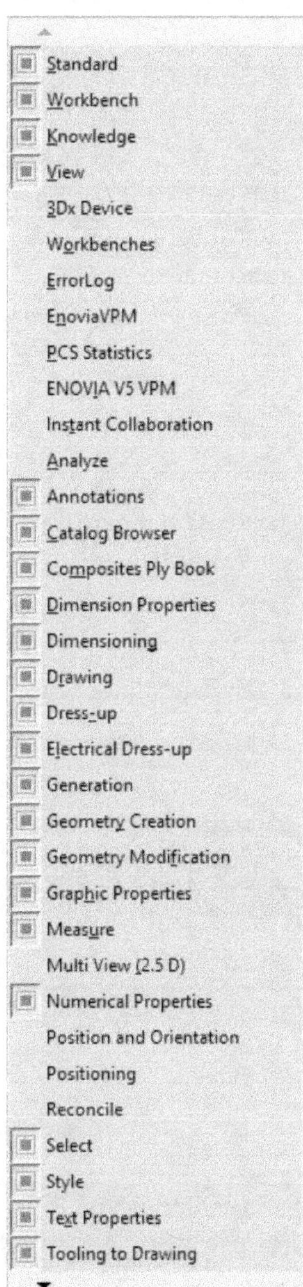

Status bar

This is available below the graphics window. It shows the prompts and the action taken while using the commands.

1 element selected

Specification Tree

Contains the list of operations carried while constructing a part.

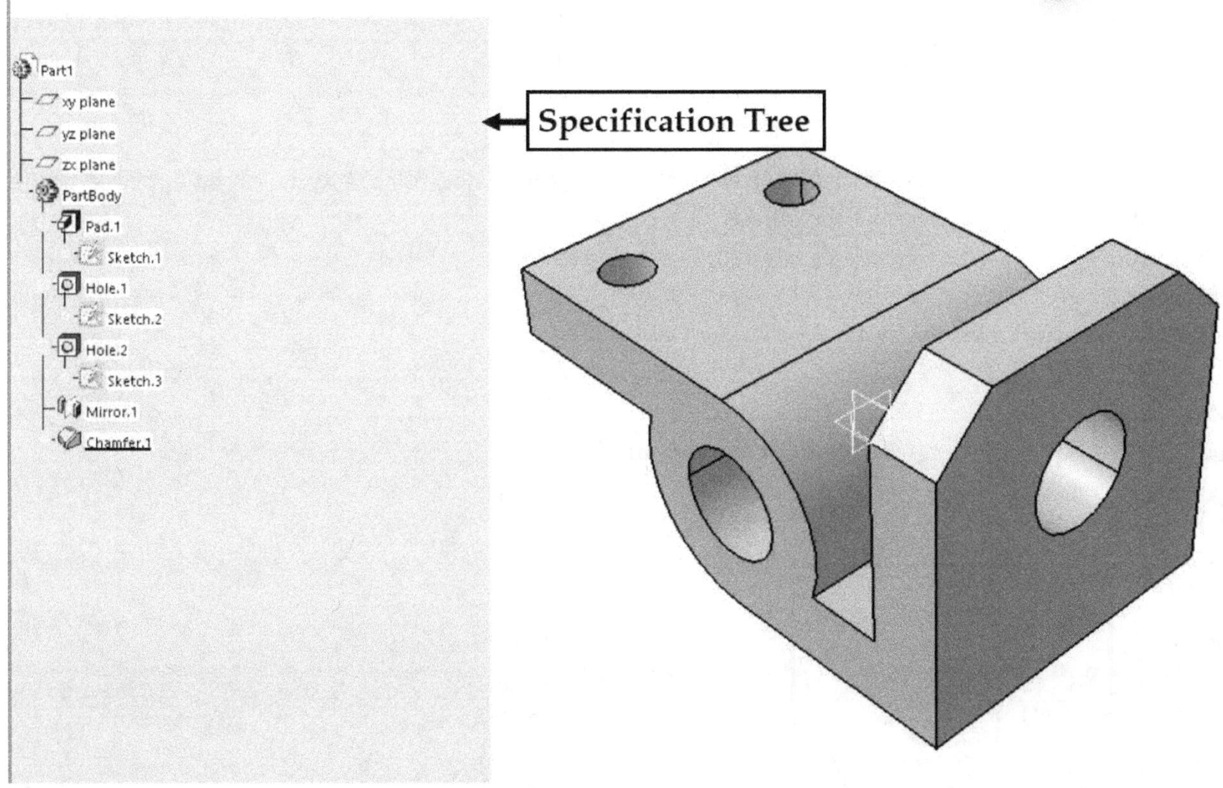

Dialogs

When you execute any command in CATIA V5, the dialog related to it appears. A dialog has of various options. The following figure shows various components of a dialog.

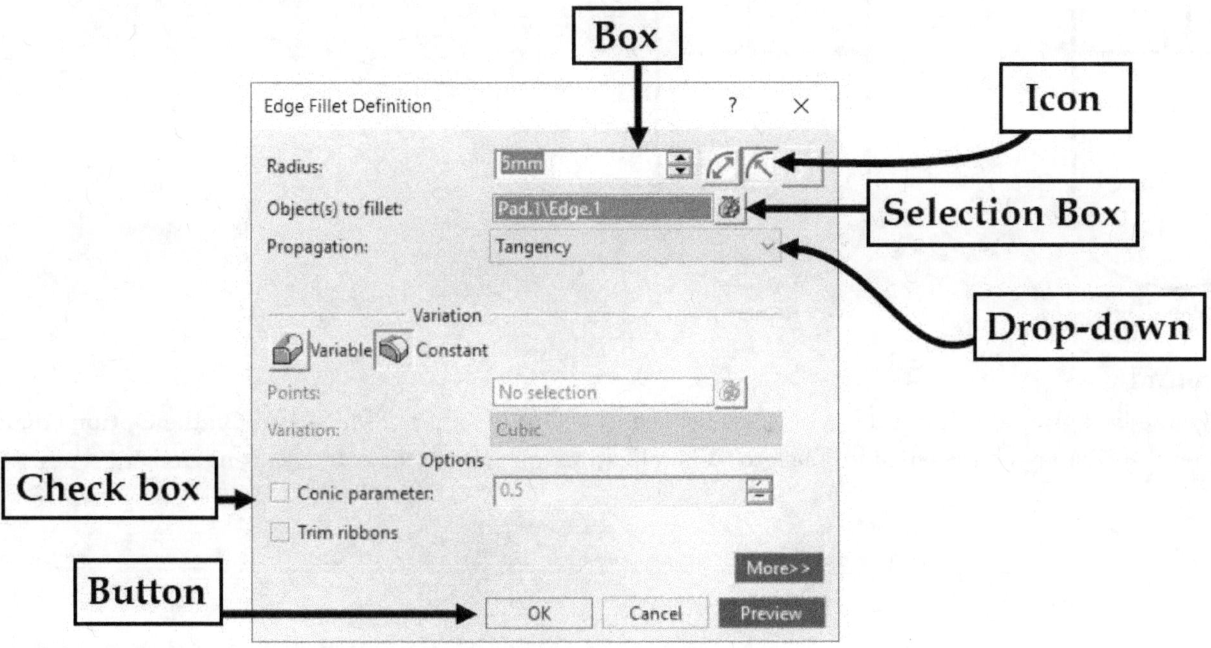

This textbook uses the default options on the dialog.

Mouse Functions

Various functions of the mouse buttons are:

Left Mouse button (MB1)

When you double-click the left mouse button (MB1) on an object, the dialog related to the object appears. Using this dialog, you can edit the parameters of the objects.

Middle Mouse button (MB2)

Press the middle mouse and drag the mouse to pan the view.

Right Mouse button (MB3)

Click this button on an object to open the shortcut menu related to it.

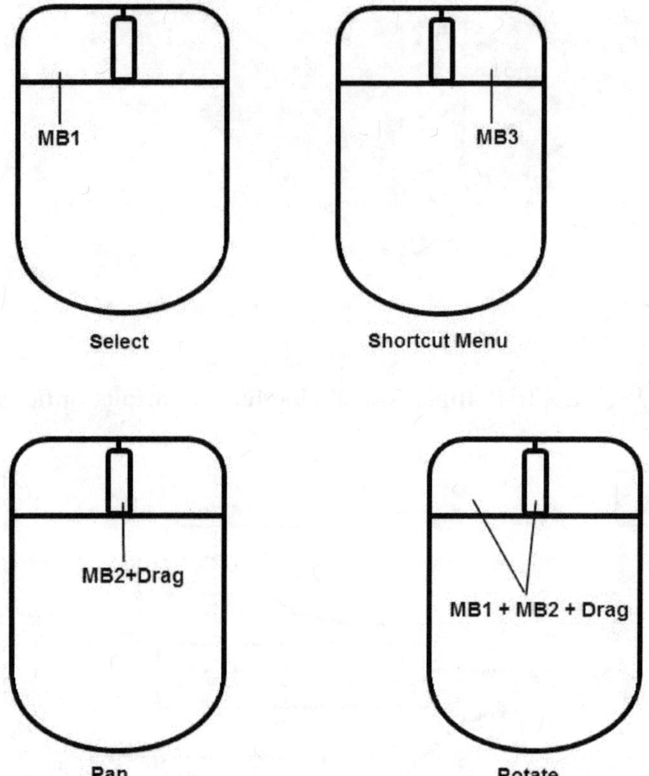

Background

To change the background color of the window, click **Tools > Options** on the Menu bar. On the **Options** dialog, click **General > Display** on the left side. Click the **Visualization** tab and set the colors various element types.

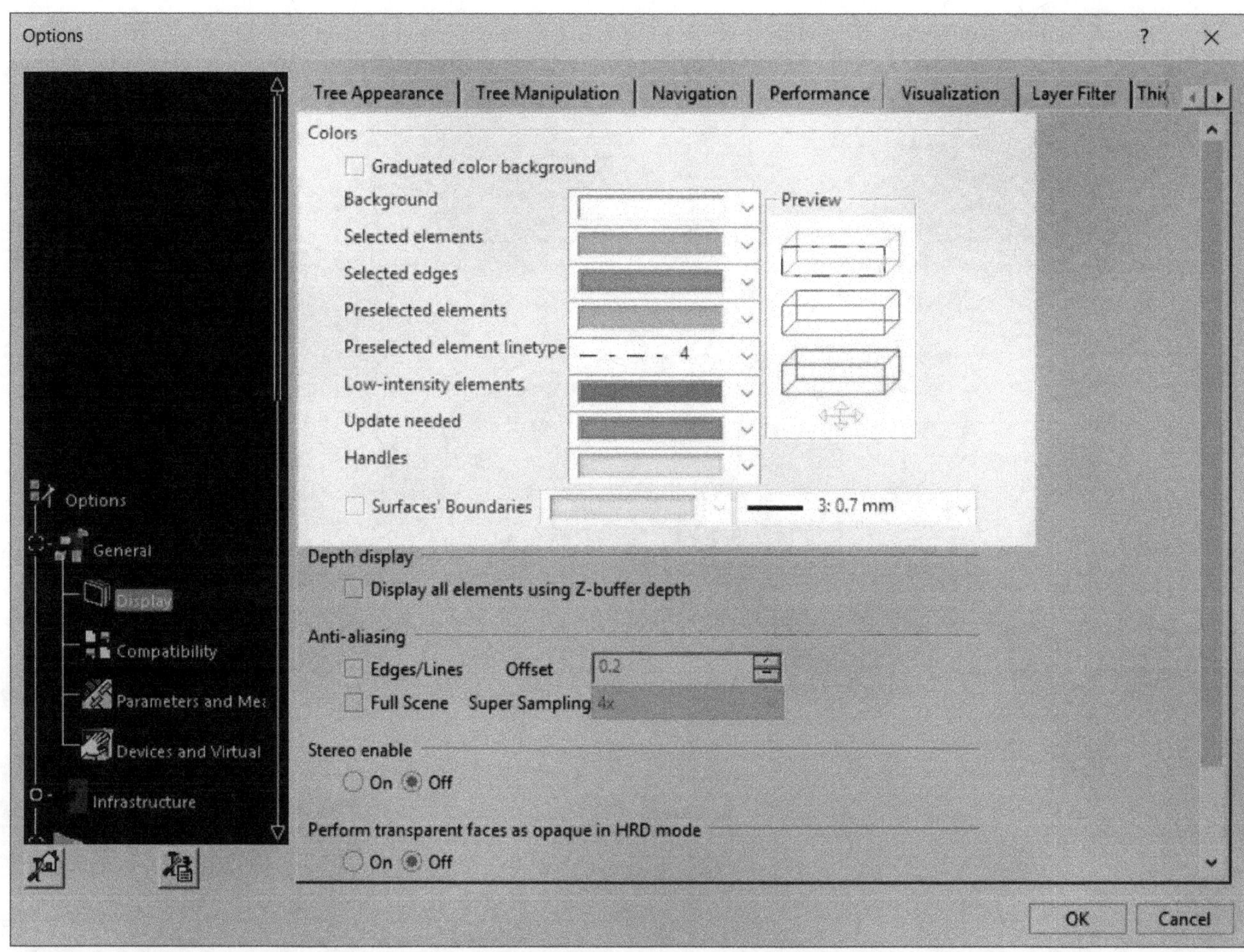

To change the color of sketch elements, click **Mechanical Design > Sketcher** on the left side, and then change the **Default color of the elements**.

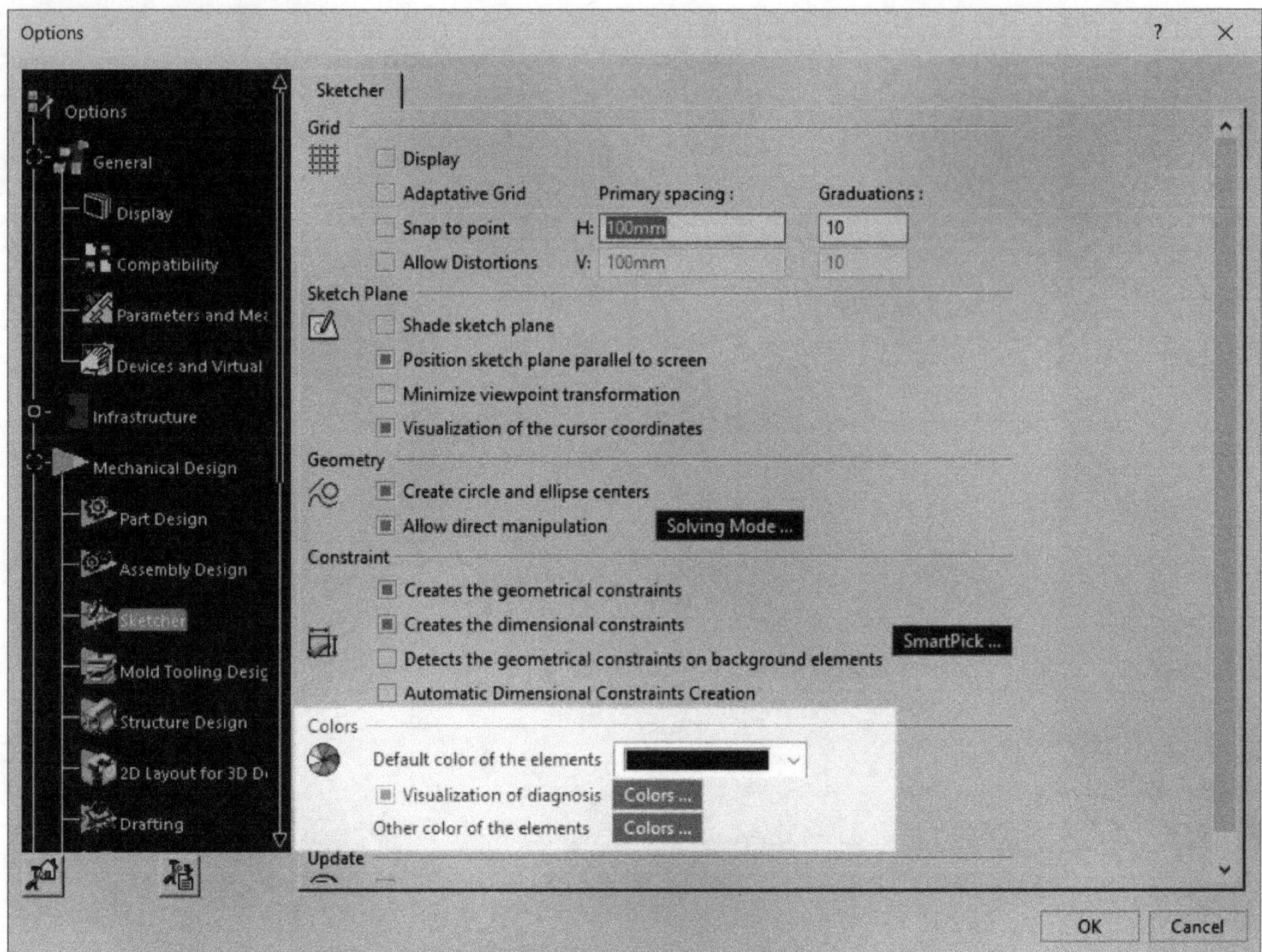

Shortcut Keys

CTRL+Z	Undo
CTRL+Y	Redo
CTRL+S	Save
F1	CATIA V5 Help
CTRL+N	New File
CTRL+O	Open File
CTRL+P	Plot
Shift+Left	Rotate To The Left
Shift+Right	Rotate To the Right
Shift+Up	Rotate Upward
Shift-Down	Rotate Downward
Alt+F8	Start Macros
Alt+F11	Visual Basic
Ctrl+Page Up	Zoom In
Ctrl+Page Down	Zoom Out
Ctrl+Left	Pan Left
Ctrl+Right	Pan Right

Ctrl+Up	Pan Up
Ctrl+Down	Pan Down
Ctrl+Shift+Left	Rotate Around Z Axis Counterclockwise
Ctrl+Shift+Right	Rotate Around Z Axis Clockwise
Ctrl+Tab	Swap Windows
Ctrl+F	Search
Ctrl+U	Update
Ctrl+X	Cut
Ctrl+C	Copy
Ctrl+V	Paste
Ctrl+F	Search
Ctrl+U	Update
Ctrl+X	Cut
Ctrl+C	Copy

Questions

1. Explain how to display the hidden toolbars.
2. What is design intent?
3. Give one example of where you would establish a constraint between part's features.
4. Explain the term 'associativity' in CATIA V5.
5. Explain the procedure to access CATIA V5 Help.
6. Explain the procedure to change the background color of the graphics window.
7. How can you activate the shortcut menu?
8. How is CATIA V5 a parametric modeling application?

Chapter 2: Sketcher Workbench

This chapter covers the methods and commands to create sketches used in the Sketcher Workbench. In CATIA V5, you can create sketches in the Sketcher Workbench. You will learn to create sketches in this Workbench.

In CATIA, you create a rough sketch, and then apply dimensional and geometric constraints that define its shape and size. The dimensional constraints define the length, size, and angle of a sketch element, whereas geometric constraints define the relations between sketch elements.

The topics covered in this chapter are:

- Sketching in Sketcher Workbench
- Use geometric and dimensional constraint to control the shape and size of a sketch
- Learn sketching commands
- Learn commands and options that help you to create sketches easily

Sketching in the Sketcher Workbench

Creating sketches in the Sketcher Workbench is very easy. You have to activate the **Sketch** command, and then define a plane on which you want to create the sketch.

1. On the **Sketcher** toolbar, click the **Sketch** icon (or) click **Insert > Sketcher > Sketch** on the menu.

2. Click on any of the reference planes located at the center of the graphics window.

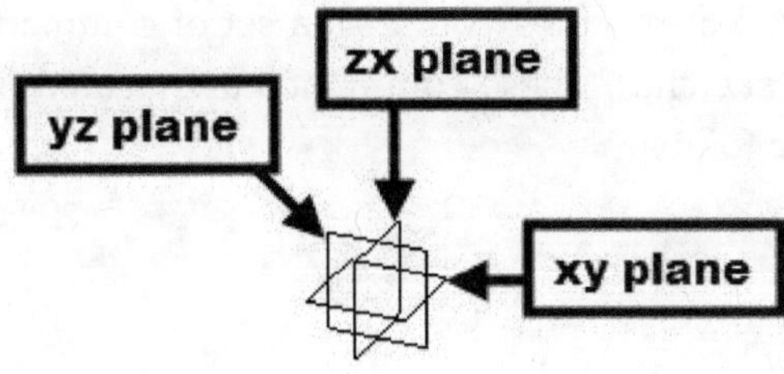

Note: By default, the edges of the reference planes are white in color. As a result, the reference planes will not be visible if the background of the graphics window is changed to white. You need to change the color of the plane edges to black to make them visible. To do this, press and hold the Ctrl key, and then select the three planes from the Specification Tree. Right click on anyone of the selected planes, and then select **Properties**.

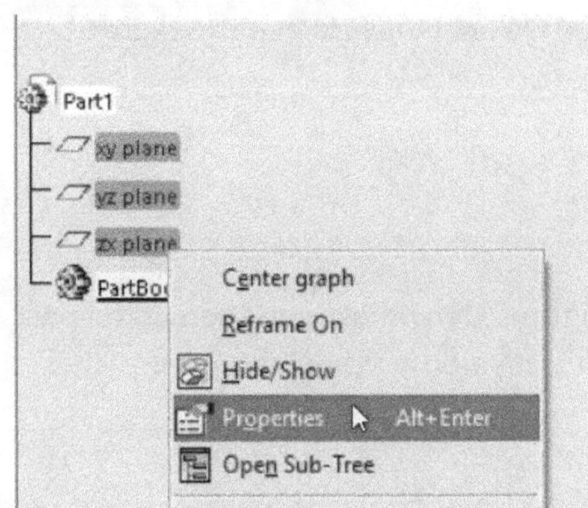

On the **Properties** dialog, click the **Graphics** tab, and then change the color of **Lines and Curves** to **Black**.

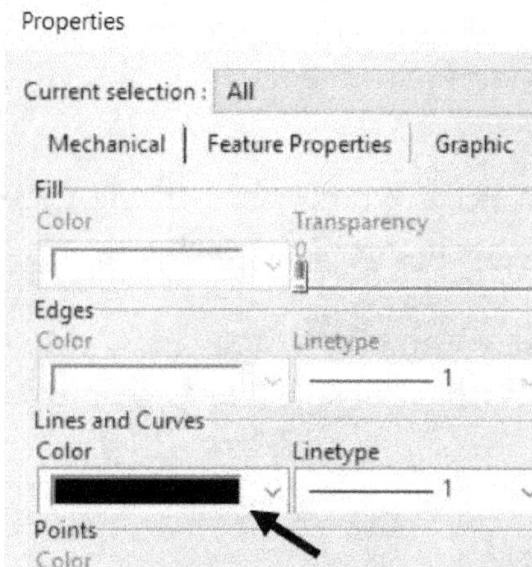

3. You can now start drawing sketches on the selected plane.

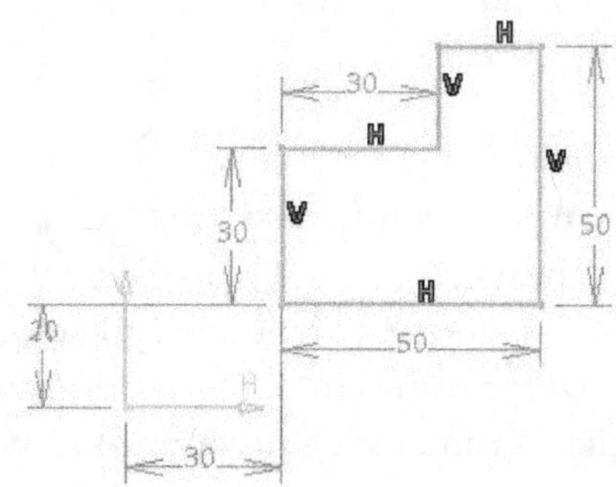

4. After creating the sketch, click **Workbenches** Toolbar **> Exit Workbench** to exit the sketch.

The following figures show the orientation of the part when the sketch is created on three different planes.

XY plane

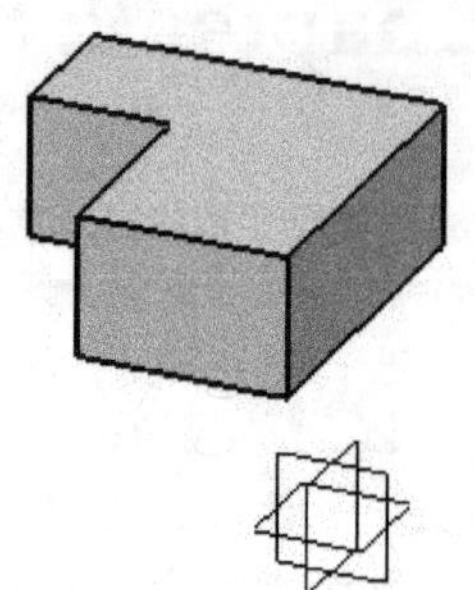

YZ Plane

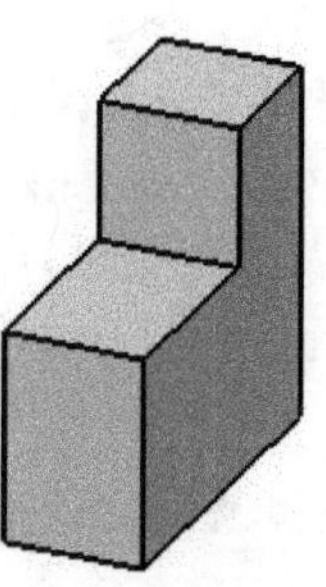

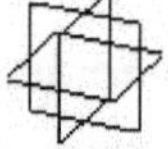

ZX Plane

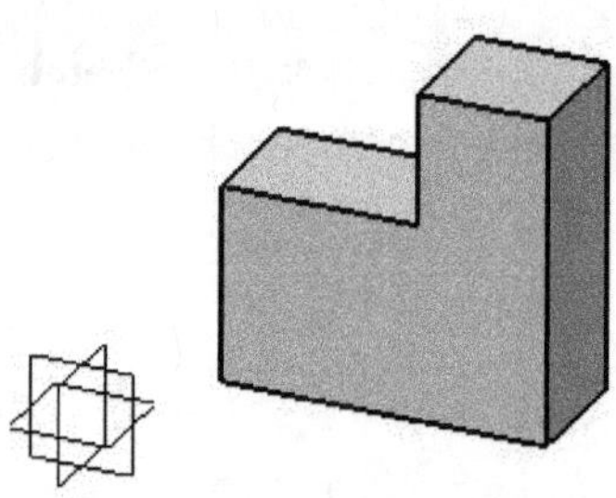

Draw Commands

CATIA V5 provides you with a set of commands to create sketches. These commands are located on the **Profile** toolbar.

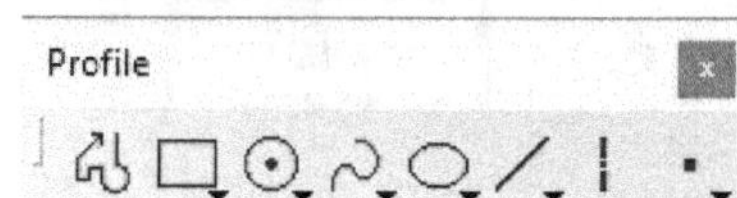

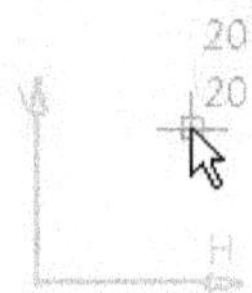

The Profile command

This is the most commonly used command while creating a sketch.

1. To activate this command, click the **Profile** button on the **Profile** toolbar (or) click **Insert > Profile > Profile** on the menu. As you move the pointer in the graphics window, you will notice the X and Y coordinates of the pointer.

2. To create a line, click in the graphics window, move the pointer and click again. After clicking for the second time, you can see an end point is added and another line segment is started. This is a convenient way to create a chain of lines.

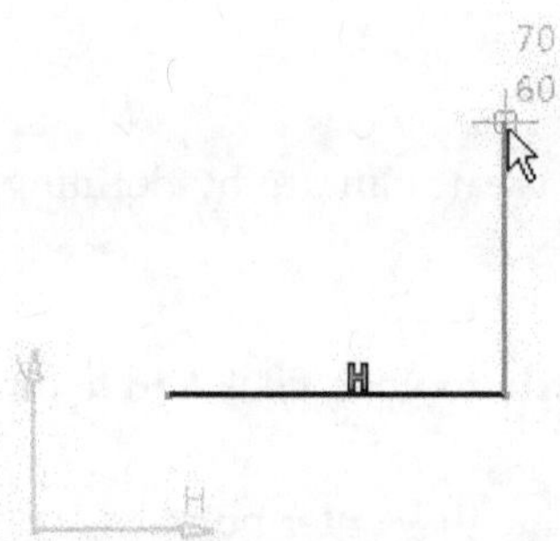

3. Continue to click to add more line segments.

The **Profile** command can also be used to draw arcs continuous with lines.

4. On the **Sketch Tools** toolbar, click the **Tangent Arc** button.

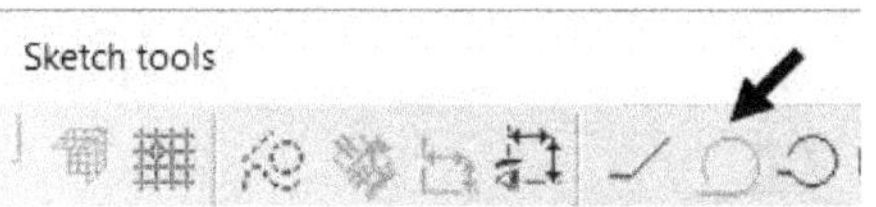

5. Move the pointer and click to draw an arc tangent to the previous line.

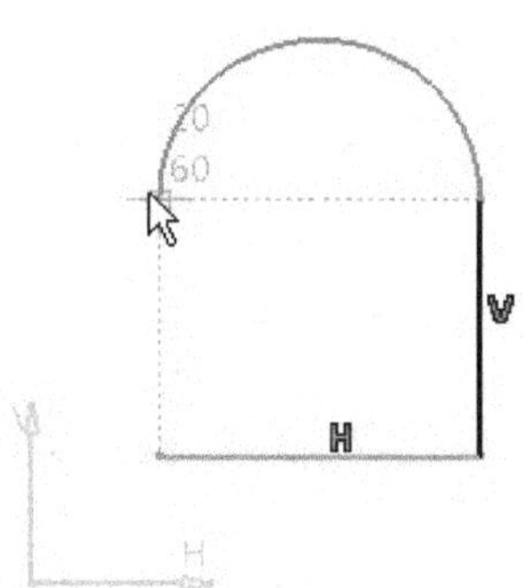

6. On the **Sketch Tools** toolbar, click the **Three Point Arc** button to create an arc normal to the previous line.

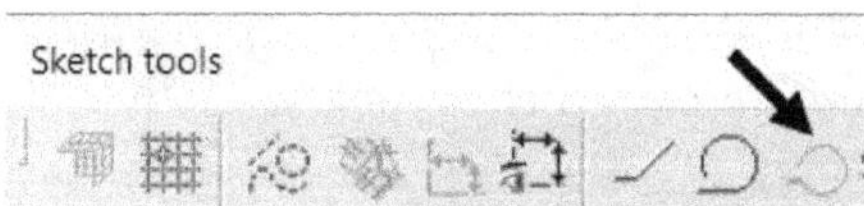

Note that the end point of the previous line is defined as the first point of the arc.

7. Define the second and third points of the arc.

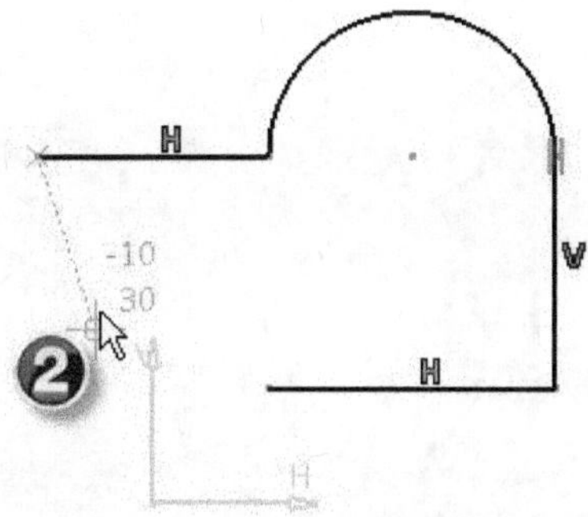

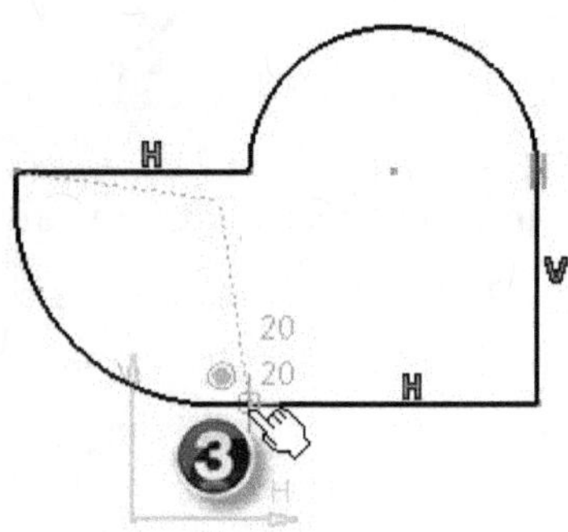

To delete a line, select it and press the **Delete** key. To select more than one line, press the Ctrl key and click on multiple line segments; the lines will be highlighted. You can also select multiple lines by dragging a box from left to right. Press and hold the left mouse button and drag a box from left to right; the lines inside the box boundary will be selected.

Three Point Arc

This command creates an arc by clicking three points in the graphic window.

1. On the **Profile** toolbar, click **Circle** drop-down > **Three Point Arc**.

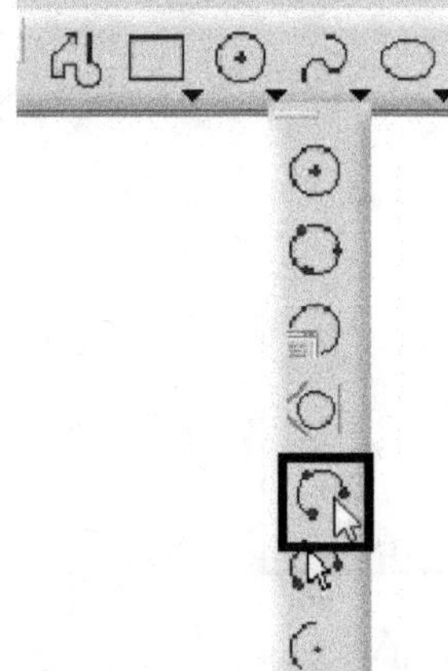

2. Click to define the start point of the arc.
3. Move the pointer and click to define a point on the periphery of the arc.
4. Again, click to define the end point.

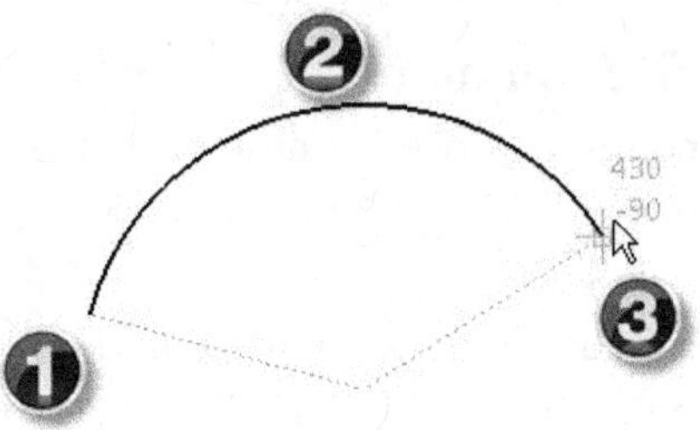

Three Point Arc Starting with Limits

This command creates an arc by defining its start, end, and radius.

1. On the **Profile** toolbar, click **Circle** drop-down > **Three Point Arc Starting with Limits**.
2. Click to define the start point of the arc.
3. Move the pointer and click again to define the end point.
4. After defining the start and end of the arc, you need to the define size of the arc. Move the pointer and click to define the radius of the arc.

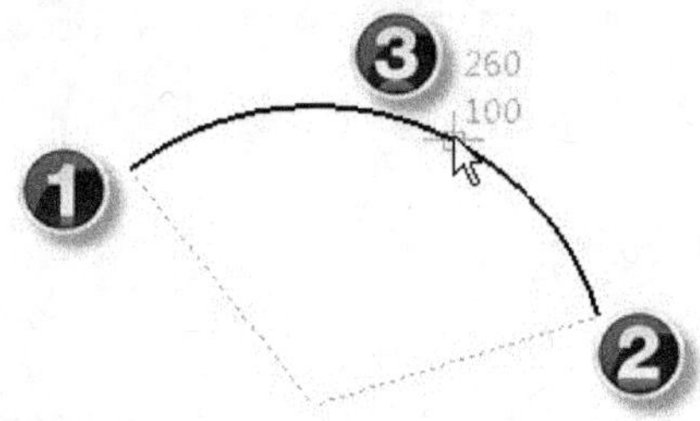

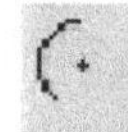

Arc

This command creates an arc by defining its center, start and end.

1. On the **Profile** toolbar, click **Circle** drop-down > **Arc**.
2. Click to define the center point.
3. Next, move the pointer and you will notice that a circle appears attached to the pointer. This defines the radius of the arc.
4. Now, click to define the start point of the arc and move the pointer; you will notice that an arc is drawn from the start point.
5. Once the arc appears the way you want, click to define its end point.

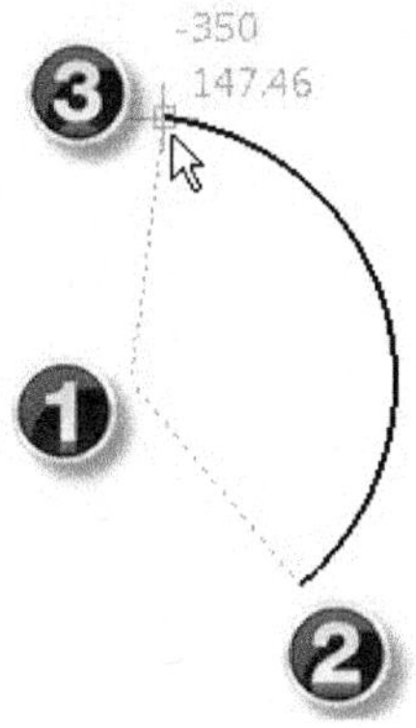

Circle

This is the most common way to draw a circle.

1. Click the **Circle** icon on the **Profile** toolbar, (or) click **Insert > Profile > Circle > Circle** on the menu.
2. Click to define the center point of the circle.
3. Drag the pointer, and then click again to define the diameter of the circle.

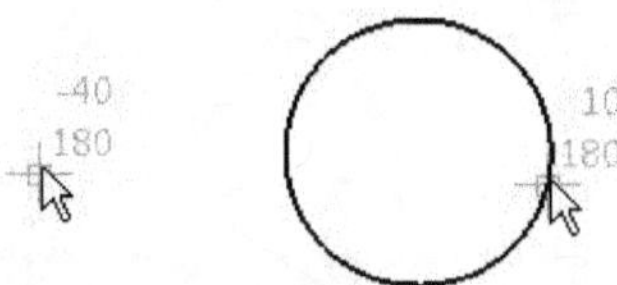

Three Point Circle

This command creates a circle by using three points.

1. On the **Profile** toolbar, click **Circle** drop-down > **Three Point Circle**.
2. Select three points from the graphics window. You can also select existing points from the sketch geometry. The first two points define the location of the circle and the third point defines its diameter.

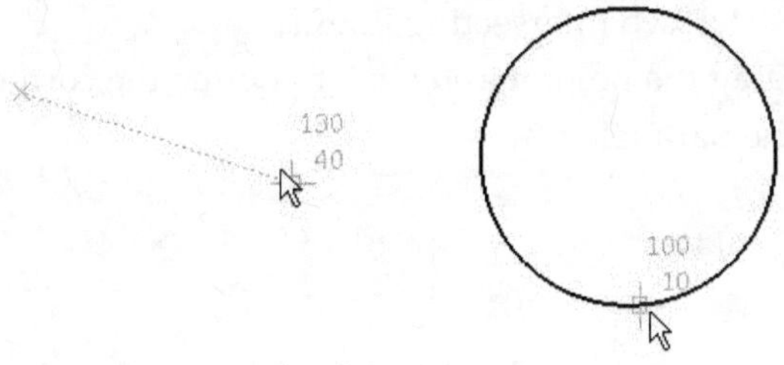

Tri-Tangent Circle

This command creates a circle tangent to three lines, arcs, or circles.

1. On the **Profile** toolbar, click **Circle** drop-down > **Tri-Tangent Circle**.
2. Select three lines, arcs or circles. This creates a circle tangent to selected lines.

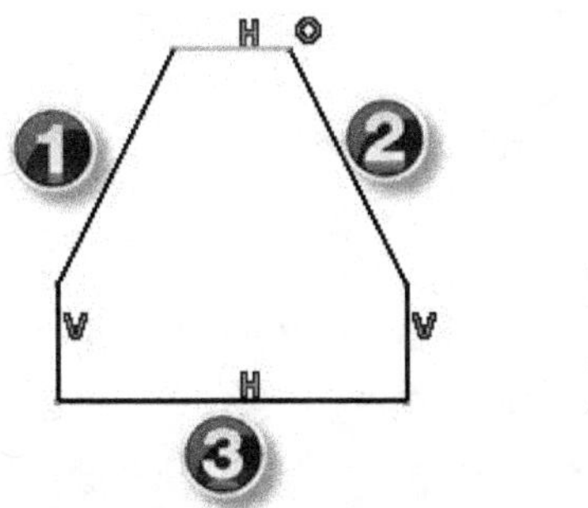

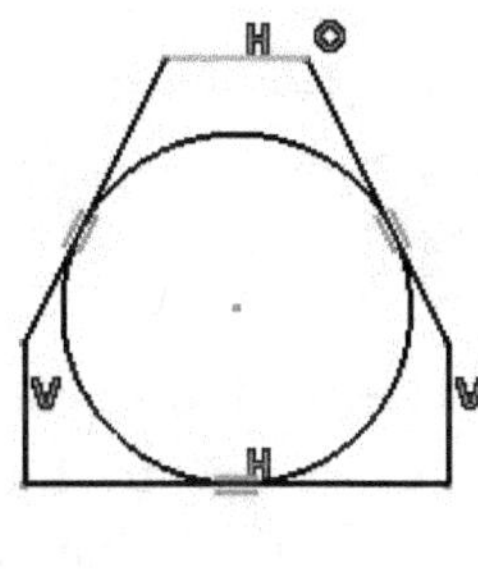

Circle Using Coordinates

This command creates a circle by using the coordinate values of its center point and the radius value that you specify.

1. On the **Profile** toolbar, click **Circle** drop-down > **Circle Using Coordinates**.
2. On the **Circle Definition** dialog, type-in values in the **X**, **Y**, and **Radius** boxes.

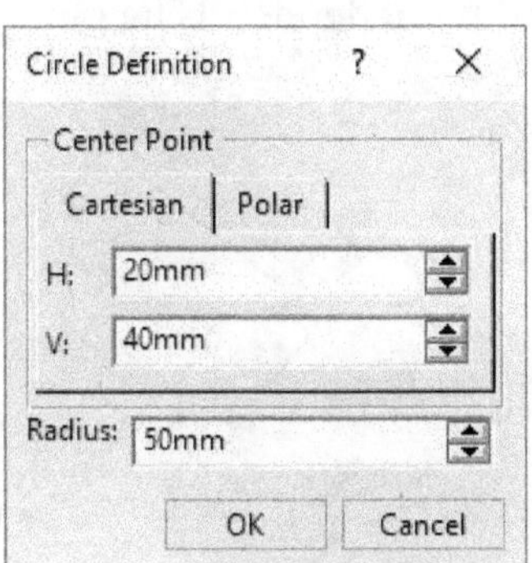

3. Click **OK** to create the circle.

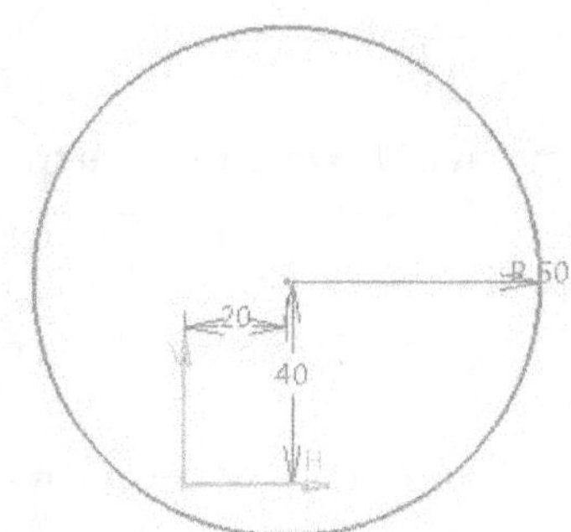

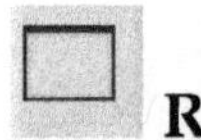

Rectangle

This command creates a rectangle by defining its diagonal corners.

1. On the **Profile** toolbar, click the **Rectangle** icon.
2. Click to define the first corner.
3. Drag the pointer and click to define the second corner.

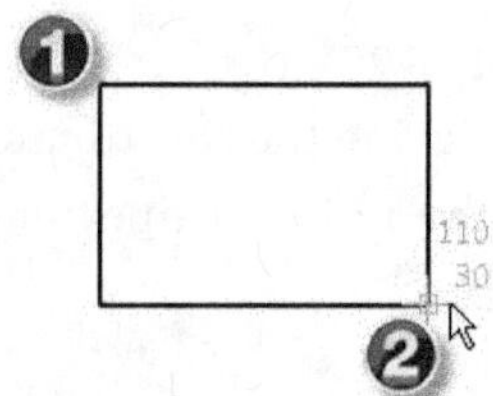

Oriented Rectangle

This command creates an inclined rectangle. The first two points define the width and inclination angle of the rectangle. The third point defines its height.

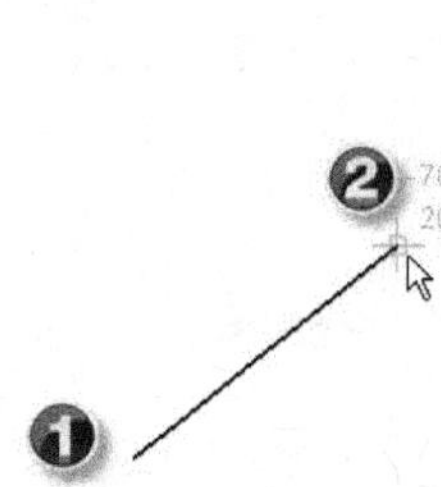

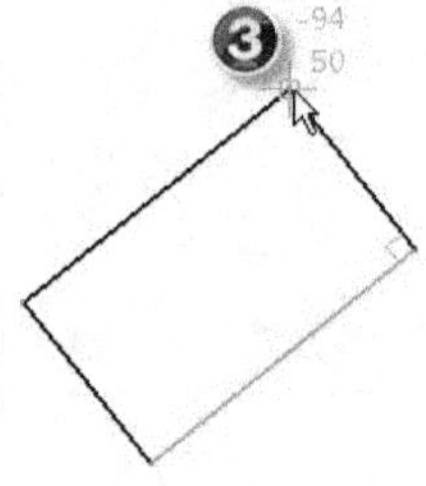

Centered Rectangle

This command creates a rectangle by defining two points: center of the rectangle and its corner.

1. On the **Profile** toolbar, click **Rectangle** drop-down **> Centered Rectangle**.
2. Click to define the center of the rectangle.
3. Move the pointer and click again to define the corner point.

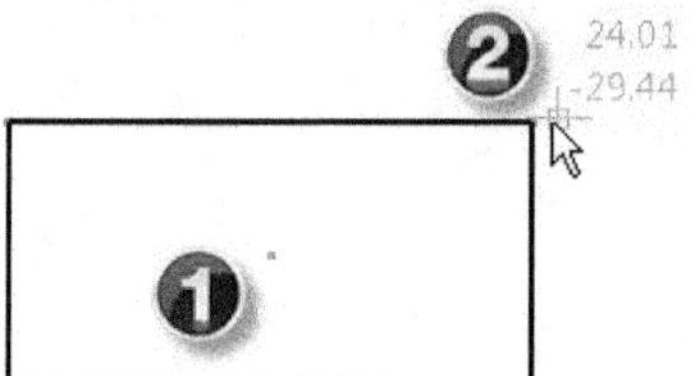

Parallelogram

This command creates a parallelogram by using three points that you specify.

1. On the **Profile** toolbar, click **Rectangle** drop-down > **Parallelogram**.
2. Select two points to define the width of the parallelogram.
3. Drag the pointer and click to define the height of parallelogram.

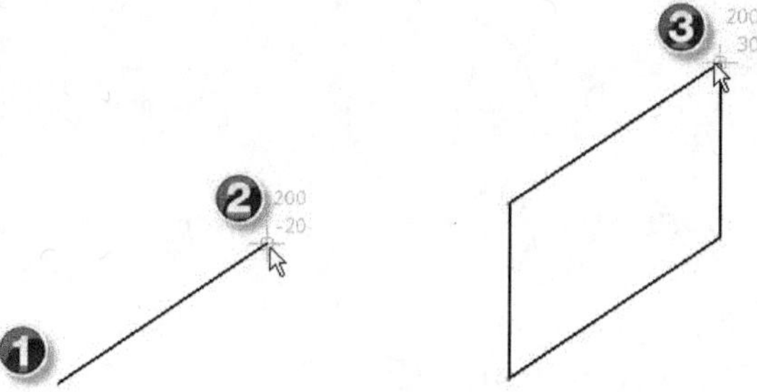

Centered Parallelogram

This command creates a parallelogram by selecting two intersecting lines. The point of intersection will become the center of the parallelogram.

1. On the **Profile** toolbar, click **Rectangle** drop-down **> Centered Parallelogram**.
2. Select two intersecting lines.
3. Drag the pointer and click to define the corner of the parallelogram.

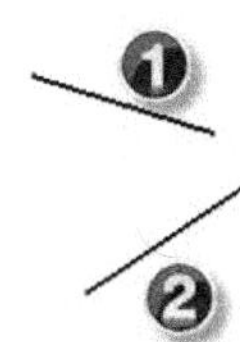

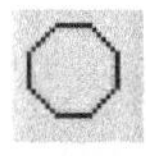

Polygon

This command provides a simple way to create a closed profile with equal length sides.

1. On the **Profile** toolbar, click **Rectangle** drop-down **>** **Polygon**.
2. Click to define the center point of the polygon.
3. Click the **Circum Circle** option on the **Sketch Tools** toolbar. The pointer will be on one of the vertices of the polygon.
4. Click the **In Circle** icon on the **Sketch Tools** toolbar. The pointer will be on one of the flat sides of the hexagon.
5. On the **Sketch Tools** toolbar, deactivate tgthe **Lock** icon next to the **Number of Sides** box.

6. Drag the pointer and click to define the size and angle of the polygon.
7. Type a value in the **Number of Sides** box on the **Sketch Tools** toolbar, and then press Enter.

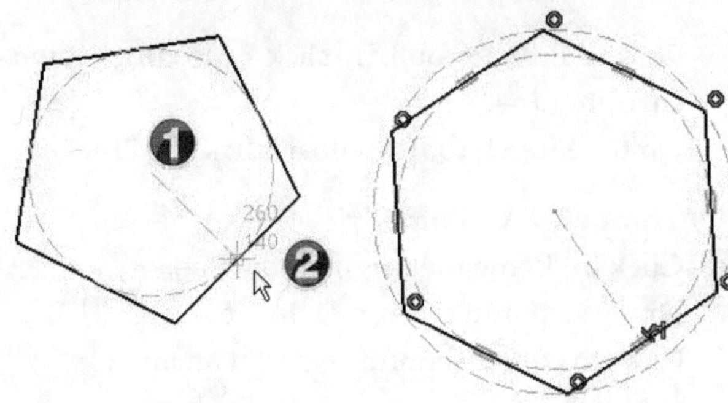

Elongated Hole

This command creates a straight slot by defining its centerline and radius.

1. On the **Profile** toolbar, click **Rectangle** drop-down > **Elongated Hole**.
2. Click to define the start point of the slot.
3. Drag the pointer and click to define the end-point. This creates the centerline of the slot.
4. Now, drag the pointer and click to define the radius of the slot.

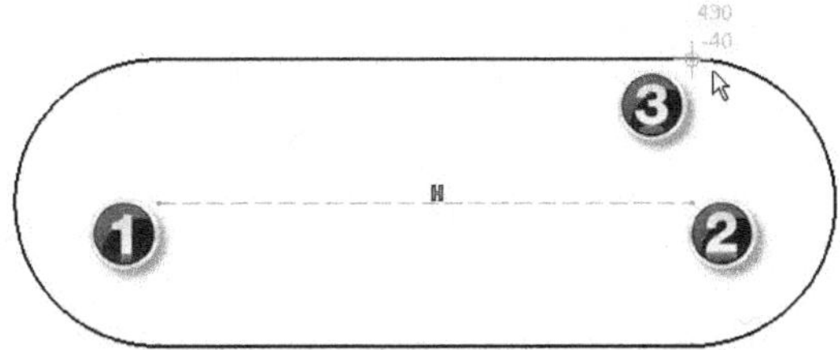

Cylindrical Elongated Hole

This command creates a curved slot by defining the curve radius and slot radius. First, you have to create an arc, and then create a slot along the arc.

1. On the **Profile** toolbar, click **Rectangle** drop-down **>** **Cylindrical Elongated Hole**.
2. Click to define the center point of the arc.
3. Drag the pointer and define the start and end points of the arc. This defines the radius and size of the center arc.
4. Now, drag the pointer and click to define the radius of the slot.

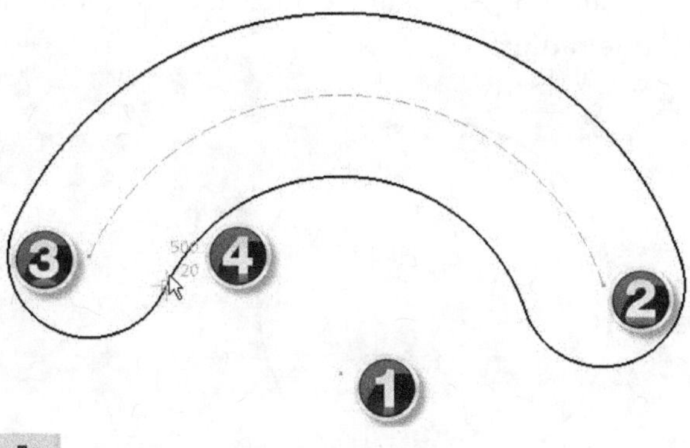

Keyhole Profile

This command creates a keyhole profile. A keyhole profile has a large and small arcs connected through a slot.

1. On the **Profile** toolbar, click **Rectangle** drop-down **> Keyhole Profile**.
2. Click to define the center point of the large arc.
3. Drag the pointer and click to define the center point of the small arc.

4. Now, drag the pointer and click to define the small radius.

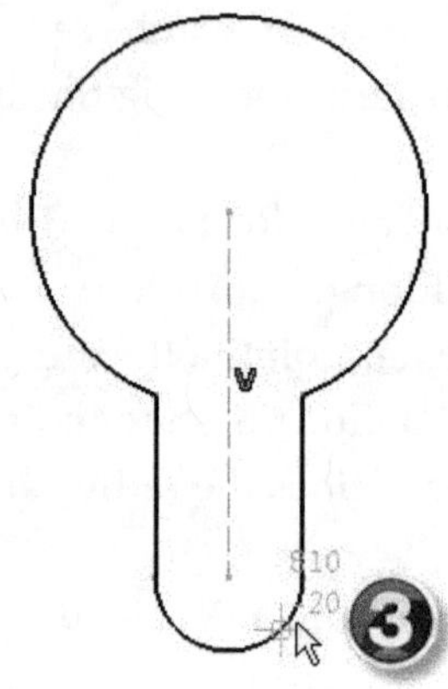

5. Again, drag the pointer and click to define the large radius.

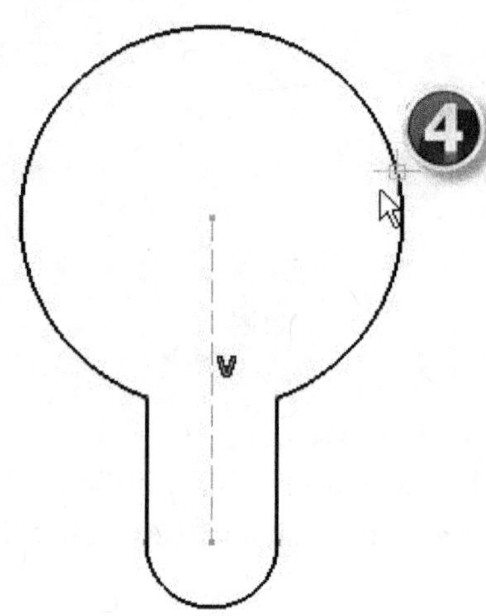

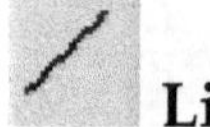

Line

This command creates a line using the start and endpoints that you select.

1. On the **Profile** toolbar, click **Line** drop-down **> Line**.
2. Click the start and endpoints of the line.

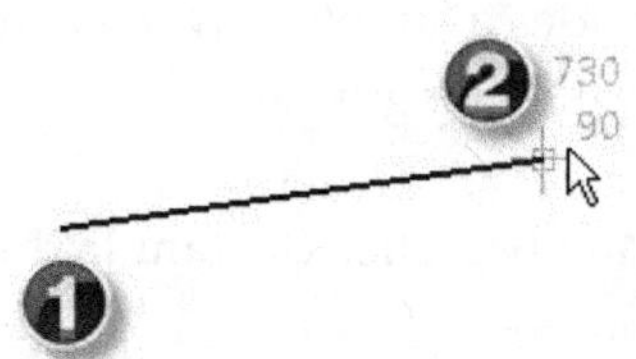

 If you want to define its midpoint and endpoint, then click **Symmetrical Extension** on the **Sketch tools** toolbar. Define the mid and endpoints of the straight line.

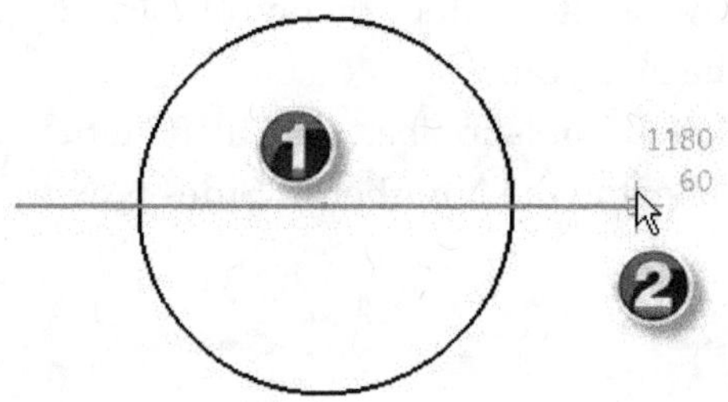

Infinite Line

This command creates a line with infinite length.

1. On the **Profile** toolbar, click **Line** drop-down > **Infinite Line**.
2. On the **Sketch tools** toolbar, click the **Line Through Two Points** icon.
3. Click to define the origin of the line.
4. Drag the pointer to rotate the line.
5. Click to create an infinite line at an angle.

If you want to create a horizontal or vertical infinite line, click the **Horizontal** or **Vertical** button on the **Sketch tools** toolbar.

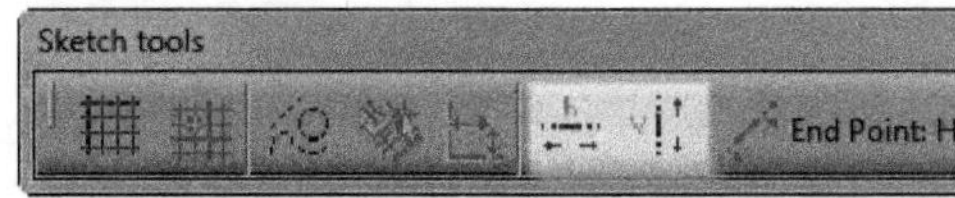

Bi-Tangent Line

This command creates a line tangent to two circles or arcs.

1. On the **Profile** toolbar, click **Line** drop-down > **Bi-Tangent Line**.
2. Select two circles or arcs. This creates a line tangent to the selected elements.

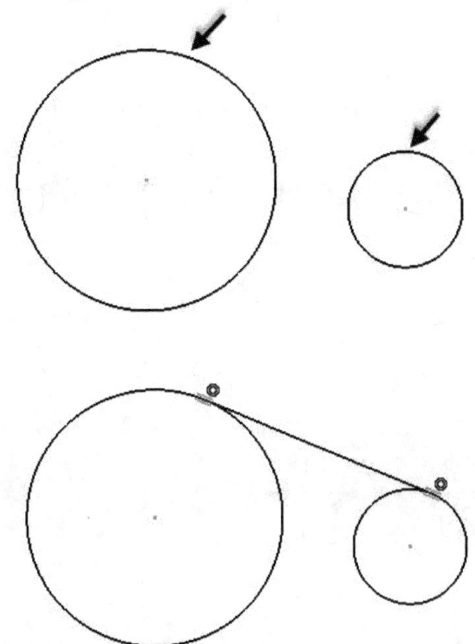

Bisecting Line

This command creates an infinite line passing through the intersection of two lines. In case of parallel lines, an infinite line will be created at the center and parallel to both the lines.

1. On the **Profile** toolbar, click **Line** drop-down > **Bisecting Line**.
2. Select two lines.

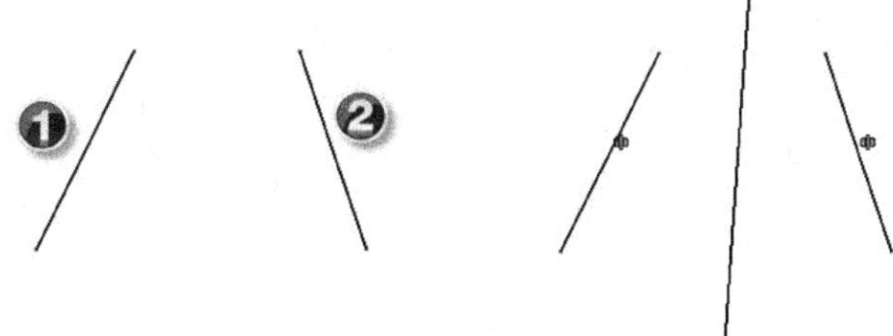

Line Normal to Curve

This command creates a line normal to arc, ellipse, circle, spline or any other curve.

1. On the **Profile** toolbar, click **Line** drop-down > **Line Normal to Curve**.
2. Click on the curve to draw a normal line.
3. Drag the pointer and click to define the endpoint of the line.

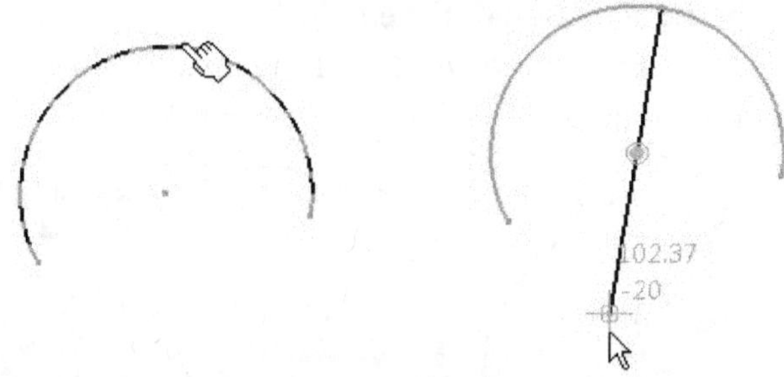

Axis

This command creates a sketch axis, which can be used while creating the revolved feature.

1. On the **Profile** toolbar, click the **Axis** icon.
2. Define the start and endpoints of the axis.

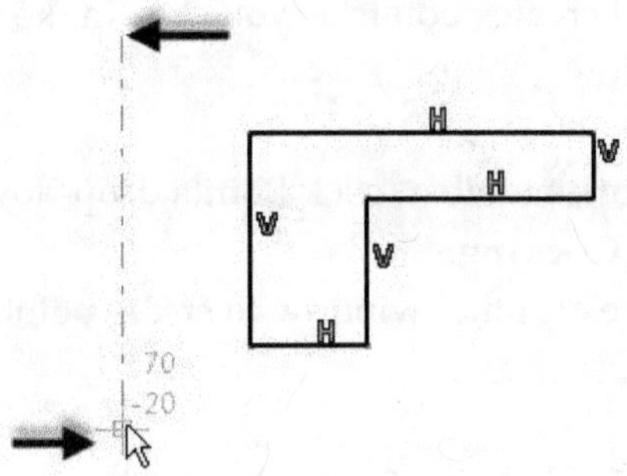

You can also convert an existing line into an axis by selecting it and clicking the **Axis** icon on the **Profile** toolbar. Next, click **Yes** on the **Axis Creation** dialog.

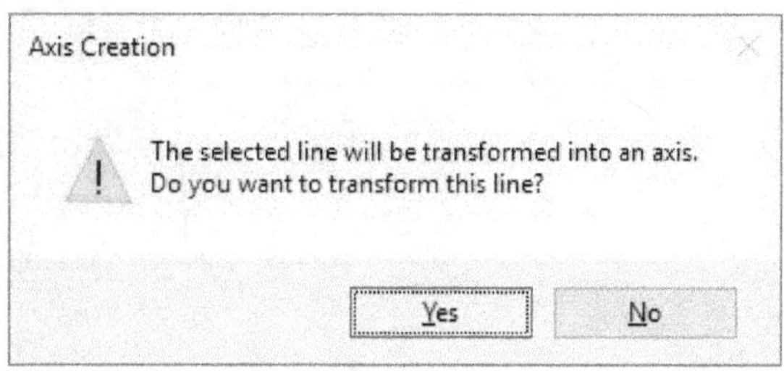

Ellipse

This command creates an ellipse using a center point, and major and minor axes.

1. On the **Profile** toolbar, click **Ellipse** drop-down > **Ellipse**.
2. Click to define the center of the ellipse.
3. Drag the pointer and click to define the major axis and orientation of the ellipse.
4. Drag the pointer and click again to define the minor axis.

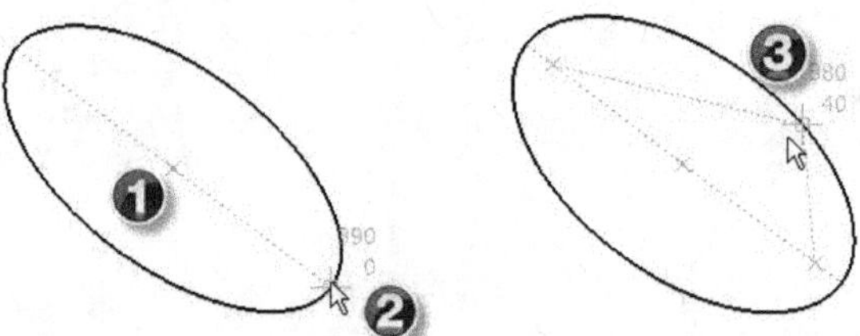

On the **Sketch tools** toolbar, you can also type-in values in the **Major Radius, Minor Radius**, and **A** (angle) boxes.

Points by Clicking

This command creates points as you click in the graphics window.

1. On the **Profile** toolbar, click **Points** drop-down > **Points by Clicking**.
2. Click in the graphics window to create points.

Point by Using Coordinates

This command creates a point by entering its coordinate values in the Cartesian or Polar coordinate system.

1. On the **Profile** toolbar, click **Points** drop-down > **Points by Using Coordinates**.
2. On the **Point Definition** dialog, click the **Cartesian** tab and type-in values in the **H** and **V** boxes.

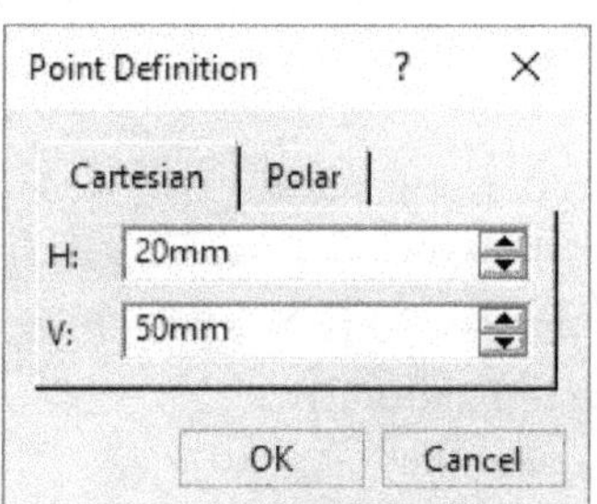

3. If you want to enter the coordinate values in the Polar coordinate system, then click the **Polar** tab and type-in values in the **Radius** and **Angle** boxes.

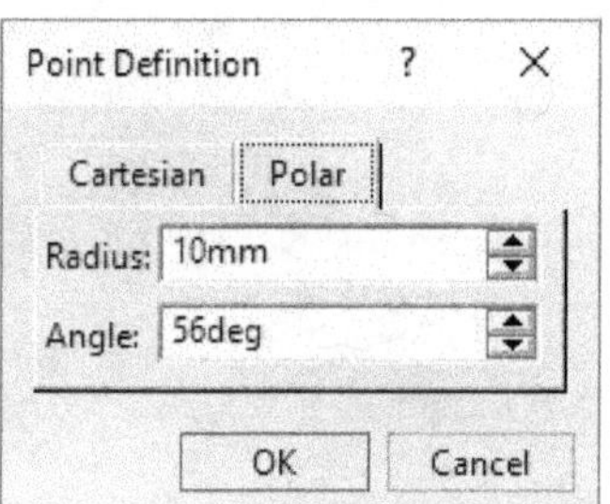

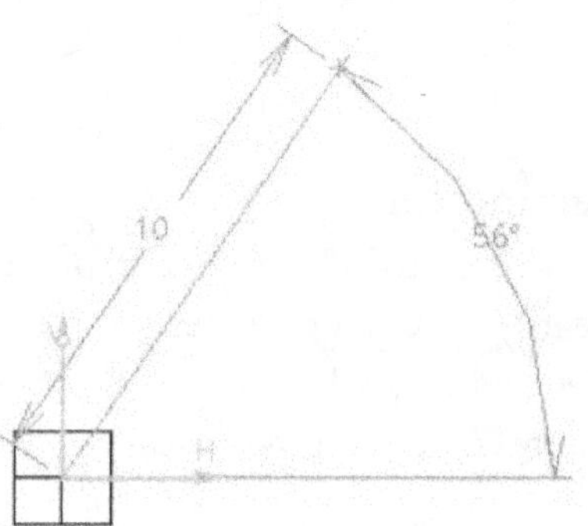

Equidistant Points

This command creates equidistant points on a selected sketch element.

1. On the **Profile** toolbar, click **Points** drop-down > **Equidistant Points**.
2. Select a sketch element.

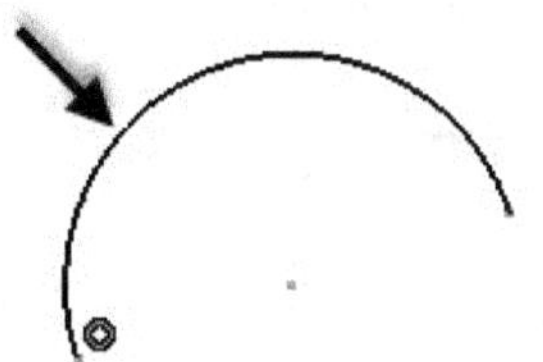

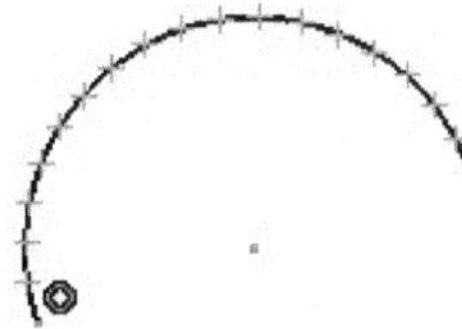

3. On the **Equidistant Point Definition** dialog, type-in a value in the **New Points** box.
4. If you want to reverse the side of point creation, then click the **Reverse Direction** button.

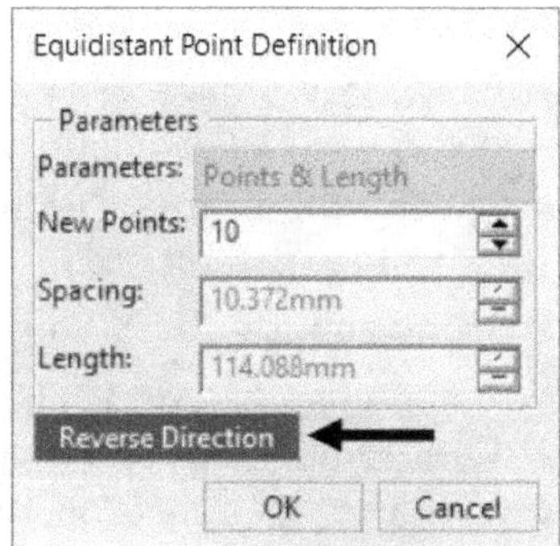

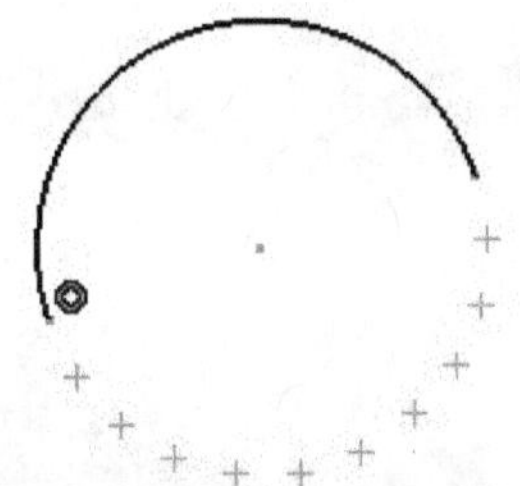

5. Click **OK** to complete the point creation.

Intersection Point

This command creates a point at the intersection of two elements.

1. On the **Profile** toolbar, click **Point** drop-down > **Intersection Point**.
2. Click on two intersecting elements.

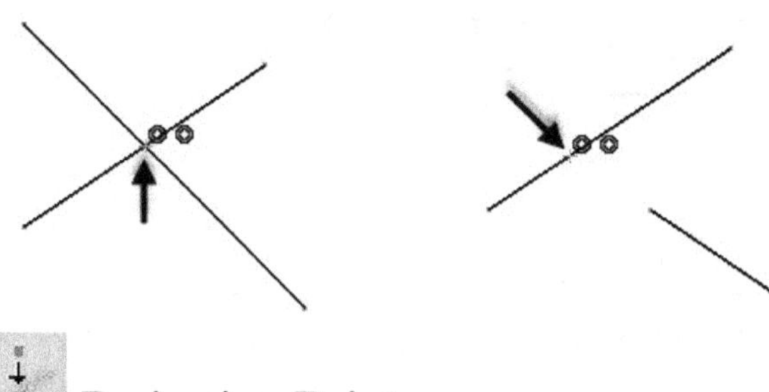

Projection Point

This command creates a new point by projecting a point onto a sketch element.

1. On the **Profile** toolbar, click **Point** drop-down > **Projection Point**.
2. Click on the point to be projected.
3. Click on the sketch element onto which the point will be projected.

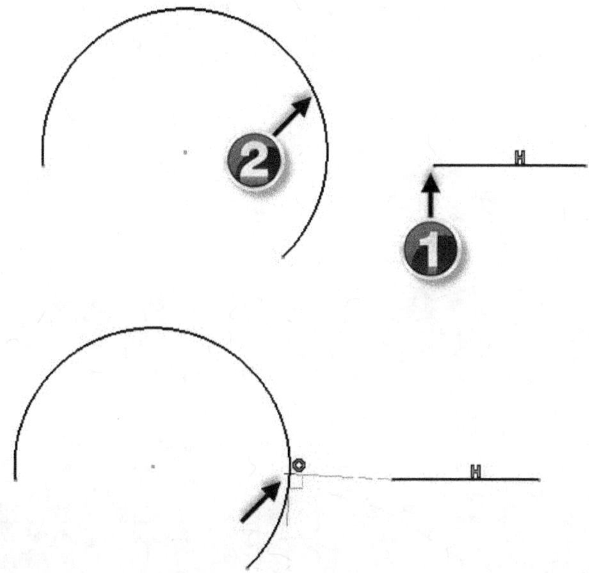

Align Points

This command aligns a point along a straight line.

1. On the **Profile** toolbar, click **Point** drop-down > **Align Points**.
2. Click on the point to be aligned.
3. Select another point or click to define the alignment direction. A straight construction line is created and the selected point is aligned along the line.

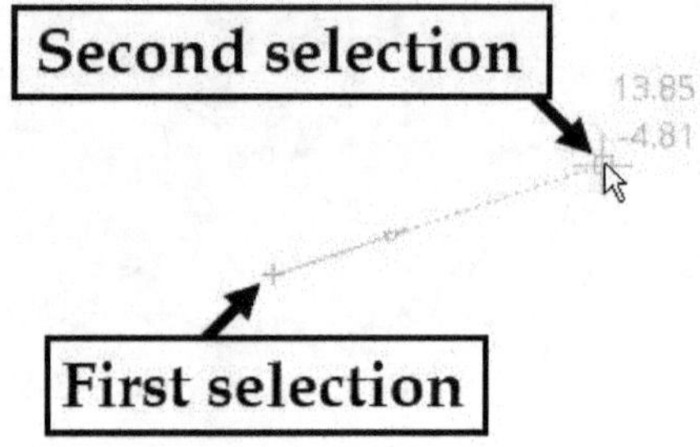

Spline

This command creates a smooth B-spline curve passing through the points you select.

1. On the **Profile** toolbar, click **Spline** drop-down > **Spline**.
2. Click to define points in the graphics window. This creates a spline passing through the selected points.
3. Press Esc to deactivate this command.

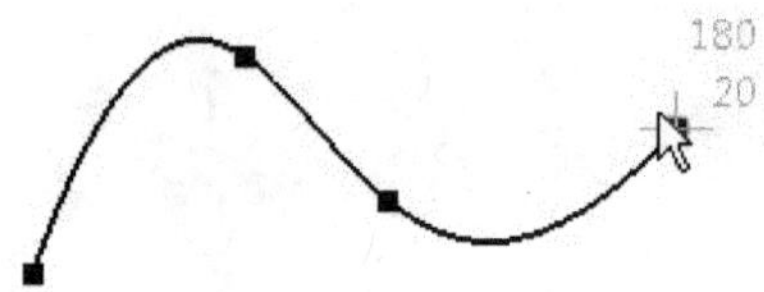

If you want to create a closed spline, then click the right mouse button and select **Close spline**.

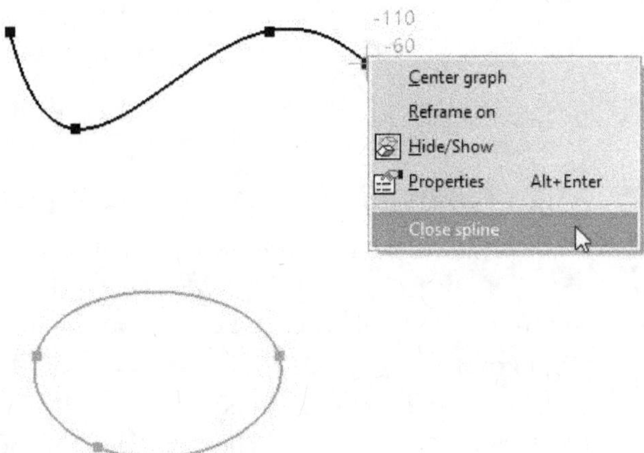

Connect

This command connects two splines or curves.

1. On the **Profile** toolbar, click **Spline** drop-down > **Connect**.
2. Click on two open curves to connect them.

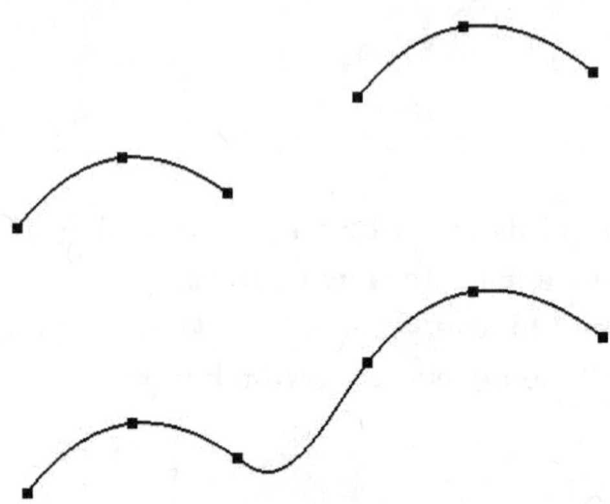

On the **Sketch tools** toolbar, you can define the type of connecting curve by using the **Connect with an Arc** and **Connect with a Spline** button. If you click the **Connect with a Spline** button, then you can define the continuity of the bridge curve using the **Continuity in point**, **Continuity in tangency**, and **Continuity in curvature** buttons. The following examples show the continuity types.

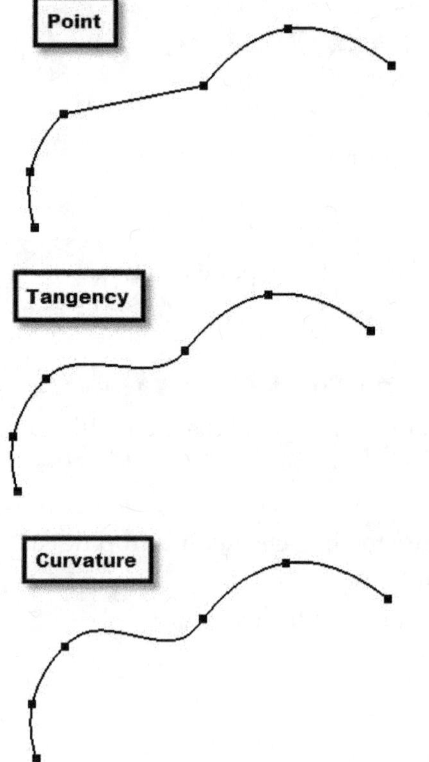

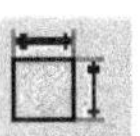

The Constraint command

It is generally considered a good practice to ensure that every sketch you create is fully constrained before moving on to creating features. The term, 'fully-constrained' means that the sketch has a definite shape and size. You can fully-constrain a sketch by using dimensions and constraints. You can add dimensions to a sketch by using the **Constraint** command (on the **Constraint** toolbar, click **Constraint** drop-down > **Constraint**). You can use this command to add all types of dimensional constraints such as length, angle, and diameter and so on. This command creates a dimension based on the geometry you select. For instance, to dimension a circle, activate the **Constraint** command, and then click on the circle. Next, move the pointer and click again to position the dimension.

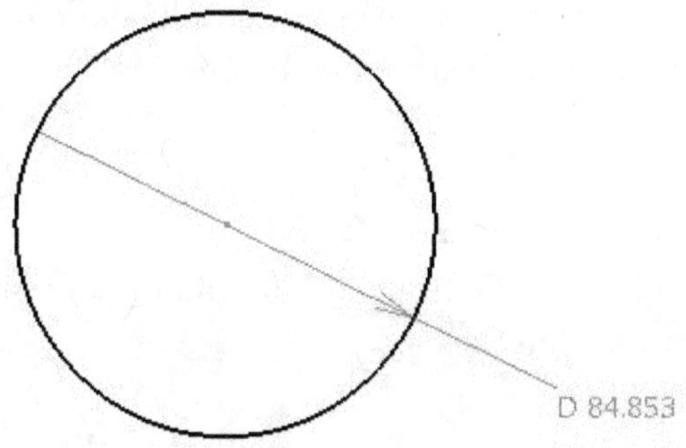

Now, you can change the size of the sketch element by modifying the dimension value. To do this, double-click on the dimension. You will notice that the **Constraint Definition** dialog pops up. Type-in a value in this box, and click **OK** to update the dimension.

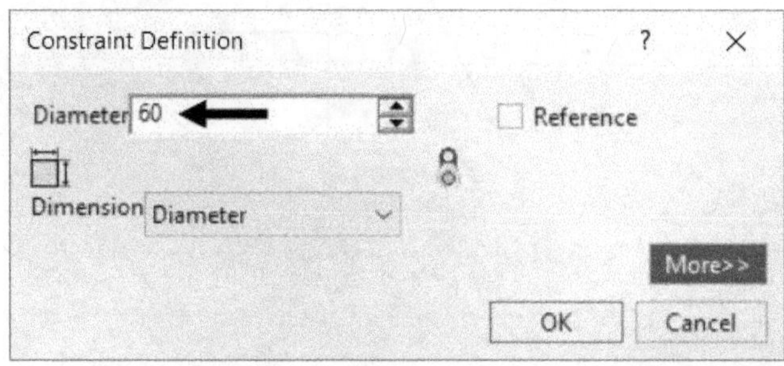

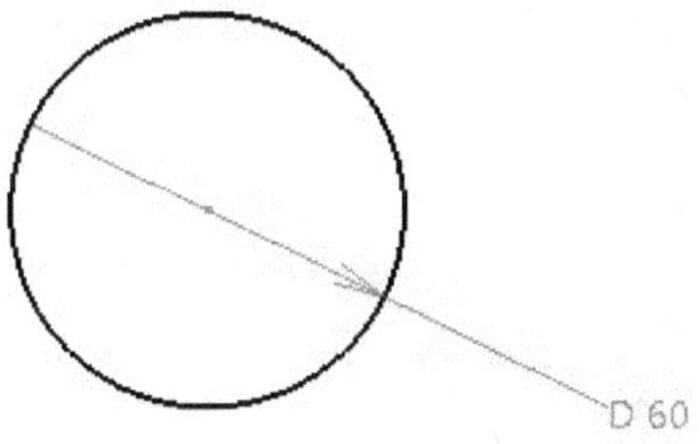

If you click a line, this command automatically creates a linear dimension. Click once more to position the dimension.

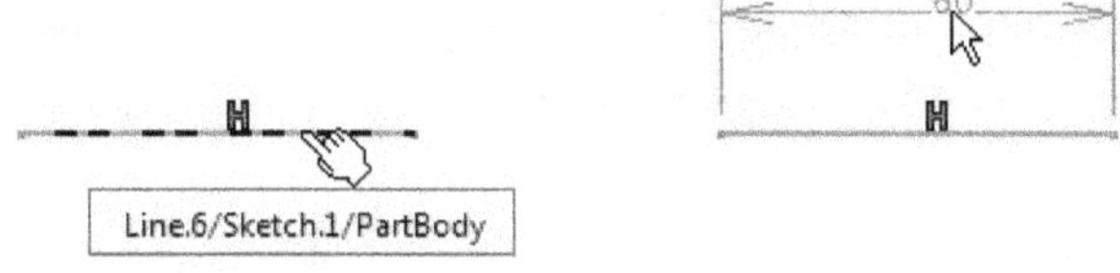

If you click on an inclined line, this command creates a dimension parallel to the line.

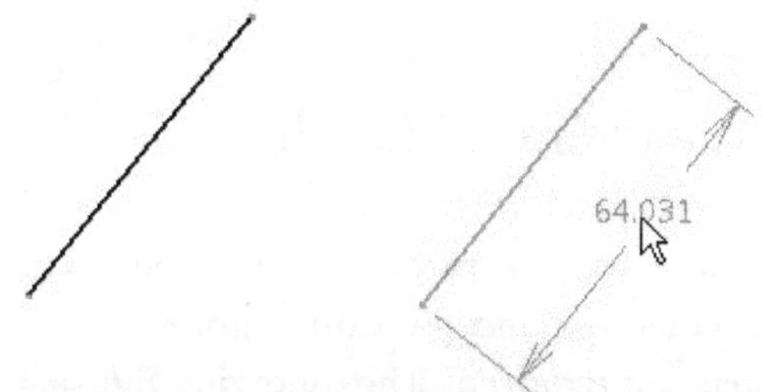

If you want to apply a horizontal dimension to the selected line, then click the right mouse button and select **Horizontal Measure Direction**.

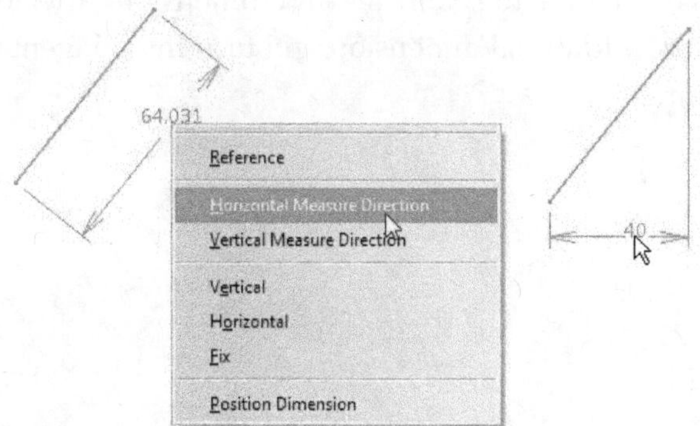

Likewise, if you want to apply a vertical dimension to the selected line, then click the right mouse button and select **Vertical Measure Direction**.

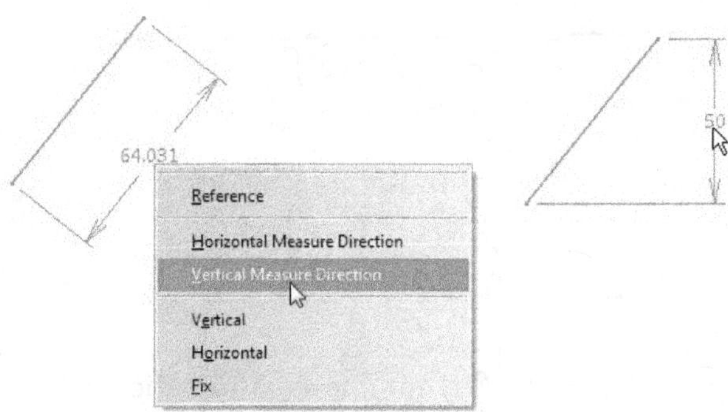

If you want to create an angle dimension between two elements, then activate the **Constraint** command and select the elements. Next, move the pointer and position the dimension.

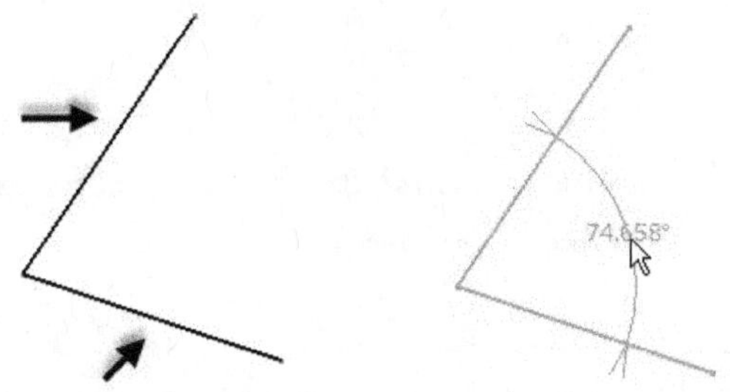

Over-constrained Sketch

When creating sketches for a part, CATIA V5 will not allow you to over-constrain the geometry. The term 'over-constrain' means adding more dimensions than required. The following figure shows a fully constrained sketch. If you add another dimension to this sketch (for example, add a diagonal dimension by selecting the corner points of the rectangle), the elements and dimensions affected by the additional dimension will turn into magenta color.

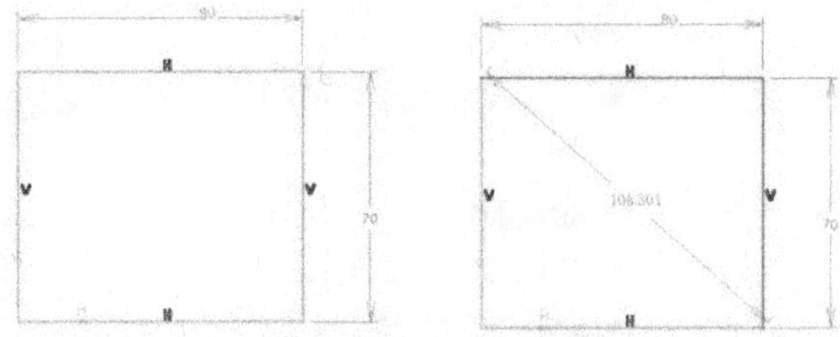

Now, you have to deactivate one of the dimensions. Click the right mouse button on the diagonal dimension and select **object > Deactivate** to deactivate the dimension. The deactivated dimension will be in black color.

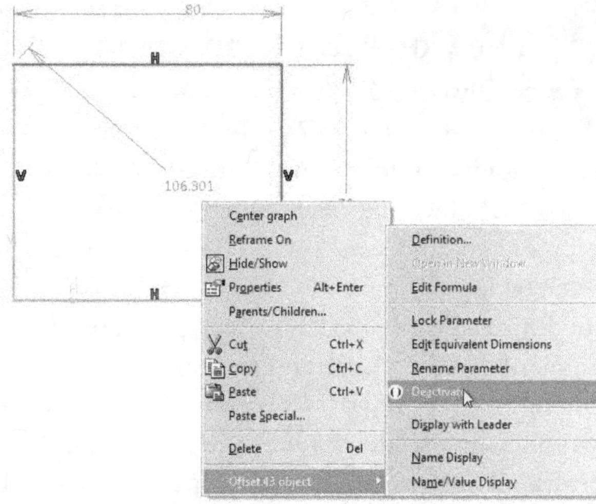

Now, if you change the value of the width, the inactive dimension along the diagonal updates, automatically. Also, note that the dimensions, which are initially created, will be driving dimensions, whereas the dimensions created after fully defining the sketch are over constraining dimensions.

Auto Constraint

This command automatically creates dimensions and fully constrains the sketch.

1. On the **Constraint** toolbar, click **Fix together > Auto Constraint**.
2. Press the left mouse button and drag a selection box around the sketch.

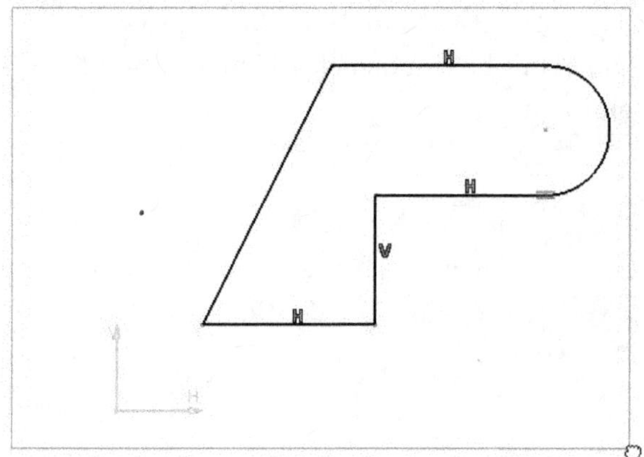

3. Click **OK** on the **Auto Constraint** dialog.

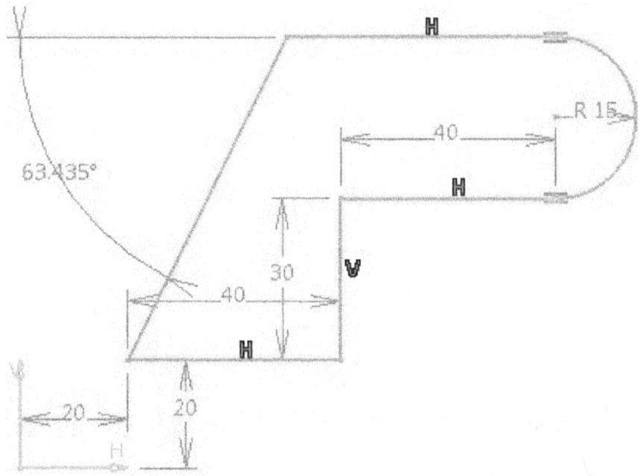

If you want to create chained dimensions, then select the complete sketch and click in the **Reference elements** selection box. Click on the longest element of the sketch to define the reference element. On the **Auto Constraint** dialog, select **Constraint mode > Chained** to create chained dimensions.

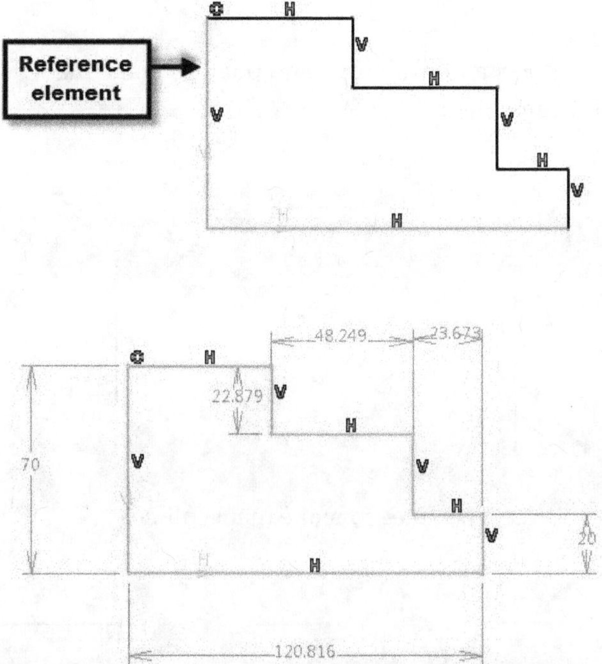

Likewise, use **Constraint Mode > Stacked** to create stacked dimensions. The procedure to create stacked dimensions is same as that of chain dimensions.

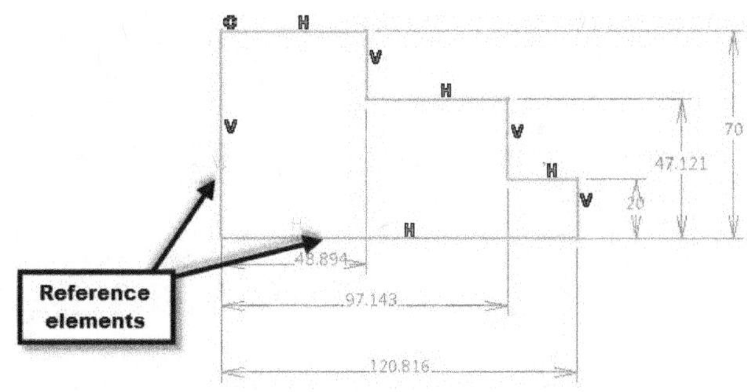

Edit Multi-Constraint

This command modifies all the constraints in a sketch using the **Edit Multi-Constraint** dialog.

1. On the **Constraint** toolbar, click the **Edit Multi-Constraint** icon.
2. On **Edit Multi-Constraint** dialog, select the dimensions and type-in a value in the **Current Value** box. For example, to change the radius value of the arc shown in figure, select the **Radius** dimension and type-in a new value in the **Current value** box.

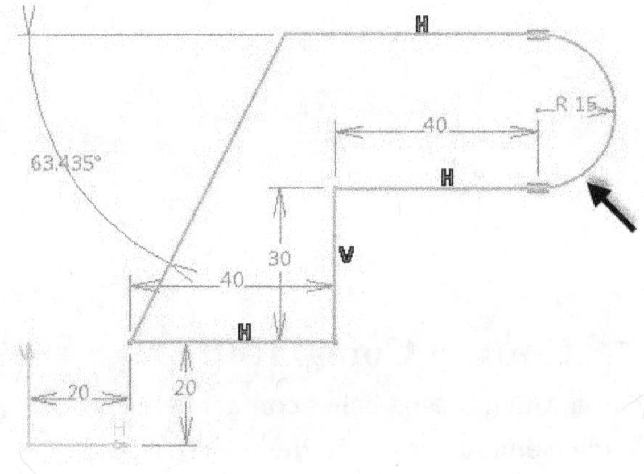

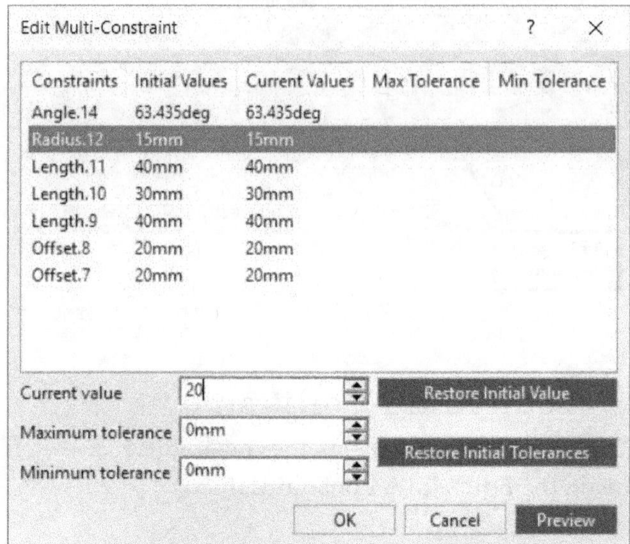

3. If required, you can type-in the maximum and minimum tolerance values.
4. Click **OK** to update the dimension.

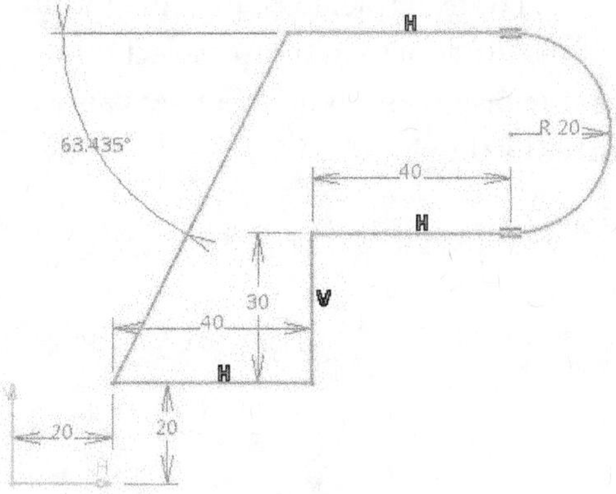

Contact Constraint

This command establishes contact between the sketch elements based on the selection.

1. On the **Constraint** toolbar, click Constraint > **Contact Constraint**.
2. Select two points to make them coincident.

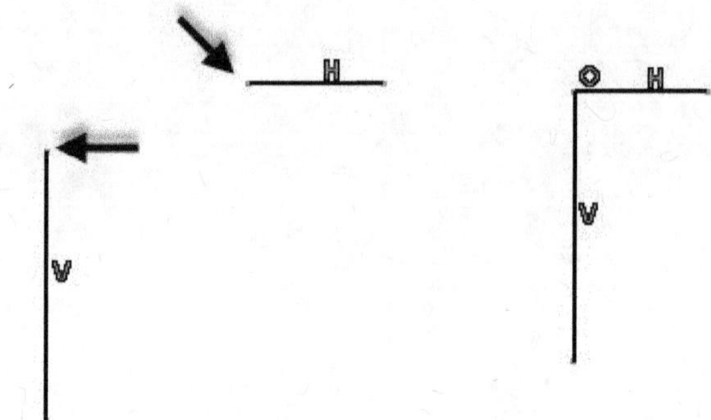

3. Select a curve and line to make them tangent to each other.

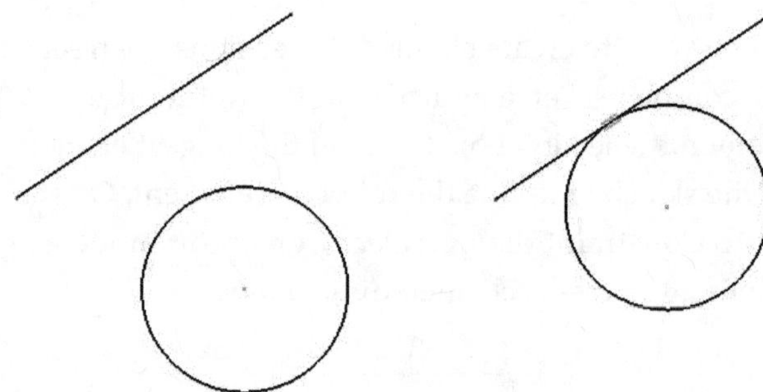

4. Select a line or curve and point to make them coincident.

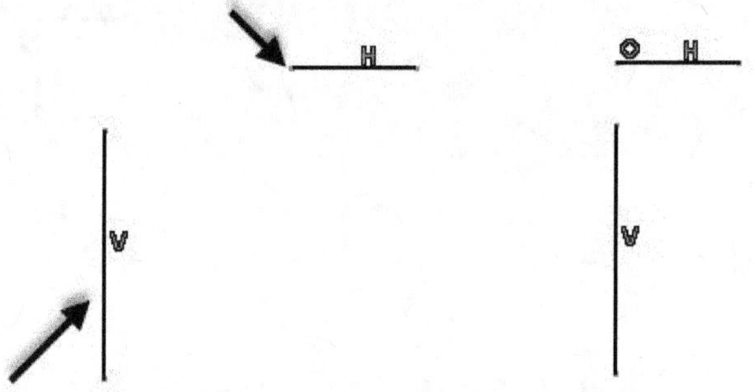

5. Select two lines to make them collinear.

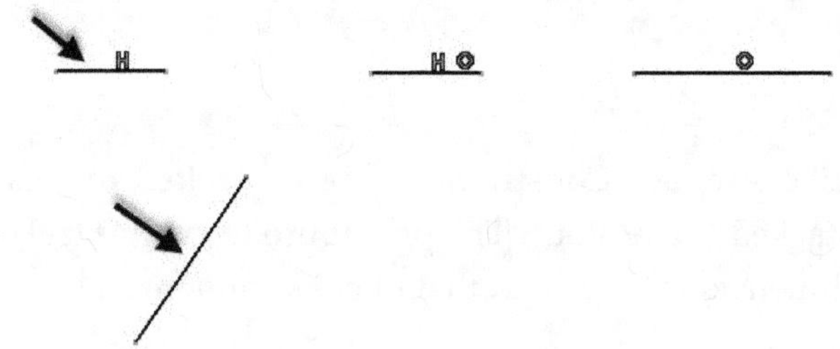

6. Select two circles or arcs to make them concentric.

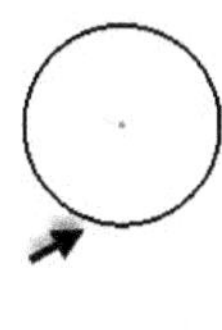
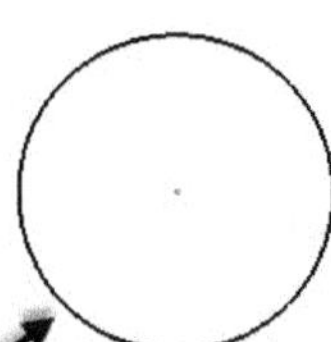
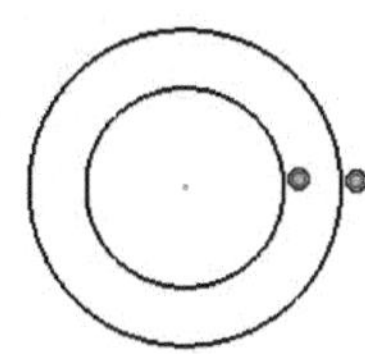

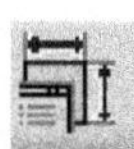

Constraints Defined in Dialog

In addition to dimensional and contact constraints, there are other constraints, which you can establish between the sketch elements. You can do this using the **Constraints Defined in Dialog** command.

1. Press and hold the Ctrl key and click on two points.
2. On the **Constraint** toolbar, click the **Constraints Defined in Dialog** icon.
3. On the **Constraint Definition** dialog, check the **Distance** option to establish a distance constraint between two points.

4. If you want to make the two points coincident with each other, then uncheck the **Distance** option.
5. Check the **Coincidence** option.

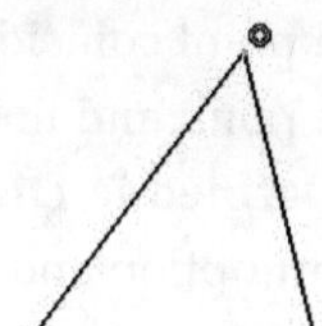

To fix a sketch element (or elements) at its current location, select it and activate the **Constraints Defined in Dialog** command.

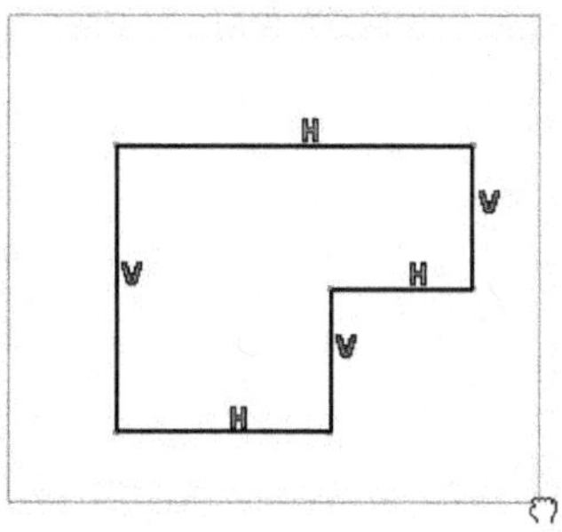

On the **Constraint Definition** dialog, check the **Fix** option.

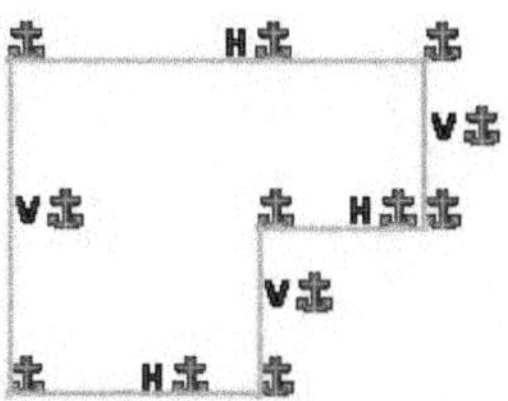

To apply the **Length** constraint, select a linear element and activate the **Constraint Defined in Dialog** command. Check the **Length** option on the **Constraint Definition** dialog.

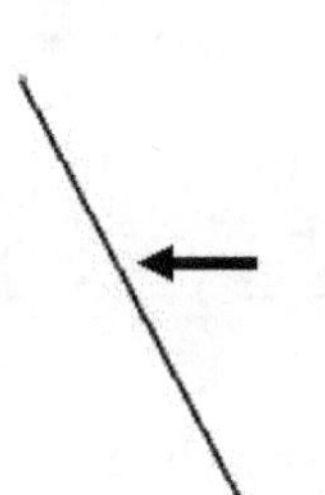
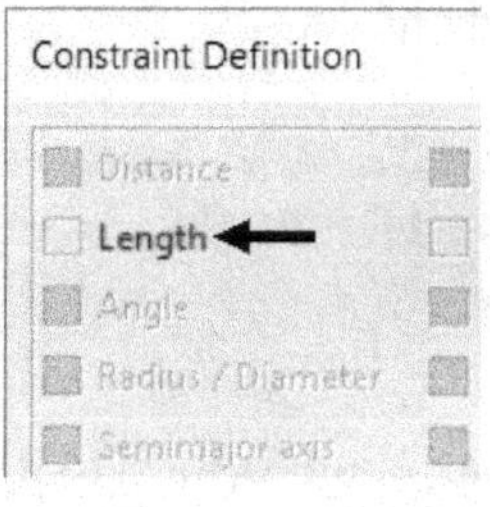

To apply the **Horizontal** constraint, select a linear element and activate **Constraint Defined in Dialog** command. Check the **Horizontal** option.

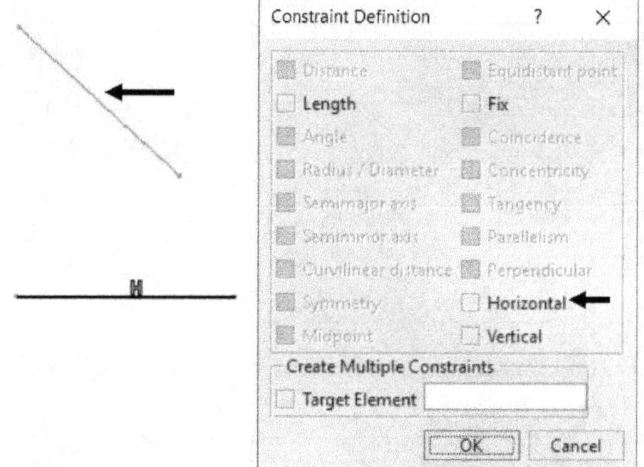

Likewise, use the **Vertical** option to make a line vertical.

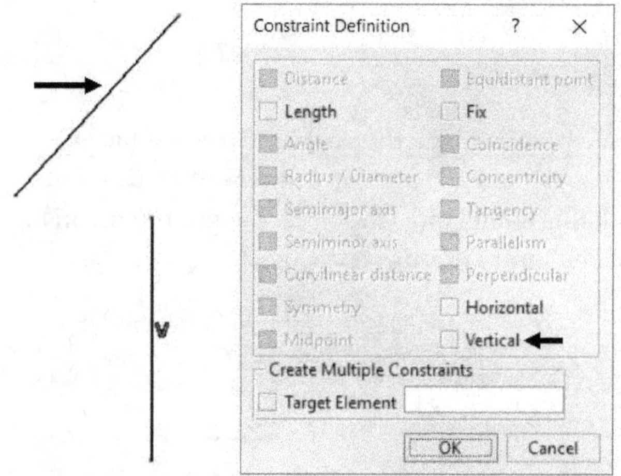

Use the **Parallelism** option to make two lines parallel to each other.

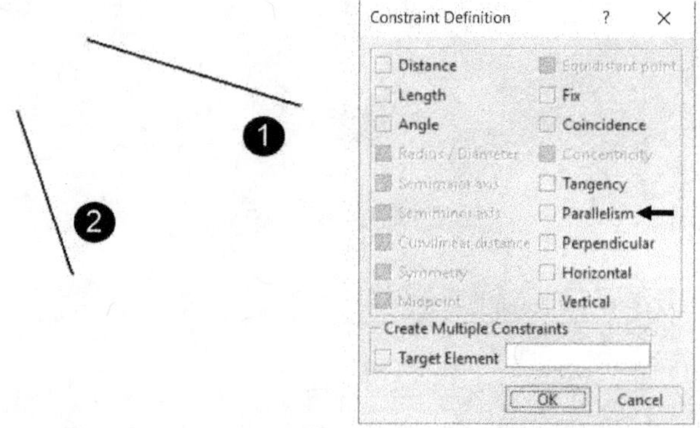

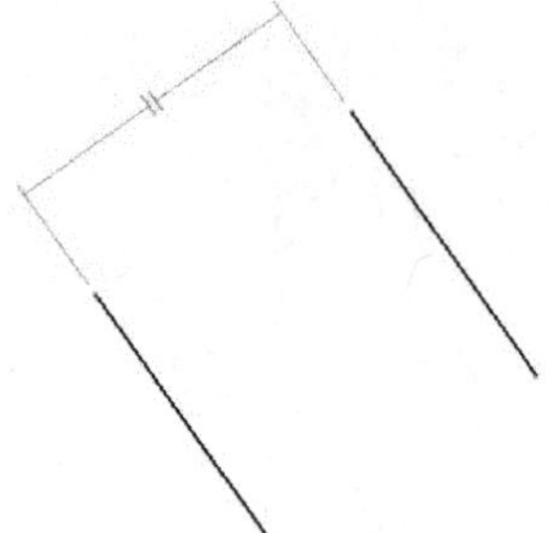

Use the **Perpendicular** option to make two lines perpendicular to each other.

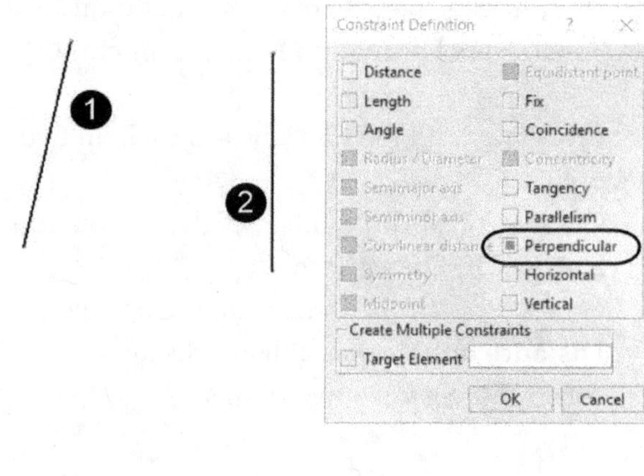

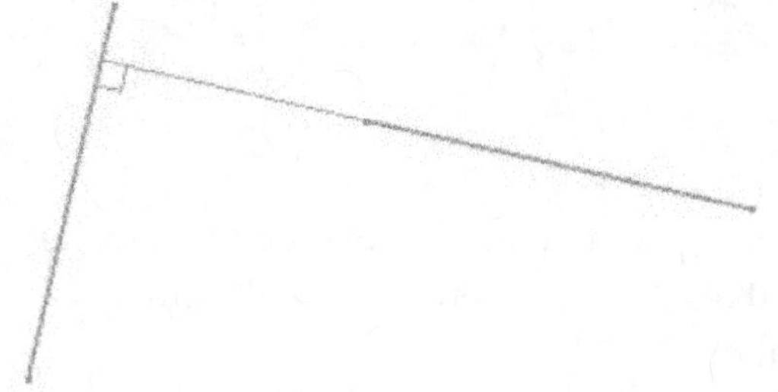

Use the **Midpoint** option to make a point coincide with the midpoint of a line. Select a point and line, and then activate the **Constraints Defined in Dialog** command. Next, check the **Midpoint** option and click **OK**.

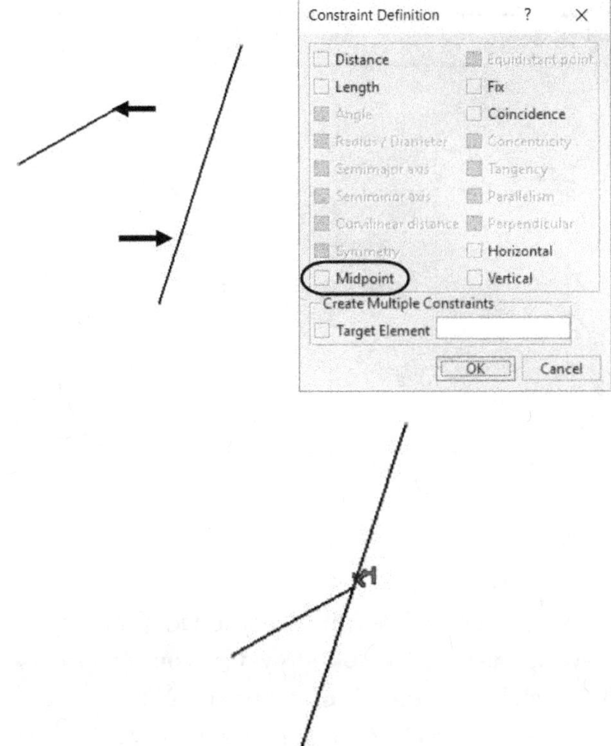

Use the **Symmetry** option to make two sketch elements symmetric about a centerline. Press the Ctrl key and click on the elements to make symmetric. Click on the symmetric line and activate the **Constraint Defined in Dialog** command.

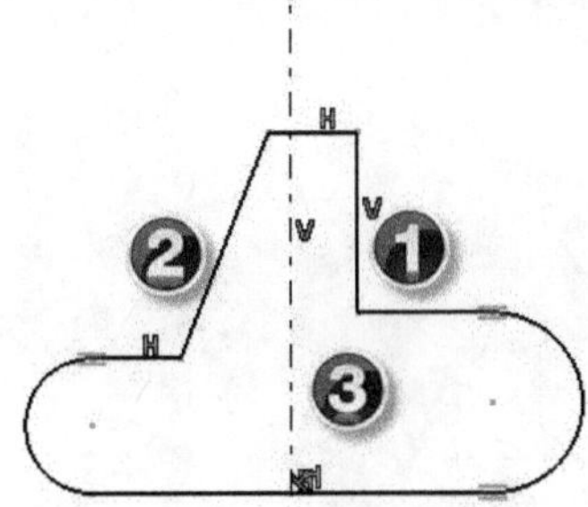

On the **Constraint Definition** dialog, check the **Symmetry** option and click **OK**.

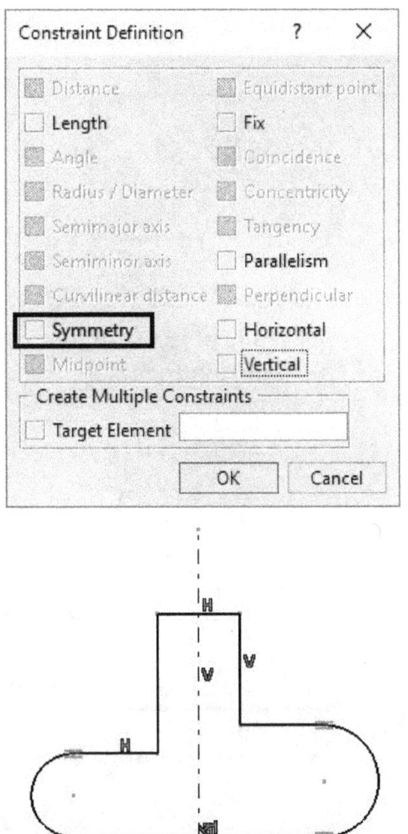

You can also create multiple constraints between two elements. To do so, check the **Target Element** option, click in **Target Element** selection box, and select the target element. Select the constraints from the **Constraint Definition** dialog.

The Fix Together command

This relation makes the selected elements act as a single unit.

1. On the **Constraint** toolbar, click the **Fix Together** icon.
2. Select two or more elements from the sketch.
3. Click **OK** on the **Fix Together Definition** dialog. The selected objects will form a rigid set.

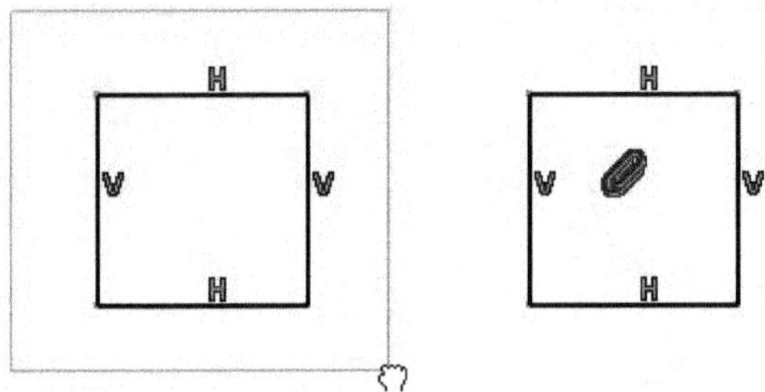

Now, click and drag anyone of the object from the rigid set. You will notice that entire set will be dragged.

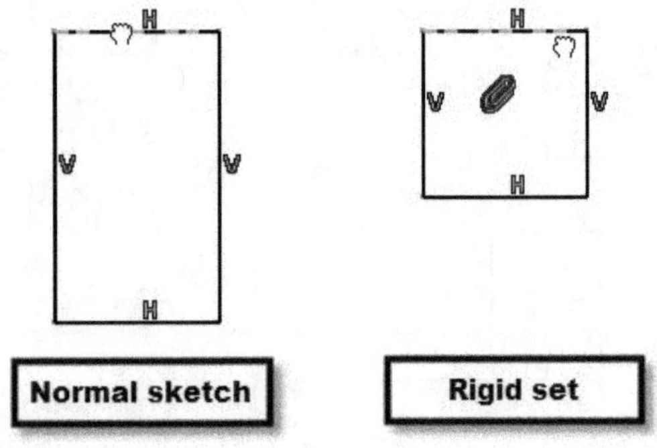

Display Geometrical Constraints

As constraints are created, they can be shown or hidden using the **Geometrical Constraints** icon on the **Visualization** toolbar. When dealing with complicated sketches involving numerous constraints, you can deactivate this button to turn off the display of all geometrical constraints.

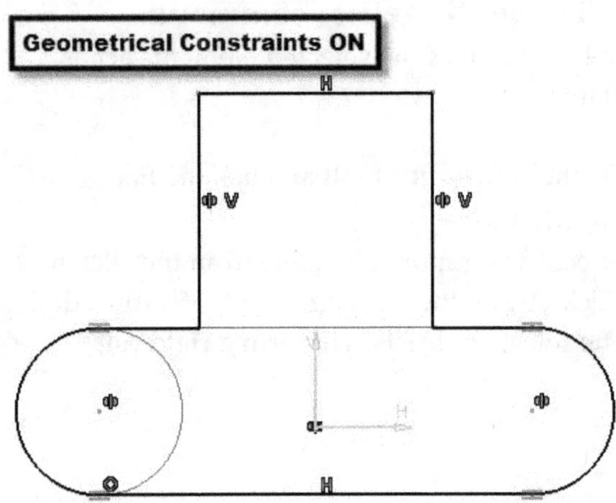

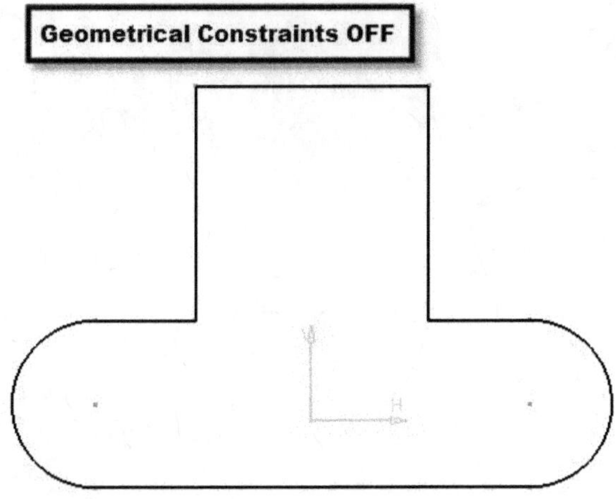

Sketch Solving Status

At any stage of the design process, you can check whether the sketch is fully constrained or not by viewing the sketch color. However, you can also use the **Sketch Solving Status** command to check the status of the sketch. Activate this command (On the **Tools** toolbar, click the **Sketch Solving Status** icon) to view the sketch status.

Sketch Analysis

This command can be used to analyse the sketch. For example, the following figure shows an over-constrained sketch.

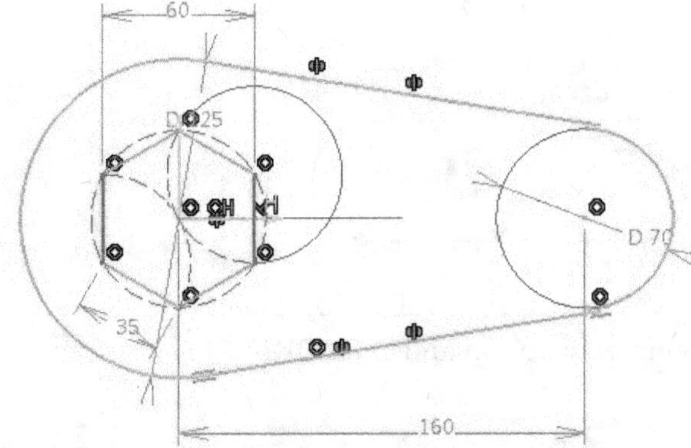

1. To analyse this sketch, activate the **Sketch Analysis** command (on the **Tools** toolbar, click **2D Analysis** drop-down > **Sketch Analysis**).
2. On the **Sketch Analysis** dialog, click the **Diagnostics** tab.

3. Under the **Solving Status** section, select the constraint marked as Over-constrained.
4. Under the **Action** section, click the **Delete geometry or constraint** button.
5. Close the dialog.

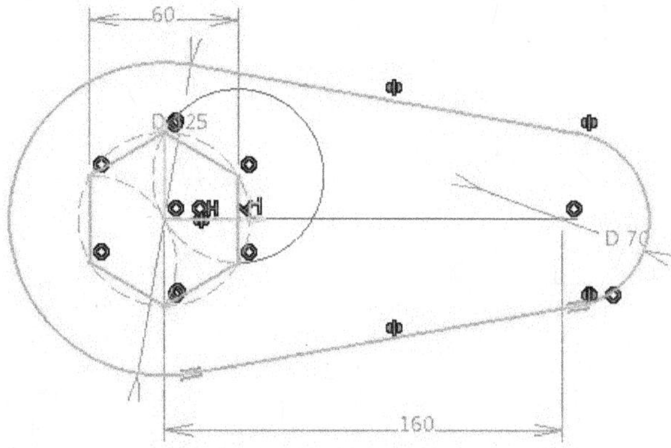

Construction/Standard Element

This command converts a standard sketch element into a construction element. Construction elements support you to create a sketch of a desired shape and size. To convert a standard sketch element to construction element, click on it and select **Construction/Standard Element** on the **Sketch tools** toolbar.

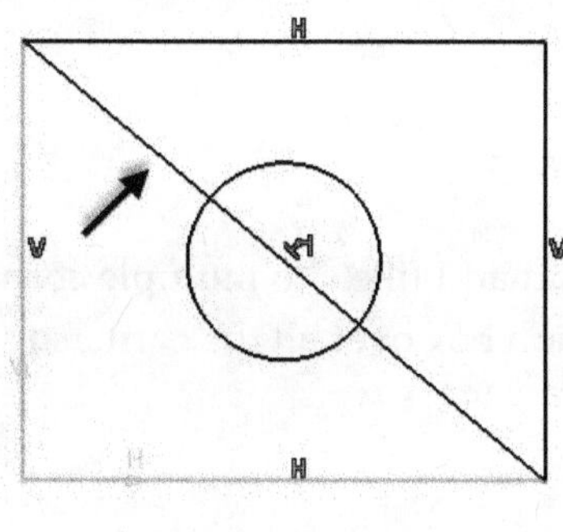

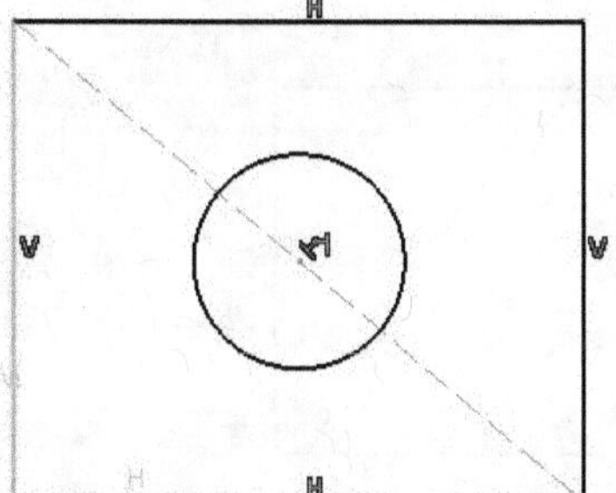

You can also convert it back to a standard sketch element by right clicking on it and selecting **Geometrical Element**.

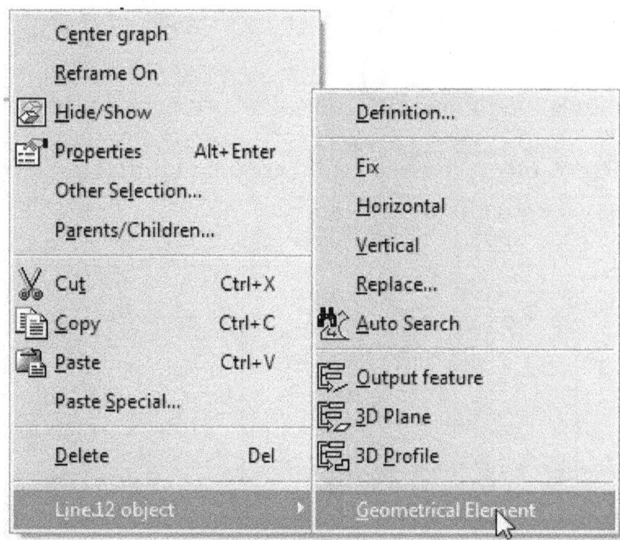

The Corner command

This command rounds a sharp corner created by intersection of two lines, arcs, circles, and rectangle or polygon vertices.

1. On the **Operation** toolbar, click the **Corner** icon (or) click **Insert > Operation > Corner > Corner**.
2. Select the intersecting elements to add a corner.

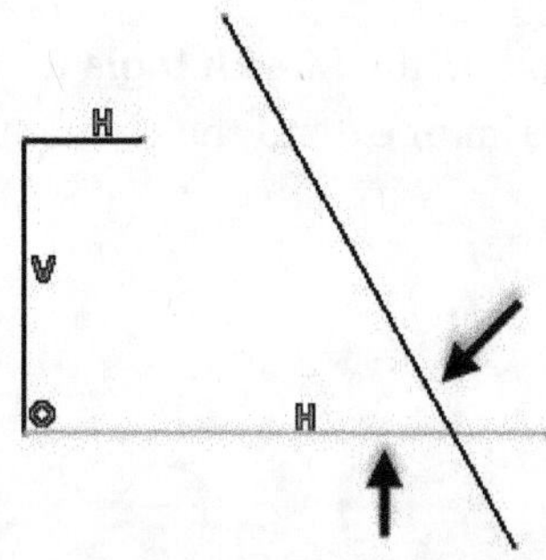

3. Type-in a radius value in the **Radius** box available on the **Sketch tools** toolbar.
4. Press Enter.

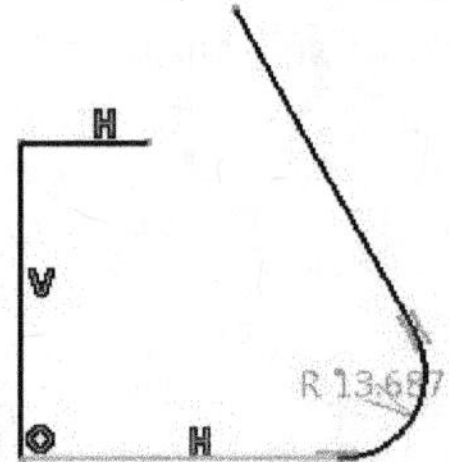

The elements to be cornered are not required to touch each other.

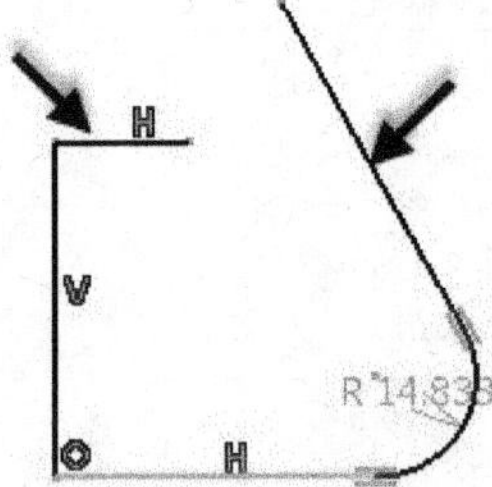

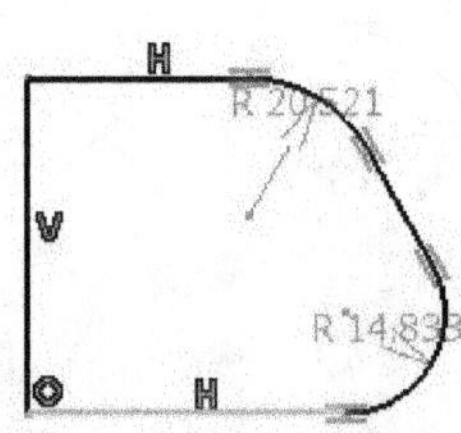

By default, the elements are automatically trimmed or extended to meet the end of the new corner radius. You can use the **Trim first Element** option on the **Sketch tools** toolbar, if you want to trim only the first element.

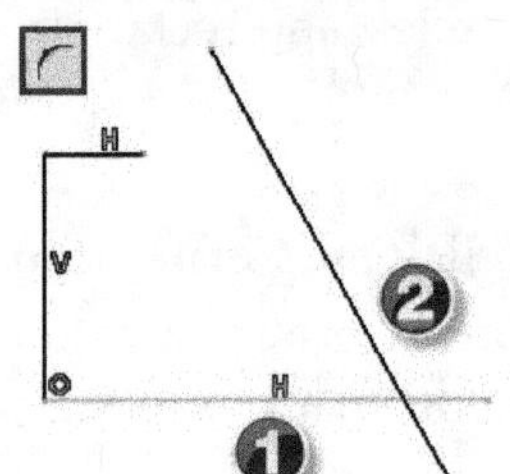

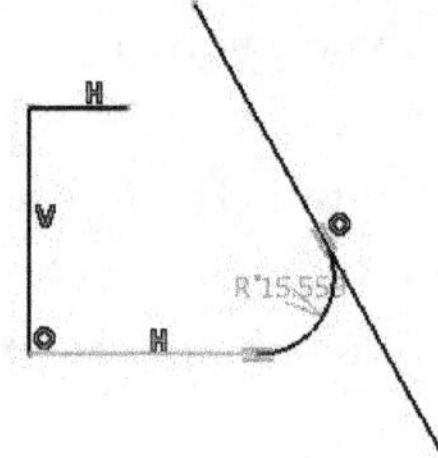

Use the **No Trim** option on the **Sketch tools** toolbar, if you do not want to trim or extend the elements as necessary.

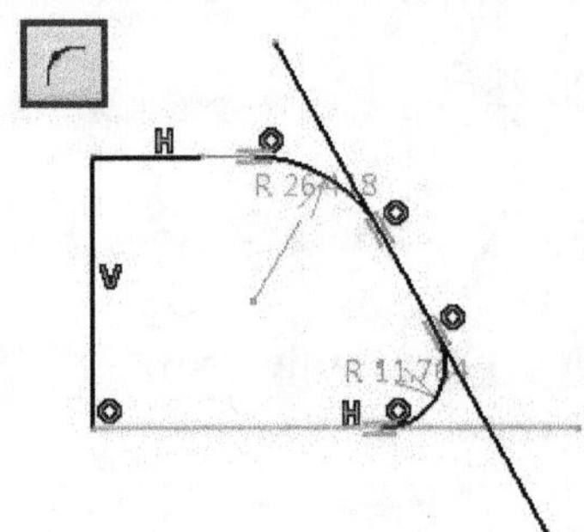

The other trim options are:

Standard Lines Trim

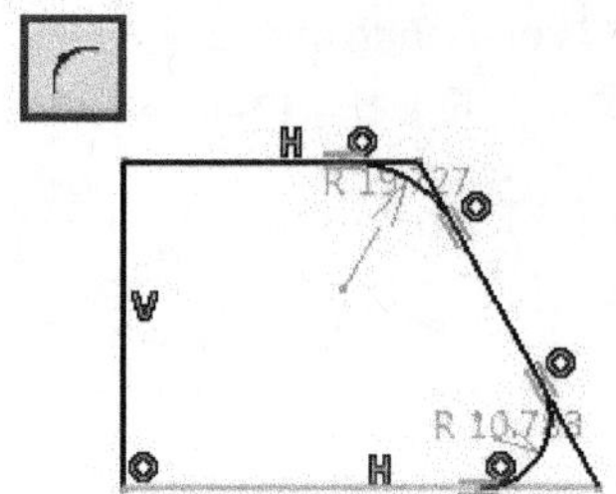

Construction Lines Trim

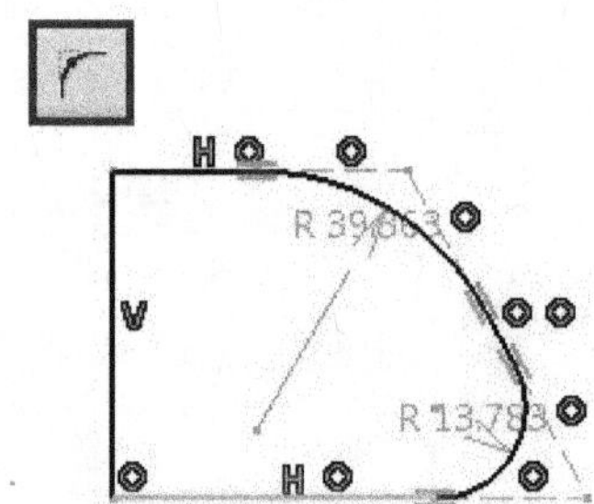

Construction Lines No Trim

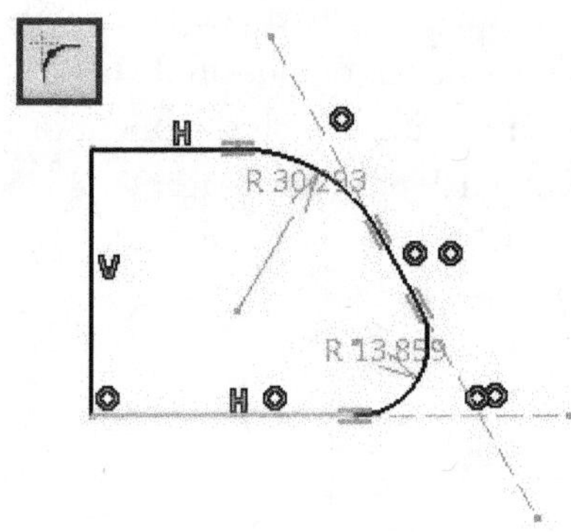

In CATIA V5, you can add fillets to multiple corners by dragging a selection box over all the corners to be filleted.

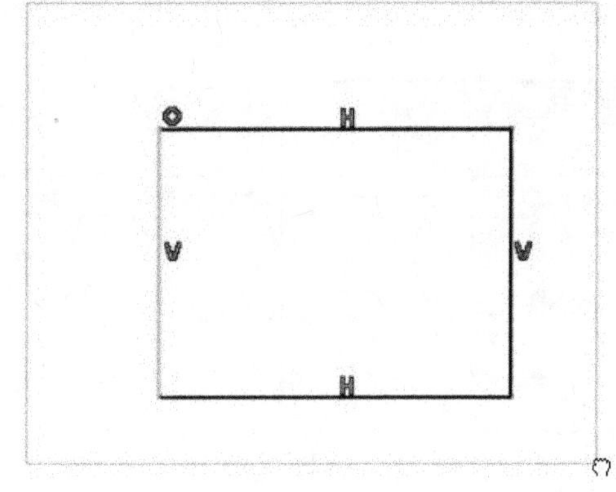

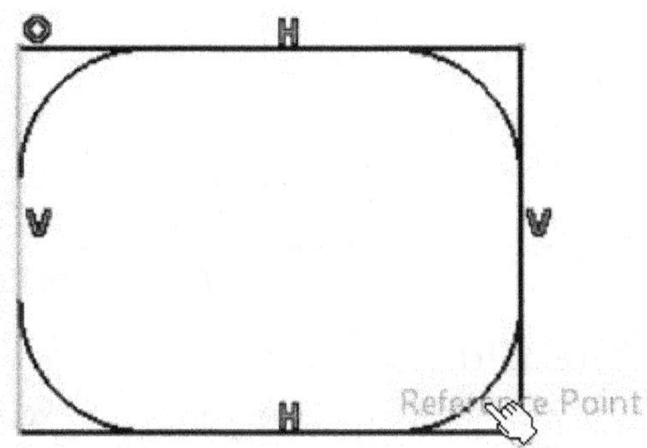

The Chamfer command

This command replaces a sharp corner with an angled line.

1. On the **Operations** toolbar, click the **Chamfer** icon.
2. Select the select the elements' ends to be chamfered.

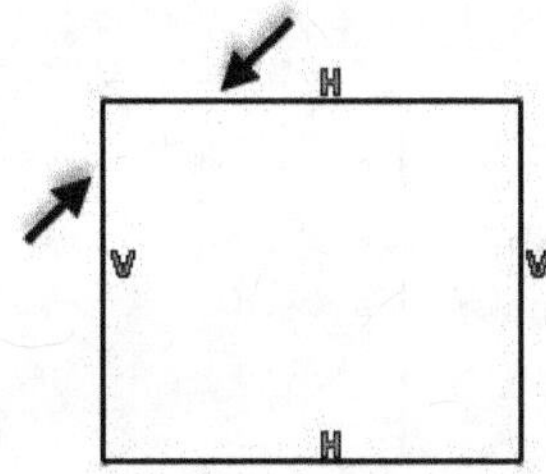

3. Type-in the chamfer angle and length in the **Angle** and **Length** boxes on the **Sketch Tools** toolbar, respectively.
4. Press Enter to create the chamfer.

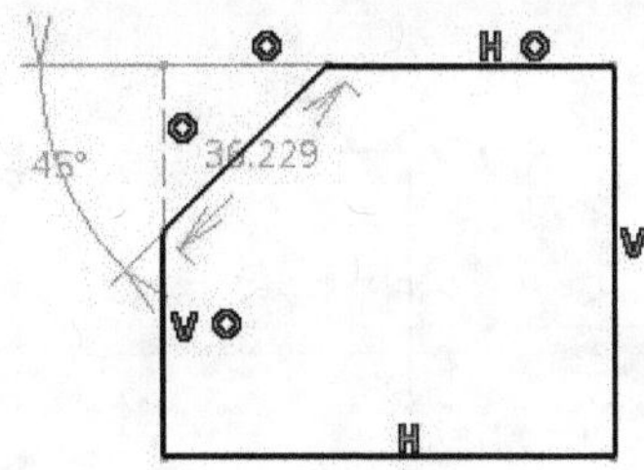

The Quick Trim command

This command trims the end of an element back to the intersection of another element.

1. On the **Operations** toolbar, click **Relimitations** drop-down > **Quick Trim**.
2. Click on the element to trim.

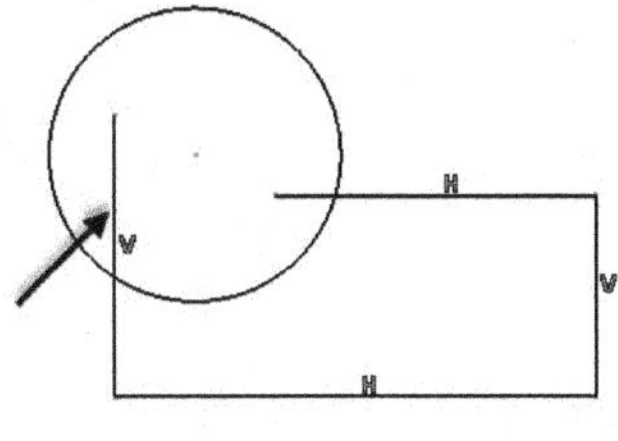

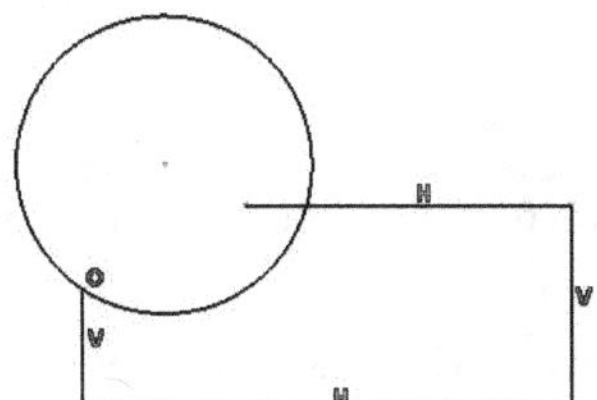

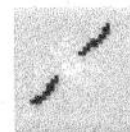

The Break command

This command breaks a sketch element at a selected point.

1. On the **Operations** toolbar, click **Relimitations** drop-down > **Break**.
2. Select the element to break.
3. Click to define the break point.

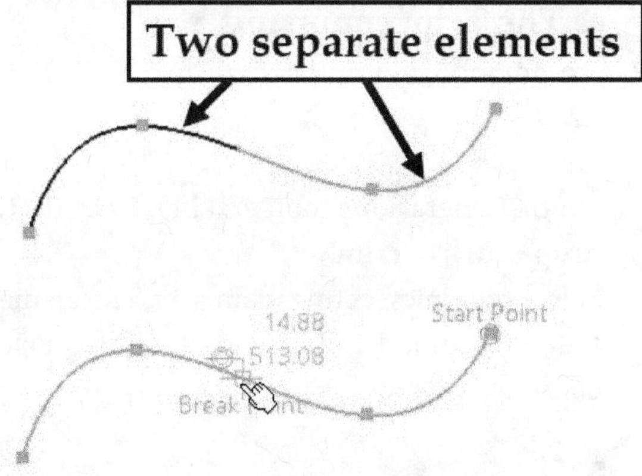

The Close Arc command

This command closes the open arc.

1. On the **Operations** toolbar, click **Relimitations** drop-down > **Close Arc**.
2. Click on an arc to convert it into a circle.

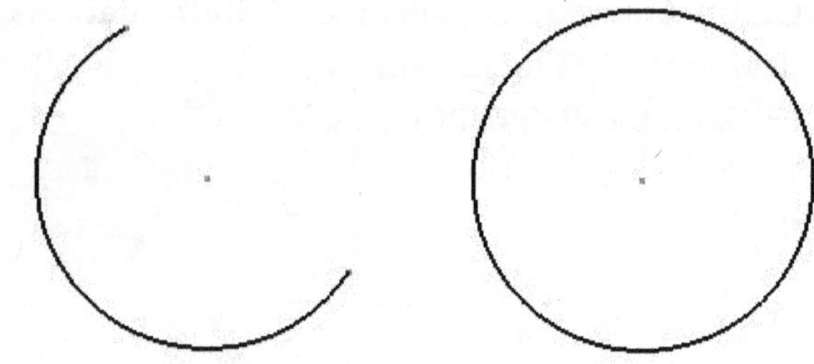

The Complement command

This command shows the complementary side of an arc.

1. On the **Operations** toolbar, click **Relimitations** drop-down > **Complement**.
2. Click on an arc to show the complementary side of it.

The Trim command

This command trims and extends elements to form a corner.

1. On the **Operations** toolbar, click **Relimitations** drop-down > **Trim**.
2. Select two intersecting elements. The elements will be trimmed and extended to form a closed corner.

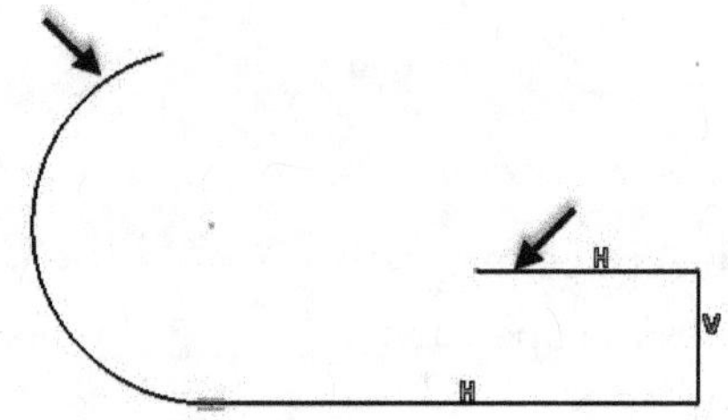

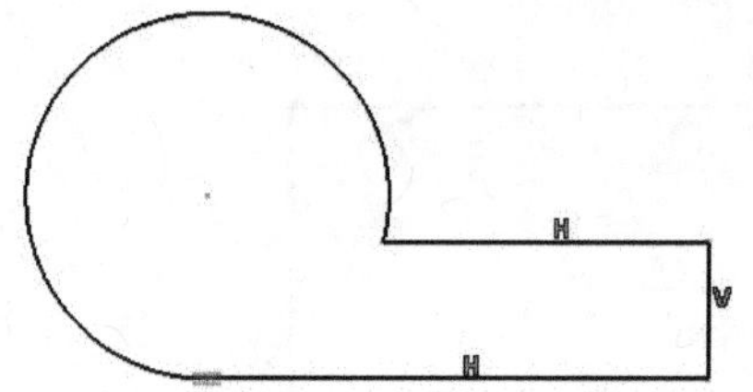

The Mirror command

This command creates a mirror copy of the selected sketch elements.

1. On the **Operations** toolbar, click **Transformation** drop-down > **Mirror**.
2. Drag a selection box and select the elements to mirror.

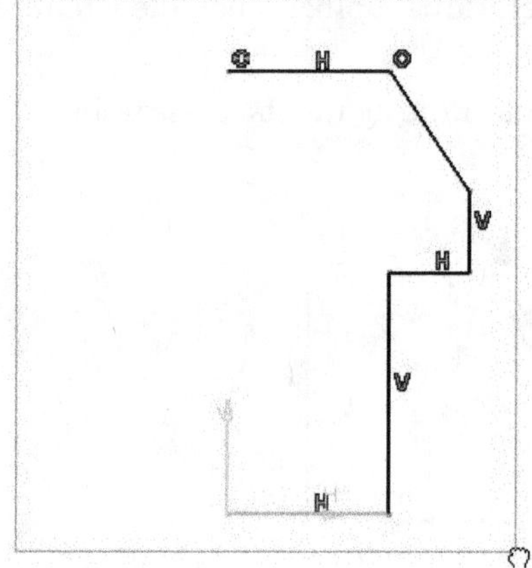

3. Click on a line or axis to define the mirror line.

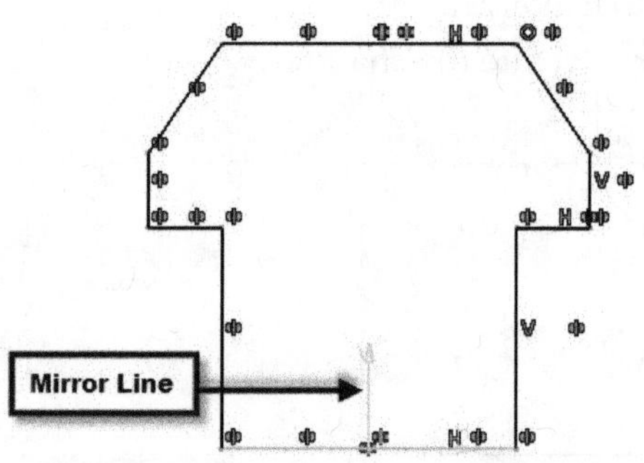

The Symmetry command

This command creates a mirror image of selected sketch elements without copying them.

1. On the **Operations** toolbar, click **Transformation** drop-down > **Symmetry**.
2. Click on the element to mirror (or) drag a selection box to select multiple elements at a time.
3. Click on the line or axis about which the element will be mirrored.

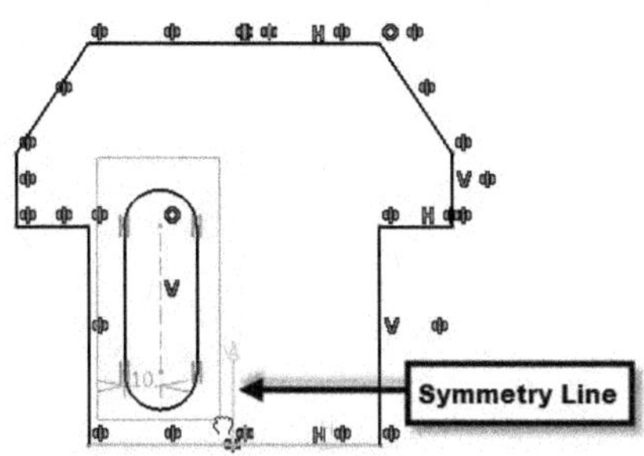

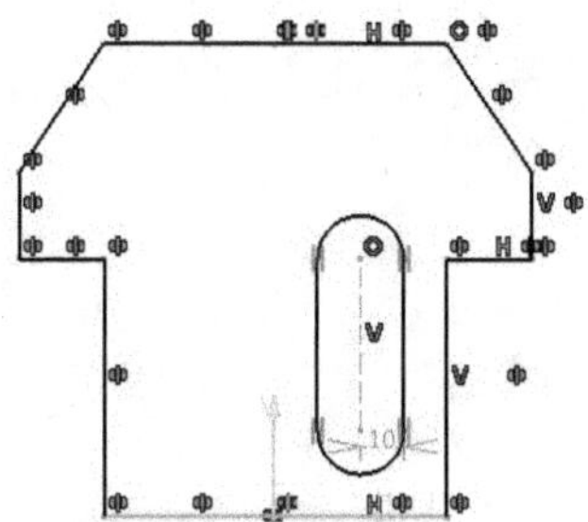

The Translate command

This command relocates one or more elements from one position in the sketch to any other position you specify.

1. On the **Operations** toolbar, click **Transformation** drop-down > **Translate**.
2. Click on the elements to translate.
3. Click to define the start point of the translation.

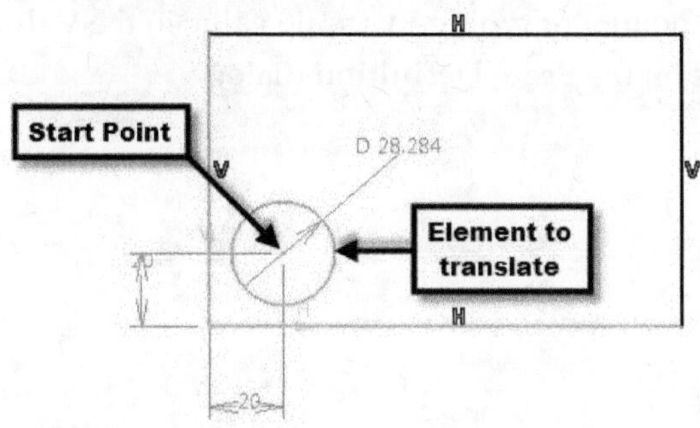

4. On the **Translation Definition** dialog, check the **Duplicate mode** if you want to copy and move the selected element(s). Next, type-in the number of instances to be created in the **Instance** box.

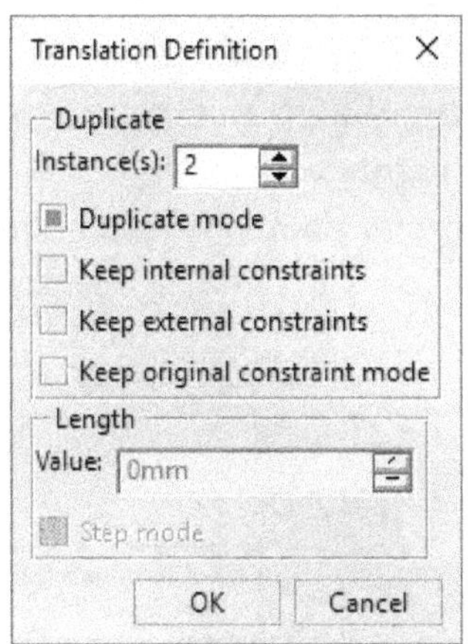

5. On the **Translation Definition** dialog, check the **Keep internal constraints** and **Keep external constraints** options to copy the constraints of the selected element as well. Check the **Keep original constraint mode** option, if you want to copy the element with it original constraints.
6. Move the pointer and click to define the translation distance (or) type-in a value in the **Value** box in the **Length** section of the **Translation Definition** dialog.

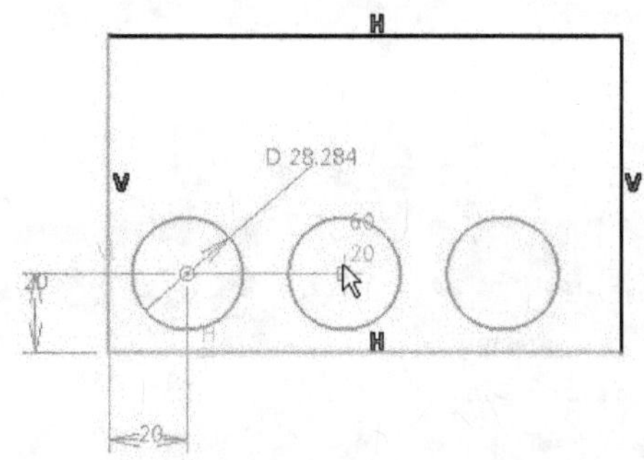

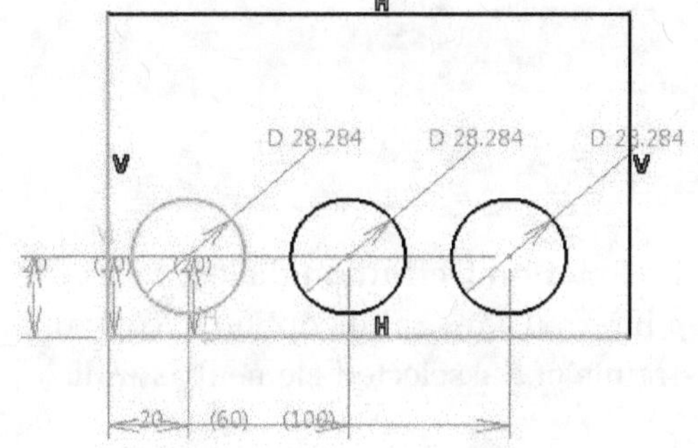

The Rotate command

This command rotates the selected elements to any position.

1. On the **Operations** toolbar, click **Transformation** drop-down > **Rotate**.
2. Select the elements to rotate.
3. Click to define the center point of the rotation.
4. Move the cursor and click to define a reference line for rotation angle.

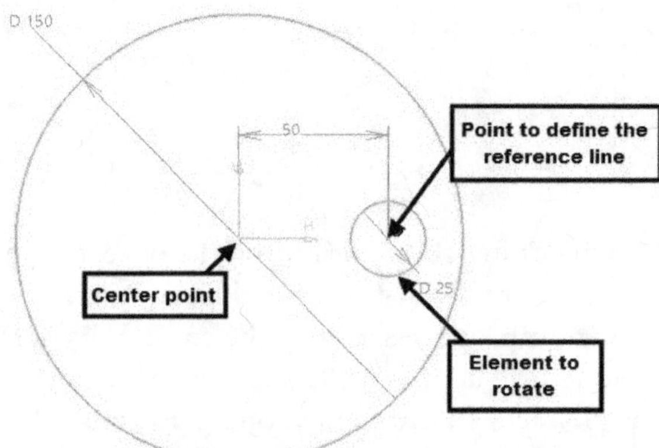

5. On the **Rotation Definition** dialog, check the **Duplicate mode** if you want to copy and rotate the selected element(s). Next, type-in the number of instances to be created in the **Instance** box.

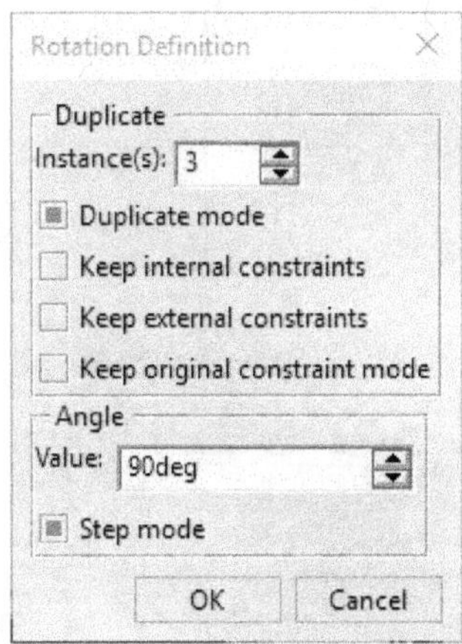

6. On the **Rotation Definition** dialog, check the **Keep internal constraints** option to copy the constraints of the selected element as well.
7. Move the pointer and click to define the rotation angle (or) type-in a value in the **Value** box on the **Rotation Definition** dialog.

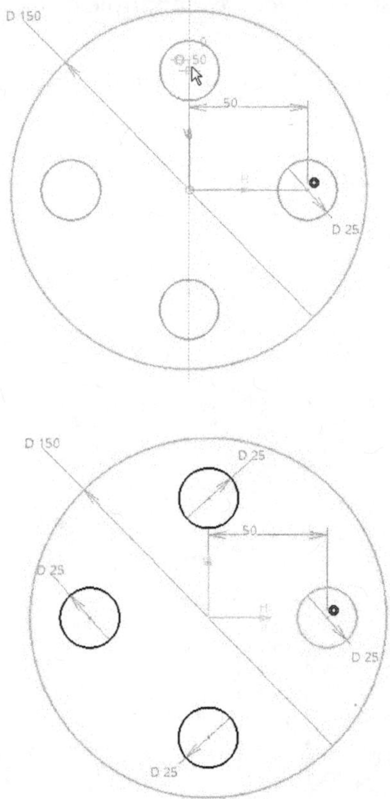

The Scale command

This command increases or decreases the size of elements in a sketch.

1. On the **Operations** toolbar, click **Transformation** drop-down > **Scale**.
2. Select the elements to scale.
3. Select a base point.
4. Scale the size of the selected elements by moving the pointer or typing-in a scale value in the **Value** box on the **Scale Definition** dialog.

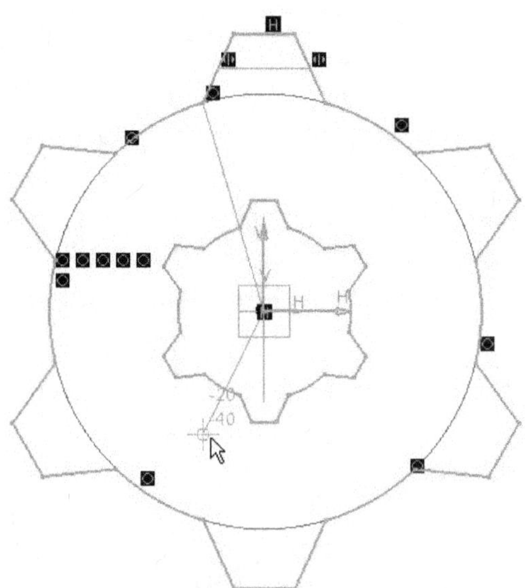

The Offset Curve command

This command creates a parallel copy of a selected element or chain of elements.

1. On the **Operations** toolbar, click **Transformation** drop-down **> Offset**.
2. Click on the sketch element to offset.

Use the **No Propagation** option on the **Sketch tools** toolbar to select a single element.

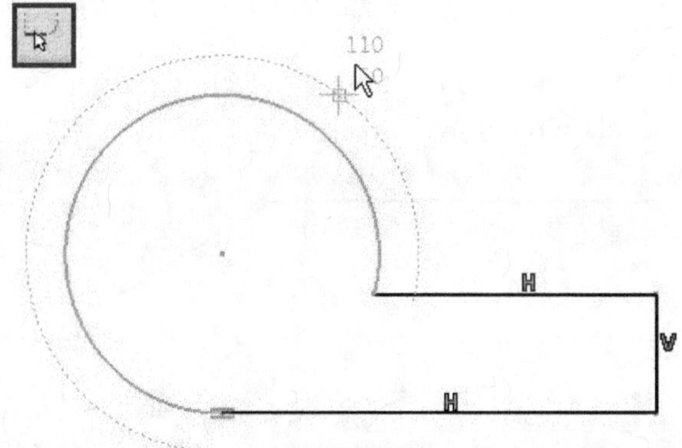

Use the **Tangent Propagation** option to select tangentially connected elements.

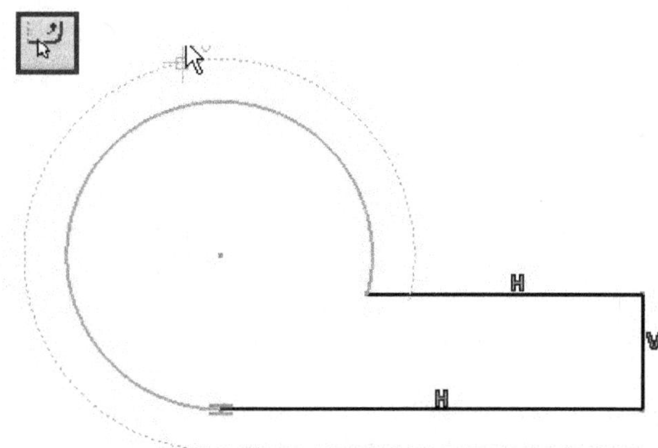

Use the **Point Propagation** option to select all the connected elements in a single click.

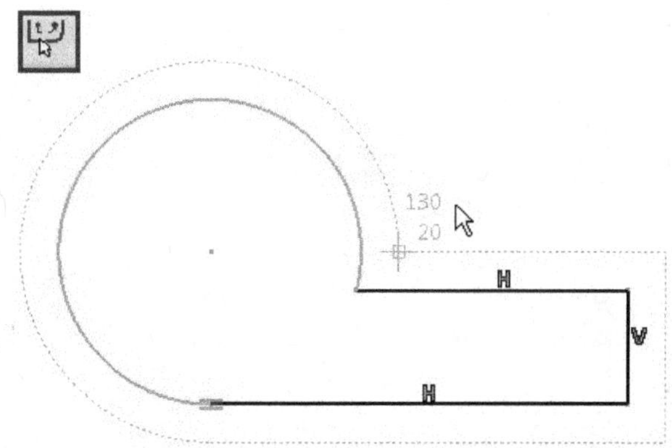

Use the **Both Sides** offset option to offset the sketch elements on both sides.

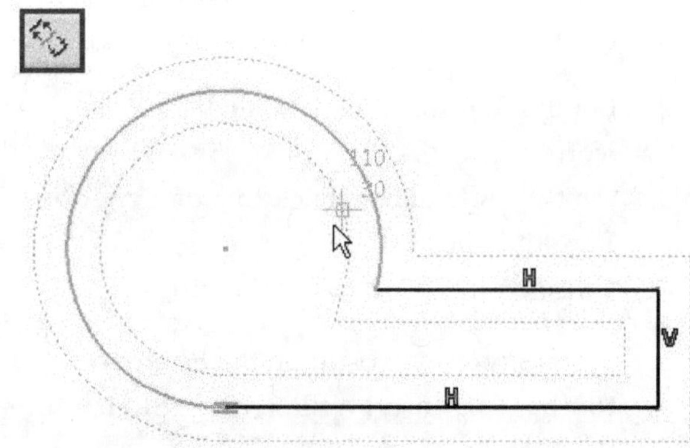

3. Type-in a value in the **Offset** box available on the **Sketch tools** toolbar.
4. If you want to create more than one offset copy, then type-in a value in the **Instance** box available on the **Sketch tools** toolbar.
5. Press Enter to create the offset copy.

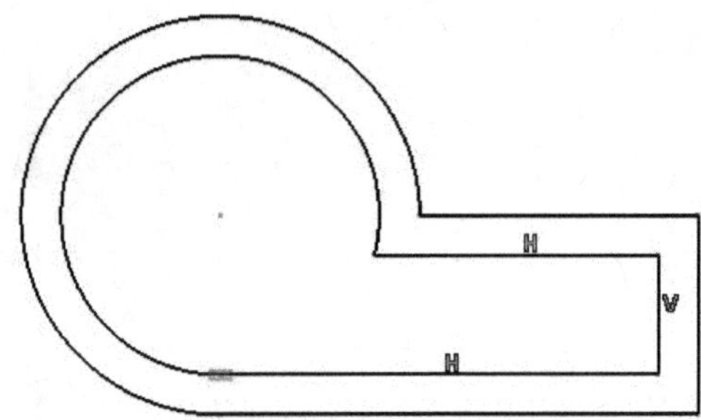

Examples

Example 1

In this example, you will draw the sketch shown below.

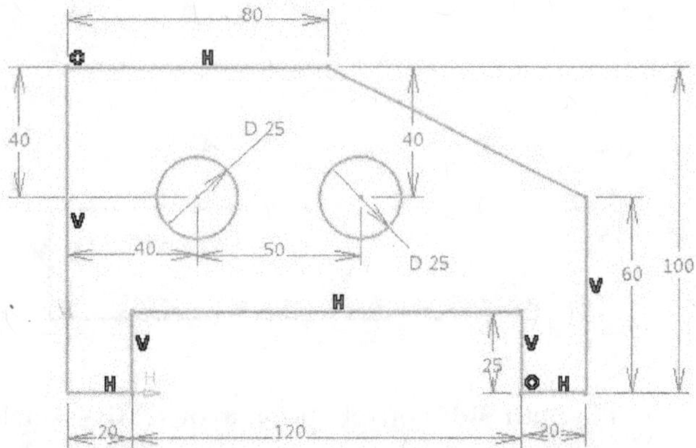

1. Start **CATIA V5-6R2017** by clicking the **CATIA V5-6R2017** icon on your desktop.
2. On the **Standard** toolbar, click the **New** icon.
3. On the **New** dialog, click **List of Types > Part** and click **OK**.
4. Click **OK** on the **New Part** dialog.
5. Click **Sketch** icon on the **Sketcher toolbar** (or) **Insert > Sketcher > Sketch** on the Menu.
6. Click on the YZ plane to start the sketch.

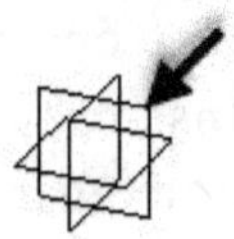

7. On the **Sketch tools** toolbar, deactivate the **Snap to Point** icon
8. On the **Profile** toolbar, click the **Profile** icon.
9. Click on the origin point to define the first point of the line.
10. Move the pointer rightwards and click.

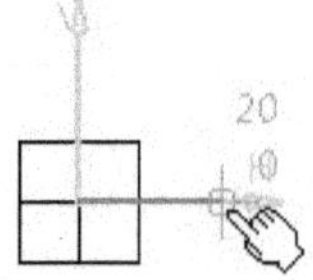

11. Move the pointer upwards and click.

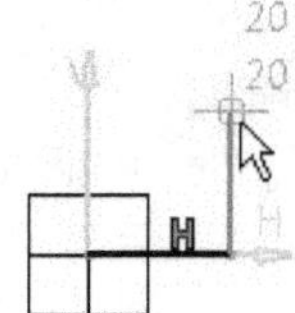

12. Move the pointer rightwards and click.

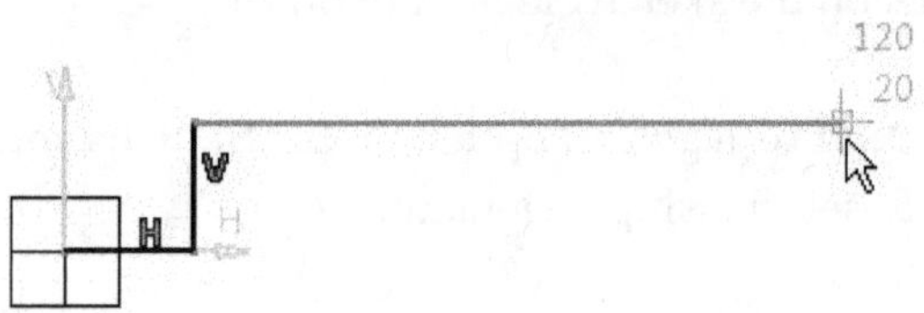

13. Create a closed loop by selecting points, as shown below.

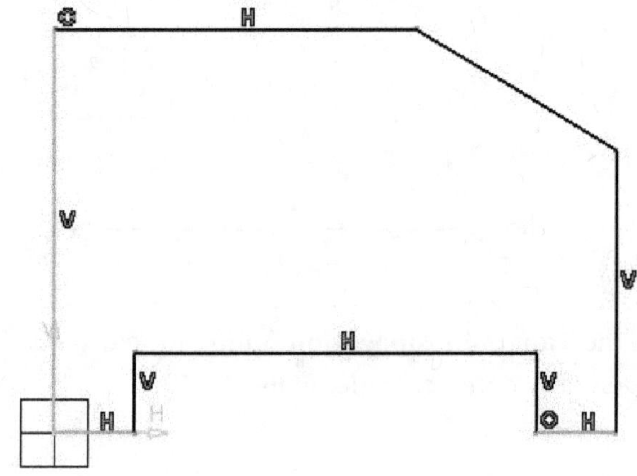

14. On the **Constraints** toolbar, click the down arrow next to the **Constraints** icon and select the **Contact Constraint** icon (or) **Insert > Constraint > Constraint Creation > Contact Constraint** on the Menu.
15. Click on the two horizontal lines at the bottom; they become collinear.

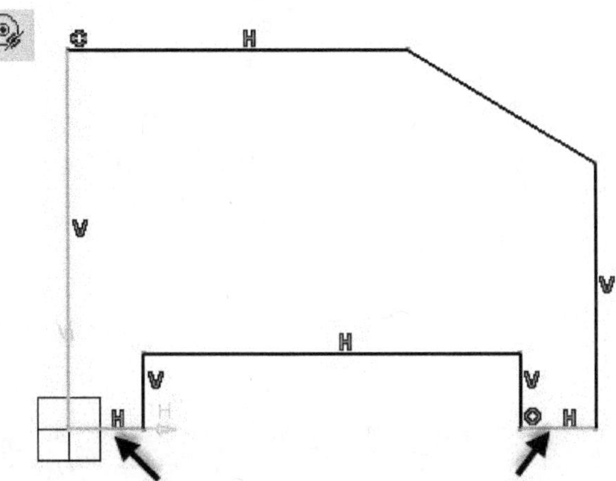

16. On the **Constraint** toolbar, double-click the **Constraint** icon and click on the lower horizontal line.
17. Move the pointer downward and click to position the dimension.

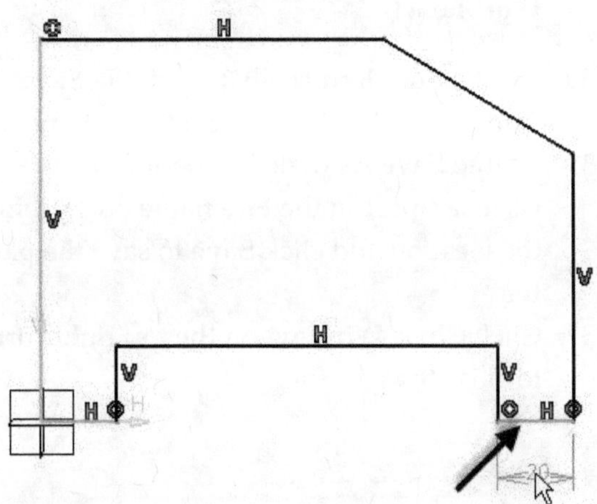

18. Click on the small vertical line.
19. Move the pointer and click to position the dimension.

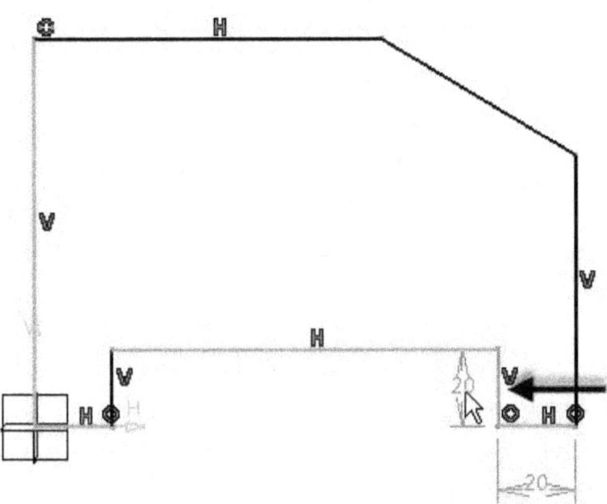

20. Likewise, create other dimensions, as shown below.

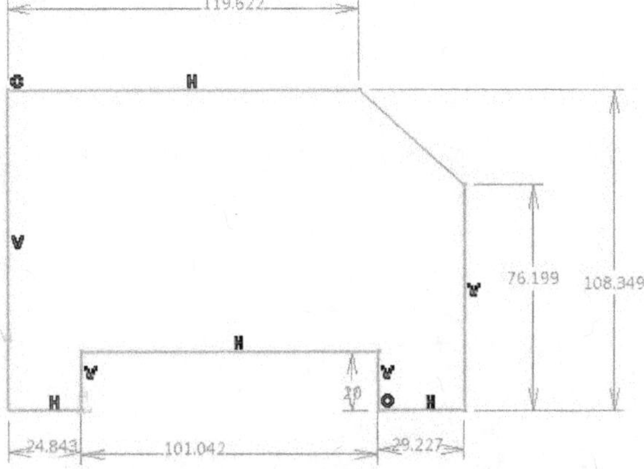

21. On the **Constraints** toolbar, click the **Edit Multi-Constraint** icon.
22. Click on the horizontal dimension, as shown in figure.

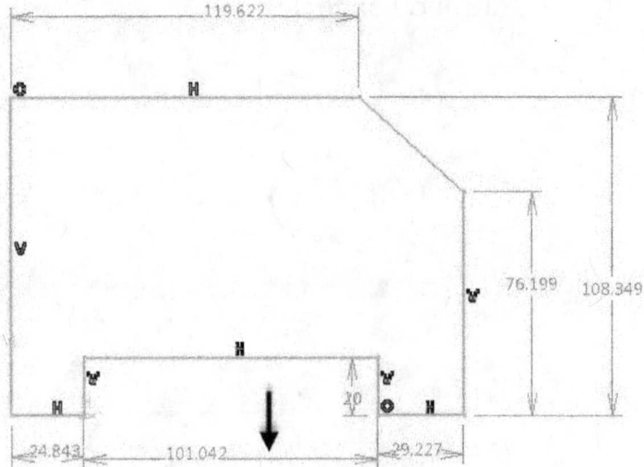

23. Type **120** in the **Current Value** box and click the **Preview** button.

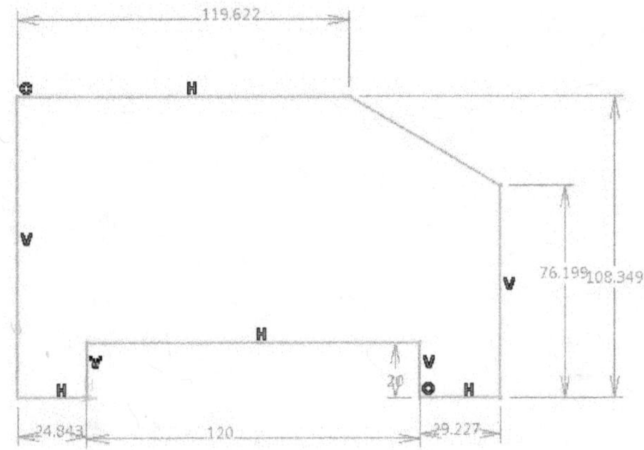

24. Likewise, change the other dimensional values. Click **OK** on the dialog.

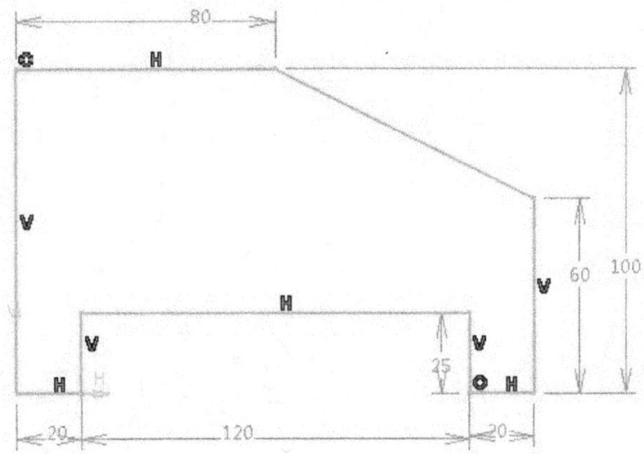

25. On the **Profile** toolbar, click **Circle** icon.
26. Click inside the sketch region to define the center point of the circle. Move the pointer and click to define the diameter. Likewise, create another circle.

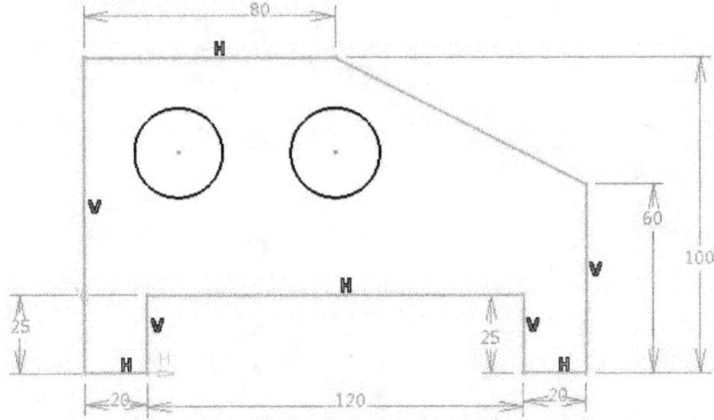

27. On the **Constraints** toolbar, click the **Constraints** icon and apply dimensions to fully constraint the circles.

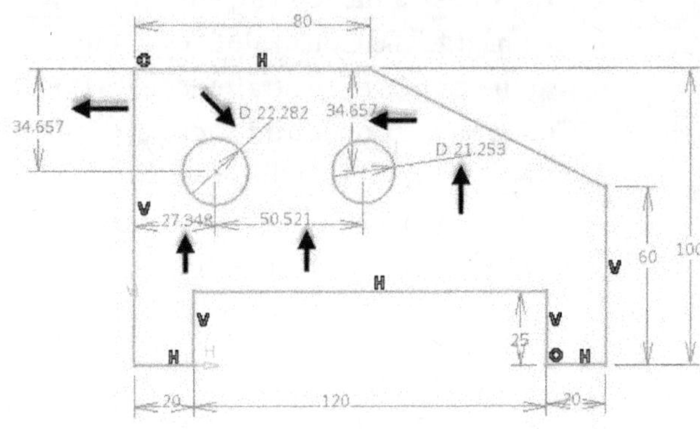

28. Activate the **Edit Multi-Constraint** command and modify the dimension values of the circles.

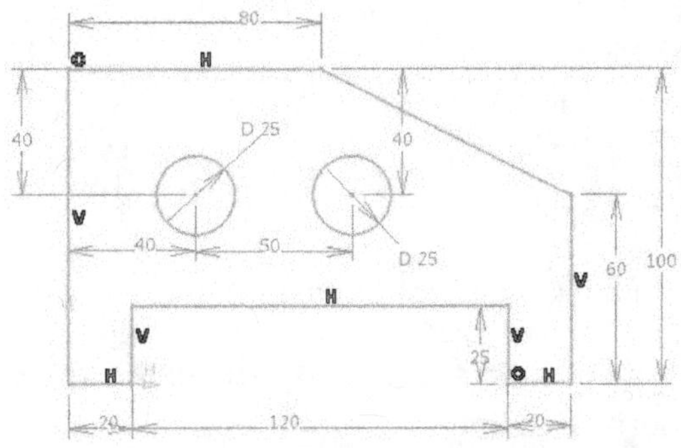

29. On the **Workbench** toolbar, click **Exit Workbench** .

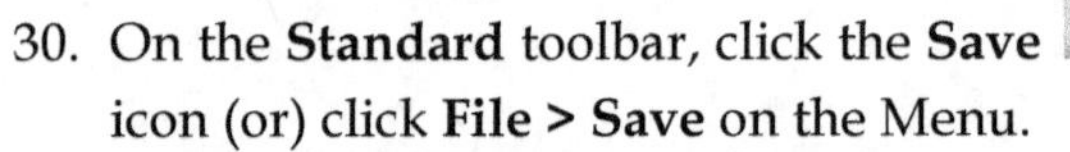

30. On the **Standard** toolbar, click the **Save** icon (or) click **File > Save** on the Menu.
31. On the **Save As** dialog, type-in **C2_example1** in the **File name** box. Define the location and click **Save** to save the part file.

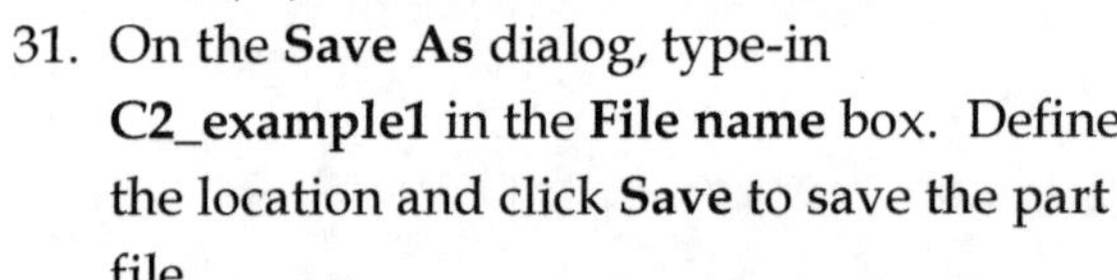

32. Click **Close Window** on the top right corner to close the part file.

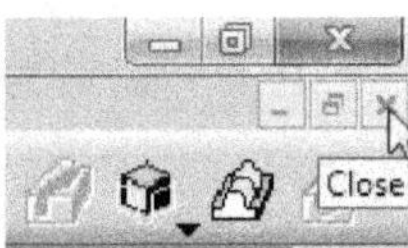

Example 2

In this example, you will draw the sketch shown below.

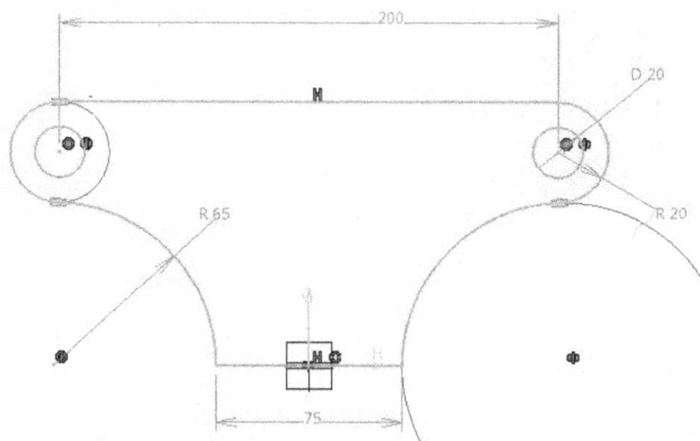

1. Start **CATIA V5-6R2017** by clicking the **CATIA V5-6R2017** icon on your desktop.
2. On the **Standard** toolbar, click the **New** icon.
3. On the **New** dialog, click **List of Types > Part** and click **OK**.
4. Click **OK** on the **New Part** dialog.
5. To start a new sketch, click the **Sketch** icon on the **Sketcher** toolbar.
6. Click on the XY Plane to start the sketch.

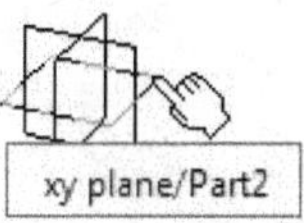

7. On the **Profile** toolbar, click the **Profile** icon.
8. Click in the second quadrant of the coordinate system to define the start point of the profile. Drag the pointer horizontally and click to define the endpoint.

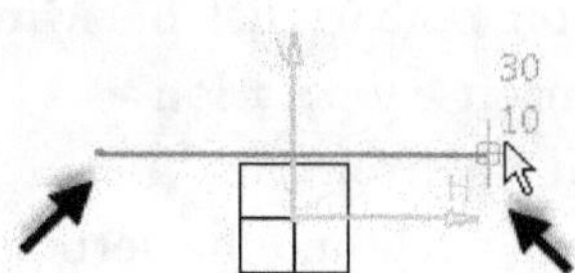

9. On the **Sketch tools** toolbar, click the **Three Point Arc** icon.
10. Move the pointer upwards right and click to define the second point of the arc.

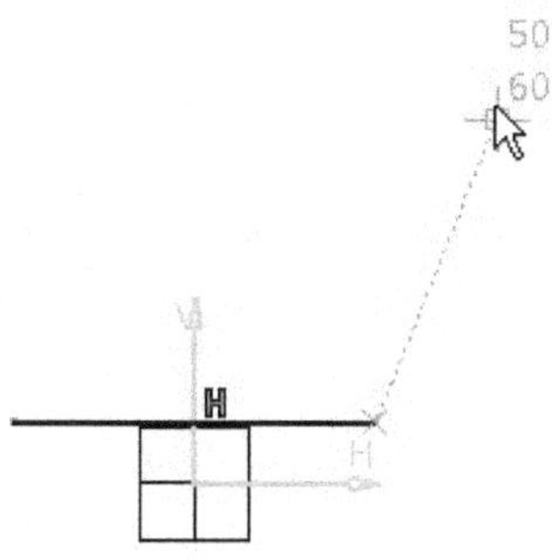

11. Move the pointer and click to define the third point of the arc, as shown.

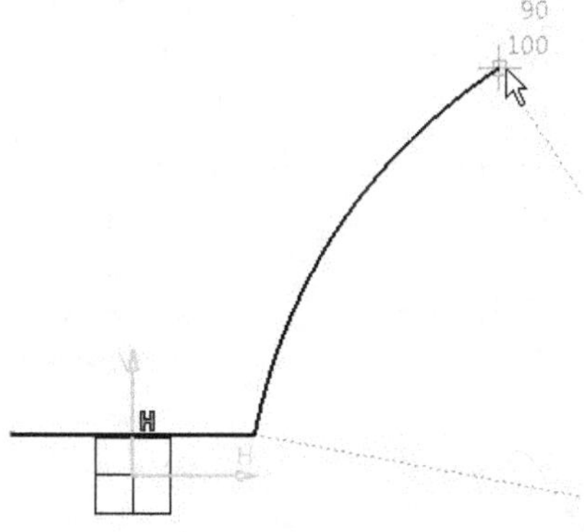

12. On the **Sketch tools** toolbar, click the **Tangent Arc** icon.
13. Move the pointer upwards and click to create an arc tangent to the previous arc.

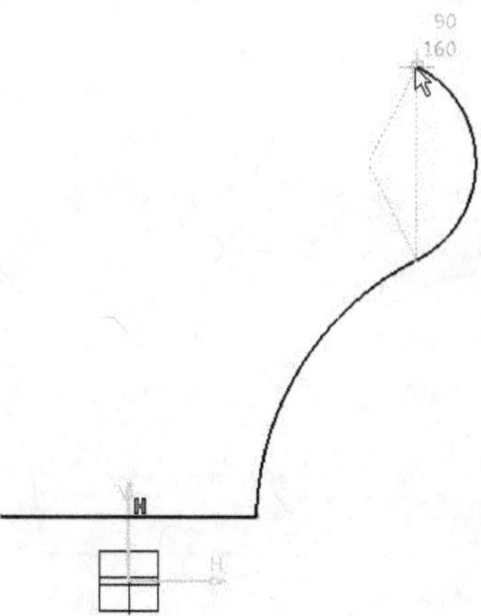

14. Move the pointer toward left and click to create a horizontal line.

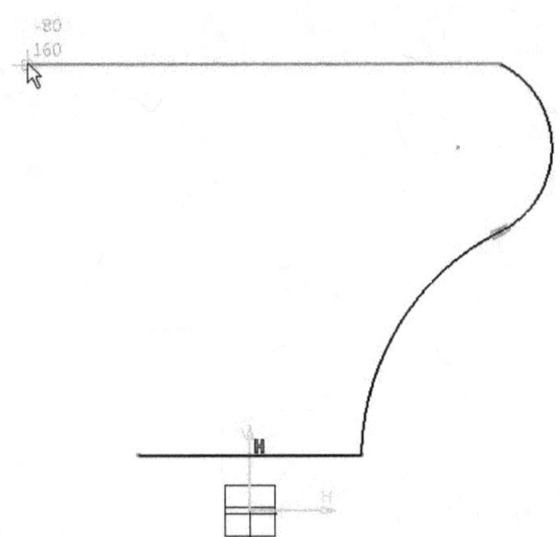

15. Click the **Tangent Arc** icon the **Sketch tools** toolbar.
16. Move the pointer downwards and click when a vertical dotted line appears, as shown below.

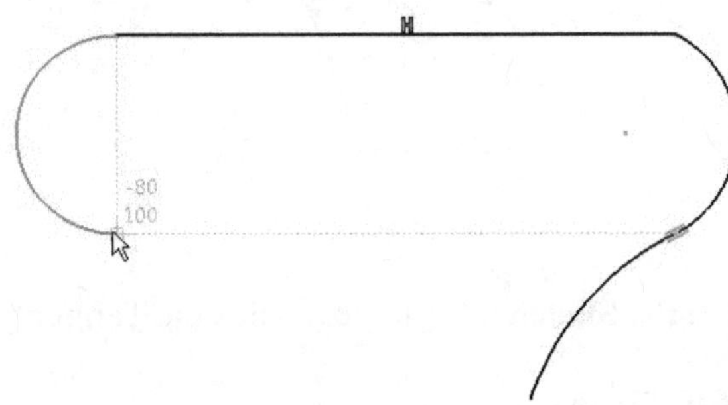

17. Click the **Tangent Arc** icon on the **Sketch tools** toolbar. Move the pointer downward right and click on the origin to close the sketch.

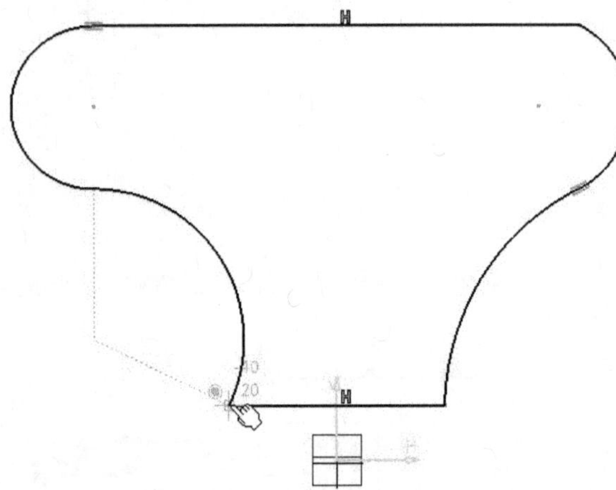

18. Press Esc to deactivate the **Profile** command.
19. Activate the **Circle** command and draw a circle on the right side.
20. Press the Ctrl key and click on the circle and the small arc.

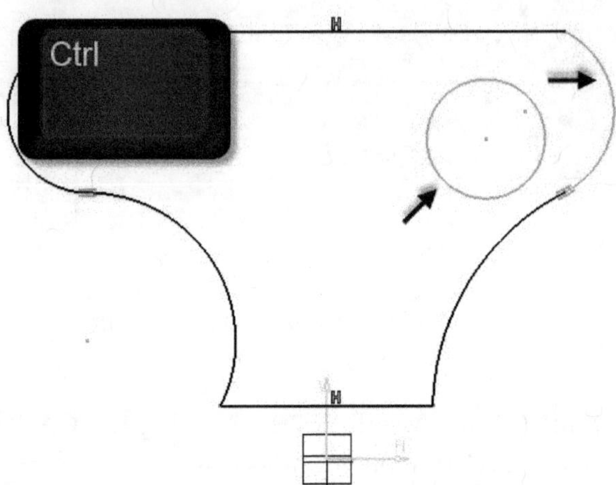

21. On the **Constraints** toolbar, click the **Constraints Defined in Dialog** icon.
22. On the **Constraints Definition** dialog, check the **Concentricity** option and click **OK**. The circle and arc are made concentric.

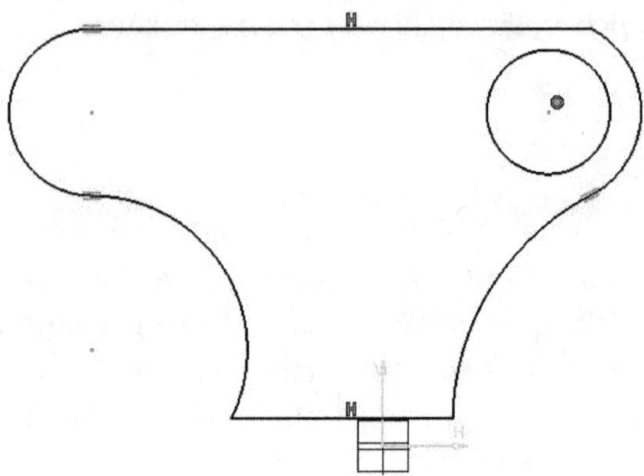

23. On the **Operation** toolbar, click the **Mirror** icon (or) click **Insert > Operation > Transformation > Mirror**.
24. Click on the small circle and the vertical axis. A mirror copy of the circle is created.

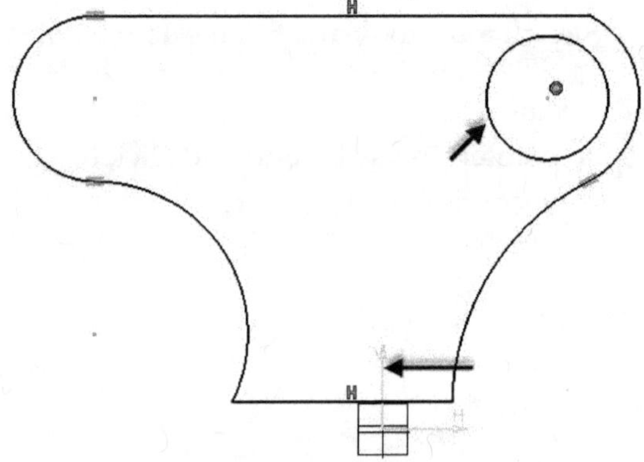

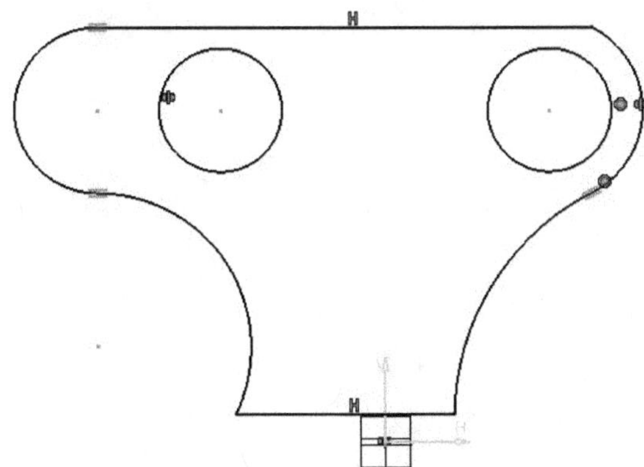

25. Apply the **Concentricity** constraint between the new circle and arc on left side.

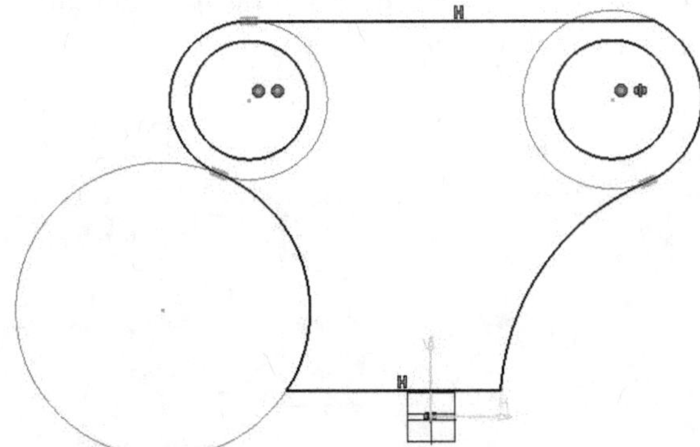

26. Press the Ctrl key and select the small arcs, and then click on the vertical axis.

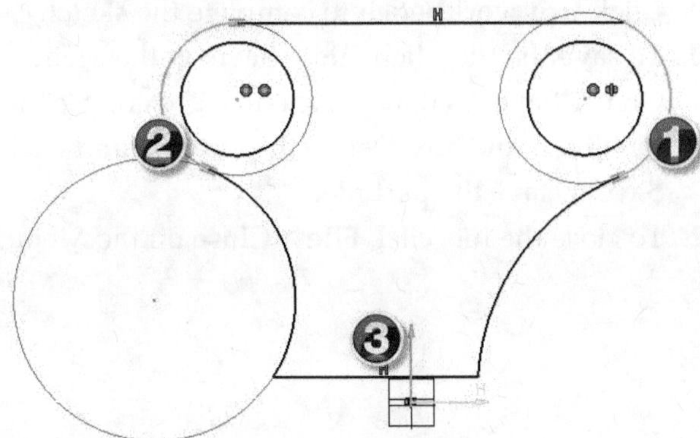

27. On the **Constraints** toolbar, click the **Constraints Defined in Dialog** icon.
28. On the **Constraints Definition** dialog, check the **Symmetry** option and click **OK**. The two arcs are made symmetric about the vertical axis.

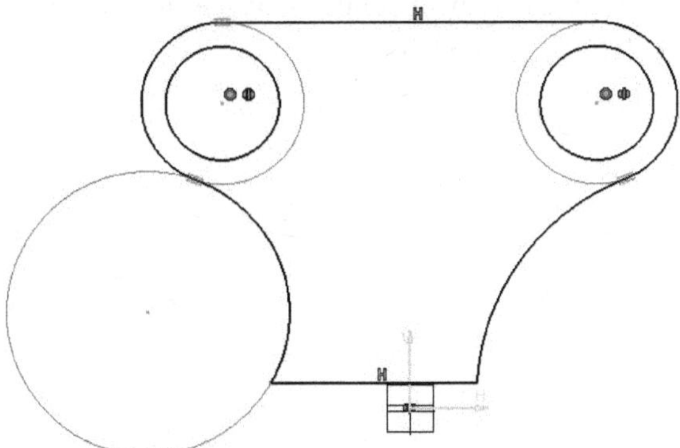

29. Likewise, make the large arcs symmetrical about the vertical axis.

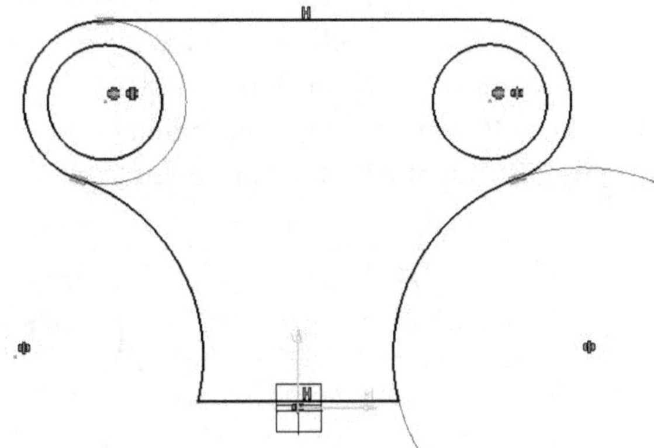

30. Press the Ctrl key and click the bottom horizontal line and the horizontal axis.
31. Activate the **Constraints Defined in Dialog** command and check the **Coincidence** option on the **Constraint Definition** dialog.
32. Click **OK** to make the horizontal line coincide with the horizontal axis.

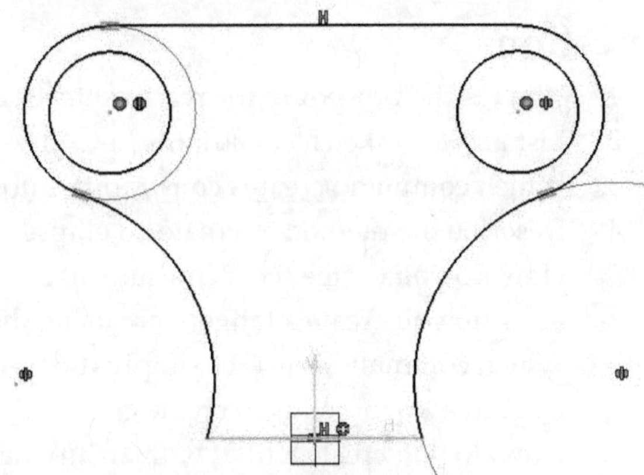

33. Press and hold the Ctrl key.

34. Click on the center point of the large arc and the horizontal line at the bottom.

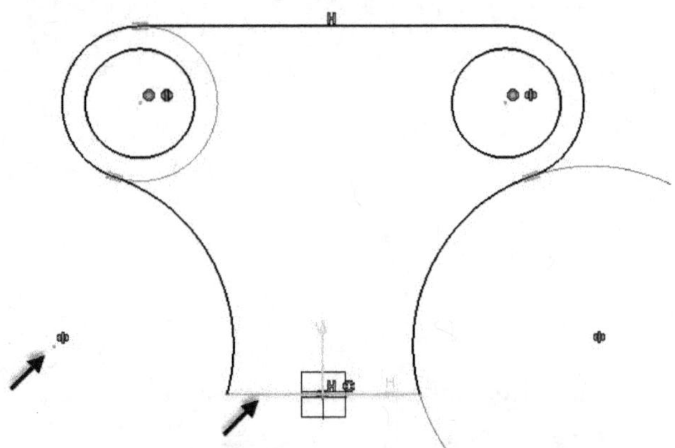

35. Activate the **Constraints Defined in Dialog** command and check the **Coincidence** option on the **Constraint Definition** dialog.
36. Click **OK** to make the center point of the large arc coincident with the horizontal line,

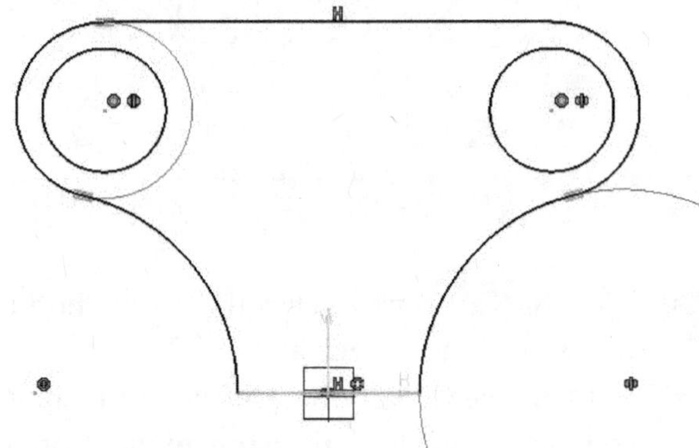

37. On the **Constraints** toolbar, double-click the **Constraints** icon and apply dimensions to the sketch, as shown below.

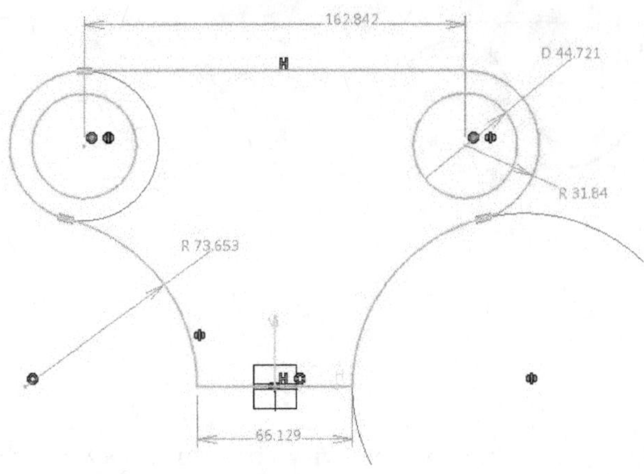

38. Activate the **Edit Multi-Constraint** command and change the dimensional values.

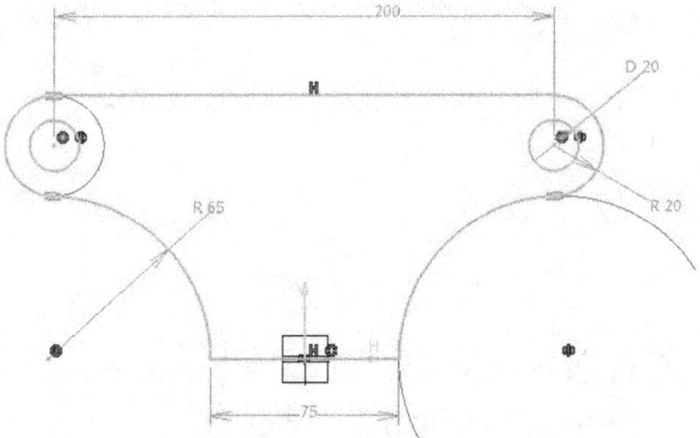

39. Click **Exit workbench** to complete the sketch.
40. To save the file, click **File > Save** on the Menu.
41. On the **Save As** dialog, type-in **C2_example2** in the **File name** box. Define the location and click **Save** to save the part file.
42. To close the file, click **File > Close** on the Menu.

Questions

1. What is the procedure to create sketches in CATIA V5?
2. List any two sketch constraints in CATIA V5.
3. Which command creates constraints automatically?
4. Describe the method to create an ellipse.
5. How do you define the shape and size of a sketch?
6. How do you create a tangent arc using the **Profile** command?
7. Which command is used to apply different types of dimensional constraints to a sketch?
8. List any two methods to create circles.
9. How do you create a fillet with an alternate solution?
10. What is the difference between the **Mirror** and **Symmetry** command?

Exercises

Exercise 1

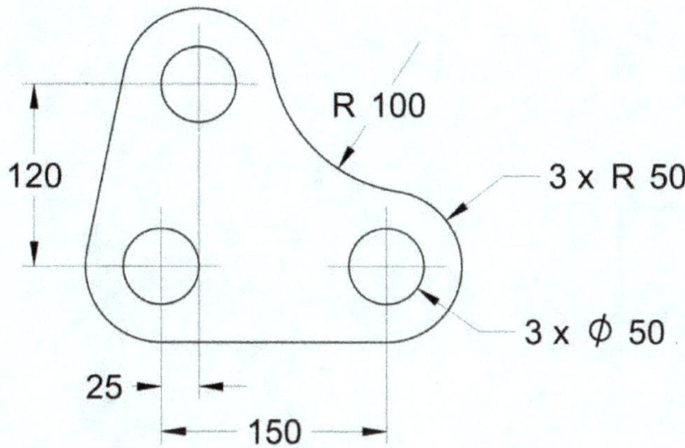

Exercise 2

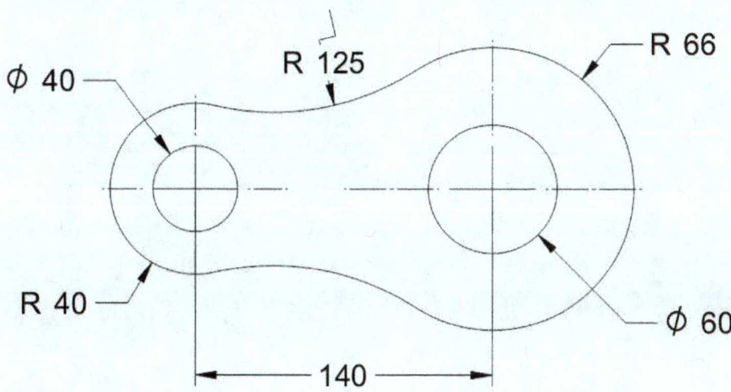

Exercise 3

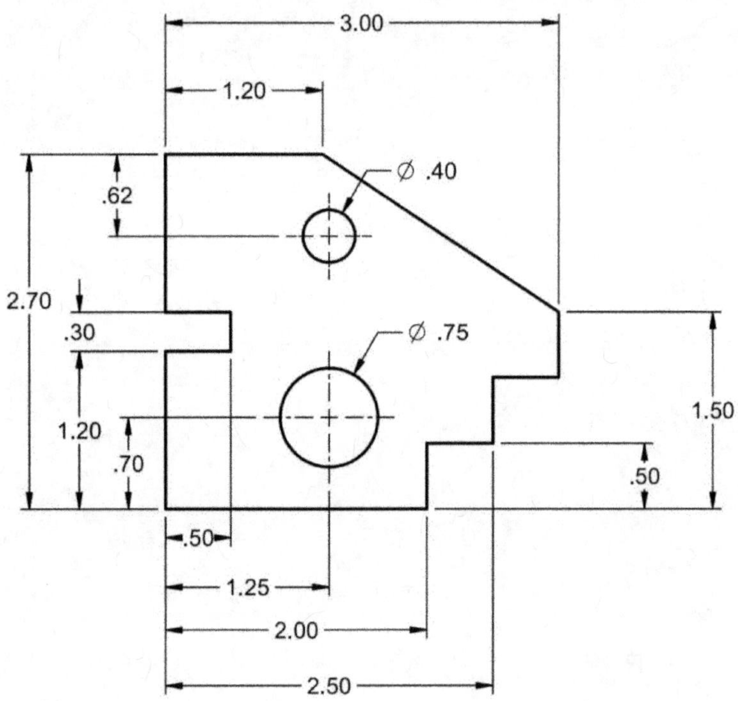

Chapter 3: Basic Sketch Based Features

Sketch-Based features are used to create basic and simple parts. Most of the times, they form the base for complex parts as well. These features are easy to create and require a single sketch. Now, you will learn the commands to create these features.

The topics covered in this chapter are:

- *Pad Features*
- *Shaft Feature*
- *Pocket Features*
- *Reference Planes*
- *More Options in the Pad and Shaft commands*
- *View commands*

 Pad

Pad is the process of taking a two-dimensional profile and converting it into 3D feature by giving it some thickness. A simple example of this would be taking a circle and converting it into a cylinder.

1. Once you have created a sketch profile or profiles you want to *Pad*, activate the **Pad** command (On the **Sketch-Based Features** toolbar, click **Pads** drop-down > **Pad** (or) click **Insert > Sketch-Based Features > Pad** on the Menu).
2. Click on the sketch profile to add thickness to it.

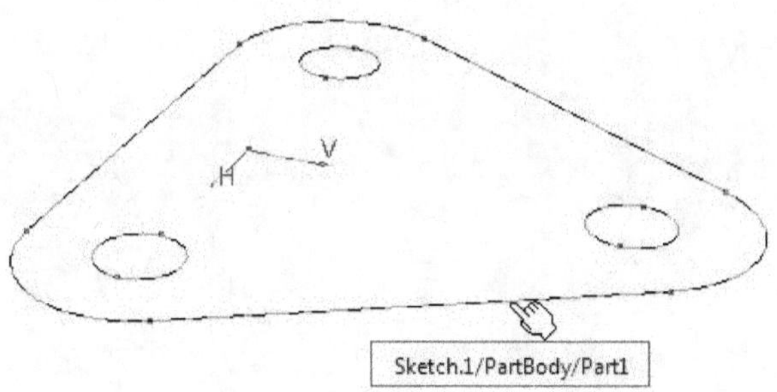

3. On the **Pad Definition** dialog, type-in a value in the **Length** box.

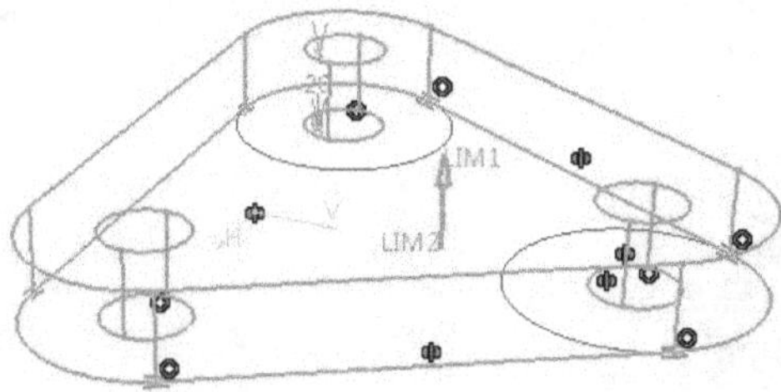

4. If you want to add equal thickness on both sides of the sketch, then check the **Mirror extent** option.
5. Click the **Preview** button to view how the model would look when completed.

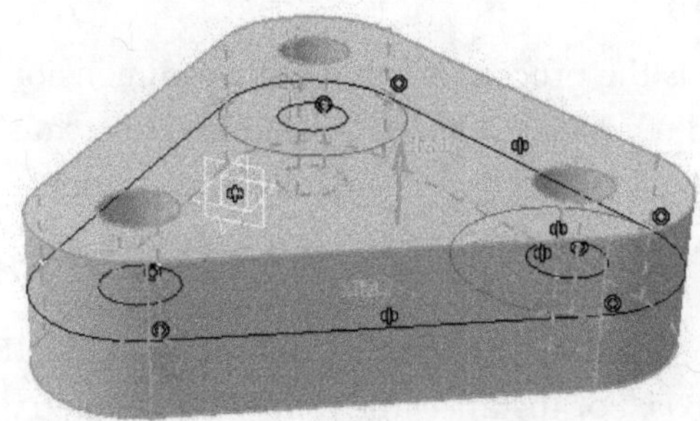

6. Click **OK** to complete the *Pad* feature.

While creating a *Pad* feature, CATIA adds material in the direction normal to the sketch.

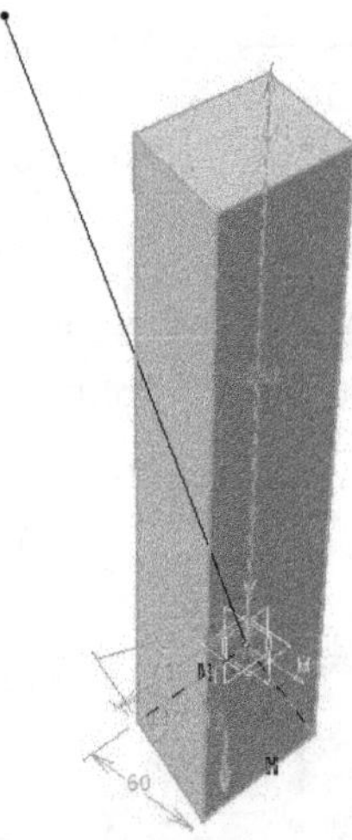

If you want to manually define the direction in which the material will be added, then click the **More** button on the **Pad Definition** dialog. Click in the **Reference** selection box and select a line.

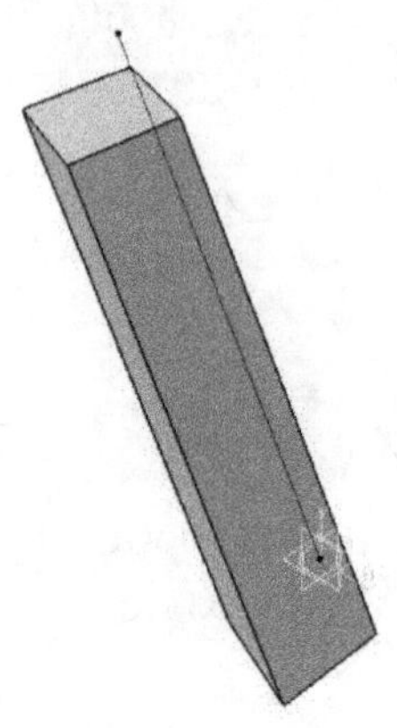

 Shaft

Revolving is the process of taking a two-dimensional profile and revolving it about a centerline to create a 3D geometry (shapes that are axially symmetric). While creating a sketch for the *Shaft* feature, it is important to think about the cross-sectional shape that will define the 3D geometry once it is revolved about an axis. For instance, the following geometry has a hole in the center.

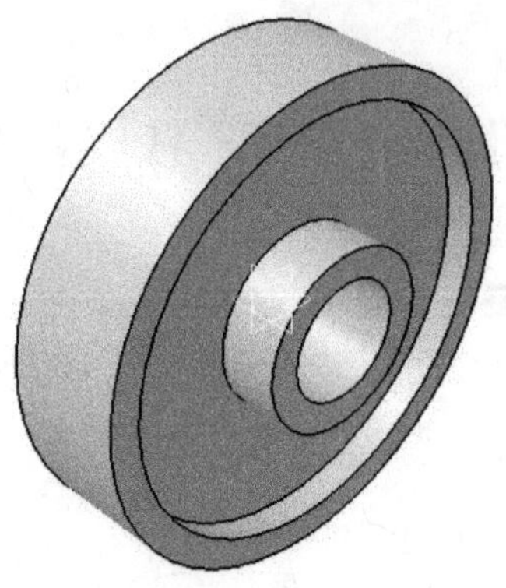

This could be created with a separate *Pocket* or *Hole* feature. But in order to make that hole part of the *Shaft* feature, you need to sketch the axis of revolution so that it leaves a space between the profile and the axis.

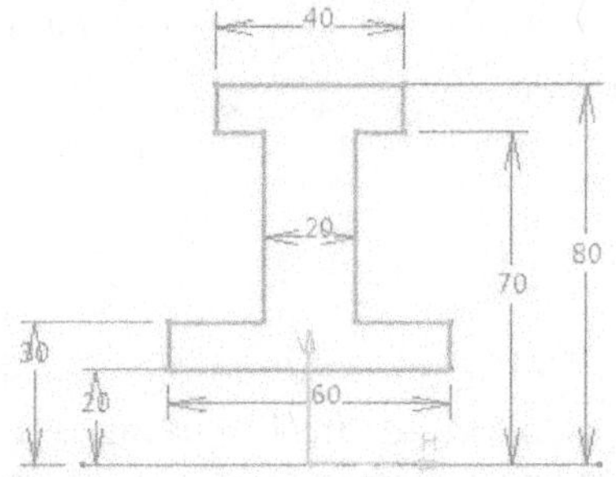

1. After completing the sketch, activate the **Shaft** command (On the **Profile** toolbar, click the Shaft icon (or) click **Insert > Sketch-Based Features > Shaft** on the Menu).
2. The sketch will be revolved by full 360 degrees.

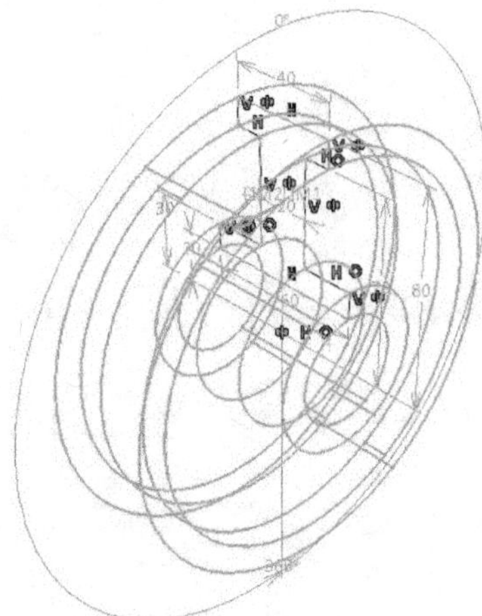

3. If you want to enter an angle of revolution, type-in a value in the **First Angle** box.

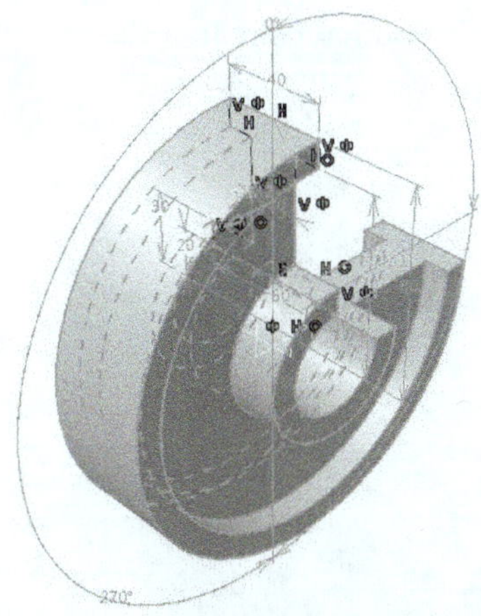

4. On the dialog, click **OK** to complete the *Shaft* feature.

Project 3D Elements

This command projects the edges of a 3D geometry onto a sketch plane.

1. Activate the Sketcher Workbench by selecting a plane or model face.
2. On the **Operations** toolbar, click **3D Geometry** drop-down > **Project 3D Elements** (or) click **Insert > Operations > 3D Geometry > Project 3D Elements** on the Menu.
3. Click on the edges of the model geometry to project them on to the sketch plane.
4. Click **OK** on the **Projection** dialog.

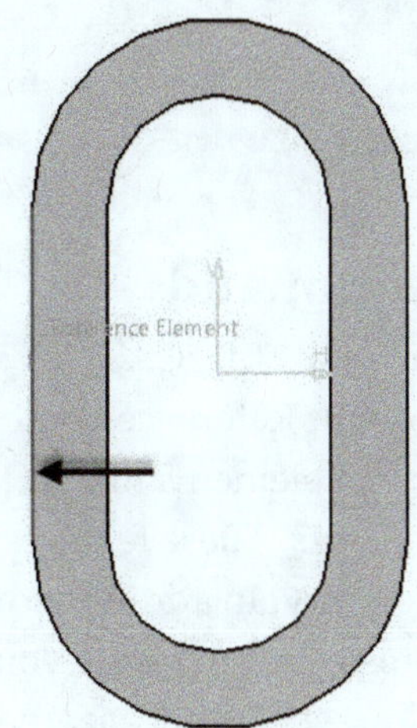

The projected element will be yellow in color and fully constrained. If you want to convert it into a normal sketch element, then right click on it and select **Mark.object > Isolate**.

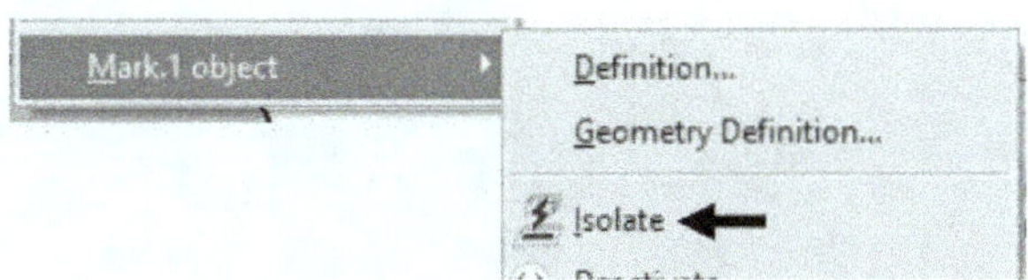

5. Complete the sketch and exit the workbench.

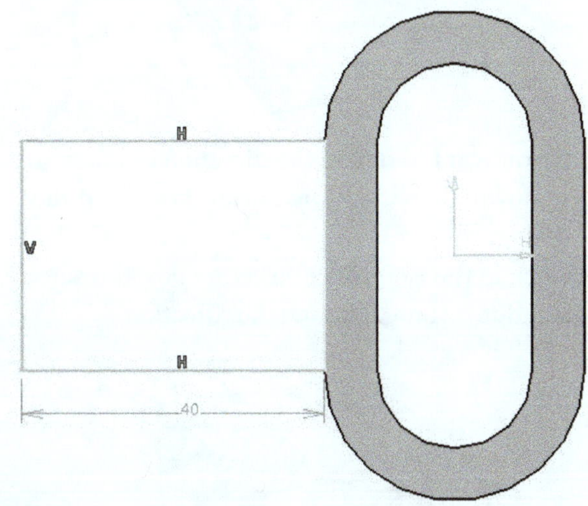

The Pocket command

This command removes material from the geometry by extruding a sketch. It functions on the same lines of the **Pad** command.

1. Draw a sketch on a plane or a model face.
2. On the **Sketch-Based Features** toolbar, click the **Pocket** icon (or) click **Insert > Sketch-Based Features > Pocket** on the Menu.
3. Select the sketch.

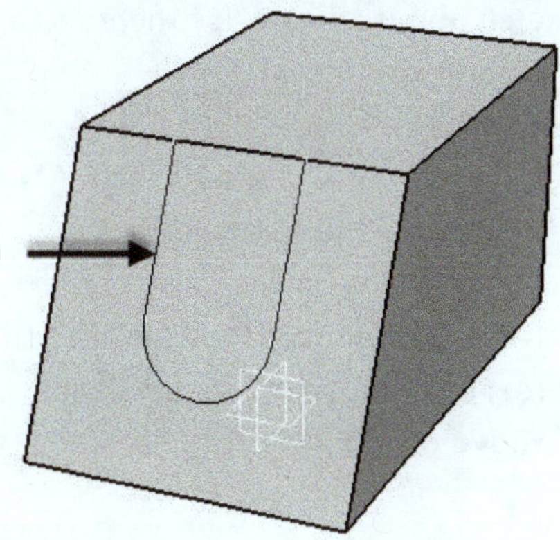

4. On the **Pocket Definition** dialog, type-in a value in the **Depth** box and click **Preview**.

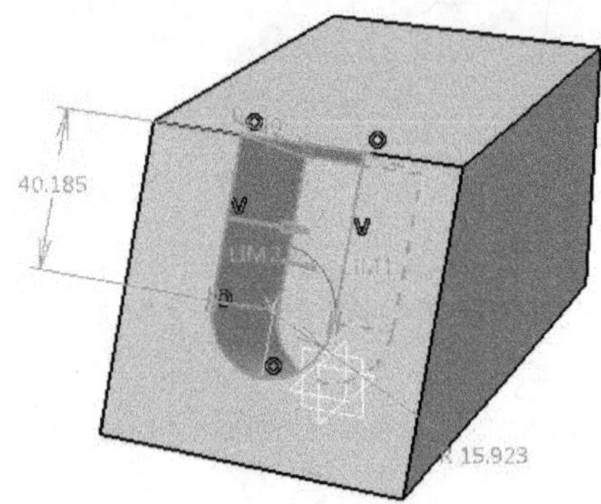

5. If you want to define the direction of material removal, then the **More** button to expand the dialog.
6. Click in the **Reference** selection box and select an edge or line to define the direction.

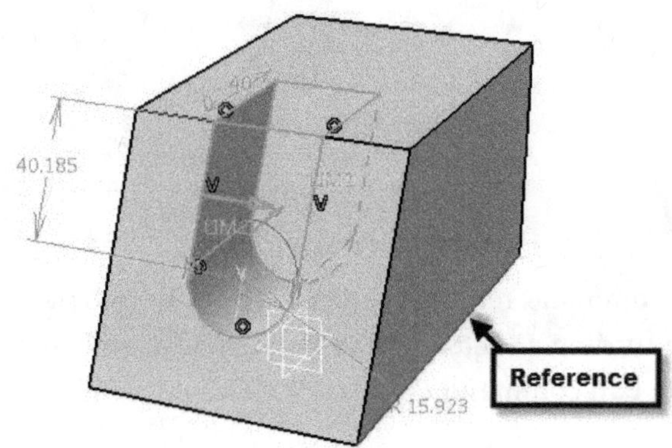

7. Click **OK** to complete the pocket feature.

 The Groove command

This command removes material from the geometry by revolving a sketch about an axis. It functions in a way similar to the **Shaft** command.

1. Draw a sketch on a plane or a model face. Also, draw a centerline using the **Centerline** command.
2. On the **Sketch-Based Features** toolbar, click the **Groove** icon (or) click **Insert > Sketch-Based Features > Groove** on the Menu.
3. Select the sketch. If you have created the centerline, then groove will be created automatically.

4. On the **Groove Definition** dialog, type-in values in the **First angle** and **Second angle** boxes.
5. Click **OK** to complete the groove feature.

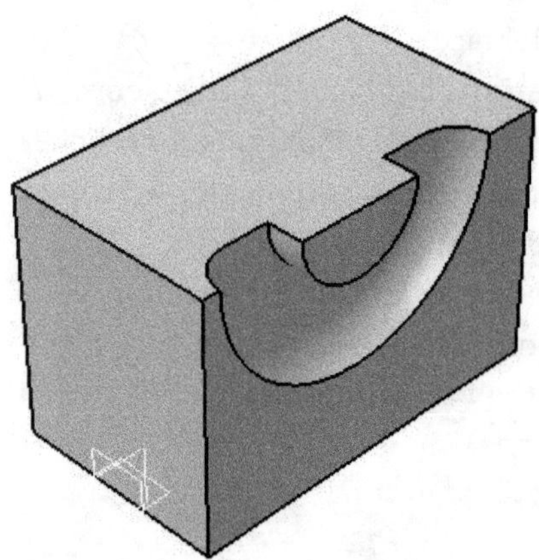

 The Plane command

Each time you start a new part file, CATIA V5 automatically creates default Reference planes. Planes are a specific type of elements in CATIA V5, known as Reference Elements. These features act as supports to your 3D geometry. In addition to the default Reference features, you can create your own additional planes. Until now, you have learned to create sketches on any of the default reference planes (XY, YZ, and XZ planes). If you want to create sketches and geometry at locations other than default reference planes, you can create new reference planes manually. You can do this by using the **Plane** command.

Offset from plane

This method creates a reference plane, which will be parallel to a face or another plane.

1. Activate the **Plane** command (On the **Reference Elements** toolbar, click the **Plane**).
2. On the **Plane Definition** dialog, select **Plane type > Offset from plane**.

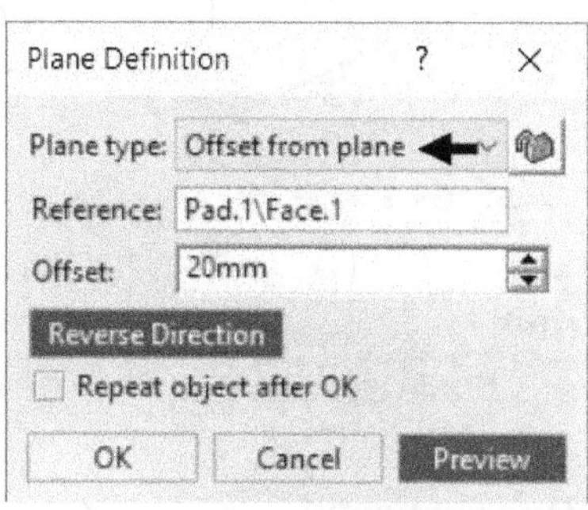

3. Select flat face.

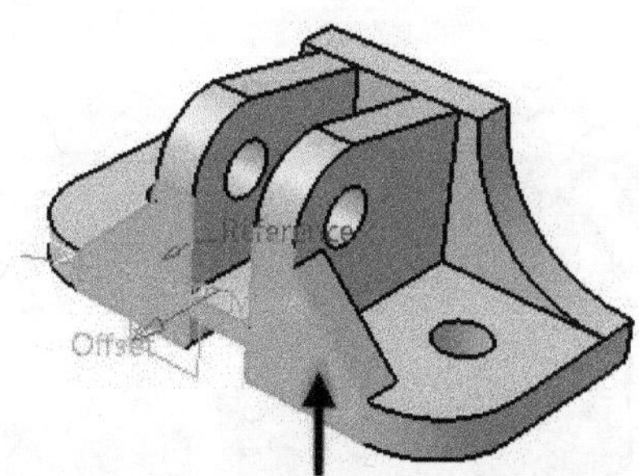

4. Drag the Offset arrow that appears on the plane (or) type-in a value in the **Offset** box to define the offset distance.
5. On the dialog, you can click the **Reverse Direction** button to flip the plane to other side of the model face.
6. If you want to create more than one offset plane, then check the **Repeat object after OK** option and click **OK**.
7. On the **Object Repetion** dialog, type-in a value in the **Instance (s)** box.
8. Check the **Create a new body** option, if you want to create the repeated planes as a separate body.

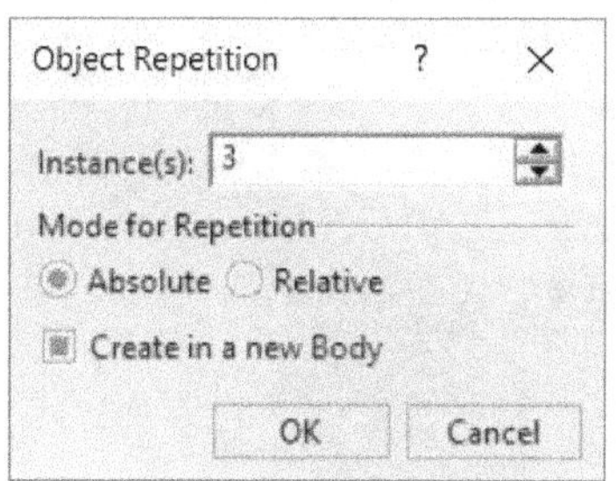

9. Click **OK** to create

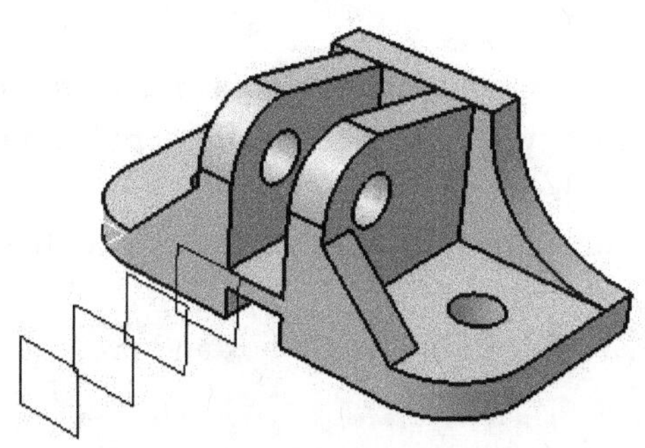

Parallel through Point

This method creates a plane parallel to a flat face at a selected point.

1. Activate the **Plane** command.
2. On the **Plane Definition** dialog, select **Plane type > Parallel through point,** and then select a flat face.
3. Select a point to define the parallel plane location.

Angle/Normal to plane

This method creates a plane, which will be positioned at an angle to a face or plane.

1. Activate the **Plane** command.

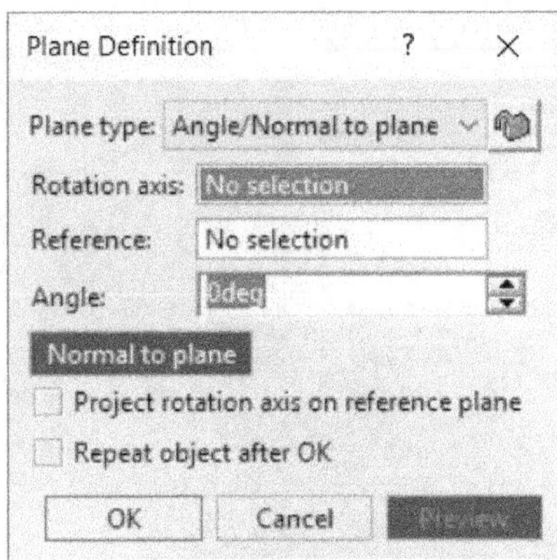

2. Select a flat face or plane to define the reference.
3. Select **Plane type > Angle/Normal to plane** on the **Plane Definition** dialog.
4. Click on an edge of the part geometry to define the rotation axis.
5. Type-in a value in the **Angle** box and press Enter.

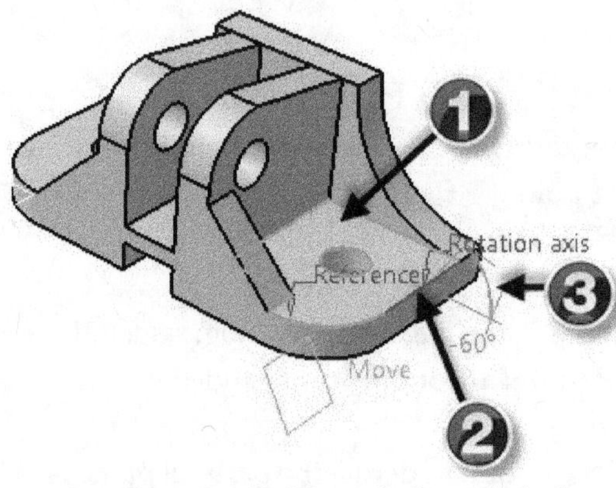

6. On the **Plane Definition** dialog, click the **Normal to plane** button to create a plane normal to the reference.
7. Click **OK**.

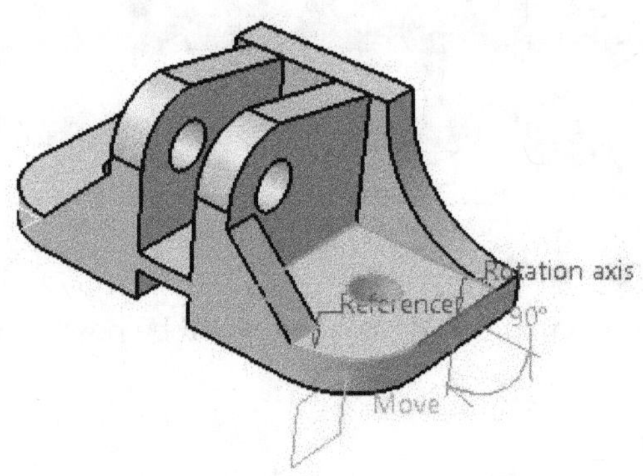

Through three points

This method creates a plane by selecting three points.

1. Activate the **Plane** command.
2. Select three points from the model geometry.
3. Click **OK** to create a plane passing through the points.

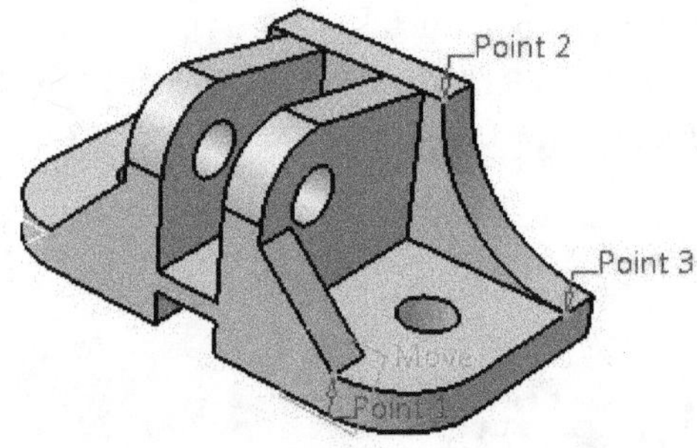

Through two lines

This method creates a plane by selecting two lines.

1. Activate the **Plane** command.
2. Select two lines from the model geometry.
3. Click **OK**.

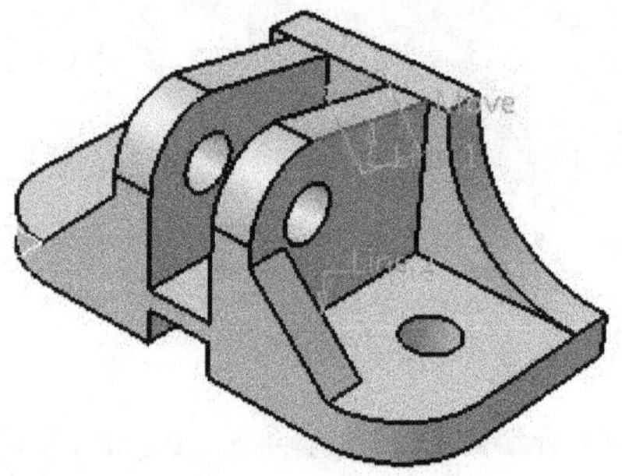

Through point and line

This method creates a plane by selecting a point and line.

1. Activate the **Plane** command.
2. Select a point and line.
3. Click **OK**.

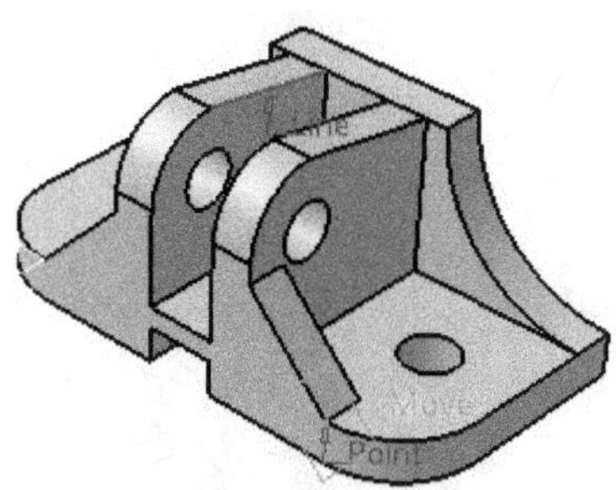

Through planar curve

This method creates a plane by selecting a non-linear planar curve.

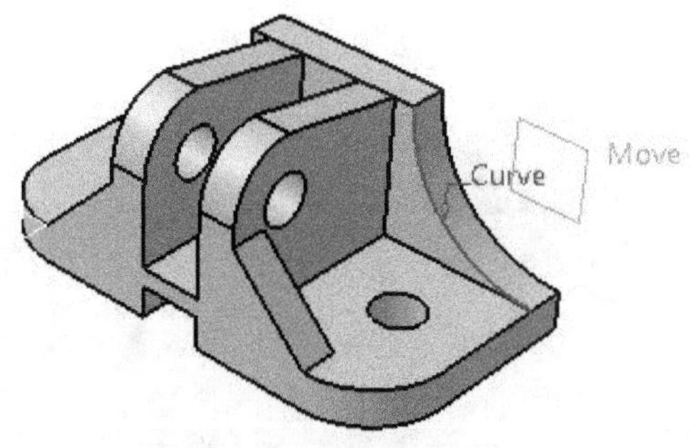

Normal to curve

This method creates a reference plane, which will be normal (perpendicular) to a line, curve, or edge.

1. On the **Plane Definition** dialog, click **Plane type > Normal to Curve** and select an edge, line, curve, arc, or circle.
2. Click on a point to define the location of the plane.
3. Click **OK**.

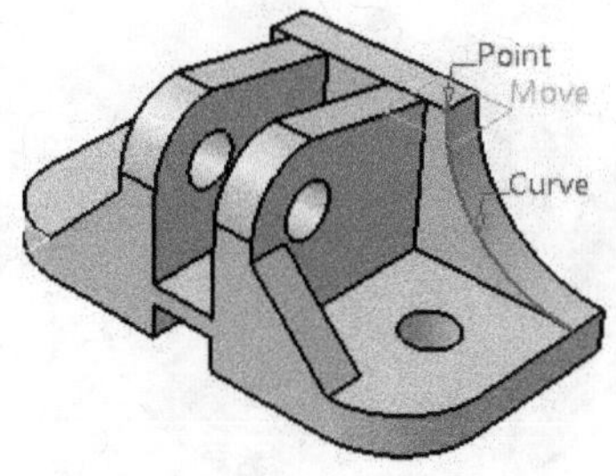

Tangent to surface

This method creates a plane tangent to a curved face.

1. On the **Plane Definition** dialog, click **Plane type > Tangent to surface** and select a curved face.
2. Click on a point. A plane tangent to the selected face appears.

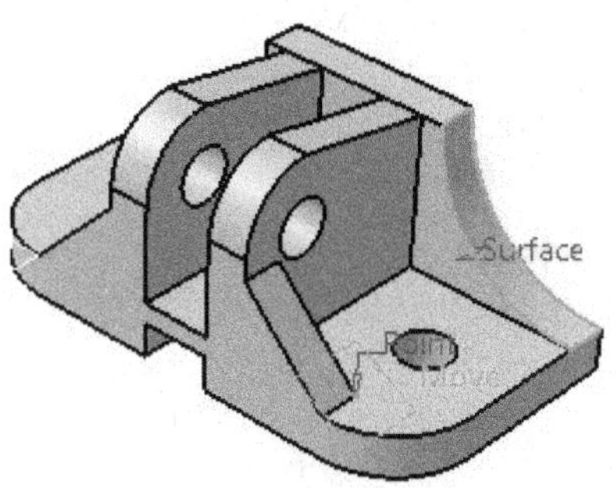

Equation

This method creates a plane using the equation Ax+By+Cz=D. You have to type-in A, B, C, and D values.

1. On the **Plane Definition** dialog, click **Plane type > Equation**.
2. Type-in values in the **A**, **B**, **C**, and **D** boxes on the **Plane Definition** box. The x, y, z coordinates will be calculated automatically and a plane will be created at the origin passing though the x, y, z coordinates.

If you want to create a plane normal to the compass, then click the **Normal to compass** button and type-in values in the **C** and **D** boxes. A plane normal to the compass will be created at distance **D/C** from the origin.

Click the **Parallel to Screen** button to create a plane parallel to screen.

Mean through points

This method creates a plane passing through points.

1. On the **Plane Definition** dialog, click **Plane type > Mean through points**.
2. Select multiple points to create a plane.

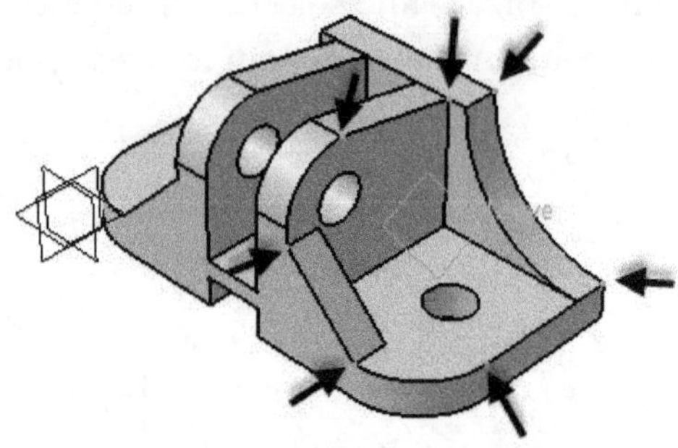

Point

The **Point** command creates points in the 3D space using seven different methods. Following sections explain you to create points using these methods.

Coordinates

This method creates a point in the 3D space by using the X, Y, Z coordinates that you specify.

1. Activate the **Point** command (on the **Reference Elements** toolbar, click the **Point** icon).
2. On the **Point Definition** dialog, click **Point type > Coordinates**.
3. On the **Point Definition** dialog, type-in the X, Y, Z coordinates.

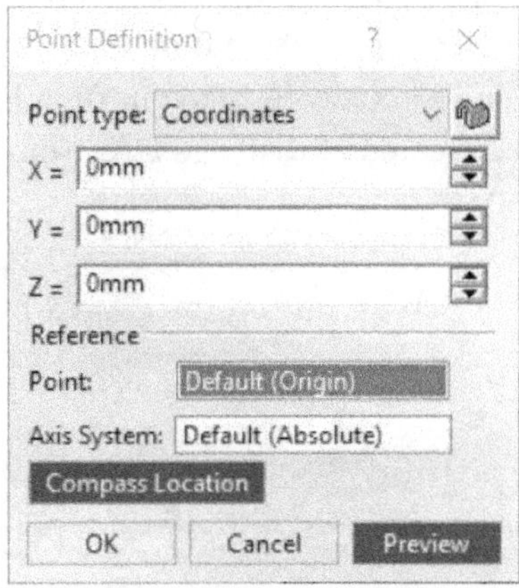

A point will be created with reference to origin (0, 0, 0).

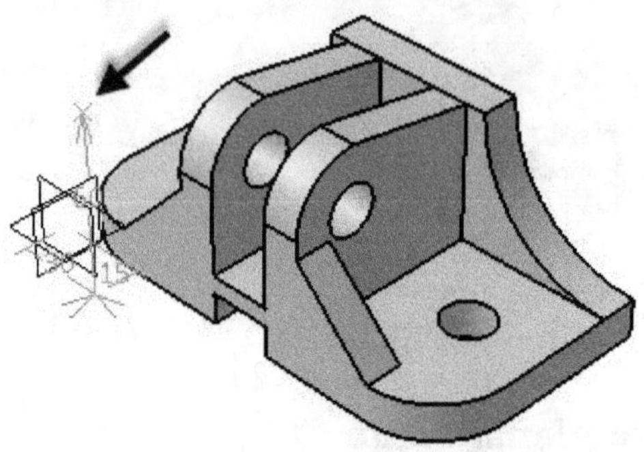

If you want to create a point with reference to a point other than the origin, then select a point from the graphics window.

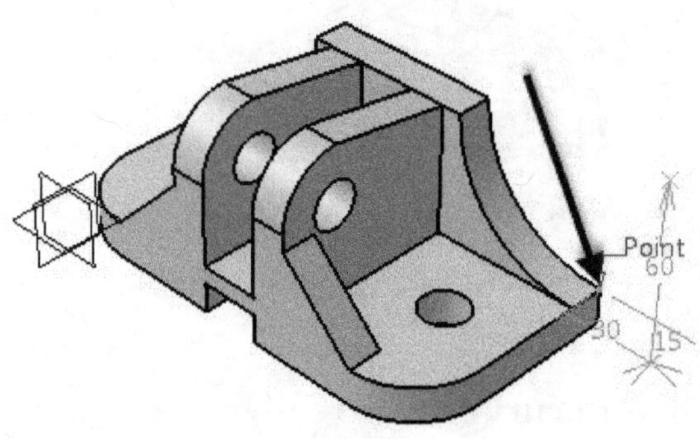

On curve

This method creates a point on a curve.

1. Activate the **Point** command and click on a curve or edge.
2. Select **Distance on curve** from the **Distance to reference** section.
3. Move the pointer and click to define the location of the point on the curve.

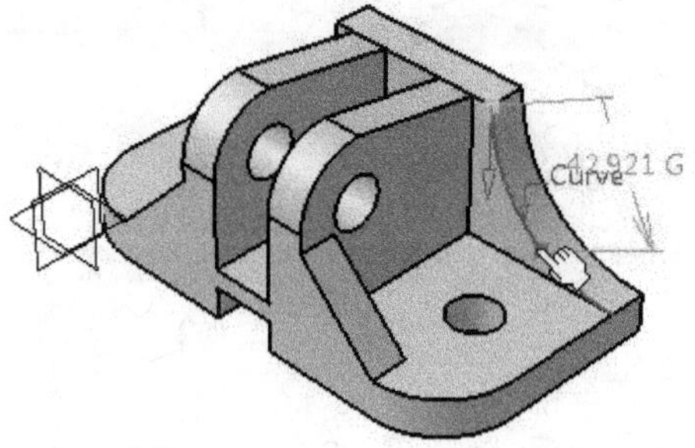

You can also define the location of the point on the curve using the **Distance along direction** and **Ratio of curve length** options.

If you select the **Distance along direction** option, you need to select a line, plane, or face to define the direction reference. Next, type in a value in the **Offset** box available on the dialog; the point will be placed at the specified offset value from the end point of the curve.

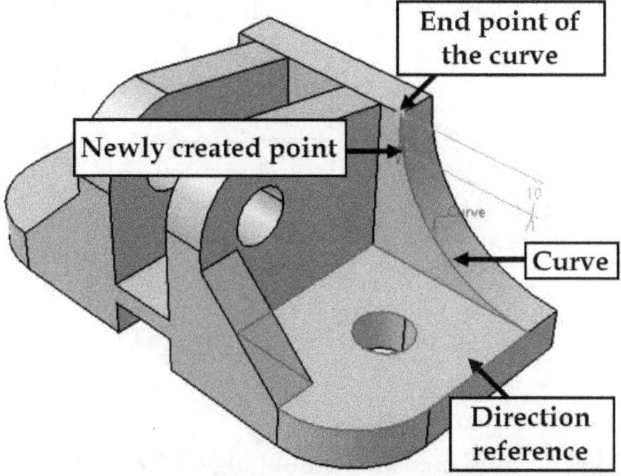

If you select the **Ratio of curve length** option, you need to type-in a value (between 0 and 1) in the **Ratio** box; the point will be placed at the length calculated based on the ratio specified. For example, if you specify 0.1 in the **Ratio** box, the point will be positioned at a distance which is one tenth of the total curve length.

On Plane

This method creates point on a planar face.

1. Activate the **Point** command and click on a planar face or plane.

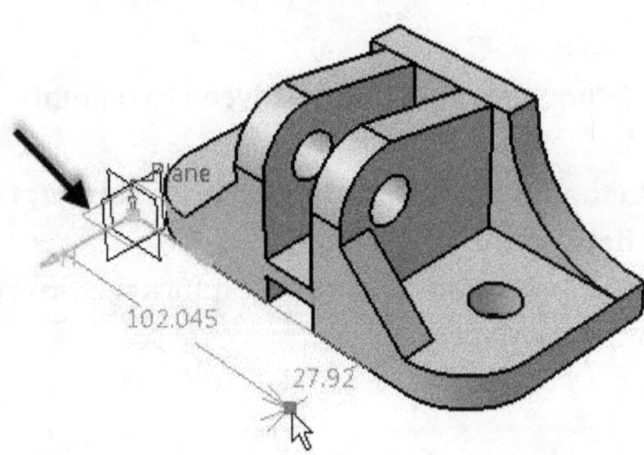

If you want to create the point with reference to a point other than the origin, then click in the **Point** selection box on the **Point Definition** dialog and click to define a reference point.

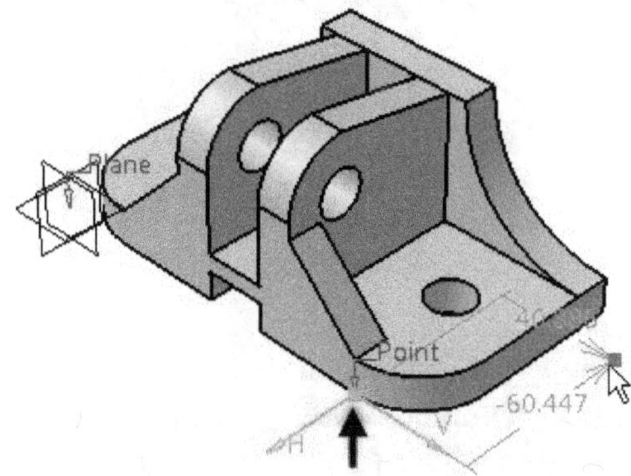

If you want to project the new point on to a surface, then click in the **Surface** selection box and select a surface.

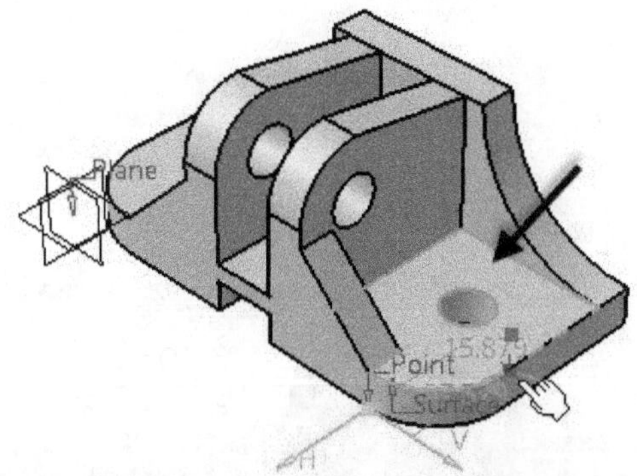

2. Move the pointer and click to define the location of the point (or) type-in values in the H and V boxes on the **Point Definition** dialog.

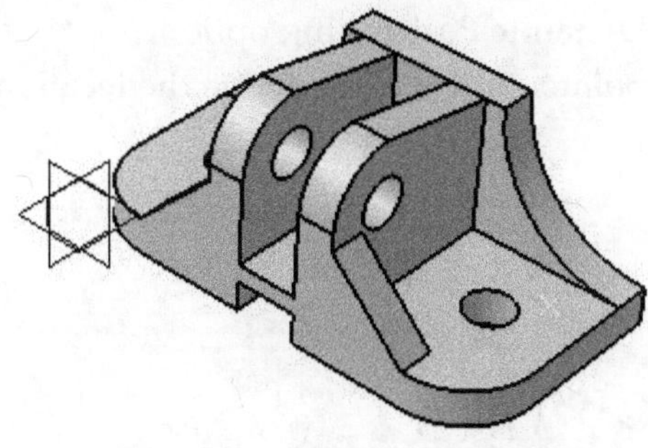

On Surface

This method creates point on a surface.

1. Activate the **Point** command and click on a surface.

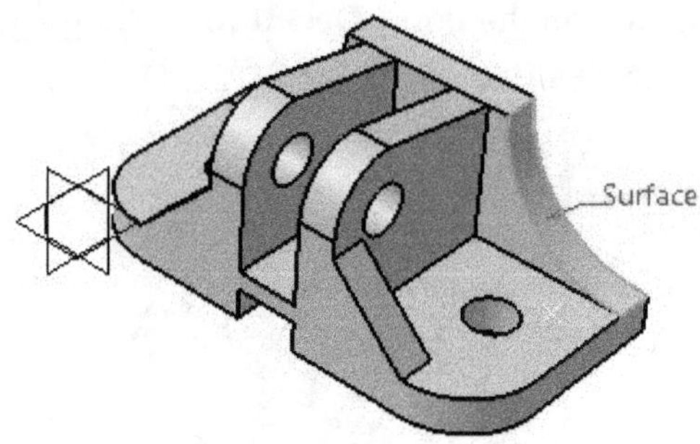

2. On the **Point Definition** dialog, click in the **Point** selection box and define a reference point on the selected surface.
3. On the **Point Definition** dialog, right click in the **Direction** selection box and select an option to define the direction of the point. For example, select **Y Component** to create the point in the Y-direction.

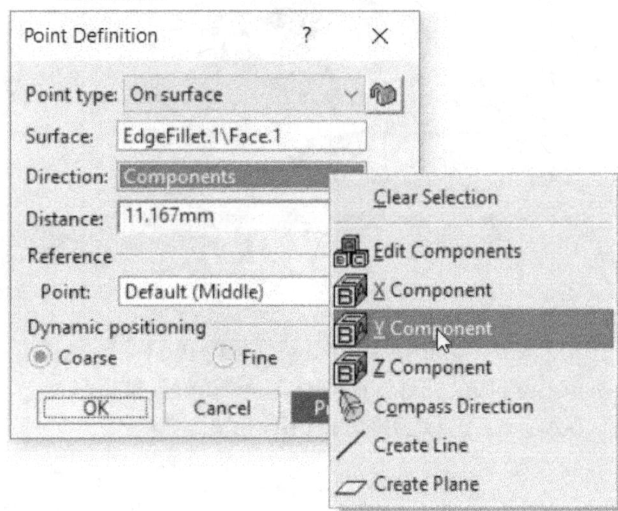

4. Select the **Dynamic Positioning** option.
5. Move the pointer and click to define the location of the point.

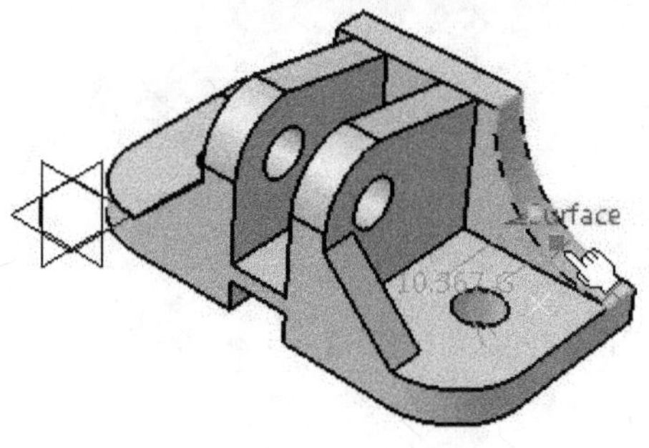

Circle/Sphere/Ellipse center

This method creates a point at the center of an arc, circle, sphere or ellipse.

1. On the **Point Definition** dialog, click **Point type > Circle/Sphere/Ellipse center**.
2. Click on an arc, circle, sphere, or elliptical entity.

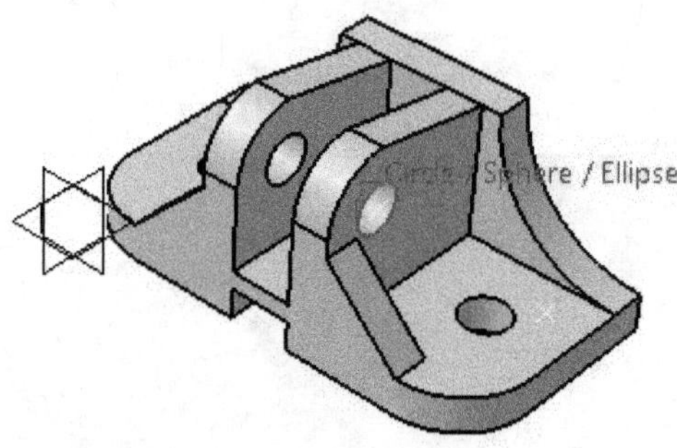

Tangent on curve

This method creates a point tangent to a curve.

1. On the **Point Definition** dialog, click **Point type > Tangent on curve**.
2. Click on an edge or curve.
3. Click on an edge or right click and select an option to define the tangential direction.
4. Click **OK** to create the point.

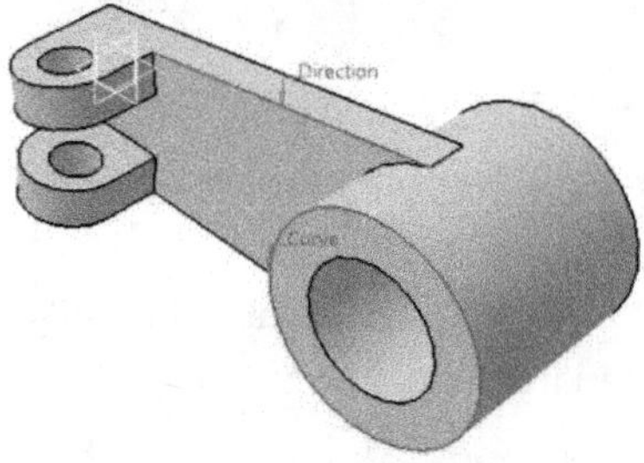

Between

This method creates a point between two points.

1. On the **Point Definition** dialog, click **Point type > Between**.
2. Select two points from the graphics window or model geometry.

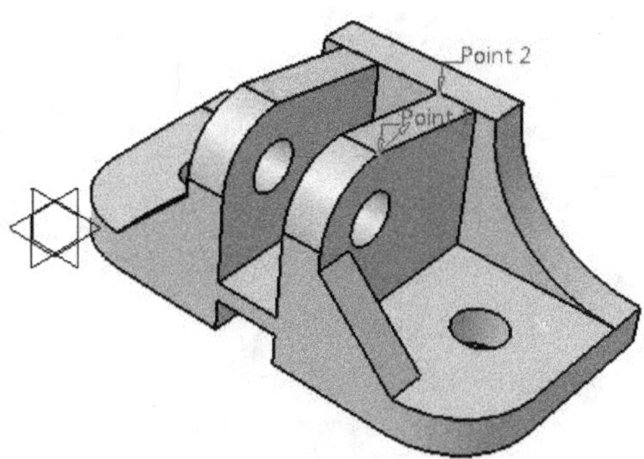

3. Type-in a value in the **Ratio** box. For example, if you type-in 0.5, the point will be created at the midpoint.
4. Click on the face, curve, or edge to define the supporting element.
5. Click **OK** to create the point.

 Line

The **Line** command (on the **Reference Elements** toolbar, click the **Line** icon) creates a line in the 3D space. The methods to create lines using this command are explained next.

Point-Point

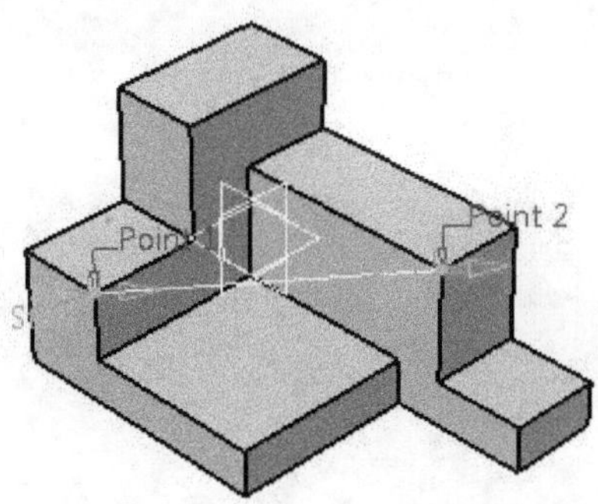

Point-Direction

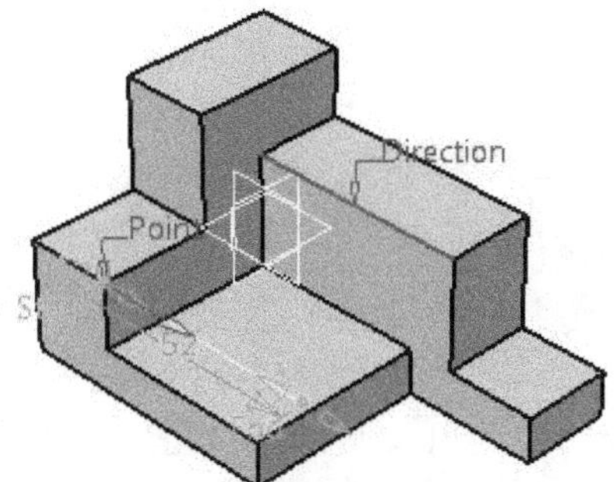

Angle/Normal to curve

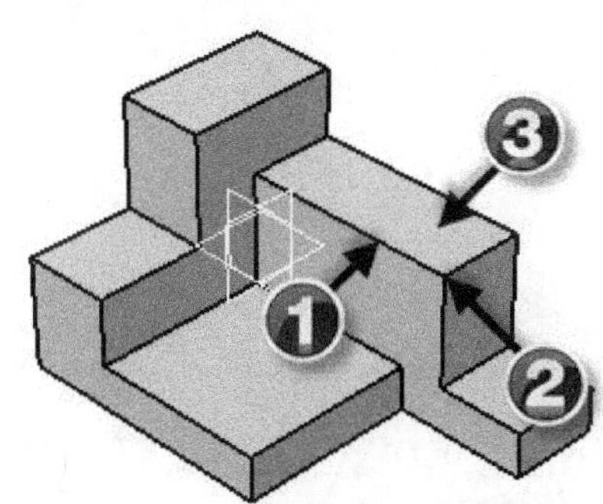

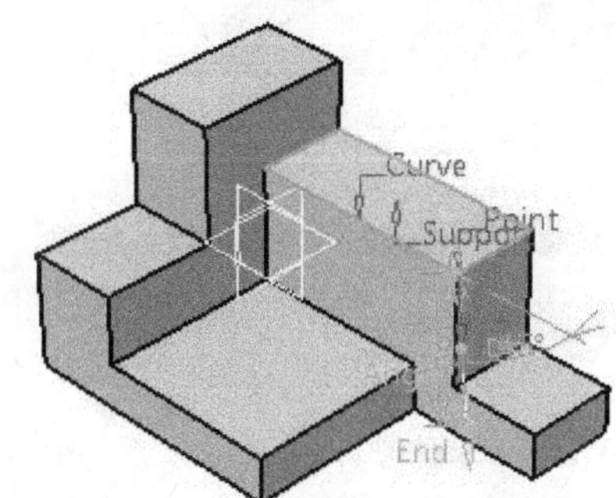

Tangent to curve

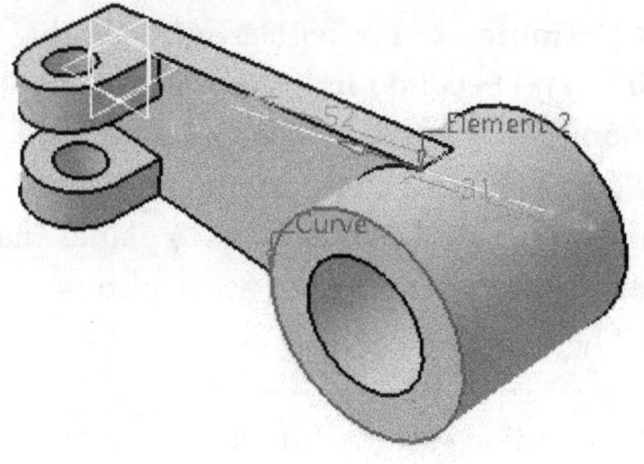

Normal to surface

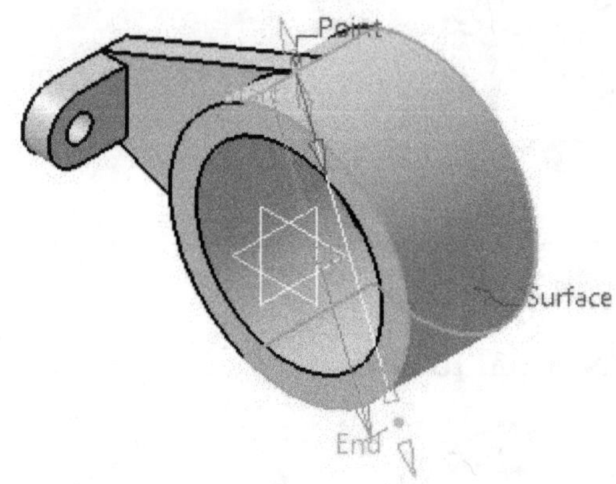

Bisecting

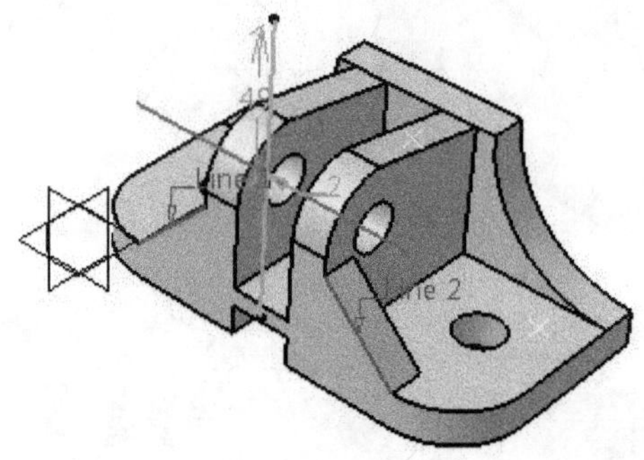

Additional options of the Pad and Pocket commands

The **Pad** and **Pocket** commands have some additional options to create a 3D geometry, complex features, and so on.

Limits

On the **Pad Definition** or **Pocket Definition** dialog, the **First Limit** and **Second Limit** sections have various options to define the start and end limits of the *Pad* or *Pocket* feature. These options are **Dimension, Up to next, Up to last, Up to plane,** and **Up to surface** (note that these options are also available in Shaft and Groove feature).

The **Up to next** option extrudes the sketch through the face next to the sketch plane.

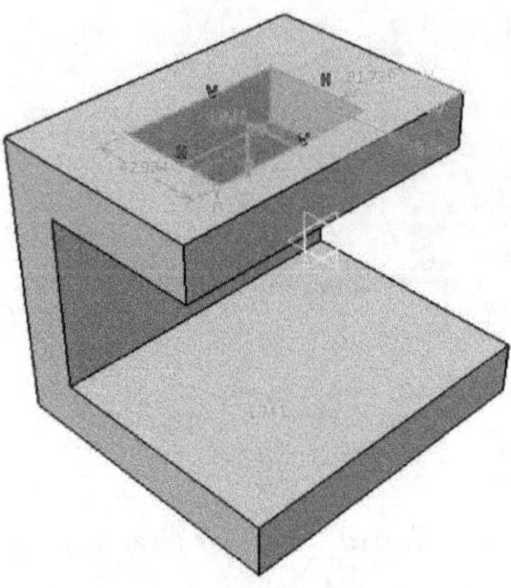

The **Up to surface** option extrudes the sketch up to a selected surface.

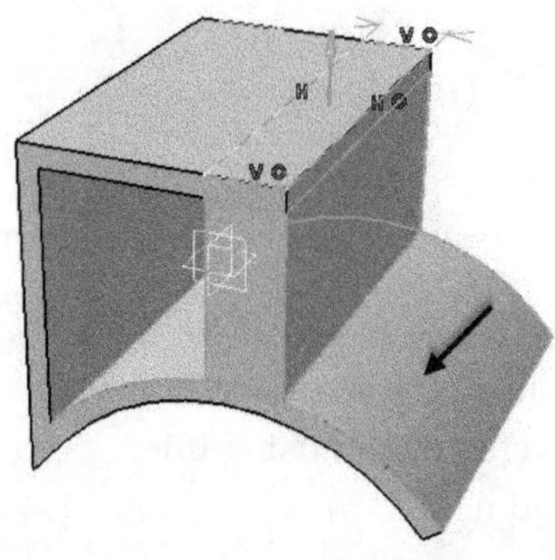

The **Up to plane** option extrudes the sketch from the sketch plane up to a selected planar face.

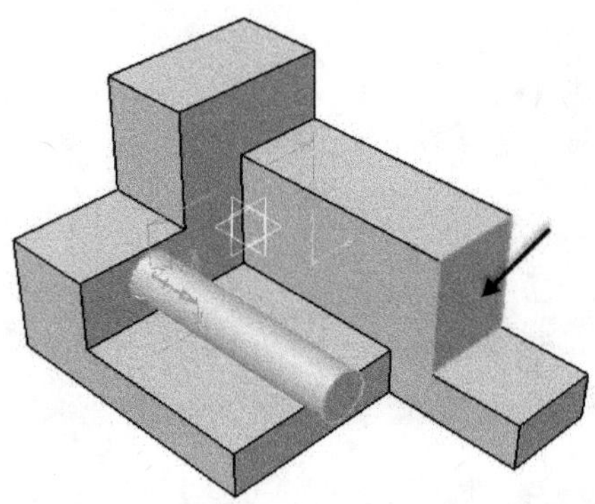

The **Up to last** option extrudes the sketch throughout the 3D geometry.

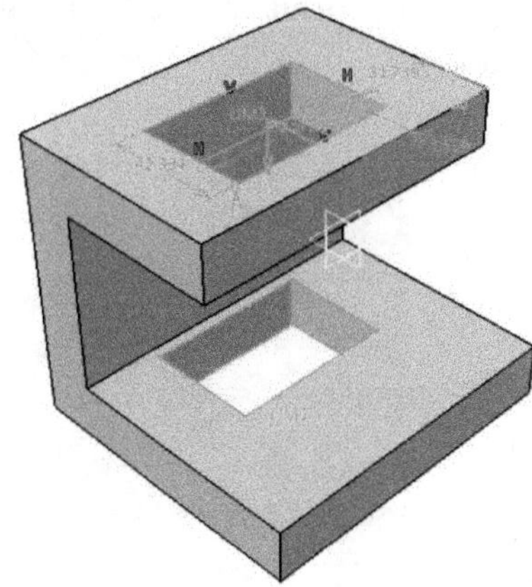

Thick

The **Thick** option will help you to add thickness to the selected sketch. Check this option on the **Pad Definition** or **Revolve Definition** dialog to add thickness to the sketch. Click the **More** button to view the **Thickness 1** and **Thickness 2** boxes. Type-in thickness values in these boxes. Check the **Neutral Fiber** option, if you want to add thickness symmetrically on both sides of the sketch.

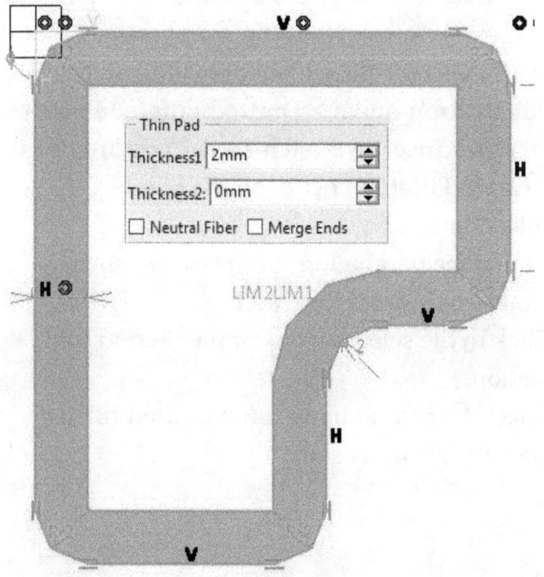

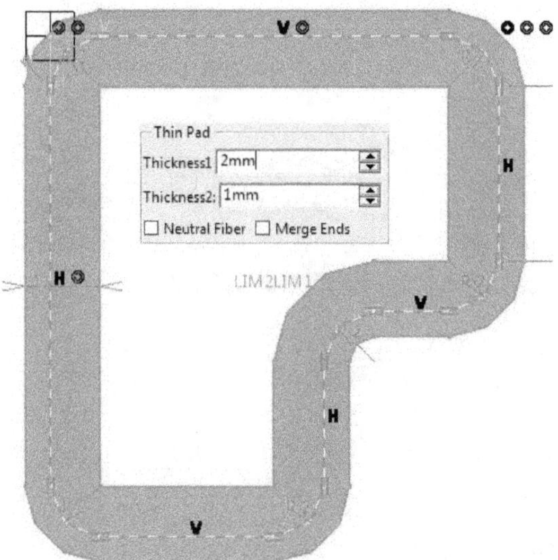

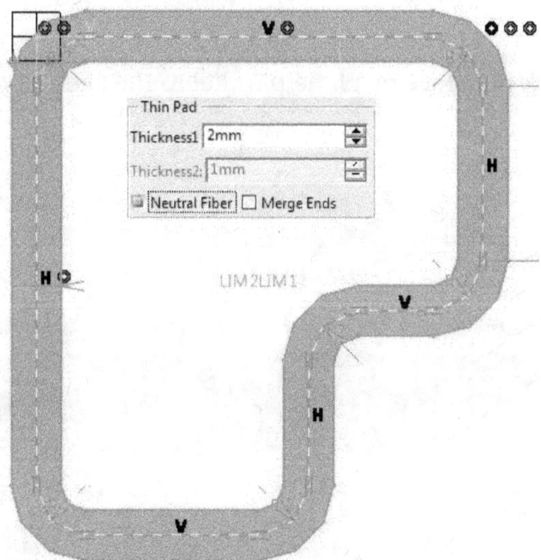

The Drafted Filleted Pad command

This command creates a drafted pad feature with fillets.

1. Draw the sketch and exit the workbench.
2. On the **Sketch-Based Features** toolbar, click **Pads** drop-down **> Drafted Filleted Pad** (or) click **Insert > Sketch-Based Features > Drafted Filleted Pad** on the Menu.
3. On the **Drafted Filleted Pa1d Definition** dialog, define the First Limit, Draft, and Fillets.

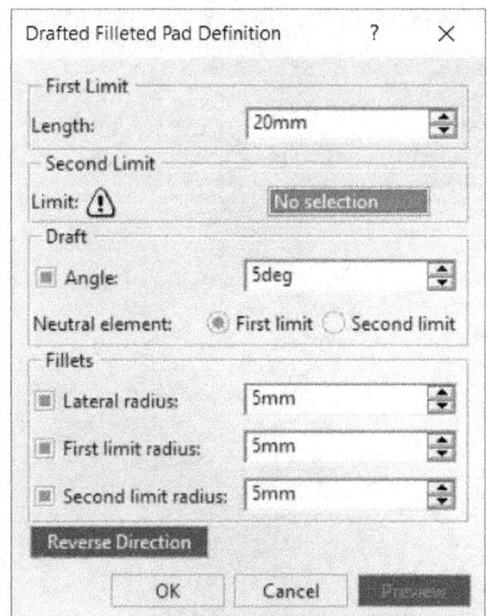

4. Click on a face or plane parallel to the sketch plane.

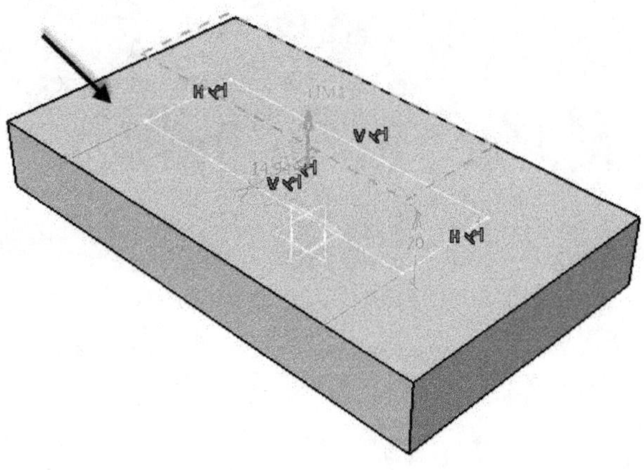

5. Click **OK**.

You will notice that the pad, draft, and fillets are created as separate features.

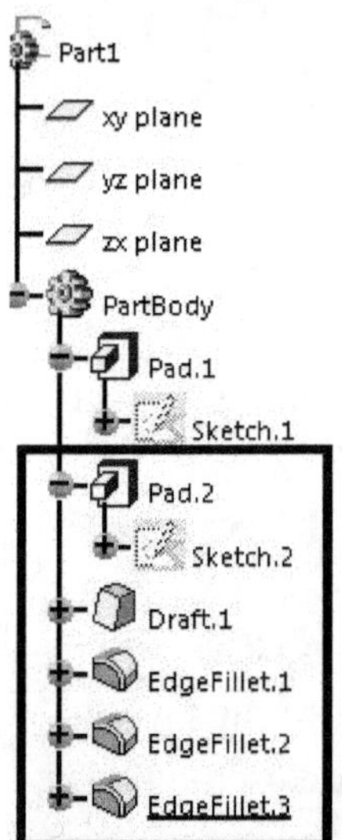

The Drafted Filleted Pocket command

This command creates a drafted pocket with fillets.

1. Draw a sketch and exit the workbench.
2. On the **Sketch-Based Features** toolbar, click **Pokets** drop-down **> Drafted Filleted Pocket** (or) click **Insert > Sketch-Based Features > Drafted Filleted Pocket** on the Menu.
3. Select the closed sketch.
4. Define the parameters on the dialog such as Draft Angle and Fillet radii.
5. Click in the selection box of the Second limit section.
6. Select the second limit of the drafted filleted pocket feature, as shown.

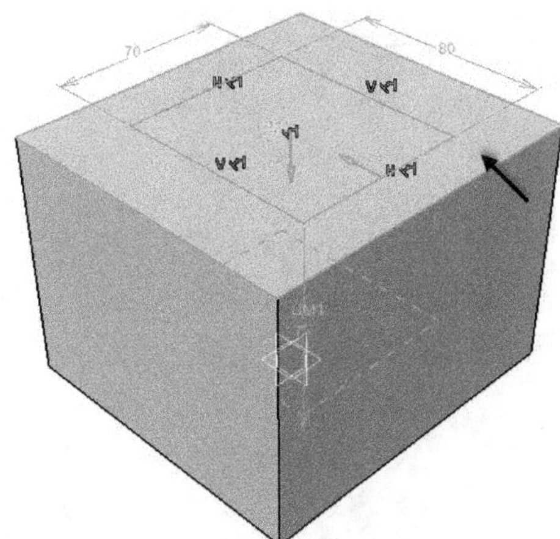

7. Click **OK**.

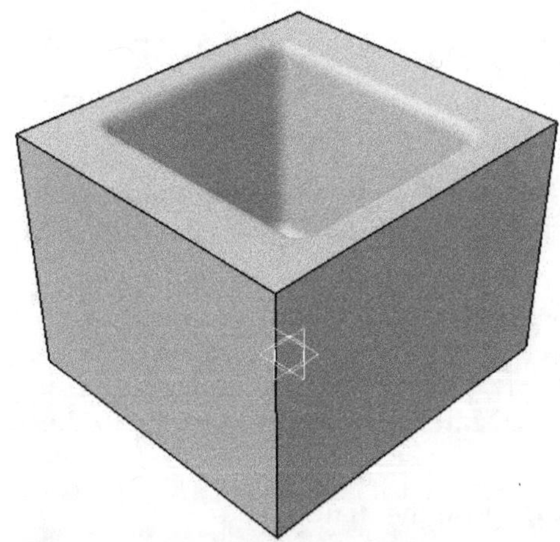

The Multi-Pad command

This command takes a sketch with internal loops and adds multiple thicknesses to it.

1. Draw a sketch, which contains internal loops. Exit the workbench.

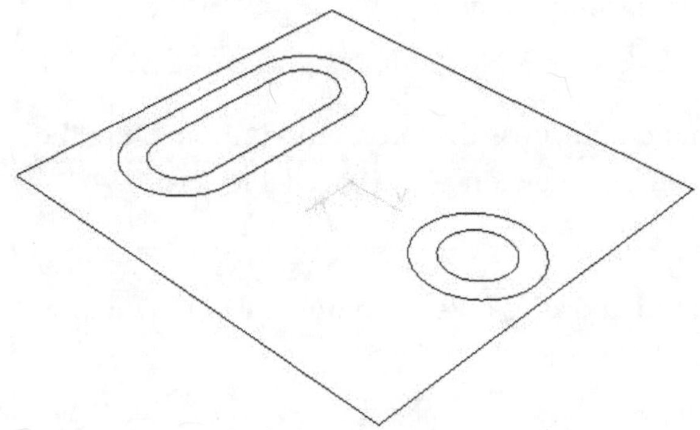

2. On the **Sketch-Based Features** toolbar, click **Pads** drop-down **> Multi-Pad** (or) click **Insert > Sketch-Based Features > Multi-Pad** on the Menu.
3. On the **Multi-Pad Definition** dialog, click on the Extrusion Domains one-by-one and type-in values in the **Length** box.
4. If you want to extrude the loops in both the directions, then click the **More** button on the dialog and define parameters in the **Second Limit** section.
5. You can also define the direction of the extrusion using the **Direction** section.
6. Click **OK**.

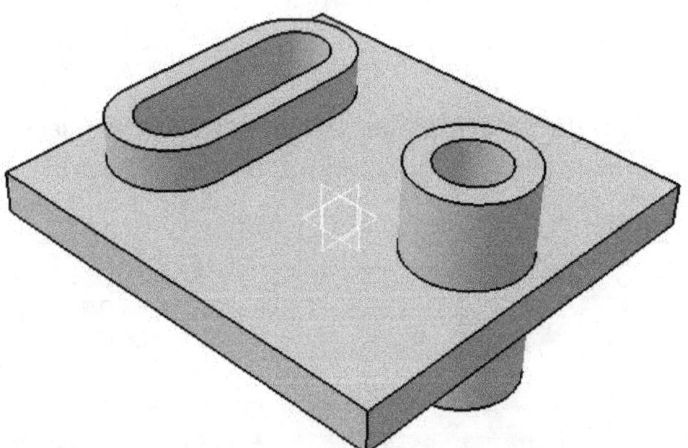

The Multi-Pocket command

This command uses a multi-loop sketch to remove material with multiple depths.

1. Draw a sketch, which contains internal loops. Exit the workbench.

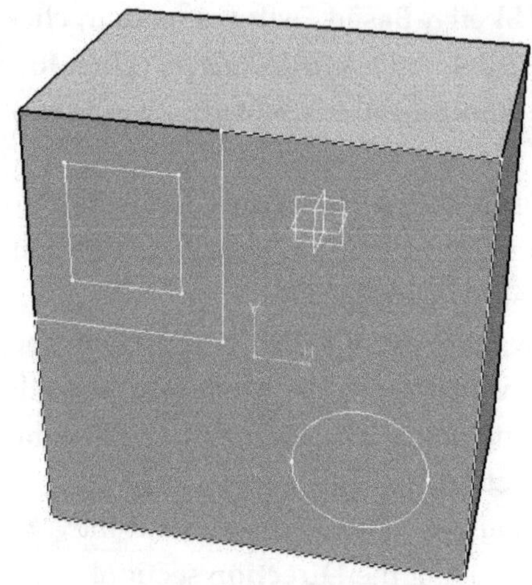

2. On the **Sketch-Based Features** toolbar, click **Pokets** drop-down > **Multi-Pocket** (or) click **Insert > Sketch-Based Features > Multi-Pocket** on the Menu.
3. On the **Multi-Pocket Definition** dialog, select the extrusion domains and define the pocket depth.
4. Click **OK**.

The Apply Material command

This command applies material to the solid geometry.

1. Activate this command by clicking the **Apply Material** button on the **Apply Material** toolbar.
2. Click on a tab on the **Library** dialog.
3. Select the material from the dialog, and then click on the part geometry.
4. Click **Apply Material** to apply material to the geometry.
5. Click **OK** to close the dialog.

View commands

The model display in the graphics window can be determined using various view commands. Most of these commands are located on **View** toolbar or on the **View** menu. The following are some of the main view commands:

	Fit All In	The model will be fitted in the current size of the graphics window so that it will be visible, completely.
	Pan	Activate this command and press the left mouse button. Drag the pointer to move the model view on plane parallel to screen.
	Rotate	Activate this command and press the left mouse button. Drag the pointer to rotate the model view.
	Zoom In	Click this button to zoom in to the geometry.

	Zoom Out	Click this button to zoom out of the geometry.
	Normal View	Activate this command and click on a plane or face. The plane will become normal to the screen.
	Shading with Edges	This represents the model with shades along with visible edges. 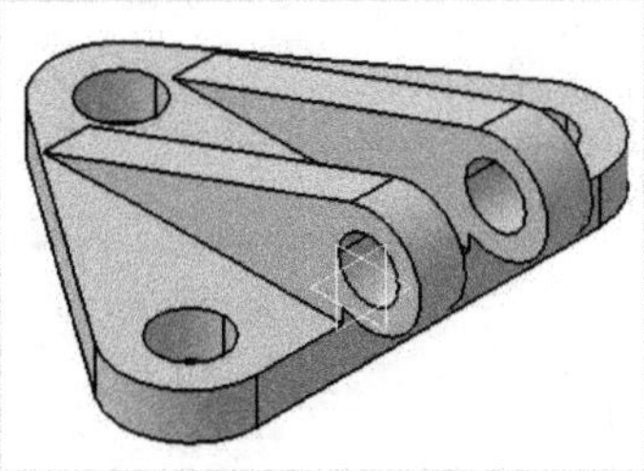
	Shading with Edges without Smooth Edges	This represents the model with shades along with visible edges. The smooth edges of the curved faces will be hidden. 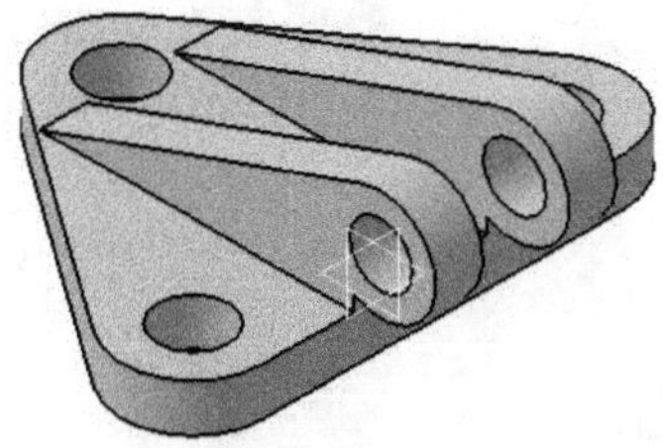
	Shading	This represents the model with shades without visible edges. 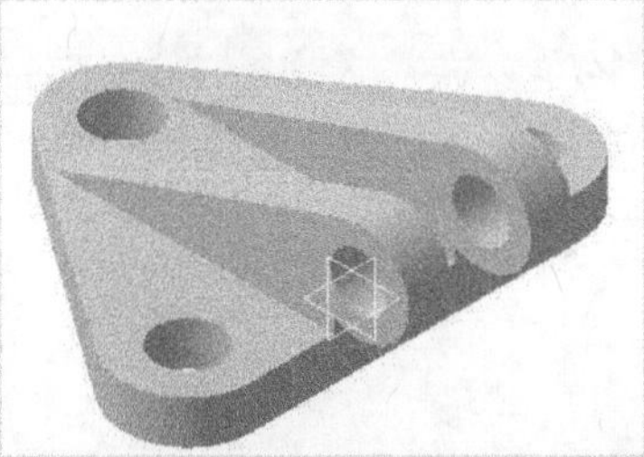
	Shading with Material	This represents the model with shades of the applied material. 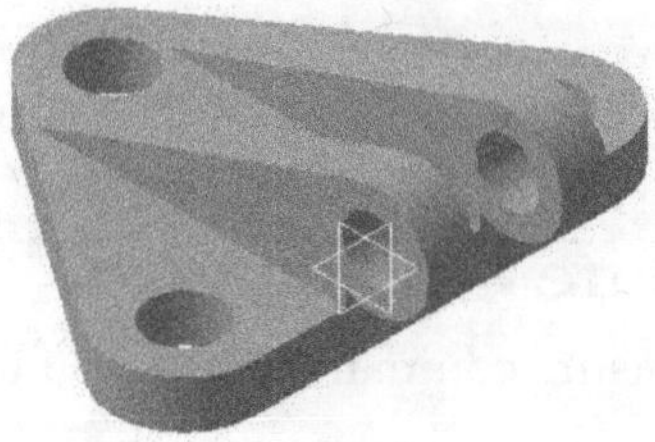

	Wireframe (NHR)	This represents the model in wireframe.	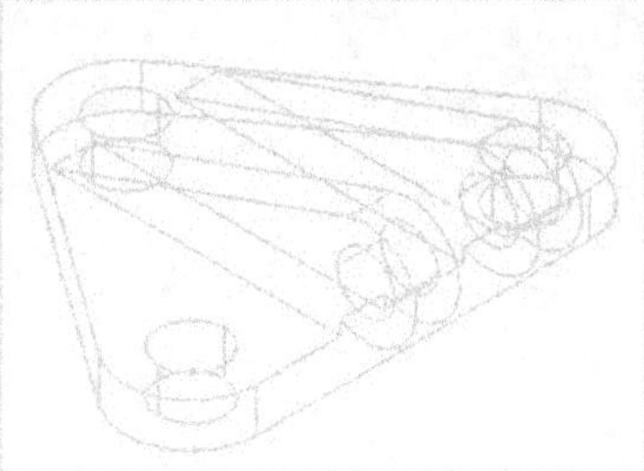
	Customize view Parameters	This command is used to create your own render style by customizing the view parameters.	
	Shading with Edges and Hidden Edges	This represents the model in shades along with hidden edges	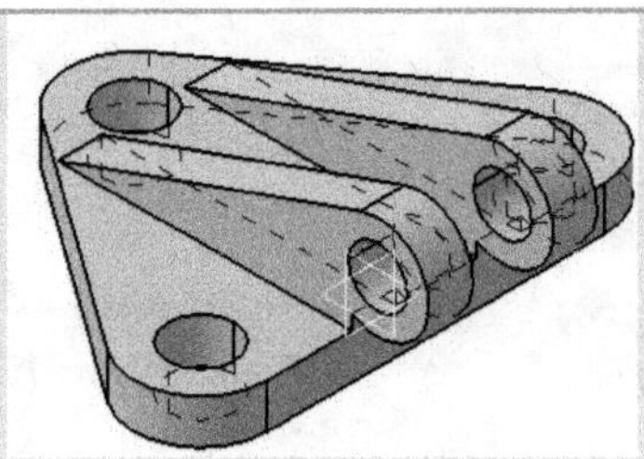
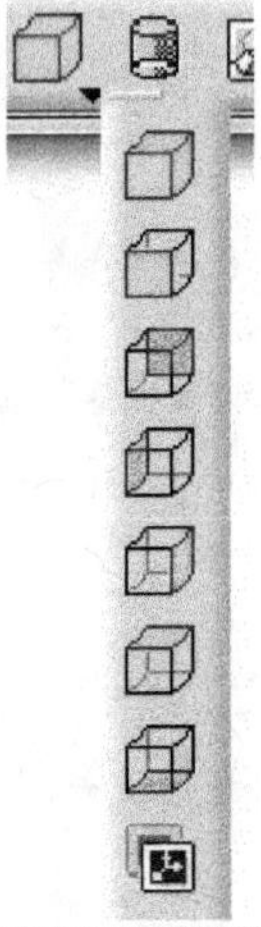	**Quick View Drop-down**	Use this drop-down to change the model view orientation.	

Measure Commands

The measure commands help you to measure the physical properties of geometry. These commands are explained next.

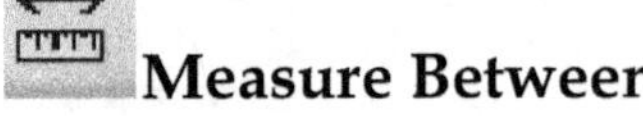

Measure Between

This command measures the distance or angle between two elements.

1. On the **Measure** toolbar, click the **Measure Between** button.
2. Click on the two elements. The distance between the two elements will appear.
3. Click **OK**.

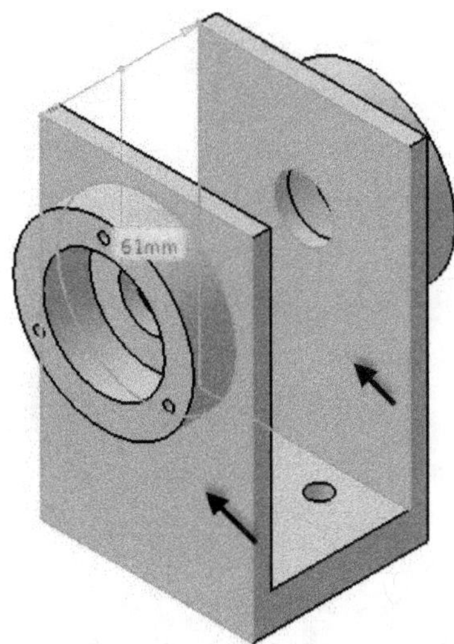

Measure Item

This command displays the physical properties of the selected element based on the element type. For example, if you select a linear edge, it displays the length of the linear edge.

1. On the **Measure** toolbar, click the **Measure Item** button.
2. Click on an element to display the measurements of the element.
3. Click **OK**.

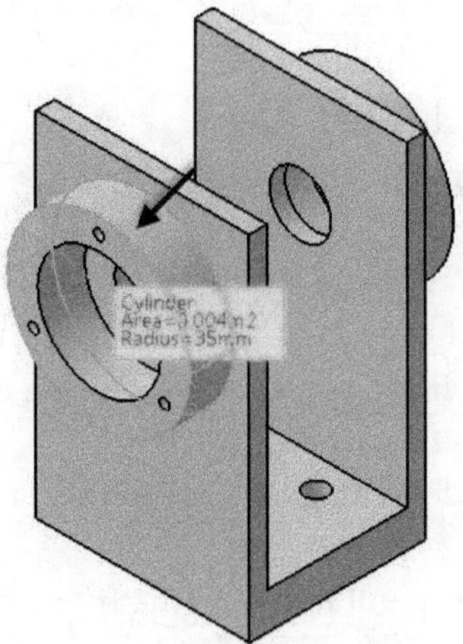

Measure Inertia

This command displays the physical properties of a part body such as volume, inertia, mass, center of gravity, and so on.

1. On the **Measure** toolbar, click the **Measure Inertia** button.

2. Click on the part body. The **Measure Inertia** dialog appears showing the properties of the body.

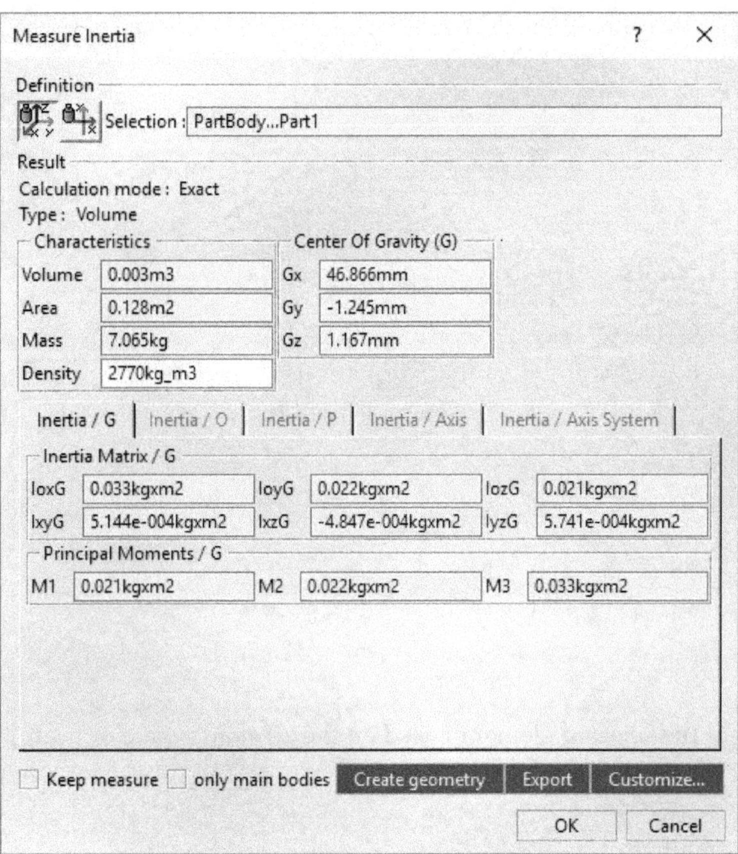

3. On this dialog, click the **Measure Inertia 2D** button, if you want to view the properties in a 2D plane.

Examples

Example 1

In this example, you will create the part shown below.

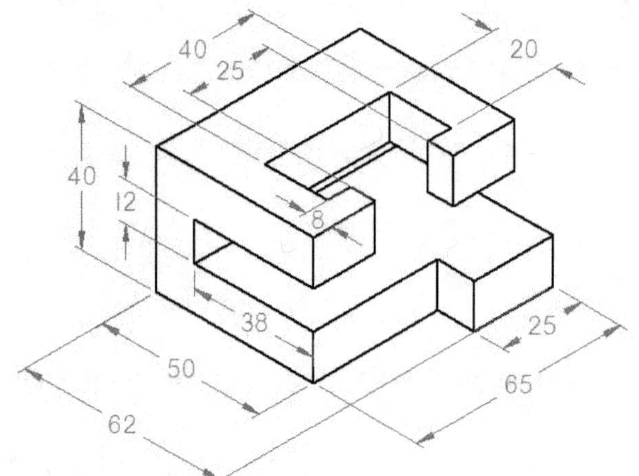

1. Start **CATIA V5-6R2017**.
2. On the Menu, click **File > New**.
3. On the **New** dialog, select **List of Types > Part**, and then click **OK**.
4. On the **New Part** dialog, type-in **C03-Example1**, and then click **OK**.
5. On the **Sketcher** toolbar, click the **Sketch** icon.
6. Click YZ plane to start the sketch.
7. On the **Profile** toolbar, click **Predefined Profile > Rectangle**.
8. Click the origin point to define the first corner of the rectangle.
9. Move the pointer toward top right and click to define the second corner.
10. Apply dimensions to the rectangle.

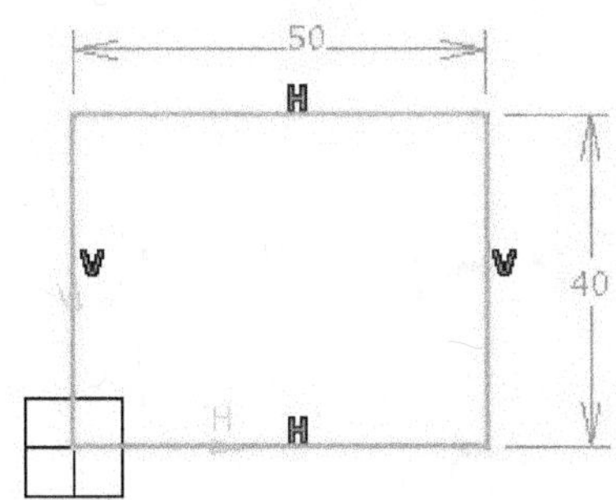

11. On the **Workbench** toolbar, click **Exit workbench**.
12. On the **Sketch-Based Features** toolbar, click **Pads** drop-down > **Pad**.
13. On the **Pad Definition** dialog, click **Type > Dimension**.
14. On the dialog, type-in **32.5** in the **Length** box.
15. Check the **Mirror extent** option and click **OK** to complete the *Pad* feature.

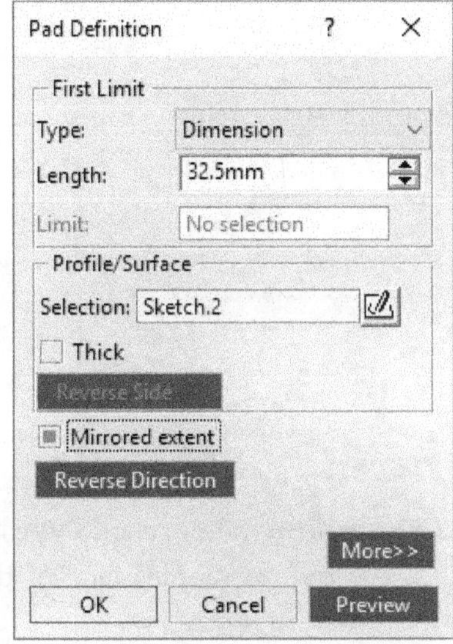

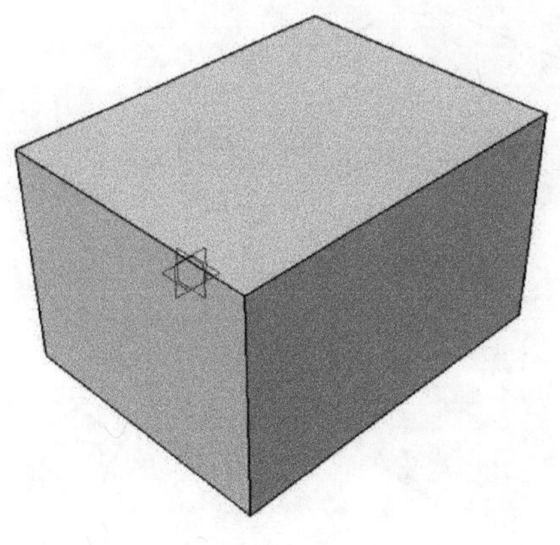

16. On the **Sketch-Based Features** toolbar, click **Pockets** drop-down > **Pocket**.
17. On the **Pocket Definition** dialog, under the **Profile/Surface** section, click the **Sketch** icon.
18. Click on the front face of the part geometry.

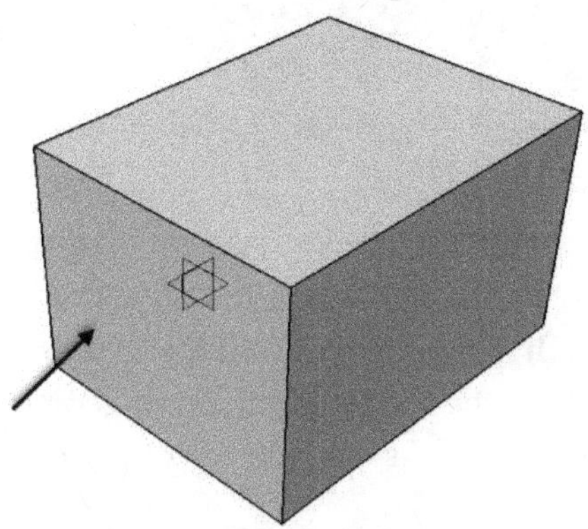

19. Activate the **Rectangle** command and draw a rectangle touching the right edge of the front face.
20. Apply constraints to it.

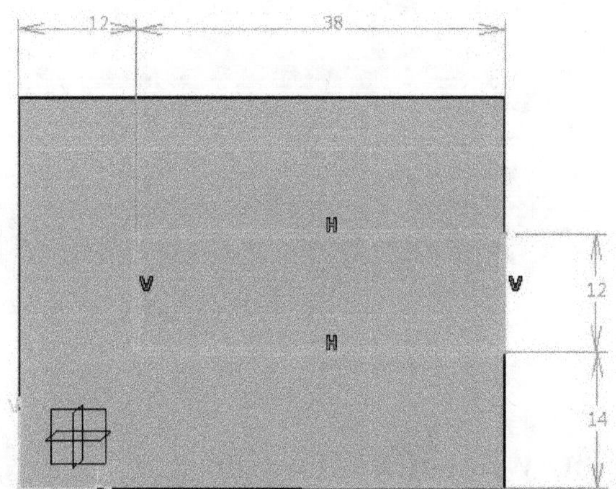

21. On the **Workbench** toolbar, click **Exit workbench**.
22. On the **Pocket Definition** dialog, select **Type > Up to last**.
23. Click **OK** to create the cut throughout the part geometry.

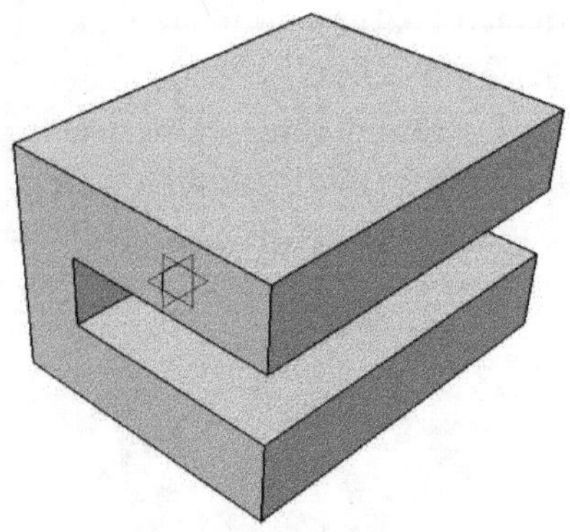

24. Activate the **Pocket** command and click the **Sketch** icon on the **Pocket Definition** dialog.
25. Click on the top face of the part geometry.
26. Draw a closed sketch on the top face.

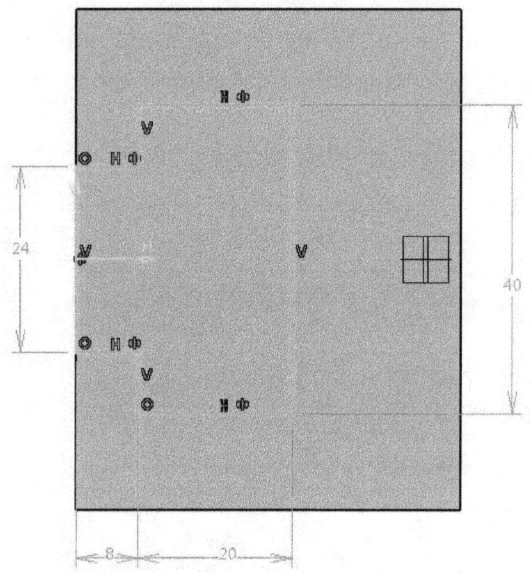

27. On the **Workbench** toolbar, click **Exit workbench**.
28. On the **Pocket Definition** dialog, click **Type > Up to next**.
29. Click **OK** to create the *Pocket* feature until the surface next to the sketch plane.

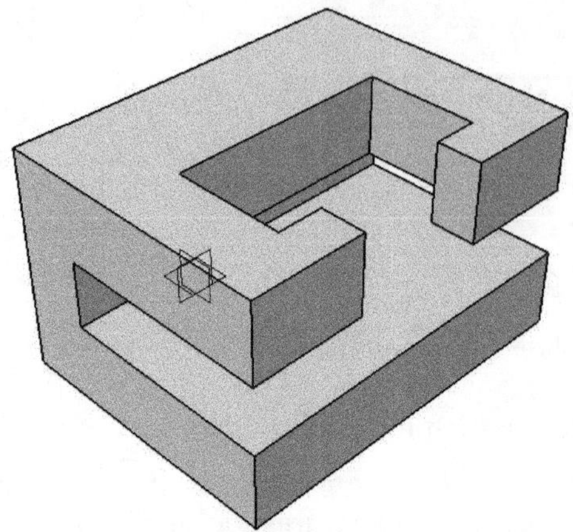

30. Activate the **Pad** command and click the **Sketch** icon on the **Pad Definition** dialog.
31. Click on the XY plane.
32. Draw a closed sketch. Apply dimensions and finish the sketch.

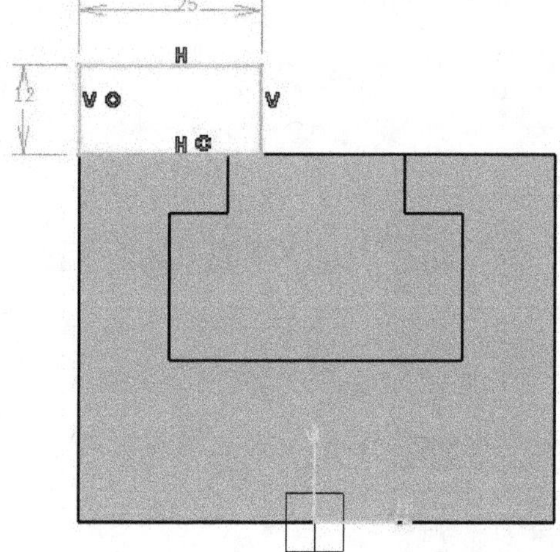

33. On the **Pad Definition** dialog, click **Type > Up to plane** and select the horizontal face of the part geometry, as shown in figure.

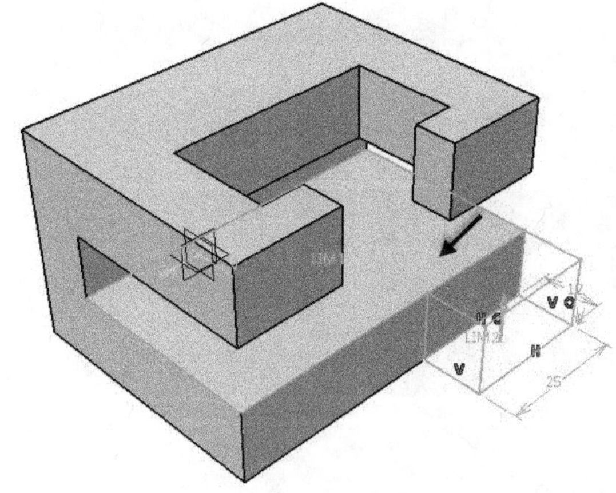

34. Click **OK** to complete the part.

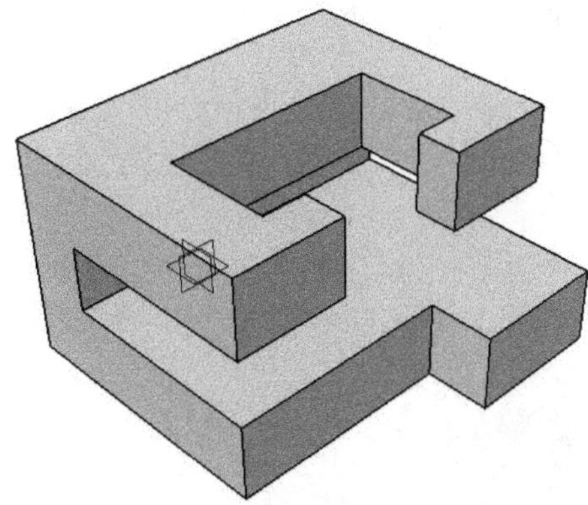

35. Save and close the file.

Example 2

In this example, you will create the part shown below.

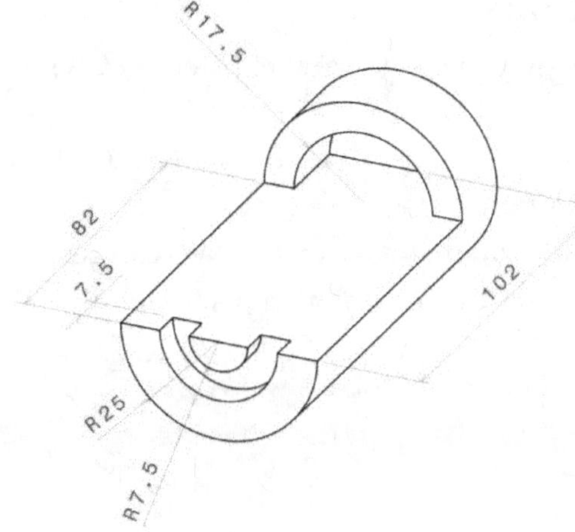

1. Start **CATIA V5-6R2017**.
2. On the Menu, click **File > New**.
3. On the **New** dialog, select **List of Types > Part**, and then click **OK**.
4. On the **New Part** dialog, type-in **C03-Example2**, and then click **OK**.
5. Draw a sketch on the XY plane, as shown below.

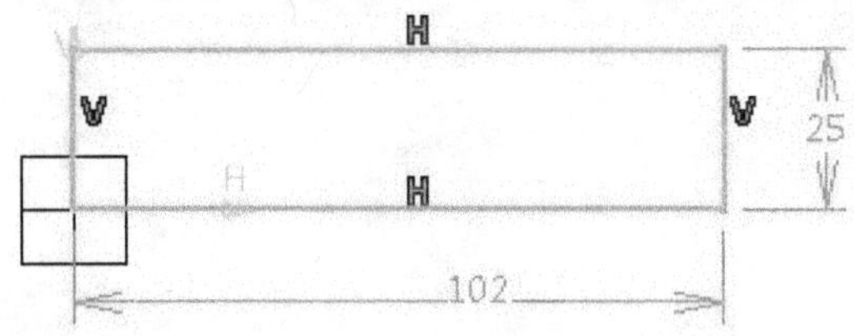

6. Exit the **Sketcher** Workbench.
7. On the **Sketch-Based Features** toolbar, click the **Shaft** icon.
8. Select the sketch and click on the line passing through the origin.

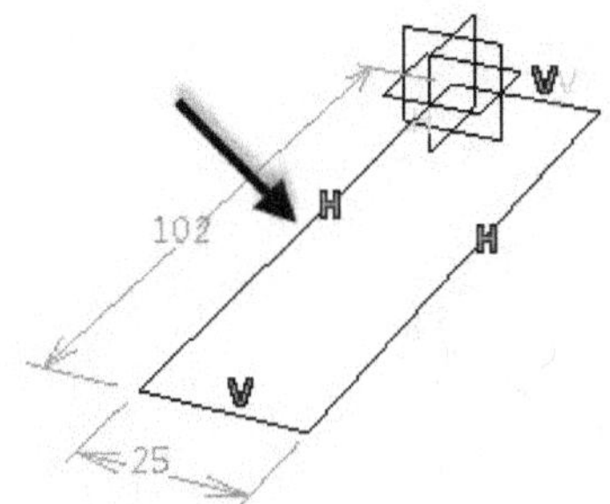

9. On the **Shaft Definition** dialog, type-in 0 and 180 in the **First angle** and **Second angle** boxes, respectively.
10. Click **OK** to create the *Shaft* feature.

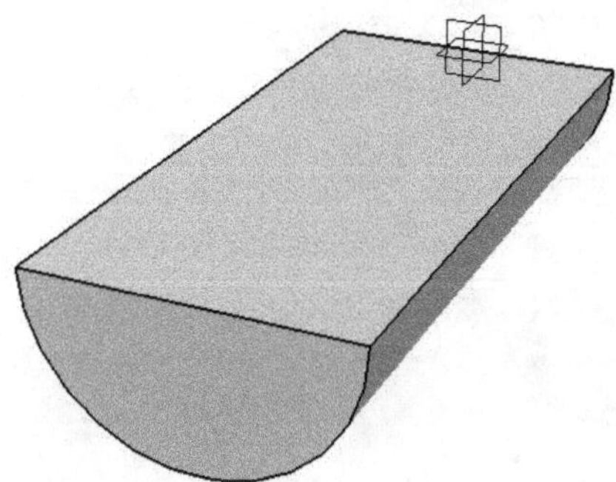

11. On the **Sketch-Based Features** toolbar, click the **Groove** icon (or) click **Insert > Sketch-Based Features > Groove** on the Menu.
12. On the **Groove Definition** dialog, click the **Sketch** icon and select the top face of the part geometry.
13. Draw the sketch on top face and apply dimensions. Make sure that you draw the axis of the revolution. Exit the sketch.

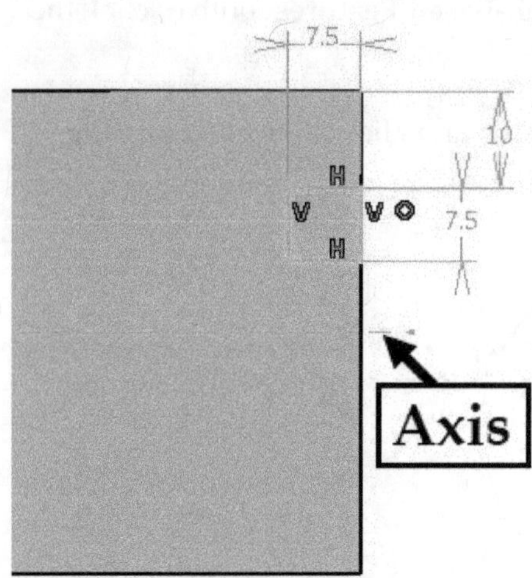

14. Type-in **0** and **180** in the **First angle** and **Second angle** boxes.
15. Click **OK** to create the revolved groove.

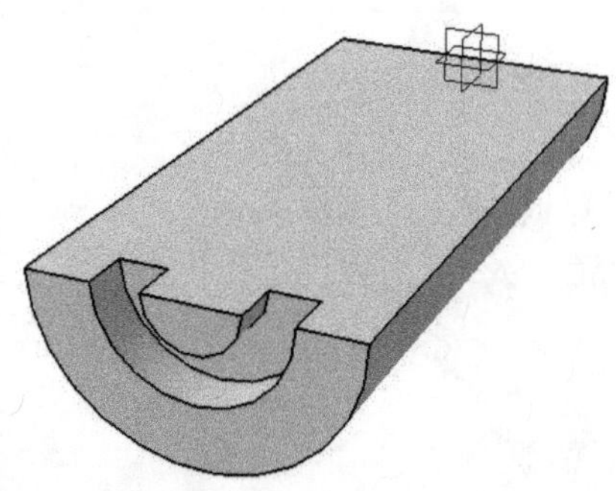

16. Activate the **Shaft** command and click the **Sketch** icon on the **Shaft Definition** dialog.
17. Click on the top face of the part geometry.
18. Draw a sketch and click **Exit workbench**.

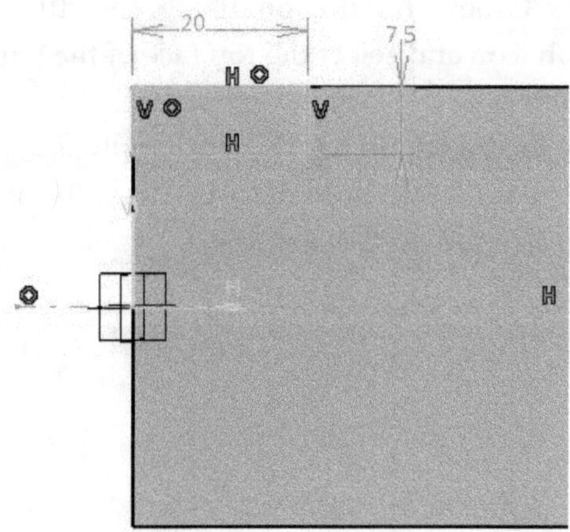

19. Type-in the **180** and **0** in the **First angle** and **Second angle** boxes, respectively.
20. Click **OK** to add the *Shaft* feature to the geometry.

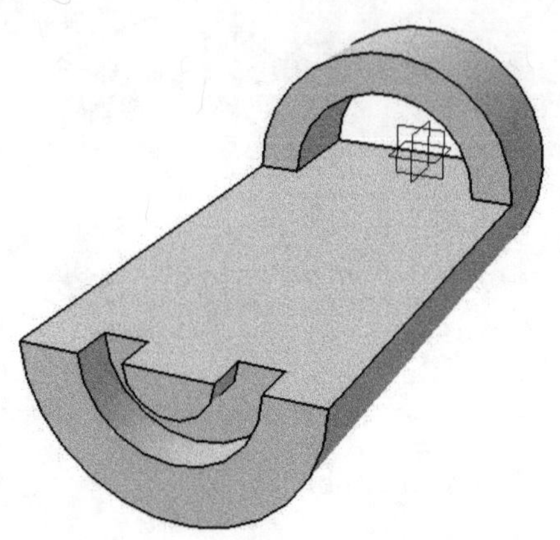

21. Save and close the file.

Questions

1. How do you create parallel planes in CATIA V5?
2. List any two-limit types available on the **Pad Definition** dialog.
3. List the commands to create pad features.
4. How do you create angled planes in CATIA V5?

Exercises

Exercise 1

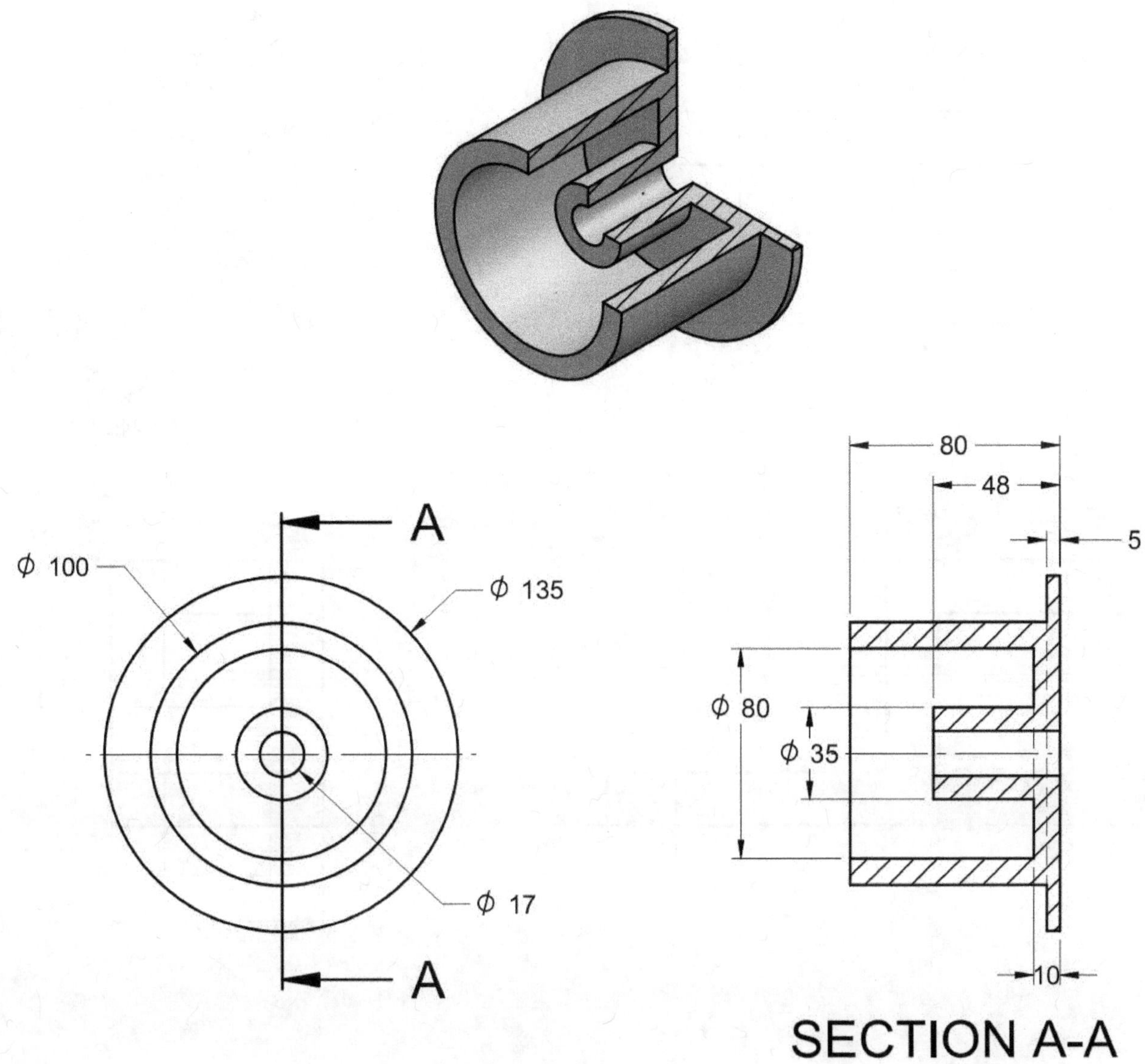

Exercise 2

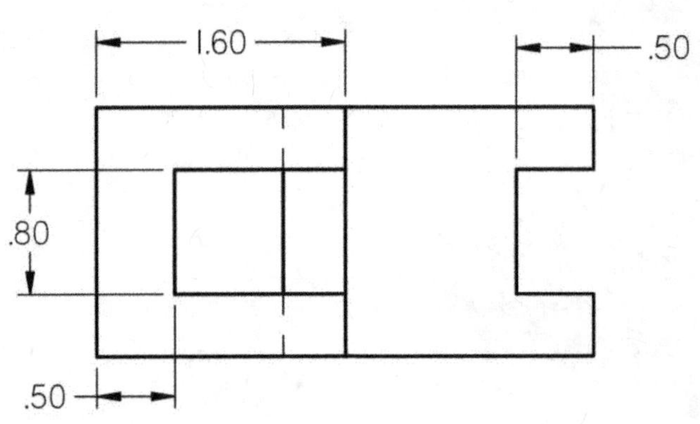

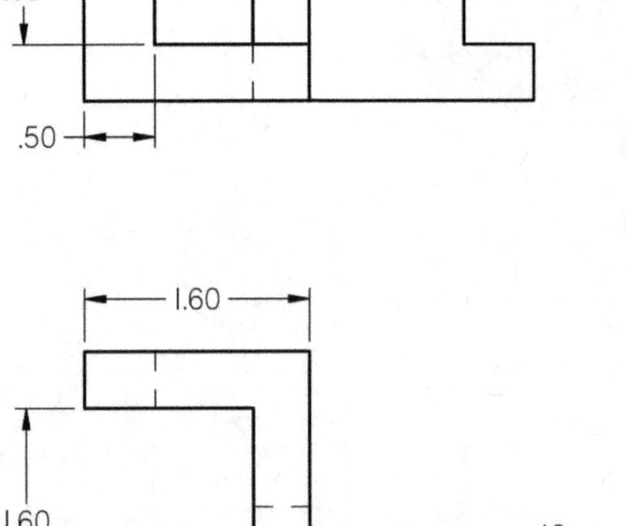

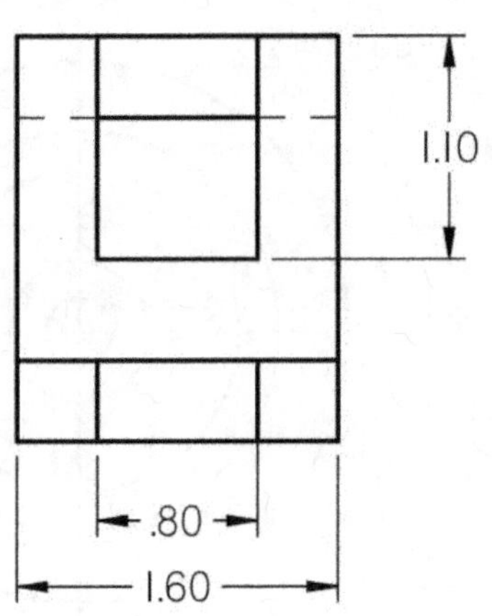

Exercise 3

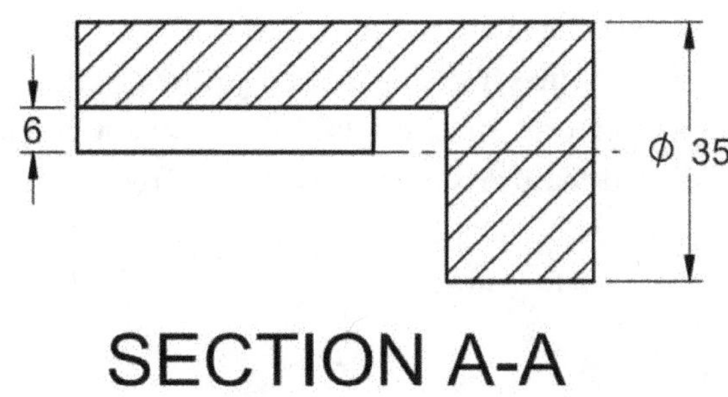

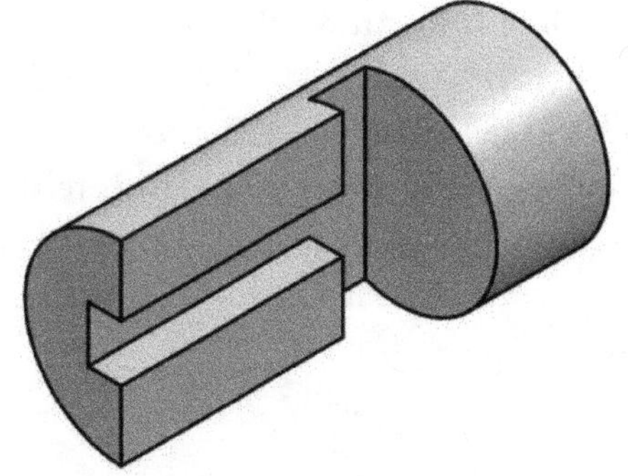

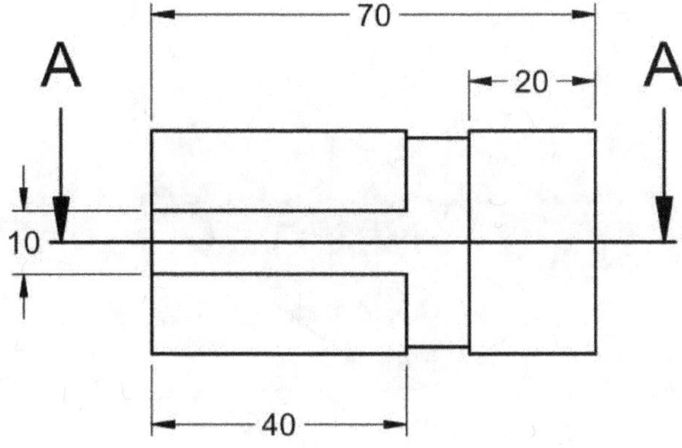

Chapter 4: Holes and Dress-Up Features

So far, all of the features that were covered in the previous chapter were based on two-dimensional sketches. However, there are certain features in CATIA V5 that do not require a sketch at all. Features that do not require a sketch are called Dress-Up features. You can simply place them on your models. However, you must have some existing geometry to add these features. Unlike a sketch-based feature, you cannot use a Dress-Up feature for a first feature of a model. For example, to create a *Fillet* feature, you must have an already existing edge. In this chapter, you will learn how to add Holes and Dress-Up features to your design.

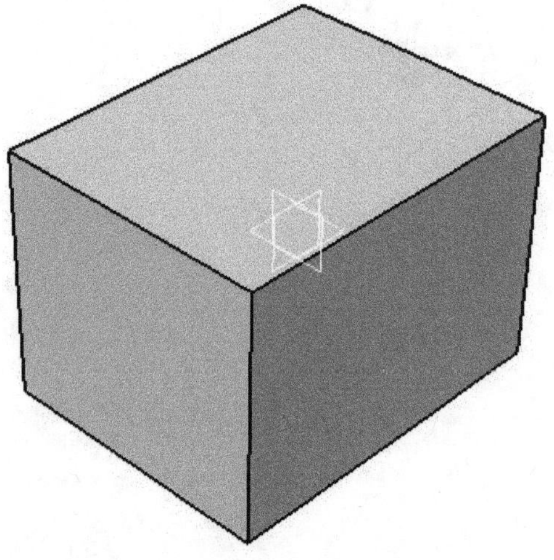

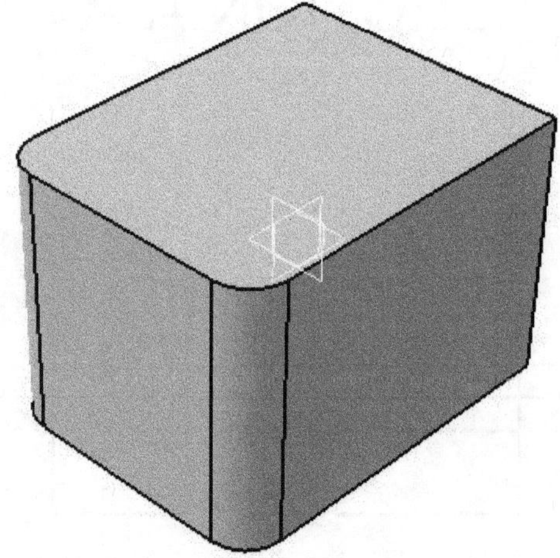

The topics covered in this chapter are:

- *Holes*
- *Threads*
- *Fillets*
- *Chamfers*
- *Drafts*
- *Shells*

 Hole

As you know, it is possible to use the *Pocket* command to create cuts and remove material. But, if you want to drill holes that are of standard sizes, the **Hole** command is a better way to do this. The reason for this is it has many hole types already predefined for you. All you have to do is choose the correct hole type and size. The other benefit is when you are going to create a 2D drawing, CATIA V5 can automatically place the correct hole annotation. Activate this command (On the **Sketch Based Features** toolbar, click the **Hole** icon) and click on a face to a add hole. You will notice that a dialog pops up. There are options in this dialog that make it easy to create different types of holes.

Simple Hole

1. To create a simple hole feature, select **Type > Simple** on the **Hole Definition** dialog.

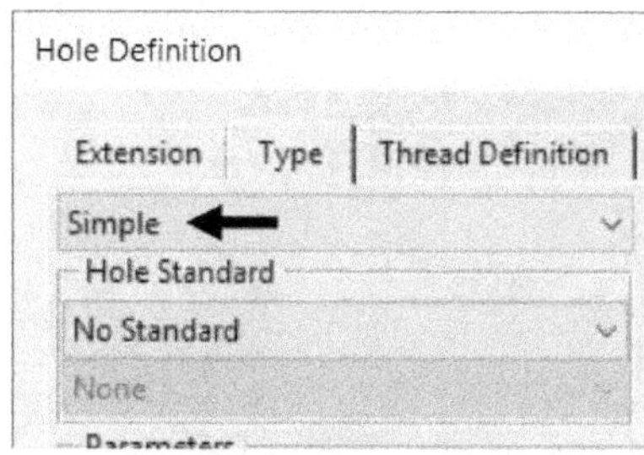

2. Under the **Extension** tab, type-in a value in the **Diameter** box and select the extension type.
3. If you want a through hole, click **Extension** drop-down > **Up To Last**. If you want a blind hole, then select **Blind** from the **Extension** drop-down. Next, type-in a value in the **Depth** box.
4. If you want a V-bottom hole, then select **Bottom > V-Bottom** and type-in a value in the **Angle** box.

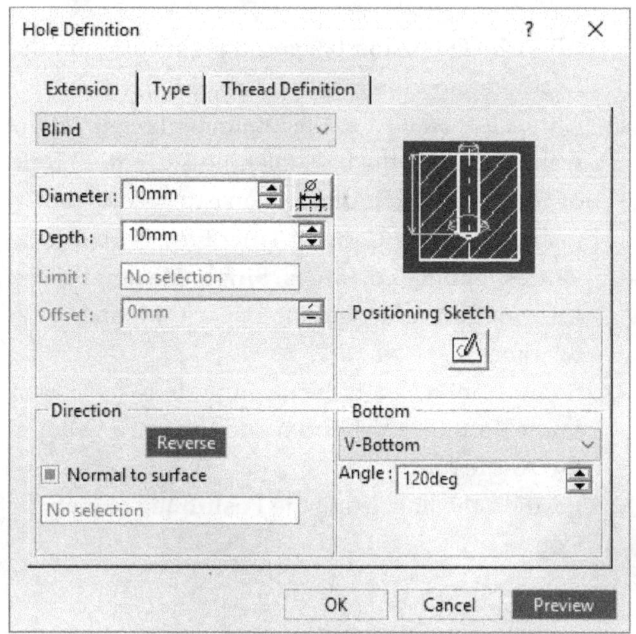

5. On the dialog, click **Positioned Sketch**, to activate the Sketcher Workbench.
6. Add dimensions to define the hole position.

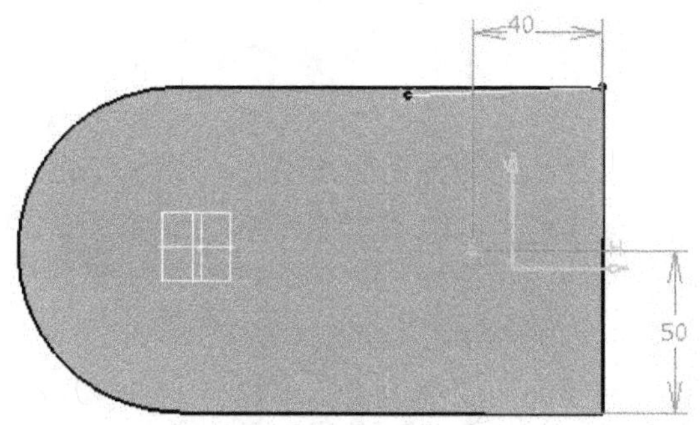

7. On the **Workbench** toolbar, click the **Exit Workbench** icon.

The hole will be created normal to the selected face.

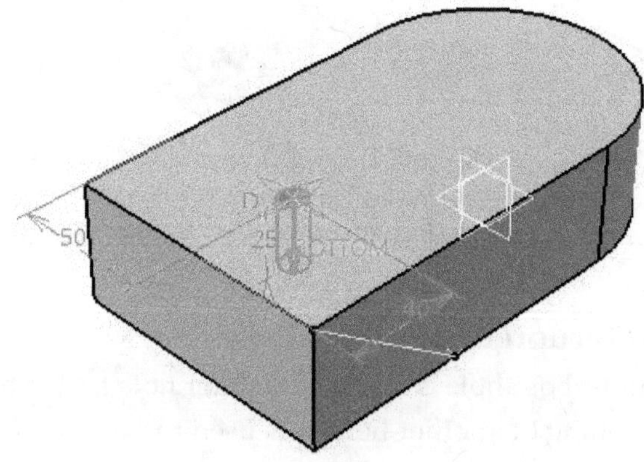

8. If you want to create holes at an angle or along a reference line, then uncheck the **Normal to Surface** option and select a reference line or edge. The hole will be created along the selected line or edge.

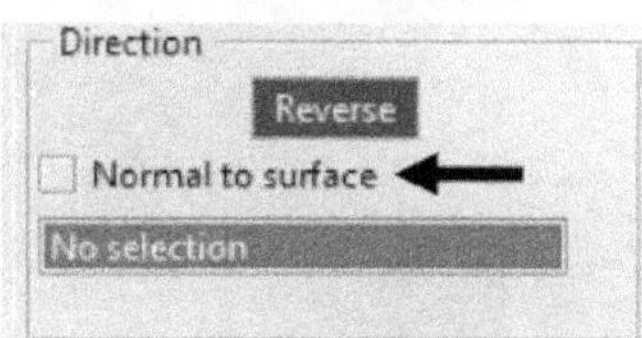

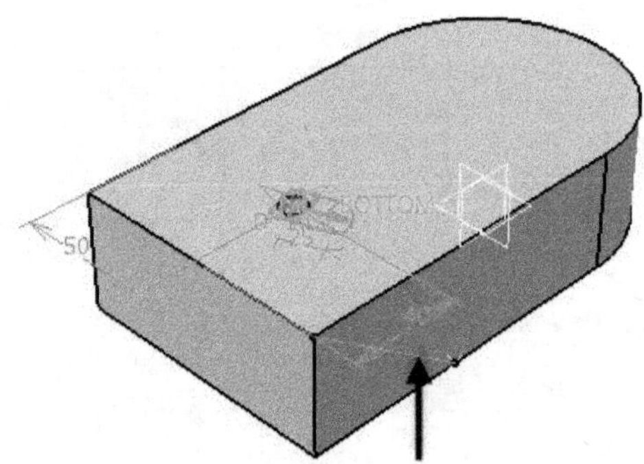

9. Click **OK** to create the holes.

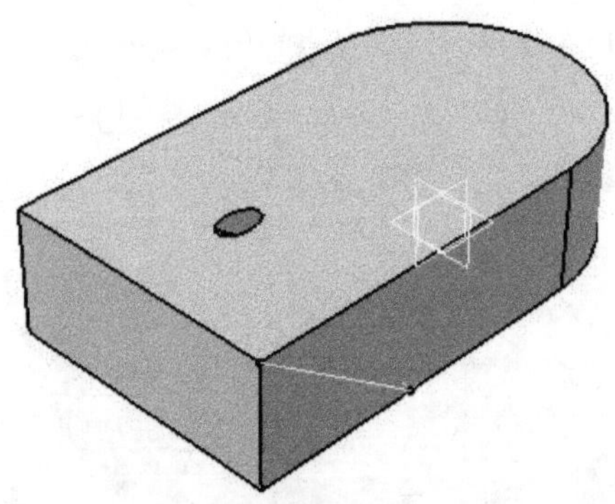

Counterbored Hole

A counterbore hole is a large diameter hole added at the opening of another hole. It is used to accommodate a fastener below the level of work piece surface.

1. To create a counterbore hole, select **Type> Counterbored** from the dialog.
2. Next, define the counterbore diameter and counterbore depth.

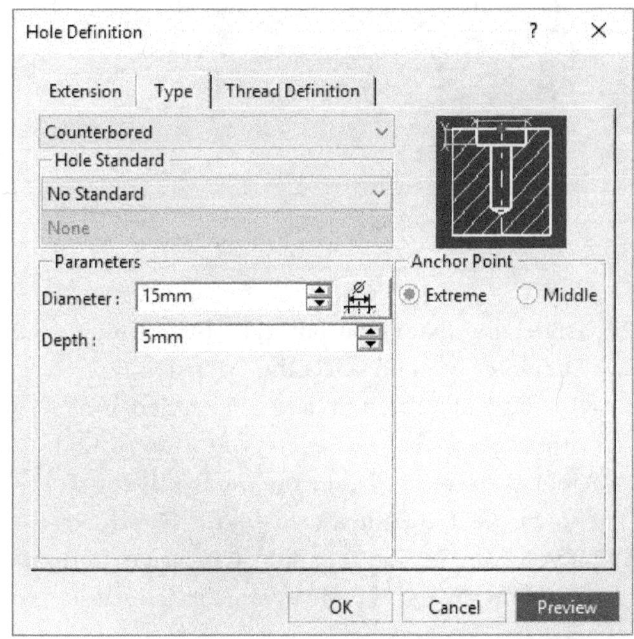

3. Click the **Extension** tab and type-in values in the **Diameter** and the **Depth** boxes.
4. Click the icon next to the **Diameter** box, if you want to specify the hole tolerances. On the **Limit of Size Definition** dialog, you can specify the tolerances using **General Tolerance**, **Numerical values**, **Tabulated values**, **Single Limit**, or **Information**. Click **OK** after specifying the tolerances.
5. If you want a V-bottomed counterbore hole, then select **Bottom > V-Bottom** and type-in a value in the **Angle** box.
6. Position the hole using the **Positioned sketch** icon.

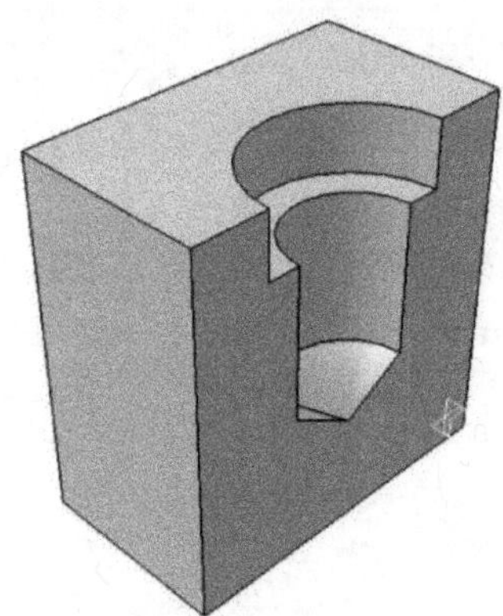

You can also create a standard counterbored hole using the **Hole Standard** drop-down available in the **Type** tab of the **Hole** dialog. You can select

Metric_cap_screws or **Socket_Head_Cap_Screws** hole standard. Next, select the hole size from the drop-down available below the **Hole Standard** drop-down.

Countersunk Hole

A countersunk hole has an enlarged V-shaped opening to accommodate a fastener below the level of work piece surface.

1. To create a countersunk hole, select **Type > Countersunk**.
2. Under the **Parameters** section, select **Mode > Depth & Angle** or **Depth & Diameter** or **Angle & Diameter**. For example, if you select **Angle & Diameter**, you must specify the Countersink diameter and angle.
3. Type-in values in the **Parameters** section.

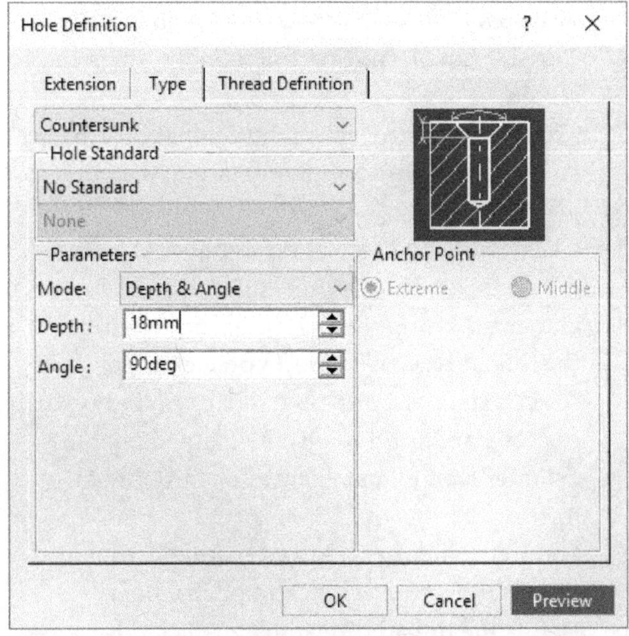

7. Click the **Extension** tab, specify the diameter, depth, and end condition of the hole.
8. Position the hole using the **Positioned sketch** icon.
9. Click **OK** on the dialog.

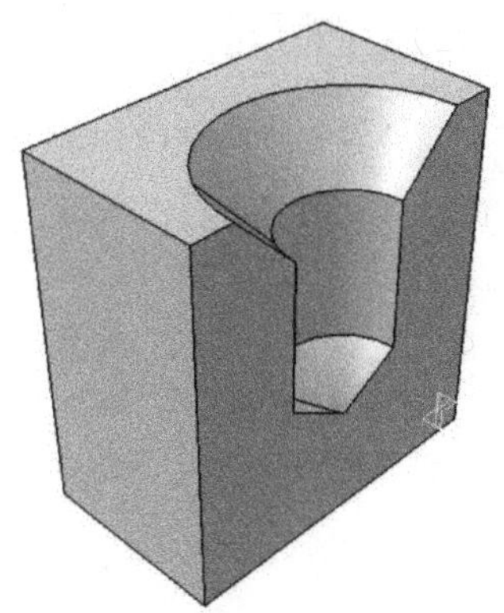

Tapered Hole

Tapering is the process of decreasing the hole diameter toward one end. A tapered hole has a smaller diameter at the bottom.

1. To create a tapered hole, select **Type > Tapered** on the **Hole Definition** dialog.
2. Type-in the taper angle value in the **Angle** box.
3. Select the **Anchor Point** to define the bottom or top diameter.

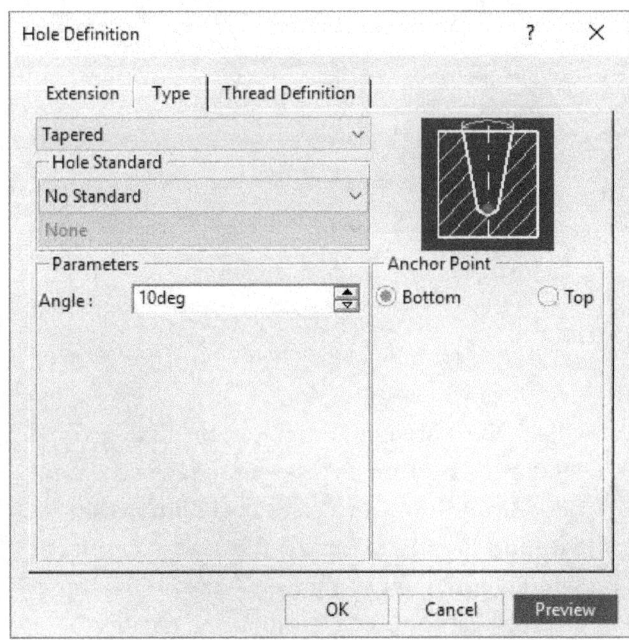

4. Specify the **Extension** parameters and hole position.
5. Click **OK** to create the tapered hole.

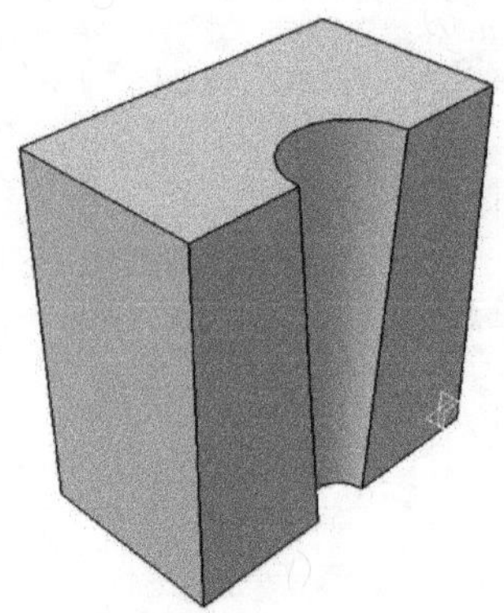

Threaded Hole

1. To create a threaded hole feature, click the **Thread Definition** tab on the **Hole Definition** dialog.

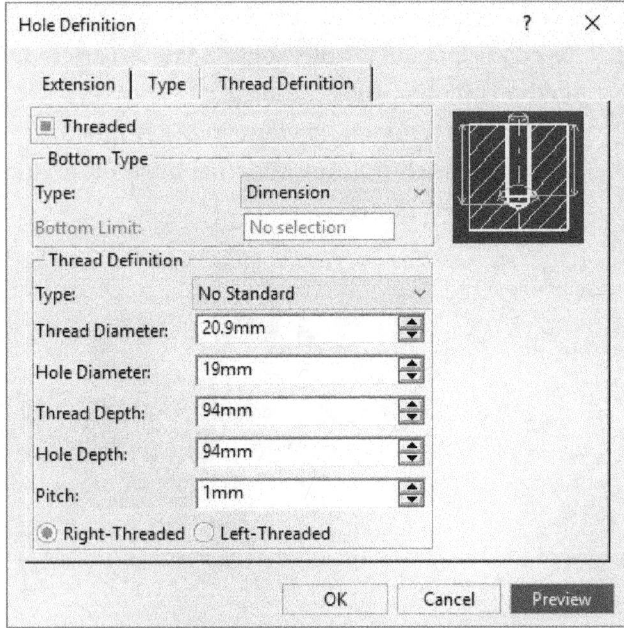

2. Check the **Threaded** option on the dialog.
3. Under the **Bottom Type** section, select the type of end condition. You can select **Dimension**, **Support Depth**, or **Up-To-Plane**. If you select **Dimension**, then you have to type-in the thread depth. The **Support Depth** option creates the thread throughout the hole. The **Up-To-Plane** option creates the thread up to a plane.
4. Under the **Thread Definition** section, select the type of the thread. You can select standard or non-standard threads. If you select standard threads, then you have to select the thread size from the **Thread Description** menu. All thread size and pitches will be calculated, automatically. If you select **No Standard** thread, then you have to type-in the thread diameter, hole diameter, and pitch.
5. Define the thread direction by select the **Right-Threaded** or **Left-Threaded** option.

The Thread/Tap command

This command adds a thread/tap feature to a cylindrical face. A thread is added to the outer cylindrical face, whereas a tap is added to the inner cylindrical face (holes). You add thread/tap features to a 3D geometry so that when you create a 2D drawing, CATIA V5 can automatically place the correct thread annotation.

1. On the **Dress-Up Features** toolbar, click the **Thread/Tap** button (or) click **Insert > Dress-Up Features > Thread/Tap** on the Menu bar. The **Thread/Tap Definition** dialog pops up on the screen.
2. To create a thread, select the **Thread** option and click on the outer cylindrical face of the part geometry.
3. Click on the end face of the cylindrical feature to define the limiting face.
4. Under the **Numerical Definition** section, select the thread type from the **Type** menu. You can select a standard or non-standard thread type. In case of standard threads, the diameter of the cylinder should match any standard thread format.
5. For non-standard threads, type-in the thread diameter, thread depth, and pitch values.
6. Define the thread direction and click **OK**.

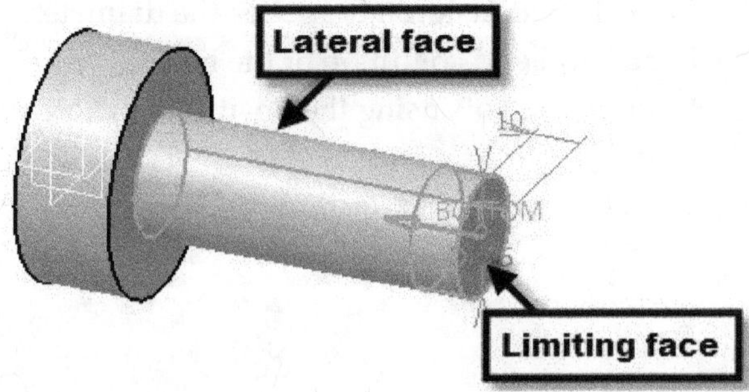

The Edge Fillet command

This command breaks the sharp edges of a model and blends them. You do not need a sketch to create a fillet. All you need to have is model edges.

1. On the **Dress-Up Features** toolbar, click the **Edge Fillet** button (or) click **Insert > Dress-Up Features > Edge Fillet** on the Menu bar. The **Edge Fillet Definition** dialog pops up on the screen.
2. Select the edges to fillet. You can also select all the edges of a face by simply clicking on the face. By mistake, if you have selected a wrong edge you can deselect it by selecting the edge again.

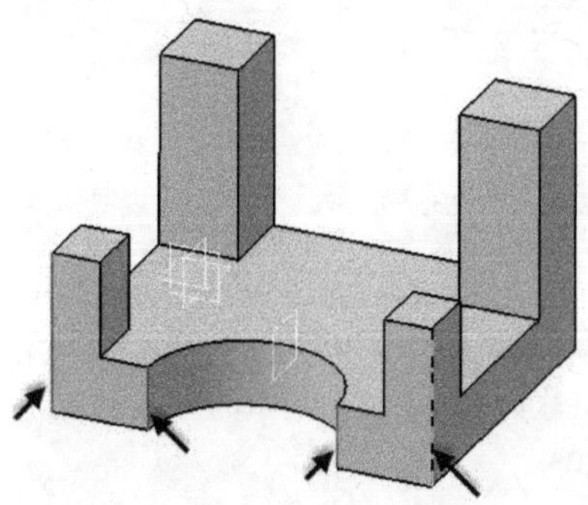

3. You can change the radius by typing a value in the **Radius** box available on the **Edge Fillet Definition** dialog. As you change the radius, all the selected edges will be updated. This is because they are all part of one instance. If you want the edges to have different radii, you must create rounds in separate instances. Select the required number of edges and click **OK** to finish this feature. The *Edge Fillet* feature will be listed in the Specification Tree.

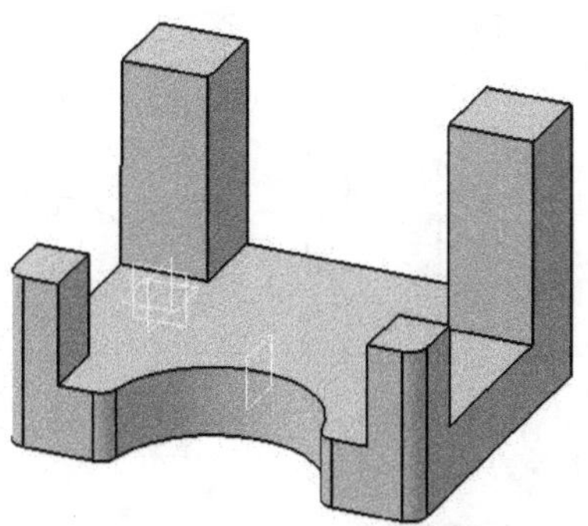

If you want to select all the edges that are tangentially connected, then select **Propagation > Tangency** on the dialog. Next, click on anyone of the tangentially connected edges; the edge fillet will be applied to all the tangentially connected edges.

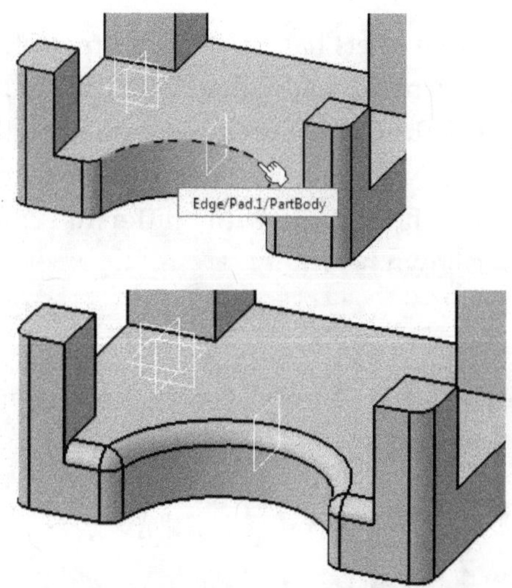

If you select **Propagation > Minimal** on the dialog, the selected will be filleted ignoring the connected ones.

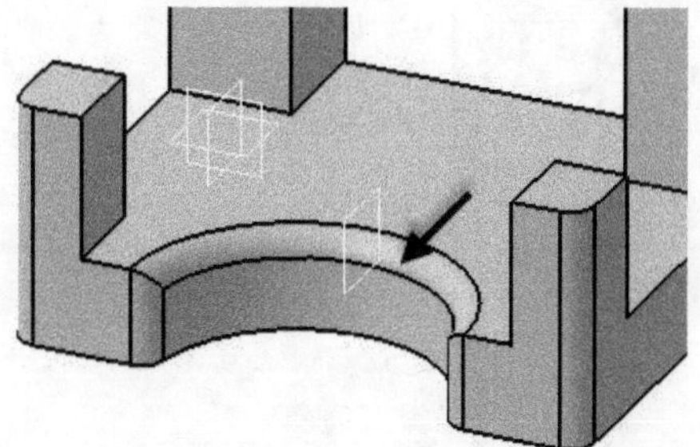

If you select **Propagation > Intersection**, then you can fillet the intersections between two features of the geometry.

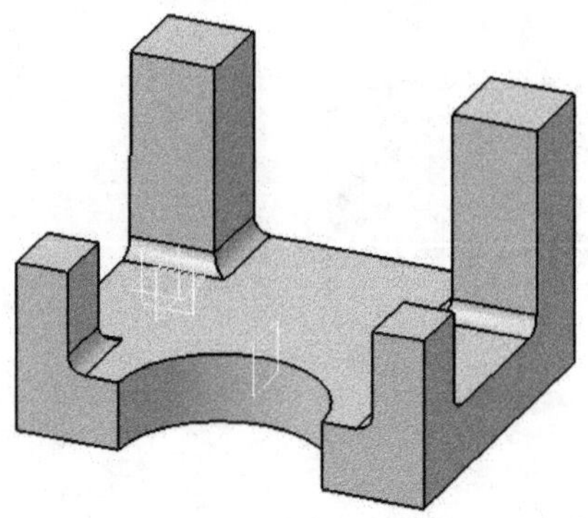

Select **Propagation > Intersection with selected features.** Next, select two features to fillet the intersections between them.

Conic fillets

By default, the edge fillets have a circular arc profile. However, if you want to create a fillet with conical arc profile, then check the **Conic parameter** option on the **Edge Fillet** dialog. Next, type-in a value in the **Conic parameter** box. The fillets with different conic parameters are shown below.

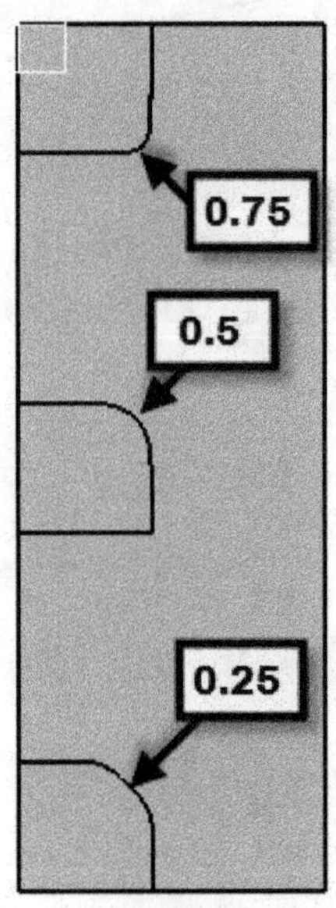

Trim ribbons

If you are creating fillets, which intersect each other, then you need to check the **Trim ribbons** option. This trims the intersecting portion.

Edge(s) to keep

If you create fillets, which intersect with the adjacent edges, then this may deform the edges.

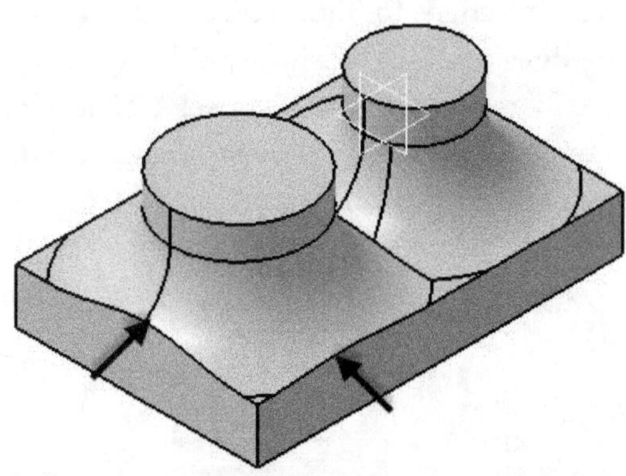

To avoid this, click the **More** button on the dialog and click in the **Edge(s) to keep** selection box. Now, select the adjacent edges.

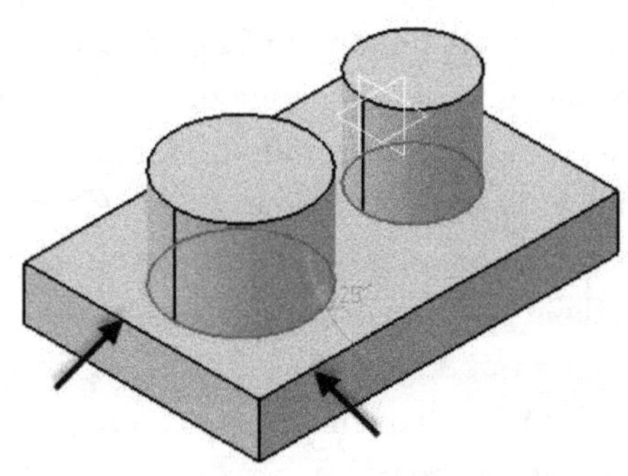

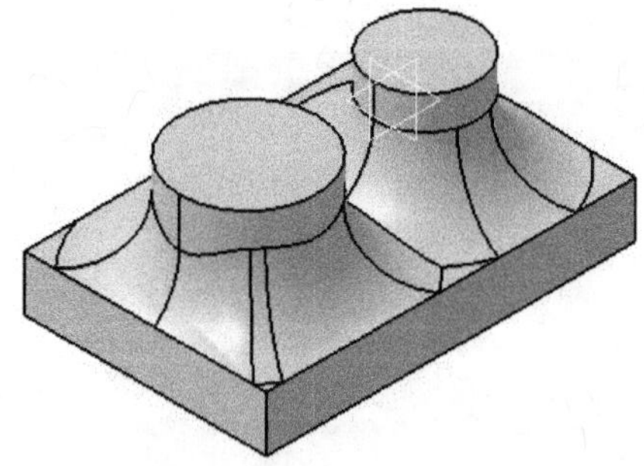

Limiting element(s)

If you want to create an edge fillet only up to some distance, then expand the **Edge Fillet Definition** dialog and click in the **Limiting element(s)** selection box. Click on a reference element (plane or point) to define the limiting elements. If there is no reference element available, then click the right mouse button in the **Limiting element(s)** selection box and create one.

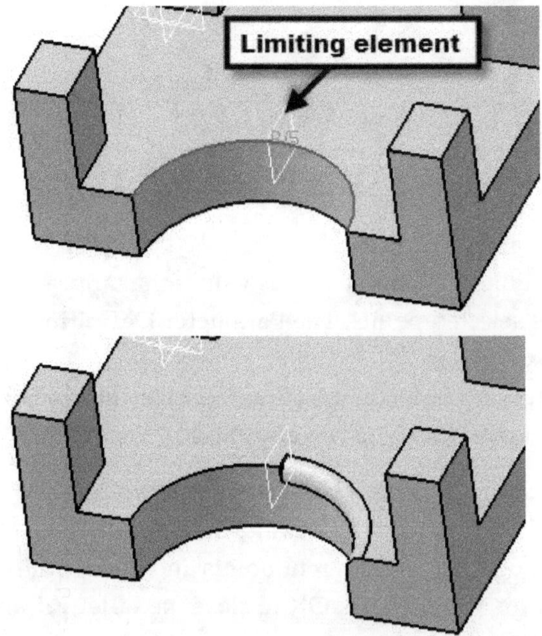

You can also limit the edge fillet between two limiting elements. To do this, click in the **Limiting elements(s)** box, and then select limiting elements. Make sure that the arrows on the selected elements point in the opposite direction. You can click on the arrows to change their direction.

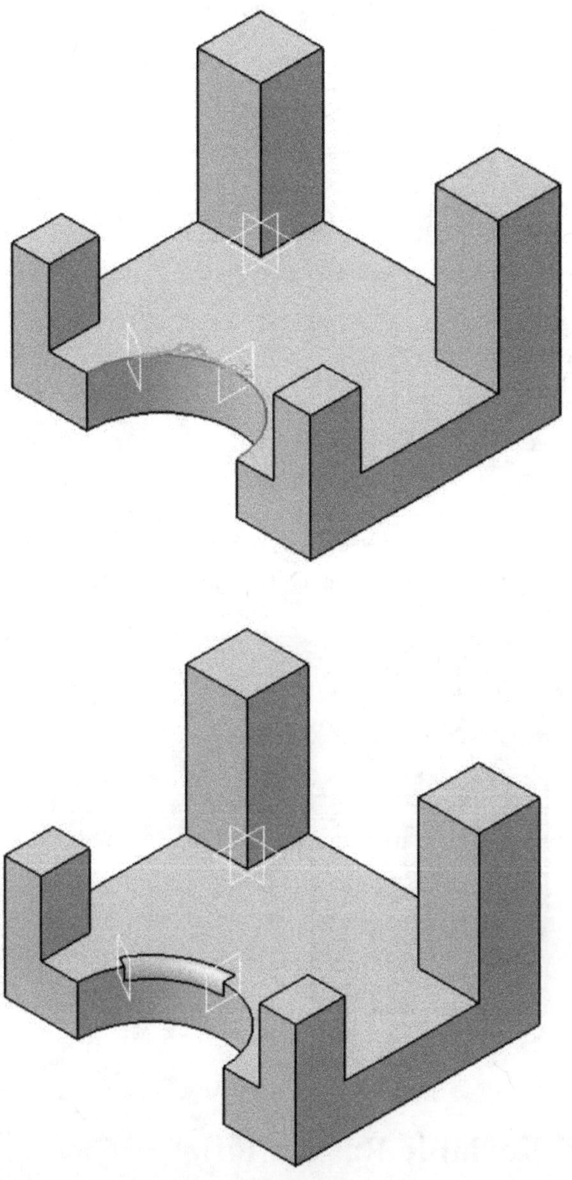

Blend corner(s)

If you create an edge fillet on three edges that come together at a corner, you have the option to control how these three fillets are blend together. Activate the **Edge Blend** command and select the three edges that meet together at a corner, refer to figure given next. On the **Edge Fillet Definition** dialog, click the right mouse button in the **Blend corner(s)** selection box, and then select **Create by edges or vertex**. If you select **Create by edges**, then the corner point will be selected, automatically. You can also select the vertex where the three fillets meet. You will notice that three setback distances appear at the corner.

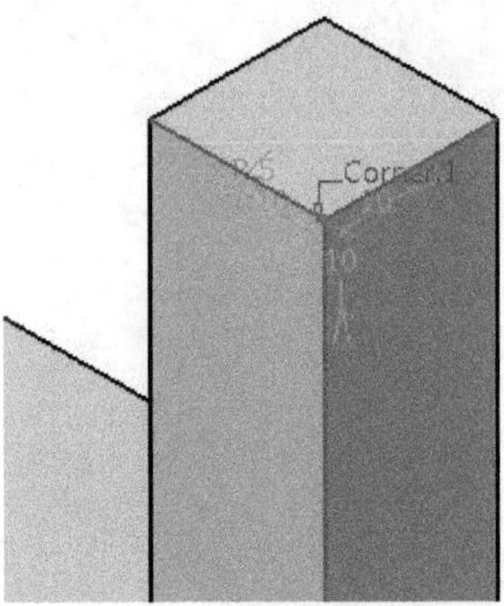

Double-click on the setback distances and type-in values in the **Parameter Definition** boxes.

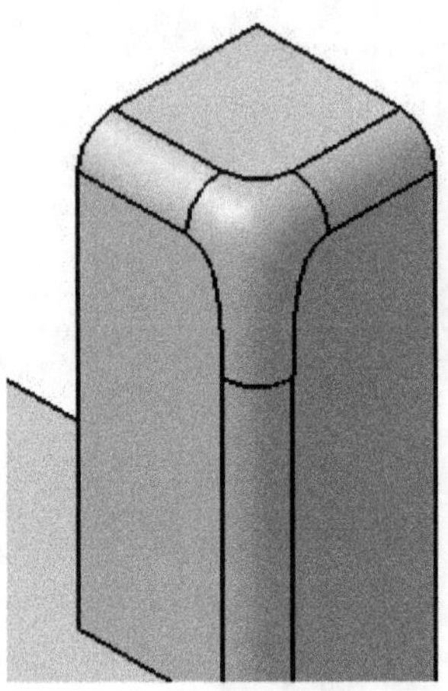

Variable Radius Fillet

CATIA V5 allows you to create a fillet with a varying radius along the selected edge.

1. On the **Dress-Up Features** toolbar, click **Fillets** drop-down > **Edge Fillet** (or) click **Insert > Dress-Up Features > Edge Fillet** on the Menu bar.
2. On the **Edge Fillet Definition** dialog, click the **Variable** icon.
3. Click on the edge to fillet.
4. Click in the **Points** selection box to select variable radius points.
5. On the selected edge, select points to define variable radius. You will notice that radius values appear on the selected points.

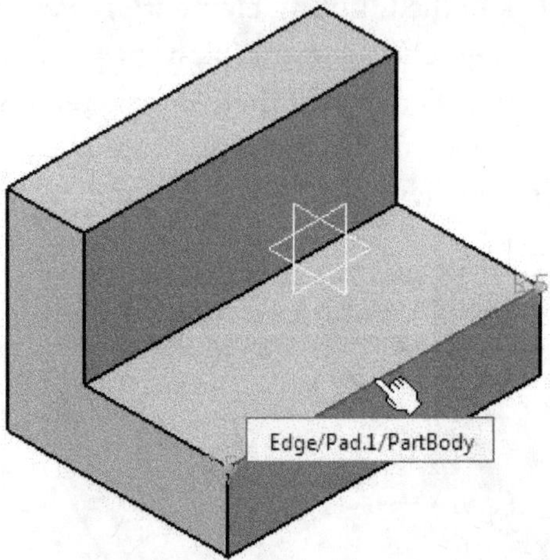

6. Double-click on the radius values that appear on the selected points. The **Parameter Definition** box appears.
7. Type-in a value in the **Parameter Definition** box and click **OK**. You can also modify the radii by clicking the button next to the **Radius** box. This displays the **Fillet values** dialog. On this dialog, click on different points and change the radius values. Click **OK** to close the **Fillet values** dialog.
8. Click **Preview** to see how the variable radius fillet would look.
9. On the dialog, click **Variation > Cubic** to get a smooth fillet. Click **Variation > Linear** to get a straight transition fillet.

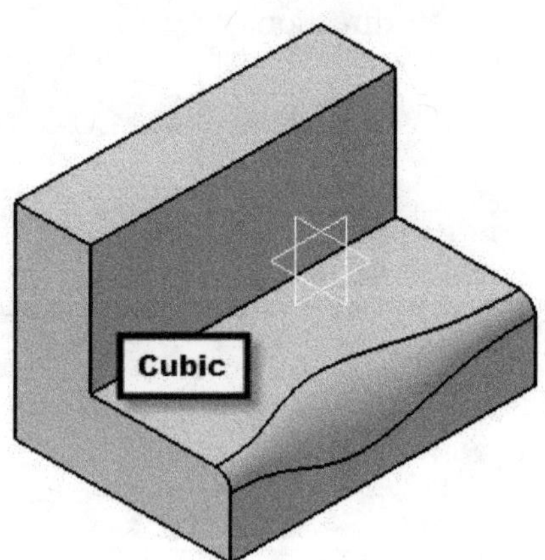

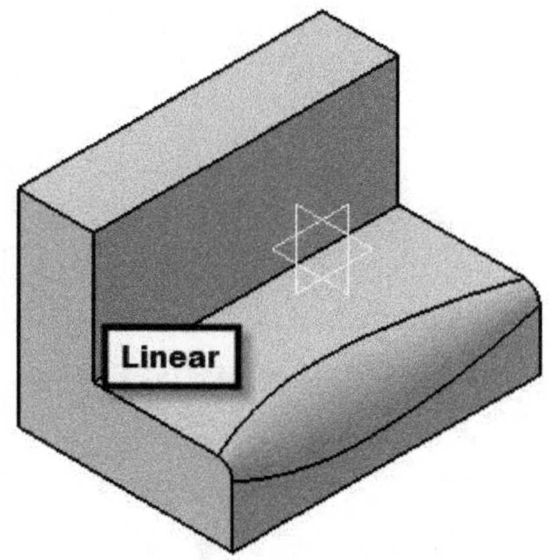

10. Click **OK** to create the variable radius fillet.

Chordal Fillet

This option helps you to create a fillet by specifying its chord length instead of a radius. The chord length is the distance between the endpoints of the fillet profile.

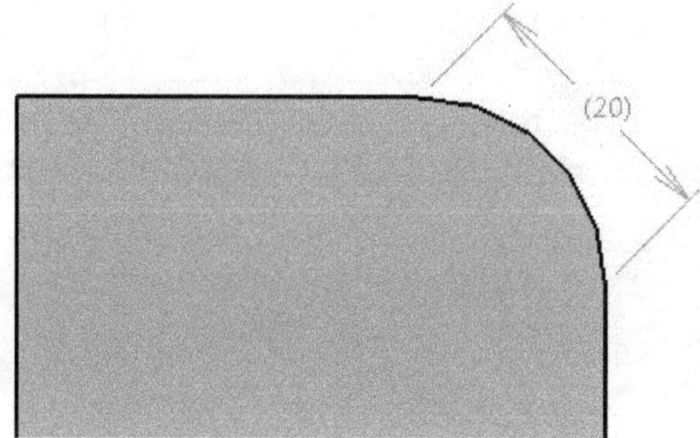

1. On the **Dress-Up Features** toolbar, click **Fillets** drop-down > **Edge Fillet** (or) click **Insert > Dress-Up Features > Edge Fillet** on the Menu bar.
2. On the **Edge Fillet Definition** dialog, click the **Chordal Length** icon available next to the **Radius** box.
3. Click on the edge to fillet.
4. Type-in a value in the **Chordal Length** box.
5. If you want to create a variable radius fillet, then click the **Variable** icon and select multiple points on the edge. Change the chordal length values of the points.

Face-Face Fillet

This command creates a fillet between two faces. The faces are not required to be connected with each other.

1. On the **Dress-Up Features** toolbar, click **Fillets** drop-down > **Face-Face Fillet** (or) click **Insert > Dress-Up Features > Face-Face Fillet** on the Menu bar.
2. Click on two faces.

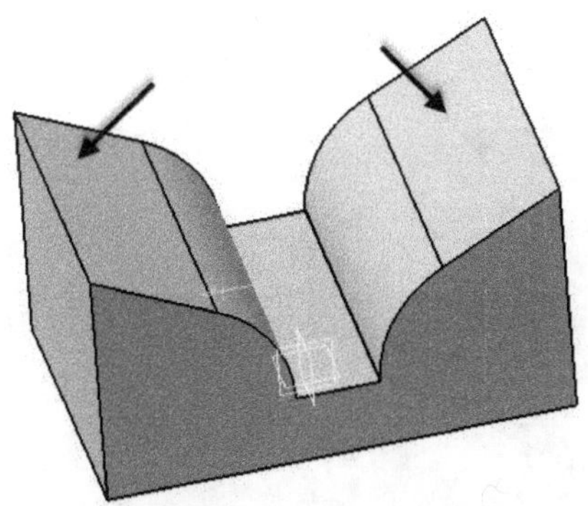

3. Type-in a value in the **Radius** box.
4. Click **OK**.

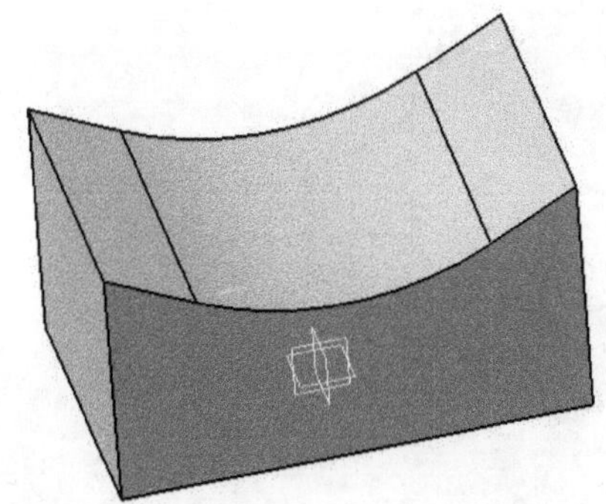

Tritangent Fillet

This command creates a fillet between three faces. It replaces the middle face with a fillet.

1. On the **Dress-Up Features** toolbar, click **Fillets** drop-down > **Tritangent Fillet** (or) click **Insert > Dress-Up Features > Tritangent Fillet** on the Menu bar.
2. Click on three faces of the model geometry.
3. Click **OK** to replace the middle face with a fillet.

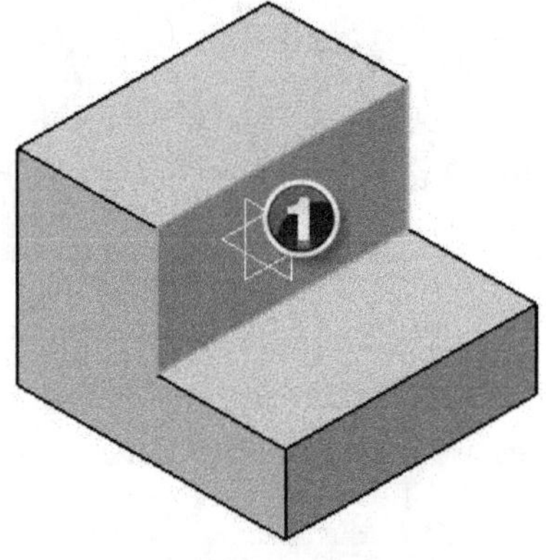

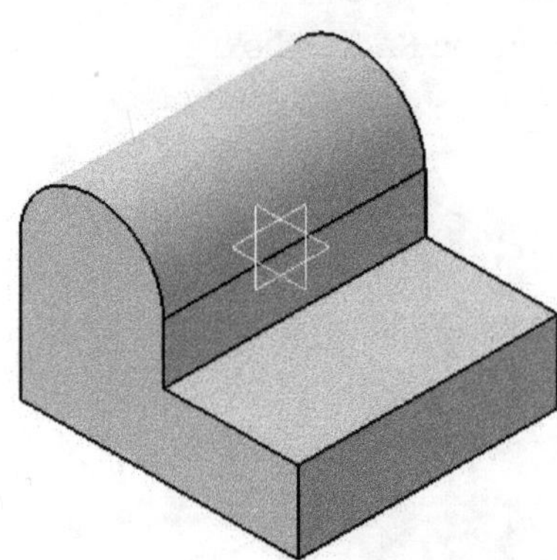

 The Chamfer command

The **Chamfer** and **Edge Fillet** commands are commonly used to break sharp edges. The difference is that the **Chamfer** command adds a bevel face to the model. A chamfer is also a placed feature.

1. On the **Dress-Up Features** toolbar, click the **Chamfer** button (or) click **Insert > Dress-Up Features > Chamfer** on the Menu bar.
2. On the **Chamfer Definition** dialog, select chamfer **Mode**. You can select **Length1/Angle**, **Length1/Length2**, **Chordal Length/Angle**, or **Height/Angle**.

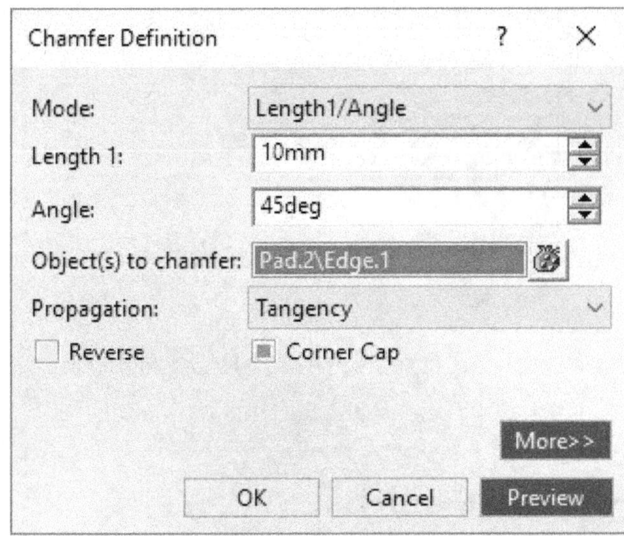

3. If you select **Mode > Length1/Angle**, then type-in the length and angle values of the chamfer.
4. Click on the edge(s) to chamfer.
5. Click **OK**.

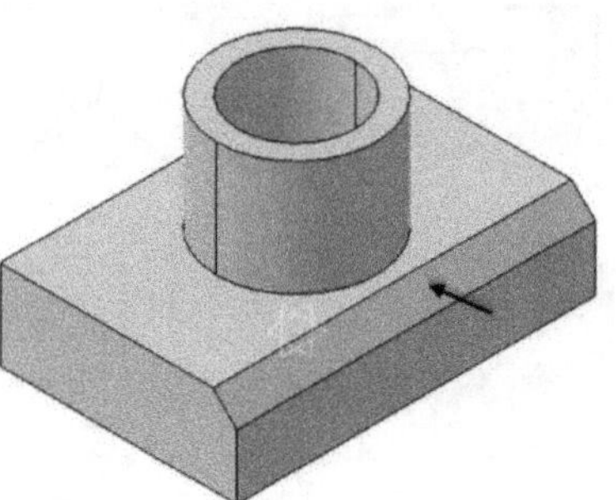

 Draft Angle

When creating cast or plastic parts, you are often required to add draft on them so that they can be molded. A draft is an angle or taper applied to the faces of parts to make it easier to remove them from a mold. When creating *Drafted Filleted Pad* features, you can predefine the draft angle. However, most of the time, it is easier to apply the draft after the features are created.

1. On the **Dress-Up Features** toolbar, click **Drafts** drop-down > **Draft Angle** (or) click **Insert > Dress-Up Features > Draft** on the Menu bar.
2. On the **Draft Definition** dialog, select **Draft Type > Constant**.

3. Click on the faces to draft.
4. Under the **Neutral Element** section, click in the **Selection** box and select a flat face or plane. This defines the neutral plane. The draft angle will be measured with reference to this face.

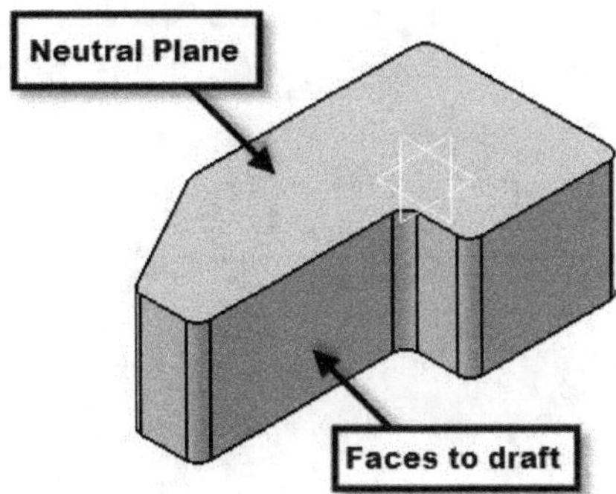

5. Type-in a value in the **Angle** box. This defines the draft angle.
6. Click **Preview**.

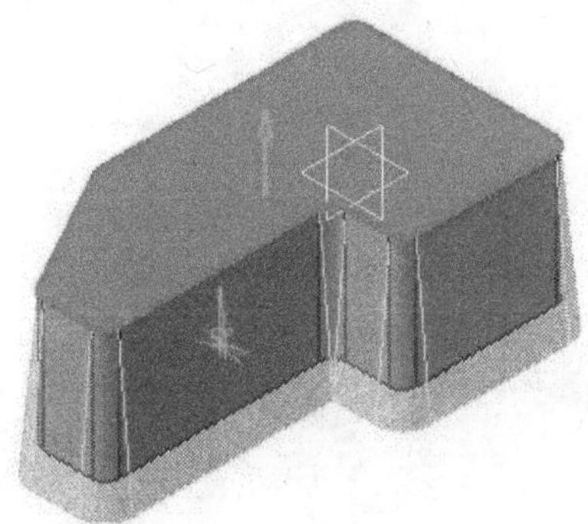

7. If you want to reverse the draft direction, then click the arrow that appears on the geometry.
8. Click **OK** to apply draft.

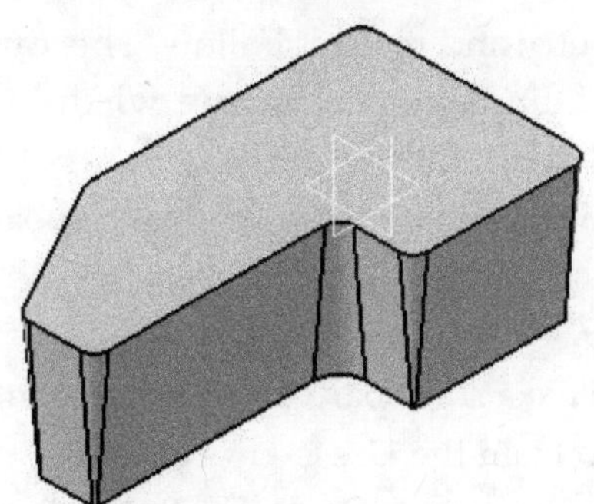

Parting=Neutral

If you want to add draft only up to a certain height, then create a plane at that height. Activate the **Draft Angle** command and select the faces to draft. Click in the **Neutral Element** selection box and select the plane. On the dialog, click the **More** button and check the **Parting=Neutral** option.

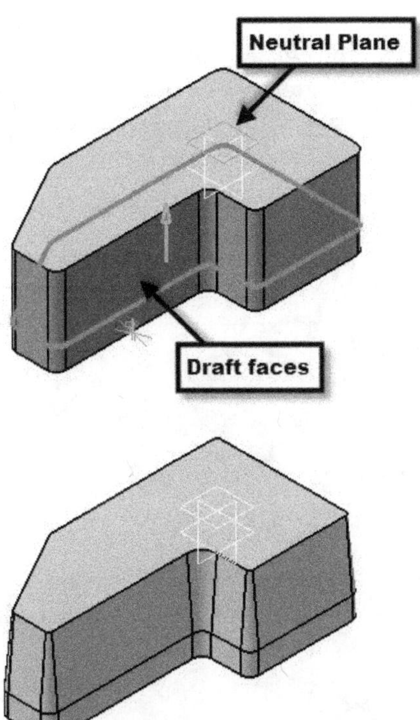

If you check the **Draft both sides** option, the draft will be applied on both sides of the parting plane.

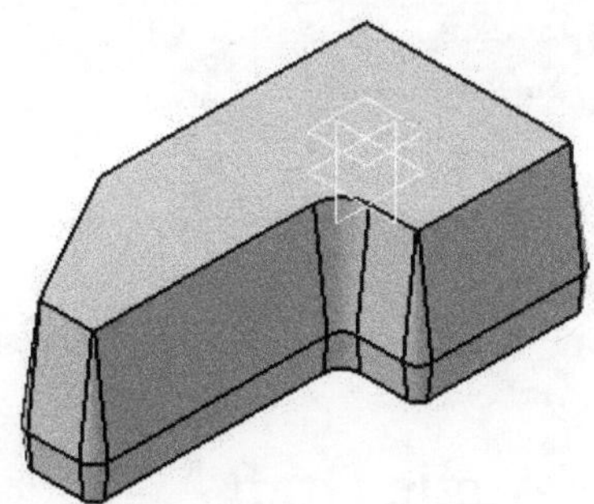

 Draft Reflect Line

This command creates a draft by using the silhouette edges (reflected lines) of the curved feature.

1. On the **Dress-Up Features** toolbar, click **Drafts** drop-down > **Draft Reflect line** (or) click **Insert > Dress-Up Features > Draft reflect line** on the Menu bar.
2. Select a curved face to define the drafting face.

3. Click in the **Pulling Direction** selection box and select a flat face or plane. This defines the pulling direction.
4. Click the **More** button on the dialog and check the **Define parting element** option.
5. Select a flat face or plane to define the parting element.

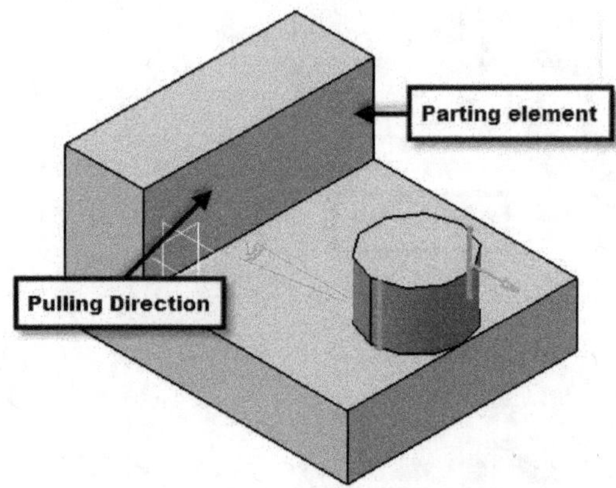

6. Type-in a value in the **Angle** box, and then click **OK**.

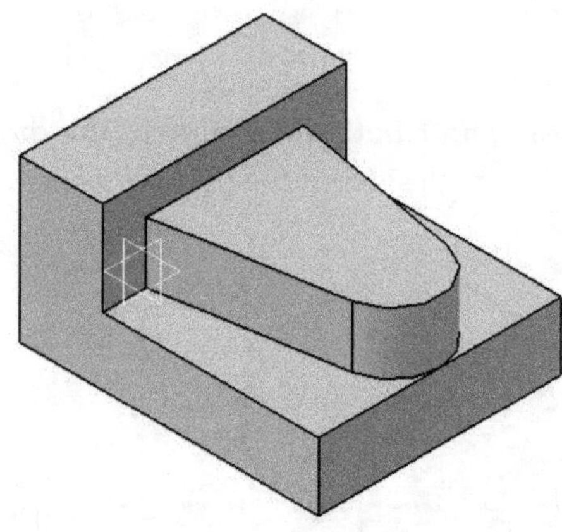

 Variable Angle Draft

This command creates a variable angle draft.

1. On the **Dress-Up Features** toolbar, click **Drafts** drop-down > **Variable Angle Draft** (or) click **Insert > Dress-Up Features > Variable Angle Draft** on the Menu bar.
2. Click on the face to draft. If you select multiple faces, you have to make sure that they are connected, tangentially.
3. Click in the **Neutral element** box and select a flat face or plane.
4. Click in the **Points** box and select multiple points to define different angles. You will notice that angle values appear on the selected points.
5. Double-click on the angle values to change them.

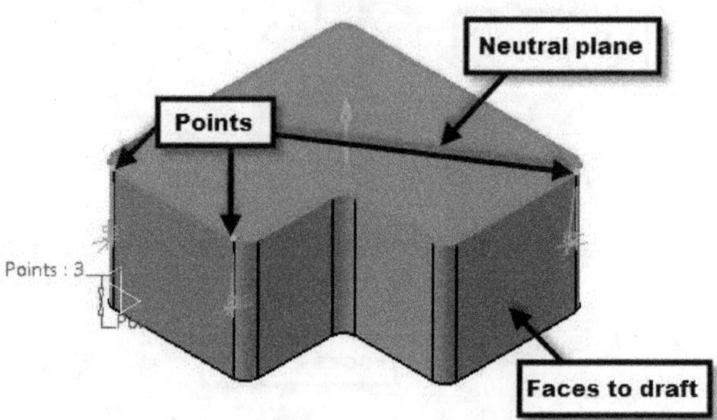

6. Click **OK**.

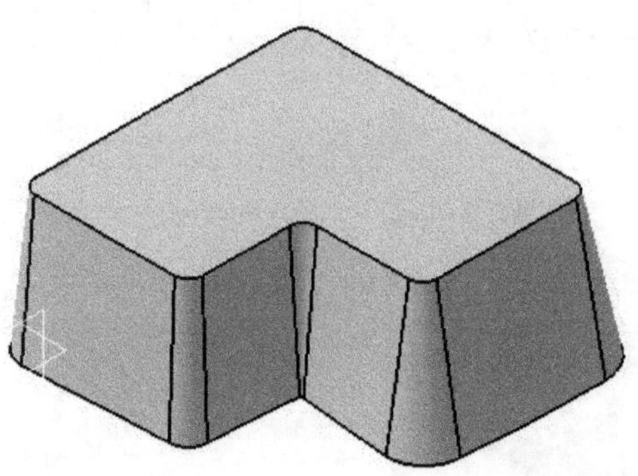

 Shell

The **Shell** is another useful feature that can be applied directly to a solid model. It allows you to take a solid geometry and make it hollow. This can be a powerful and timesaving technique, when designing parts that call for thin walls such as bottles, tanks, and containers. This command is easy to use.

1. You should have a solid part, and then activate this command from the **Dress-Up Features** toolbar (or) click **Insert > Dress-Up Features > Shell** on the Menu bar.
2. Select the faces to remove.
3. Type-in the wall thickness in the **Default inside thickness** box.

4. If you want to add outside thickness, then type-in a value in the **Default outside thickness** box.
5. If you want add different thickness to some faces, then click in the **Other thickness faces** box, and then select the faces to add different thickness. You will notice that a thickness value appears on the selected face. Double-click on the value and change it.

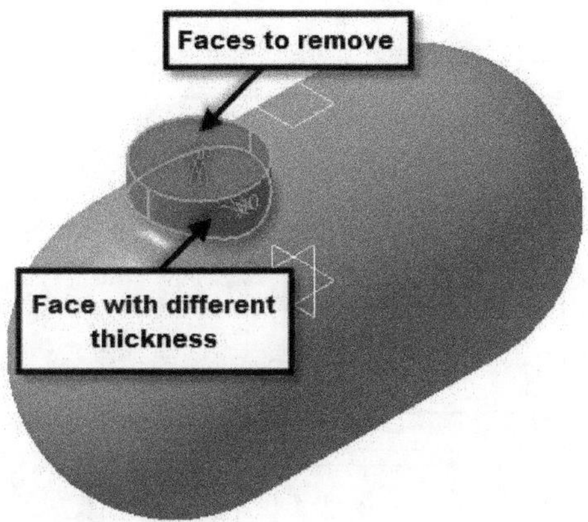

6. Click **OK** to finish the feature.

If you want to shell the solid body without removing any faces, then simply type-in a value in the **Default inner thickness** box and click **OK**. This creates the shell without removing the faces. Change the **Render style** to **Wireframe** or **Shading with Edges and Hidden Edges** to view the shell.

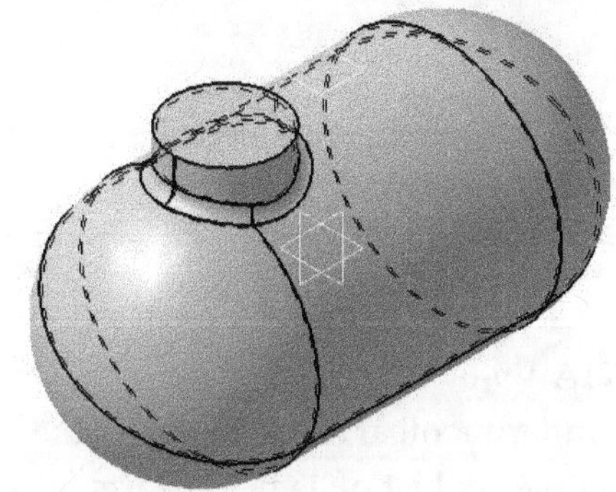

Examples

Example 1

In this example, you will create the part shown next.

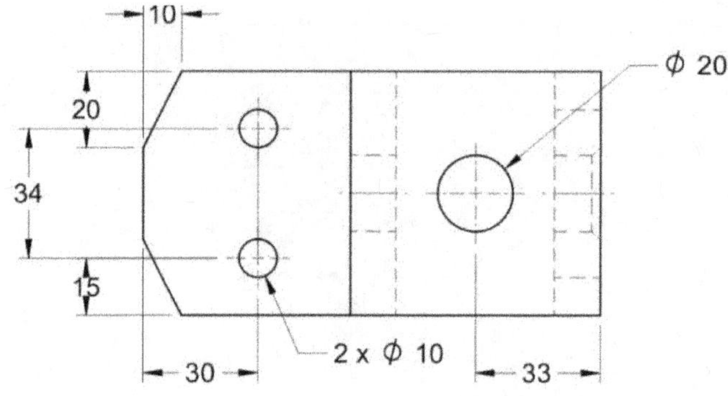

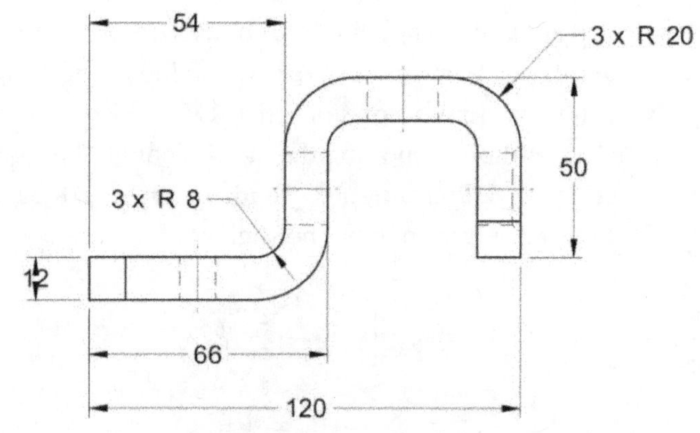

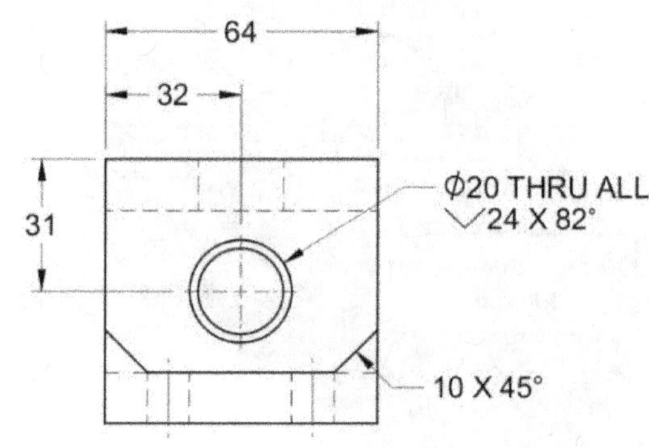

1. Start **CATIA V5-6R2017**.
2. On the **Standard** toolbar, click **New**. On the **New** dialog, select **List of Types > Parts**. Click **OK**.
3. On the **New Part** dialog, type-in **C04-Example1** and check the **Enable hybrid design** option. Click **OK**.
4. On the **Sketch Based Features** toolbar, click the **Pad** icon.
5. On the **Pad Definition** dialog, click the **Sketch** icon and select the YZ plane. Draw the sketch shown in figure and create the pad feature of 64 mm thickness.

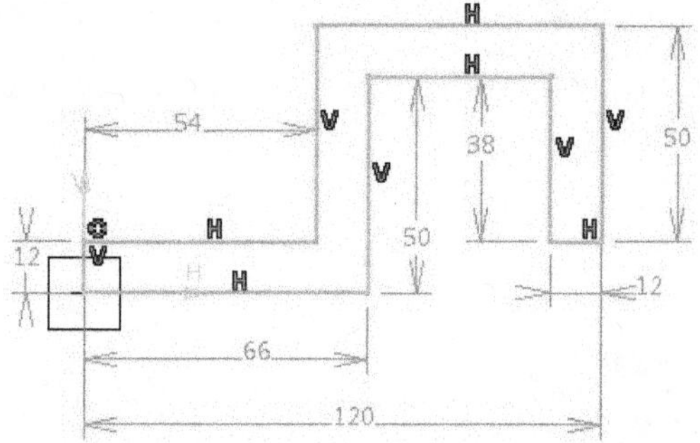

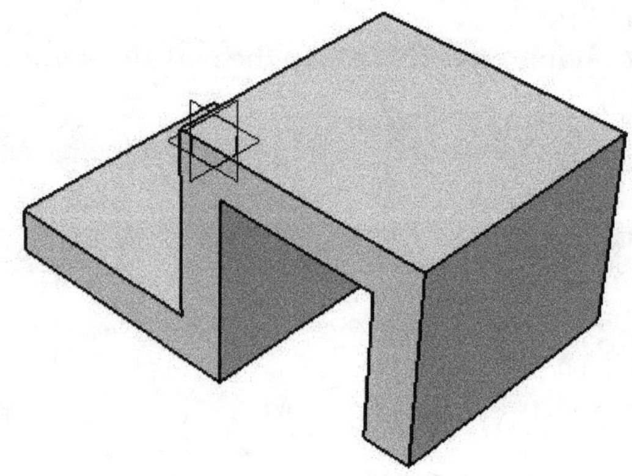

6. On the **Sketcher** toolbar, click the **Sketch** icon, and then select the right-side face.

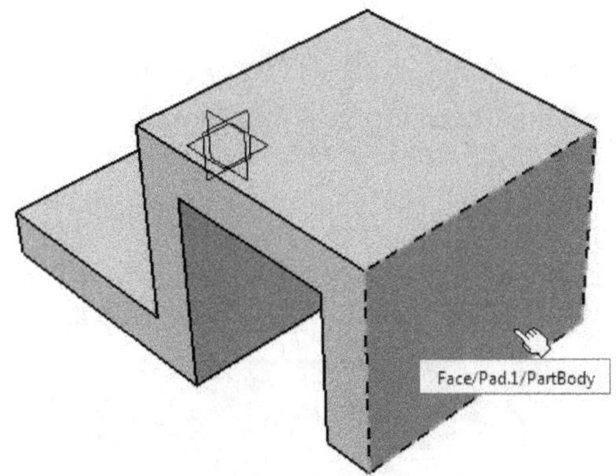

7. On the **Profile** toolbar, click **Points** drop-down > **Point by clicking** and place a point.
8. Add dimensions to locate the point.

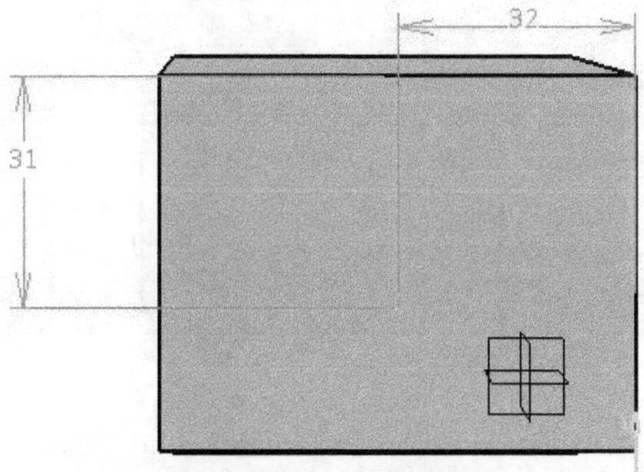

9. Click **Exit Workbench**.
10. On the **Sketch Based Features** toolbar, click the **Hole** icon and select the sketch point.
11. Click on the right-side face.
12. On the **Hole Definition** dialog, select **Extension > Up to Last**.
13. Type-in 20 in the **Diameter** box.
14. Click the **Type** tab and **Countersunk** from the drop-down.
15. Under the **Parameters** section, select **Mode > Angle & Diameter**.
16. Set the **Angle** and **Diameter** values to **82** and **24**, respectively.

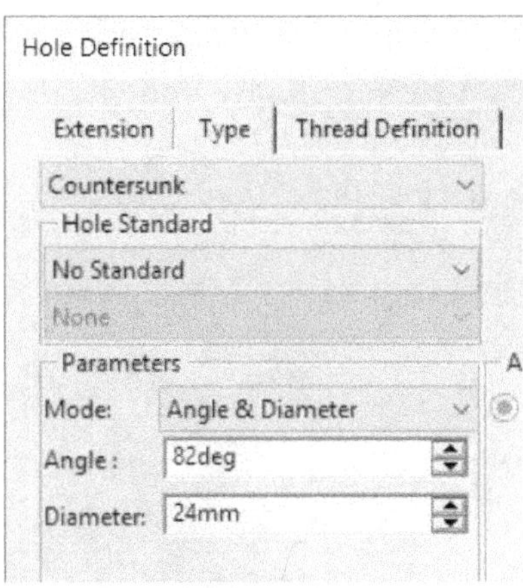

17. Click **OK** to complete the hole feature.

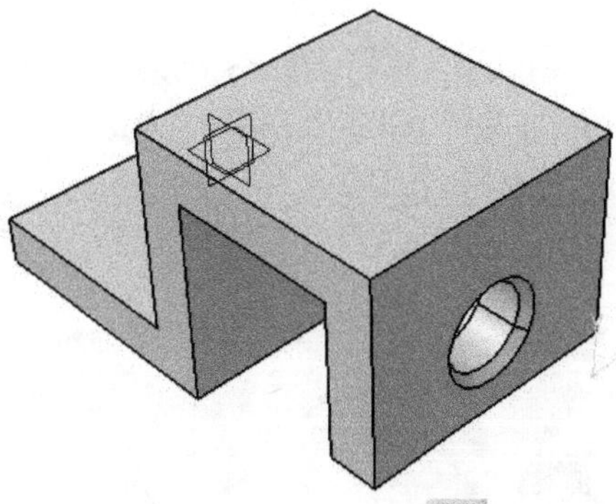

18. Activate the **Hole** command and click on the top face of the part geometry.
19. On the **Hole Definition** dialog, click the **Positioned Sketch** icon to activate the **Sketcher** Workbench.
20. Add dimensions to the sketch point and exit the **Sketcher** Workbench.

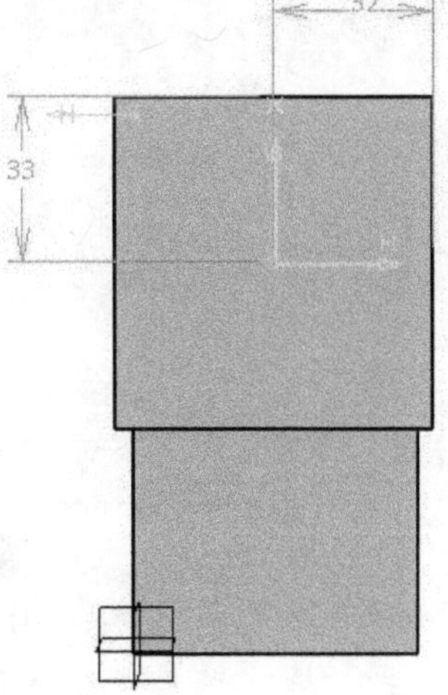

21. On the **Hole Definition** dialog, click the **Type** tab and select **Simple** from the drop-down.
22. Click **OK** to close the dialog.

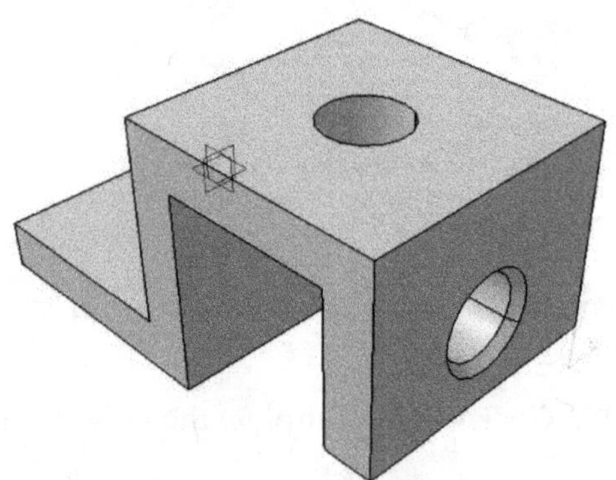

23. On the Menu bar, click **View > Compass**.
24. On the top-right corner of the graphic window, double-click the Z-axis of the Compass.

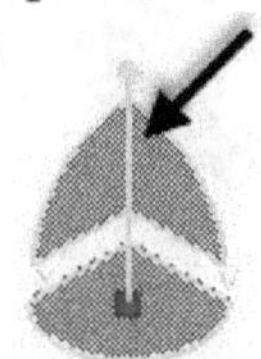

25. On the **Parameters for Compass Manipulation** dialog, type-in **90** in the **Rotation Increment** box along the W axis.
26. Click the rotation in positive direction button. Click **Close** to close the dialog.

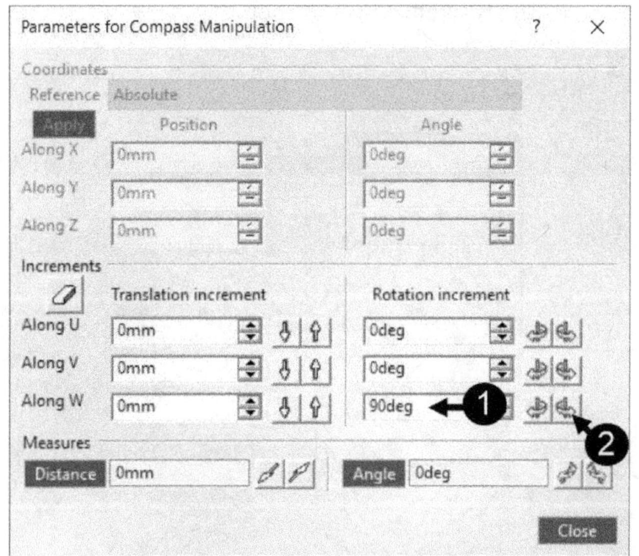

27. On the **View** toolbar, click the **Fit All In** icon to fit the geometry in the graphics window.
28. Activate the **Sketch** command and click on the lower top face of the model geometry.
29. Activate the **Points by clicking** command and place two points.
30. Add dimensions to position the points.

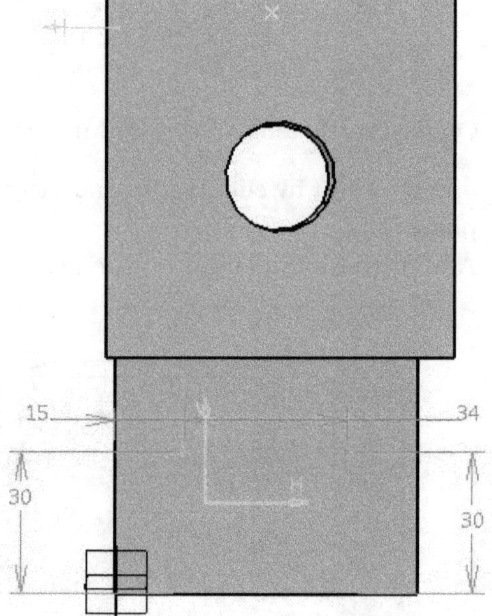

31. Exit the **Sketcher** Workbench.
32. Activate the **Hole** command and select anyone of the sketch points.
33. Click on the lower top face of the model geometry.
34. On the **Hole Definition** dialog, select **Extension > Up To Last**.
35. Type-in **10** in the **Diameter** box and click **OK**.
36. Create another hole using the remaining sketch point.

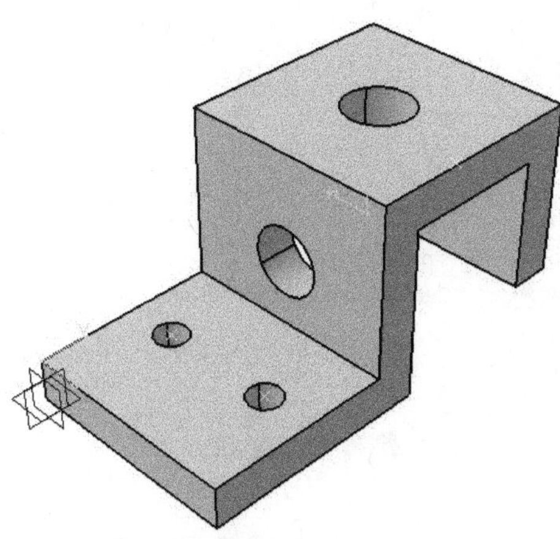

Chamfer Edges

1. On the **Dress-Up Features** toolbar, click the **Chamfer** icon (or) click **Insert > Dress-Up Features > Chamfer**.
2. On the **Chamfer Definition** dialog, select **Mode > Length1/Length2**.
3. Set the **Length1** and **Length 2** values to **20** and **10**, respectively.
4. Click on the side vertical edges, as shown in figure.

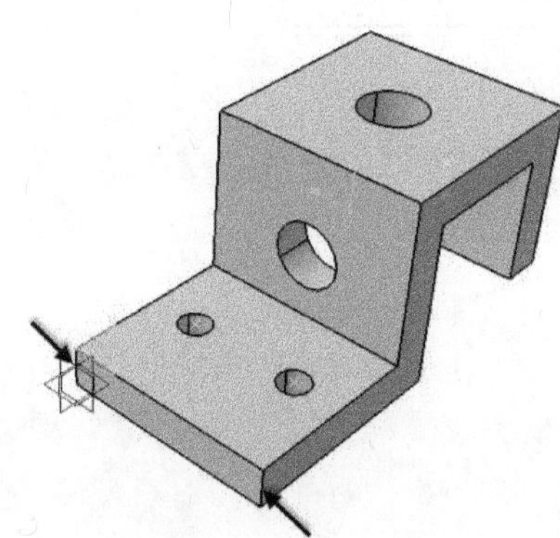

5. Click **OK** to apply chamfers.

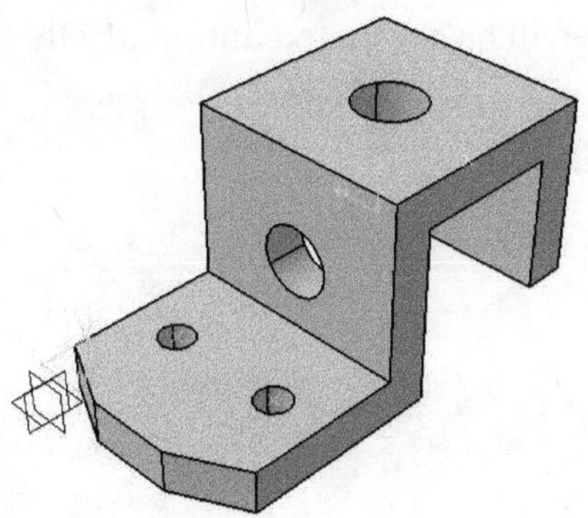

6. On the **Dress-Up Features** toolbar, click the **Edge Fillet** icon (or) click **Insert > Dress-Up Features > Edge Fillet**.
7. On the **Edge Fillet Definition** dialog, type-in **8** in the **Radius** box.
8. On the **View** toolbar, click **View Mode** drop-down > **Wireframe (NHR)** .
9. Click on the horizontal edges of the geometry, as shown below.

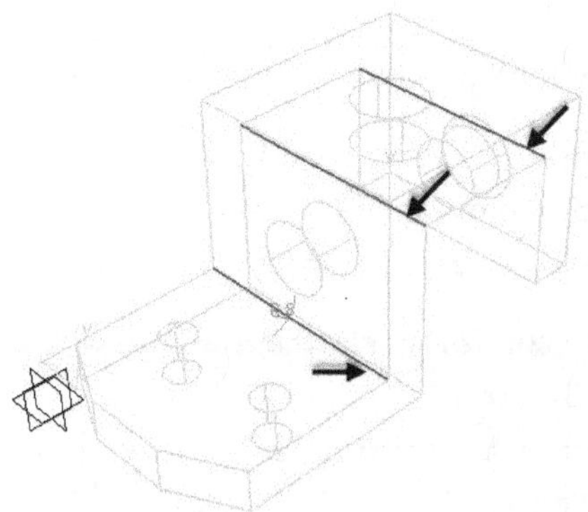

10. Click **OK** to add edge fillets.
11. Activate the **Edge Fillet** command and type-in 20 in the **Radius** box.
12. Click on the outer edges of the model, as shown below. Click **OK** to complete the edge fillet feature.

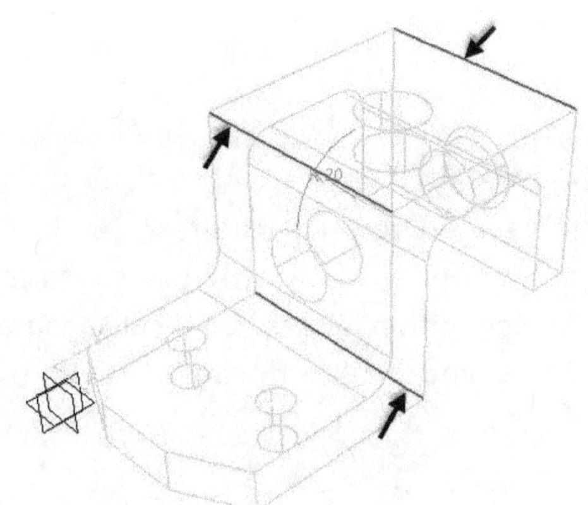

13. On the **View** toolbar, click **View Mode** drop-down > **Shading with Edges** .

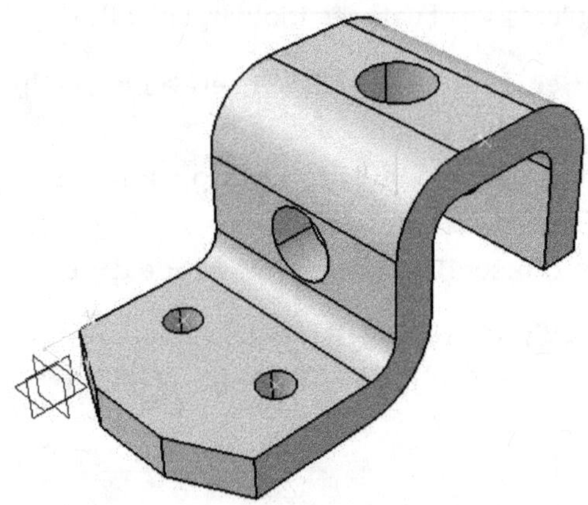

14. On the **View** toolbar, click **Quick View Drop-down > Isometric View** to change the orientation of the model view to Isometric.
15. On the **Dress-Up Features** toolbar, click the **Chamfer** icon (or) click **Insert > Dress-Up Features > Chamfer**.
16. On the **Chamfer Definition** dialog, select **Mode > Length1/Angle**.
17. Click on the lower corners of the part geometry.

18. Type-in **10** and **45** in the **Length** and **Angle** boxes, respectively. Click **OK** to chamfer the edges.

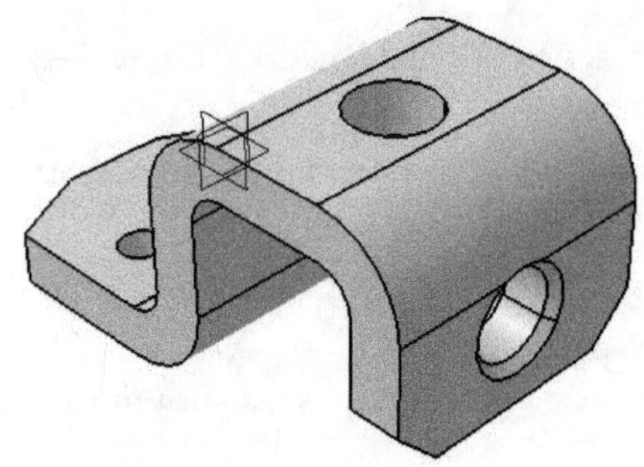

19. Save and close the file.

Questions

1. What are **Dress-Up** features?
2. Which option allows you to create a chamfer with unequal setbacks?
3. Which option allows you create a variable radius blend?
4. When you create a thread on a cylindrical face, the thread diameter will be calculated automatically or not?

Exercises

Exercise 1

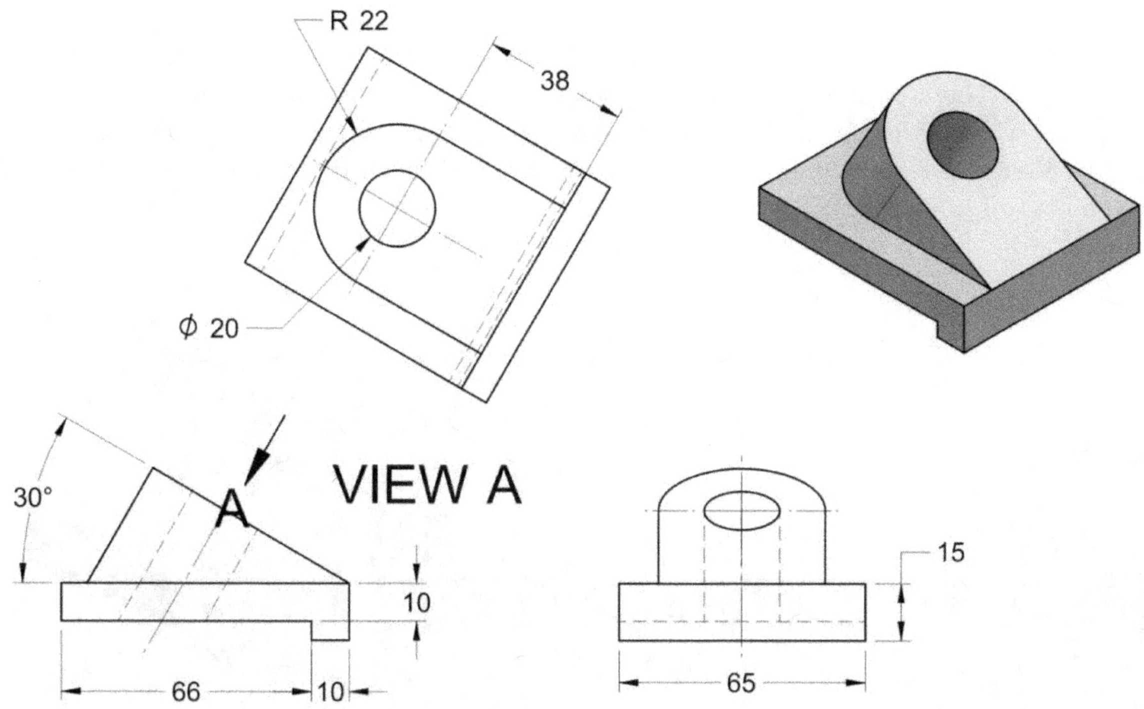

Exercise 2

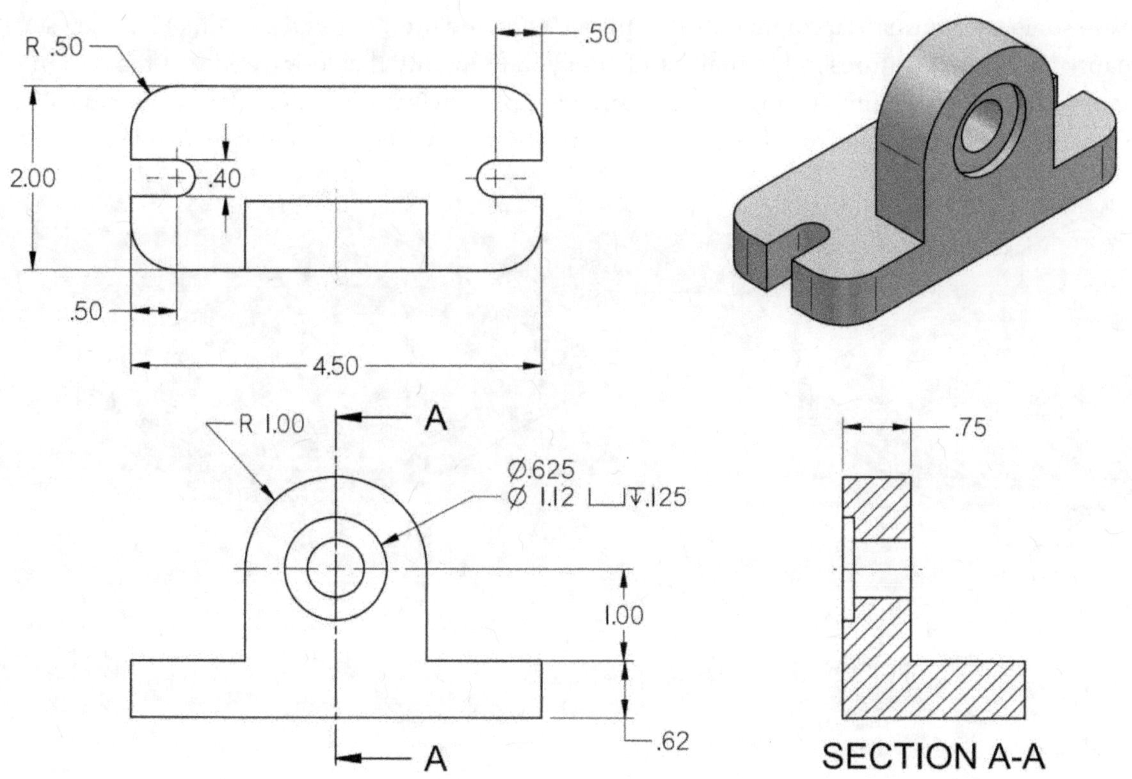

Chapter 5: Patterned Geometry

When designing a part geometry, oftentimes there are elements of symmetry in each part or there are at least a few features that are repeated multiple times. In these situations, CATIA V5 offers you some commands that save your time. For example, you can use mirror features to design symmetric parts, which makes designing the part quicker. This is because you only have to design a portion of the part and use the mirror feature to create the remaining geometry.

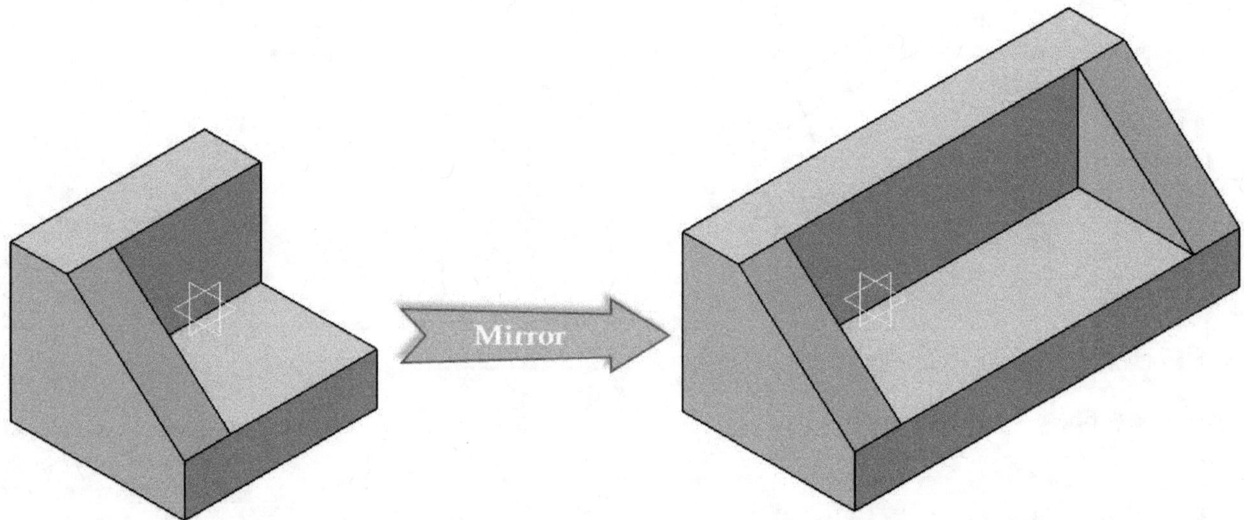

In addition, there are some transformation commands to replicate a feature throughout a part quickly. They save you time from creating additional features individually and help you to modify the design easily. If the design changes, you only need to change the first feature and the rest of the pattern features will update, automatically. In this chapter, you will learn to create mirrored and pattern geometries using the commands available in CATIA V5.

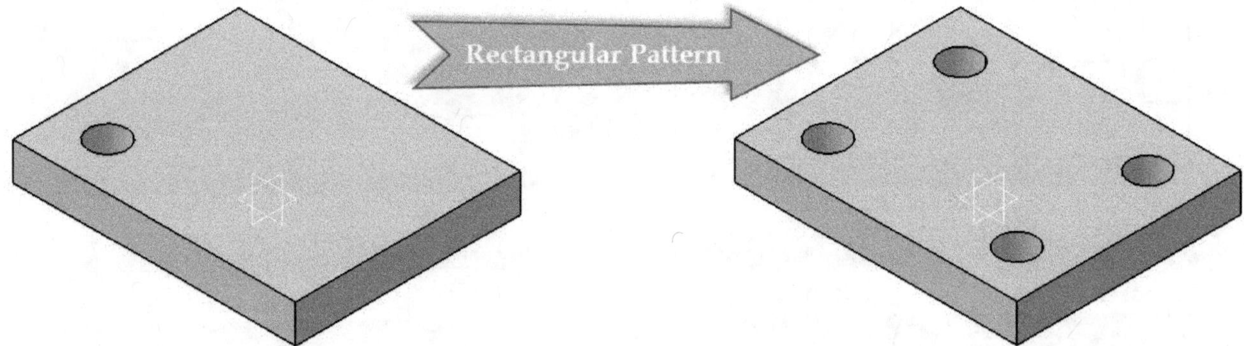

The topics covered in this chapter are:

- *Mirror* features
- *Rectangular Patterns*
- *Circular Patterns*
- *User Patterns*
- *Fill Patterns*

 The Mirror command

If you are designing a part that is symmetric, you can save time by using the **Mirror Feature** command. Using this command, you can replicate individual features of the entire body. To mirror features (3D geometry), you need to have a face or plane to use as a mirroring element. You can use a model face, default plane, or create a new plane, if it does not exist where it is needed.

1. On the **Transformation Features** toolbar, click the **Mirror** button (or) click **Insert > Transformation Features > Mirror** on the Menu bar.
2. Select the reference plane about which the features are to be mirrored.
3. Click in the **Object to mirror** box and click on the features to mirror.

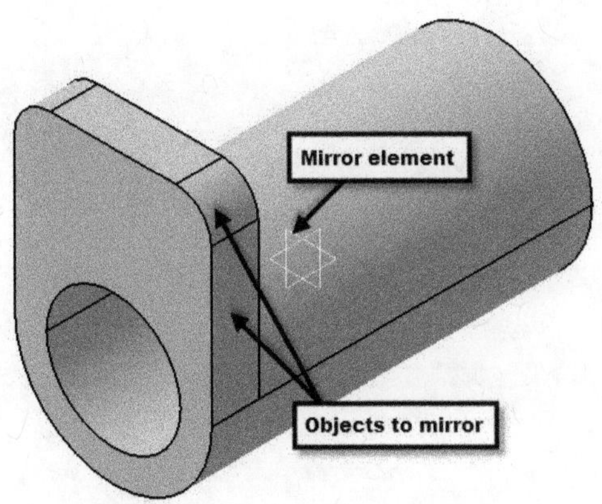

4. Click **OK**.

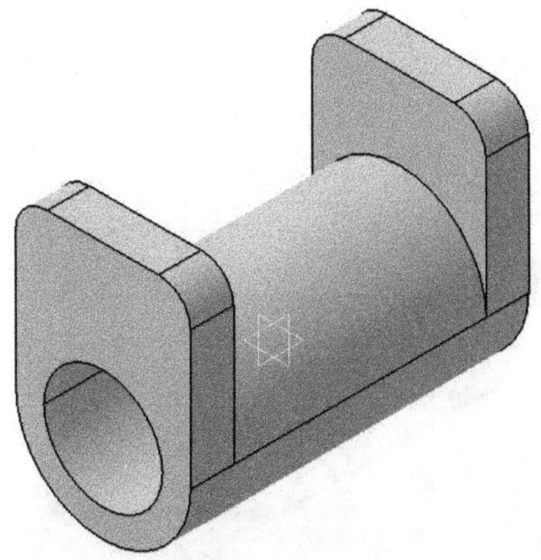

Now, if you make changes to original feature, the mirror feature will be updated automatically.

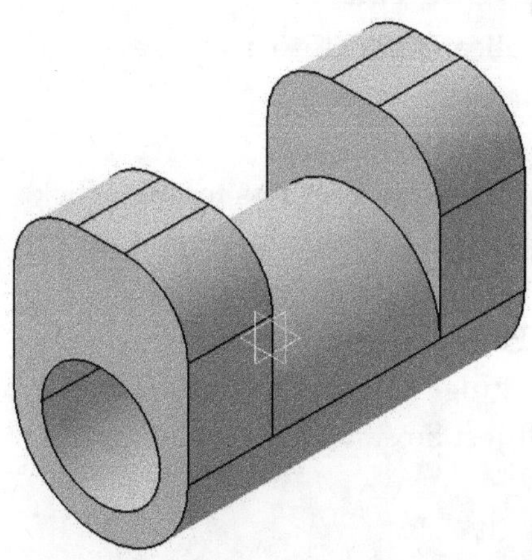

If the part you are creating is completely symmetric, you can save more time by creating half of it and mirroring the entire geometry rather than individual features. Activate the **Mirror** command and click on the mirror element. As the solid body is selected by default, you just need to click **OK** to mirror the complete body.

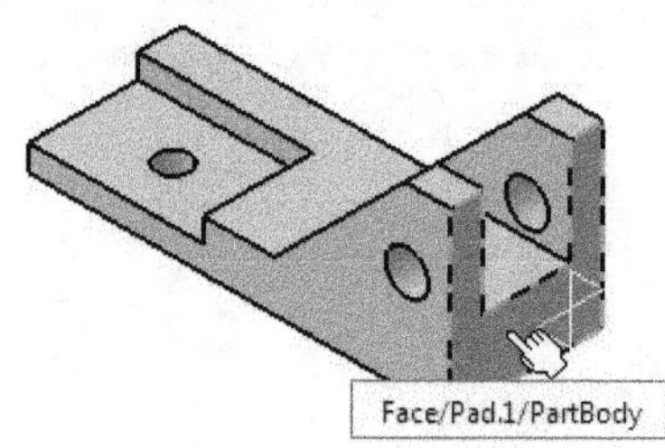

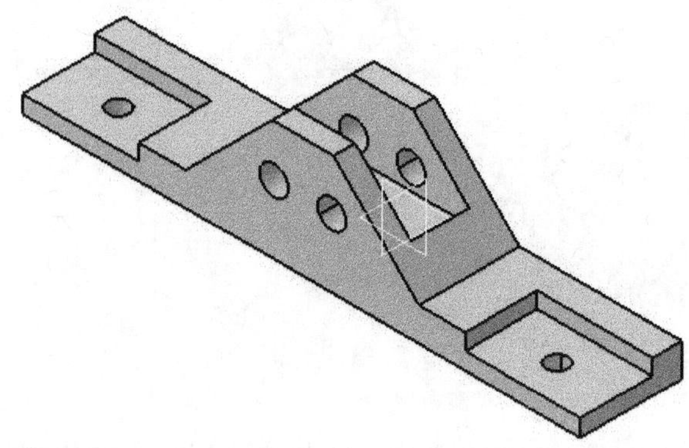

Rectangular Pattern

This command replicates a feature using a rectangular layout.

1. On the **Transformation Features** toolbar, click **Patterns** drop-down > **Rectangular Pattern** (or) click **Insert > Transformation Features > Rectangular Pattern** on the Menu bar.
2. On the **Rectangular Pattern Definition** dialog, click in the **Object** box and select the object to pattern.

In the CATIA V5, you can also create a hole or a sketch based feature inside the **Rectangular Pattern** command. To do this, right click in the **Object** box, and then select the required command from the menu.

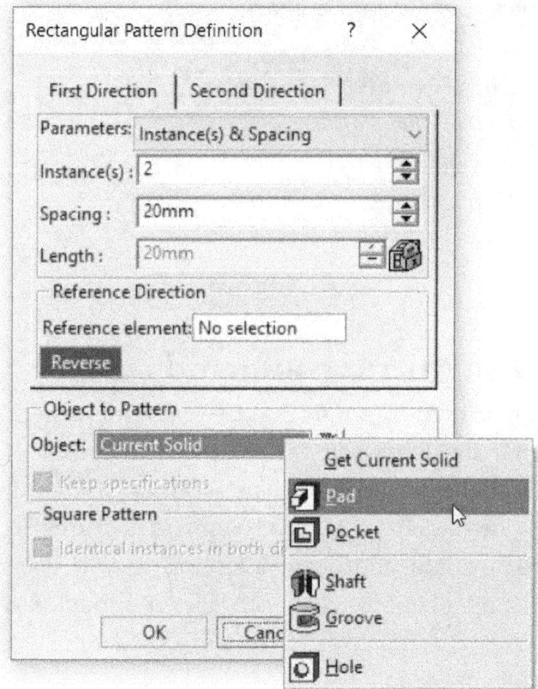

3. Click in the **Reference element** box and click on an edge to define the first direction of the rectangular pattern. You will notice that a pattern preview appears on the model.
4. Now, select **Parameters > Instance(s) & Spacing** on the dialog and set the parameters of the pattern (**Instance(s)** and **Spacing**).
5. Click the **Reverse** button, if you want to reverse the pattern direction.

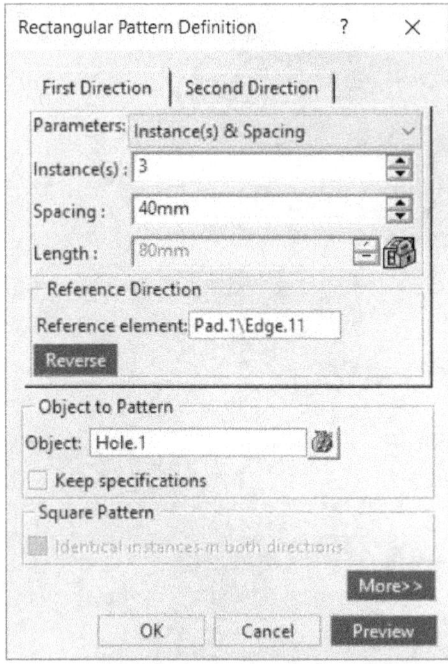

6. Click the **Second Direction** tab on the dialog.
7. Click in the **Reference element** box and click on an edge to define the second direction of the pattern.
8. Set the parameters (**Instance(s)** and **Spacing**) of pattern in the second direction.
9. Click the **Reverse** button, if you want to reverse the pattern direction.

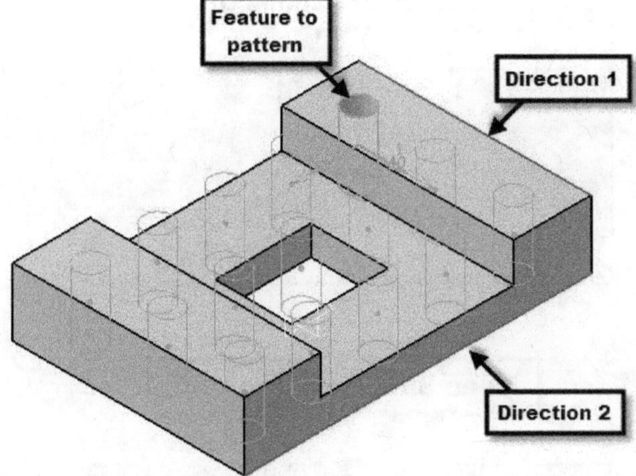

10. Click **Preview**.

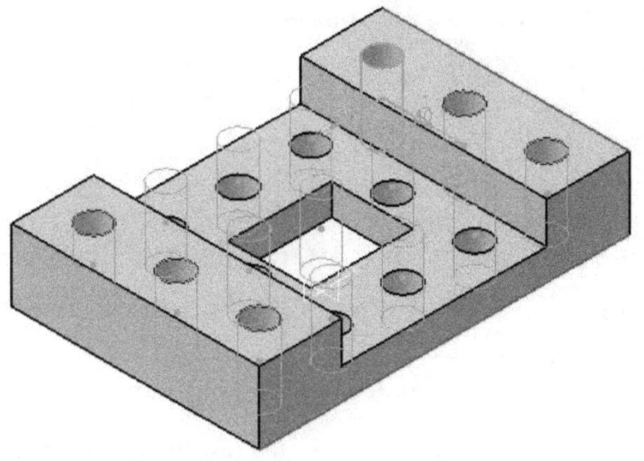

If you want to suppress an instance of the pattern, then click on the orange dot on it. This suppresses the instance. If you want to unsuppress the instance, then click the orange dot again.

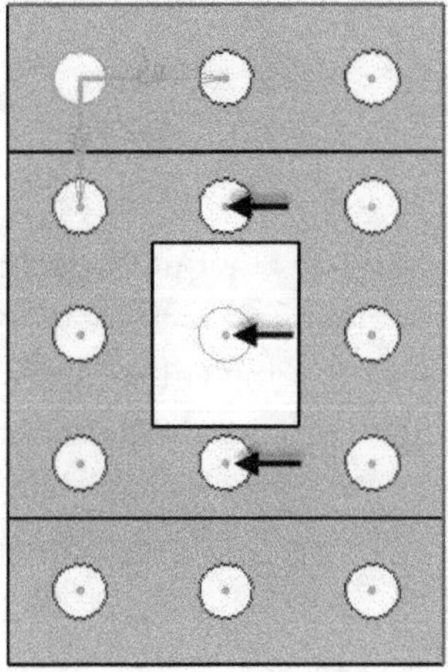

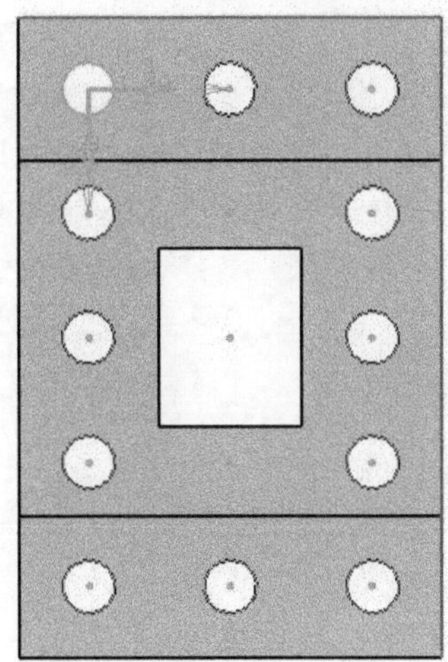

Select **Parameters > Instance(s) & Length** on the **Rectangular Pattern Definition** dialog, if you want to enter instance(s) and total length along the direction 1 or direction 2.

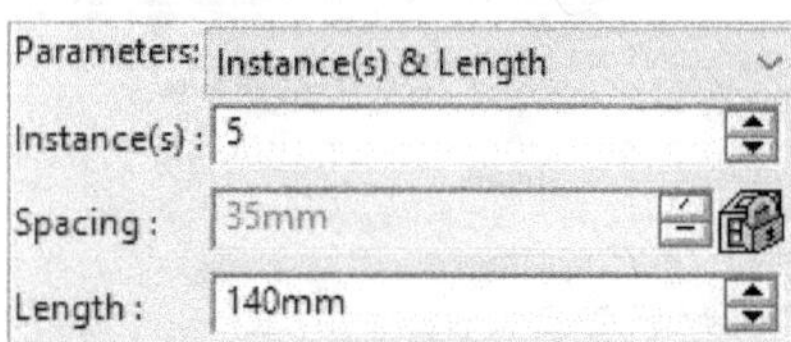

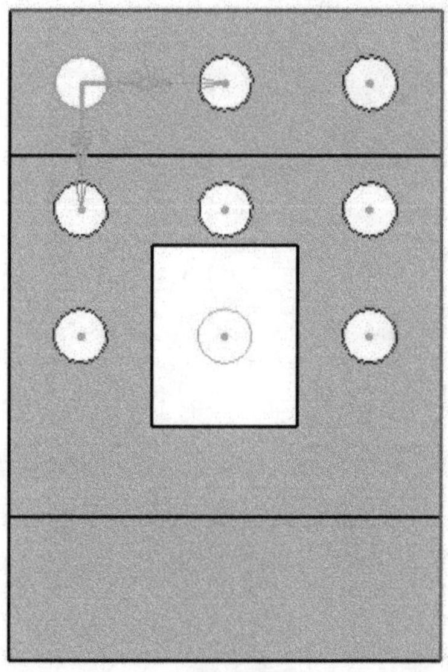

Select **Parameters > Spacing & Length**, if you want to enter the distance between individual instances of the pattern and total length along the directions.

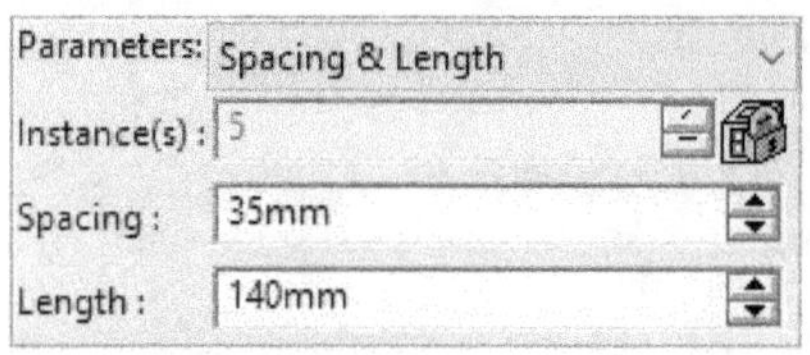

Select **Parameters > Instance(s) & Unequal Spacing** to define different spacing values for each instance. You will notice that individual spacing values appear on the pattern. Double-click on these values and change them.

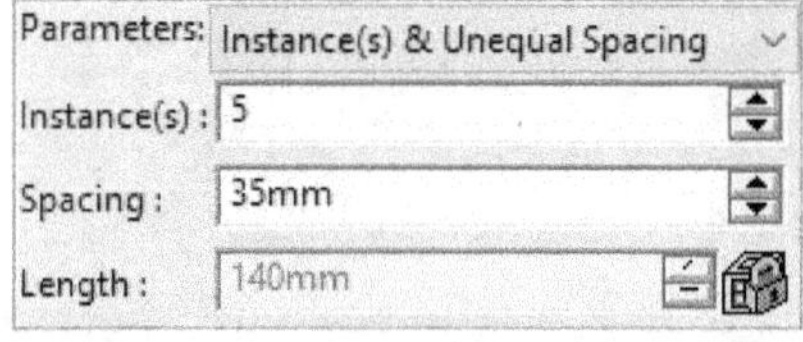

If you want to create a square pattern, then check **Identical instances in both directions** under the **Square Pattern** section.

Keep Specifications

This option creates the rectangular pattern by keeping the specifications of the original feature. For example, if the original feature of pattern is created by extruding up to an irregular surface, then the **Keep Specifications** option in the **Object to Pattern** section of the **Rectangular Pattern** dialog creates all the features of the rectangular pattern by maintaining the extrusion condition.

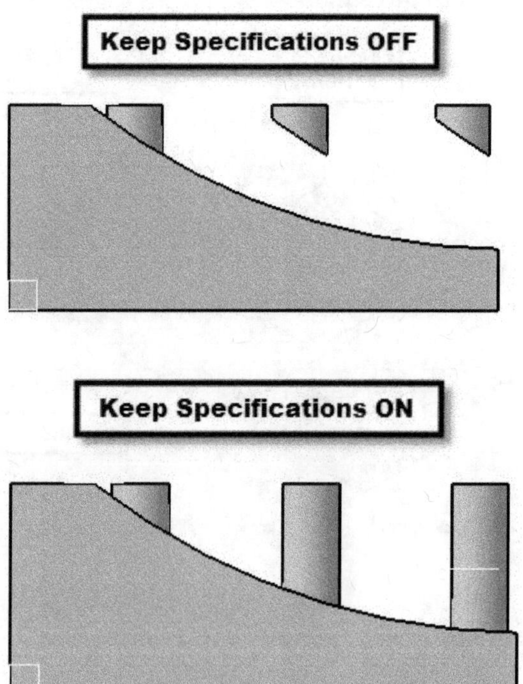

Patterning the entire geometry

Patterning the entire geometry of a part is easier than patterning features. You need to activate the **Rectangular Pattern** command and define the direction, instant count, and spacing between the instances. There is no need to select the geometry as the entire body is selected by default.

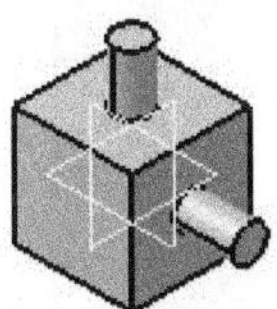

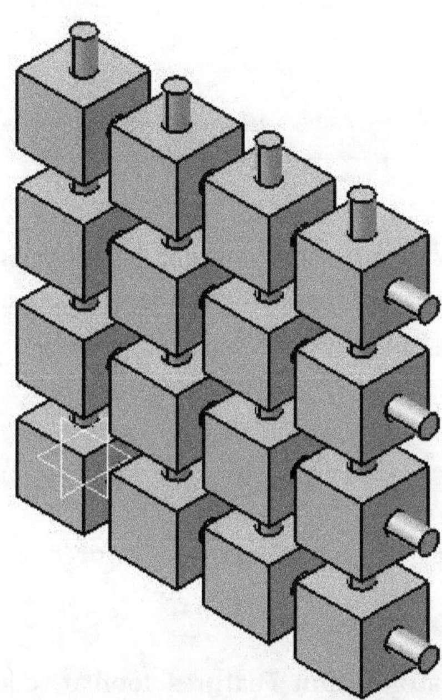

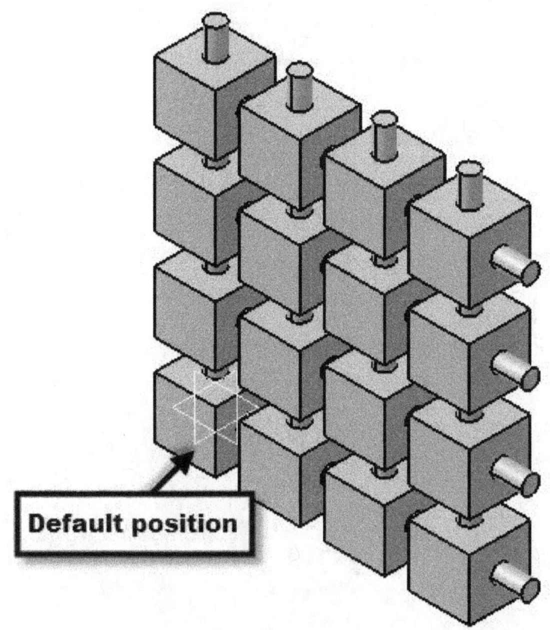

Position of Object in Pattern

On the **Rectangular Pattern Definition** dialog, there is an option to change the position of the original feature/body. Expand the **Rectangular Pattern Definition** dialog type-in values in **Row in direction 1** and **Row in direction 2** boxes. The position of the origin feature/body changes.

You can also change the angular position of the pattern feature/body by typing-in a value in the **Rotation angle** box.

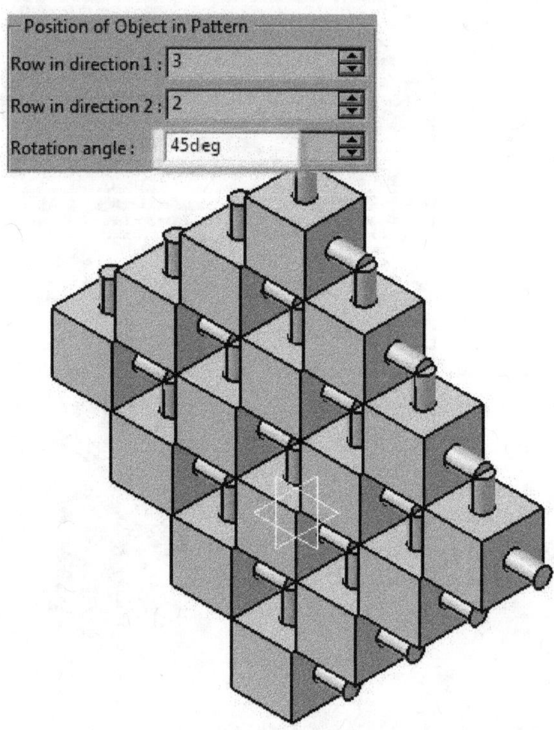

Staggered Pattern Definition

The **Rectangular Pattern** command has an option to create staggered pattern. In a staggered pattern, the position of one row is offset from another.

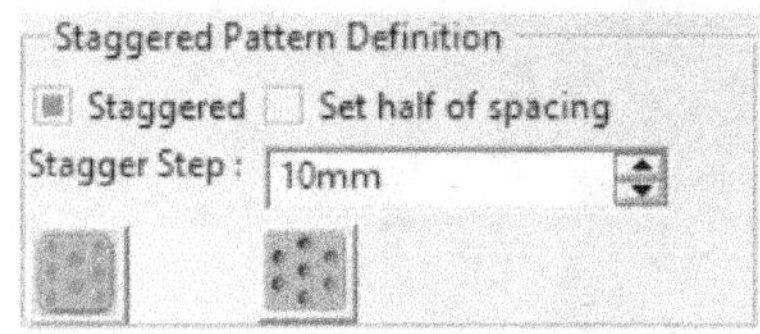

1. To create this kind of pattern, you need to activate the **Rectangular Pattern** command and select the feature to pattern.
2. Define the pattern parameters in two directions (make sure that there are more than two instances in both the directions).
3. Expand the **Rectangular Pattern Definition** dialog and check the **Staggered** option.
4. Type-in the offset value in the **Stagger Step** box (or) check the **Set half of spacing** option.
5. Click anyone of the two buttons available in the **Staggered Pattern Definition** section.
6. Click **OK** to create the staggered pattern.

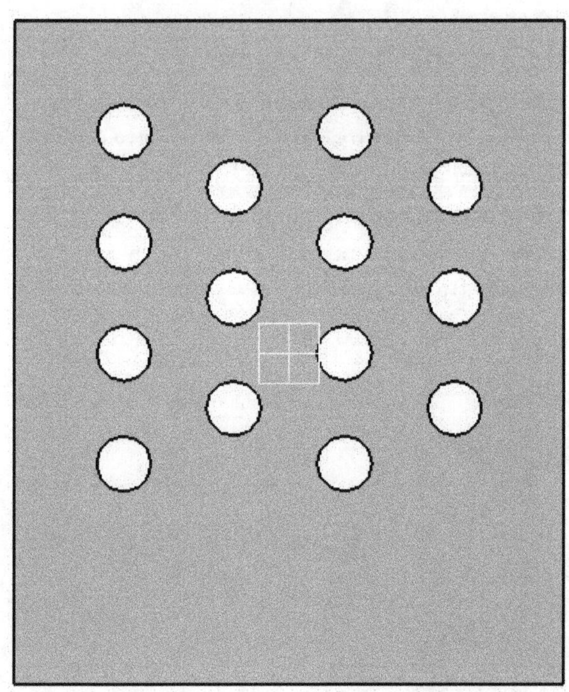

Square Pattern

The **Rectangular Pattern** command has an option to create a square pattern. Check the **Identical instances in both directions** option in the Square Pattern section to create a square pattern.

Circular Pattern

This command patterns the selected features in a circular fashion.

1. On the **Transformation Features** toolbar, click **Patterns** drop-down > **Circular Pattern** (or) click **Insert > Transformation Features > Circular Pattern** on the Menu bar.
2. Click in the **Object** box and select the feature to pattern from the model geometry.
3. Click in the **Reference element** box and select an axis, edge, plane, or cylindrical face. This defines the axis of circular pattern.
4. Select **Parameters > Complete Crown**.
5. Type-in a value in the **Instance(s)** box.

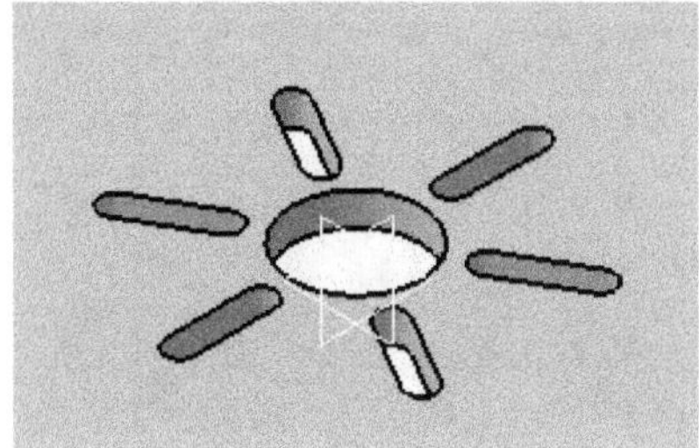

Select **Parameters > Instance(s) & angular spacing**, if you want to type-in the instance count and the angle between individual instances.

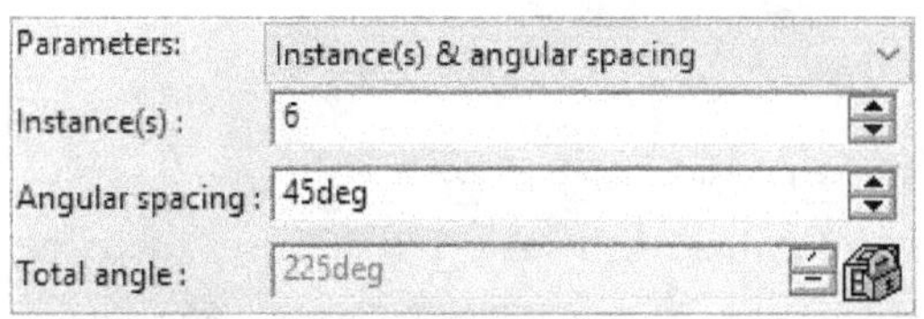

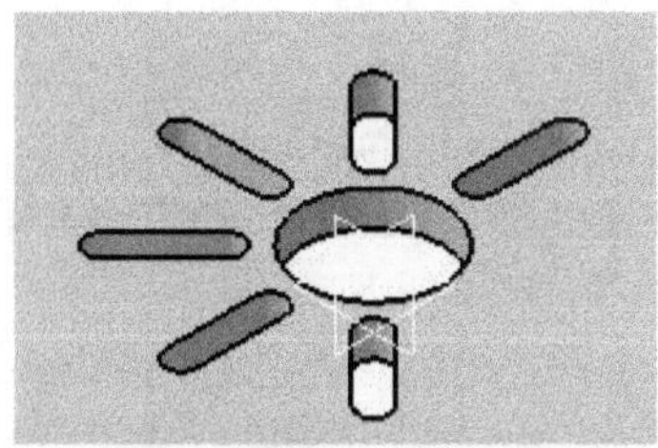

Select **Parameters > Instance(s) & total angle**, if you want to type-in the instance count and total angle. The angle between the instances will be calculated, automatically. For example, enter 5 in the Instance(s) box and 300 in the **Total angle** box. This creates five instances including the original one. The angle between the instances will be 60 (300/5). However, if you enter 6 and 360 in the **Instance(s)** and **Total angle** boxes, an error appears showing that one or more instances overlap each other.

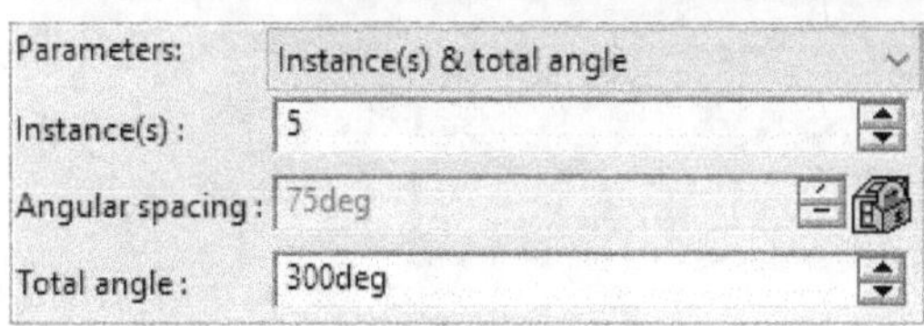

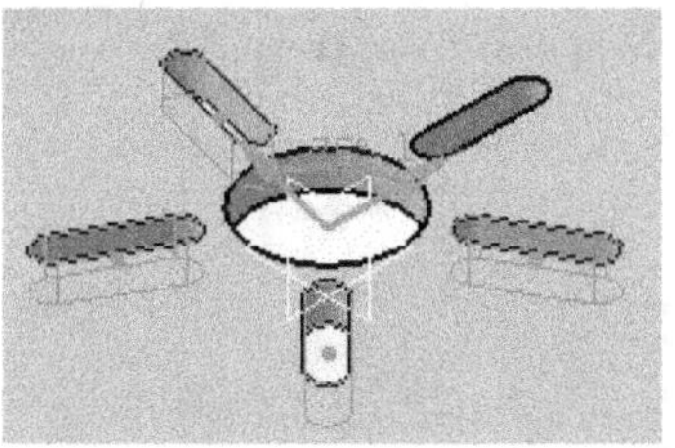

Select **Parameters > Angular spacing & total angle**, if you want to type-in the angle between individual instances and the total angle of the circular pattern.

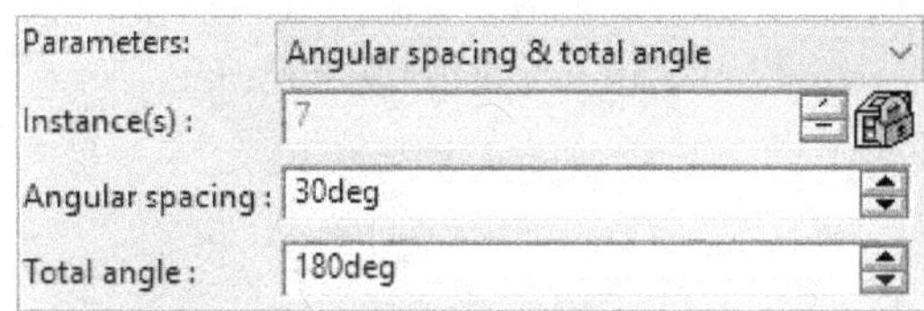

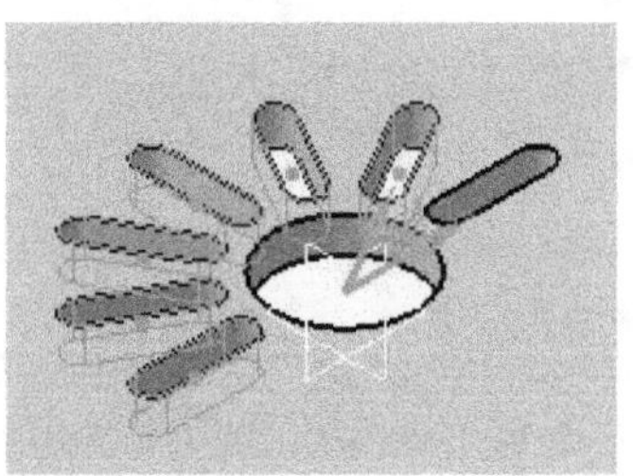

Select **Parameters > Instance(s) & unequal angular spacing**, if you want to define different angular spacing for each instance. You will notice that the individual spacing values appear on the pattern. Double-click on these values and change them.

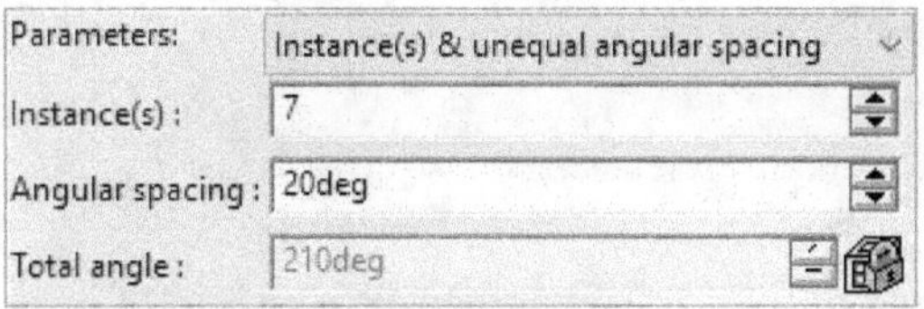

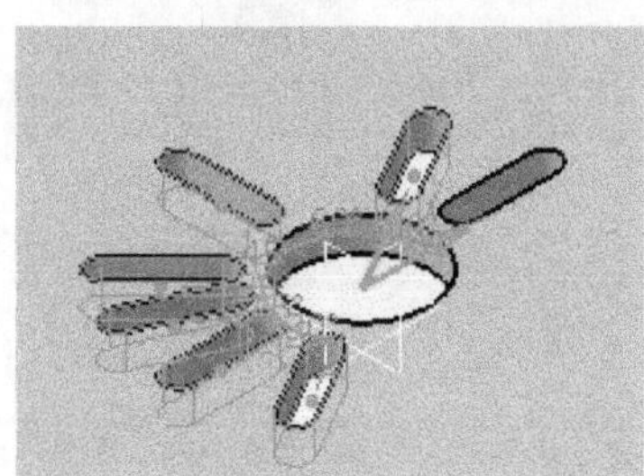

First, click on **More** button to expand the dialog. Under the **Rotation of Instance(s)** section, uncheck

Radial alignment of instance(s) to pattern the feature with the original orientation.

Check this option to change the orientation of the instances, as they are patterned in the circular fashion.

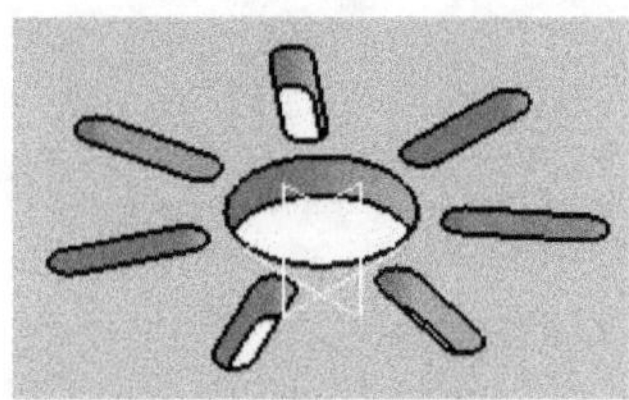

Crown Definition

The **Circular Pattern** command has options to radiate the circular pattern.

1. On the **Circular Pattern Definition** dialog, click the **Crown Definition** tab to view the options to radiate the circular pattern.
2. Select **Parameters > Circle(s) & circle spacing**.
3. Type-in values in the **Circle(s)** and **Circle spacing** boxes.

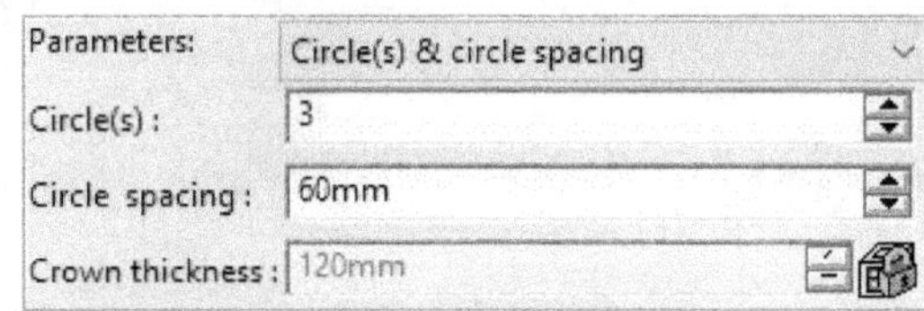

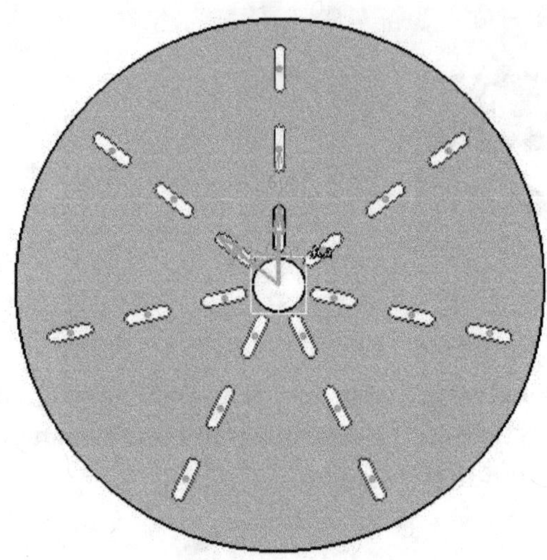

 User Pattern

This command patterns the selected features by using user-defined points.

1. On the **Transformation Features** toolbar, click **Patterns** drop-down > **User Pattern** (or) click **Insert > Transformation Features > User Pattern** on the Menu bar.
2. On the **User Defined Pattern Definition** dialog, click in the **Object** box and select the feature to pattern.
3. Click in the **Anchor** box and select a point to define the origin point of the pattern.
4. Click on individual points (or) the sketch containing points.

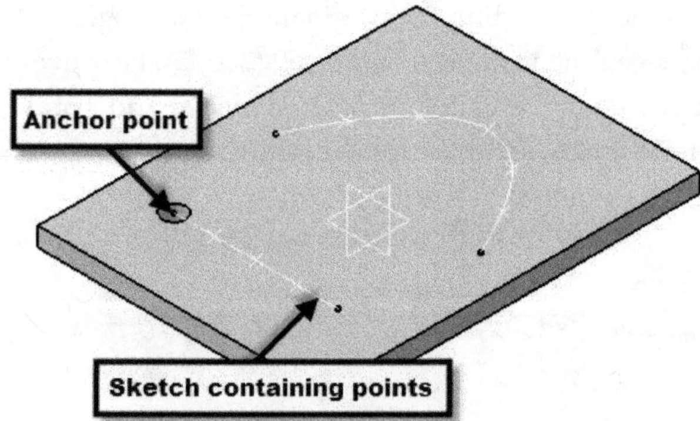

5. Click **OK** to create the pattern.

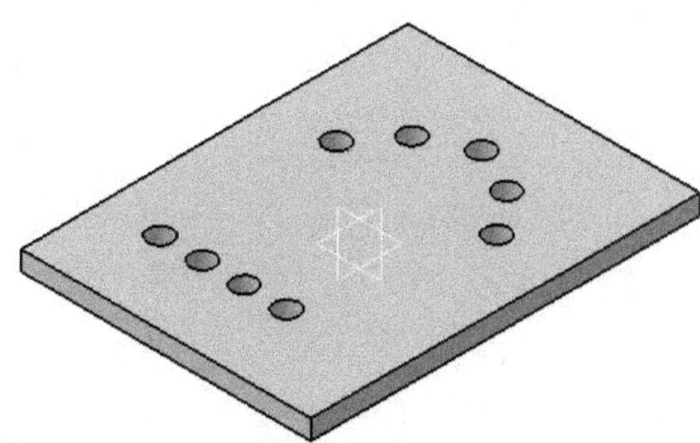

Scaling

This command scales the part geometry with reference to the face, point, or plane.

1. On the **Transformation Features** toolbar, click **Scale** drop-down > **Scaling** (or) click **Insert > Transformation Features > Scaling** on the Menu bar.
2. Click on the face or plane to define the scaling direction.
3. Type-in the scaling factor in the **Ratio** box.

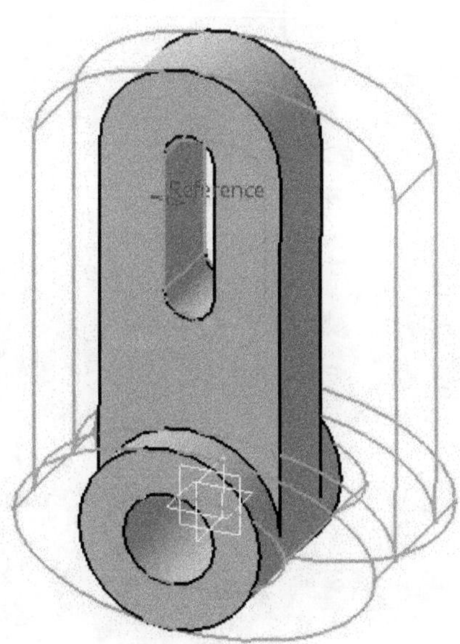

4. Click **OK** to scale the body.

Affinity

This command scales the part geometry along three directions using the coordinate values that you specify.

1. On the **Transformation Features** toolbar, click **Scale** drop-down > **Affinity** (or) click **Insert > Transformation Features > Affinity** on the Menu bar.
2. On the **Affinity Definition** dialog, type-in values in the X, Y, Z boxes.

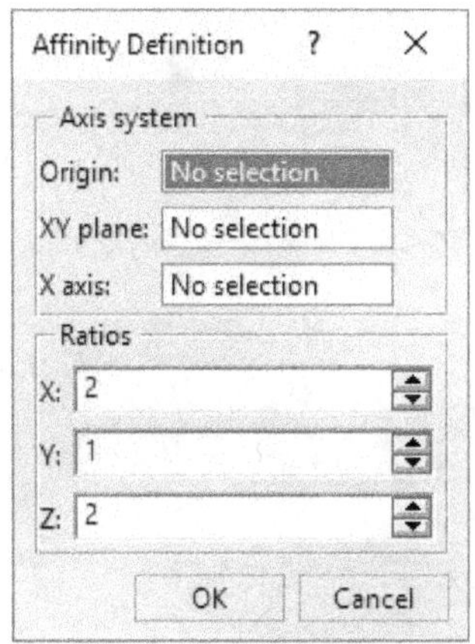

3. Click **OK**.

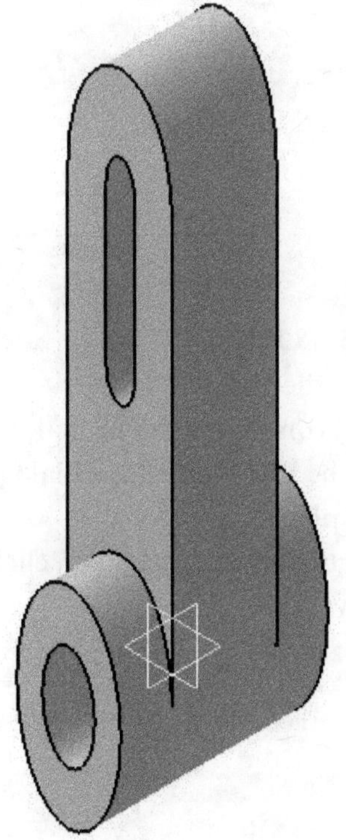

Examples

Example 1

In this example, you will create the part shown next.

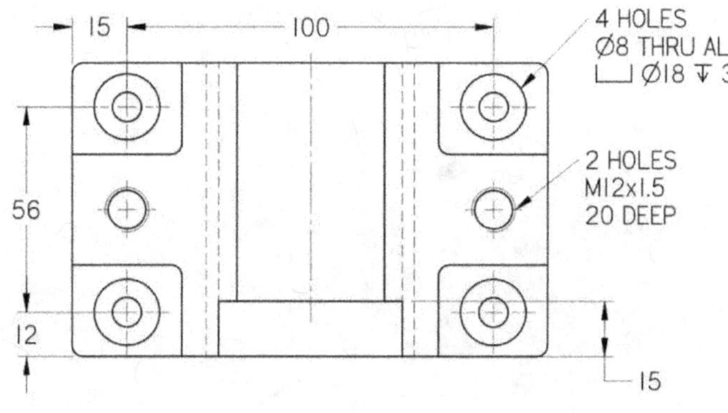

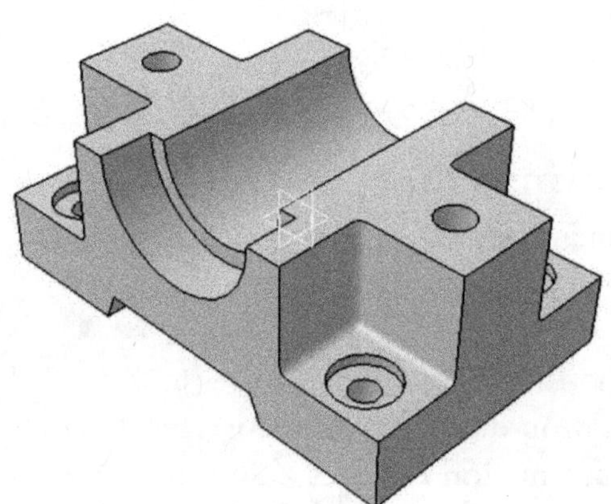

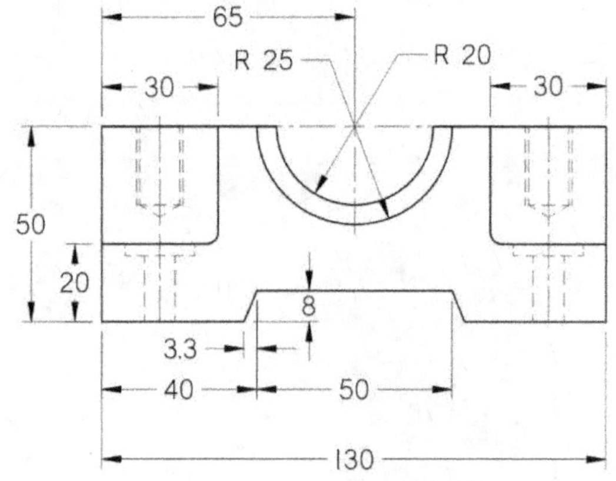

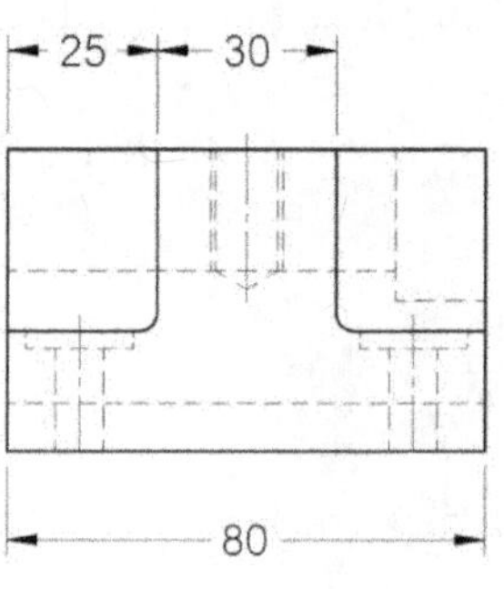

1. Start **CATIA V5-6R2017**.
2. Open a new part file.
3. Activate the **Pad** command and click the **Sketch** icon on the **Pad Definition** dialog.
4. Click on the YZ plane.
5. Create a rectangular sketch, and then click **Exit workbench**.

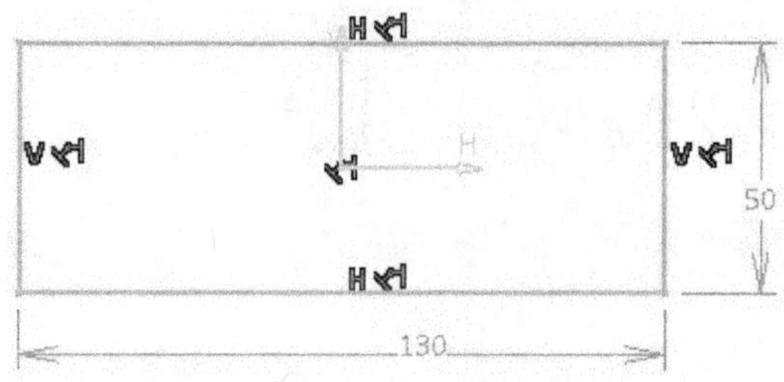

6. On the **Pad Definition** dialog, type-in **40** in the **Length** box.
7. Check the **Mirror extent** option.
8. Click **OK** to complete the *Pad* feature.

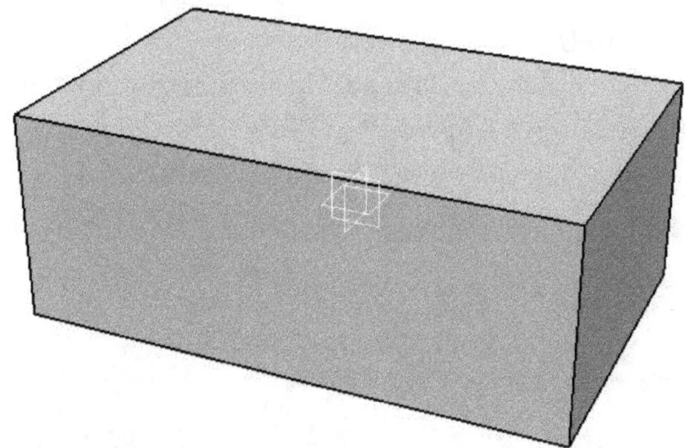

9. On the **Sketcher** toolbar, click **Sketch > Positioned Sketch**.

10. Click on the top face of the part geometry.
11. On the **Sketch Positioning** dialog, under the **Origin** section, select **Type > Intersection 2 Lines**.
12. Click on the edges of the part geometry, as shown below.

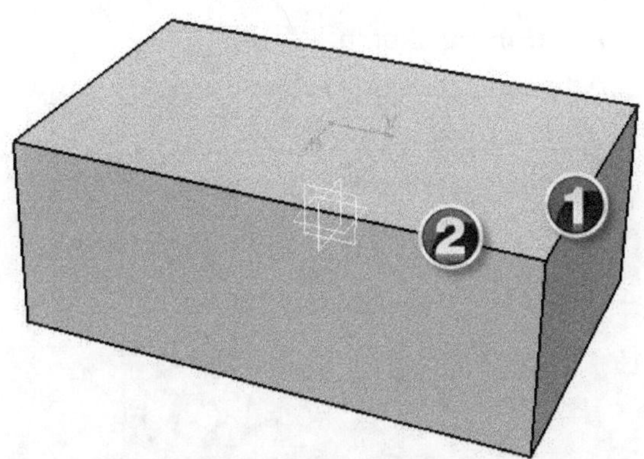

13. On the dialog, check the **Reverse H** and **Reverse V** options.
14. Click **OK** to start the sketch.
15. Create a rectangular sketch and click **Exit workbench**.

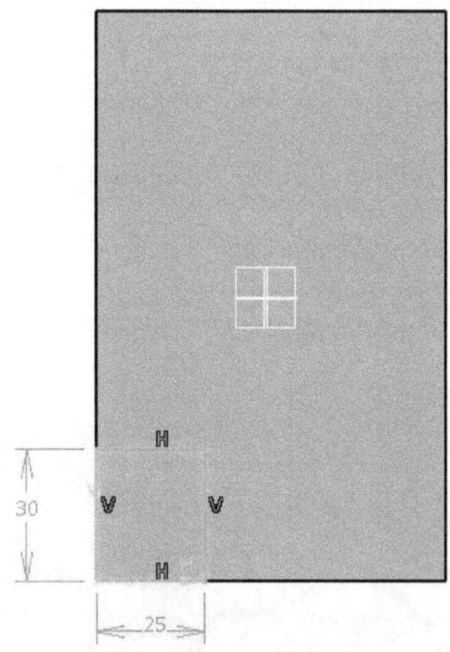

16. Activate the **Pocket** command.
17. Create the *Pocket* feature of **30 mm** depth.

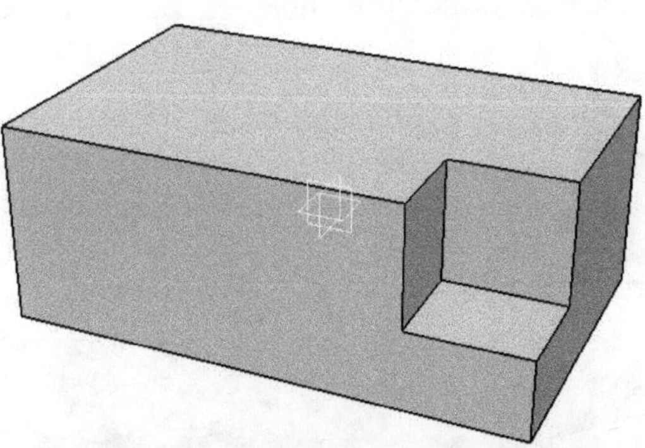

18. Activate the **Hole** command and click on the bottom face of the *Pocket* feature.

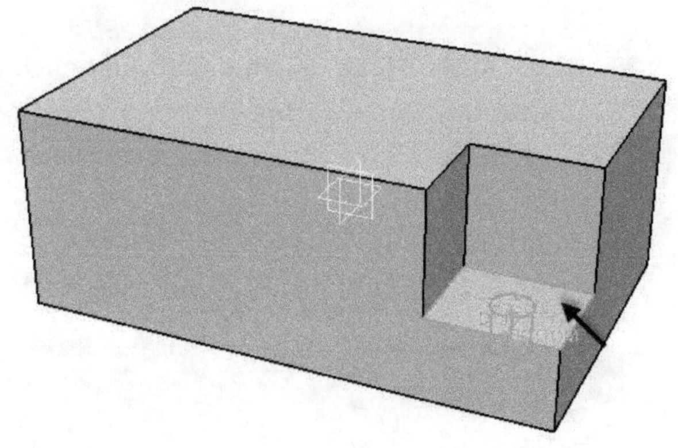

19. On the **Hole Definition** dialog, click **Extension > Up to last**.
20. Set the **Diameter** value to 8.
21. Click the **Type** tab and select **Counterbored** from the drop-down.
22. Type-in **18** and **3** in the **Diameter** and **Depth** boxes, respectively.
23. Click the **Extension** tab, and then click the **Positioning sketch** icon.
24. Apply constraints to position the hole.

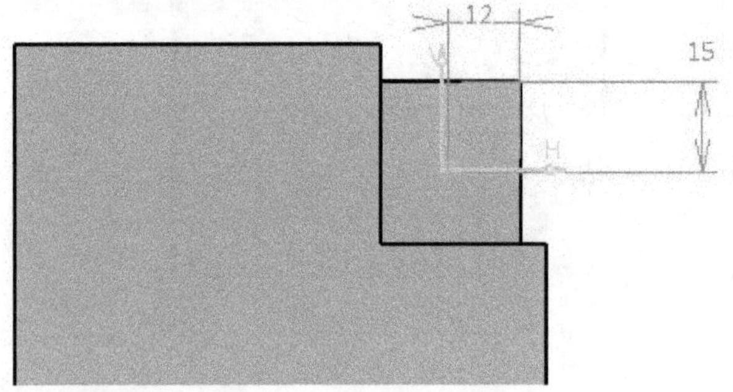

25. Click **Exit workbench**, and then click **OK** to create the counterbored hole.

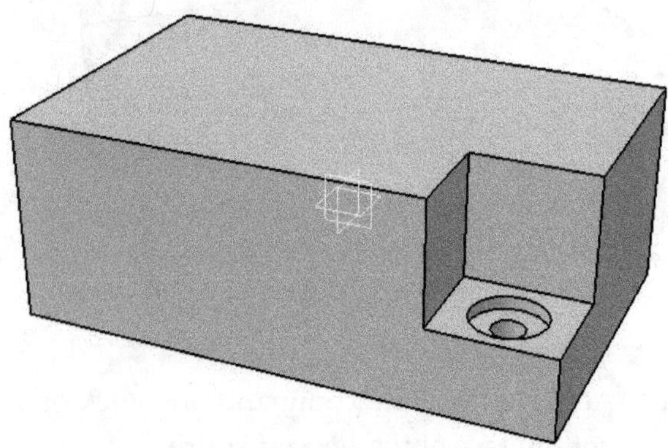

26. Activate the **Hole** command and click on the top face of the part geometry.
27. Click the **Type** tab and select **Simple** from the drop-down.
28. Click the **Thread Definition** tab and check the **Threaded** option.
29. Under the **Thread Definition** section, select **Type > Metric Thin Pitch**.
30. Click **OK** on the **Warning** message.
31. Select **Thread Description > M12X1.5**.

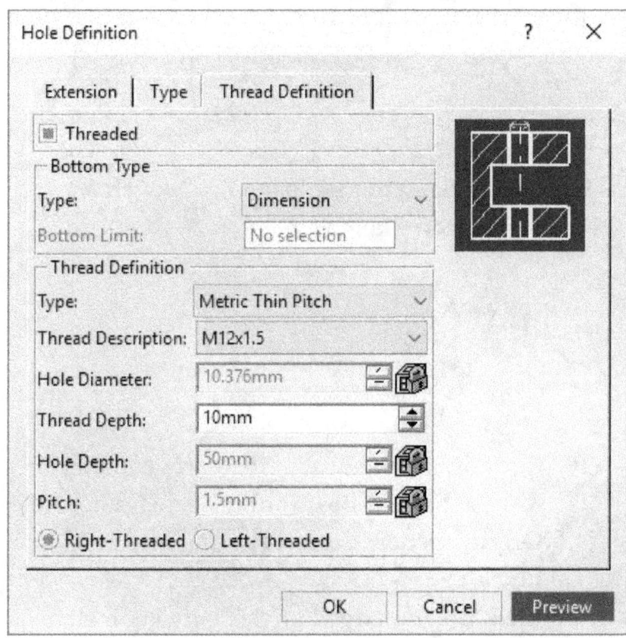

32. Click the **Extension** tab, and the click the **Positioning sketch** icon.
33. Add constraints to define the hole location.

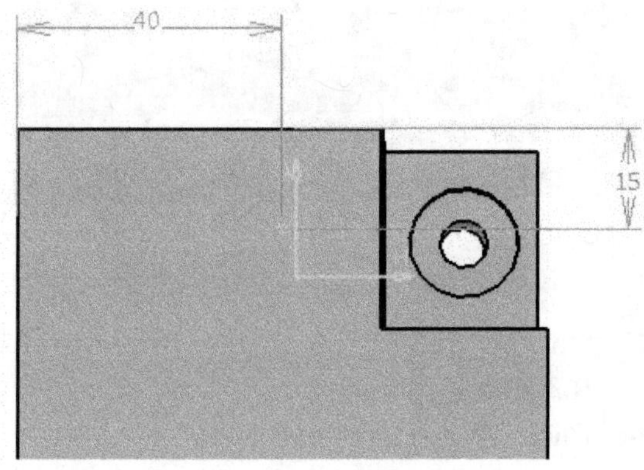

34. Click **Exit workbench**, and then click **OK** to create a threaded hole.

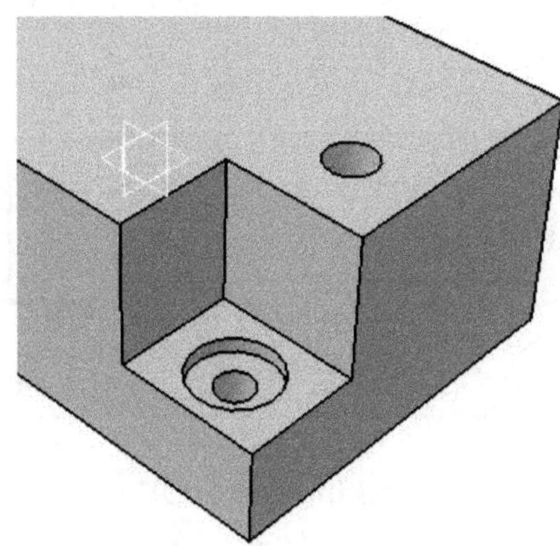

35. On the **Transformation Features** toolbar, click **Pattern** drop-down > **Rectangular Pattern** (or) click **Insert > Transformation Features > Rectangular Pattern** on the Menu.
36. On the **Rectangular Pattern Definition** dialog, under the **First Direction** tab, select **Parameters > Instance(s) & Spacing**.
37. Type-in **2** and **100** in the **Instance(s)** and **Spacing** boxes.
38. Under the **Reference Direction** section, click in the **Reference element** selection box, and then click on the top front edge of the part geometry.

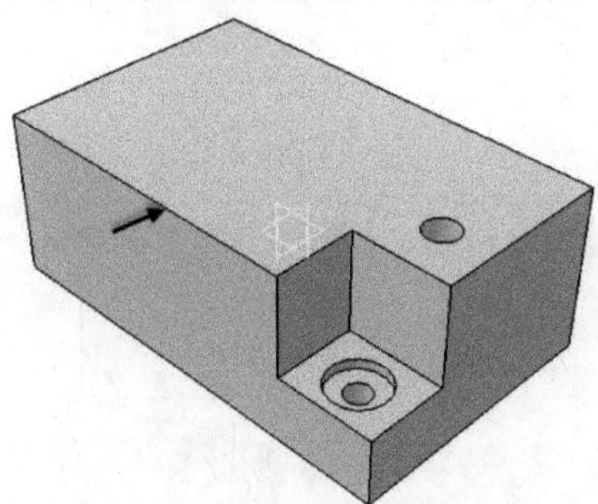

39. Under the **Object to Pattern** section, click in the **Object** selection box and select the *Pocket* feature.
40. Under the **Second Direction** section, type-in **2** and **55** in the **Instance(s)** and **Spacing** boxes, respectively.
41. Under the **Reference Direction** section, click in the **Reference element** box and click on the top side edge of the part geometry.

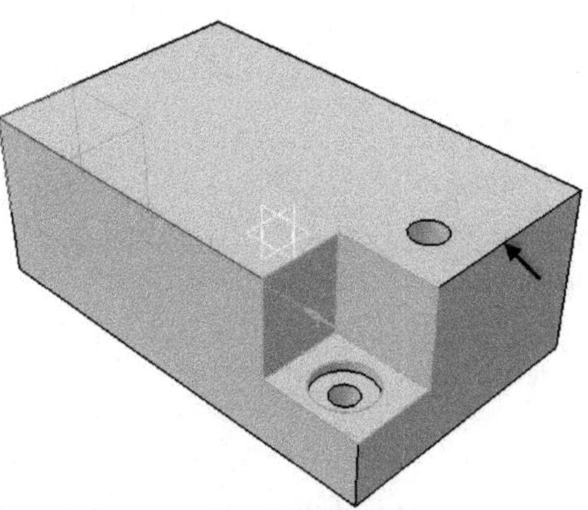

42. Click the **Reverse** button, and then click **OK** to pattern the *Pocket* feature.

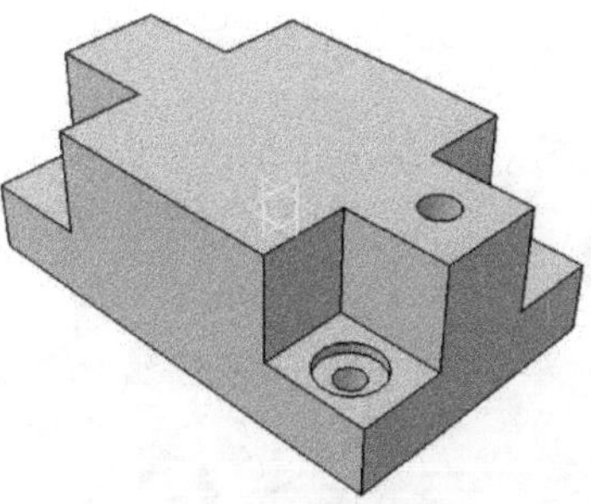

43. Likewise, pattern the counterbored hole. The pattern parameters are same.

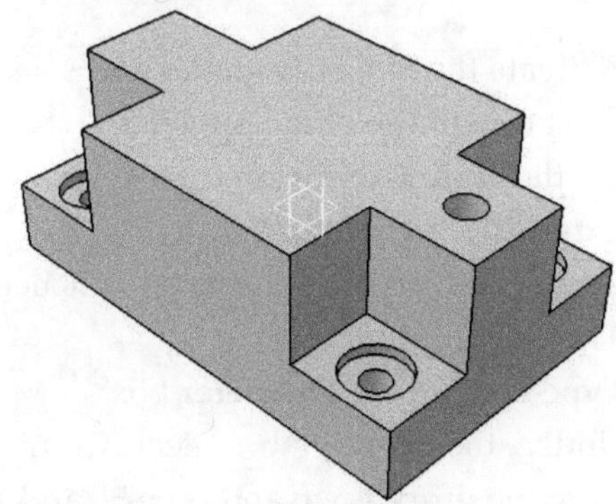

44. On the **Transformation Features** toolbar, click the **Mirror** icon (or) click **Insert > Transformation Features > Mirror** on the Menu.
45. In the Specification Tree, click the **zx plane** to define the mirror plane.

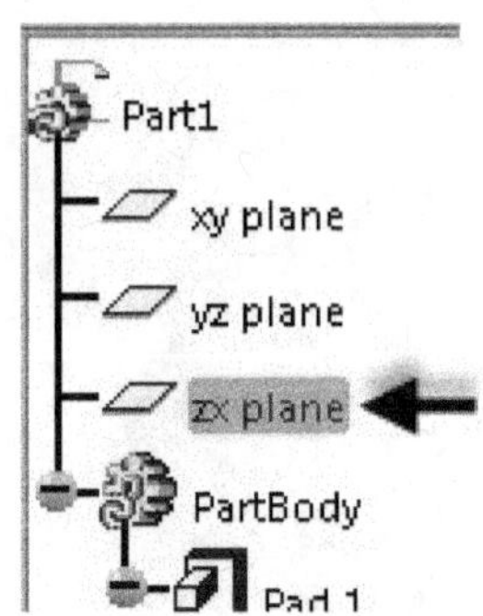

46. On the **Mirror Definition** dialog, click in the **Object to mirror** selection box and select the threaded hole feature.
47. Click **OK** to mirror the selected features.

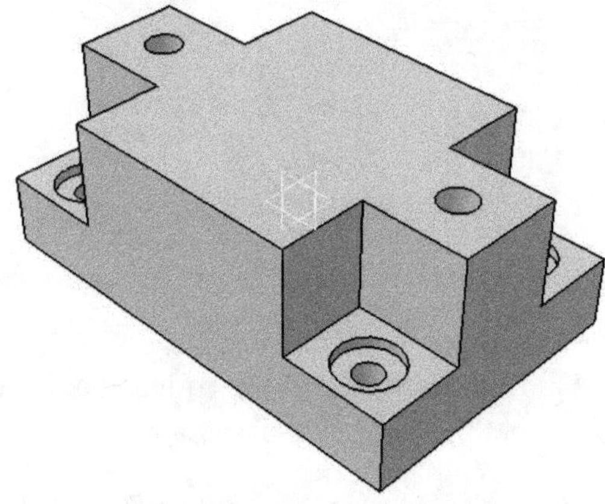

48. Activate the **Hole** command and select the front face of the part geometry.
49. On the **Hole Definition** dialog, click **Extension > Up to last**.
50. On the **Thread Definition** tab, uncheck the **Threaded** option.
51. Type-in **40** in the **Diameter** box
52. Under the **Type** tab, select **Counterbored** from the drop-down and type **50** and **15** in the **Diameter** and **Depth** boxes, respectively.
53. Click the **Thread Definition** tab and uncheck the **Threaded** option.
54. Under the **Extension** tab, click the **Positioning sketch** icon, and then add constraints to define the location of the hole.

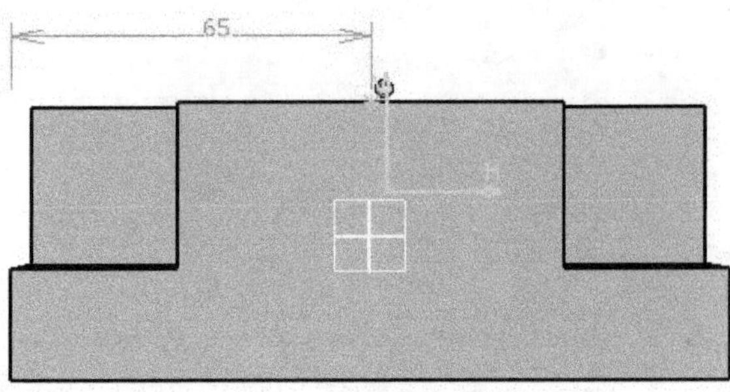

55. Exit the sketch, and then click **OK**.

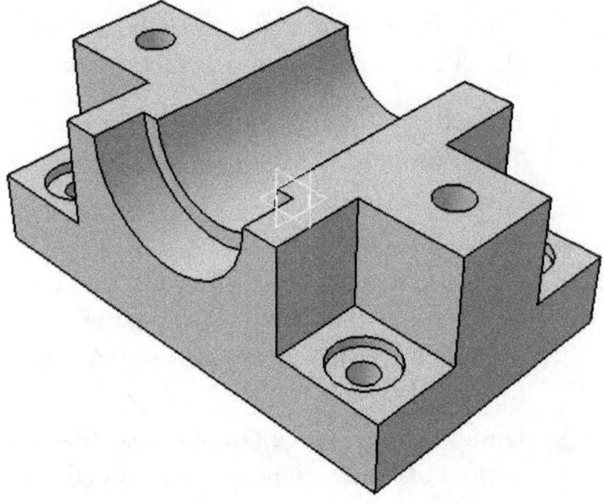

56. Draw a sketch on the front face of the pat geometry and create a *Pocket* throughout the geometry.

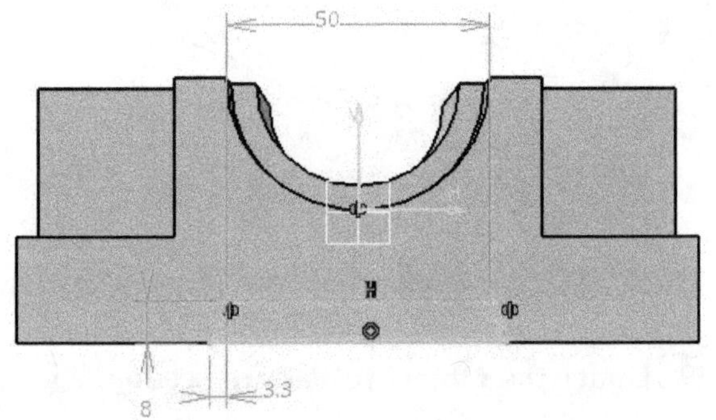

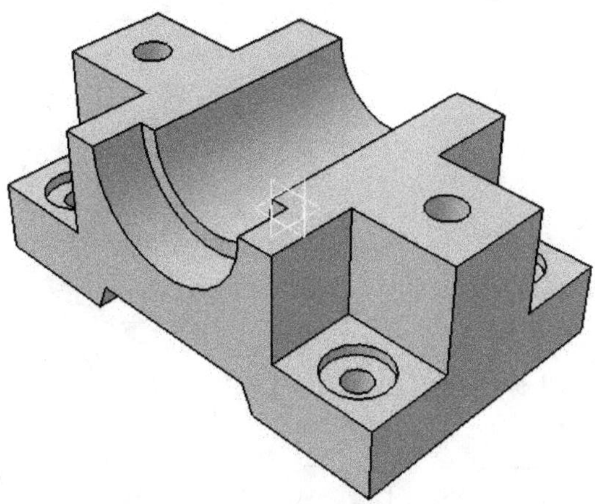

57. Fillet the sharp edges of the *Pocket* features. The fillet radius is 2 mm.

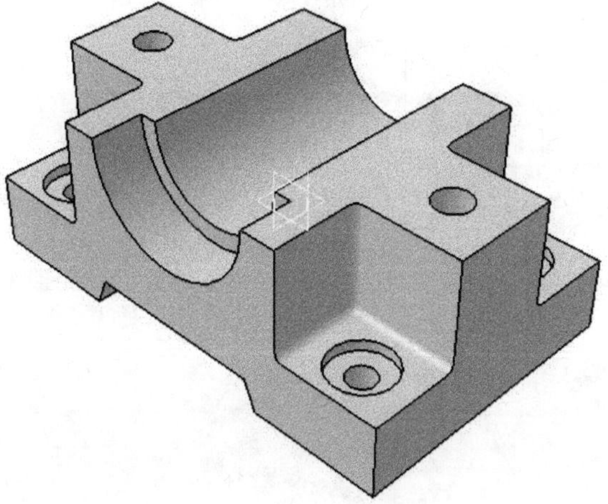

Exercises

Exercise 1

58. Save and close the part file.

Questions

1. Describe the procedure to create a mirror feature.
2. List any two layouts to create patterns.
3. What is the difference between the **Mirror Feature** and **Mirror Geometry** command?
4. Describe the procedure to create a helical pattern.
5. List the methods to define spacing in a linear pattern.

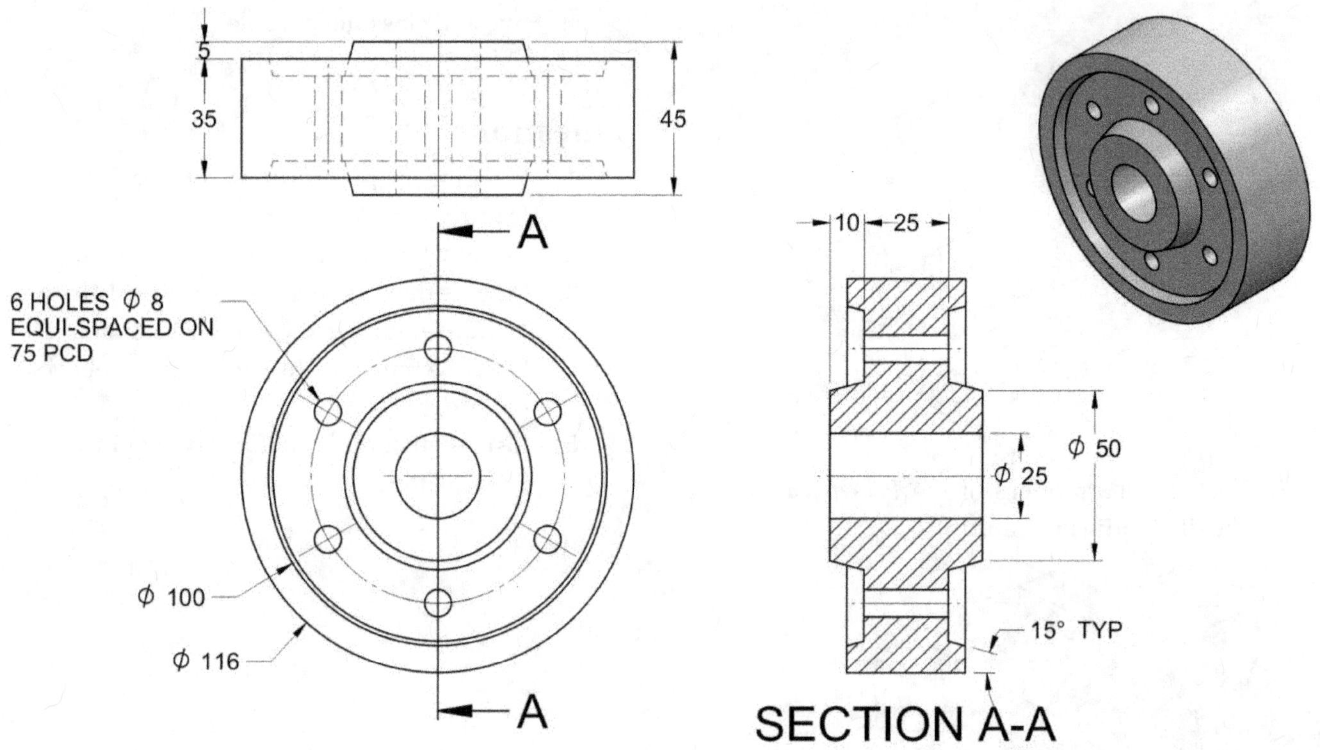
5
35
45
A
6 HOLES ϕ 8
EQUI-SPACED ON
75 PCD
ϕ 100
ϕ 116
A
10
25
ϕ 50
ϕ 25
15° TYP
SECTION A-A

Exercise 2

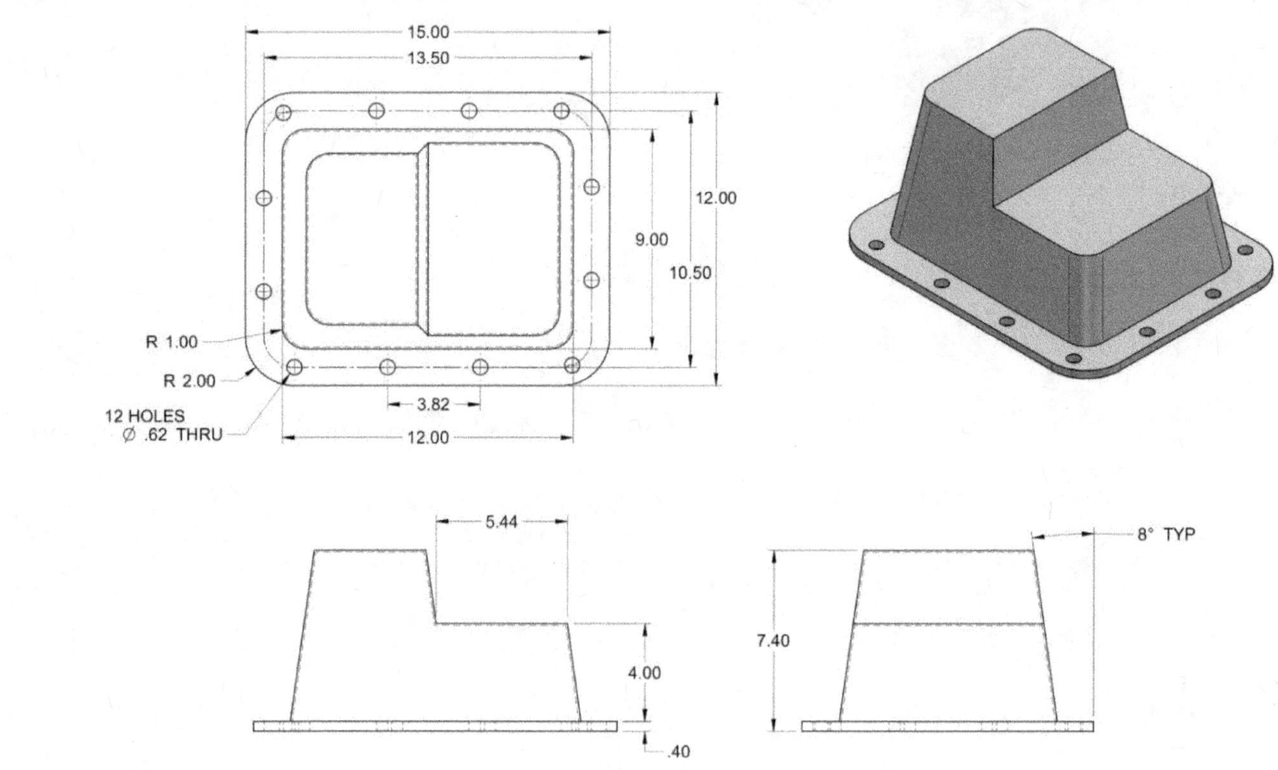
15.00
13.50
12.00
9.00
10.50
R 1.00
R 2.00
12 HOLES
Ø .62 THRU
3.82
12.00
5.44
8° TYP
7.40
4.00
.40
SHEET THICKNESS = 0.079 in

Chapter 6: Rib Features

The **Rib** command is one of the basic commands available in CATIA that allow you to generate a solid geometry. It can be used to create simple geometry as well as complex shapes. A rib is composed of two items: a cross-section and a path. The cross-section controls the shape of rib while the path controls its direction. For example, look at the angled cylinder shown in figure. This is created using a simple rib with the circle as the profile and an angled line as the path.

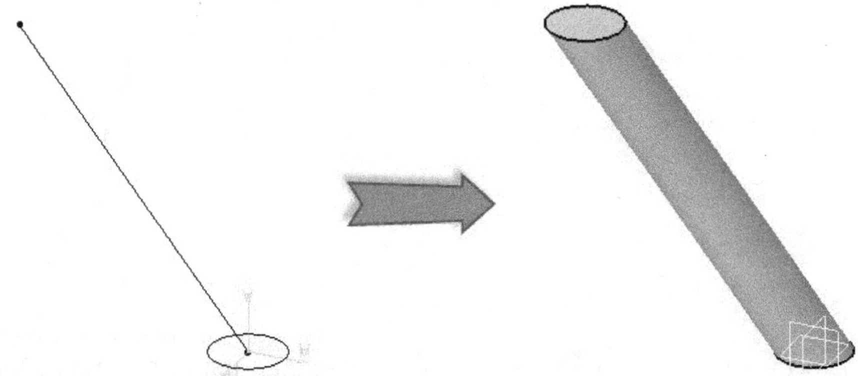

By the making the path a bit more complex, you can see that a rib allows you to create the shape you would not be able to create using commands such as Pad or Revolve.

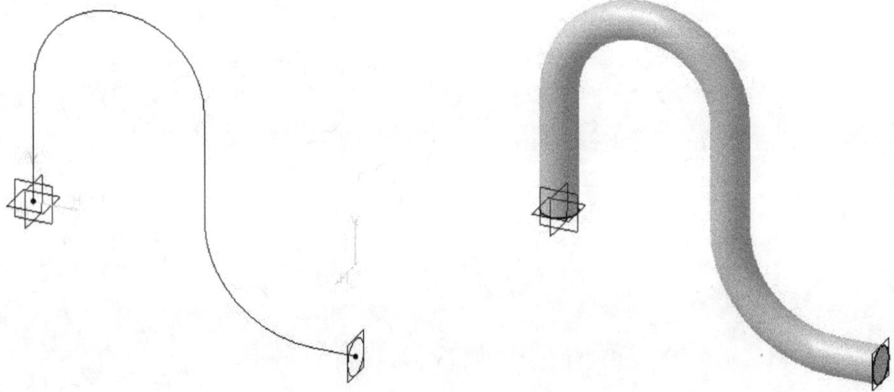

The topics covered in this chapter are:

- *Create Simple rib features*
- *Avoiding errors and intersections*
- *Various types of center curves that can be used to create rib features*
- *Merging end faces of the rib*
- *Create Slot features*

 The Rib command

This type of rib requires two elements: a center curve and profile. The profile defines the shape of the rib along the center curve. A center curve is used to control the direction of the profile and it can be a sketch or an edge.

1. To create a rib, you must first create a center curve and a profile.
2. Create a center curve by drawing a sketch. It can be an open or closed sketch.

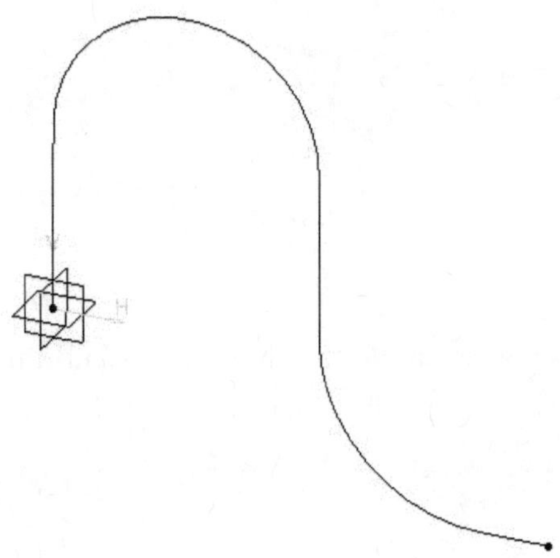

3. Activate the **Plane** command and create a plane normal to the path.
4. Sketch the profile on the plane normal to the path.

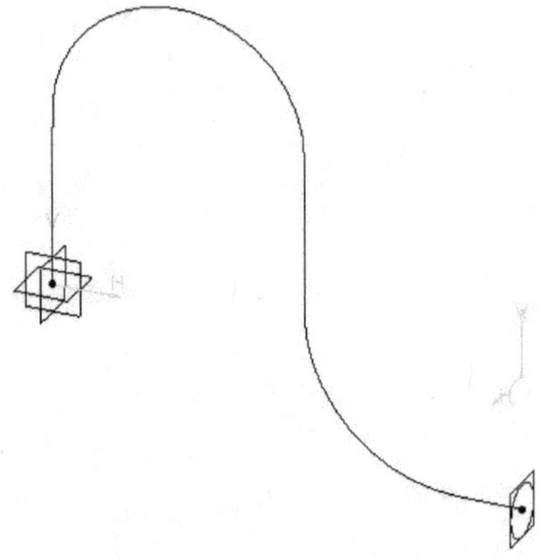

5. On the **Sketch-Based Features** toolbar, click the **Rib** button (or) click **Insert > Sketch-Based Features > Rib** on the Menu bar. As you activate the **Rib** command, a dialog appears showing different options to create the rib.
6. Select the profile and center curve.
7. Click **OK**.

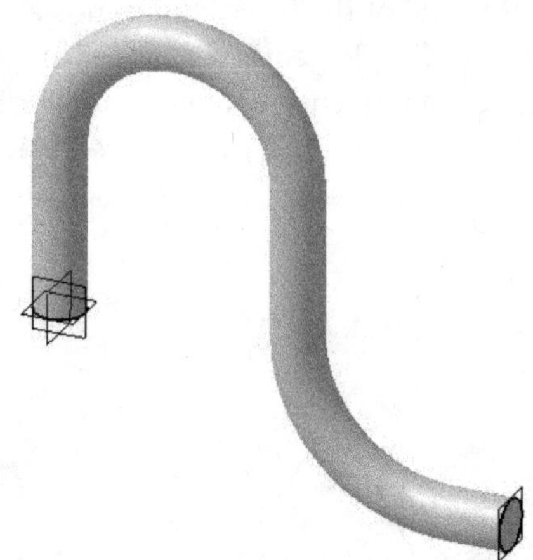

CATIA will not allow the sweep to result in a self-intersecting geometry. As the profile is swept along a path, it cannot comeback and cross itself. For example, if the profile of the sweep is larger than the curve, the resulting geometry will intersect and the sweep will fail.

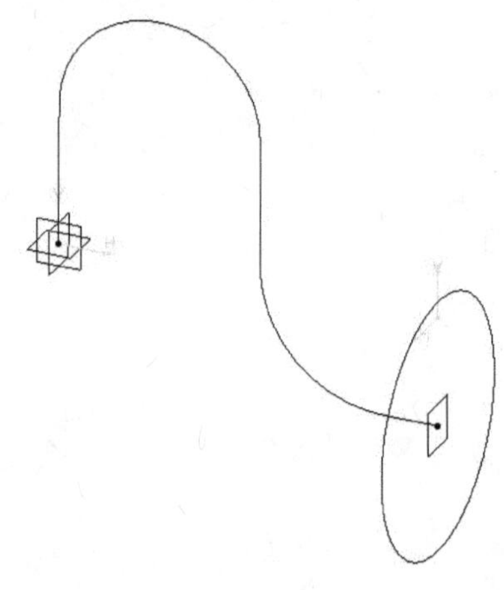

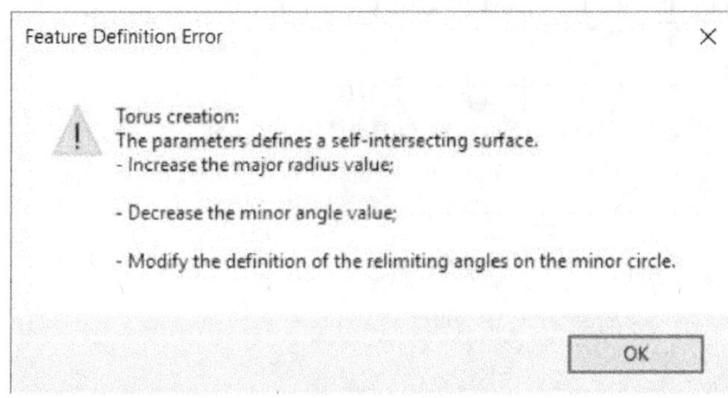

A rib profile must be created as a sketch. However, a center curve can be a sketch, curve, or edge. The following illustrations show various types of center curves and resultant rib features.

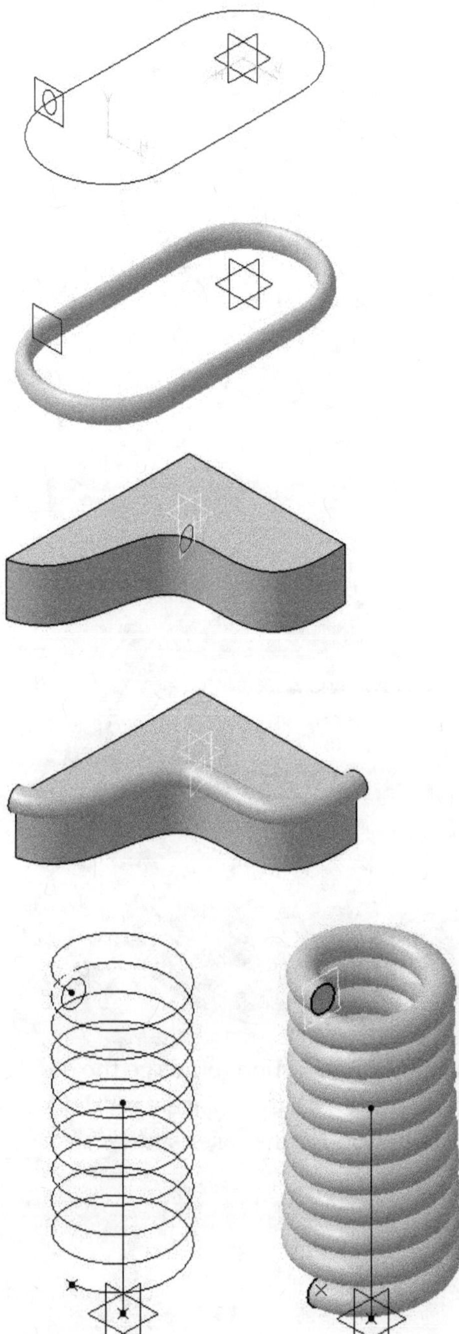

Profile Control

The profile control options define the orientation of the resulting geometry. The **Keep angle** option sweeps the profile in the direction normal to the center curve. The **Pulling Direction** option sweeps the profile along the direction that you define.

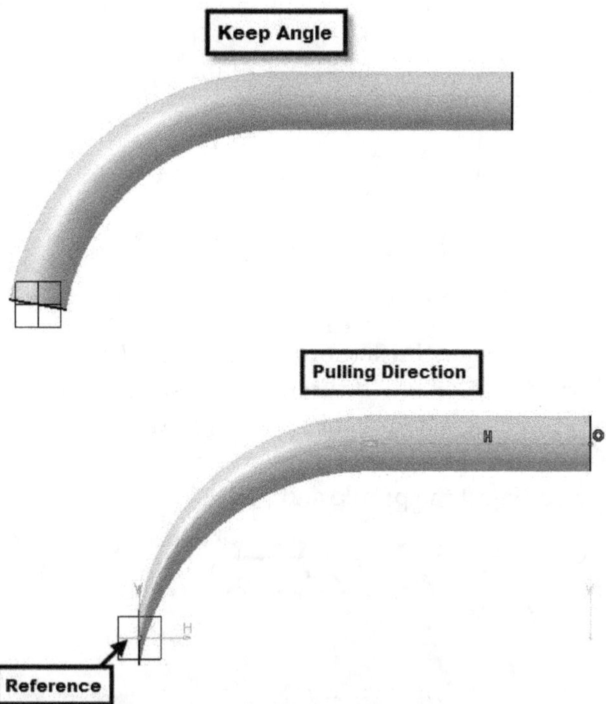

You can also use the **Pulling Direction** option to sweep the profile and path, which are not normal to each other.

1. Activate the **Rib** command and select **Profile Control > Pulling Direction**.
2. Select the plane parallel to the profile and path. This defines the pulling direction.
3. Check the **Move profile to path** option.
4. Select the profile and path.

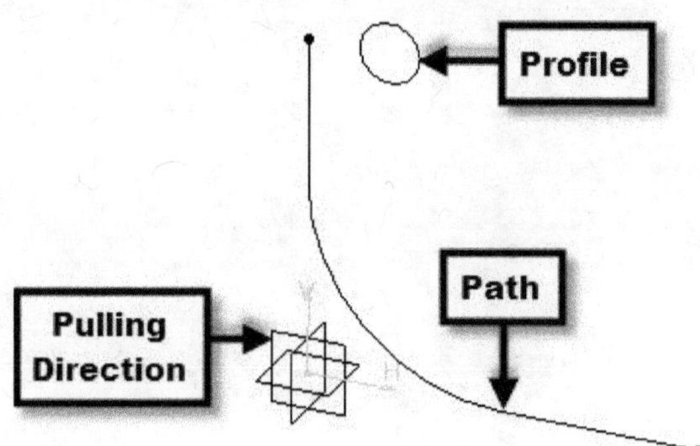

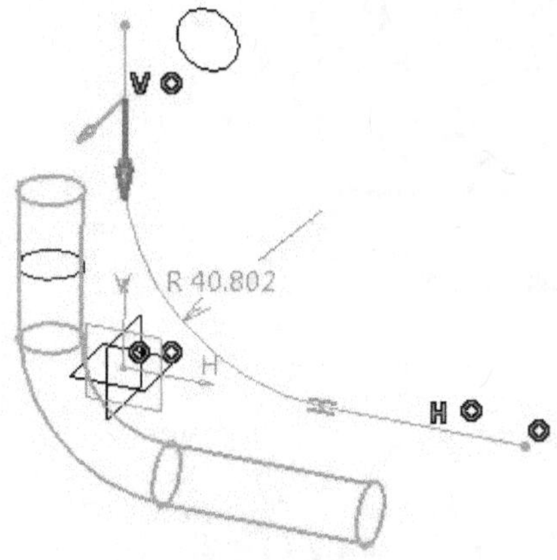

The **Reference Surface** option under the **Profile Control** section will be useful while sweeping a profile along a non-planar path. For example, define a path and cross-section similar to the one shown in figure. Select the profile and path

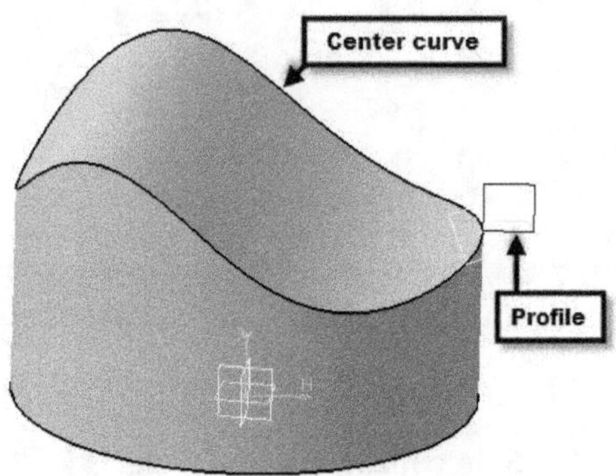

On the dialog, select **Profile Control > Reference Surface** and click on the top surface. The rib will be created by maintaining contact with the top surface.

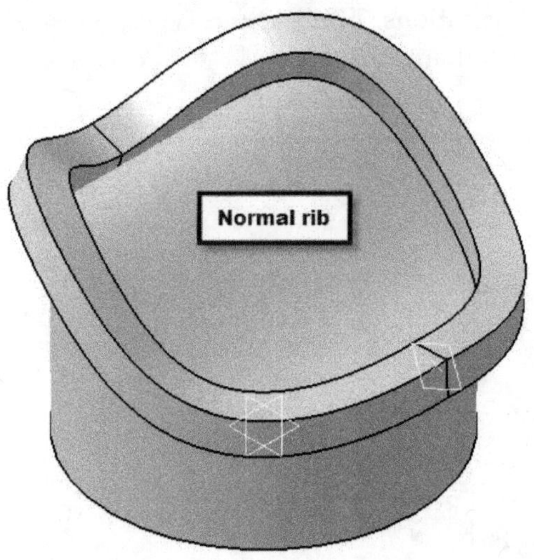

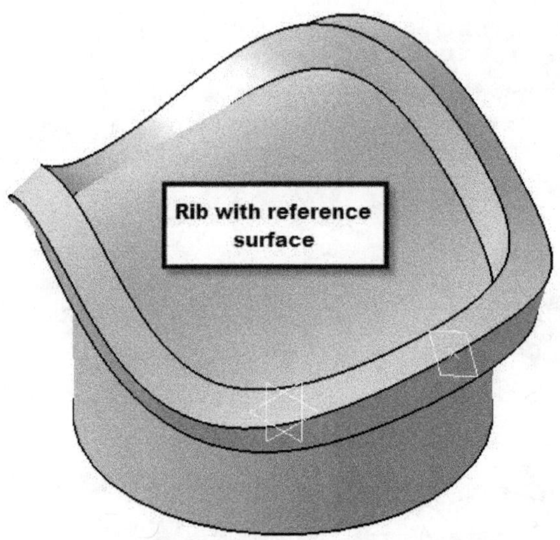

Use the **Merge end faces** option to merge the end faces of the rib feature with the adjacent model faces. You can use this option for the cases similar to the following one.

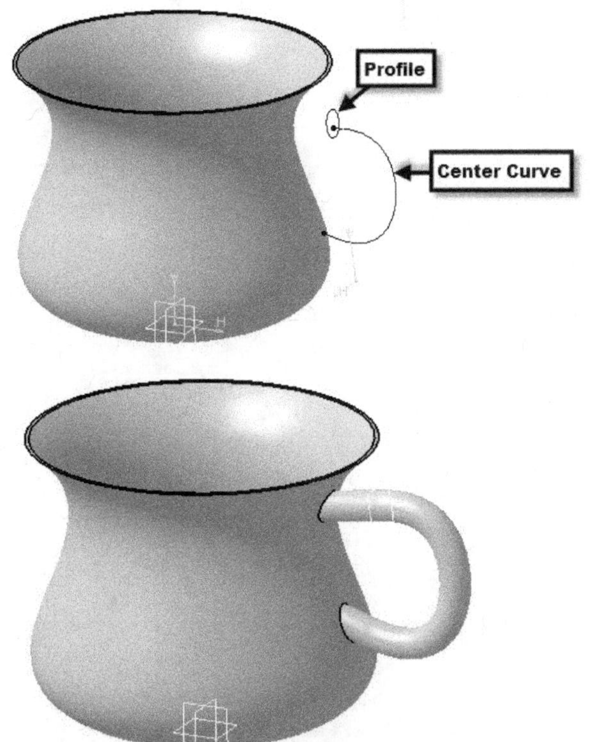

Use the **Thick Profile** option to create a shelled rib feature. This option can be used to create pipes.

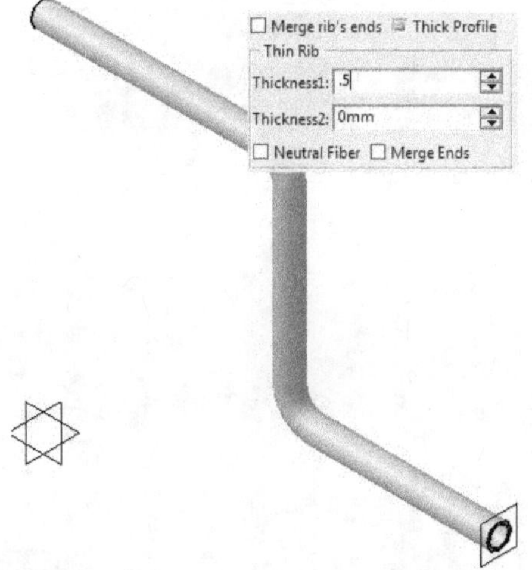

The Slot command

In addition to adding rib features, CATIA allows you to remove geometry using the **Slot** command.

1. On the **Sketch-Based Features** toolbar, click the **Slot** button (or) click **Insert > Sketch-Based Features > Slot** on the Menu bar.
2. Select the profile and center curve from the model geometry.

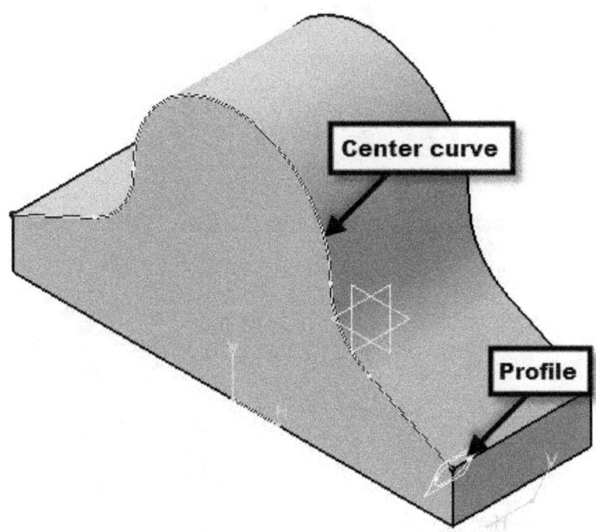

3. Click **Preview** on the dialog. You will notice that slot is not created throughout the geometry.

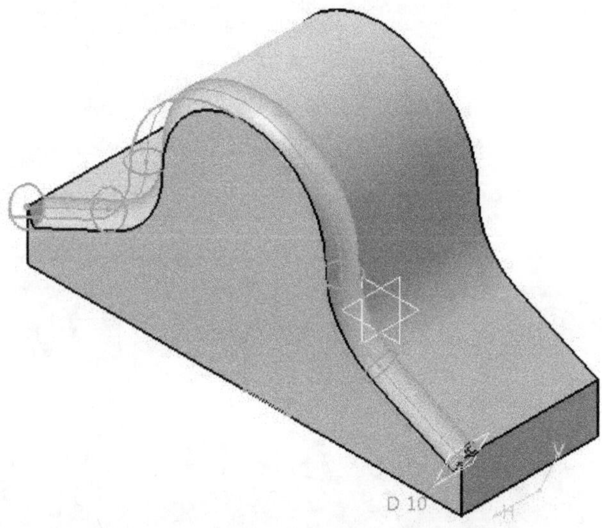

4. On the dialog, check the **Merge slot's ends** option. The resultant swept cutout will be throughout the geometry. Click **OK**.

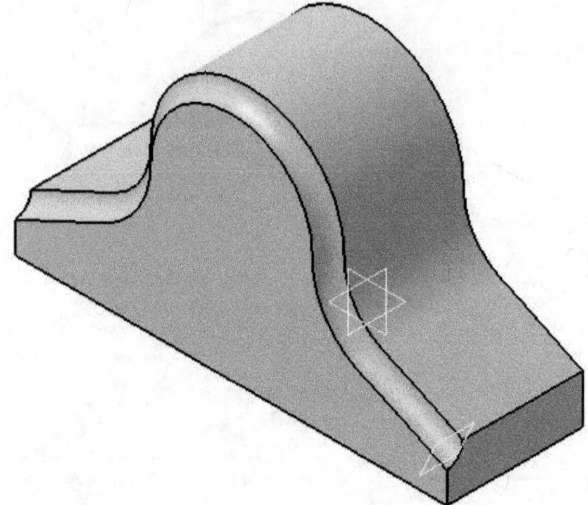

Examples

Example 1

In this example, you will create the part shown below.

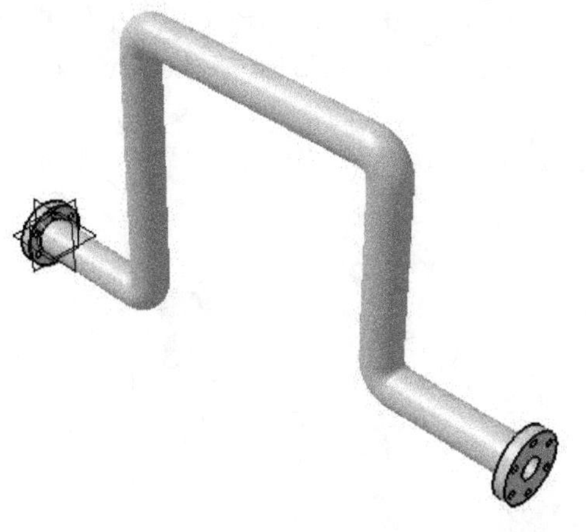

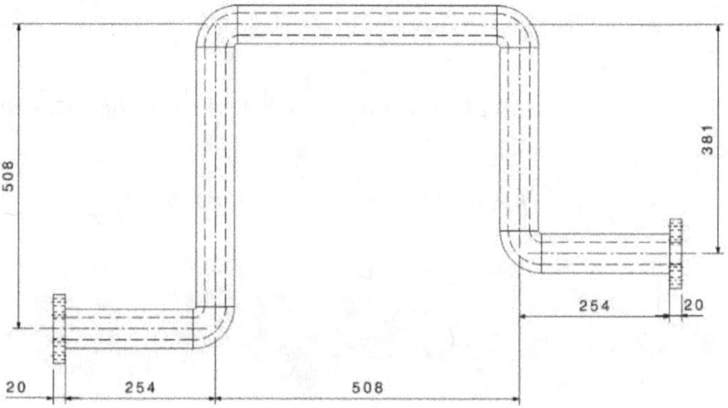

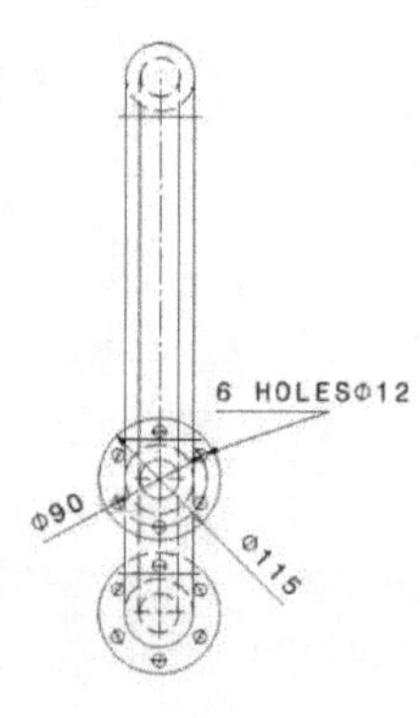

PIPE I.D. 51

PIPE O.D. 65

1. Start **CATIA V5-6R2017**.
2. Open a new part file.
3. Draw the sketch on the YZ plane, as shown in figure.
4. Click **Exit workbench** to complete the sketch.

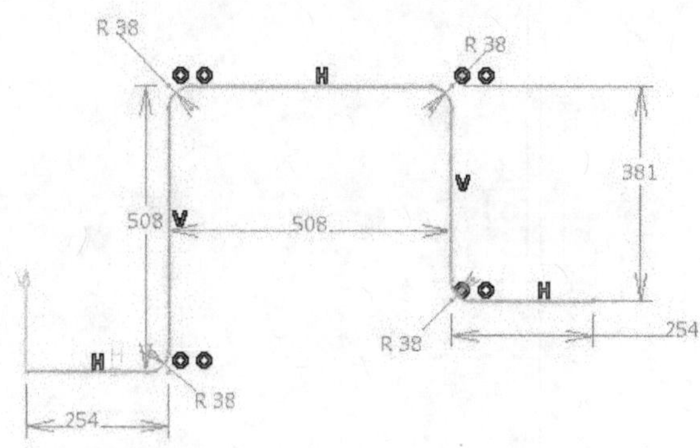

5. On the **Reference Elements** toolbar, click the **Plane** icon.

6. On the **Plane Definition** dialog, click **Plane type > Normal to curve**.
7. Click on the end-point of the sketch to define the plane location.

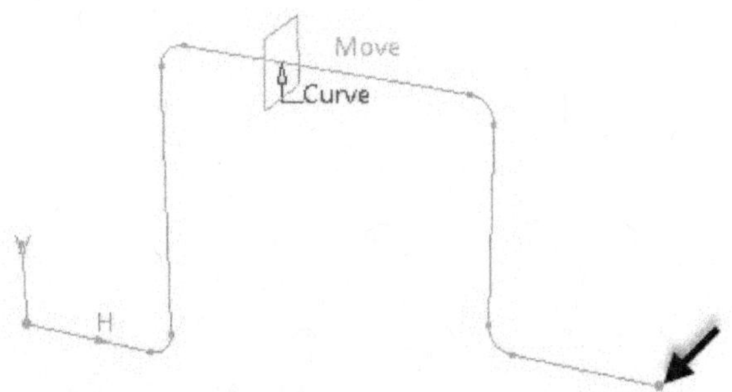

8. Click **OK** to create the plane.

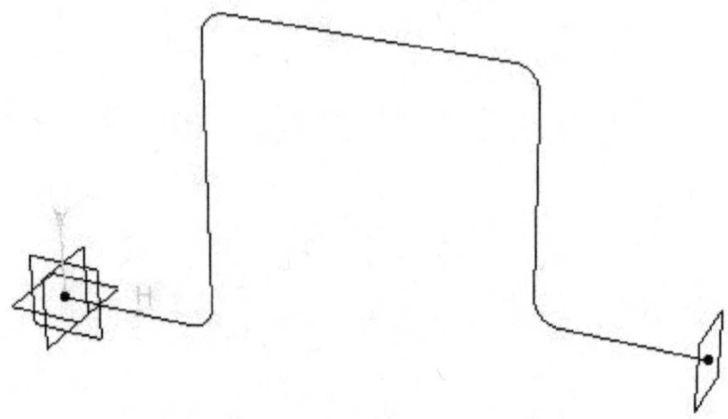

9. Start a sketch on the new plane (refer to **Chapter 2: Sketcher Workbench** to learn about starting a sketch).
10. Draw a circle and make its center coincident with endpoint of the previous sketch.

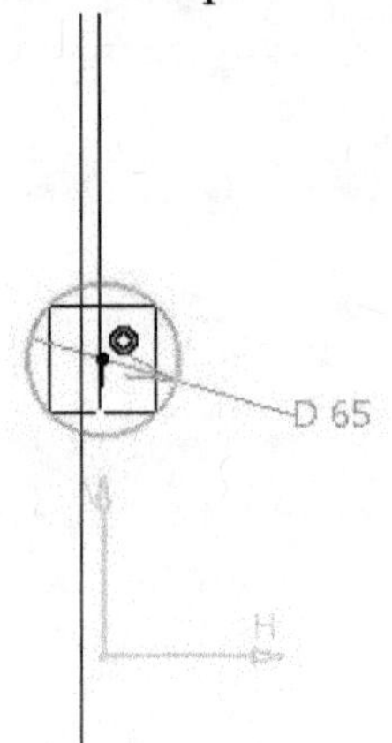

11. Click the **Exit workbench** icon.
12. On the **Sketch-Based Features** toolbar, click the **Rib** icon (or) click **Insert > Sketch-Based Features > Rib** on the Menu.
13. Select the first sketch to define the Center curve.
14. On the **Rib Definition** dialog, check the **Thick Profile** option and type-in 14 in the **Thickness 1** box.
15. Click **OK** to create the *Rib* feature.

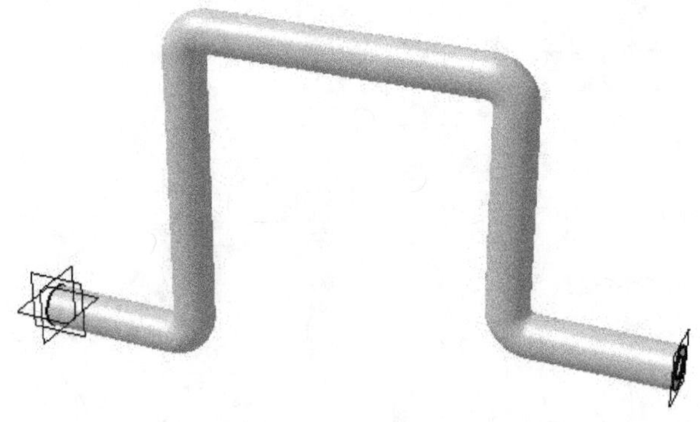

16. Activate the **Pad** command and click the **Sketch** icon
17. Click on the front-end face of the *Rib* feature.

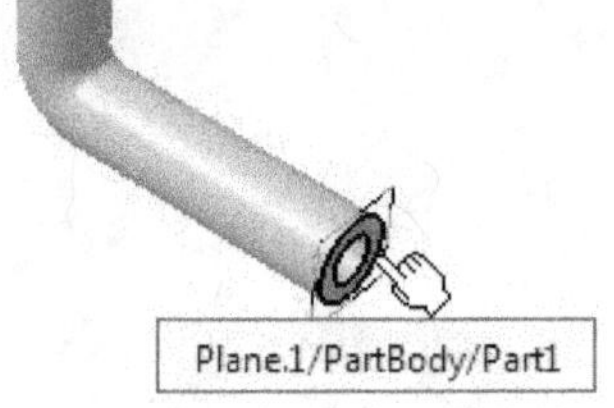

18. On the **3D Geometry** toolbar, click **Project 3D Elements** and click on the inner circular edge.

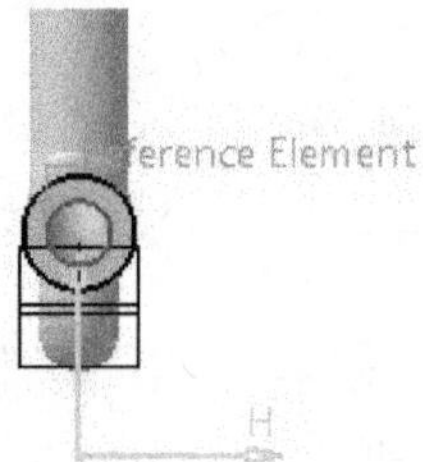

19. On the **Projection** dialog, click **OK** to project the curve onto the sketch plane.
20. Draw a circle of 115 diameter.

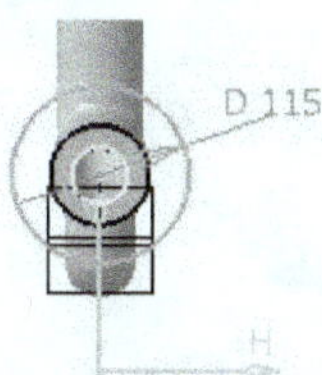

21. Click **Exit workbench** to complete the sketch.
22. Type-in **20** in the **Length** box. Click the Reverse Direction and **OK** to complete the *Pad* feature.

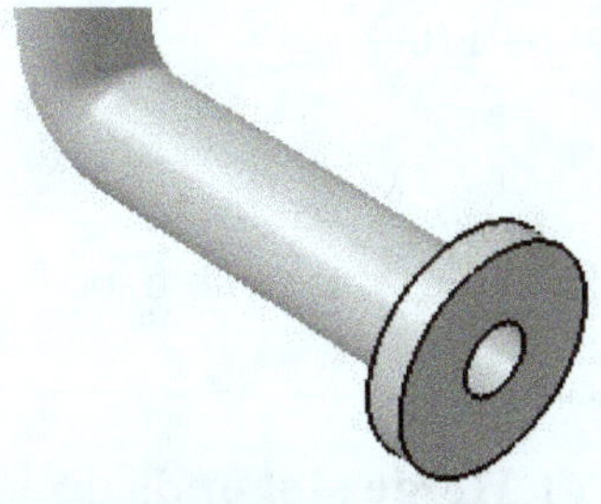

23. Create a hole of 12 diameter on the *Pad* feature.

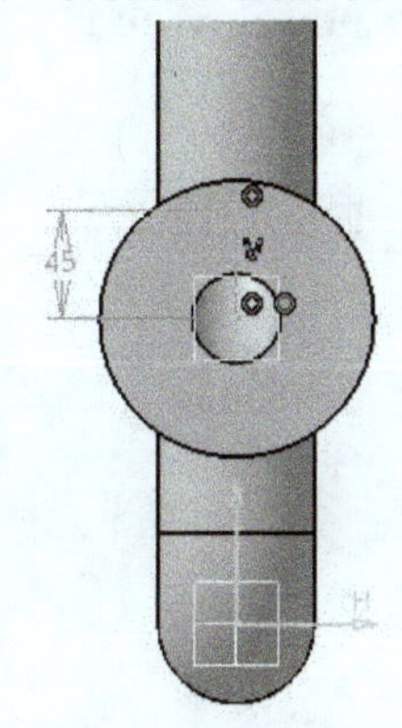

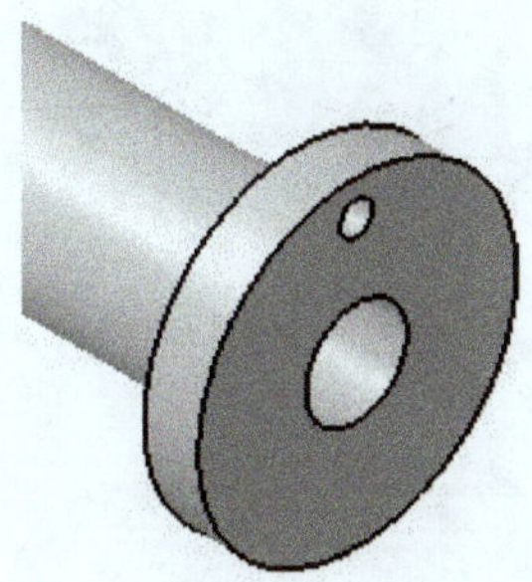

24. On the **Transformation Features** toolbar, click **Pattern** drop-down > **Circular Pattern** .
25. On the **Circular Pattern Definition** dialog, select **Parameters > Instance(s) & angular spacing**.
26. Type-in **6** and **60** in the **Instance(s)** and **Angular spacing** boxes, respectively.
27. Under the **Reference Direction** section, click in the **Reference element** box and select the outer cylindrical face of the *Pad* feature.
28. Under the **Object to Pattern** section, click in the **Object** box and select the hole.
29. Click **OK** to pattern the hole.

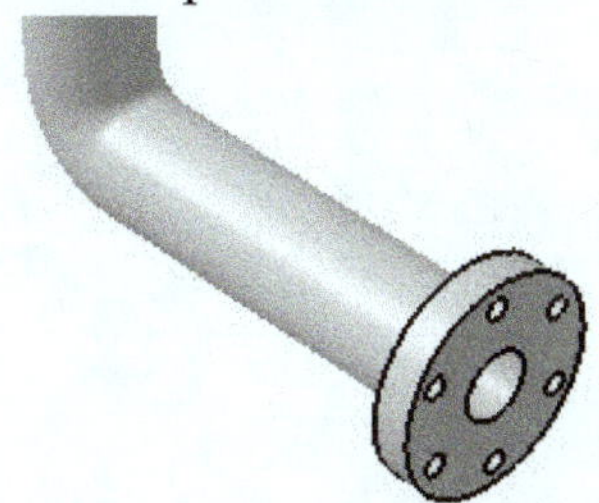

30. On the **Reference Elements** toolbar, click the **Point** icon.
31. On the **Point Definition** dialog, type-in 0, -20 and 0 in X, Y, and Z boxes and then click **OK**.
32. On the **Transformation Features** toolbar, click **Pattern** drop-down > **User Pattern** .
33. Click on the new reference point.

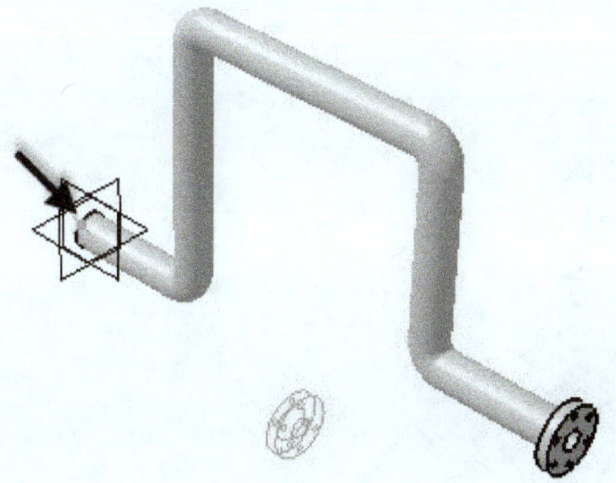

34. On the **User Pattern Definition** dialog, click in the **Object** box and select the *Pad* feature.
35. Click **OK** to pattern the *Pad* feature.

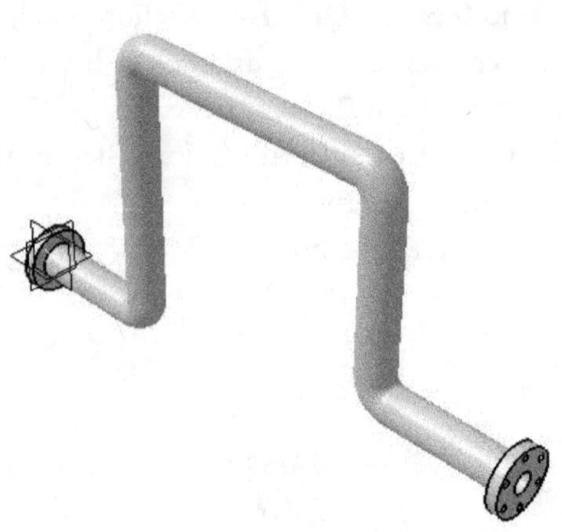

36. On the **Reference Elements** toolbar, click the **Point** icon.
37. On the **Point Definition** dialog, type-in 0, -10 and 0 in X, Y, and Z boxes and then click **OK**.
38. Activate the **User Pattern** command and select the reference point.
39. Click in the **Object** box and select the Circular pattern from the Specification tree.
40. Click **OK** to pattern the circular pattern.

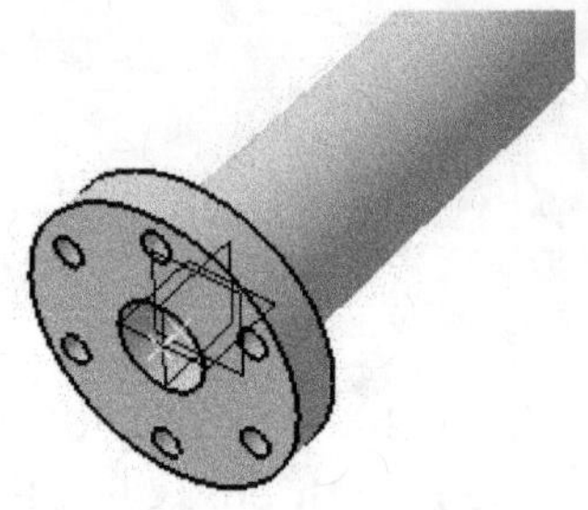

41. Change the model view orientation.
42. Save and close the part file.

Questions

1. List the types of path that can be used to create *Rib* features.
2. What is the use of **Merge slot ends** option?
3. Why do we use the **Reference Surface** option in the **Rib** command?
4. What is the use of **Pulling Direction** option?

Exercises

Exercise1

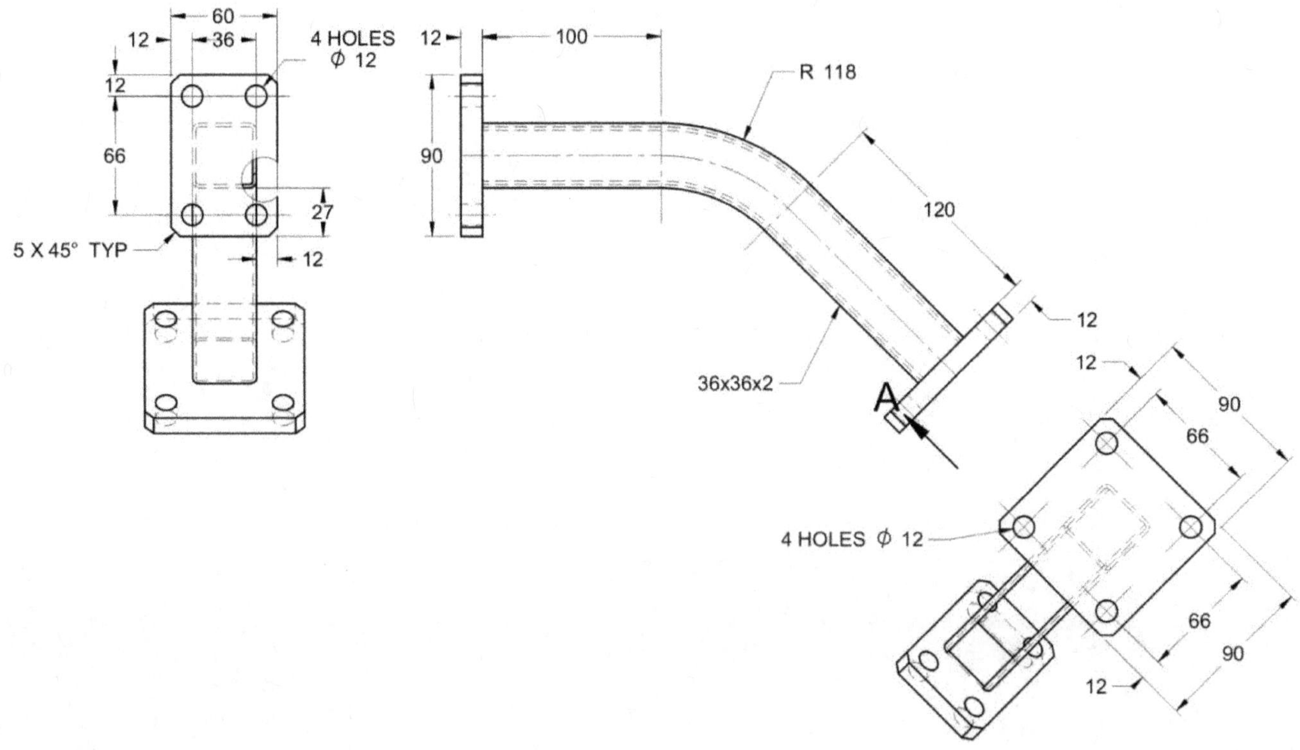
60
12
36
4 HOLES
Ø 12
12
66
27
5 X 45° TYP
12
12
100
90
R 118
120
12
36x36x2
A
12
90
66
4 HOLES Ø 12
66
90
12

Chapter 7: Multi Section Solids

The **Multi Section Solid** command is one of the advanced commands available in CATIA that allows you to create simple as well as complex shapes. A basic multi section solid is created by defining two cross-sections and joining them together. For example, if you create a loft feature between a circle and a square, you can easily change the cross-sectional shape of the solid. This ability is what separates the multi section solid feature from the rib feature.

The topics covered in this chapter are:

- *Basic Multi-sections Solid*
- *Multi Section Solids*
- *Removed Multi Section Solids*

 The Multi-sections Solid command

This command creates a solid feature between different cross-sections.

1. To create this type of feature, first create two or more sections on different planes. The planes can be parallel or perpendicular to each other.
2. On the **Sketch-Based Features** toolbar, click the **Multi-sections Solid** button (or) **Insert > Sketch-Based Features > Multi-sections Solid** on the Menu bar.
3. Select two or more sections to define the multi section solid.

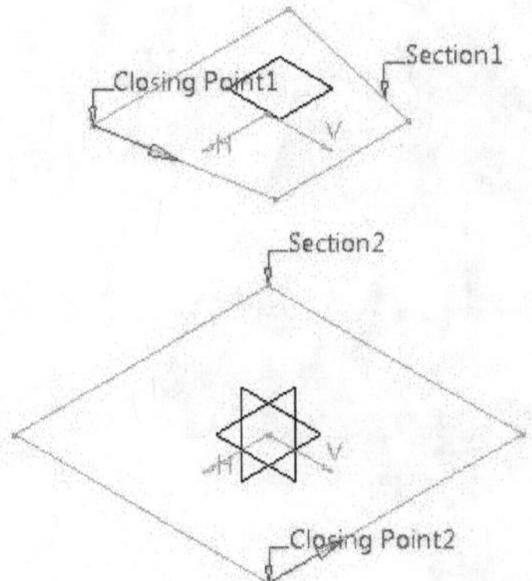

You have to ensure that the closing points of the cross-sections should be on same corners. For example, if the closing point of the first section is on the left corner, then the closing points on other cross-sections should also be on the left corner. If they are not on same corners, then click the right mouse

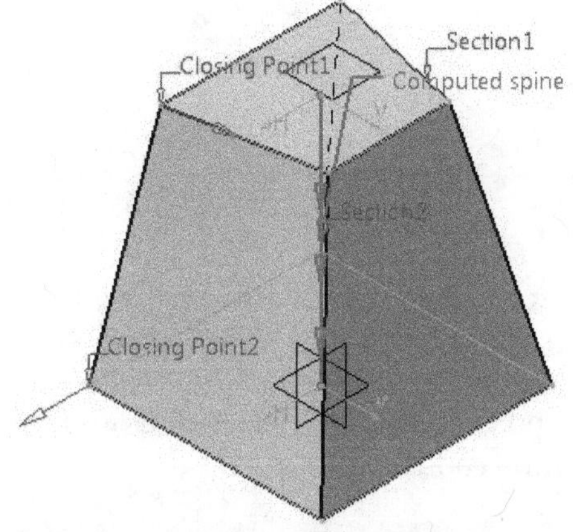

button on anyone of the cross-sections on the dialog and select **Replace Closing Point**. Click on the corner point matching with the other section.

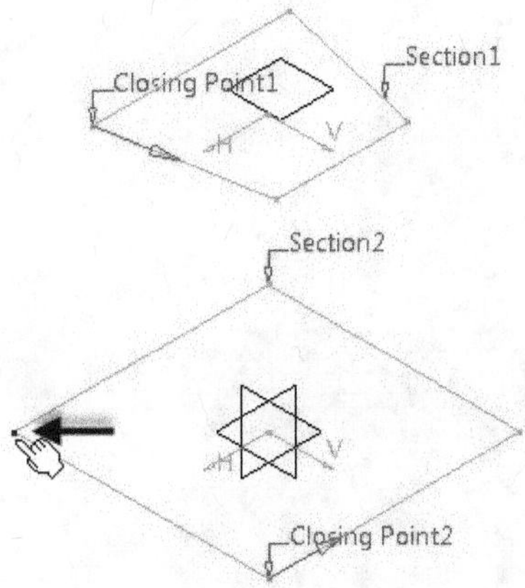

4. Click the **Preview** button. The model preview updates immediately, as shown below.

5. Now, you have to define supports for the cross-sections. Click on anyone of the sections on the

dialog and select the absolute coordinate system of the section.

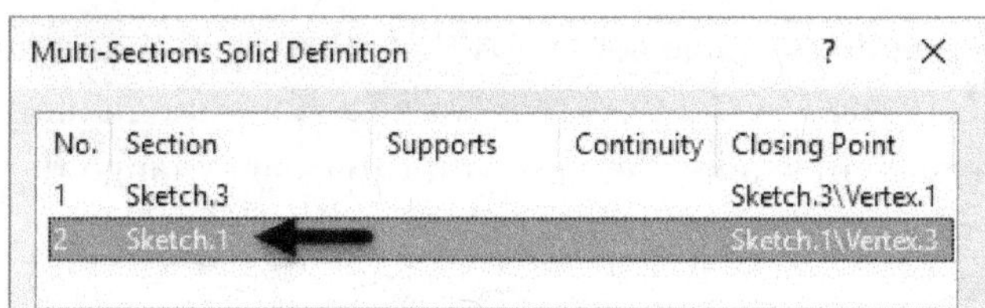

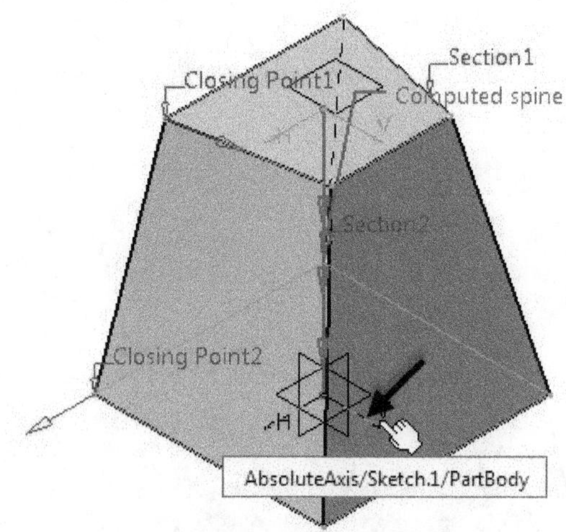

6. Likewise, and click on the other sections and click on its absolute coordinate system.

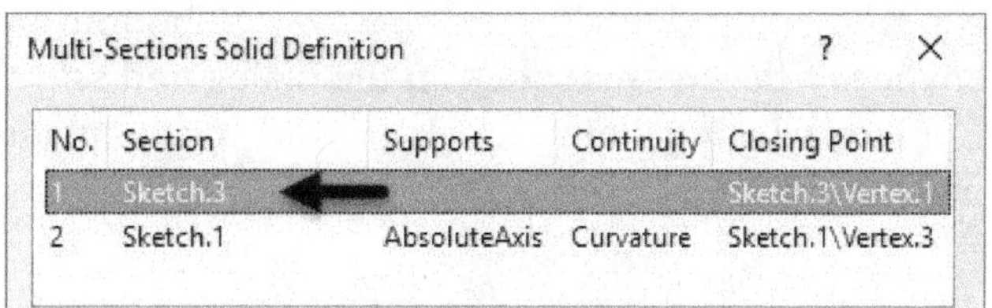

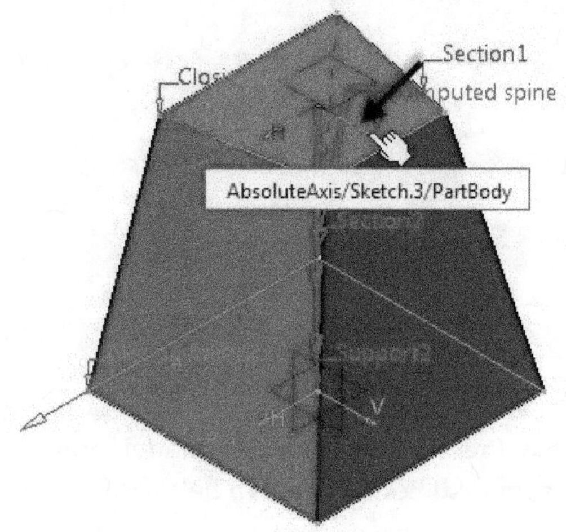

The shape of a simple multi section solid is controlled by the cross-sections and the plane location. However, the behaviour of the side faces can be controlled by the **Continuity** between the cross-sections. If you would like to change the appearance of the side faces, you can change the **Continuity** of the cross-sections of the multi section solid. For instance, click on the first cross-section in the dialog, and then select **Continuity > Tangent**. Click **Preview** to view the changes. You can notice that the beginning of the solid starts in a direction normal to the cross-section.

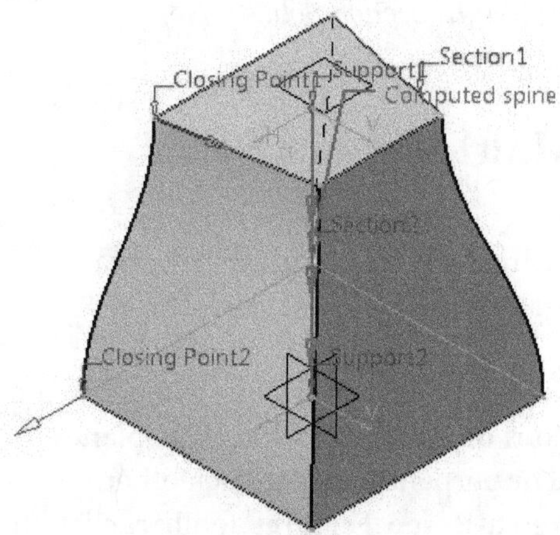

If you select **Continuity > Curvature**, the side faces will maintain curvature continuity with the first cross-section.

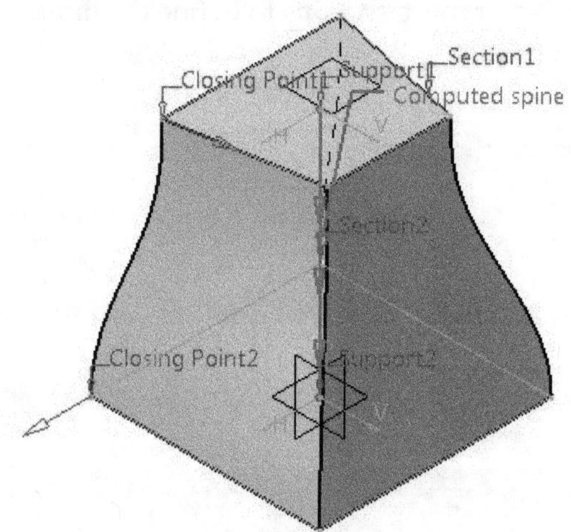

Likewise, select the second cross-section from the dialog and change the continuity type.

7. Click **OK** to complete the feature.

Types of the Cross-sections

In addition to 2D sketches, you can also use different element types to define cross-sections by using different element types. For instance, you can use existing model faces, surfaces, and curves

Couplings

Sections used for creating multi section solids should have a matching number of segments. For example, a three-sided section will loft nicely to another three-sided section despite the differences in the shape of the individual segments. The **Multi Section Solid** command does a good job of generating smooth faces to join them.

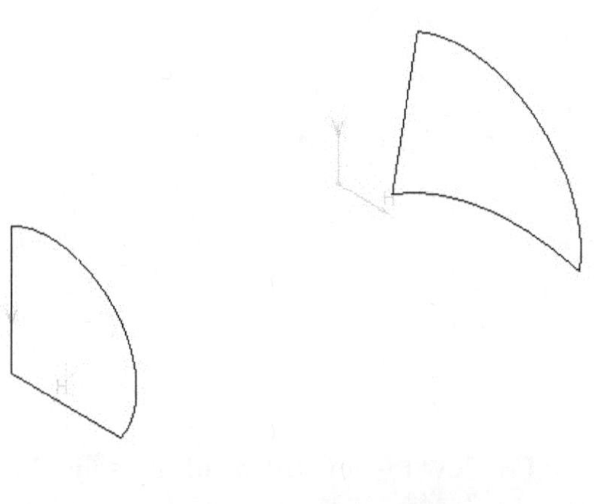

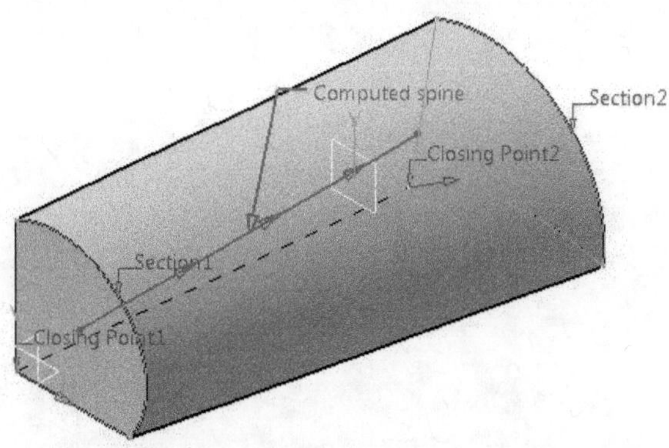

On the other hand, a four-sided section and two-sided section will result in an error.

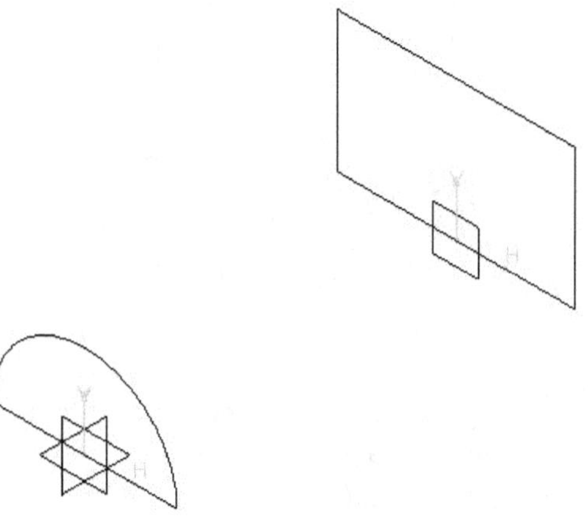

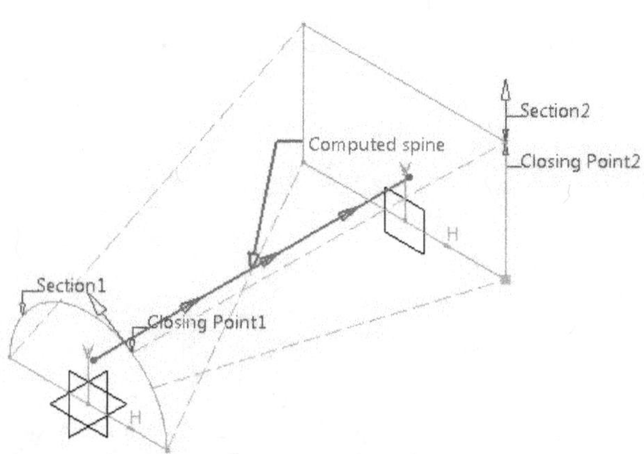

To get the desired result, you have to break one of the sections so that they have equal number of segments.

1. Click **Cancel** on the **Multi-sections Solid Definition** dialog and double-click on the arc to activate its sketch.

2. Activate the **Break** command (click **Insert > Operations > Relimitations > Break** on the Menu bar) and break the arc into three segments. You can also use dimensions to define the exact location of the split points.

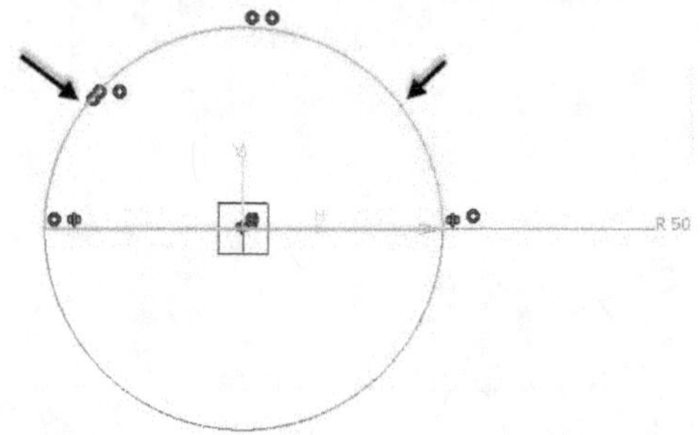

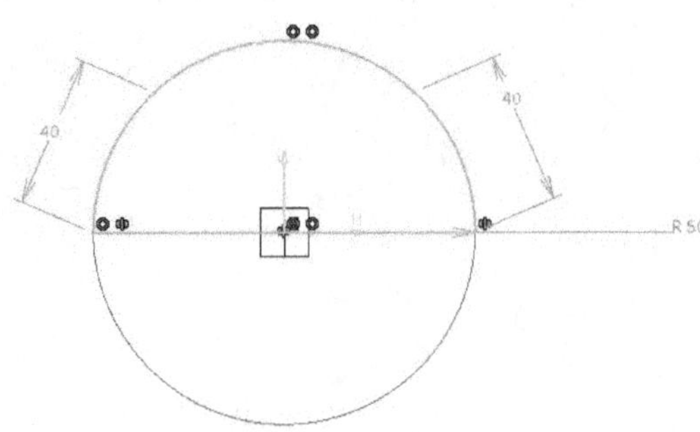

3. Now, exit the **Sketcher** workbench and activate the **Multi-sections Solid** command.
4. Select the sections one by one.
5. On the **Multi-sections Solid Definition** dialog, click the **Coupling** tab.
6. Select the vertices of the section 1 and section 2, as shown below. This creates a coupling.

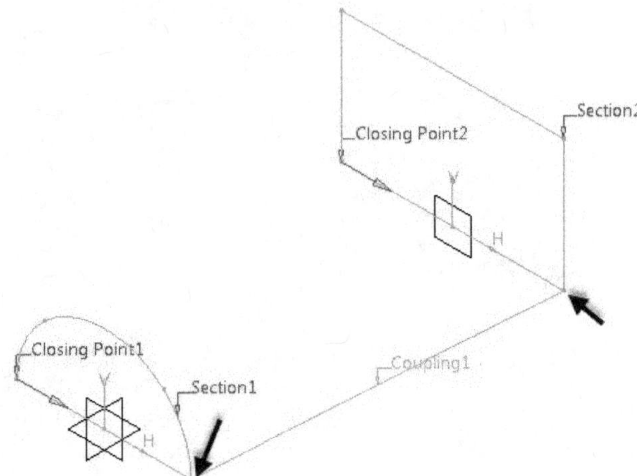

7. Likewise, create other couplings using the vertices.

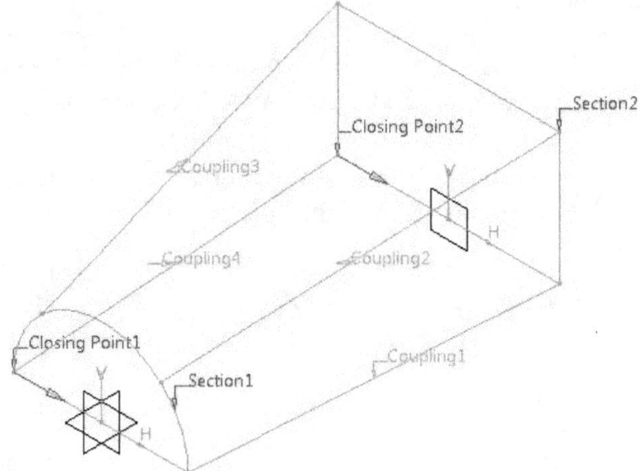

8. Click **OK** to complete the feature.

Spines

When you create a multi section solid, a spine is defined between the sections, automatically. The spine controls the way the multi section solid is transformed between the sections. You can also define the spine using a curve or sketch element.

1. Activate the **Multi-sections Solid** command and select the sections.

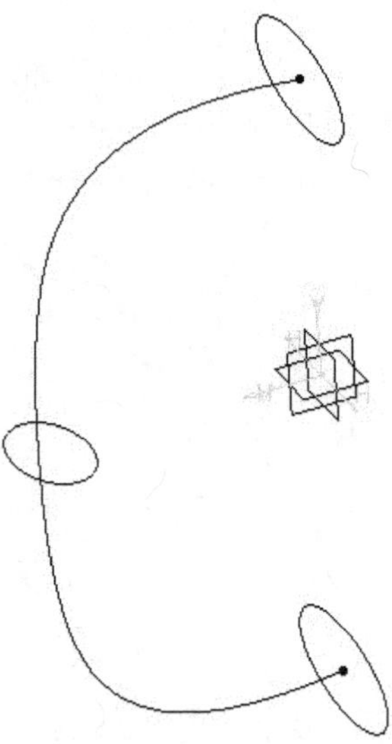

2. Click **Preview** to view the resulting solid.

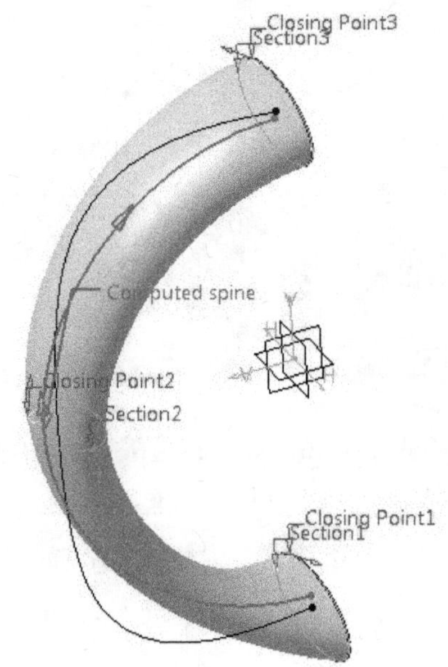

3. Click on the **Spine** tab and select the curve passing through the section. This defines the spine.
4. Click **OK** to create the solid.

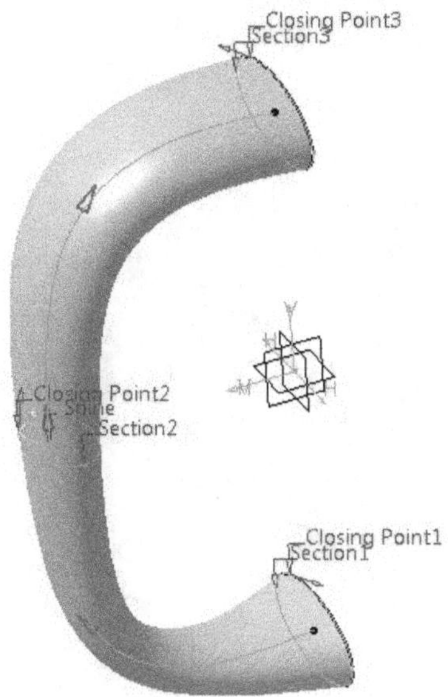

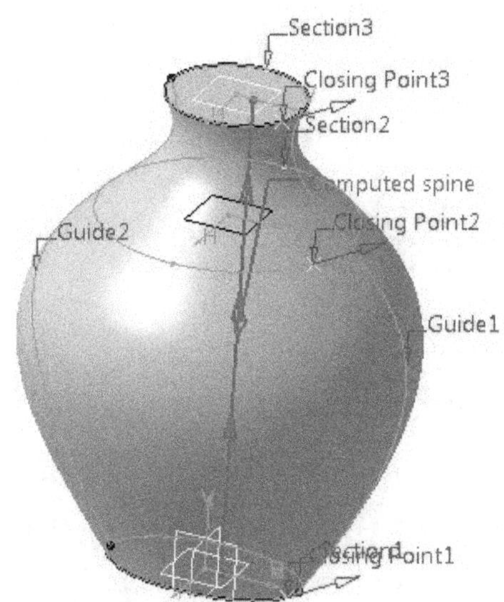

Guides

Similar to **Continuity** options, guides allow you to control the behaviour of a multi sections solid between cross-sections. You can create guides by using 2D sketches. You can also use the **3D Spline** command to create guided curves. Ensure that the guides touch the cross-sections.

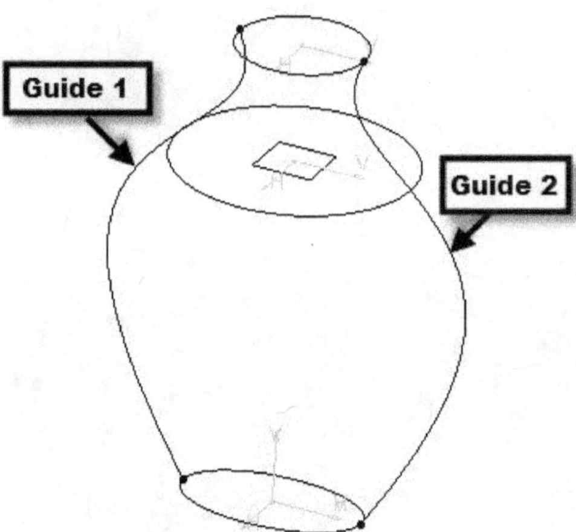

1. Now, activate the **Multi Section Solid** command and select the cross-sections.
2. To select guide curves, click the **Guides** tab on the dialog.
3. Click in the **Guides** list and select the first and second guides.
4. Click the **Preview** button. You will see that the preview updates.

Relimitation

The **Relimitation** options limits the transformation of the multi sections solids to the start and end sections, as shown below.

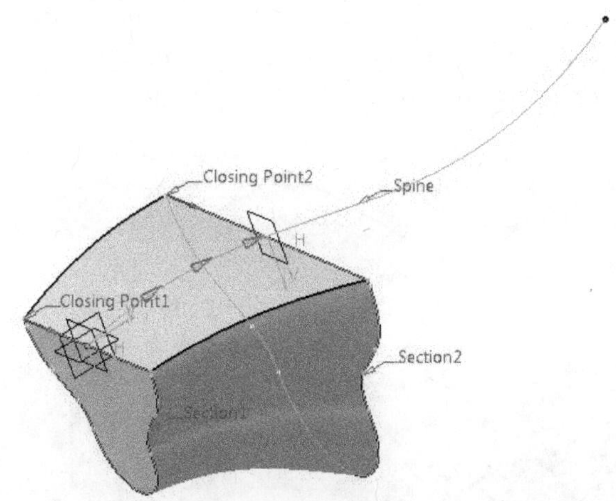

If you want to create the multi section solid up to the complete length of the spine or guides, then click the **Relimitation** tab on the dialog. Uncheck the **Relimited on start section** and **Relimited on end section** options. Click **Preview** to view the relimited solid.

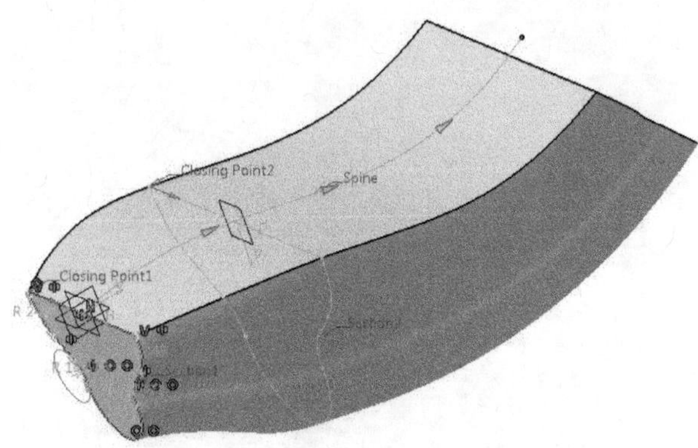

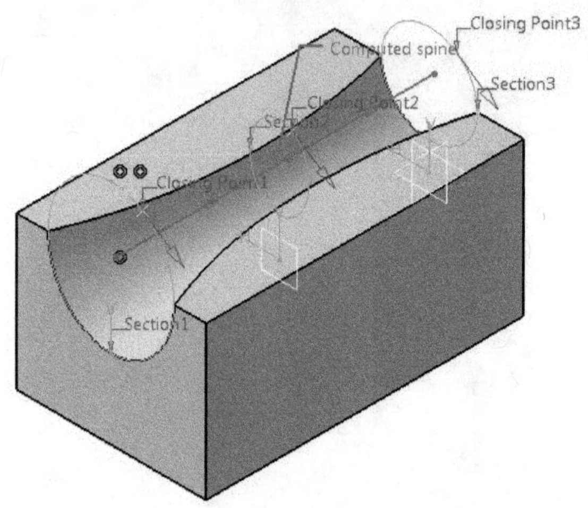

 Removed Multi-sections Solid

Like other standard features such as pad, revolve and rib, the multi-sections solid feature can be used to add material. However, it can also be used to remove material. You can do this by using the **Removed Multi-sections Solid** command. Activate this command (click the **Removed Multi-sections Solid** button on the **Sketch-Based Features** toolbar) and select the cross-sections. Ensure that the arrows on the cross-sections point in the same direction. Click **Preview** and **OK** to create the feature.

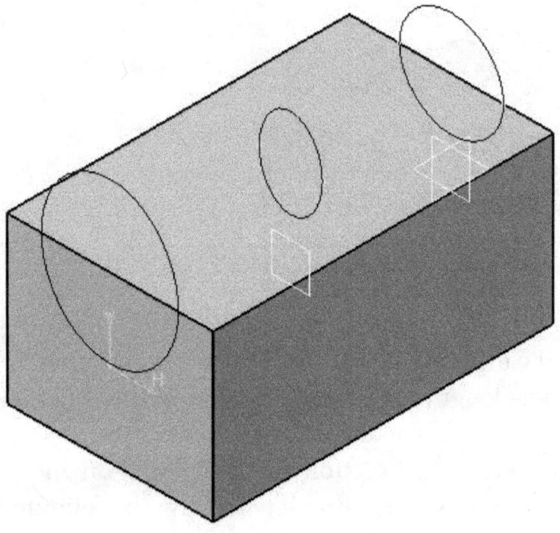

Examples

Example 1

In this example, you will create the part shown below.

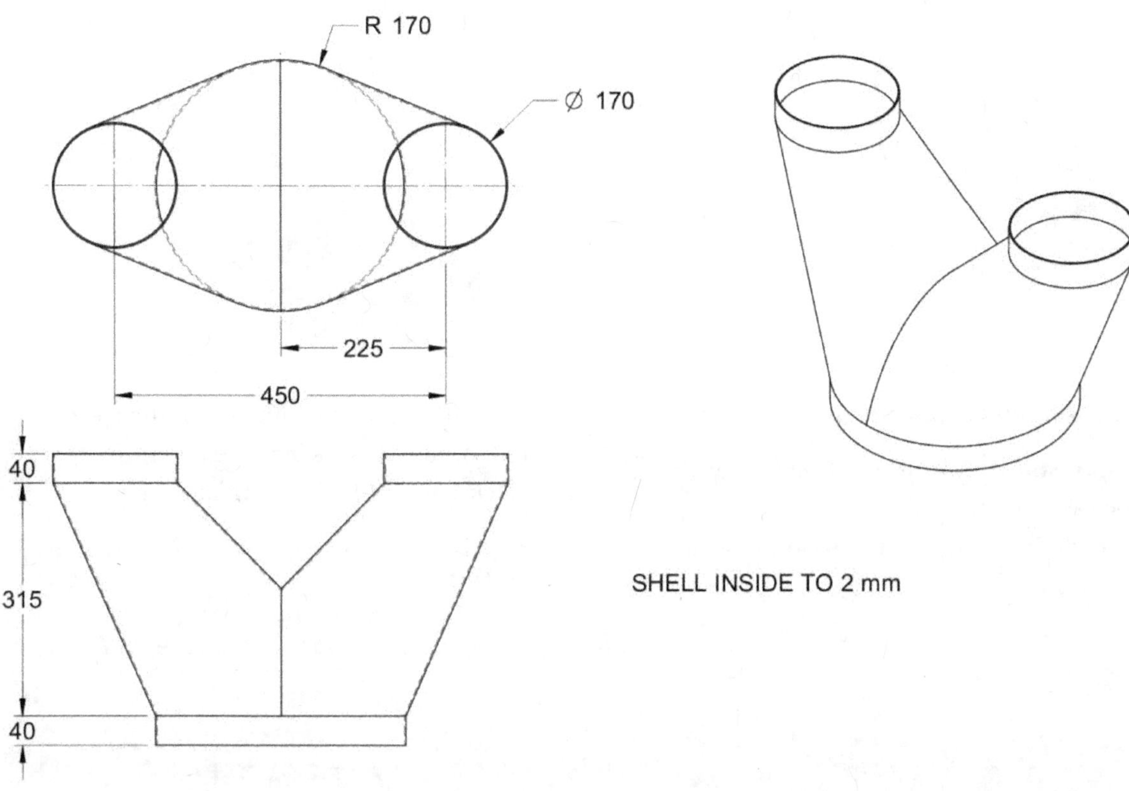

1. Start **CATIA V5-6R2017**.
2. Open a new part file.
3. Start a new sketch on the xy plane and draw a circle of 340 mm diameter.

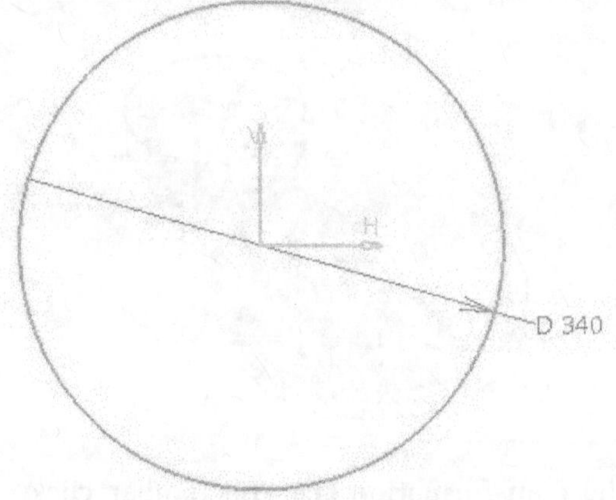

4. Exit the sketch.
5. Create the *Pad* feature with 40 mm thickness.

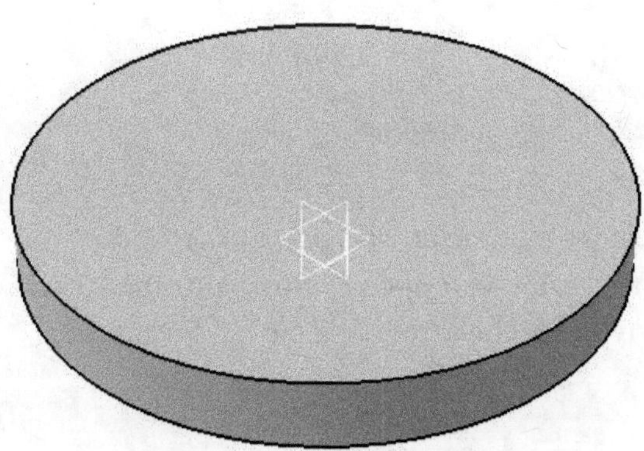

6. On the **Reference Elements** toolbar, click the **Plane** icon.
7. Click on the top face of the geometry and type-in 315 in the **Offset** box.
8. Click **OK** to create an offset plane.
9. Start a sketch on the offset plane.

10. Draw a circle of 170 mm diameter and add dimensions to it. Exit the sketch.

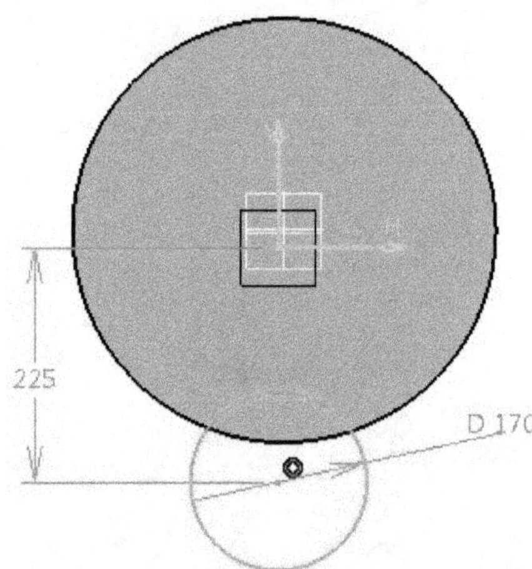

11. On the **Sketch-Based Features** toolbar, click the **Multi-sections Solid** icon. The first section will be selected, automatically.
12. Click on the circular edge of the base to define the second section.

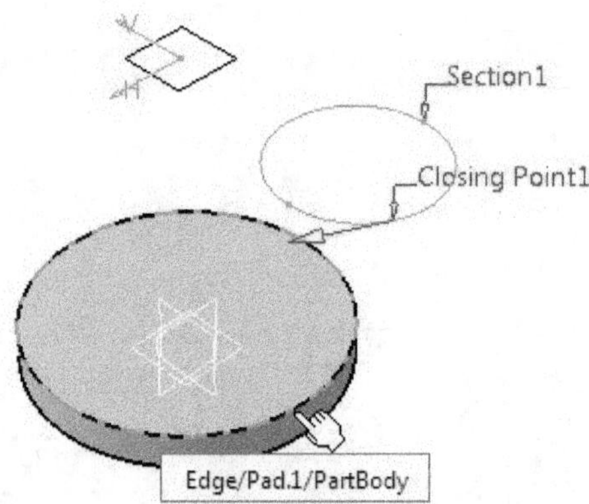

13. Ensure that the arrows point in same direction. If they point in opposite direction, then click on anyone of the arrow reverse its direction.

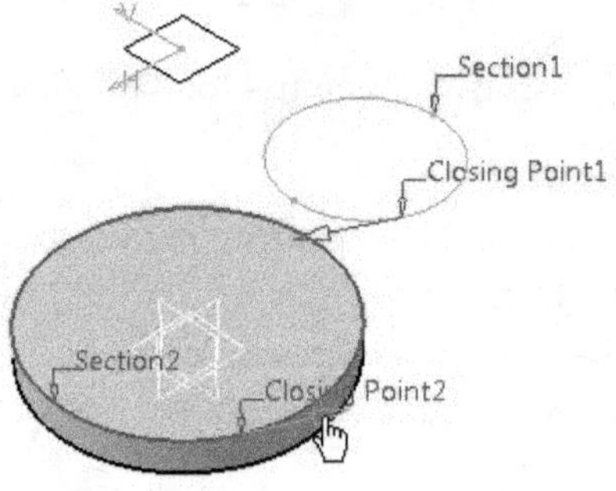

14. Click **OK** to create the *Multi-section solid* feature.

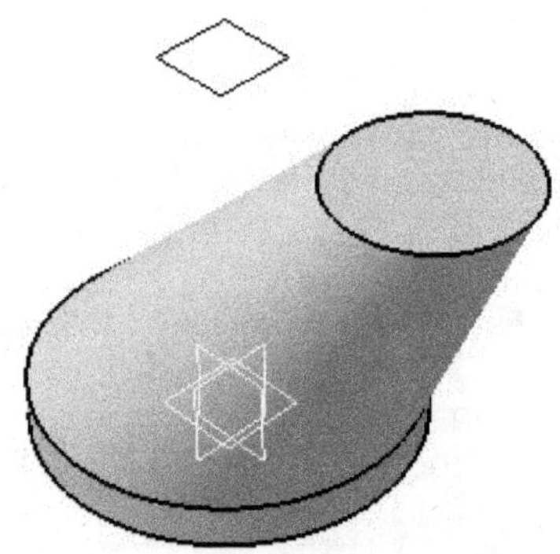

15. Activate the **Pad** command and click on the top face of the *Multi-section solid* feature.
16. Click **Yes** on the **Warning** message.

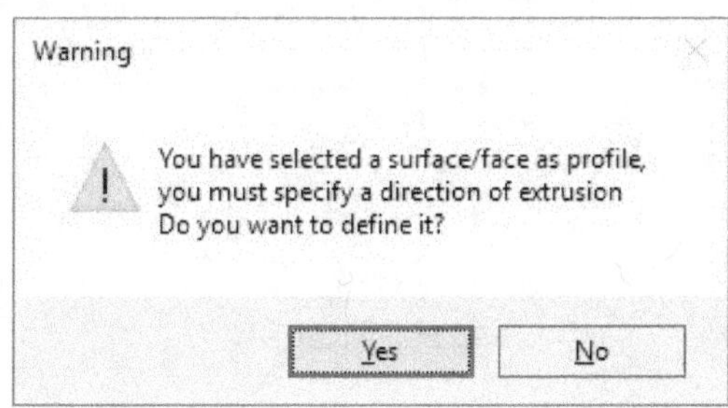

17. Select the xy plane on the Specification tree.
18. Type-in 40 in the **Length** box, and then click **OK** to create the *Pad* feature.

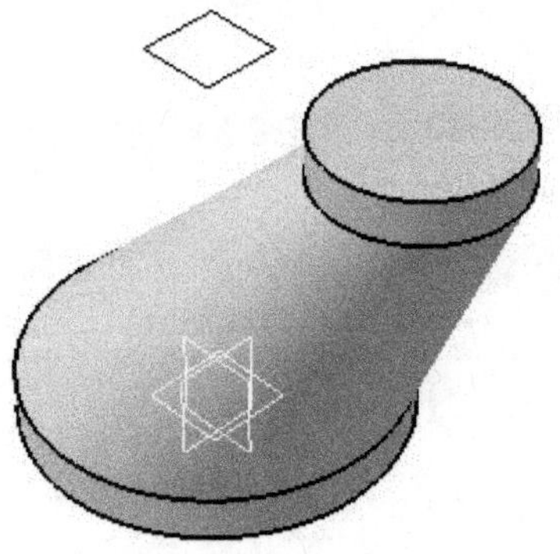

19. On the **Transformation Features** toolbar, click the **Mirror** icon, and then select the zx plane to define the mirroring element.

20. Click **OK** to mirror the entire solid body.

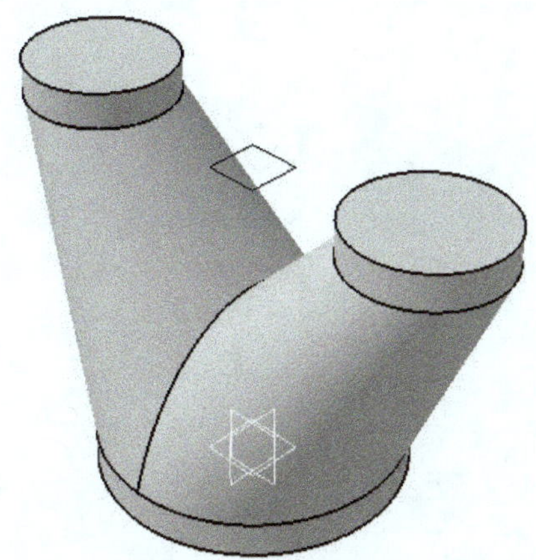

21. On the **Dress-up Features** toolbar, click the **Shell** icon.
22. Click on the flat faces of the model geometry.

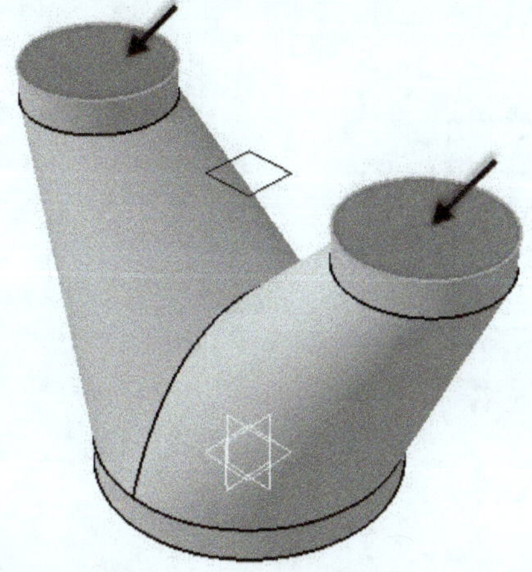

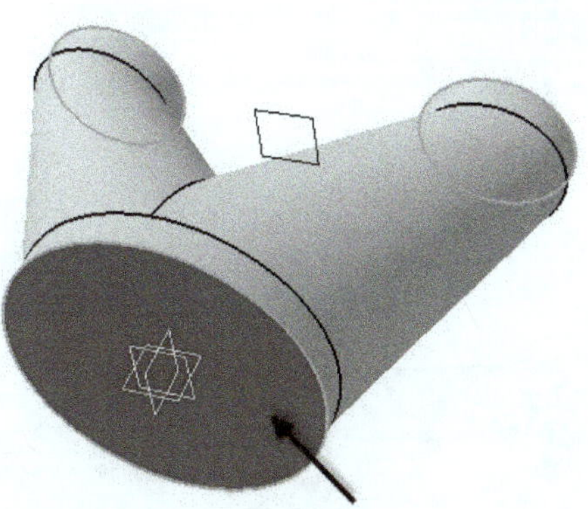

23. On the **Shell Definition** dialog, type-in 2 in the **Default inside thickness** box.
24. Click **OK**. The part geometry is shelled.

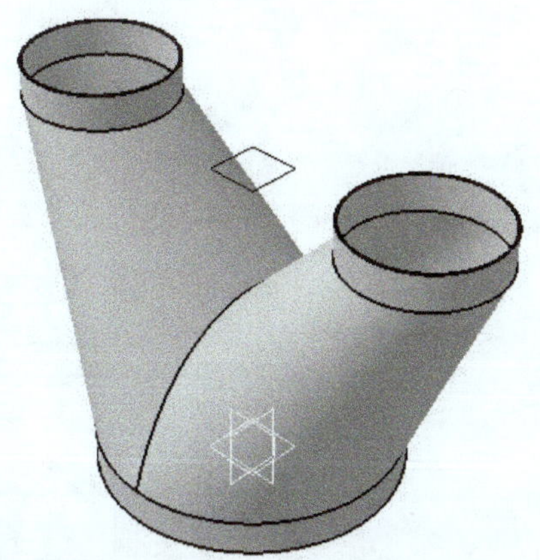

25. Save and close the part file.

Questions

1. Describe the procedure to create a *Multi-sections solid* feature.
2. List the **Continuity** options.
3. List the type of elements that can be selected to create a *Multi-sections solid* feature.

Exercises

Exercise 1

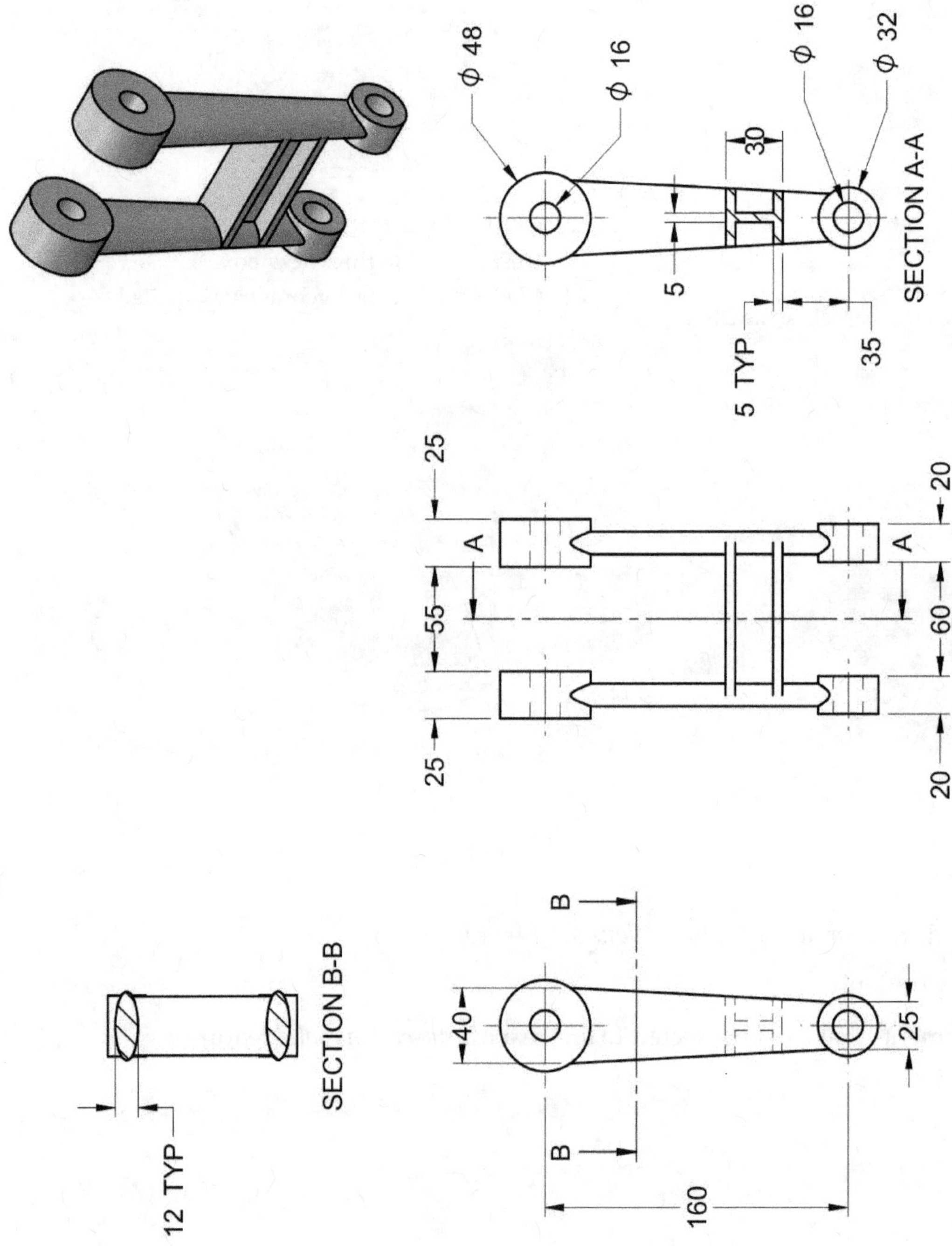

Chapter 8: Additional Features and Multibody Parts

CATIA V5 offers you some additional commands and features which will help you to create complex models. These commands are explained in this chapter.

The topics covered in this chapter are:

- *Stiffeners*
- *Solid Combine*
- *Multi-body parts*
- *Boolean Operations*

Stiffener

This command creates stiffening features to add structural stability, strength and support to your designs. Just like any other sketch-based feature, a stiffener requires a two dimensional sketch.

1. Create a sketch, as shown in figure.

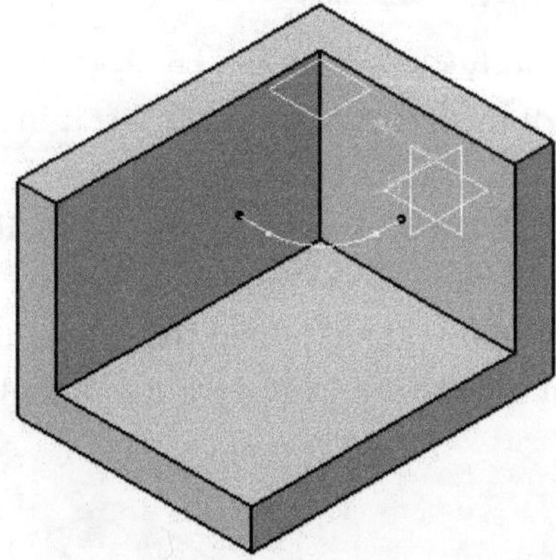

2. On the **Sketch-Based Features** toolbar, click **Advanced** drop-down > **Stiffener** (or) click **Insert > Sketch-Based Features > Stiffener** on the Menu bar.
3. Select the sketch; the preview of the geometry appears. You can add material to either side of the sketch line or evenly to both sides.
4. Check the **Neutral Fiber** option to add material to both sides of the sketch line.
5. Type-in the thickness value of the stiffener feature in the **Thickness1** box.
6. You can click the **Reverse direction** button to change the side of the material (optional).
7. You can define the direction of the rib feature by using the **From Side** or **From Top** option.

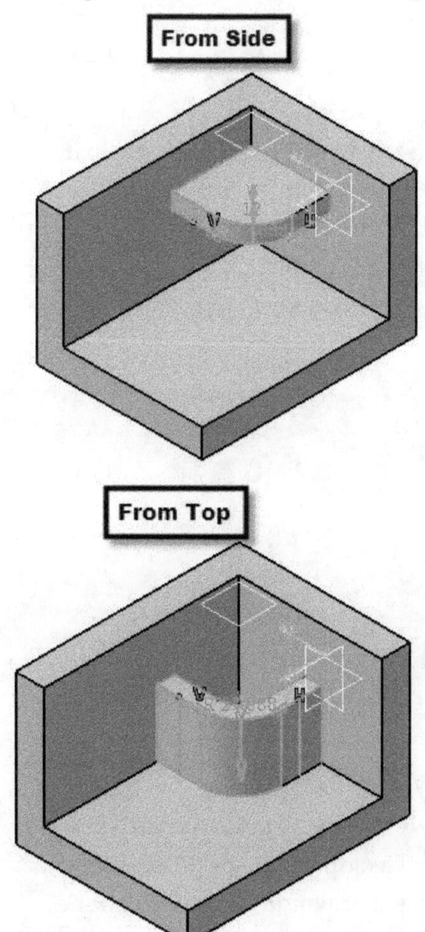

8. Click **OK** to complete the feature.

 Solid Combine

This command creates a solid body by using two sketches, which are perpendicular to each other.

1. Create two sketches, as shown in figure.

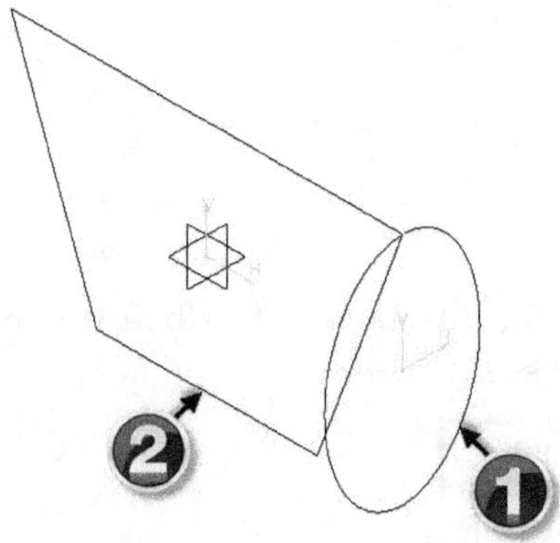

2. On the **Sketch-Based Features** toolbar, click **Advanced** drop-down > **Solid Combine** (or) click **Insert > Sketch-Based Features > Solid Combine** on the Menu bar.
3. Select the two sketches.
4. Click **OK**.

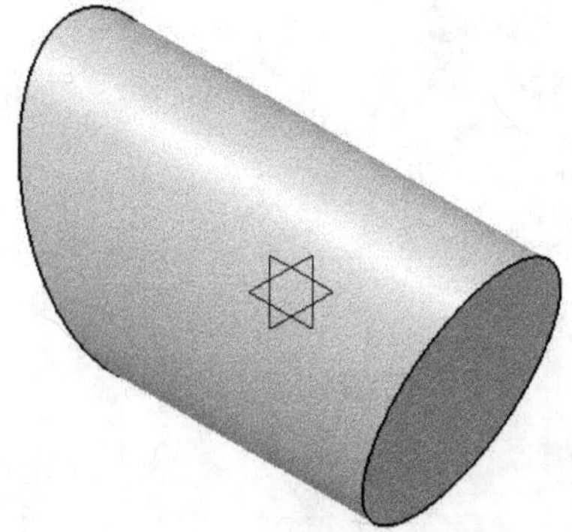

Multi-body Parts

CATIA V5 allows the use of multiple bodies when designing parts. This opens the door to several design techniques that would otherwise not be possible. In this section, you will learn some of these techniques.

Creating Multi-bodies

The number of bodies in a part can change throughout the design process. CATIA V5 makes it easy to create separate single bodies and multiple bodies, and combine multiple bodies into single bodies.

1. In order to create multiple bodies in a part, first create a solid body, and then click **Insert > Body** on the Menu bar. A new body is added to the Specification Tree and the previous body is hidden.

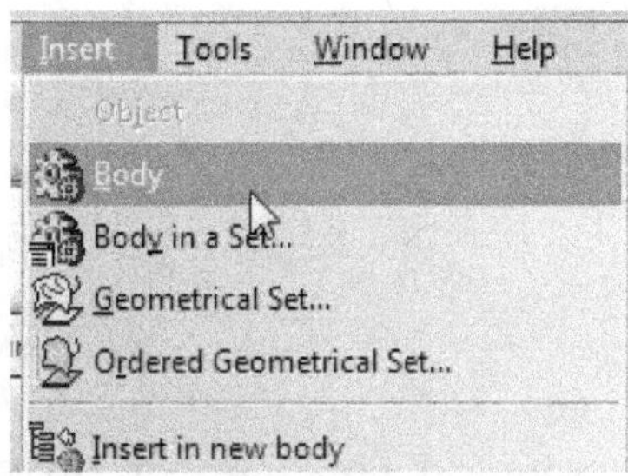

2. Now, create another solid body using anyone of the modeling tools.

Insert in new body

The **Insert in new body** command can be used to separate a feature of the body, and then insert it in a new body. This command can be used to perform local operations. For example, if you apply the shell feature to the front portion of the model shown in figure, the whole model will be shelled. To solve this problem, you must split the solid body into multiple bodies.

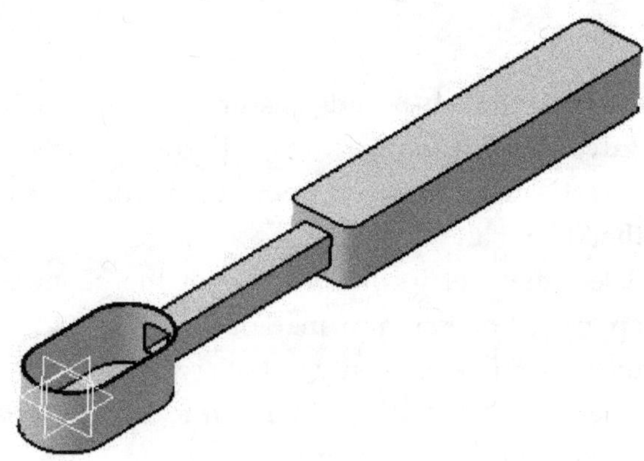

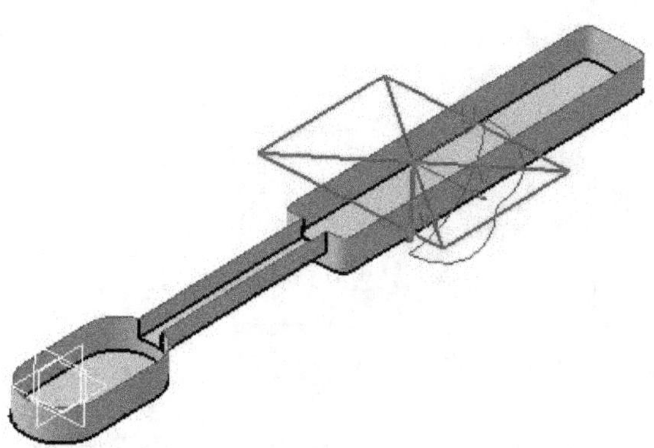

1. To perform shell operation to the front portion, you must create it as a separate feature.
2. Expand the Specification Tree and select the feature of the front portion.

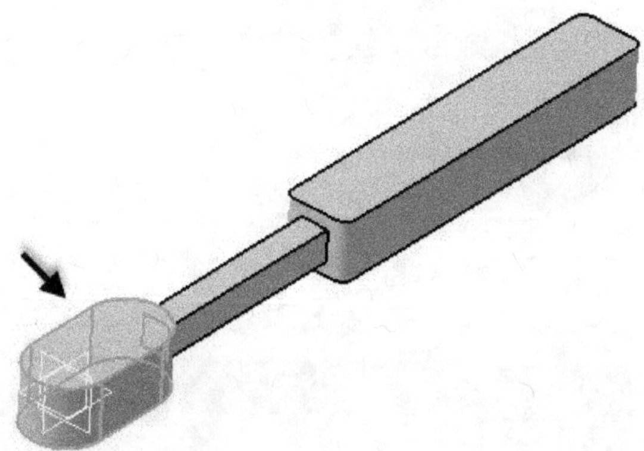

3. On the Menu bar, click **Insert > Insert in new body**.

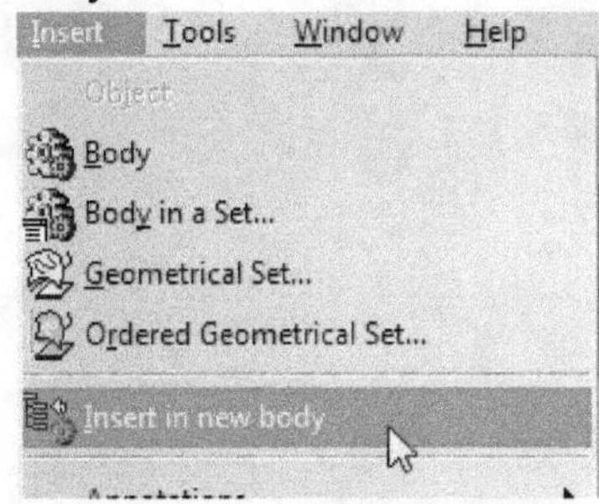

You will notice that a new body is created and the selected feature is inserted into that body. In addition, the Assemble operation is performed between the new body and main body.

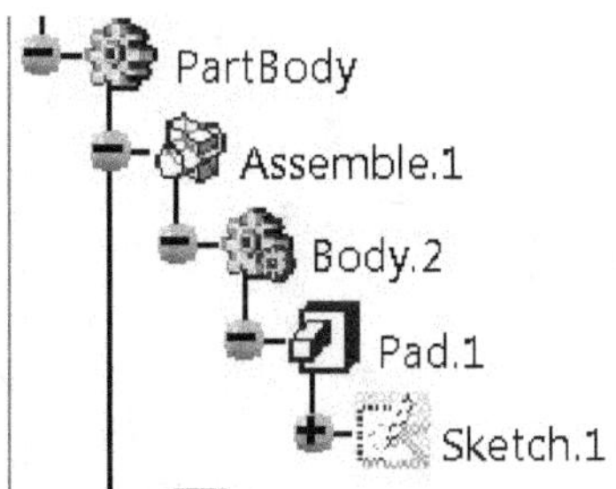

4. Now, click the right mouse button on the new body and select **Define In Work Object**. This activates the new body.

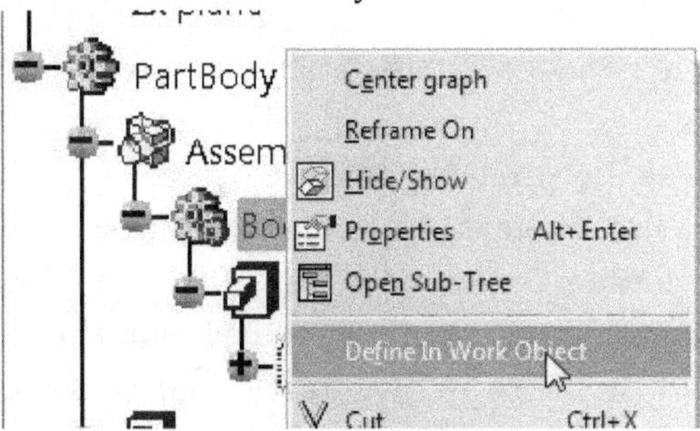

5. Now, activate the **Shell** command and perform the shell operation.

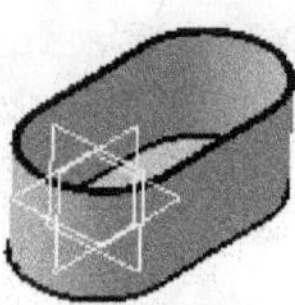

6. Click the right mouse button on the main body and select **Define In Work Object**.

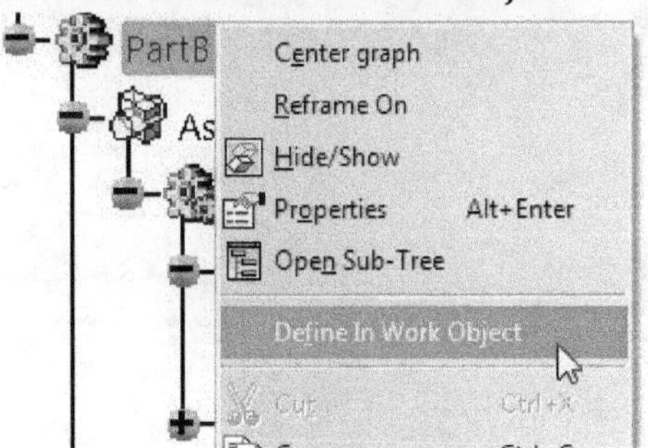

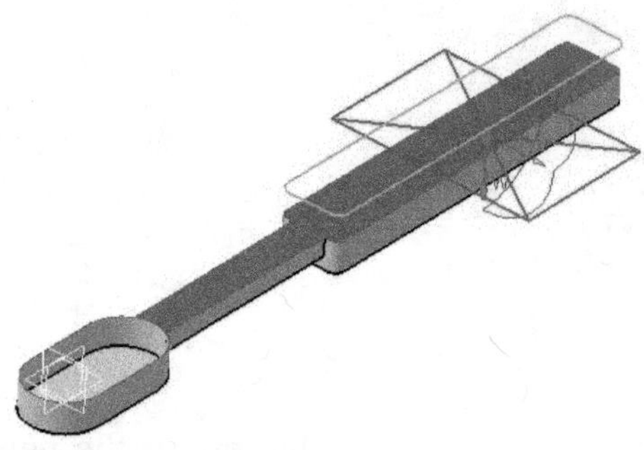

Assemble

This command assembles two bodies into a single one.

1. Create two or more bodies.
2. On the **Boolean Operations** toolbar, click the **Assemble** button (or) click **Insert > Boolean Operations > Assemble** on the Menu bar.
3. Click on the body to assemble, and then click on main body.
4. Click **OK**.

The geometry of the resultant body will depend upon the type of bodies used. For example, if you assemble, a body created using a *Pad* feature; resultant body will be the addition of two bodies.

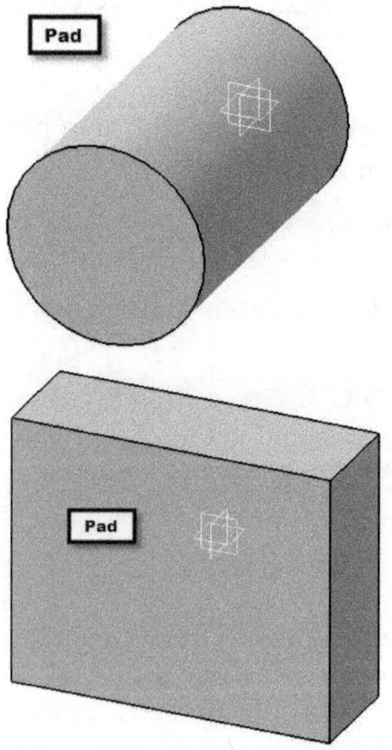

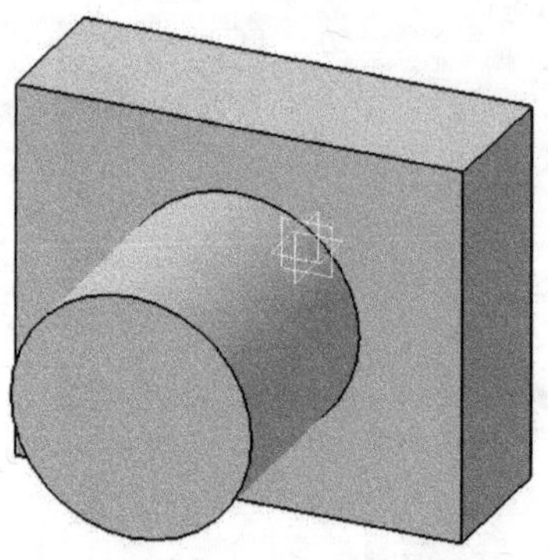

If you assemble a body created using a *Pocket* Feature, then it will result in a pocket in the resultant body.

Add

This command combines two separate bodies.

1. On the **Boolean Operations** toolbar, click **Boolean Operations** drop-down > **Add** (or) click **Insert > Boolean Operations > Add** on the Menu bar.
2. Select the two bodies and click **OK**.

Remove

This command performs the function of subtracting one solid body from another.

1. On the **Boolean Operations** toolbar, click **Boolean Operations** drop-down > **Remove** (or) click **Insert > Boolean Operations > Remove** on the Menu bar.
2. Select tool body and the target body.
   Tool

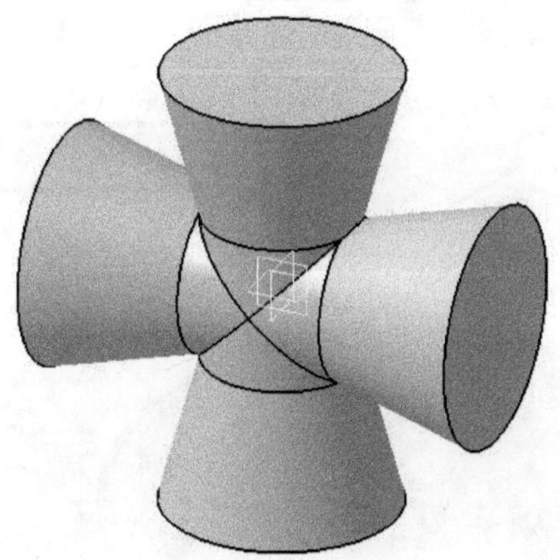

Target

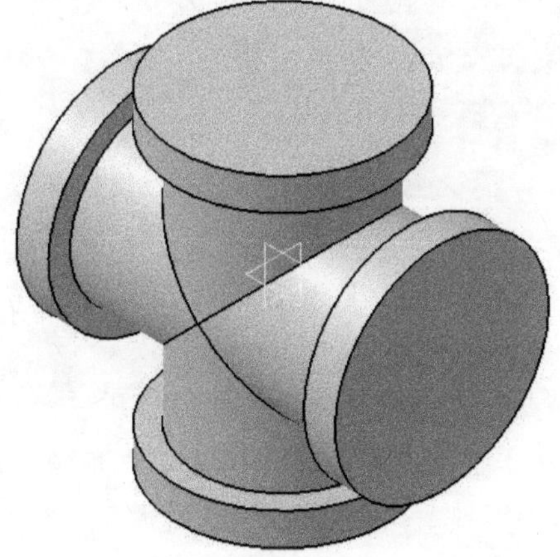

3. Click **OK** to subtract the tool body from the target.

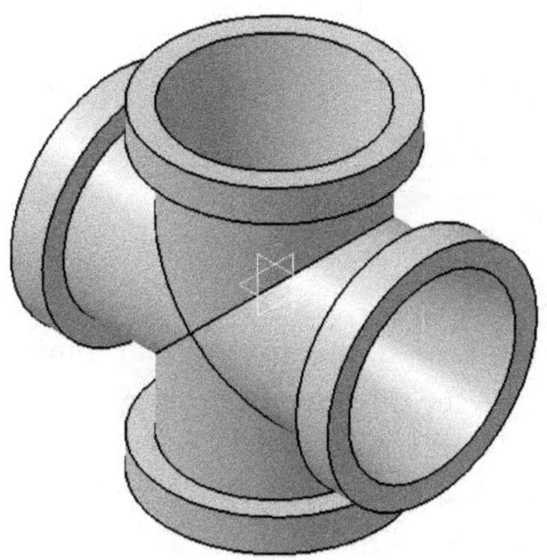

Intersect

By using the **Intersect** command, you can generate bodies defined by the intersecting volume of two bodies.

1. On the **Boolean Operations** toolbar, click **Boolean Operations** drop-down > **Intersect** (or) click **Insert > Boolean Operations > Intersect** on the Menu bar.
2. Select two bodies.

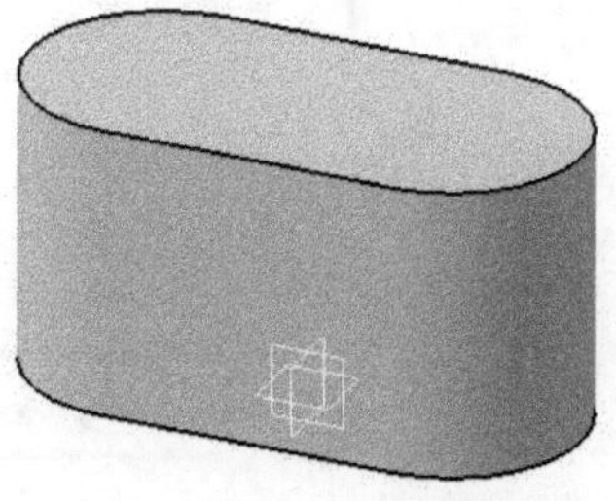

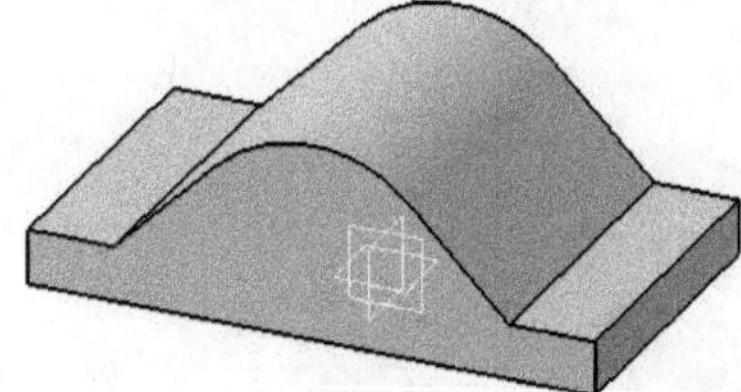

3. Click **OK** to see the resultant single solid body

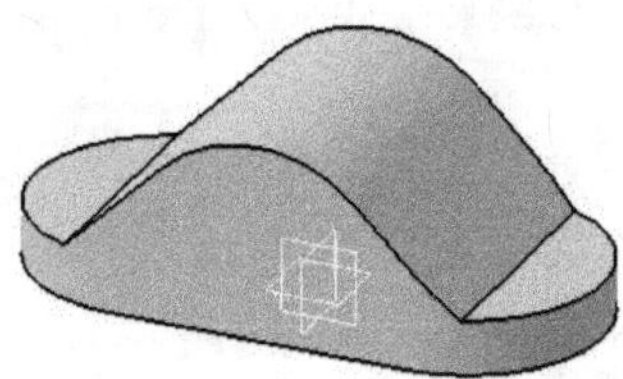

Union Trim

By using the **Union Trim** command, you can combine two bodies and trim the unwanted portion.

1. Create two bodies.
2. Ensure that the **Partbody** is not active.
3. On the **Boolean Operations** toolbar, click the **Union Trim** button (or) click **Insert > Boolean Operations > Union Trim** on the Menu bar.
4. Click on the second body. The **Trim Definition** dialog appears.
5. On the **Trim Definition** dialog, click the **Faces to remove** box and select the faces to remove.
6. Click the **Faces to Keep** box and select faces to keep.

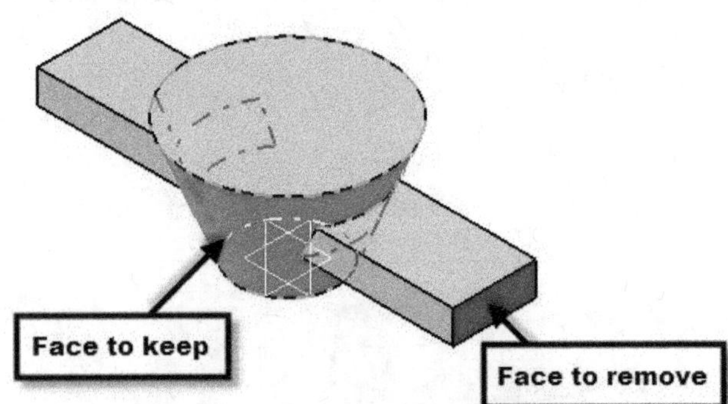

7. Click **OK**.

Remove Lump

This command trims a lump of body from the main part body.

1. Create two bodies and combine them.
2. On the **Boolean Operations** toolbar, click the **Remove Lump** button (or) click **Insert > Boolean Operations > Remove Lump** on the Menu bar.
3. Click on the part body.
4. On the **Remove Lump** dialog, click the **Faces to remove** box.
5. Select the face of the body to be trimmed.

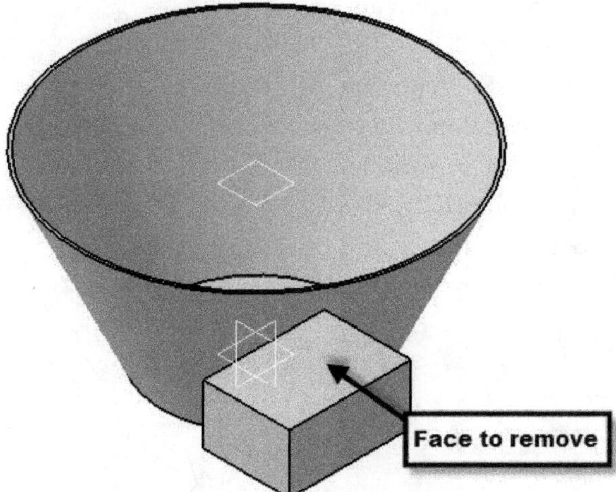

6. Click **OK**.

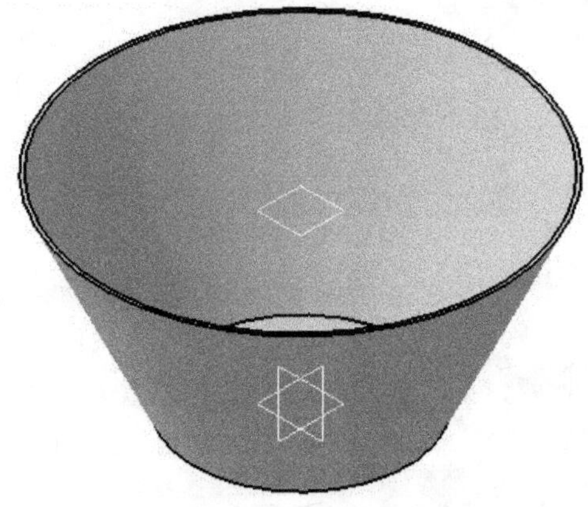

Examples

Example 1 (Millimetres)

In this example, you will create the part shown next.

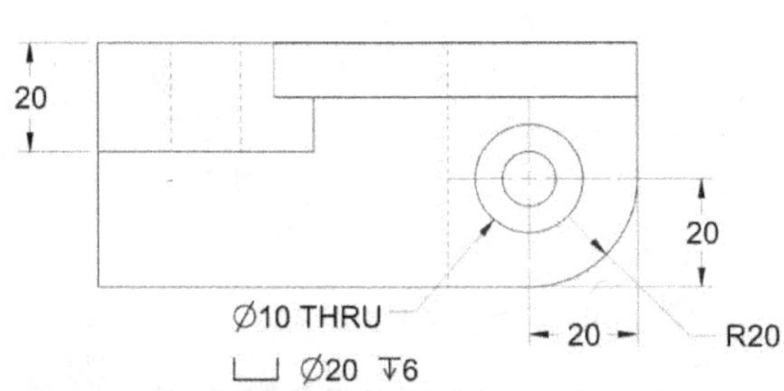

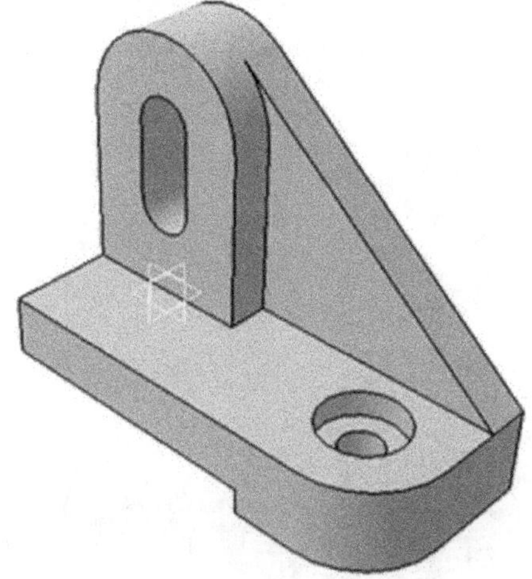

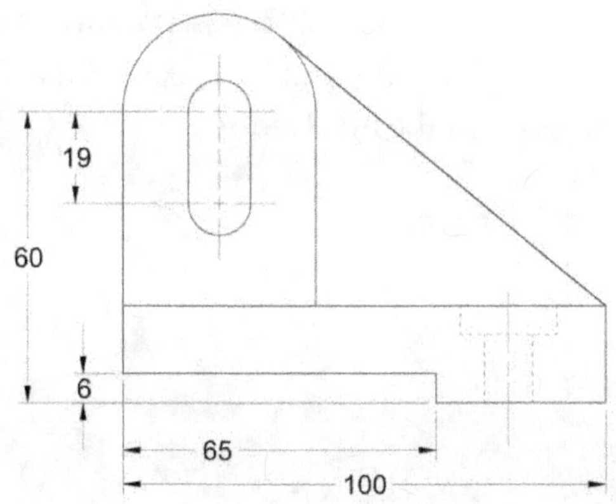

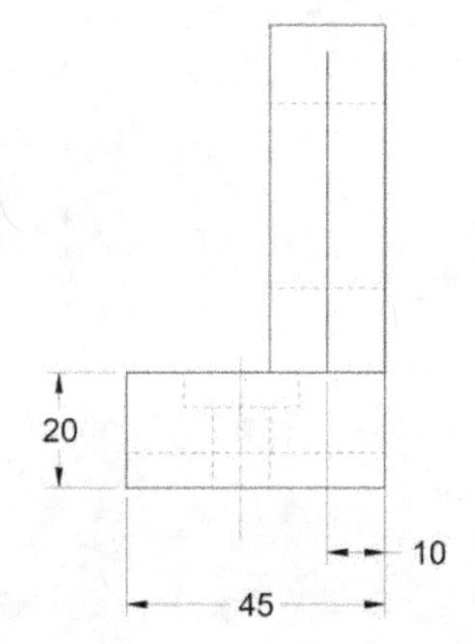

1. Start **CATIA V5-6R2017**.
2. Open a new part file.
3. Create the rectangular base on the XY plane. The extrusion depth is 20 mm.

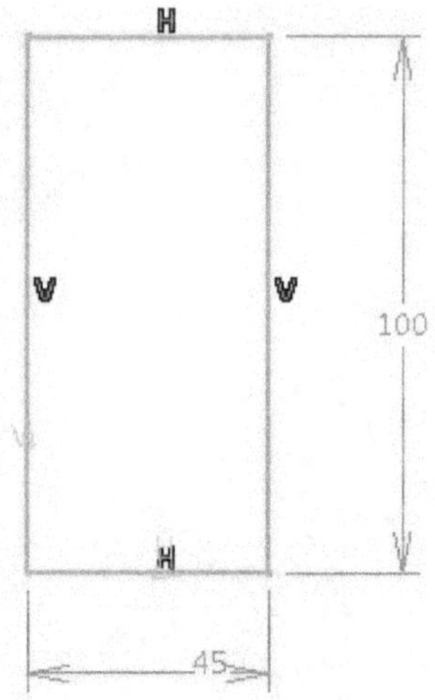

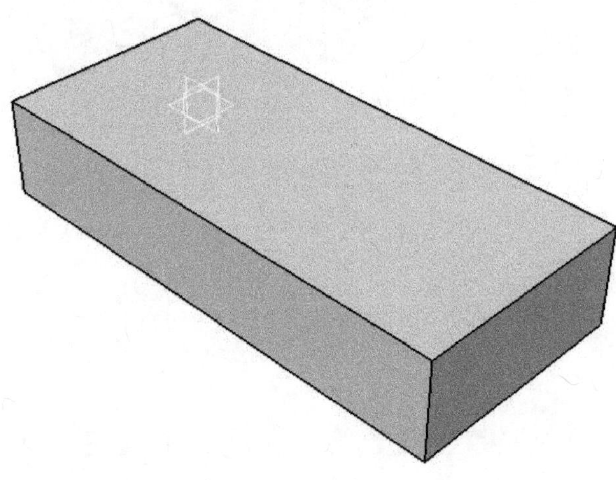

4. Construct the second feature on the YZ plane. The extrusion depth is 20 mm.

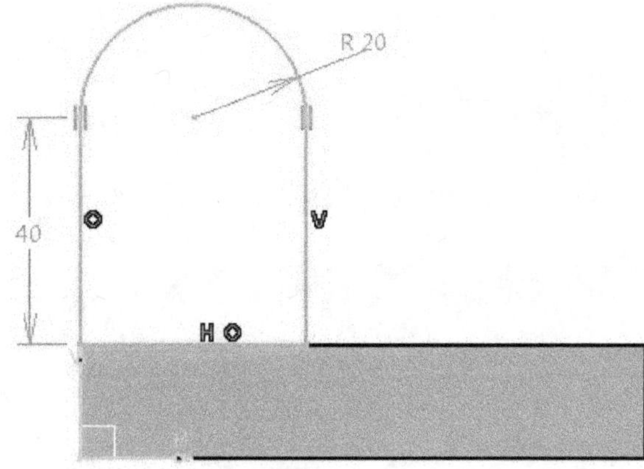

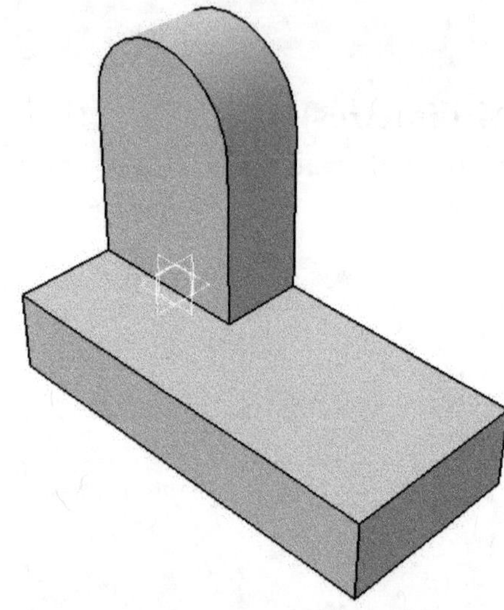

5. On the **Sketch-Based Features** toolbar, click **Advanced drop-down > Stiffener** (or) click **Insert > Sketch-Based Features > Stiffener** on the Menu.
6. On the **Stiffener Definition** dialog, click on the **Sketch** icon and select the yz plane.
7. Draw a line, which is tangent to the curved face of the second feature and connected to the top right vertex of the first feature.

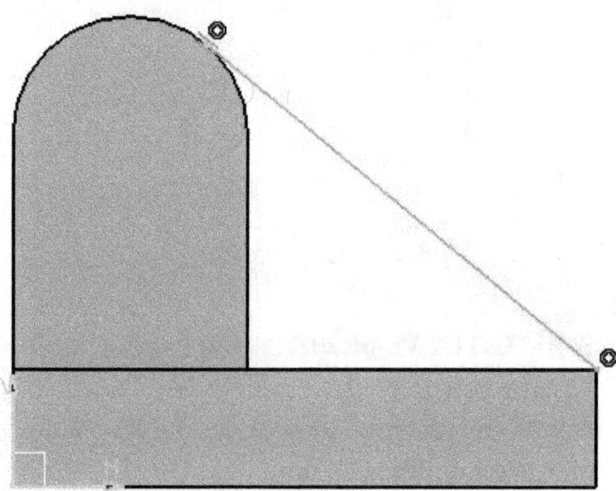

8. Click **Exit workbench**.
9. On the **Stiffener Definition** dialog, under the **Thickness** section, uncheck the **Neutral Fiber** option and click the **Reverse direction** button.
10. Type-in 10 in the **Thickness** box and click **OK** to create the stiffener.

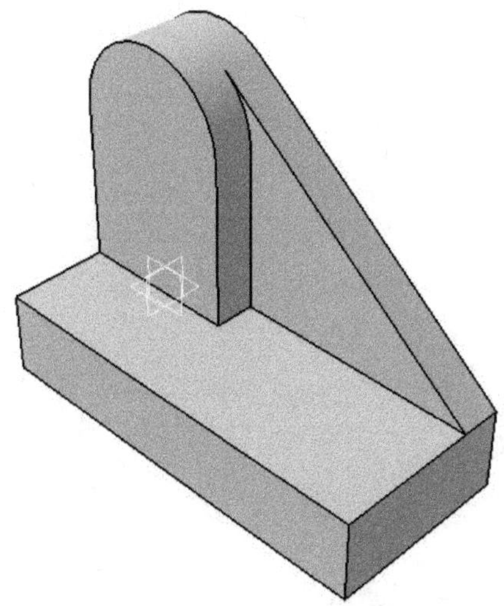

11. Activate the **Pocket** command and click the **Sketch** icon on the dialog.
12. Click on the front face of the second feature, and then draw the sketch for the slot feature.

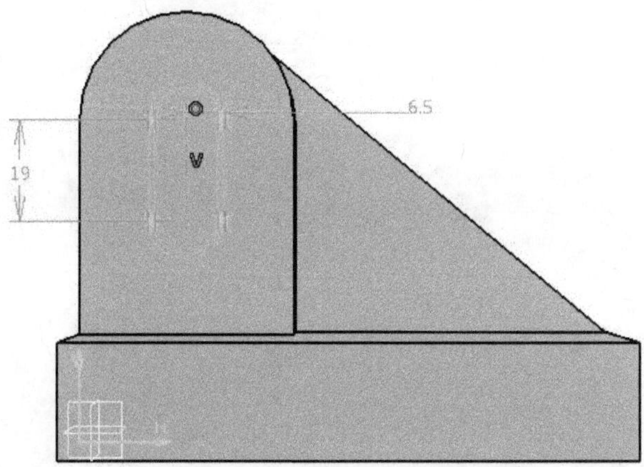

13. Exit the sketch and create the *Pocket* feature.

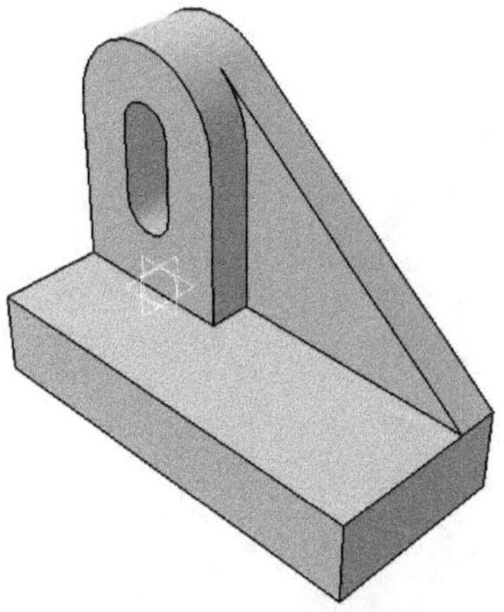

14. Create another *Pocket* feature on the front face of the base.

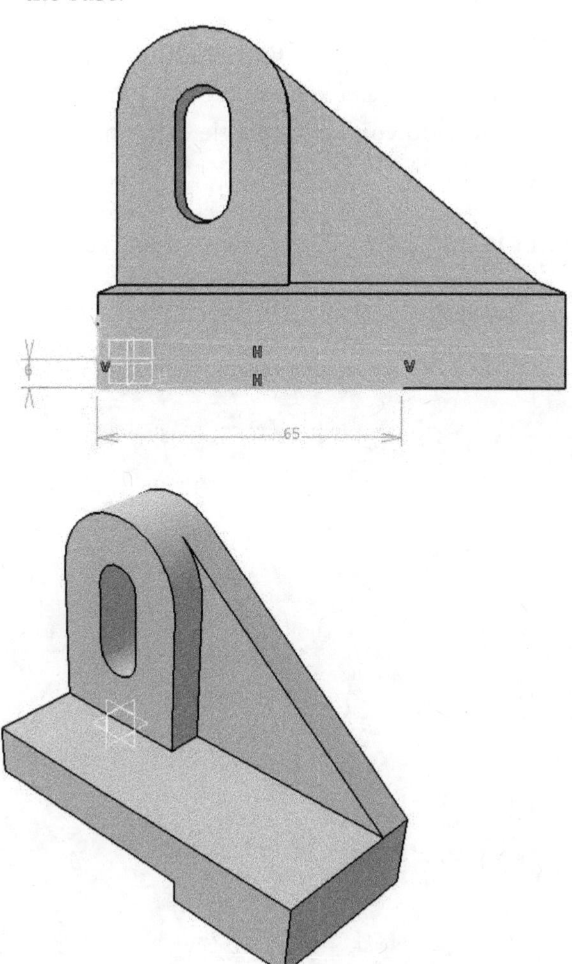

15. Add an edge fillet and counterbored hole to the model geometry.

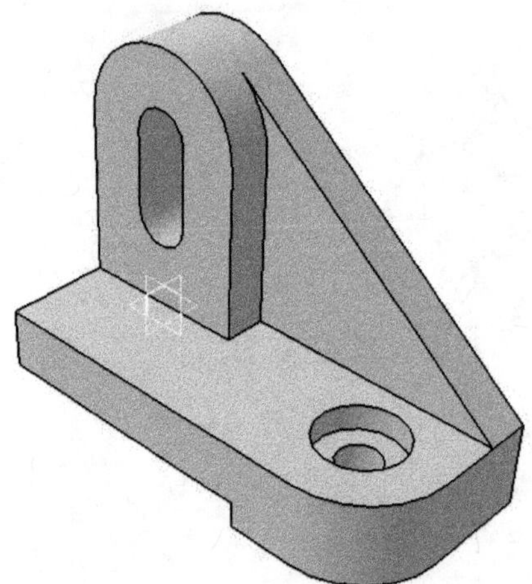

16. Save and close the file.

Questions

1. What is the use of the **Stiffener** command?
2. Why do we create multi body parts?
3. How do you split a single body into multiple bodies?

Exercises

Exercise 1

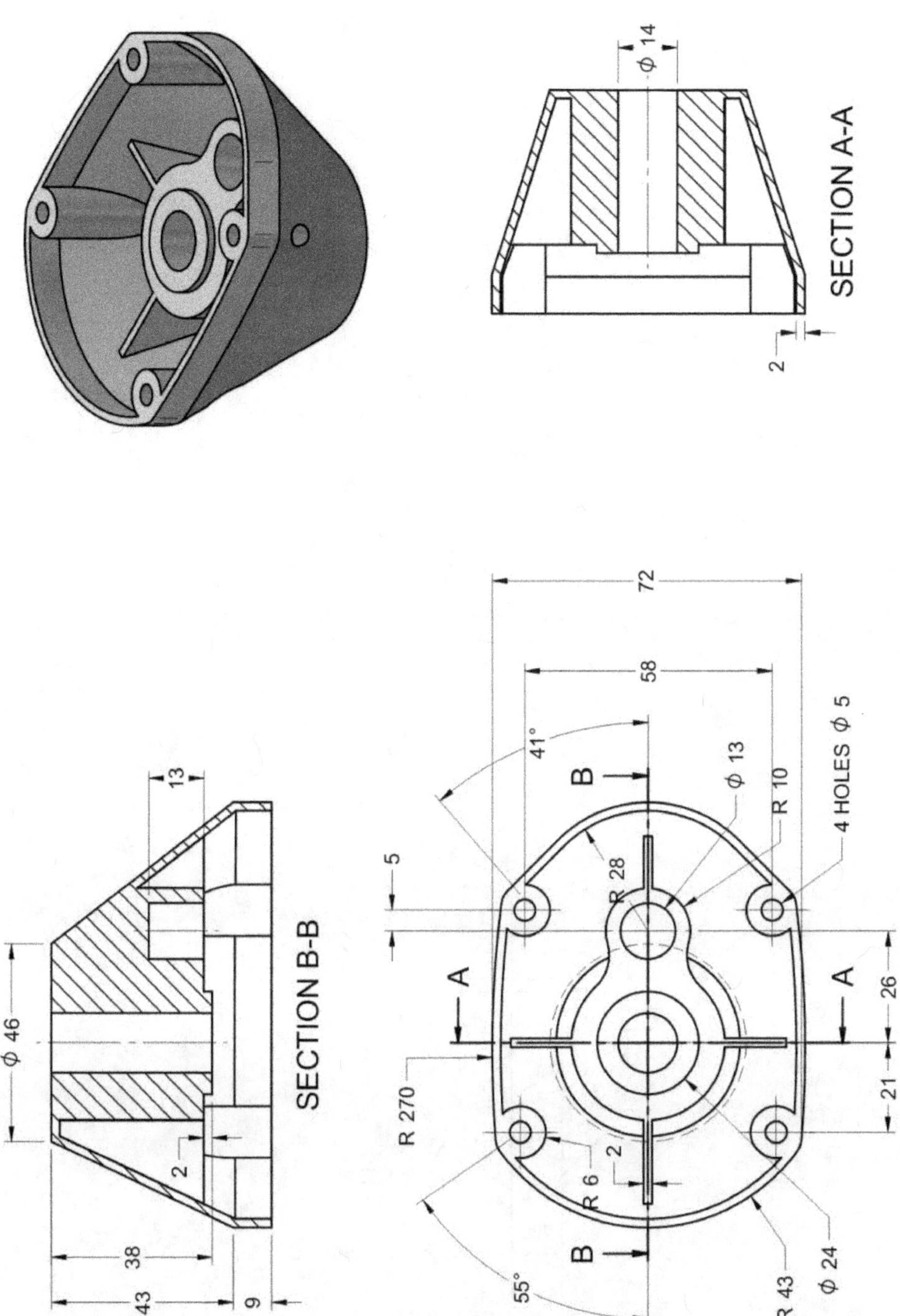
ϕ 14
SECTION A-A
2
72
58
41°
B
ϕ 13
R 10
4 HOLES ϕ 5
R 28
5
A
A
26
21
R 270
2
R 6
B
55°
R 43
ϕ 24
ϕ 46
13
2
SECTION B-B
38
43
9

Exercise 2

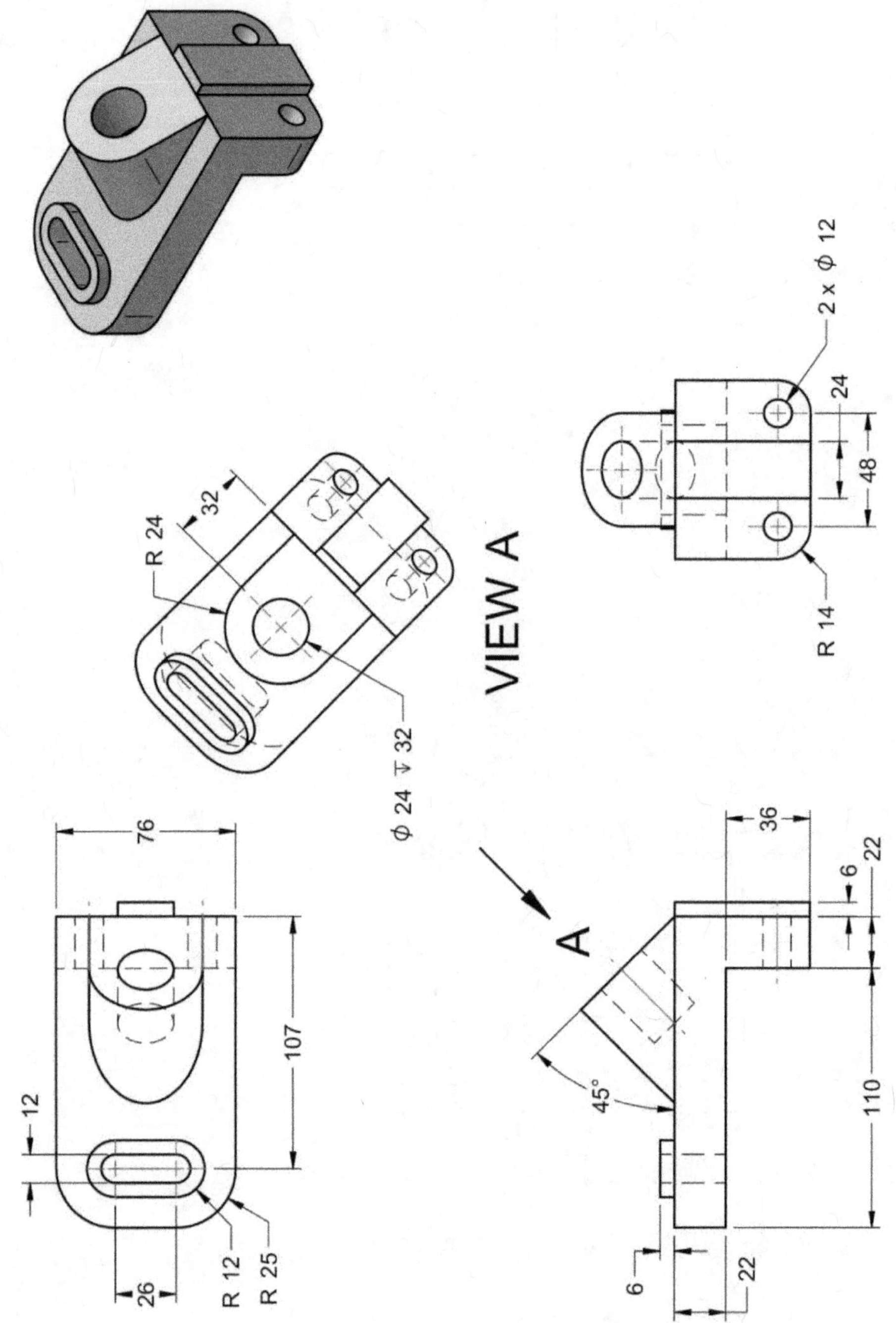

Exercise 3 (Inches)

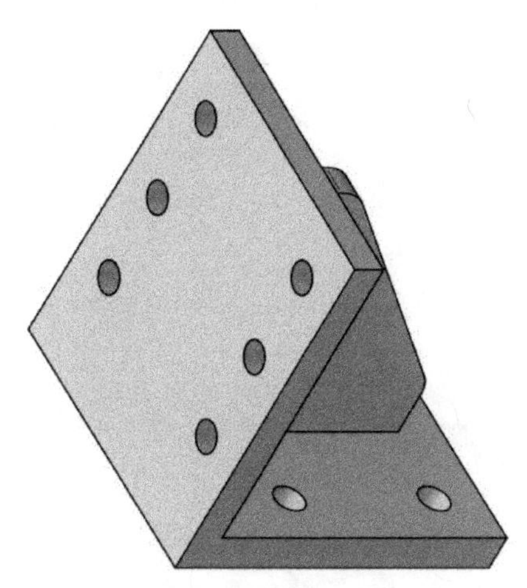

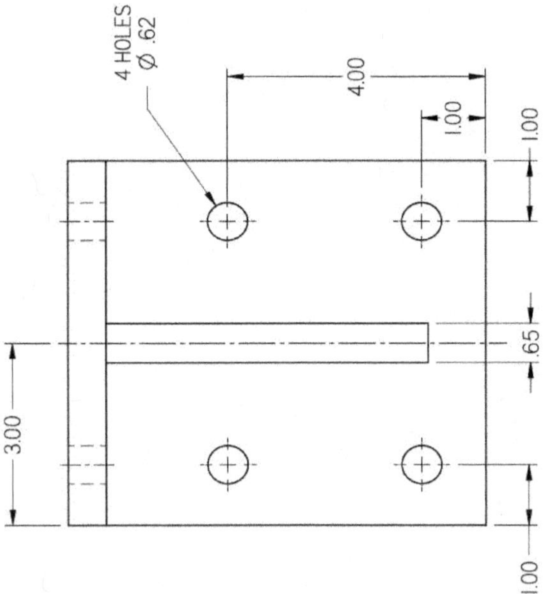
4 HOLES
Ø .62
4.00
1.00
1.00
.65
3.00
1.00

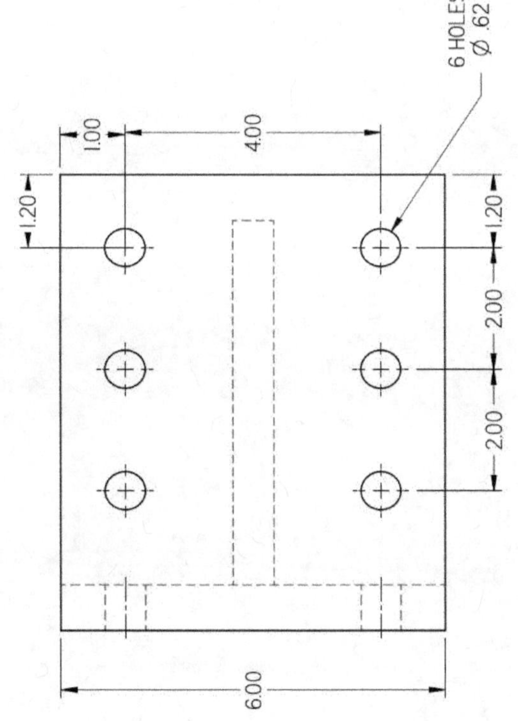
6 HOLES
Ø .62
1.00
4.00
1.20
1.20
2.00
2.00
6.00

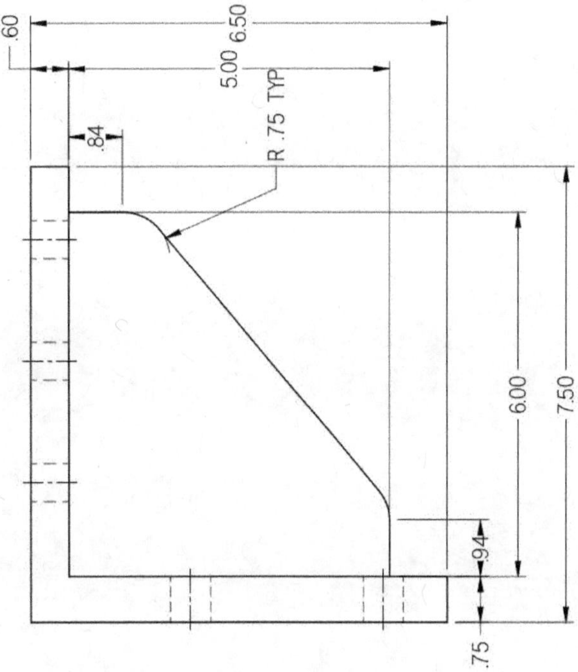
.60
6.50
5.00
R .75 TYP
.84
6.00
7.50
.94
.75

Chapter 9: Modifying Parts

In design process, it is not required to achieve the final model in the first attempt. There is always a need to modify the existing parts to get the desired part geometry. In this chapter, you will learn various commands and techniques to make changes to a part.

The topics covered in this chapter are:

- *Edit Sketches*
- *Edit Feature Parameters*
- *Edit Feature definition*
- *Deactivate and activate features*
- *Change sketch support*

Edit Sketches

Sketches form the base of a 3D geometry. They control the size and shape of the geometry. If you want to modify the 3D geometry, most of the times, you are required to edit sketches.

1. To do this, click the right-mouse button on the feature to edit and select **Featurename.object > Edit Sketch**.

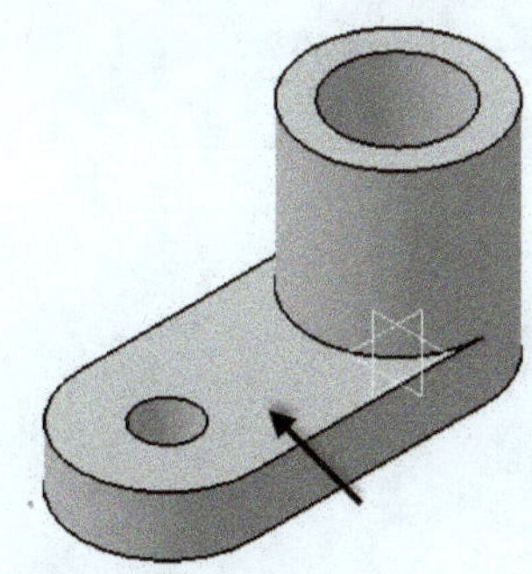

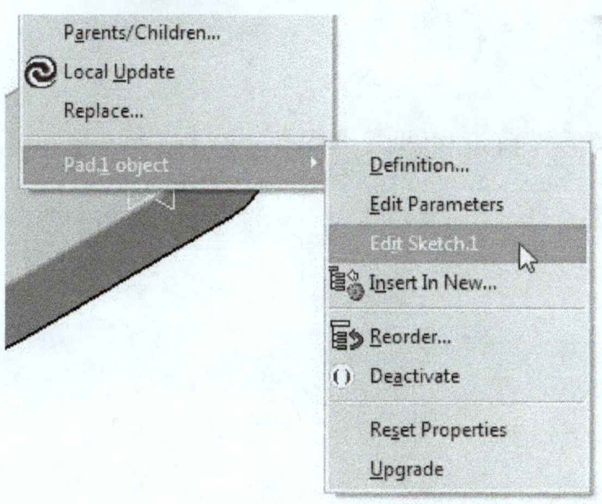

2. Now, modify the sketch and click **Exit workbench**. You will notice that the part geometry updates immediately.

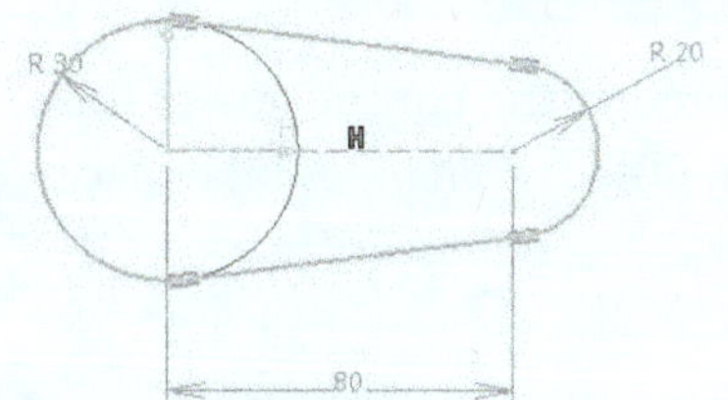

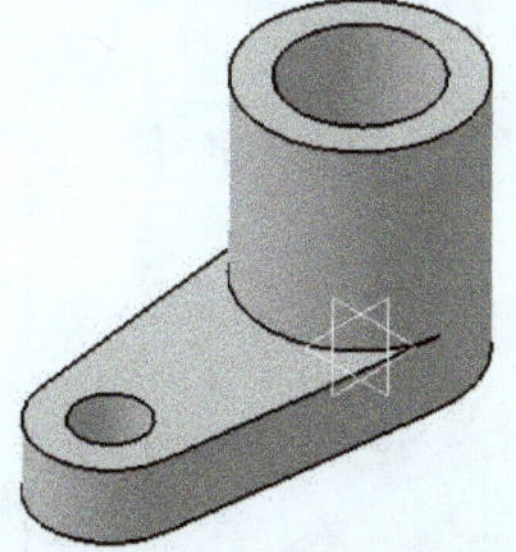

Edit Feature Definition

Features are the building blocks of model geometry.

1. To modify a feature, click the right mouse button on it and select **Featurename.object > Definition**. The dialog related to the feature appears.

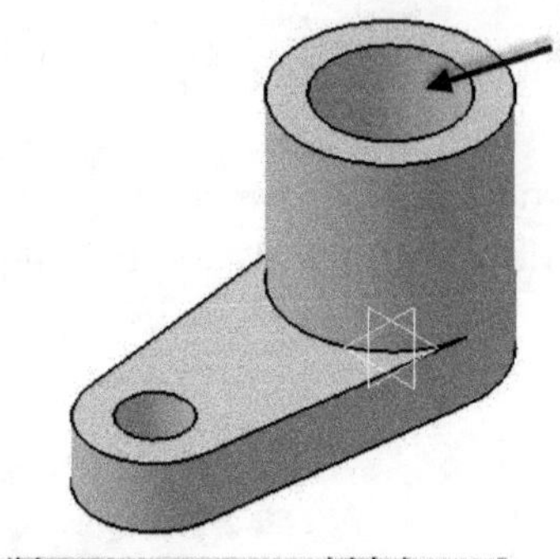

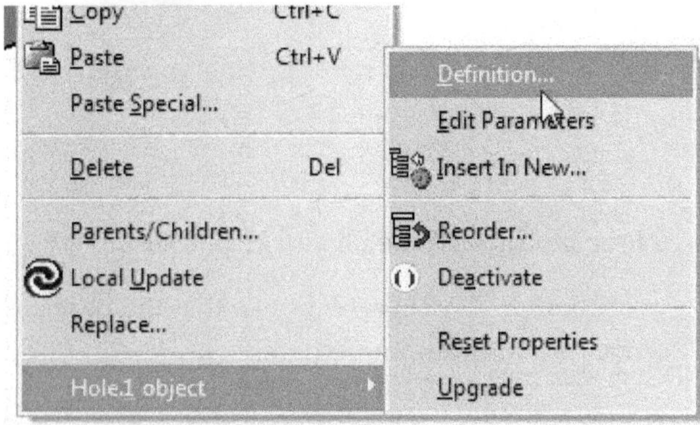

2. On this dialog, modify the parameters of the feature and click **OK**. The changes take place instantaneously.

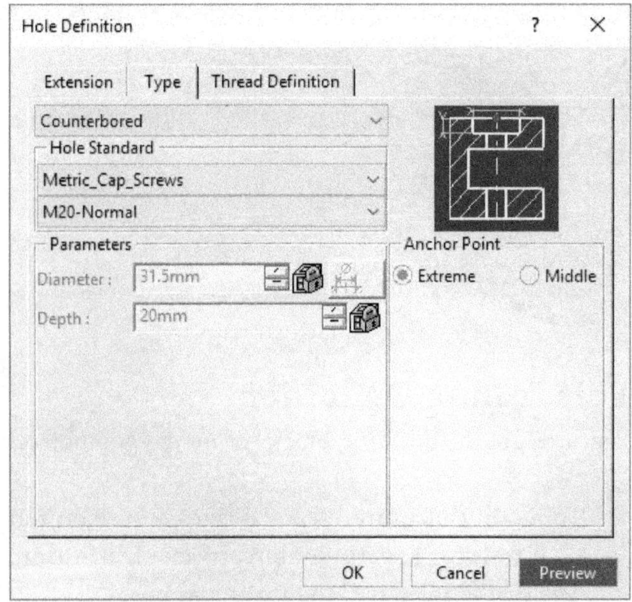

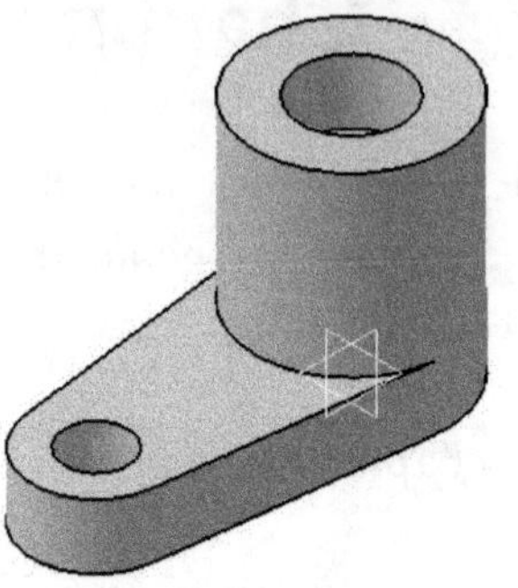

Edit Feature Parameters

CATIA V5 allows you to modify a feature by editing its parametric dimensions.

1. Click the right mouse button on it and select **Featurename.object > Edit Parameters**. The parameters of the feature appear.

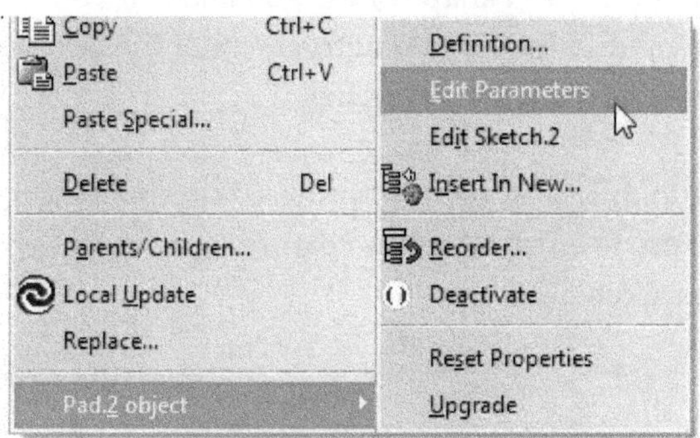

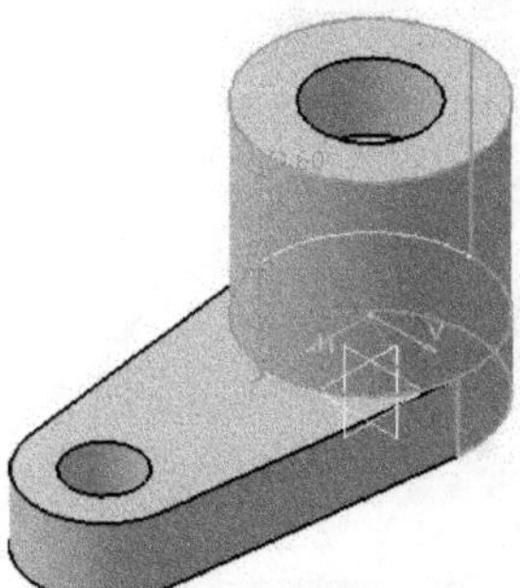

2. To edit a parameter, double-click on it and type-in a new value in the **Parameter Definition** box. Click **OK**.

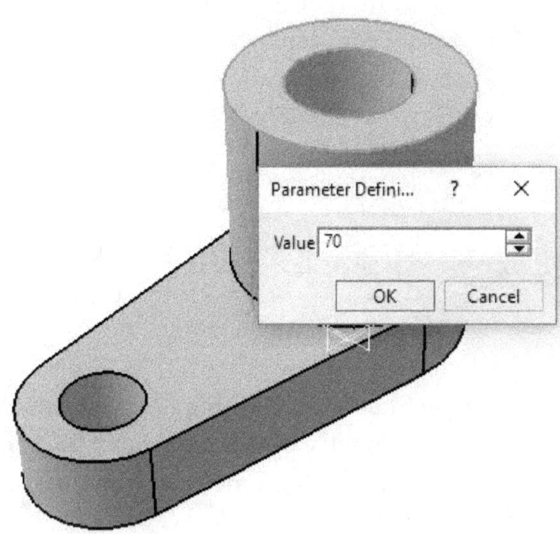

3. On the **Tools** toolbar, click the **Update All** button to update the feature.

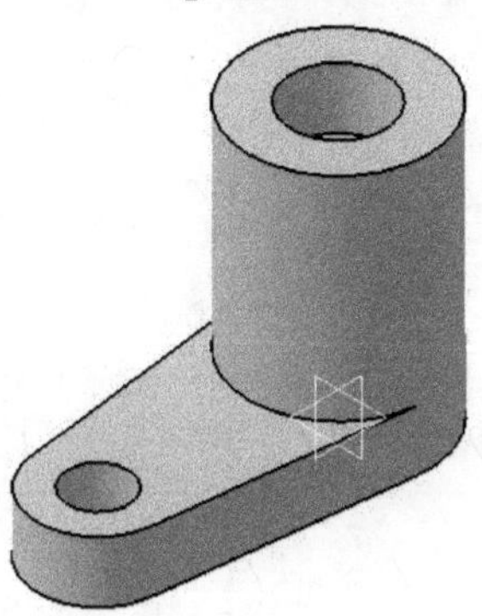

Deactivate Features

Sometimes you may need to deactivate some features of model geometry.

1. To do this, click the right mouse button on a feature and select **Deactivate**.

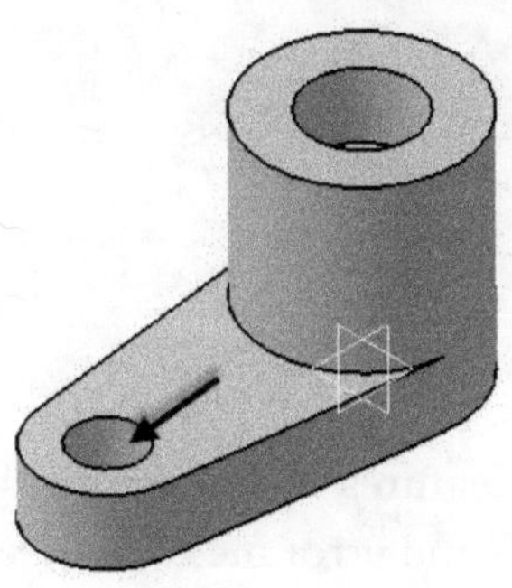

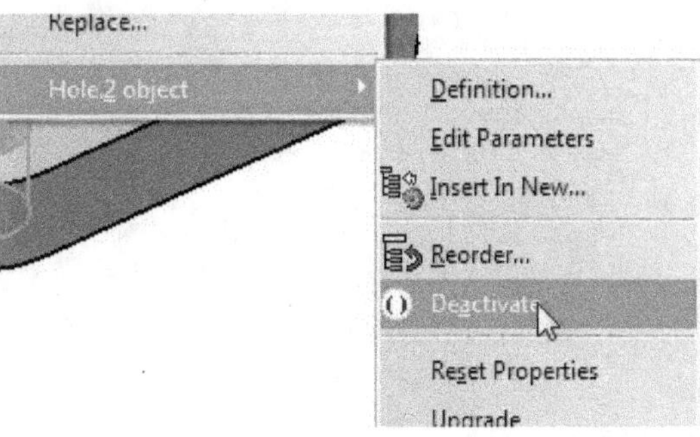

On the **Deactivate** dialog, check the **Deactivate aggregated elements** option if you want to deactivate all the sketches and references elements related to the feature. Otherwise, uncheck this option.

2. Click **OK** to deactivate the feature.

Activate Features

1. If you want to activate the deactivated features, then expand the Specification Tree.
2. Click the right mouse button on the deactivated feature and select **Featurename.object > Activate.**

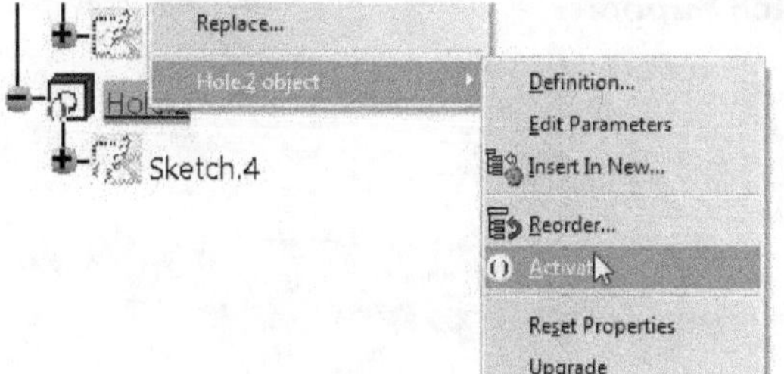

3. Click **OK**. The feature will become active again.

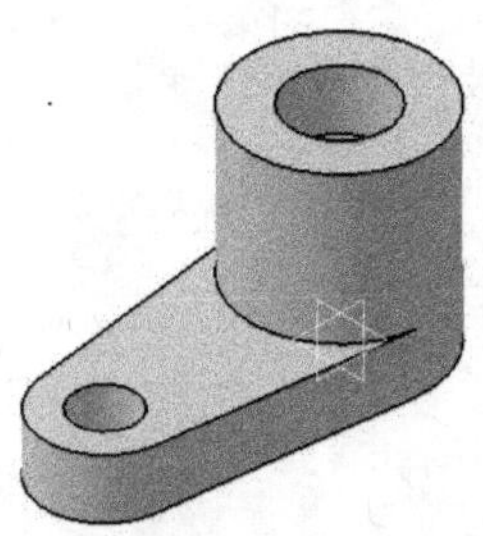

Changing the Sketch Support

CATIA V5 allows you to change the sketch support of a feature.

1. Expand the **Specification Tree** and go to the feature to modify.

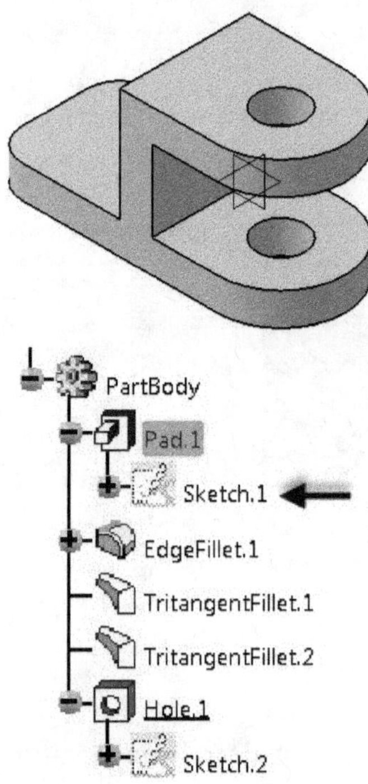

2. Click the right mouse button on the sketch of the feature and select **Sketchname.object > Change Sketch Support**.

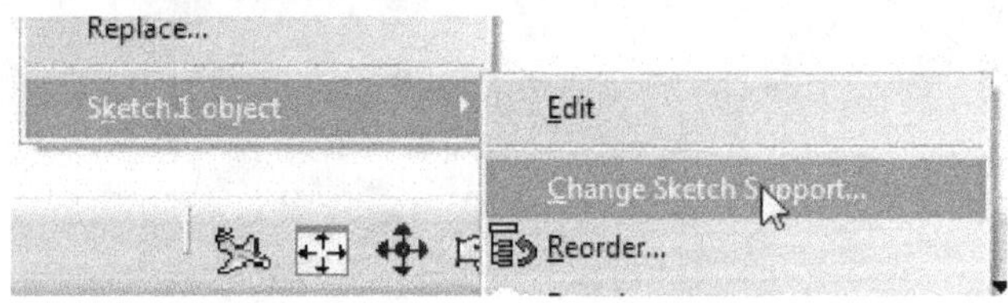

3. Select a different plane to define the new sketch support. You can select it from the graphics window or Specification Tree.

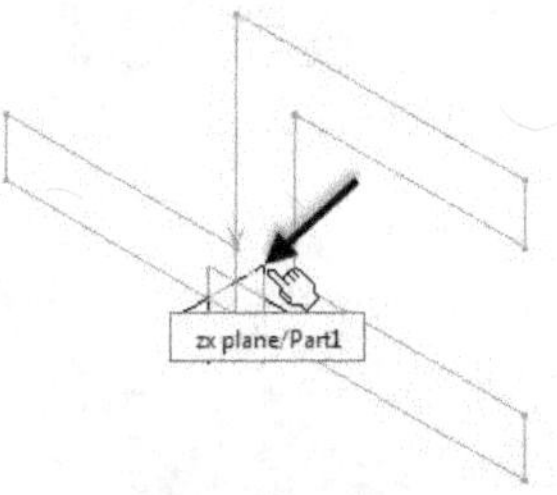

4. On the **Sketch Positioning** dialog, check the **Move Geometry** option and click **OK**. The orientation of the geometry will change accordingly.

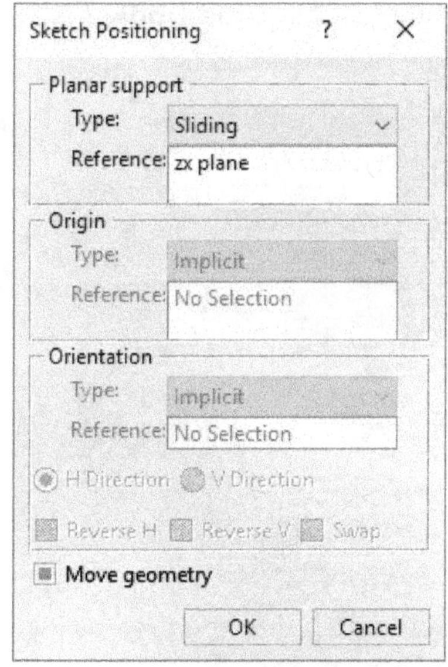

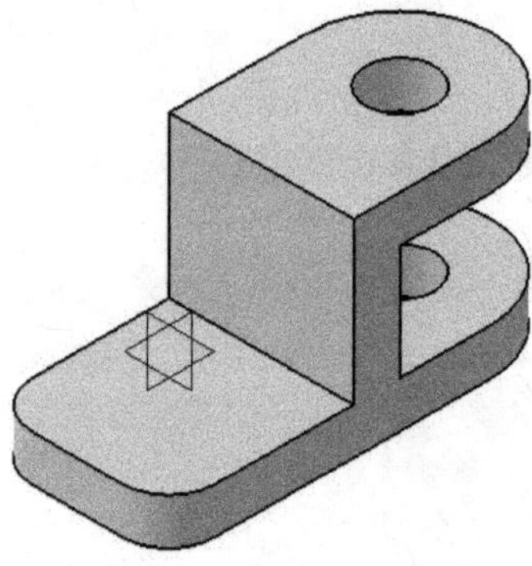

If there are any sketches or features on the geometry, it may show some warnings and error messages. You have to manually solve these problems or avoid changing the sketch support when the model becomes complex. It is recommended that you select correct plane initially based on model orientation.

Examples

Example 1

In this example, you will create the part shown below, and then modify it.

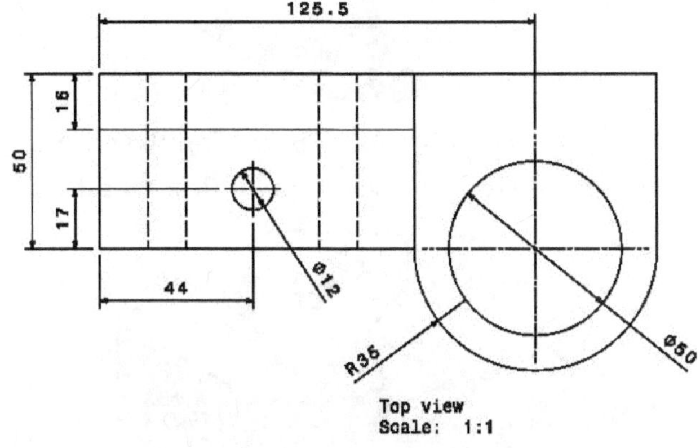

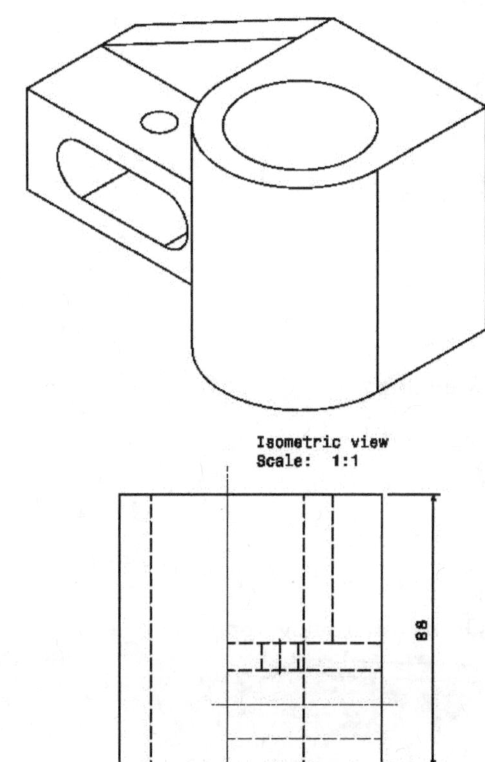

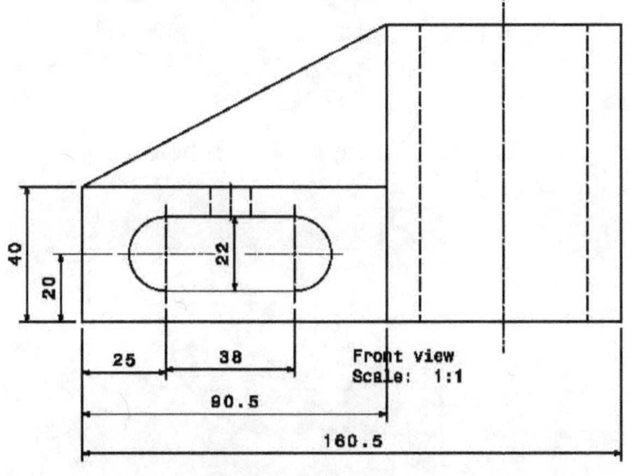

The Specification Tree of the part is given next.

1. Start **CATIA V5-6R2017** and open a part file.
2. Create the part using the tools and commands in CATIA V5.

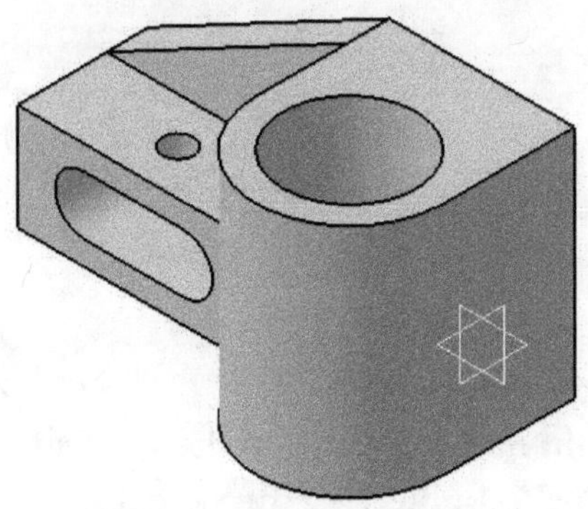

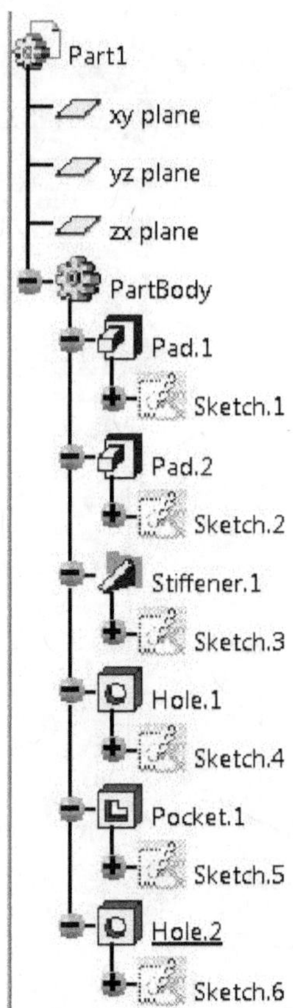

3. Double-click on the 50 mm diameter hole. The **Hole Definition** dialog appears.

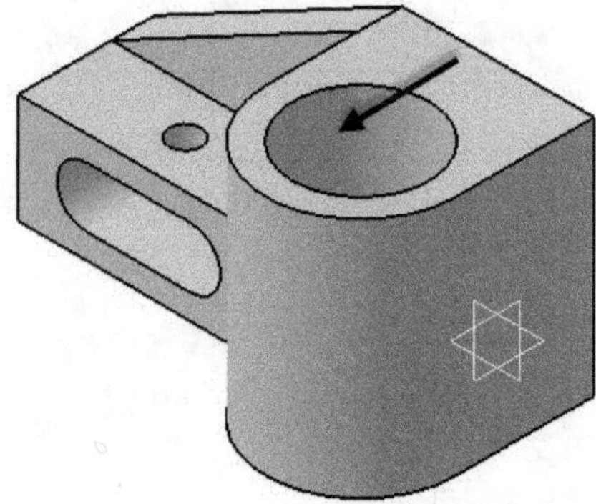

4. On the **Hole Definition** dialog, click the **Type** tab, and then select **Counterbored** from the drop-down.
5. Set the counterbore **Diameter** to **50** and **Depth** to **20**.
6. Click the **Extension** tab and set the **Diameter** to 35. Click **OK** to close the dialog.

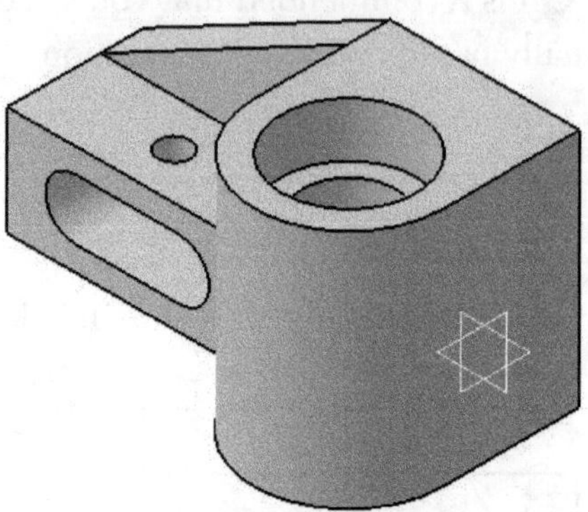

7. Click the right mouse button on the rectangular pad feature and select **Pad.object > Edit Sketch**.

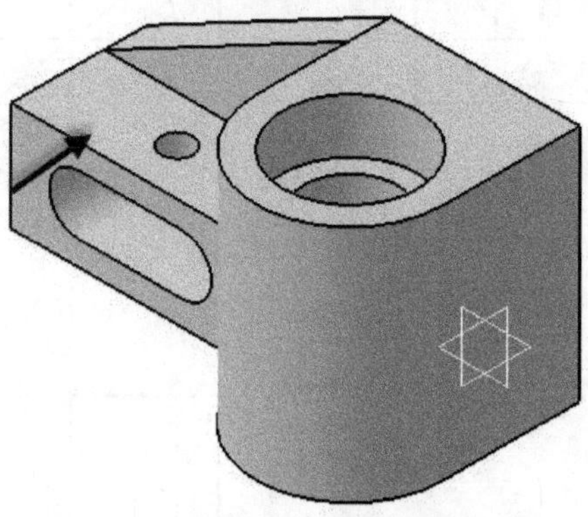

8. Modify the sketch, as shown below.

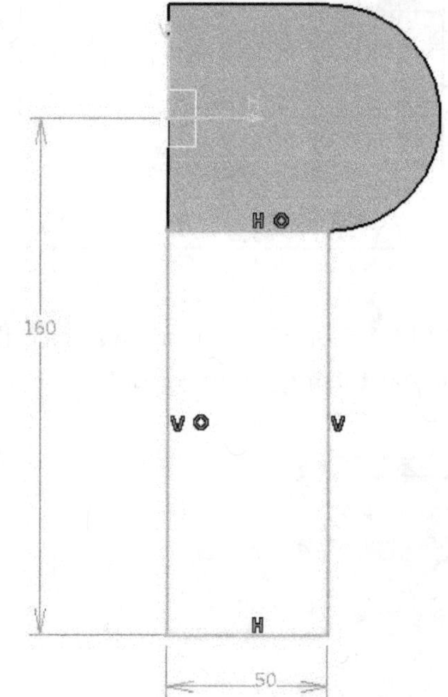

9. Exit the sketch.
10. Click the right mouse button on the slot feature and select **Pocket1.object > Edit Sketch**.

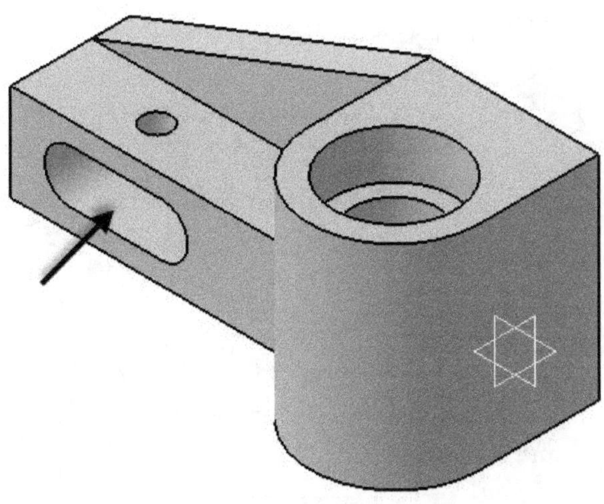

11. Delete the length dimension of the slot, and then add a new dimension between the right-side arc and right vertical edge.

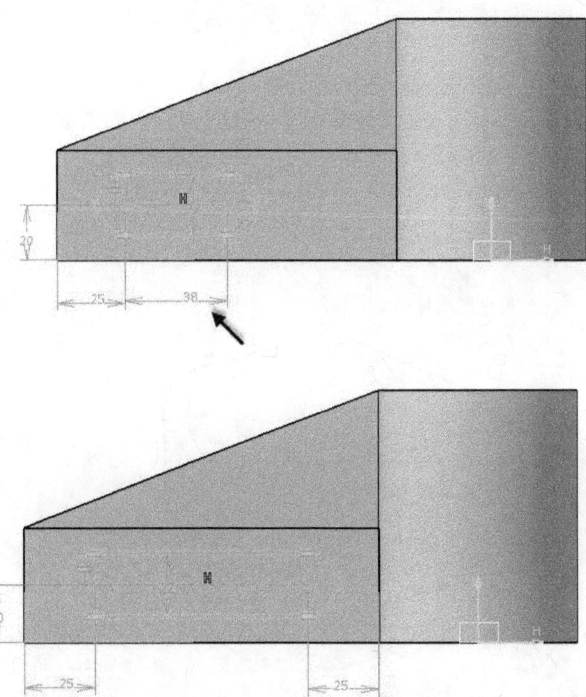

12. Exit the sketch.
13. Double-click on the small hole, and then click the **Positioned sketch** button on the dialog.

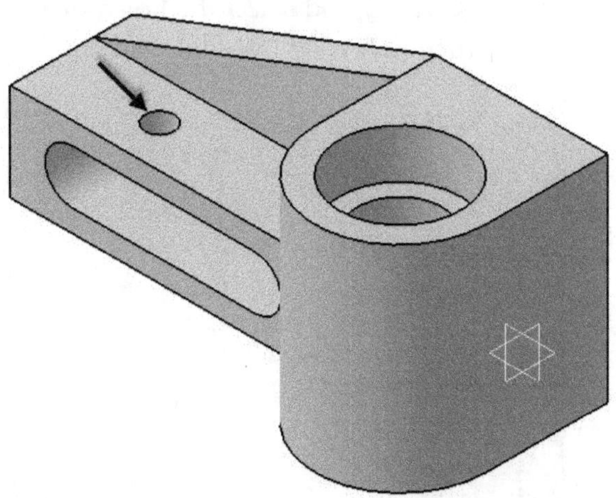

14. Delete the positioning dimensions.

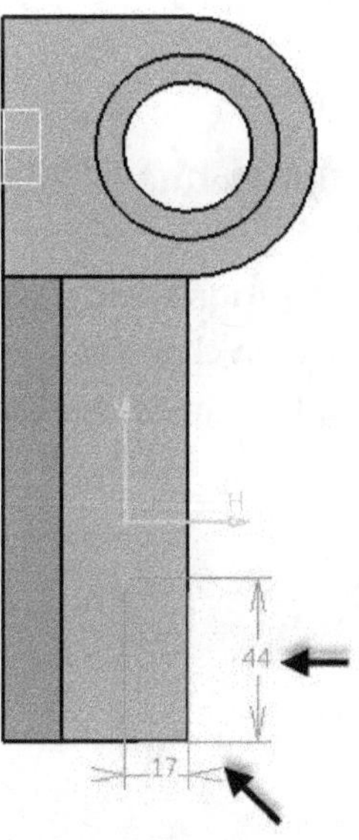

15. Create a construction line and make its ends coincident with the corners, as shown below.

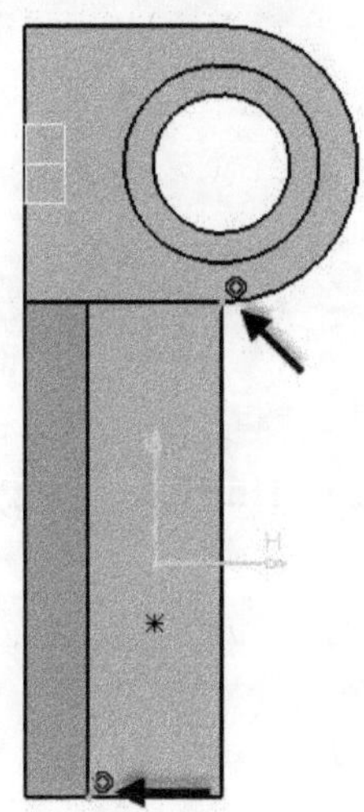

16. Press the Ctrl key and select the hole point and the construction line.

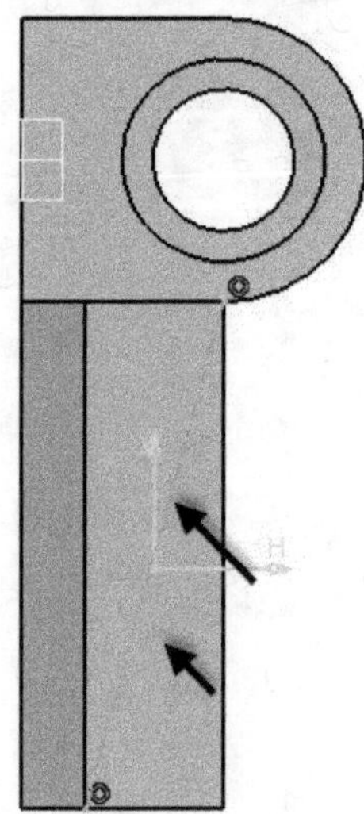

17. Activate the **Constraint Define in Dialog Box** command.
18. On the **Constraint Definition** dialog, check the **Midpoint** option, and then click **OK**. This positions the hole point on the midpoint of the construction line.

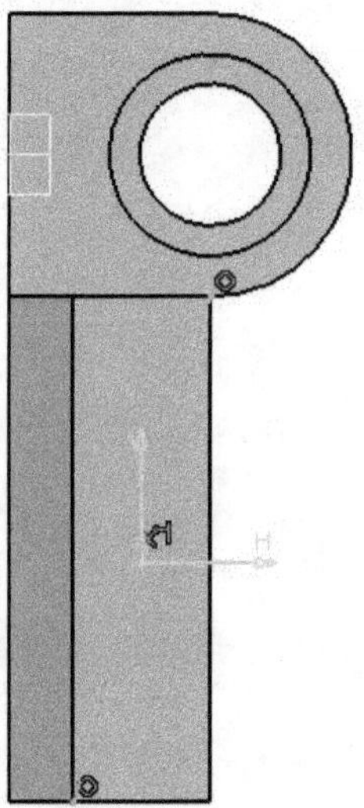

19. Exit the sketch.
20. Click **OK** on the **Hole Definition** dialog.

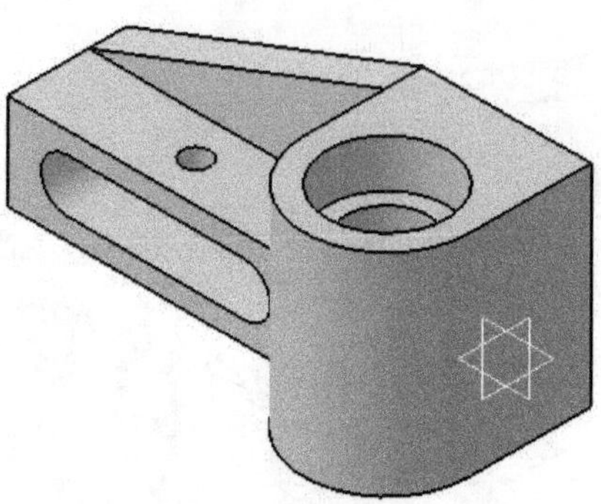

21. Now, change the size of the pad feature. You will notice that the slot and hole are adjusted automatically.

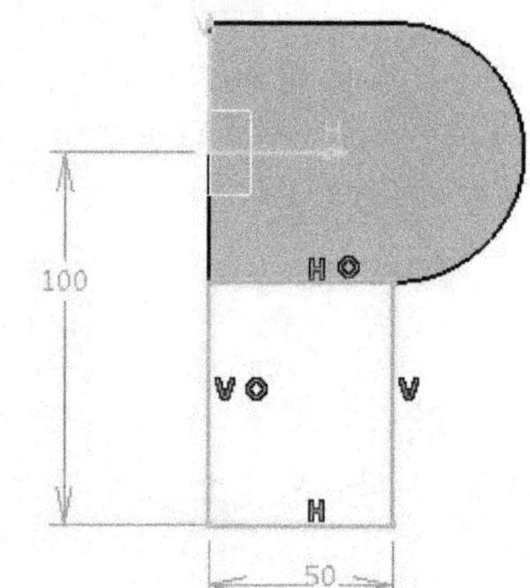

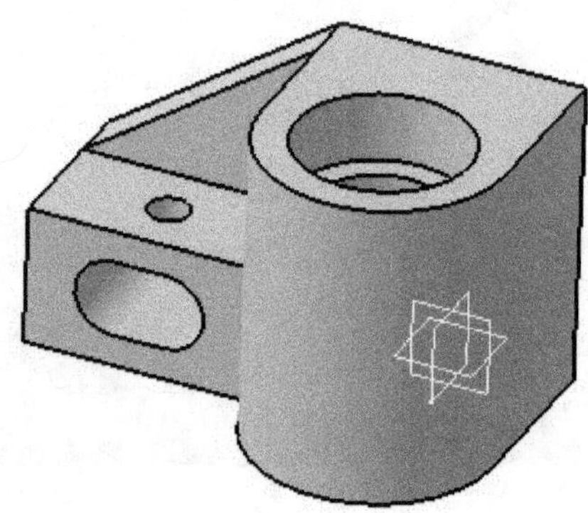

22. Save and close the file.

Questions

1. How do you modify the sketch of a feature?
2. How do you modify a feature directly?
3. How can you change the orientation of the model?

Exercises

Exercise 1

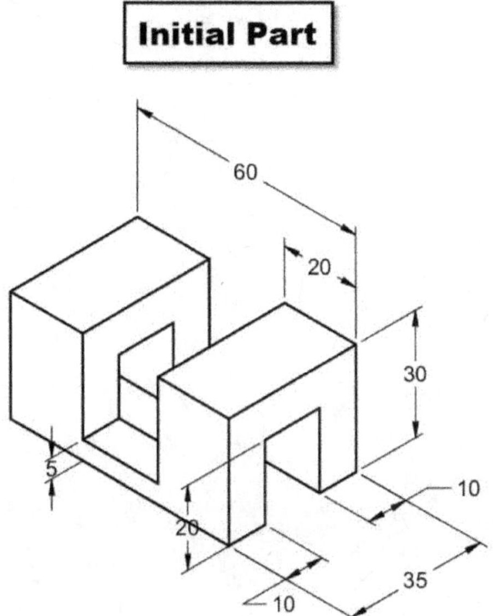

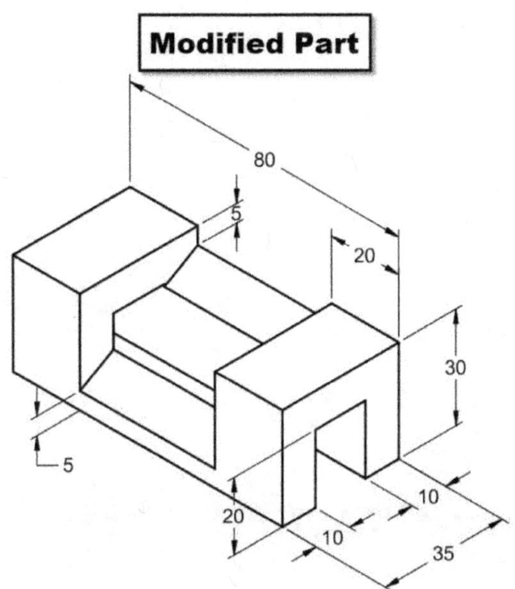

Chapter 10: Assemblies

After creating individual components, you can bring them together into an assembly. By doing so, it is possible to identify incorrect design problems that may not have been noticeable at the part level. In this chapter, you will learn how to bring components into the Assembly Design Workbench and position them.

The topics covered in this chapter are:

- *Starting an assembly*
- *Inserting Components*
- *Adding Constraints*
- *Moving components*
- *Checking Interference*
- *Editing Assemblies*
- *Replacing Components*
- *Patterning Components*
- *Creating Subassemblies*
- *Top-down Assembly Design*
- *Creating Exploded Views*

Starting an Assembly

To begin an assembly file, click **File > New** on the Menu bar, and select the **Product** template from the **New** dialog. Click **OK**.

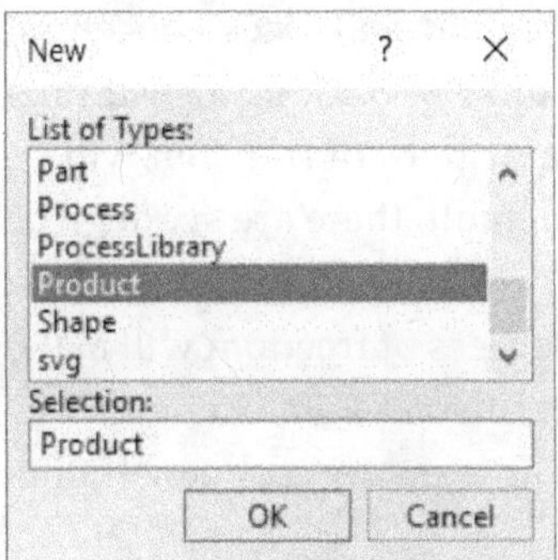

Another way to start an assembly is to click **Start > Mechanical Design > Assembly Design**. This opens the assembly environment. Now, you can add components to the assembly using the **Existing Components** command.

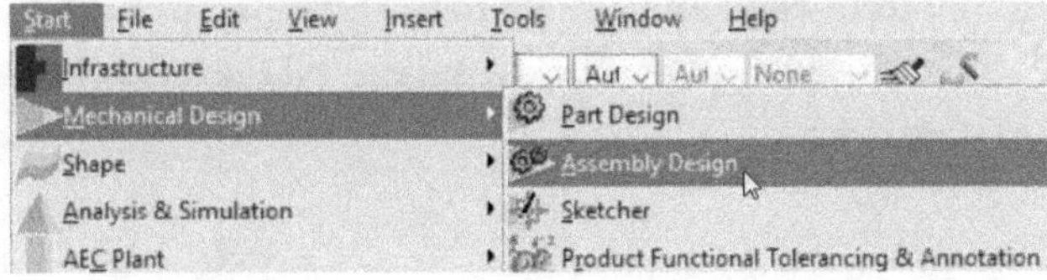

After starting an assembly file, you need to make sure that some important toolbars are displayed in the window. Some of the important toolbars that are most frequently used in assembly are **Product Structure Tools, Constraint**, and **Move** toolbars.

Click on the Product Structure Tools toolbar, press and hold the left mouse button, and the drag it toward top left corner. The toolbar is placed below the menu bar.

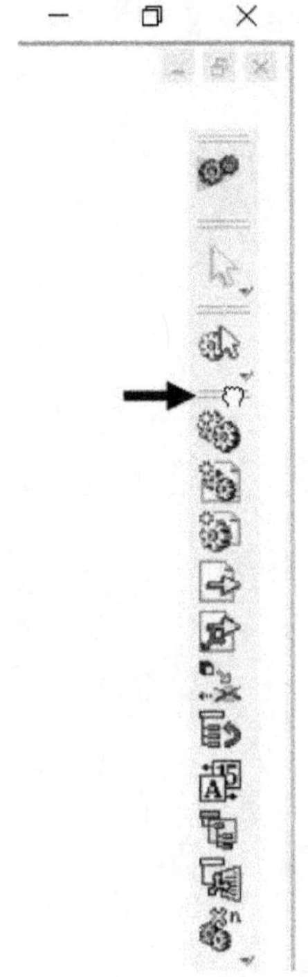

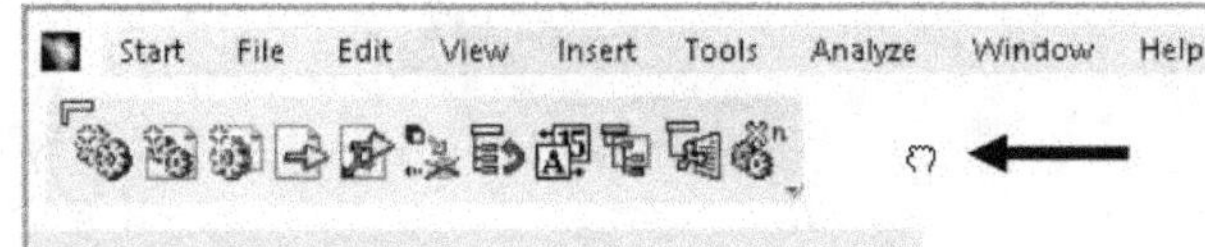

Likewise, drag the **Constraint** and **Move** toolbars, and then release them below the menu bar.

Inserting Components

There are two different methods to insert an existing part into an assembly. The first one is to insert using the **Existing Component** command.

1. On the **Product Structure Tools** toolbar, click the **Existing Component** button (or) click **Insert > Existing Component** on the Menu bar.
2. In the Specification Tree, click **Product**.

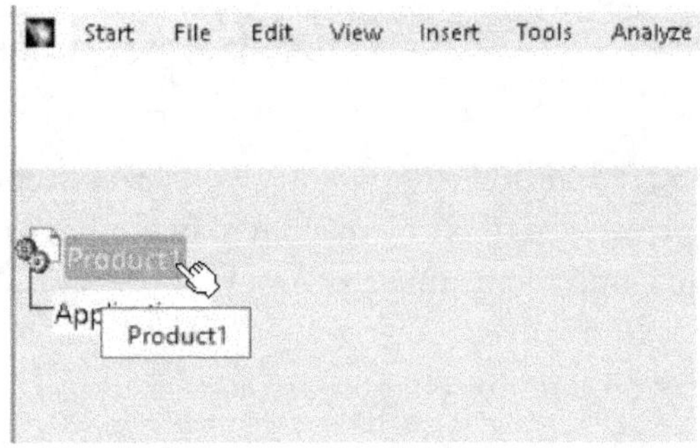

3. Browse to the Location of the component and select it.
4. Click **Open**. The component is inserted in the assembly.
5. On the **View** toolbar, click the **Isometric View** icon.

Fixing the first Component

After inserting components into an assembly, you have to define constraints between them. By applying constraints, you can make components to flush with each other or make two cylindrical faces concentric with each other, and so on. As you add constraints between components, the degrees of freedom will be removed from them. By default, there are six degrees of freedom for a part (three linear and three rotational). Eliminating degrees of freedom will make components attached and interact with each other as in real life. Now, you will learn to add constraints between components

After placing the component at the origin, it is free to move. You can check the degrees of freedom by using the **Degree(s) of freedom** command.

1. Double-click on the Part in the Specification Tree.
2. On the Menu bar, click **Analyze > Degree(s) of freedom**.

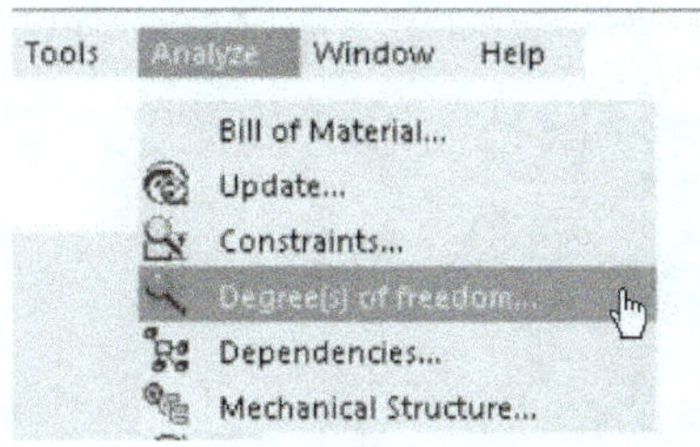

A warning message appears showing the degrees of freedom of the selected component.

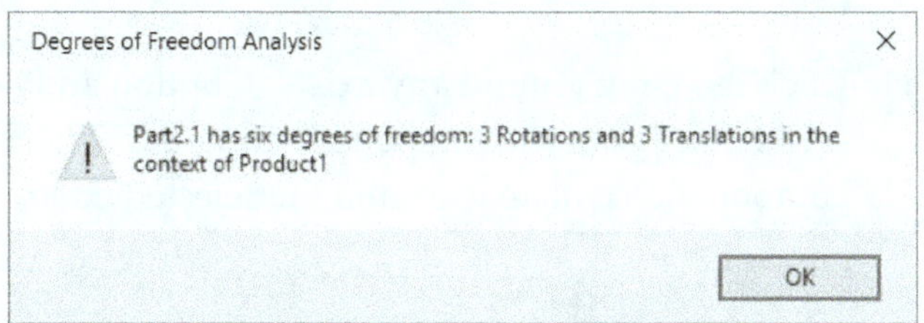

3. Click **OK** on the warning message box.
4. In order to remove the degrees of freedom of the first component, double-click on **Product1** in the Specification Tree.
5. On the **Constraints** toolbar, click the **Fix Component** button (or) click **Insert > Fix** on the Menu bar.
6. Select the first component to fix it at the origin. You will notice that the **Fix** glyph appears on the components.

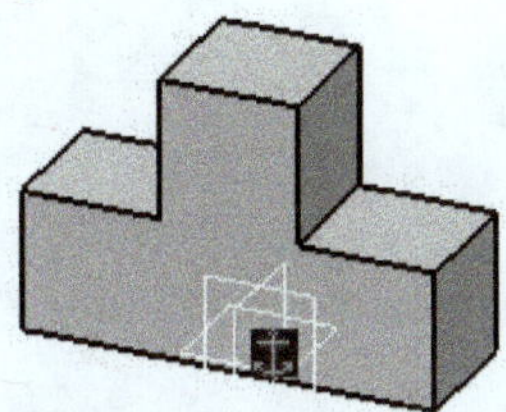

7. Double-click on Partt2 in the Specification Tree.
8. On the Menu bar, click **Analyze > Degree(s) of freedom**. You can notice that the component is fully fixed at the origin.

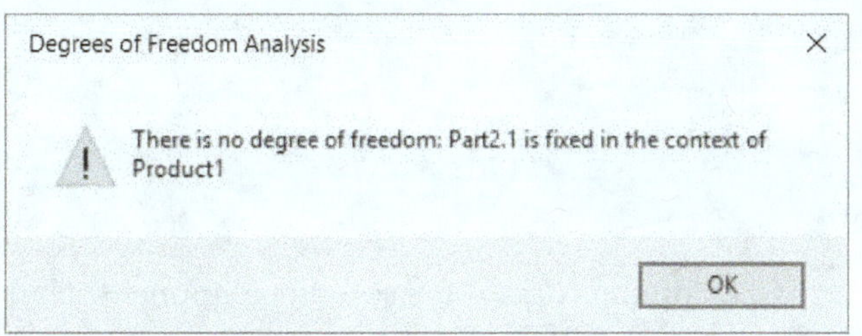

9. Click **OK** on the **Degrees of Freedom Analysis** dialog.

Inserting the Second Component

1. On the **Product Structure Tools** toolbar, click the **Existing Component With Positioning** button (or) click **Insert > Existing Component with Positioning** on the Menu bar.
2. In the Specification Tree, click **Product1** and go to the location of the second component.
3. Select the component and click **Open**. The **Smart Move** dialog appears on the screen.
4. In the **Smart Move** dialog, you can click and drag the component to the required location.

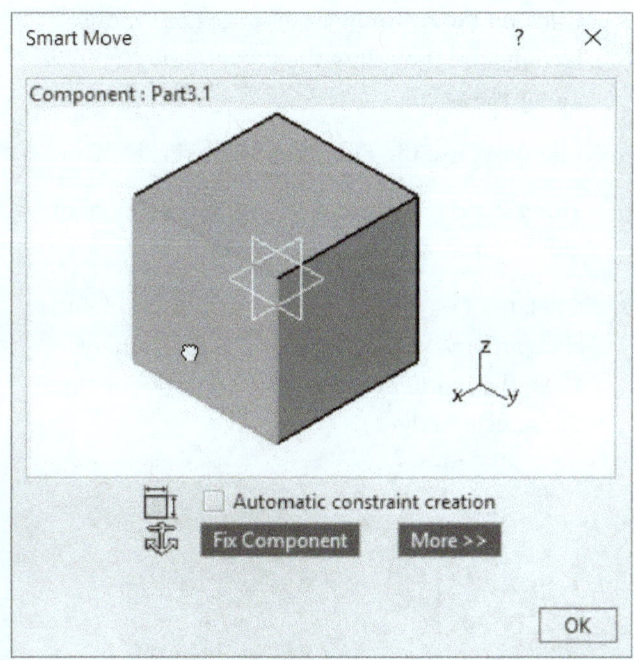

5. Click **OK**.

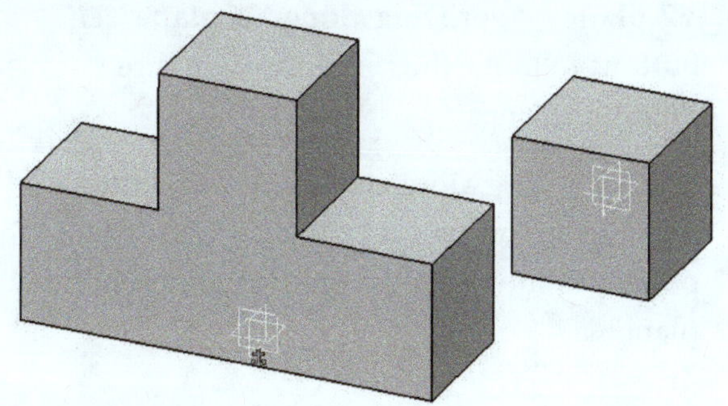

 Manipulation

After inserting components into the assembly, you can move or rotate them.

1. Double-click on **Product1** in the Specification Tree.
2. On the **Move** toolbar, click the **Manipulation** button (or) click **Edit > Move > Manipulate**.
3. If the component is constrained, then check the **With respect to constraints** option on the **Manipulation Parameters** dialog. This allows you to manipulate the component by considering the applied constraints.
4. On the **Manipulation Parameters** dialog, click the **Drag along X axis** button.
5. Click on the component, hold the left mouse button, and then drag the component; it moves along the x-axis.
6. Likewise, use the **Drag along Y axis**, **Drag along Z axis** buttons drag the component along Y and Z axes, respectively.
7. Click the **Drag along any axis** button and click anyone of the edges of the component. Drag the pointer to move the component along the selected edge.

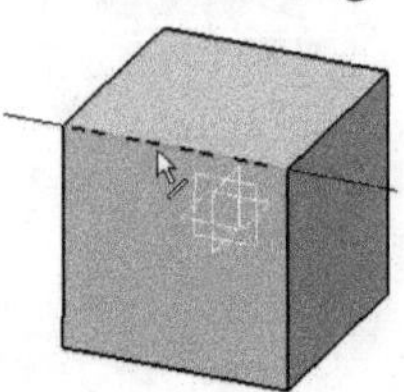

8. Use the **Drag along XY plane**, **Drag along YZ plane**, or **Drag along XZ plane** buttons to move the component on three different planes.
9. Click the **Drag along any plane** button and select a face or plane of the component. Drag the pointer to move the component on the selected plane.

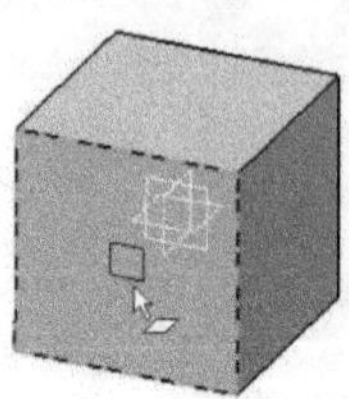

10. Use the **Drag around X axis**, **Drag around Y axis**, or **Drag around Z axis** buttons to rotate the component around three different axes .
11. Click the **Drag around any axis** button and select an edge of the component. Drag the component to rotate it around the selected edge.

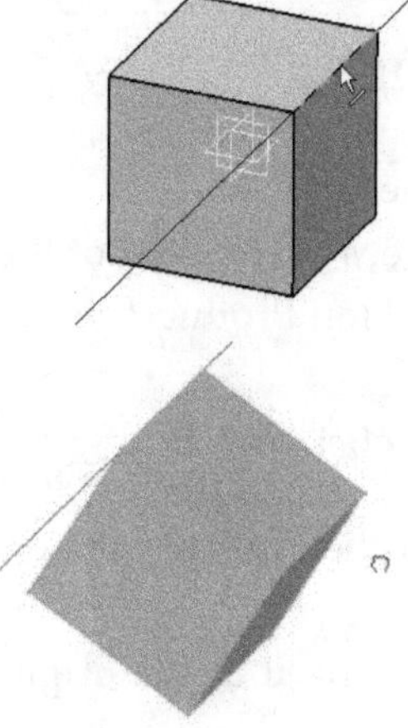

12. Click **OK**.

 Snap

This command moves a component by snaping the elements (edges, planes) of two components.

1. On the **Move** toolbar, click **Snap** drop-down > **Snap** (or) click **Edit > Move > Snap** on the Menu bar.
2. Click on the edge of the first component.

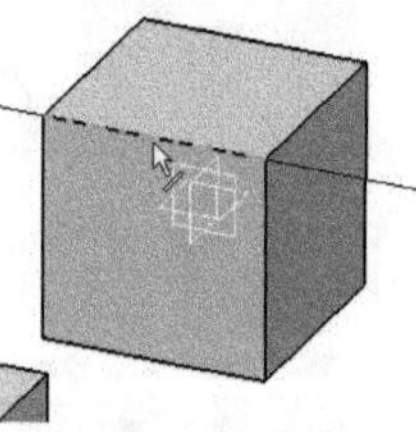

3. Click on the edge of the second component. The two edges will be aligned.

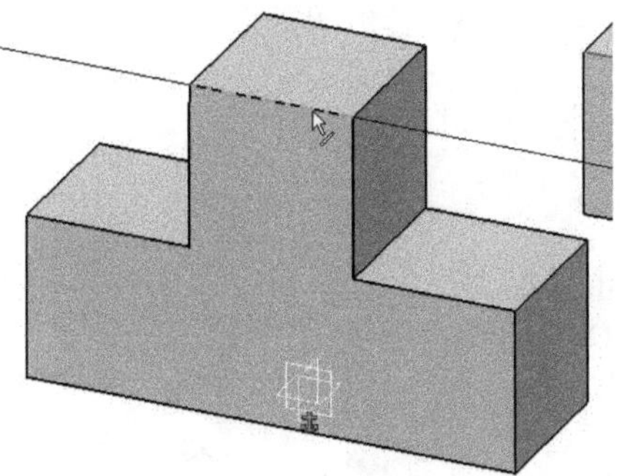

4. Click on the green arrow to reverse the alignment direction.

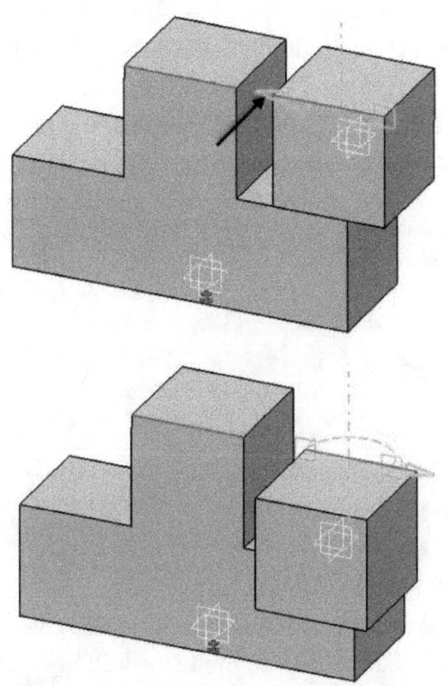

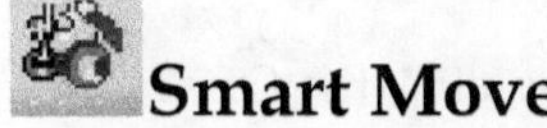 Smart Move

This command and the **Snap** command function in same way. The advantage of this command is that you can create constraints between two snapped objects.

1. On the **Move** toolbar, click **Snap** drop-down > **Smart Move** (or) click **Edit > Move > Smart Move** on the Menu bar.
2. Click on an object (edge or face) of the first component, and then drag it onto the second component. The two objects will be aligned together.

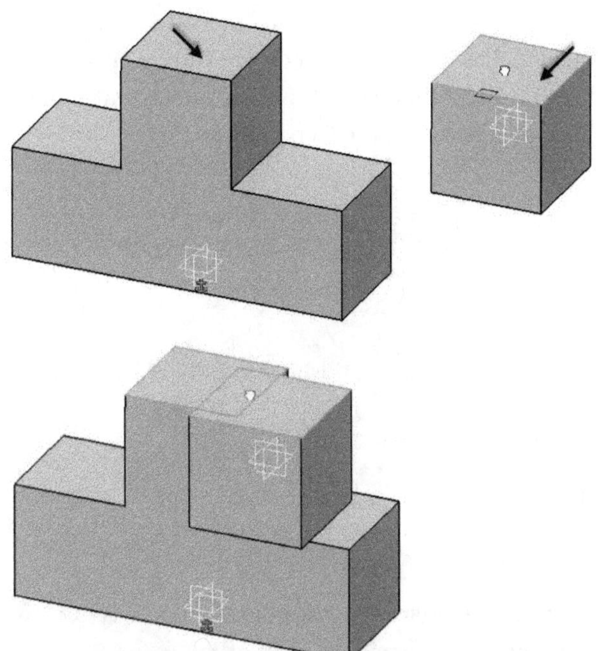

3. Click the green arrow if you want to reverse the alignment direction.
4. On the **Smart Move** dialog, check the **Automatic constraint creation** option to apply constraints between the aligned objects.
5. On the **Smart Move** dialog, click the **More** button to view the type of constraints that can be applied.
6. If you want to apply only a particular type of constraint between the two objects, then select the constraint from the list.
7. Move the constraint to the top of the list by clicking the upward arrow button.

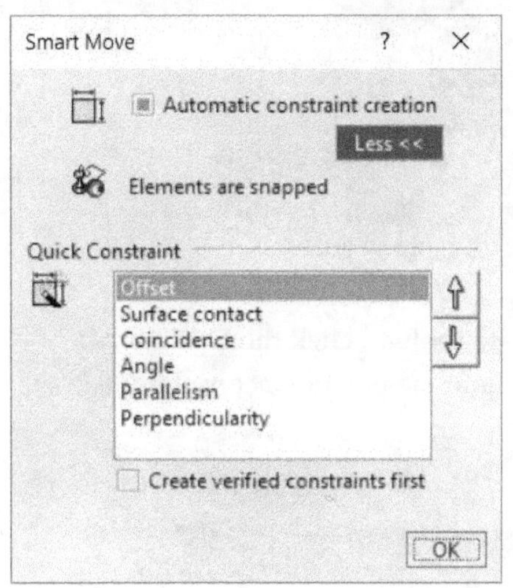

8. Check the **Create verified constraints first** option, and then click **OK**. The constraint will be applied between the two objects.

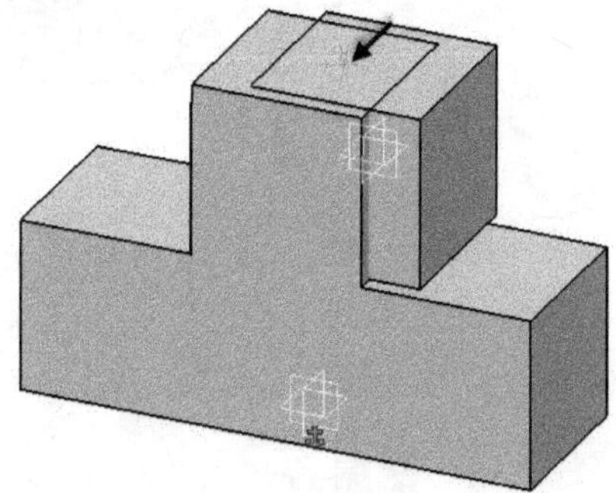

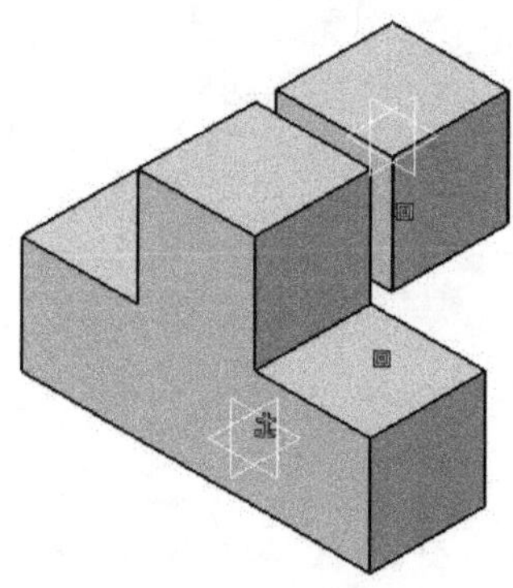

If you want to update the assembly automatically, then open the **Options** dialog (click **Tools > Options** on the Menu bar). On the **Options** dialog, click **Mechanical Design > Assembly Design** in the tree. Select **Update > Automatic** option, and then click **OK**. However, this may slow down the speed due to instant updates.

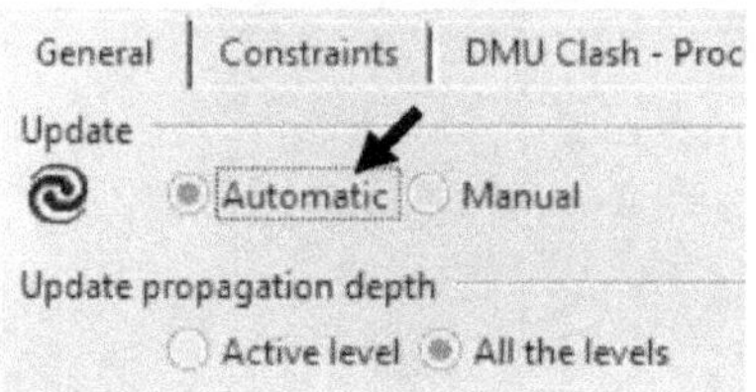

Contact Constraint

The **Contact Constraint** command makes two faces coincident and opposite to each other.

1. On the **Constraints** toolbar, click the **Contact Constraint** button (or) click **Insert > Contact** on the Menu bar. The **Assistant** dialog pops up on the screen.
2. Check the **Do not prompt in future** option, and then click **Close** on the dialog.
3. Select a face of the first part.
4. Click on a face of the second part. This creates a contact constraint between the two faces.

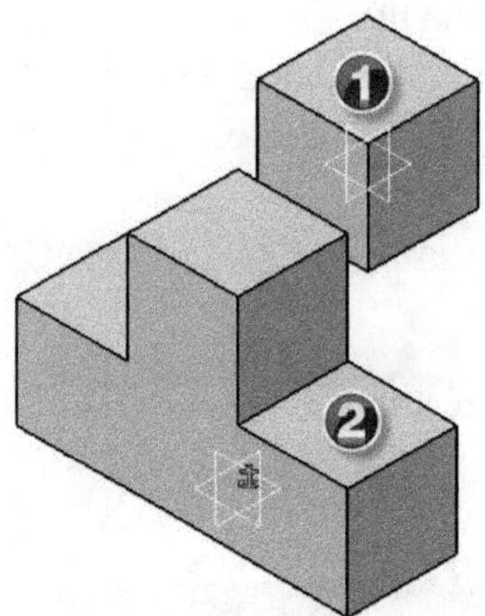

5. On the **Update** toolbar, click the **Update All** button to update the positions components.

Offset Constraint

The **Offset Constraint** command creates a distance between two faces. In addition, the faces will be parallel to each other.

1. On the **Constraints** toolbar, click the **Offset Constraint** button (or) click **Insert > Offset** on the Menu bar.
2. Select a face of the first part.
3. Click on a face of the second part.

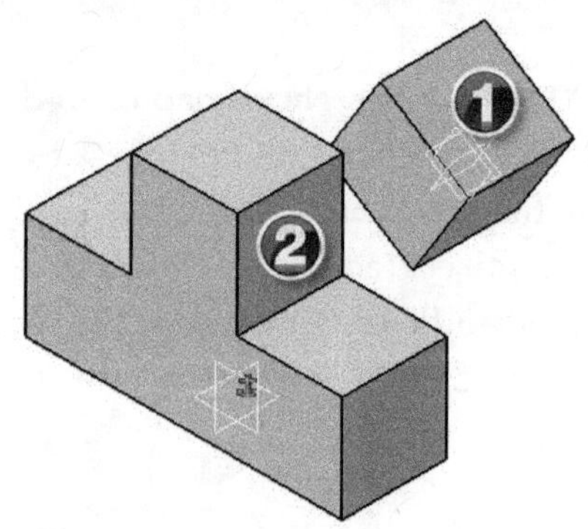

4. On the **Constraint Properties** dialog, select **Orientation > Same** to make the selected faces point in same direction.

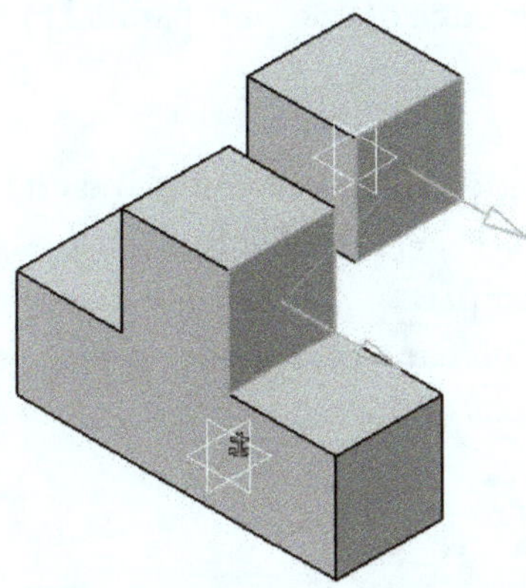

If you select **Orientation > Opposite**, the faces point in the direction opposite to each other.

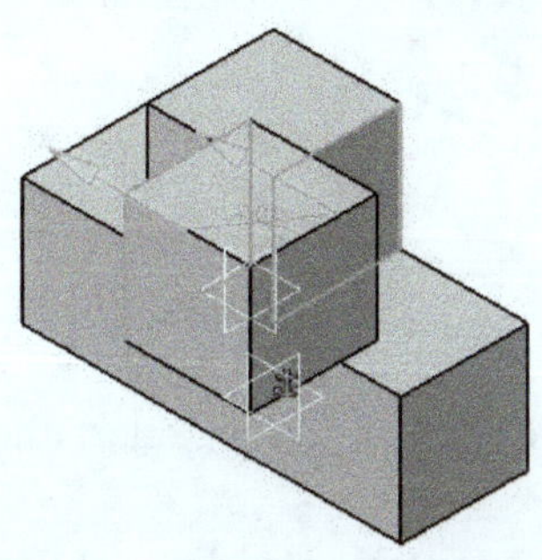

If you select **Orientation > Undefined**, the faces point in the current direction.

5. Type-in a value in the **Offset** box (or) if you check the **Measure** option, the current distance between the selected faces will be used as offset distance.

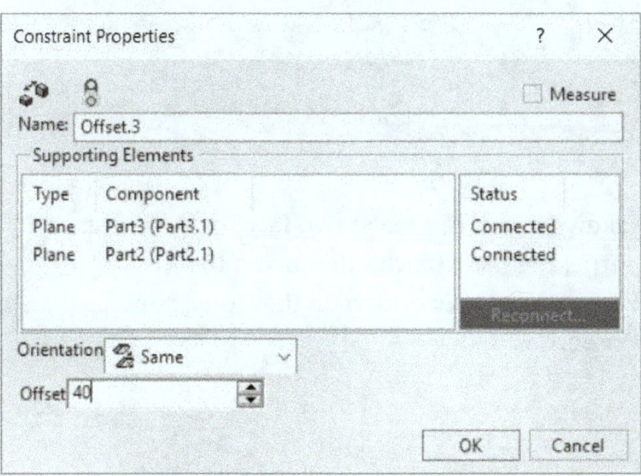

6. Click **OK**.

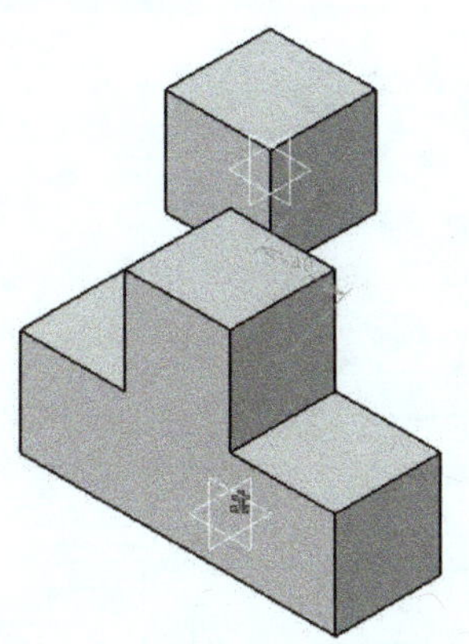

Coincidence Constraint

The **Coincidence Constraint** command makes the axes of two cylindrical faces coincide with each other.

1. On the **Constraints** toolbar, click the **Coincidence Constraint** button (or) click **Insert > Coincidence** on the Menu cbar.
2. Click on a cylindrical face, linear edge, or axis of the first part.
3. Click on a cylindrical face, linear edge, or axis of the target part. The two cylindrical axes will be aligned together.

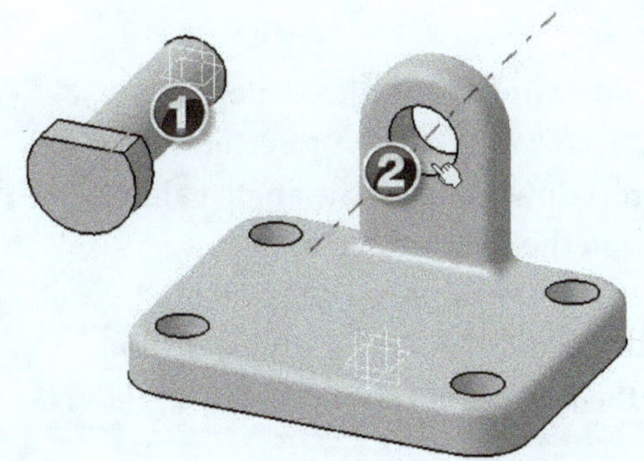

 Angle Constraint

The **Angle Constraint** command is used to position faces at a specified angle.

1. On the **Constraints** toolbar, click the **Angle Constraint** button (or) click **Insert > Angle** on the Menu bar.
2. Click on a plane or linear element of the first part.
3. Click on a plane or linear element of the second part.

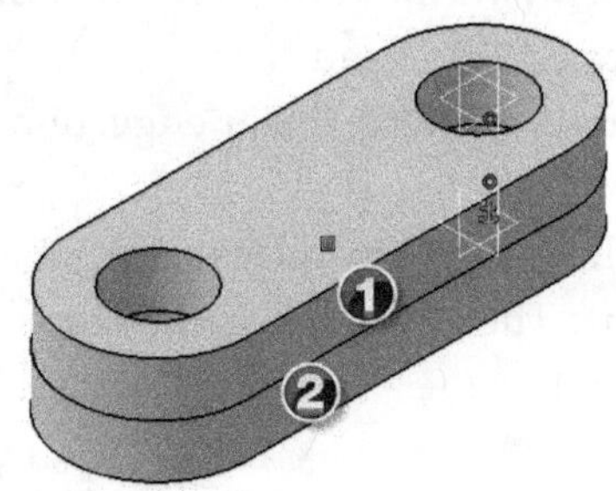

4. On the **Constraint Properties** dialog, select **Sector 1, Sector 2, Sector 3**, or **Sector 4** from the **Sector** drop-down menu. The angle value is displayed in the selected sector.
5. Type-in a value in the **Angle** box on the **Constraint Properties** dialog. Click **OK** to position the first part at the specified angle.

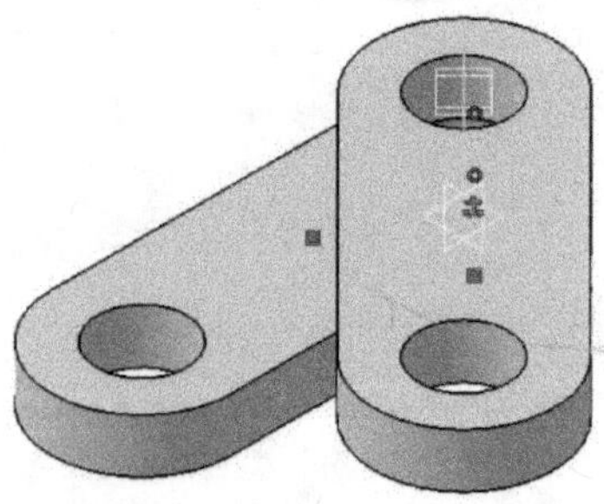

Parallelism and Perpendicularity Constraints

The **Angle Constraint** command can also be used to make an axis, face or edge of one-part parallel to that of another part.

1. Activate the **Angle Constraint** command and select a planar face, cylindrical face, linear edge, or axis of the first part.
2. Next, click on a planar face, cylindrical face, linear edge, or axis of the second part.

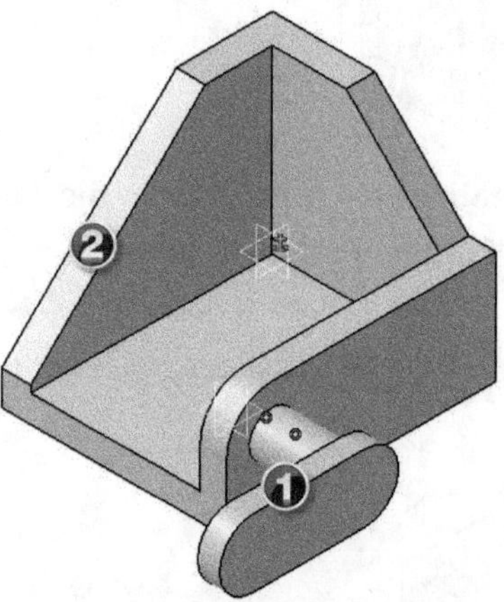

3. On the **Constraint Properties** dialog, select the **Parallelism** option.
4. On the dialog, set the **Orientation** and click **OK**. The selected elements will be parallel to each other.

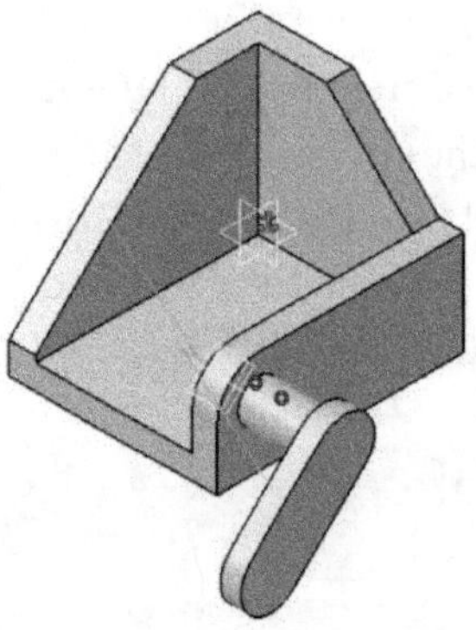

Likewise, you can make two faces, edges, or axes perpendicular to each other using the **Perpendicularity** option on the **Constraint Properties** dialog.

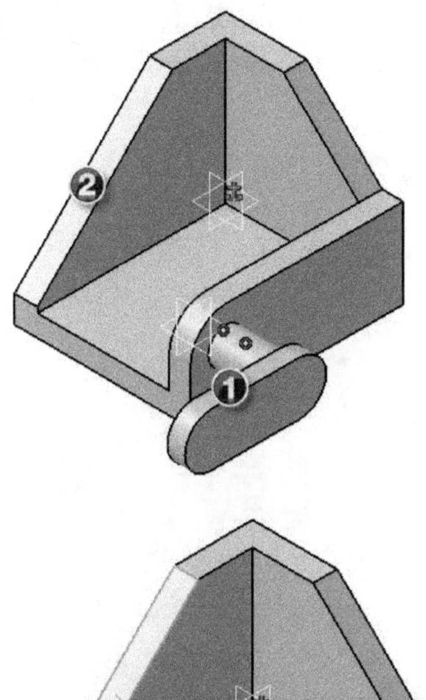

Fix Together

The **Fix Together** constraint makes components to form a rigid set. As you move a single part in a rigid set, all the other components will also be moved.

1. On the **Constraints** toolbar, click the **Fix Together** button (or) click **Insert > Fix Together** on the Menu bar.
2. Select components from the assembly window.

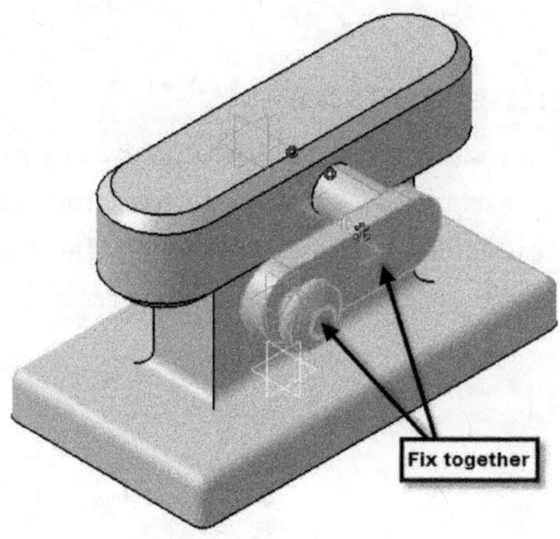

3. Click **OK** on the dialog. The selected components are fixed together.
4. Now, activate the **Manipulation** command and check the **With respect to constraints** option.
5. Rotate or move anyone of the parts, which are fixed together. You will notice that the other parts are also manipulated.

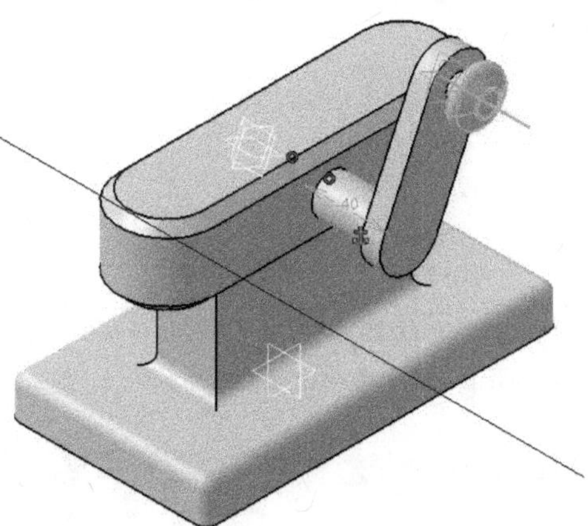

Clash

In an assembly, two or more components can overlap or occupy the same space. However, this would be physically impossible in the real world. When you add constraints between components, CATIA V5 develops real-world contacts and movements between them. However, sometimes clashes can occur. To check such errors, CATIA V5 provides you with a command called **Clash**.

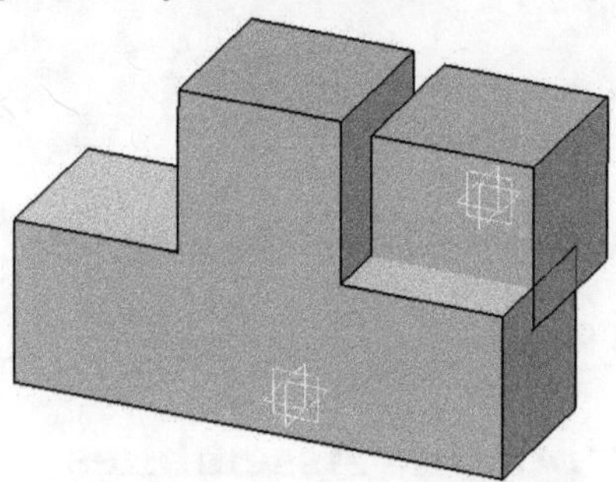

1. On the **Space Analysis** toolbar, click the **Clash** button (or) click **Analyze > Clash** on the menu bar.
2. On the **Check Clash** dialog, select the type of clash analysis. You can select **Contact + Clash** or

Clearance + Contact + Clash, Authorized Penetration, or **Clash rule**.

3. Select **Between all components** from the lower drop-down menu. You can also select **Inside one selection, Selection against all**, or **Between two selections**. This defines components between which the clash analysis is performed.

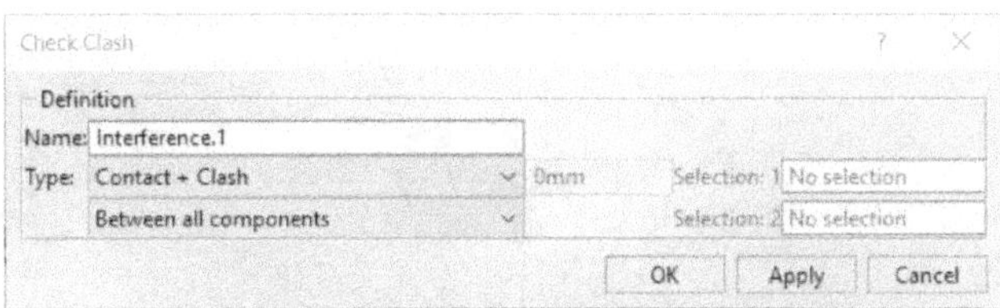

4. Click **Apply** on the dialog. The preview window appears showing the interference value.

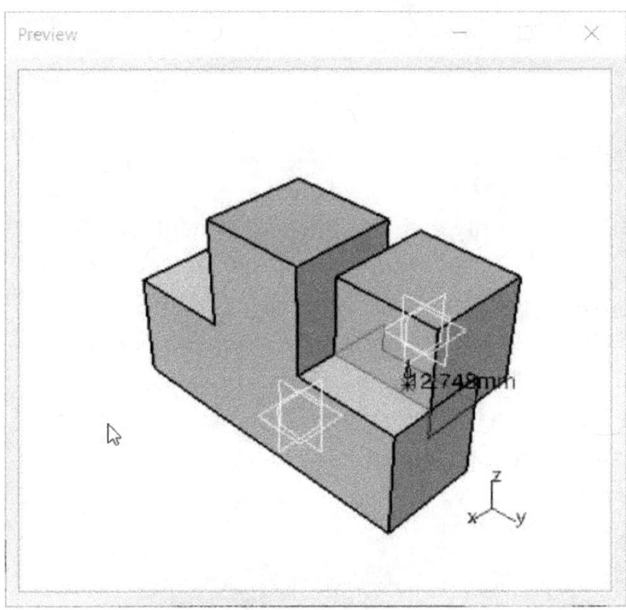

Now, you can export the clash report by using the **Export As** button.

Editing and Updating Assemblies

During the design process, the correct design is not achieved on the first attempt. There is always a need to go back and make modifications. CATIA V5, allows you to accomplish this process very easily.

1. To modify a part in an assembly, double click on it. This activates the **Part Design** workbench.

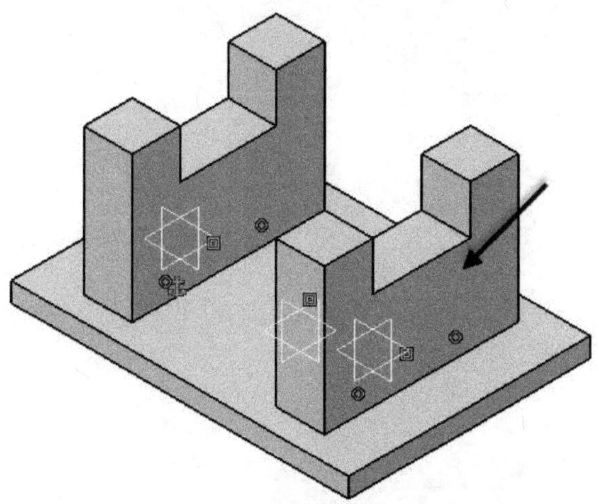

2. Now, make changes to the part.

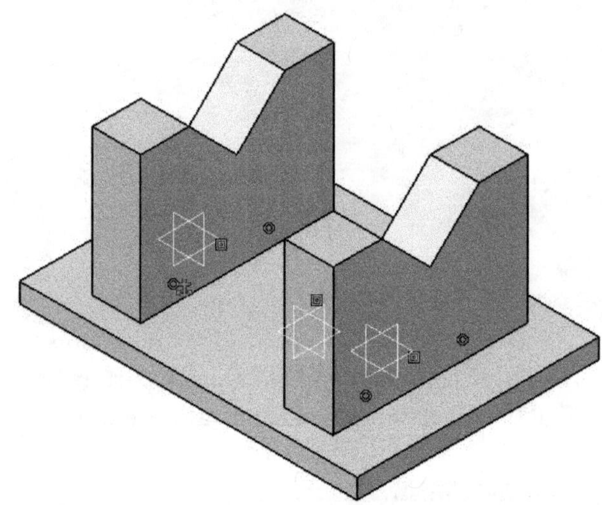

3. In the Specification Tree, double-click on **Product1** to return to the **Assembly Design** workbench.

Redefining Constraints

You can also redefine the existing constraints in an assembly. For example, if you want to change the faces that contact each other, then follow the steps given next.

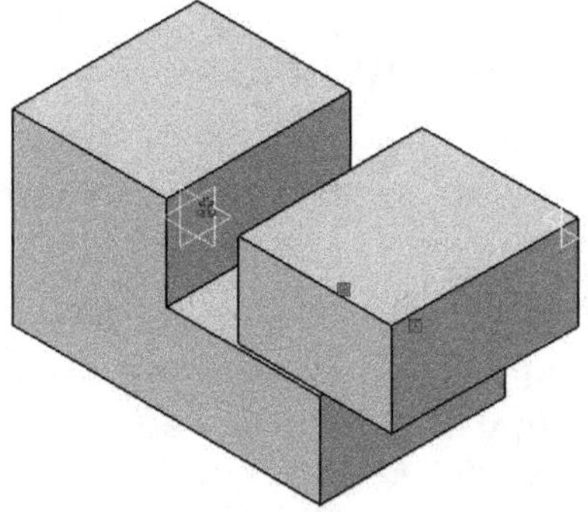

1. In the Specification Tree, expand the **Constraints** section.
2. Click the right mouse button on the **Surface contact** constraint, and then select **Surface contact.object > Definition**.

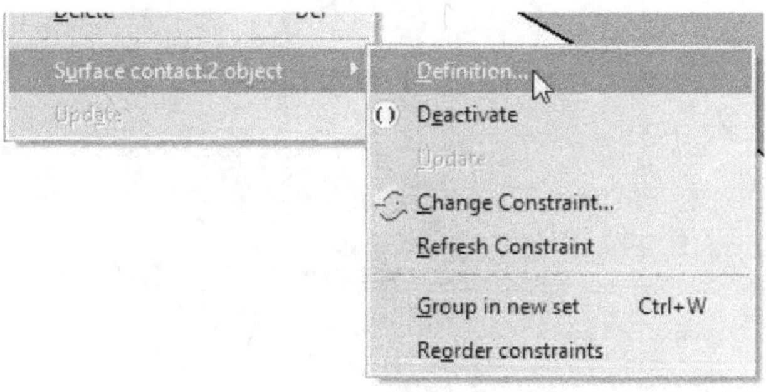

3. Click the **More** button on the **Constraint Definition** dialog.
4. On the expanded dialog, click the face to replace.

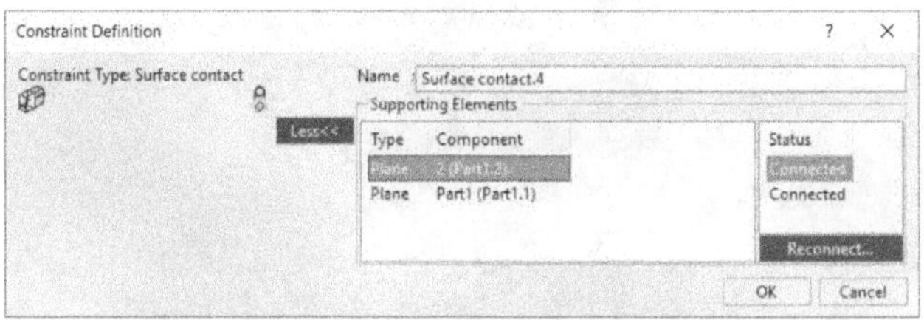

5. Click the **Reconnect** button.
6. Click on the new face.

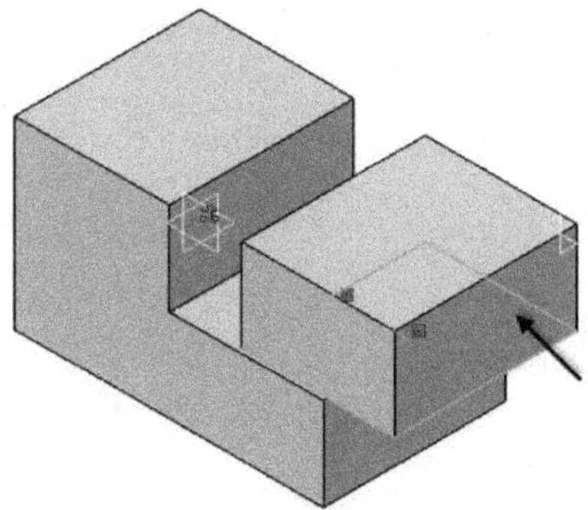

7. Click **OK**. The contact constraint will be redefined.

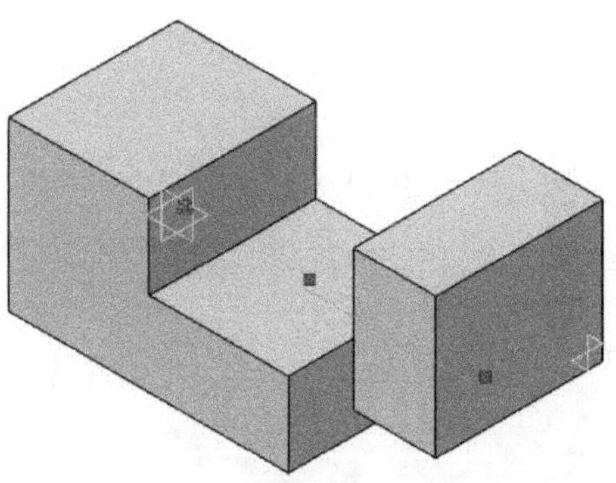

Change Constraint

You can also convert an existing constraint into another type of constraint. For example, if you want to convert the **Contact Constraint** into **Offset Constraint**, then follow the steps given next.

1. On the **Constraints** toolbar, click the **Change Constraint** button.
2. Click on the **Contact constraint** glyph that appears on the assembly. The **Possible Constraints** dialog appears.

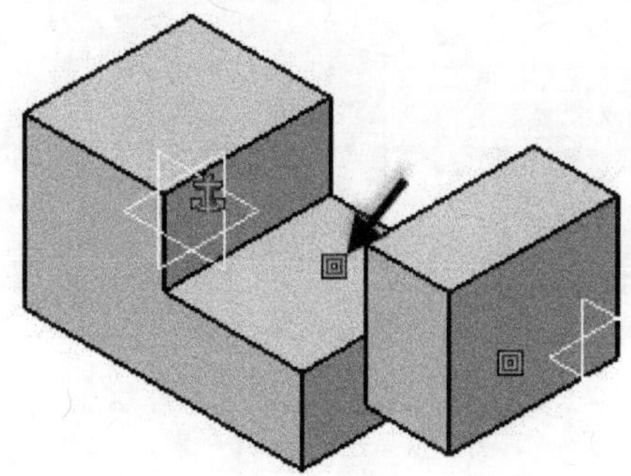

3. On the **Possible Constraints** dialog, select **Offset**, and then click **OK**. The **Contact** constraint is converted into the **Offset** constraint.

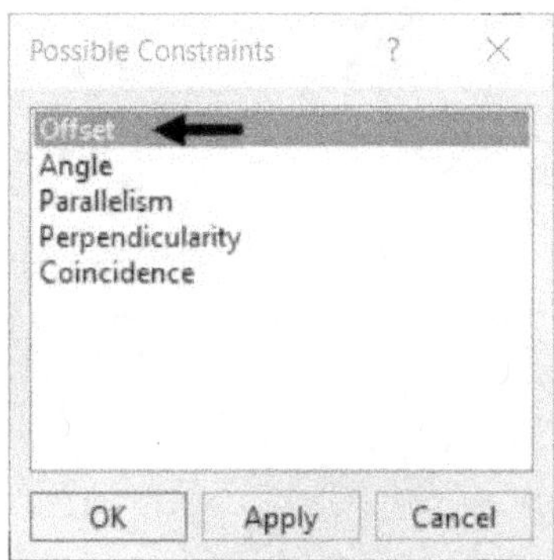

4. Now, double-click on the Offset distance value to change it.

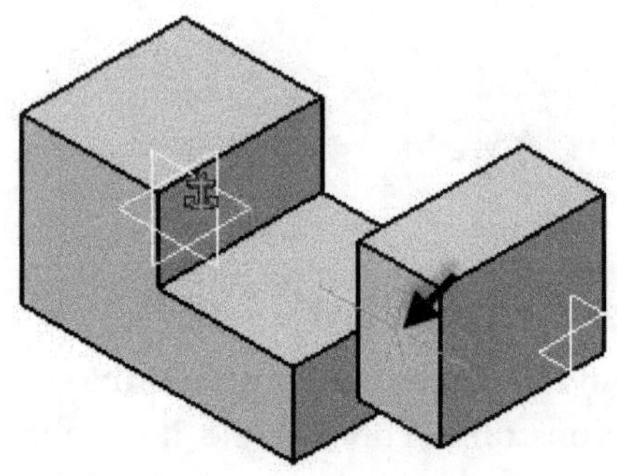

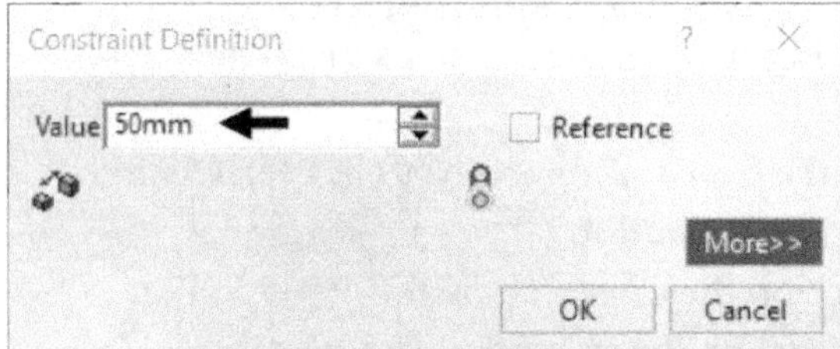

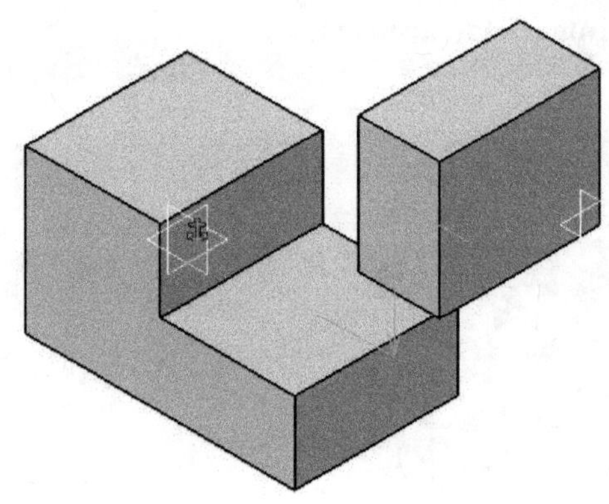

Replace Component

CATIA V5 allows you to replace any component in an assembly. To do this, follow the steps given next.

1. On the **Product Structure Tools** toolbar, click the **Replace Component** button (or) **Edit > Components > Replace Component** on the Menu bar.
2. Click on the component to replace.

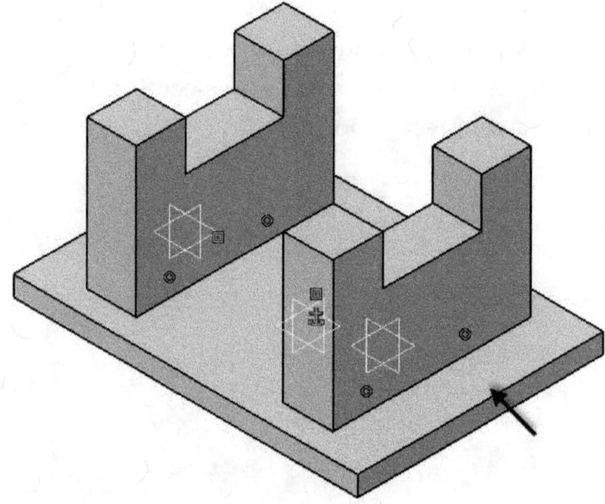

3. On the **File Selection** dialog, go to the location of the replacement part.

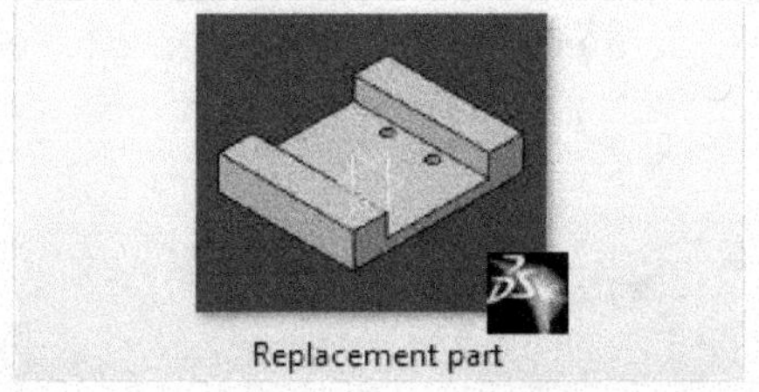

4. Select the component and click **Open**. If the new component is not similar to the old component, then the **Impacts On Replace** dialog appears. It shows the constraints that are affected.

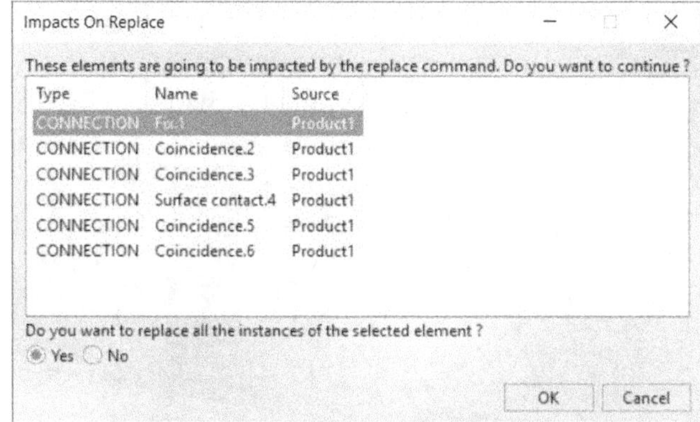
Impacts On Replace

These elements are going to be impacted by the replace command. Do you want to continue ?

Type	Name	Source
CONNECTION	Fix.1	Product1
CONNECTION	Coincidence.2	Product1
CONNECTION	Coincidence.3	Product1
CONNECTION	Surface contact.4	Product1
CONNECTION	Coincidence.5	Product1
CONNECTION	Coincidence.6	Product1

Do you want to replace all the instances of the selected element ?

Yes No

OK Cancel

5. Click **OK** to replace the component.

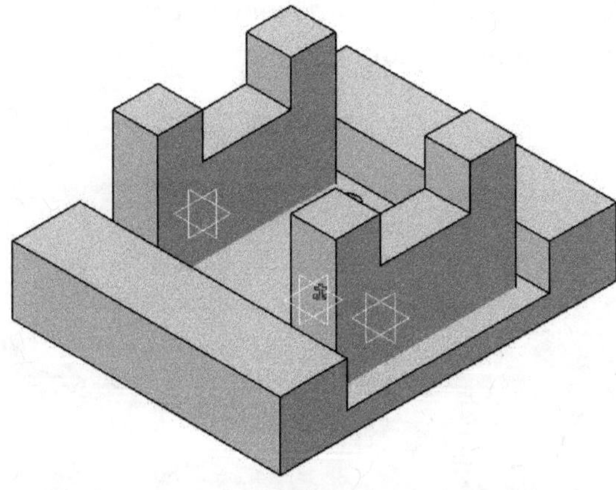

6. Now, you can redefine the existing constraints or delete them and define new constraints. In this case, you can redefine the existing constraints.

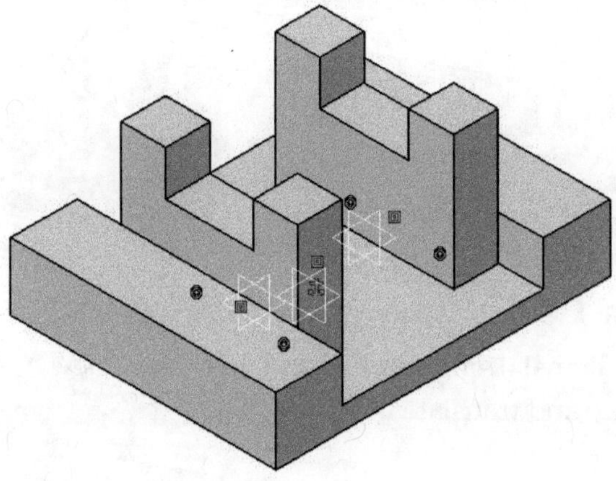

 Reuse Pattern

The **Reuse Pattern** command allows you to replicate individual components in an assembly. However, instead of defining layouts of rectangular or circular patterns, you can select an existing pattern as a reference. For example, in the assembly shown in figure, you can position one screw using constraints, and then use the **Reuse Pattern** command to place screws in the remaining holes.

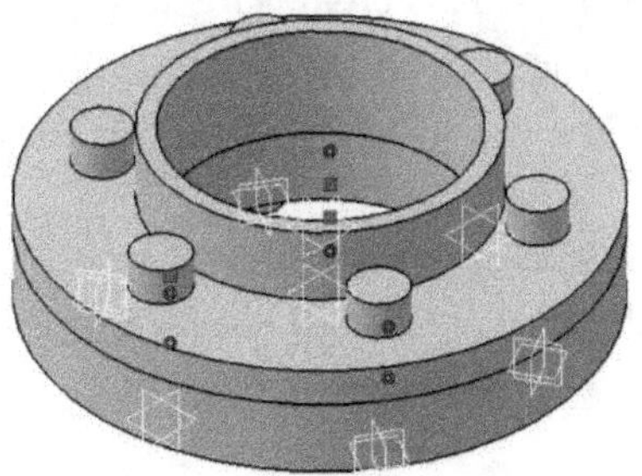

1. Position the screw in one hole using the **Coincidence Constraint**, **Contact Constraint**, and **Angle Constraint**.

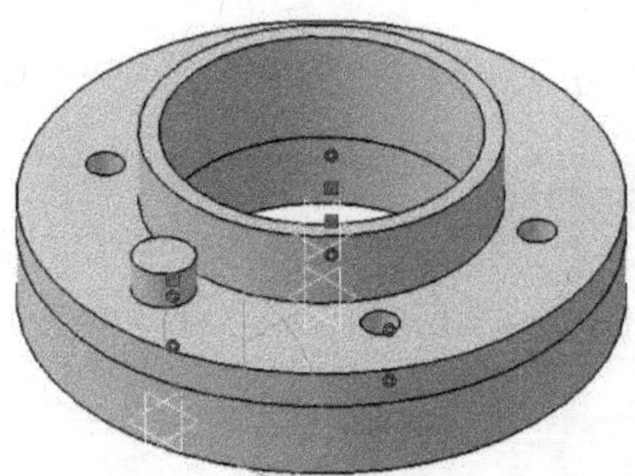

2. On the **Constraints** toolbar, click the **Reuse Pattern** button (or) click **Insert > Reuse Pattern** on the Menu bar.
3. In the Specification Tree, expand the **Constraints** section and select the **Coincidence** constraint related to the screw. The pattern preview appears.

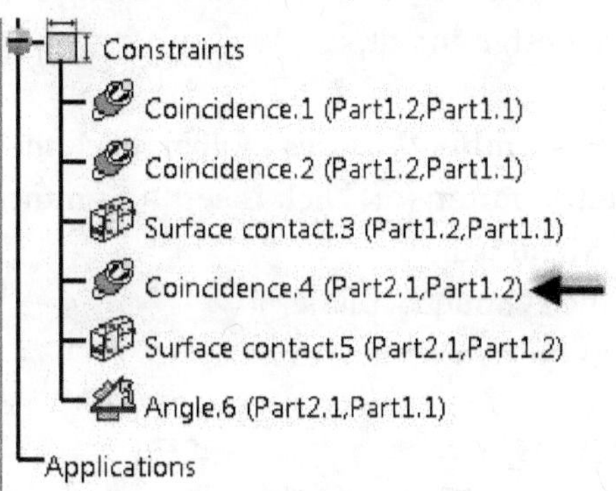

4. On the **Instantiation on a pattern** dialog, check the **Keep link with the pattern** option. This links the components with the pattern.

5. Select the **generated constraints** option to apply constraints to individual instances of the pattern.
6. Select **First instance on pattern > re-use the original component**. This creates instances at all the locations on the pattern except the original one.

If you select **create a new instance**, new instances of the component will be created at all the locations on the pattern.

If you select **cut & paste the original component**, the original component will be pasted at all the locations on the pattern.

7. Click **OK**. The screw will be replicated using the existing pattern.

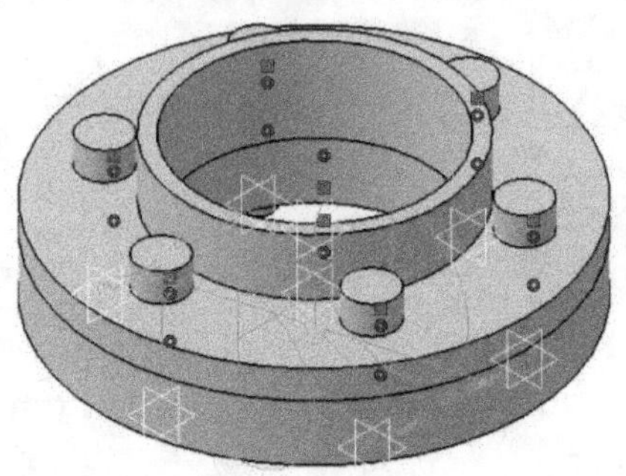

Symmetry

When designing symmetric assemblies, the **Symmetry** command will help you in saving time and capture design intent.

1. On the **Assembly Features** toolbar, click the **Symmetry** button (or) click **Insert > Symmetry** on the Menu bar.
2. Select the symmetry plane.
3. Click on the component to mirror.

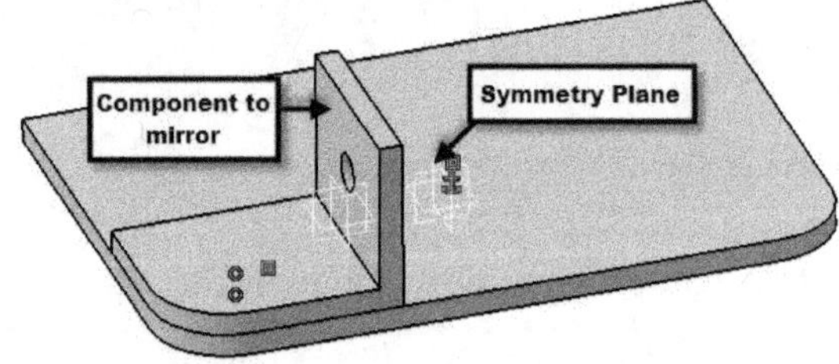

4. On the **Assembly Symmetry Wizard** dialog, select **Mirror, new component** to mirror the component about the symmetry plane.

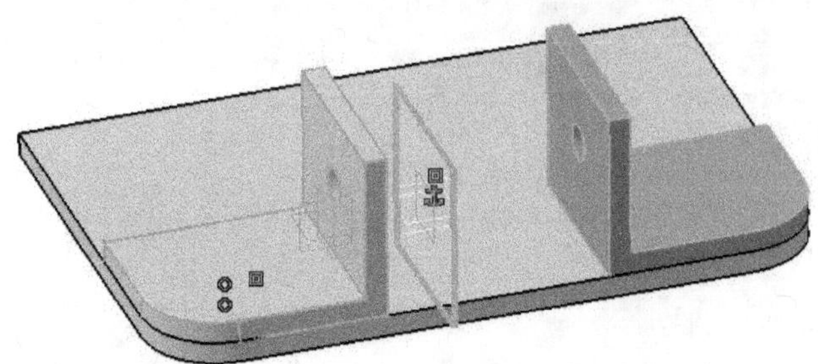

Select **Rotation, new instance** to create a new instance of the selected component and rotate it about the symmetry plane.

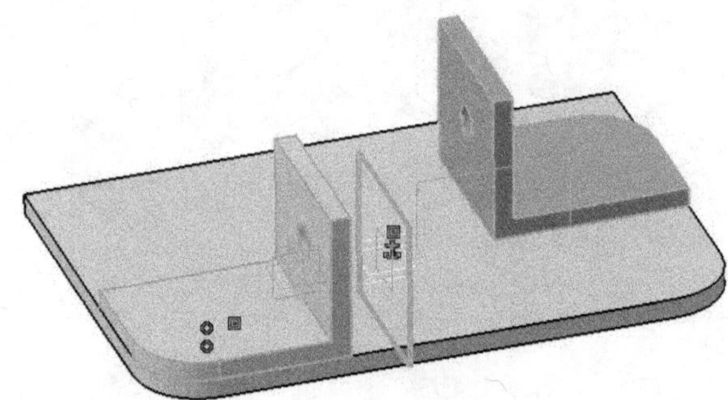

Select **Rotation, same instance** to rotate the selected instance about the symmetry plane.

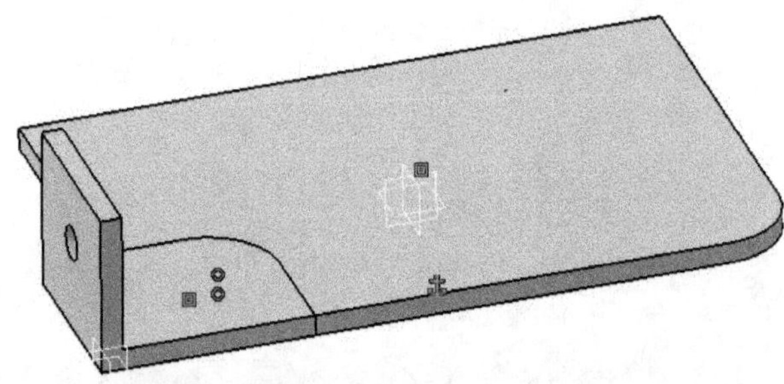

Select **Translation, new instance** to create a new instance and translate it.

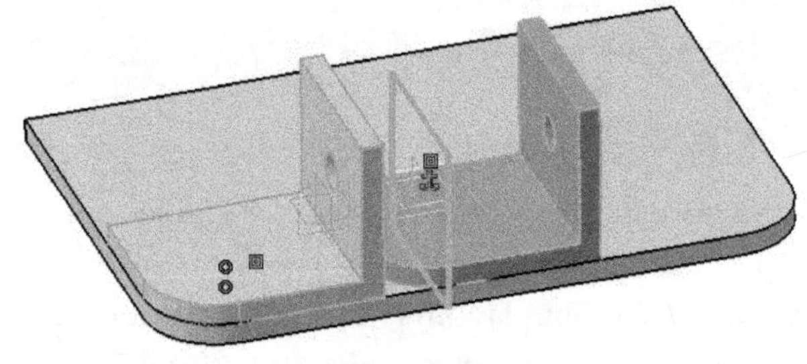

5. Select the required options under the **Geometry to be mirrored in new part**.
6. If you want to associate the mirrored component with original, then check the **Keep link with position** and **Keep link with geometry** options.
7. Click **Finish**, and then **Close**.

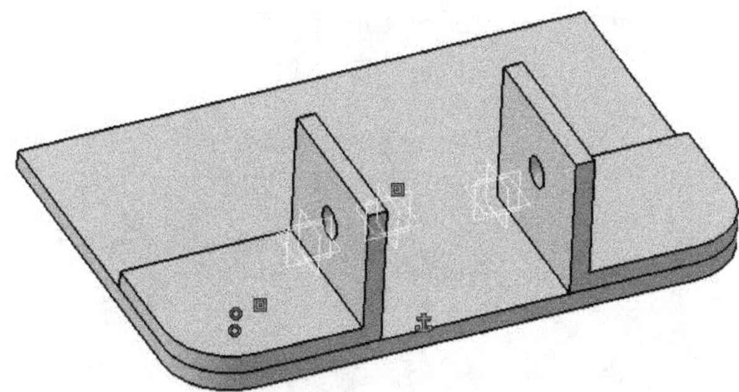

Sub-assemblies

The use of sub-assemblies has many advantages in CATIA V5. Sub-assemblies make large assemblies easier to manage. They make it easy for multiple users to collaborate on a single large assembly design. They can also affect the way you document a large assembly design in 2D drawings. For these reasons, it is important for you to create sub-assemblies in a variety of ways. The easiest way to create a sub-assembly is to insert an existing assembly into another assembly. Next, apply constraints to constrain the assembly. The process of applying constraints is also simplified. You are required to apply constraints between only one part of a sub-assembly and a part of the main assembly. In addition, you can easily hide a group of components with the help of sub-assemblies. To do this, right-click on a sub-assembly and select **Hide/Show**.

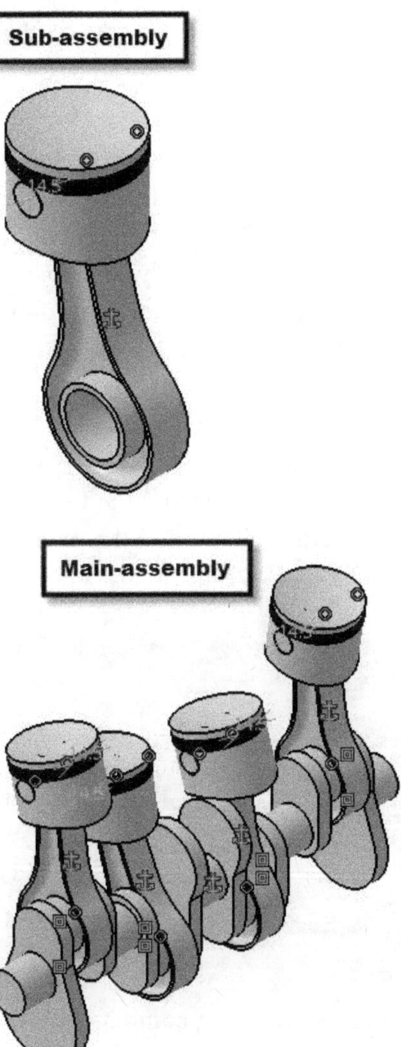

Top Down Assembly Design

In CATIA V5, there are two methods to create an assembly. The method you are probably familiar with is to create individual components, and then insert them into an assembly. This method is known as Bottom-Up Assembly Design. The second method is called Top Down Assembly Design. In this method, you will create individual components within the Assembly Design Workbench. This allows you to design an individual part while taking into account how it will interact with other components in an assembly. There are several advantages in Top-Down Assembly Design. As you design a part within the assembly, you can be sure that it will fit properly. You can also use reference geometry from the other components.

Creating a New Part

Top-down assembly design can be used to add new parts to an already existing assembly.

1. To create a part at the assembly level using the Top down Design, activate the **Part** command (click the **Part** button on the **Product Structure Tools** toolbar).
2. In the Specification Tree, click **Product1**. A part file is created.
3. In the Specification Tree, expand the Part1 section, and then double-click on the part name. This activates the **Part Design** workbench.

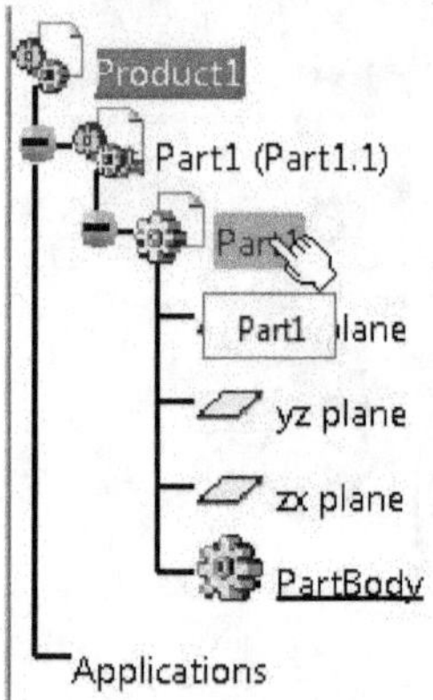

4. Now, use the part modeling commands and create the part geometry.

5. In the Specification Tree, double-click on **Product1** to switch to the Assembly Design workbench.
6. To create the second component, activate the **Part** command and select **Product1** in the Specification Tree. The **New Part: Origin Point** message appears.
7. Click **Yes** to define a new origin for the component (or) click **No** to use the assembly origin for the component.
8. If you click **Yes**, then you have to select a point or component to define the origin.

9. In the Specification Tree, expand Part2 and double-click on **Part2**.

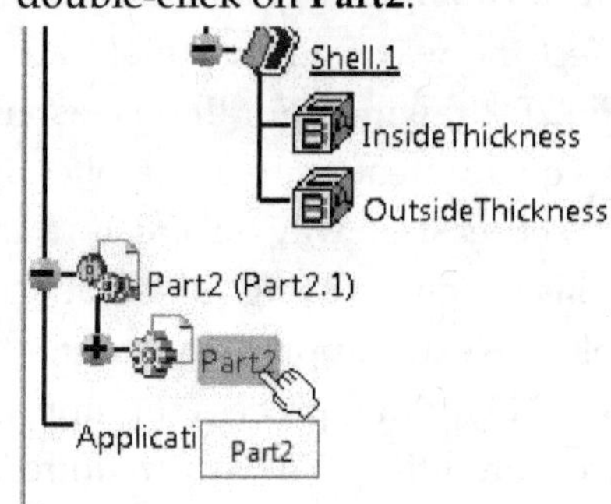

10. On the Menu bar, click **Tools > Options** to open the **Options** dialog.
11. On the **Options** dialog, click **Infrastructure > Part Infrastructure**.
12. On the **General** tab, check the **Keep Link with selected object**. Click **OK**.

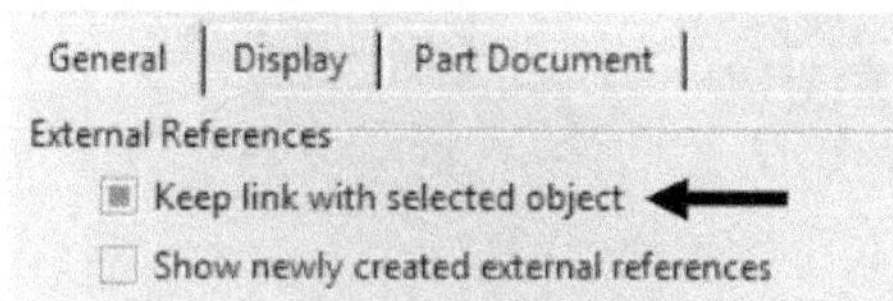

13. Now, you can create the part by using the faces and edges of the first part as reference. For example, activate the **Sketch** command and select the top face of the first part.

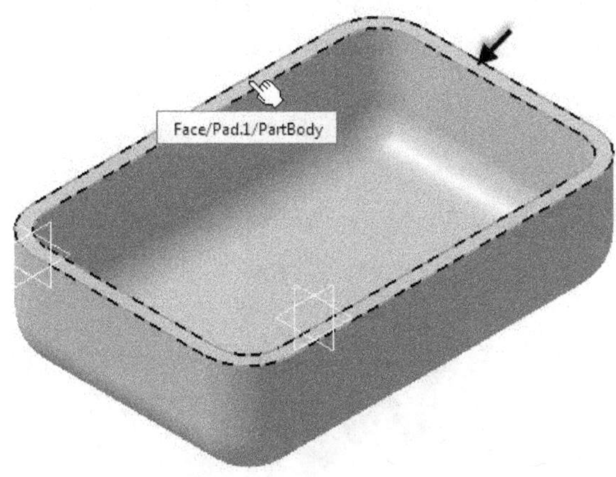

14. Activate the **Project 3D Elements** command and project the outer edges of the first component.

15. Exit the Sketcher Workbench.
16. Use the sketch to create a *Pad* feature.

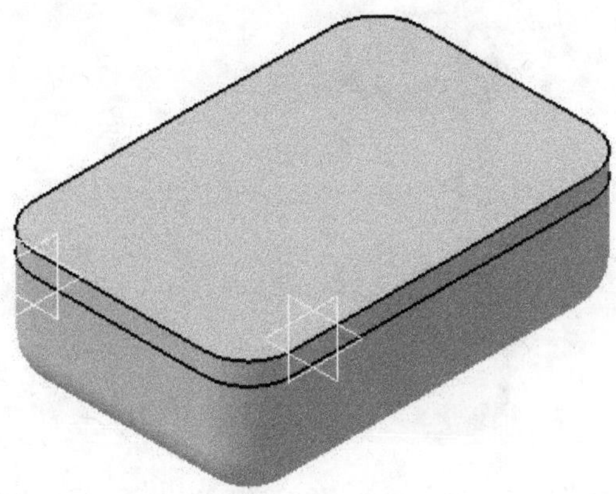

17. Activate the first component and modify the model.

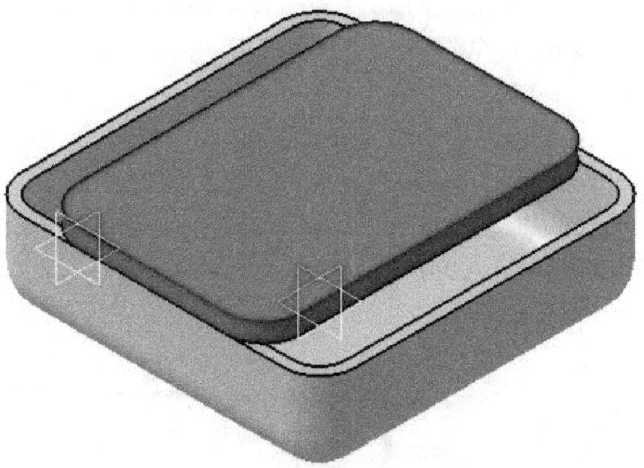

18. Return to the **Assembly Design** workbench to see that the second component is update, automatically.

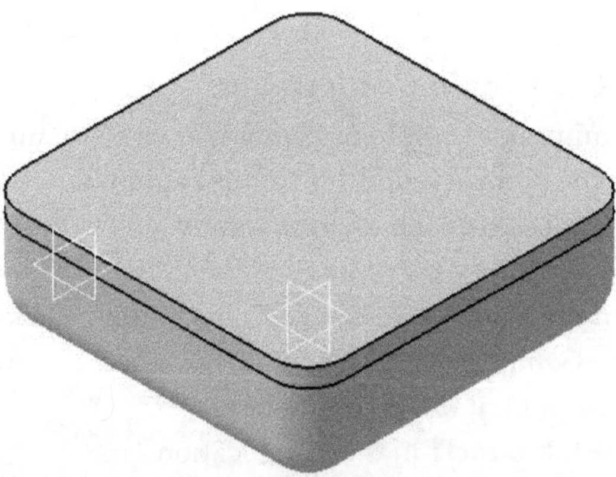

19. To save the assembly and its components, click **File > Save Management** on the Menu bar.
20. On the **Save Management** dialog, click on the Product, and then click the **Save as** button.
21. Define the location and file name of the product, and then click **Save**.
22. Likewise, save the components of the assembly.
23. Click **OK**.

Creating a Product

The **Product** command creates a new assembly inside the main assembly. The assembly and its parts will be saved as separate files.

1. On the **Product Structure Tools** toolbar, click the **Product** button (or) click **Insert > New Product** on the Menu bar.

2. In the Specification tree, click **Product1**. A new assembly will be listed inside the main assembly.
3. Double-click on **Product2** to activate it.
4. Create individual parts of the assembly.
5. Save the assembly. You will notice that separate files are created for the main assembly, sub-assembly, and parts.

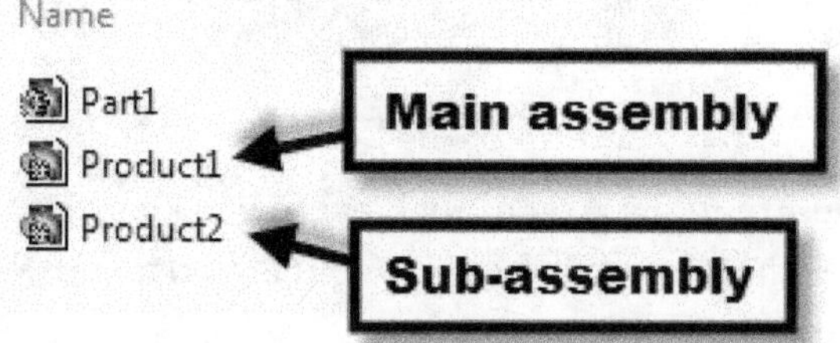

Creating a Component

The **Component** command creates a new assembly inside the main assembly. The sub-assembly will be an integral part of the main assembly.

1. On the **Product Structure Tools** toolbar, click the **Component** button (or) click **Insert > New Component** on the Menu bar.
2. Click **Product1** in the Specification Tree.
3. Create individual parts inside the sub-assembly.
4. Save the assembly. You will notice that only the files of the main assembly and parts are created. The sub-assembly file is not created.

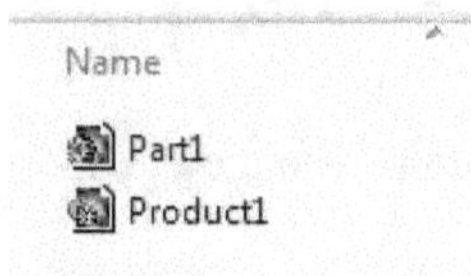

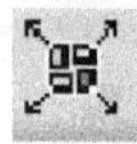

Explode

To document an assembly design properly, it is very common to create an exploded view. In an exploded view, the components of an assembly are pulled apart to show how they were assembled.

1. To create an exploded view, activate the **Explode** command (click **Explode** on the **Move** toolbar (or) click **Edit > Move Explode in assembly design**).
2. On the **Explode** dialog, click in the **Fixed product** box and select the part to be fixed at its location.

3. Select **Depth > All Levels** on the **Explode** dialog. This explodes all the parts including the one in subassemblies. If you select **Depth >First Level**, the parts in subassemblies will not be exploded.
4. Select **Type > Constrained**. This explodes the parts with respect to the constraints existing between parts.

If you select **Type > 3D**, the parts will be exploded randomly in the 3D space, as shown.

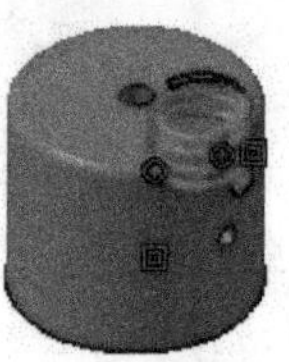

If you select **Type > 2D**, the parts will be exploded in a 2D plane parallel to the viewpoint. For example, if you set the viewpoint to front plane, the parts will be exploded in the front plane.

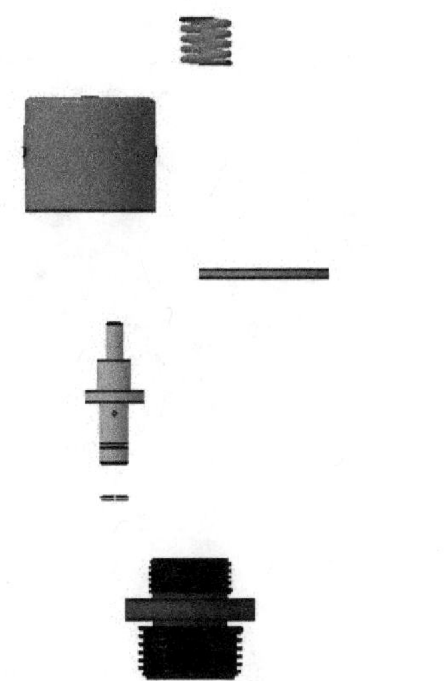

5. Click **Apply**. The **Information Box** appears. Click **OK** to close the box.

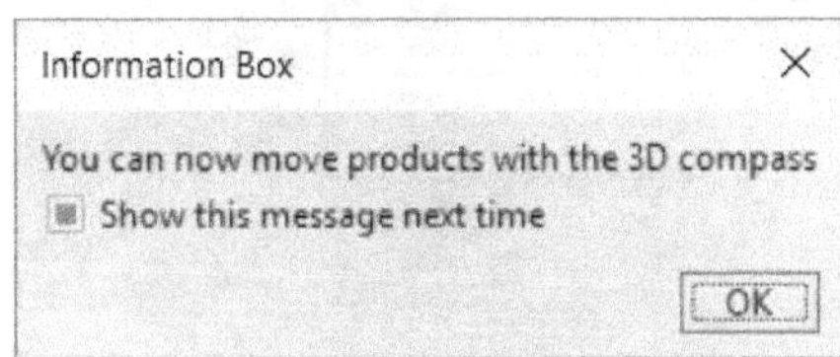

6. Drag the scroller on the **Explode** dialog to change the explode distance.

Examples

Example 1 (Bottom Up Assembly)

In this example, you will create the assembly shown next.

7. Click **OK**, and then **Yes**.

8. Click the **Update All** button to switch back to the assembled view.

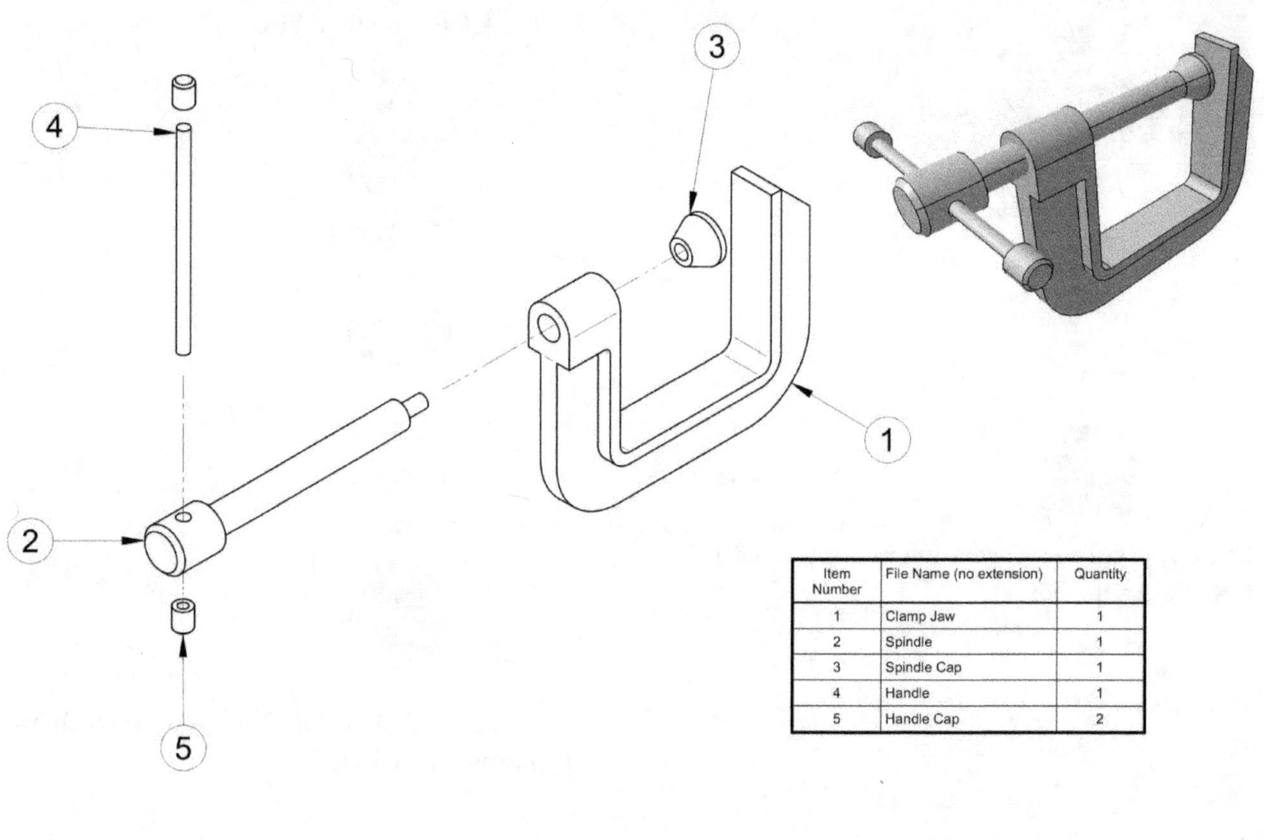

Item Number	File Name (no extension)	Quantity
1	Clamp Jaw	1
2	Spindle	1
3	Spindle Cap	1
4	Handle	1
5	Handle Cap	2

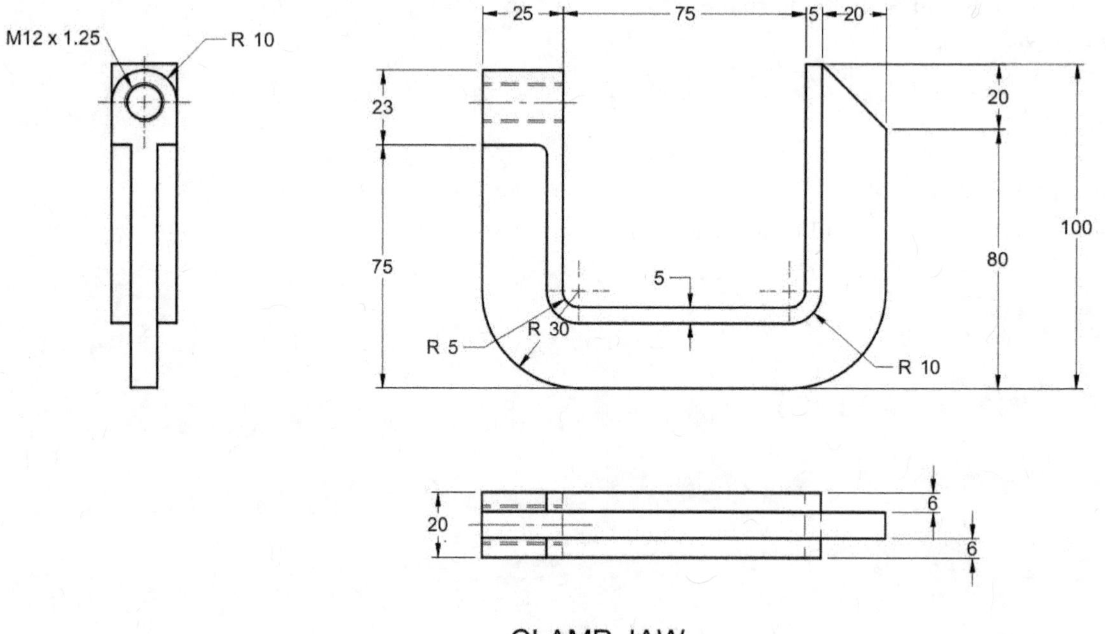

CLAMP JAW

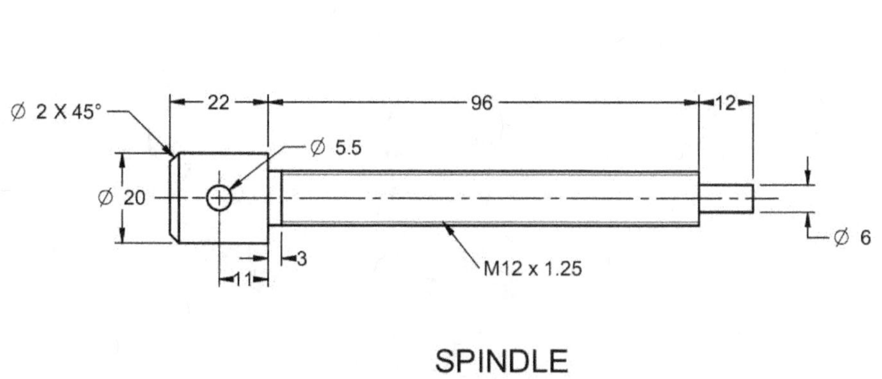

SPINDLE

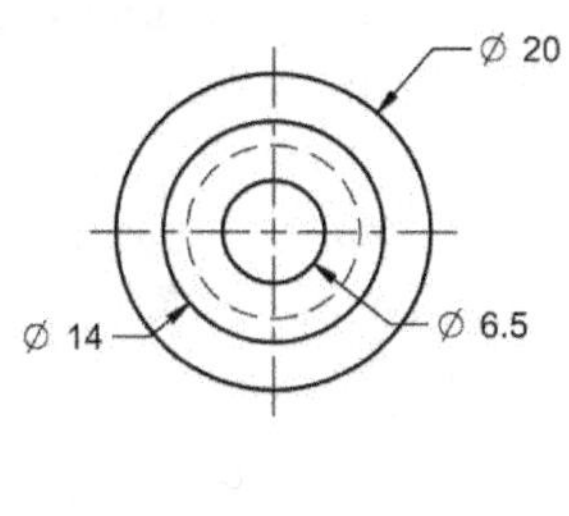

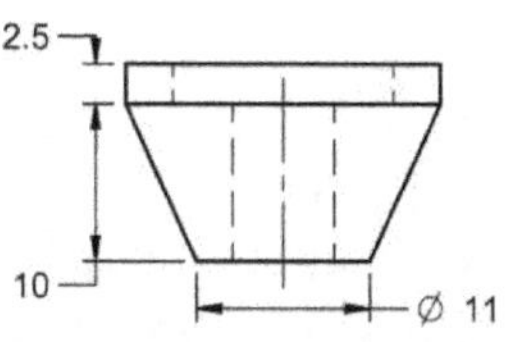

SPINDLE CAP

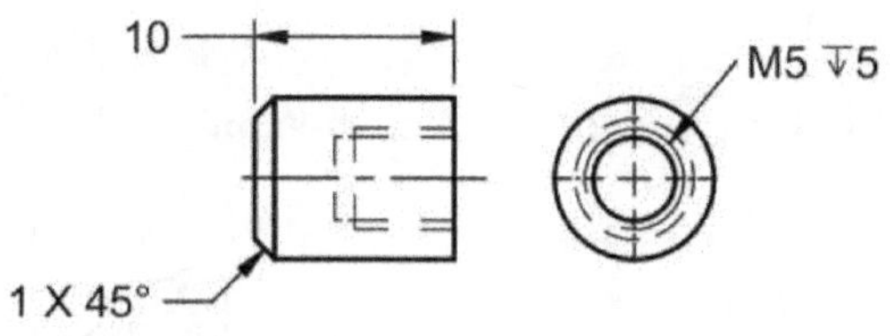

HANDLE CAP

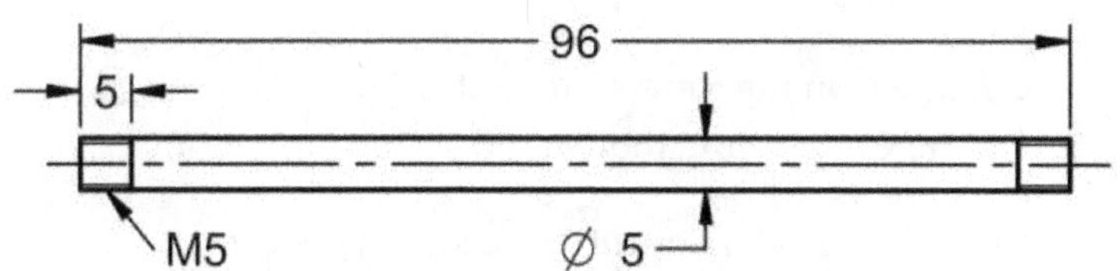

HANDLE

1. Start **CATIA V5-6R2017**.
2. Create and save all the components of the assembly in a single folder. Name this folder as *G-Clamp*. Close all the files.
3. On the Menu, click **Start > Mechanical Design > Assembly Design**.
4. On the **Product Structure Tools** toolbar, click the **Existing Component** icon (or) select **Insert > Existing Component** on the menu.
5. Click **Product1** in the Specification tree.
6. On the **File Selection** dialog, go to the *G-Clamp* folder. Select *Clamp Jaw* and click **Open**.
7. On the **View** toolbar, click **Quick View** drop-down > **Isometric View 0]0/**.
8. On the **Constraints** toolbar, click the **Fix Component** icon and select the Clamp Jaw. This fixes the component at the origin.

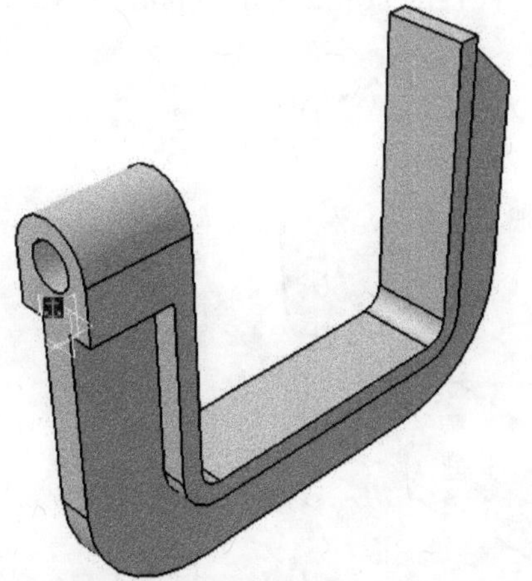

9. On the **Product Structure Tools** toolbar, click the **Existing Component With Positioning** icon (or) select **Insert > Existing Component with Positioning** on the menu.
10. Click **Product1** in the Specification tree.
11. On the **File Selection** dialog, select *Spindle*, and then click **Open**.

12. On the **Part number conflicts** dialog, click **Automatic rename**, and then click **OK**.
13. On the **Smart Move** dialog, click and drag the component so that it is positioned, as shown in figure.

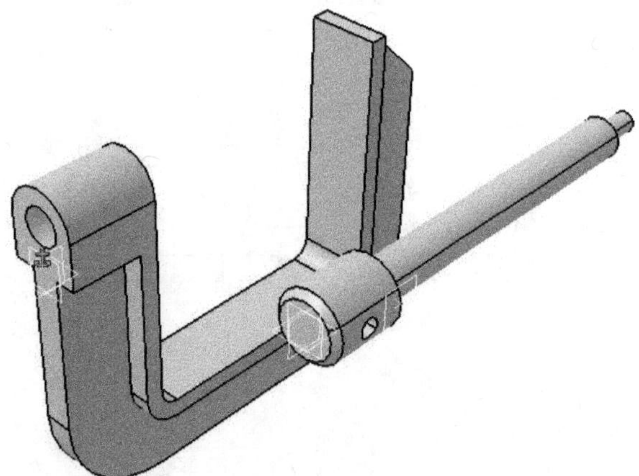

14. Click **OK** on the **Smart Move** dialog.
15. On the **Constraints** toolbar, click the **Coincidence Constraint** icon (or) select **Insert > Coincidence** on the Menu.
16. On the **Assistant** message, check **Do not prompt in future** option, and then click **Close**.
17. Select the axes of the spindle and clamp jaw.

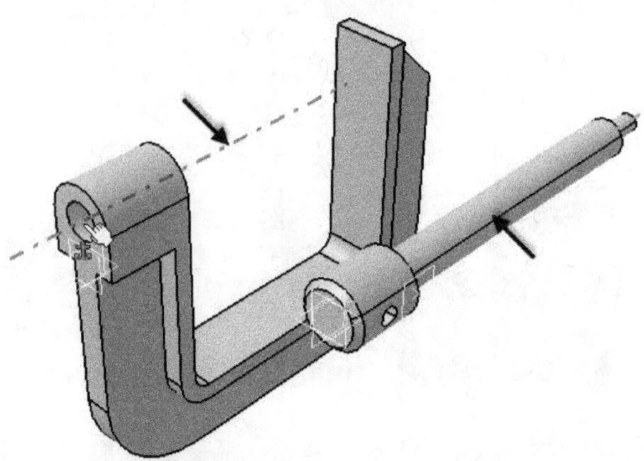

18. On the **Constraints** toolbar, click the **Offset Constraint** icon (or) click **Inset > Offset** on the Menu.
19. Click on the front face of the clamp jaw and that of the spindle.

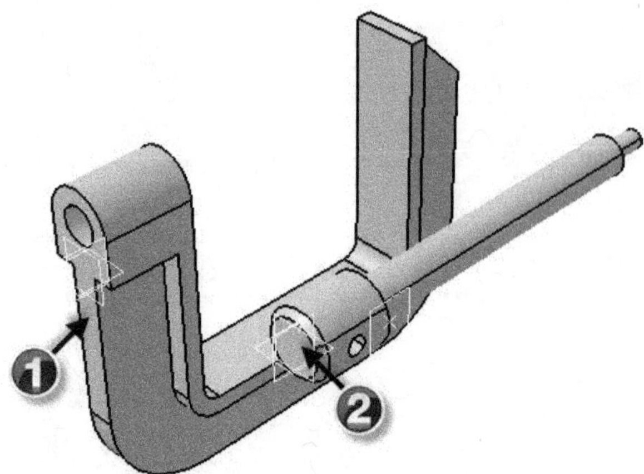

20. On the **Constraint Properties** dialog, set the **Orientation** to **Same** and type-in **40** in the **Offset** box.
21. Click **OK**.
22. On the **Update** toolbar, click the **Update All** icon.

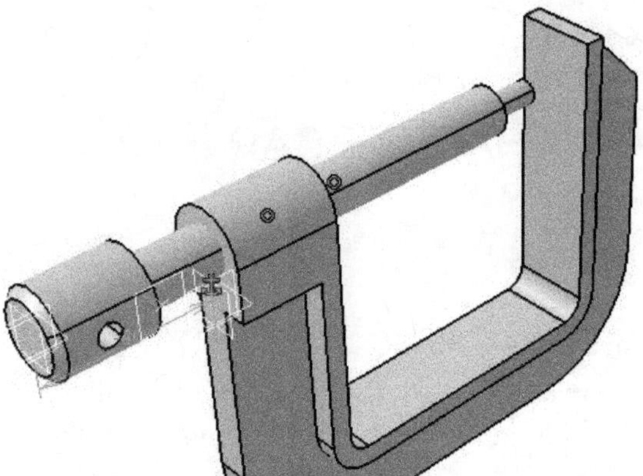

23. In the Specification tree, click the right mouse button on **Part 1.1** and select **Part1.1.1 object > Component Degrees of Freedom**.

The **Degrees of Freedom Analysis** dialog appears on the screen. It shows **Rotation** in Degrees of Freedom section. In addition, a rotation symbol appears on the spindle.

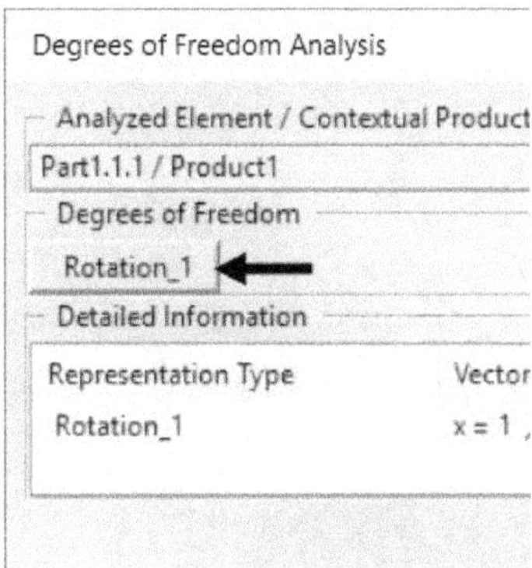

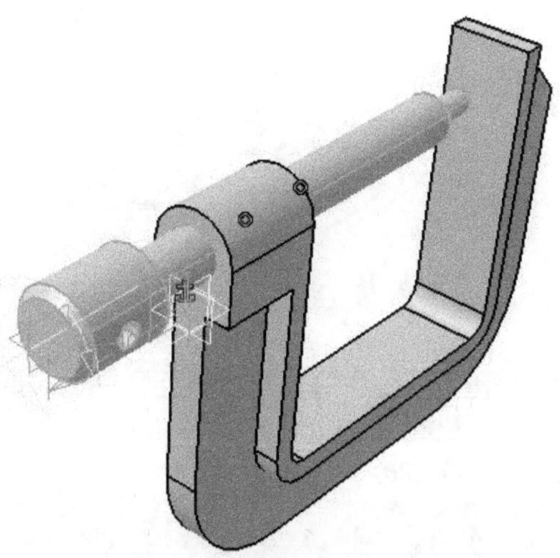

24. Close the **Degrees of Freedom Analysis** dialog.
25. On the **Constraints** toolbar, click the **Angle Constraint** icon (or) select **Insert > Angle** on the Menu.
26. Click on the XY plane of the *Spindle* and bottom flat face of the *Clamp Jaw*.

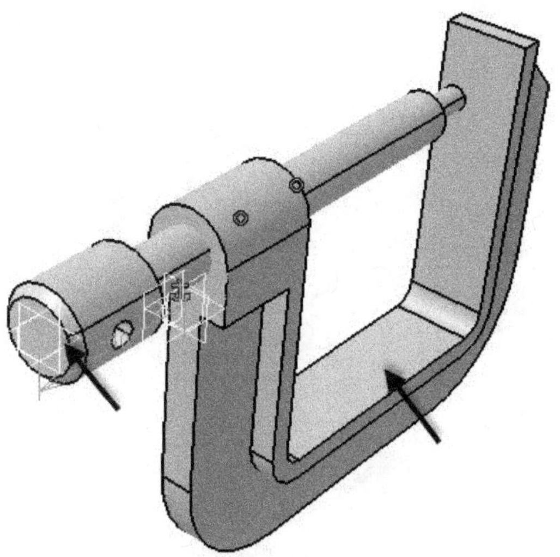

27. On the **Constraint Properties** dialog, select the **Parallelism** option and set the **Orientation** to **Same**.
28. Click **OK** to apply the parallel constraint.

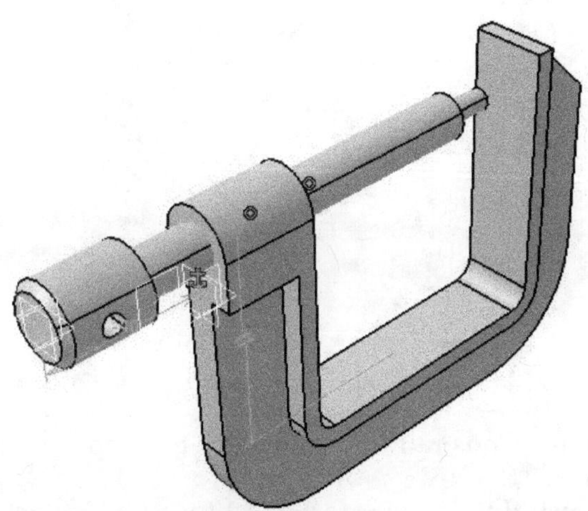

29. Now, check the degrees of freedom of the spindle. You will notice that it is fully constrained.
30. Insert the *Spindle Cap* into the assembly window.

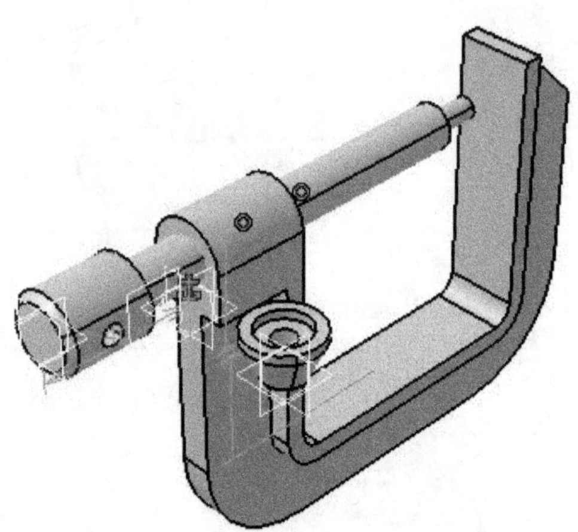

31. Activate the **Coincidence Constraint** command and click on the axes of the spindle and spindle cap.

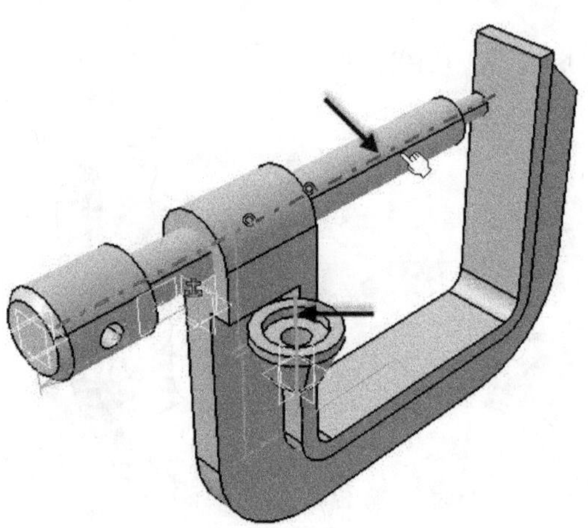

32. On the **Constraints** toolbar, click the **Contact Constraint** icon (or) select **Insert > Contact** on the Menu.
33. Rotate the assembly and click on the bottom face of the spindle cap.

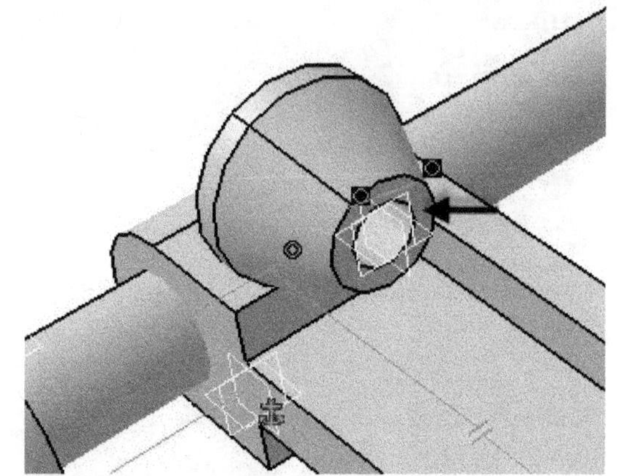

34. Rotate the assembly and click on the face, as shown below.

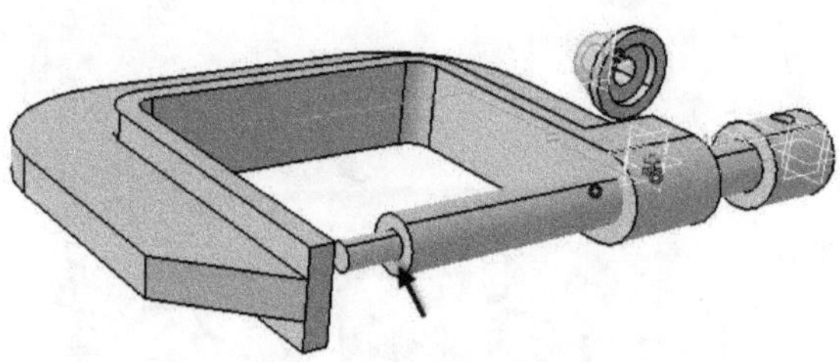

35. Activate the **Angle Constraint** command.
36. Select the zx plane of the spindle cap and that of the spindle.

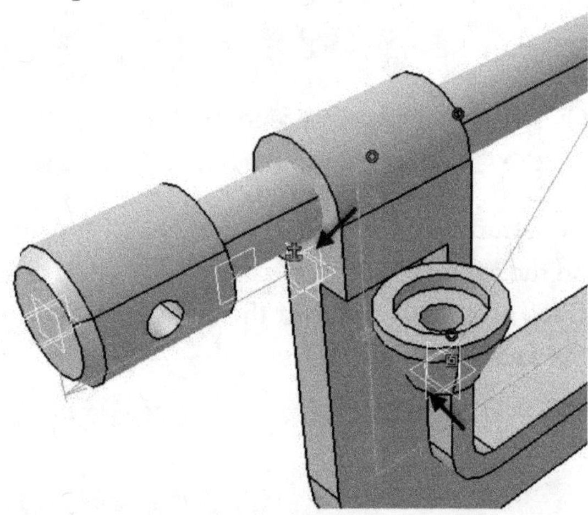

37. On the **Constraint Properties** dialog, select the **Parallelism** option and set the **Orientation** to **Same**.
38. Click **OK** to apply the parallel constraint.
39. On the **Update** toolbar, click the **Update All** icon.

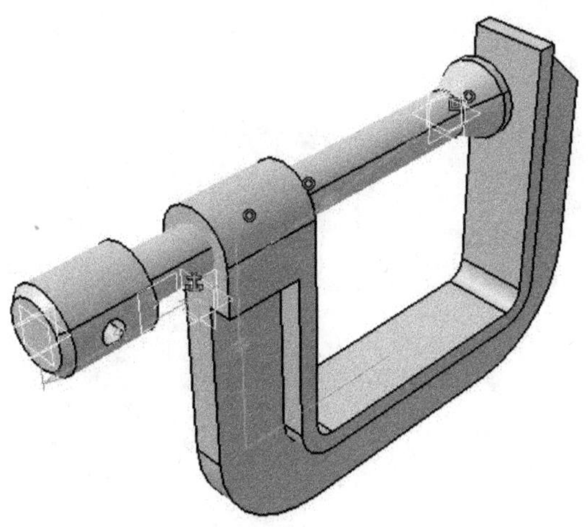

40. Insert the *Handle* into the assembly.

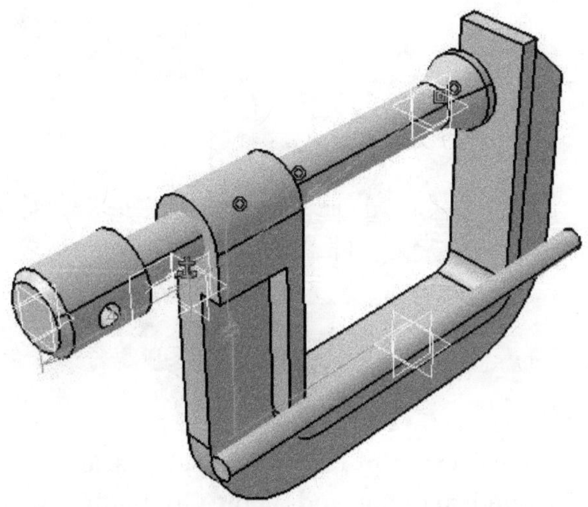

41. Activate the **Coincidence Constraint** command and select the axes of the handle and the hole on the spindle.

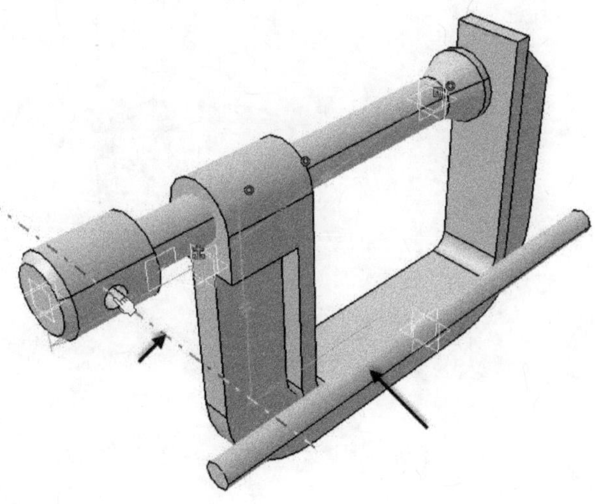

42. Activate the **Offset Constraint** command.
43. Click on the yz plane of the handle and zx plane of the spindle.

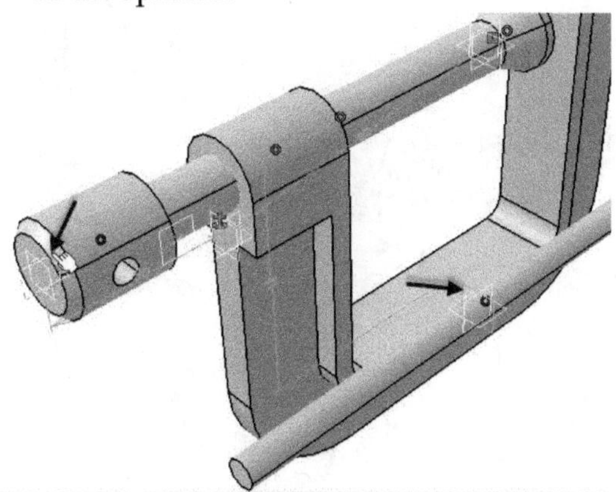

44. On the **Constraint Properties** dialog, type-in **0** in the **Offset** box and click **OK.**
45. On the **Update** toolbar, click the **Update All** icon.
46. Insert the *Handle cap* into the Assembly window.

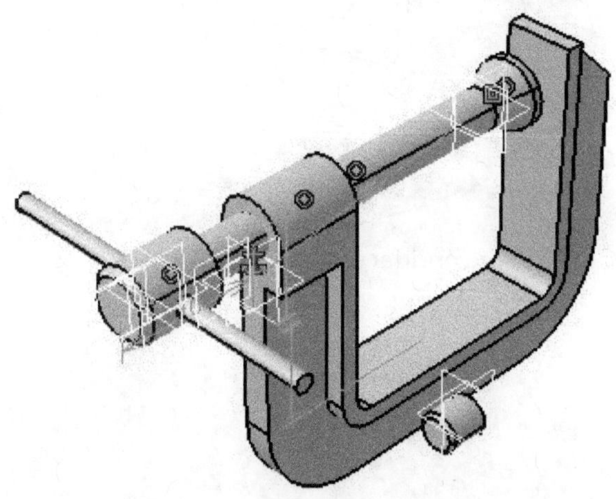

47. Activate the **Coincidence Constraint** command, and then select the axes of the handle and handle cap.

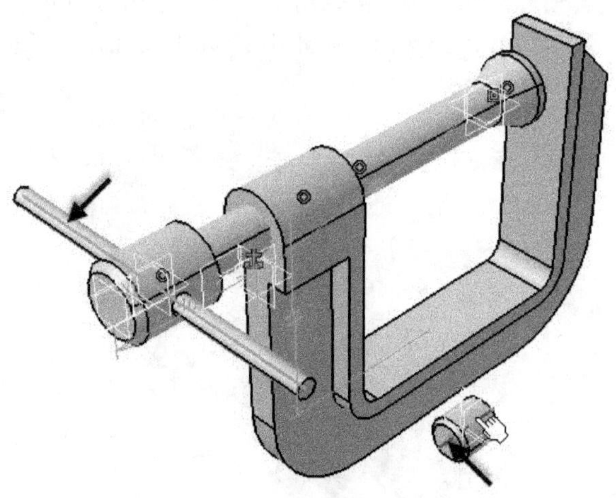

48. Activate the **Contact Constraint** command and click on the innermost flat face of the handle cap.

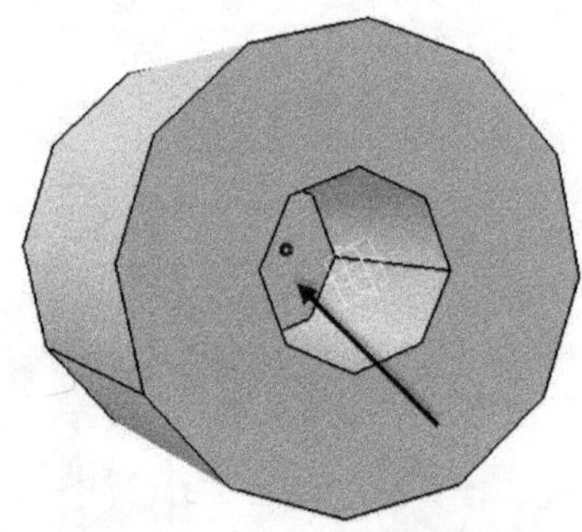

49. Click on the end face of the handle.

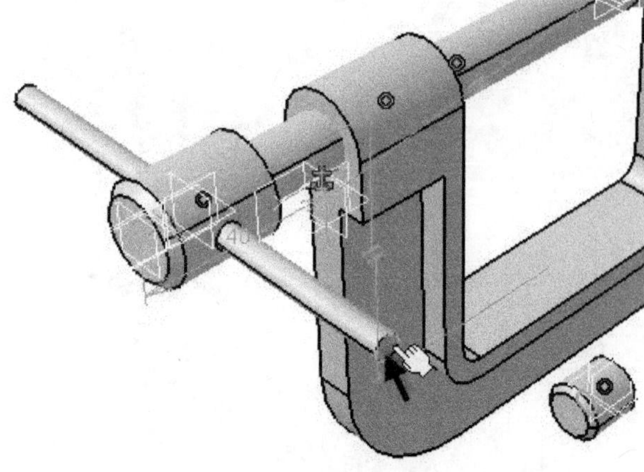

50. Activate the **Angle Constraint** command, and then select the xy planes of the handle and handle cap.

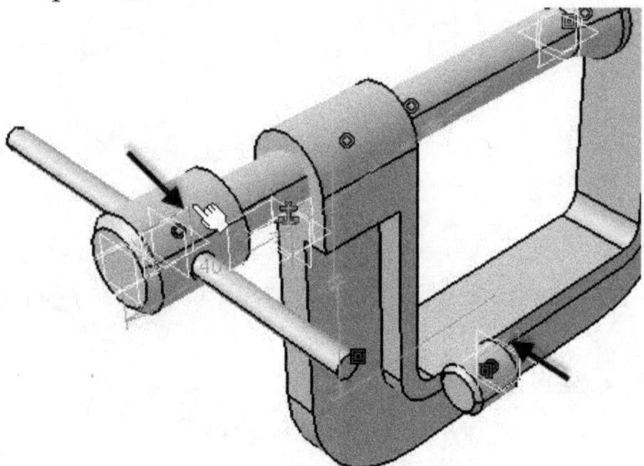

51. On the **Constraint Properties** dialog, select the **Parallelism** option and set the **Orientation** to **Same**.
52. Click **OK** to apply the parallel constraint.
53. On the **Update** toolbar, click the **Update All**  icon.

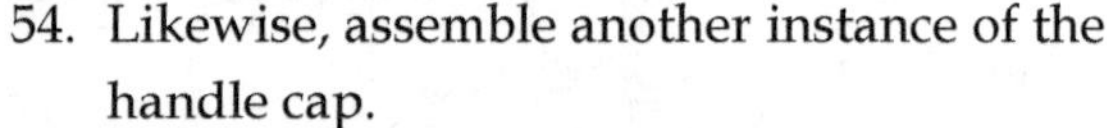

54. Likewise, assemble another instance of the handle cap.

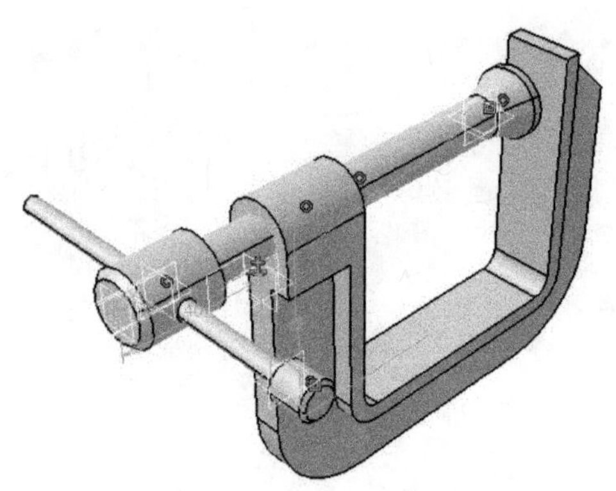

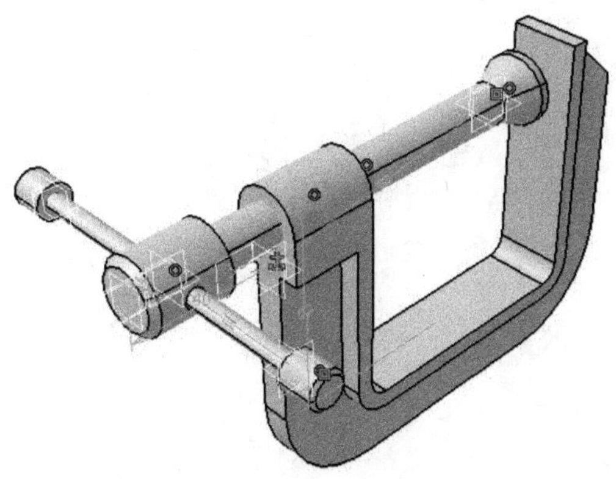

55. Save and close the assembly.

Example 2 (Top Down Assembly)

In this example, you will create the assembly shown next.

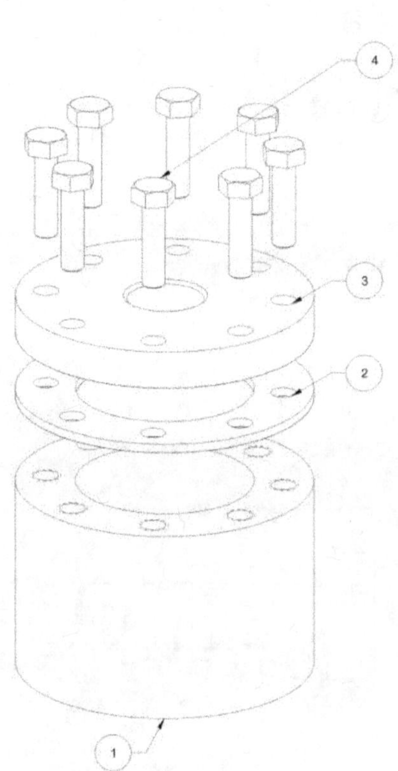

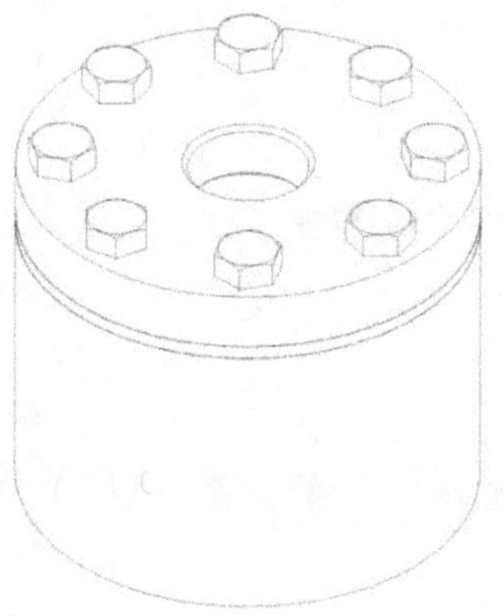

4	HEX BOLT AM,M8X1.25X30	8
3	COVER PLATE	1
2	GASKET	1
1	CYLINDER BASE	1
PC NO	PART NAME	QTY

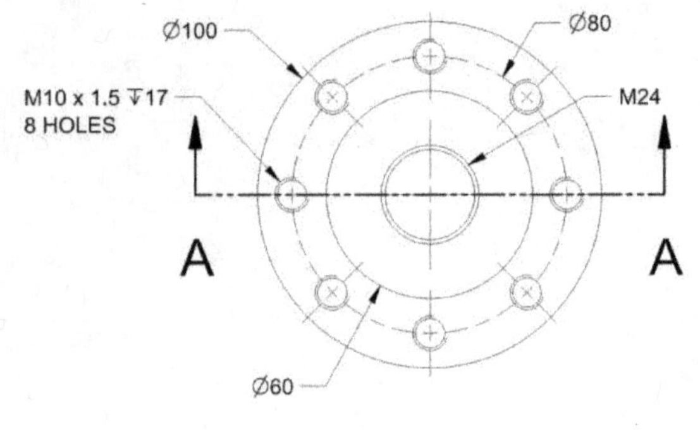

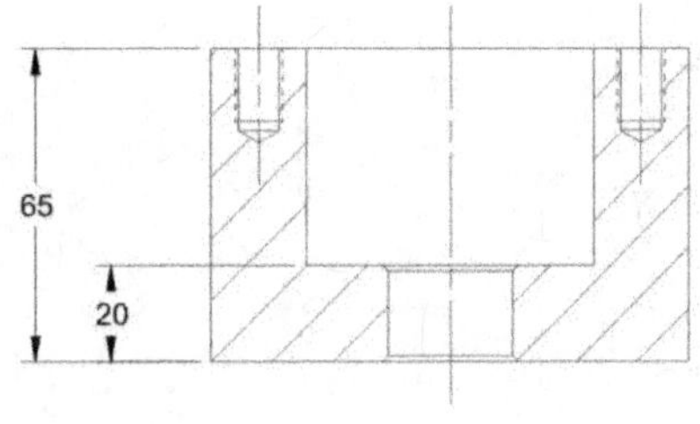

SECTION A-A

Cylinder Base

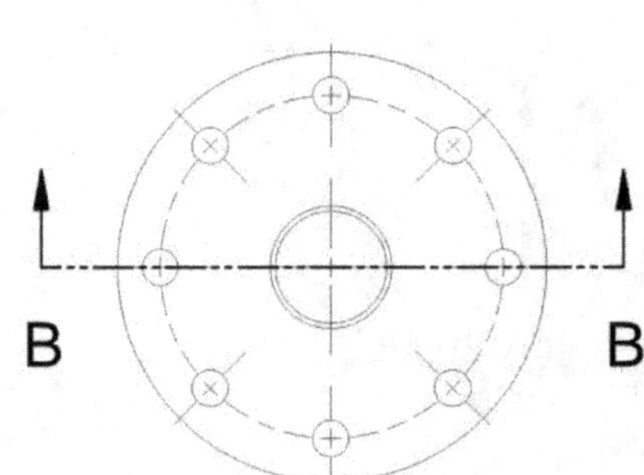

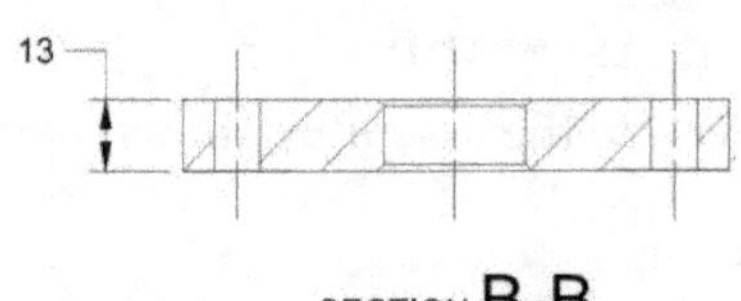

SECTION B-B

Cover Plate

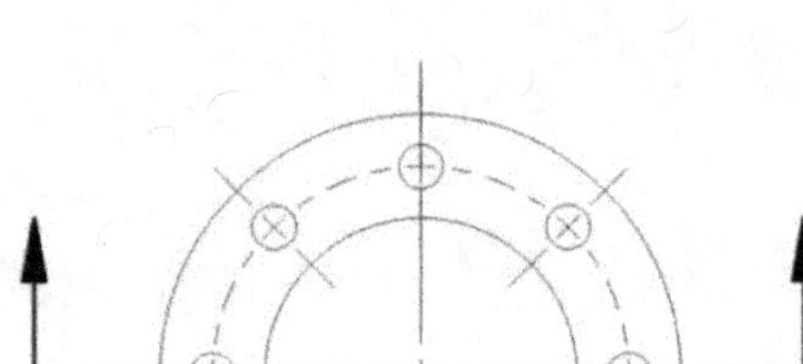

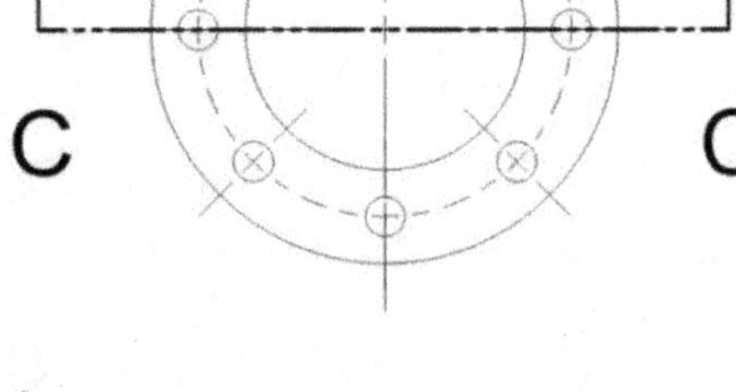

SECTION C-C

Gasket

15

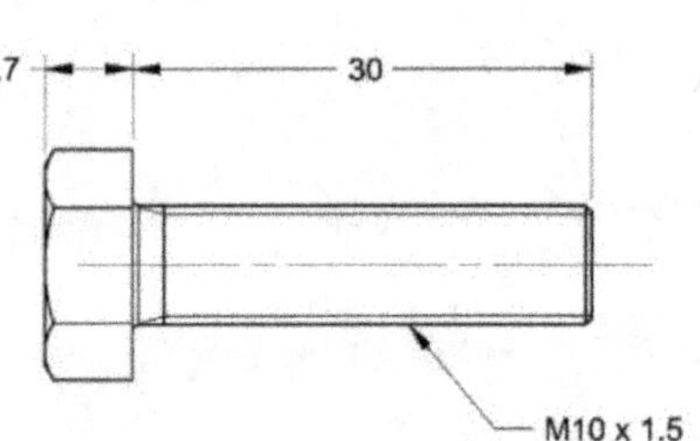

Screw

1. Start **CATIA V5-6R2017**.
2. On the Menu bar, click **File > New** to open the **New** dialog.

3. On the **New** dialog, select **List of Types > Product** and click **OK**.
4. On the **Product Structure Tools** toolbar, click the **Part** button.
5. Select **Product 1** from the Specification Tree. This creates a new part file inside the assembly.
6. In the Specification Tree, expand **Product 1 > Part 1(Part 1.1) > Part 1**.
7. Double-click on Part 1 to activate the part mode.
8. Draw a sketch on the zx plane and revolve it.

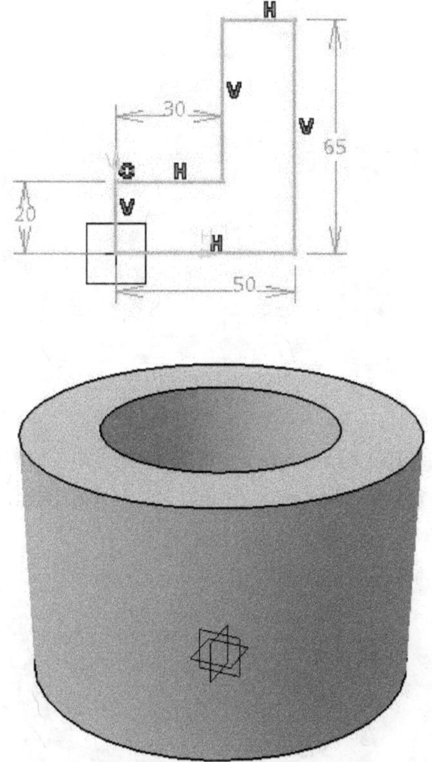

9. Create a threaded hole on the top face of the model.

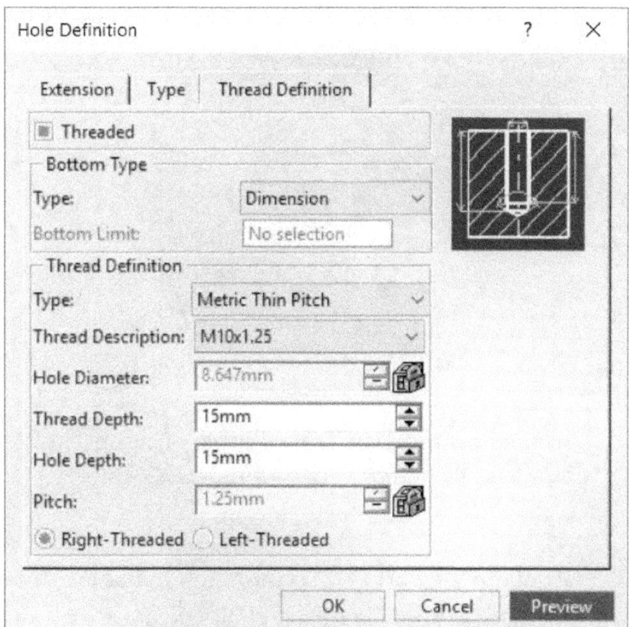

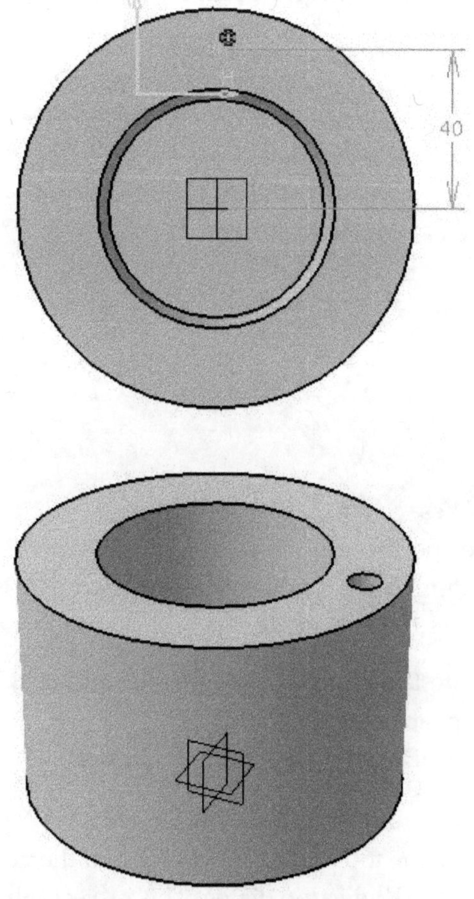

10. Create a circular pattern of the hole. The number of holes in the pattern are 8.

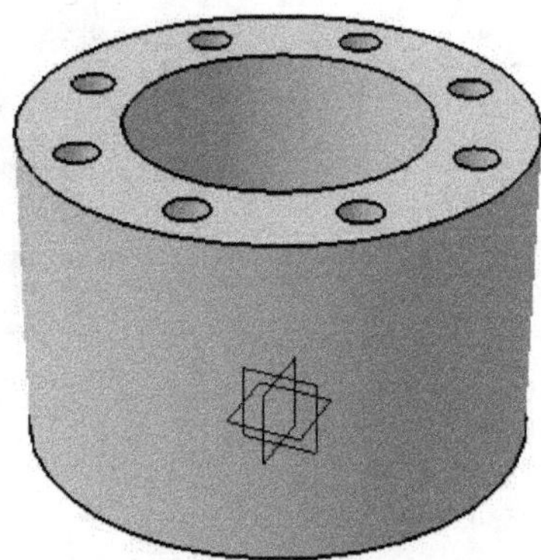

11. In the Specification Tree, double-click on **Product 1** to switch back to the Assembly mode.
12. Activate the **Part** command (On the **Product Structure Tools** toolbar, click the **Part** button) and select **Product1** from the Specification Tree. The **New Part: Origin Point** alert message pops up on the screen.

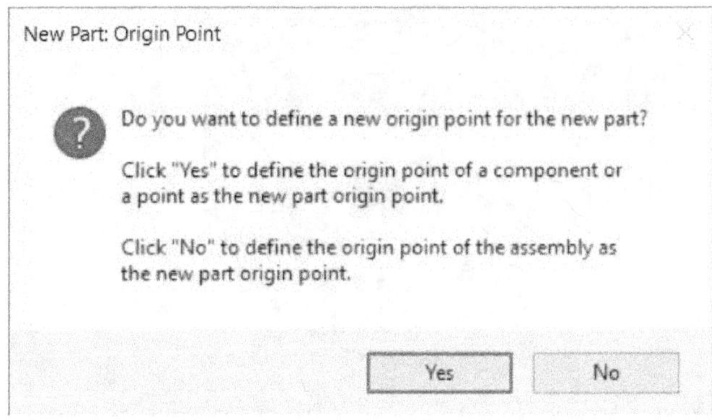

13. Click **Yes**.
14. In the Specification Tree, expand the **Part 2 (Part 2.1)** item and double-click on **Part 2**. This activates the Part mode.
15. Activate the **Sketch** command and click on the top face of the model.
16. On the **3D Geometry** toolbar, click the **Project 3D Elements** button.
17. Click on the top face of the model, and then click **OK** on the **Projection** dialog. This projects all the edges of the top face onto the sketch plane.

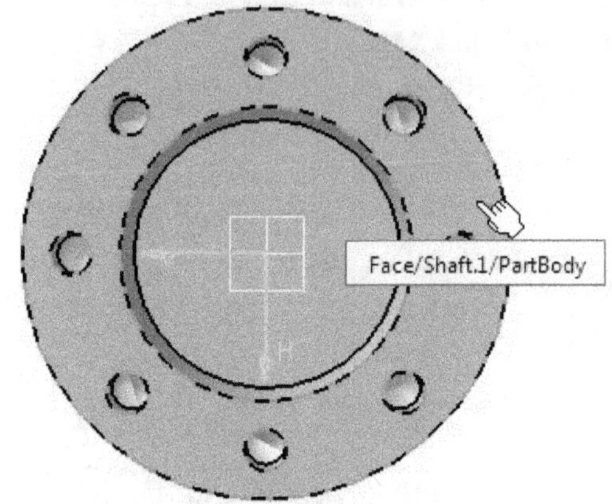

18. Exit the Sketcher workbench.
19. Extrude the sketch up to 3 mm length in the upward direction.

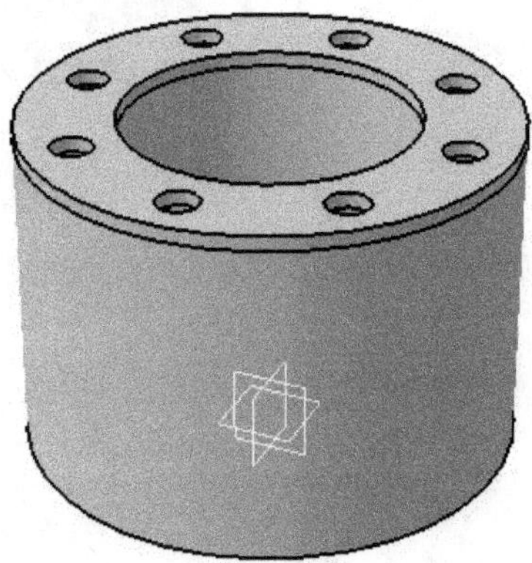

20. In the Specification Tree, double-click on **Product1** to activate the assembly mode.
21. Activate the **Part** command and create a new part file inside the assembly.

22. In the Specification Tree, double-click on Part3 to activate the part mode.
23. Start a sketch on the top face of the gasket.

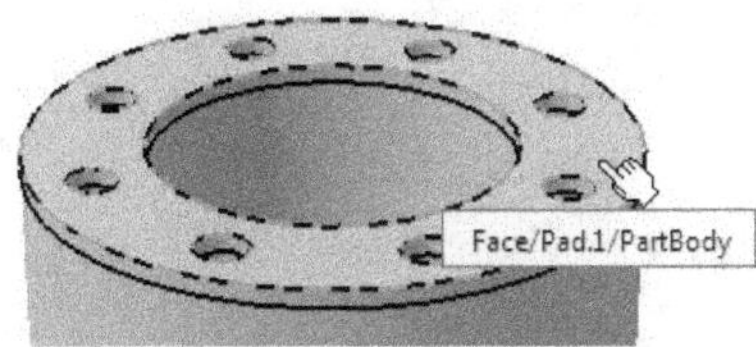

24. Project the outer circular edge and the edges of the holes.

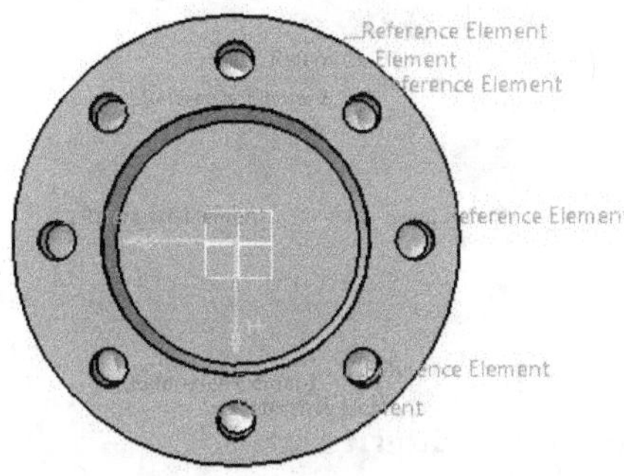

25. Exit the sketch and extrude it up to 13 mm length.

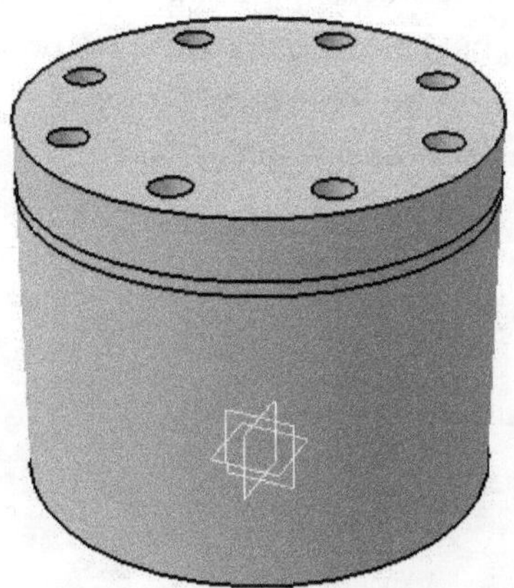

26. Activate the **Sketch** command and click on the top face of the Extruded feature.
27. On the **Profile** toolbar, click the **Point** icon, and then select the origin point.
28. Exit the Sketcher Workbench.

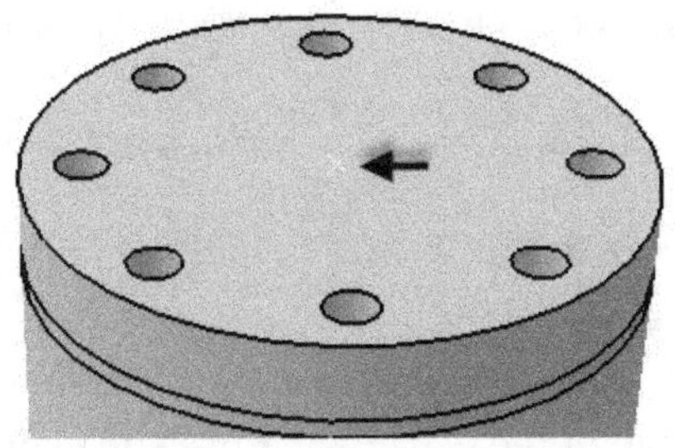

29. Activate the Assembly mode by clicking **Product1** in the Specification Tree.
30. Activate the **Part** command create a new part inside the assembly.
31. Expand the Specification Tree and double-click on Part4.
32. Start a sketch on the top face of the assembly.
33. Activate the **Project 3D Elements** command and select anyone of the circular edges of the holes.
34. Click **OK** to project the selected edge.

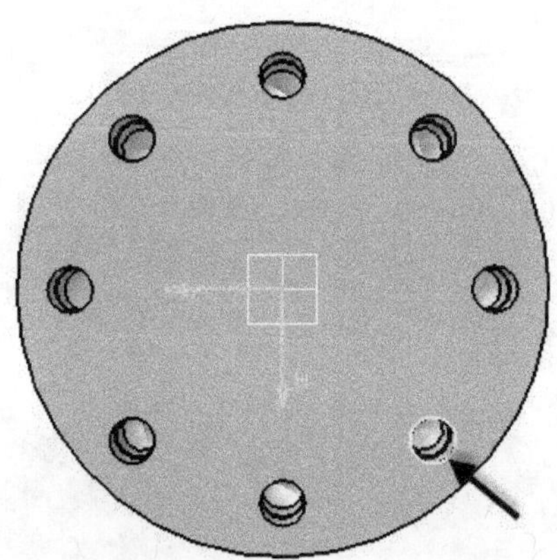

35. Exit the sketch and activate the **Pad** command.
36. Extrude the sketch up to 30 mm length in the downward direction.

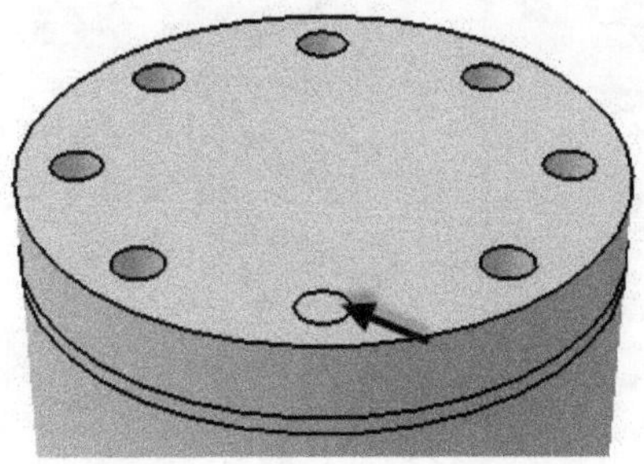

37. Start a sketch on the top face of the extrude feature.
38. On the **Profile** toolbar, click **Predefined Profile drop-down > Hexagon**, and then draw a hexagon.
39. Press and hold the Ctrl key, and then select the circle edge of the extrude feature and center point of the hexagon.
40. Click the **Constraints Defined in Dialog** icon on the **Constraint** toolbar.
41. On the **Constraint Definition** dialog, check the **Concentricity** option and click **OK**.
42. Select anyone of the edges of the hexagon.
43. Click the **Constraints Defined in Dialog** icon on the **Constraint** toolbar.
44. On the **Constraint Definition** dialog, check the **Vertical** option, and then click **OK**.
45. Add dimensional constraint to the hexagon.

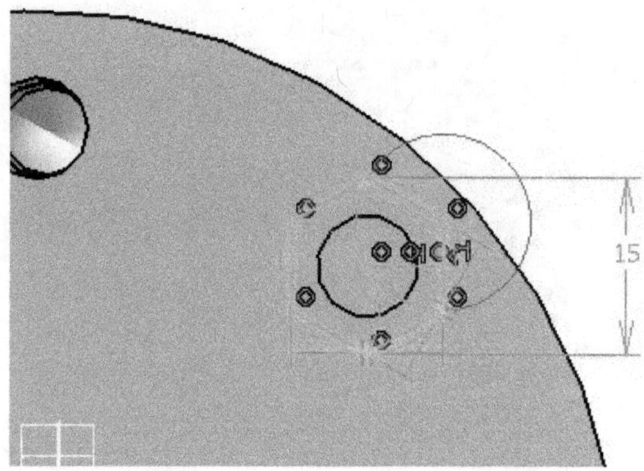

46. Exit the sketch and extrude it up to 5.7 mm length.

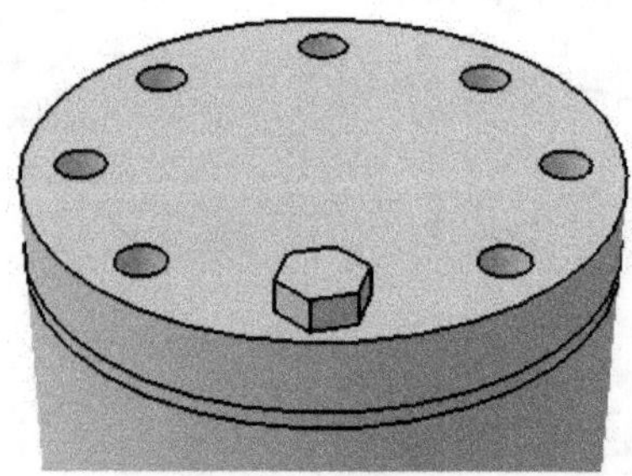

47. Activate the Assembly mode by double-clicking on **Product1**.
48. Fix the cylindrical base by using the **Fix Component** constraint.

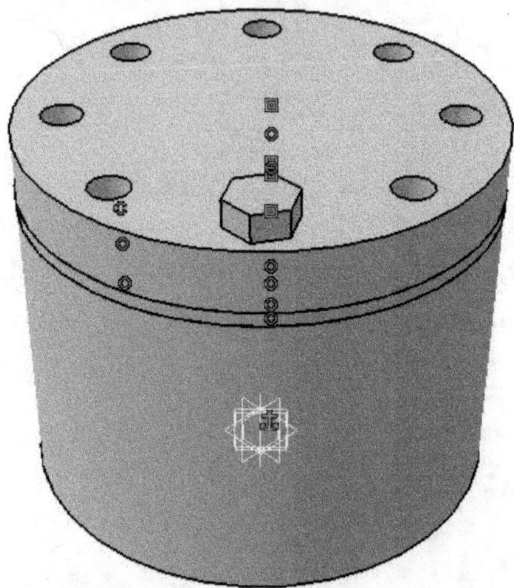

49. On the **Constraints** toolbar, click the **Reuse Pattern** button. This brings up the **Instantiation on a pattern** dialog.
50. Select the bolt to define the component to instantiate.
51. In the Specification Tree, expand Part1 and select **CircPattern1**. The pattern and the component that has the pattern are selected.
52. Click **OK** to pattern the bolts.

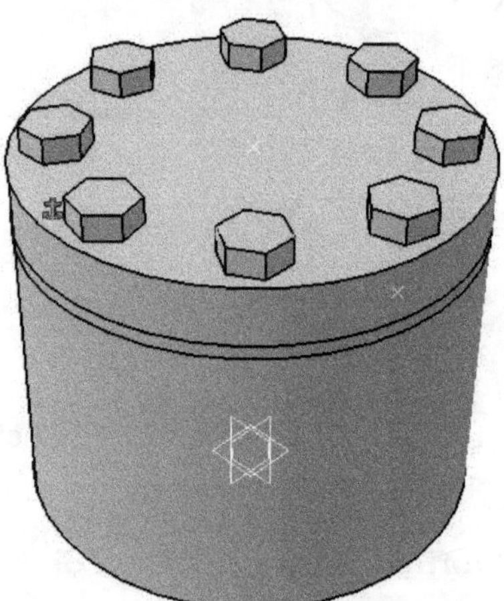

53. On the **Assembly Features** toolbar, click the **Hole** button (or) on the Menu bar, click **Insert > Assembly Features > Hole**.

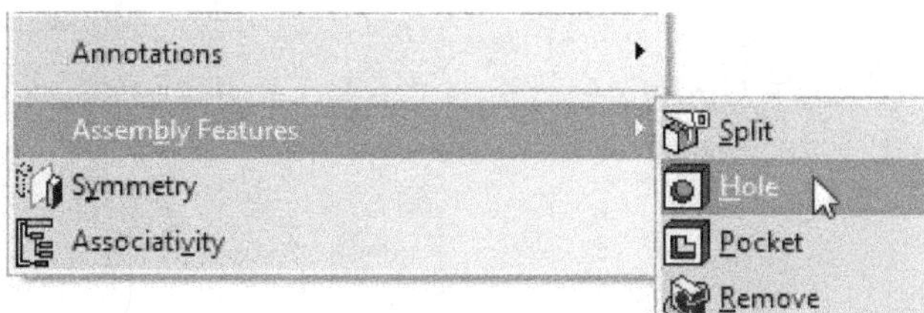

54. Select the point located on the top face of the model.
55. Click on the top face of the assembly.
56. On the **Assembly Features Definition** dialog, select the **Part1** from the **Parts possibly affected** section and click the down-arrow button.

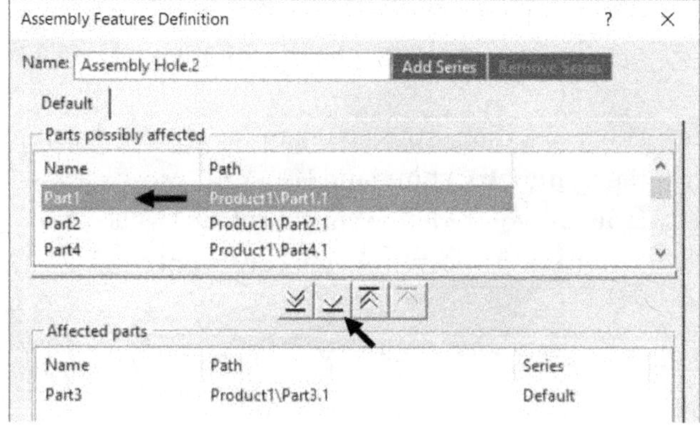

57. On the **Hole Definition** dialog, select **Extension > Blind**.
58. Type-in **81** in the **Depth** box.
59. Click the **Thread Definition** tab and check the **Threaded** option.
60. Select **Type > Metric Thick Pitch**.
61. Select **Thread Description > M24**.
62. Type-in **81** in the **Thread Depth** box.
63. Click **OK** to create the hole. You will notice a new item in the Specification Tree.

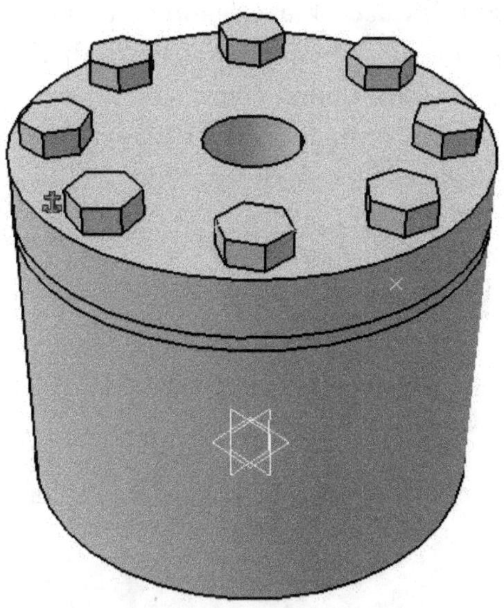

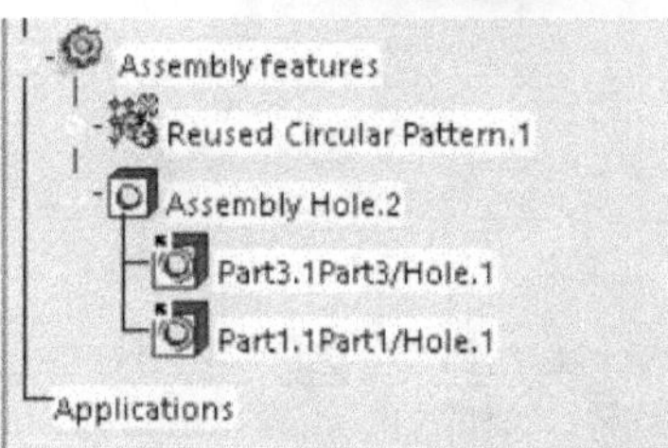

64. On the Menu bar, click **File > Save Management**.
65. Select **Product1** from the **Save Management** dialog.
66. Click **Save As**.
67. On the **Save As** dialog, browse to the required location on your hard drive.
68. Click the **New Folder** option, and then type-in **Example2** as the name of the folder.
69. Double-click on the folder.
70. Type *Pressure_cylinder* in the **File name** box, and then click **Save**.
71. Select Part1, and then click **Save As**.
72. Type *Cylinder_Base* in the **File** name box, and then click **Save**.
73. Likewise, save the **Part2**, **Part3**, and **Part4** as *Gasket*, *Cover_plate*, and *Screw*, respectively.
74. Click **OK** on the **Save Management** dialog.
75. On the **Move** toolbar, click the **Explode** button.
76. On the **Explode** dialog, click in the **Fixed product** selection box, and then select the base.

77. Click **OK** to explode the assembly. A warning message pops up showing that you are about to modify product positions. Click Yes.
78. Click the **Fit** button on the **View** toolbar. This fits the exploded state inside the graphics window.

79. Click **Update All** on the **Update** toolbar.
80. Save and close the assembly.

Questions

1. How do you start an assembly from an already opened part?
2. What is the use of the **Reuse Pattern** command?
3. List the advantages of Top-down assembly approach.
4. How do you create a sub-assembly in the Assembly Design Workbench?
5. Briefly explain how to edit components in an assembly.
6. What are the results that can be achieved using the **Symmetry** command?
7. How do you redefine constraints in CATIA V5?
8. What are the uses of **Angle** constraint?

Exercise 1

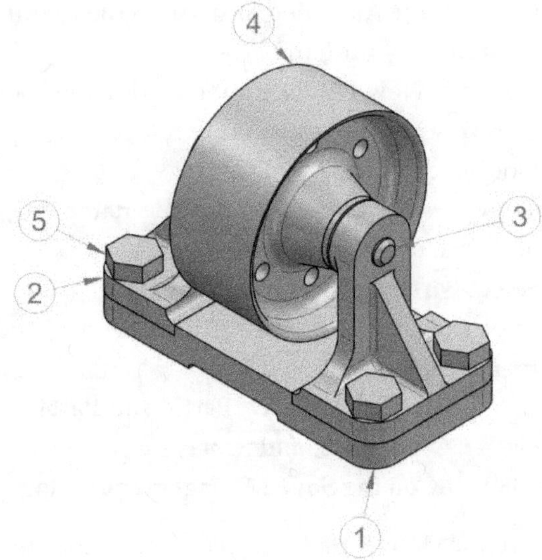

Item Number	File Name (no extension)	Quantity
1	Base	1
2	Bracket	2
3	Spindle	1
4	Roller-Bush assembly	1
5	Bolt	4

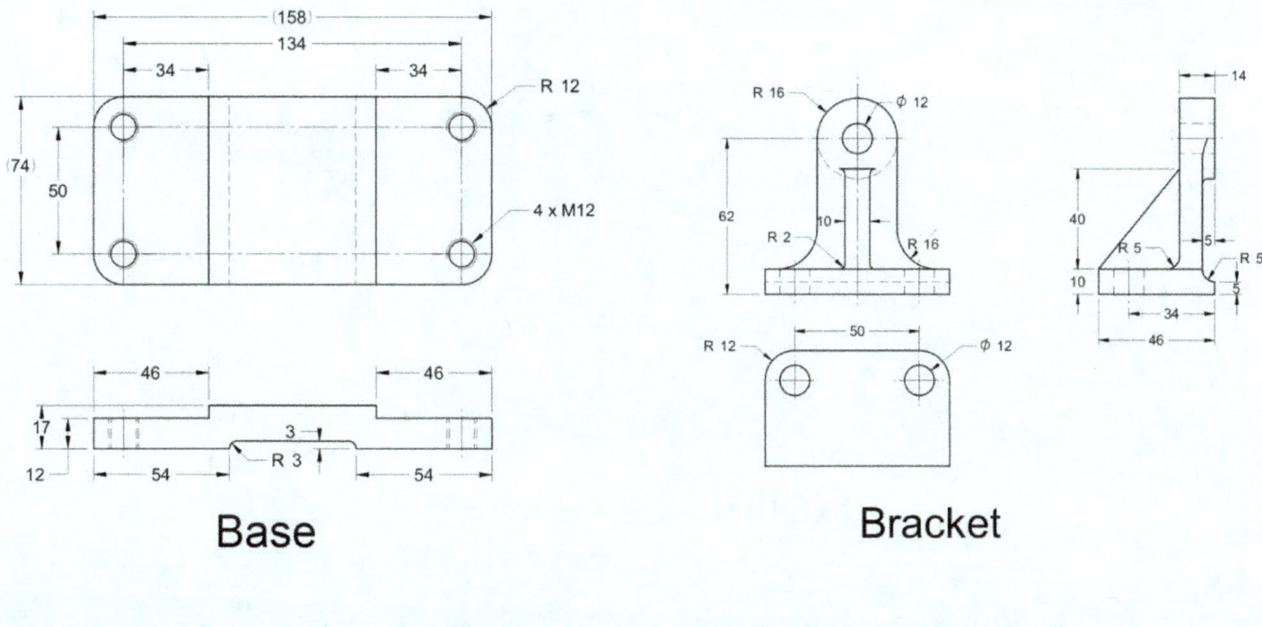

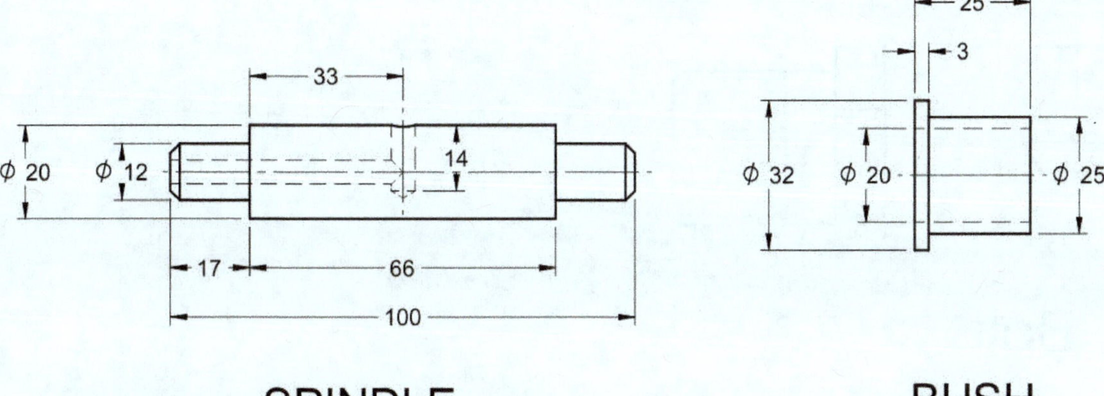

SPINDLE

BUSH

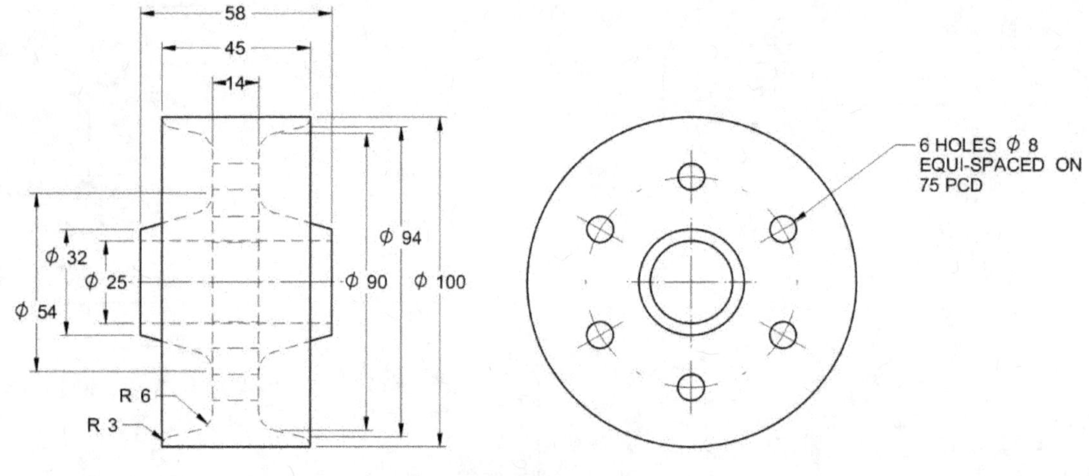
58
45
14
Φ 32
Φ 25
Φ 54
Φ 94
Φ 90
Φ 100
R 6
R 3
6 HOLES Φ 8
EQUI-SPACED ON
75 PCD

Roller

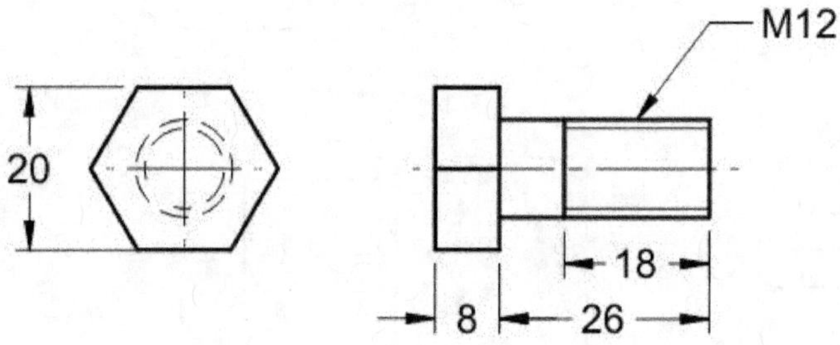
M12
20
18
8
26

Bolt

Chapter 11: Drawings

Drawings are used to document 3D models in the traditional 2D format including dimensions and other instructions useful for the manufacturing purpose. In CATIA V5, you first create 3D models and assemblies, and then use them to generate the drawing. There is a direct association between the 3D model and the drawing. When changes are made to the model, every view in the drawing will be updated. This relationship between the 3D model and the drawing makes the drawing process fast and accurate. Because of the mainstream adoption of 2D drawings of the mechanical industry, drawings are one of the three main file types you can create in CATIA V5.

The topics covered in this chapter are:

- *Front view*
- *Projected views*
- *Auxiliary views*
- *Section views*
- *Detailed views*
- *Break-out Section views*
- *View Breaks*
- *Parts List and Balloons*
- *Generate Dimensions*
- *Dimensions*
- *Centerlines*
- *Axis*
- *Notes*

Starting a Drawing

To start a new drawing, open the part or product document, which you want to document, and then follow the steps given next.

1. On the Menu bar, click **Start > Mechanical Design > Drafting**.

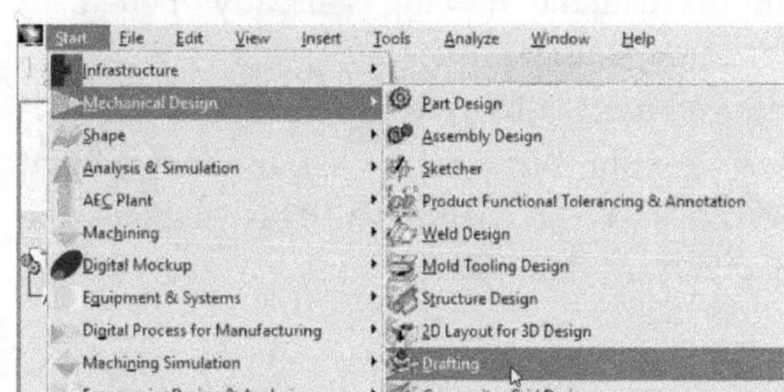

2. On the **New Drawing Creation** dialog, click the **Empty Sheet** icon to start a drawing with an empty sheet.

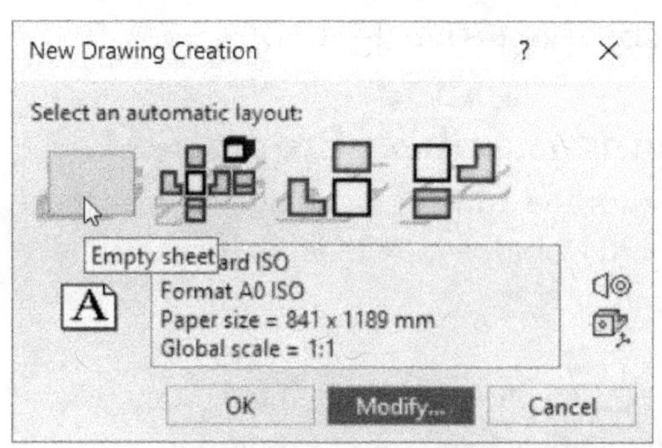

If you select the **All Views** icon, the drawing with all views of the part file will be created.

Likewise, use the **Front, Bottom and Right** 

and **Front, Top and Left** icons to start the drawing with the respective view layouts.

3. Click the **Modify** button to open the **New Drawing** dialog.
4. On the **New Drawing** dialog, set the **Standard** of the drawing.
5. Select the sheet size from the **Sheet Style** drop-down.
6. Set the drawing orientation to **Portrait** or **Landscape**.

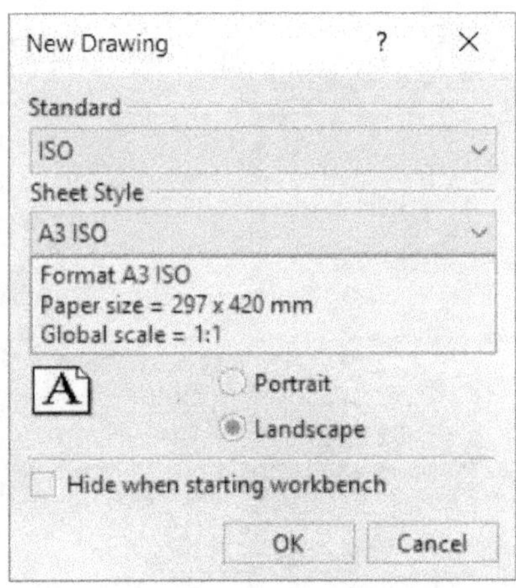

7. Click **OK** twice to start the drawing.

Modifying the Sheet Properties

Before creating the drawing, you have to check the sheet properties, and modify them as per your requirement.

1. In the Specification tree, click the right mouse button on **Sheet1** and select **Properties**.

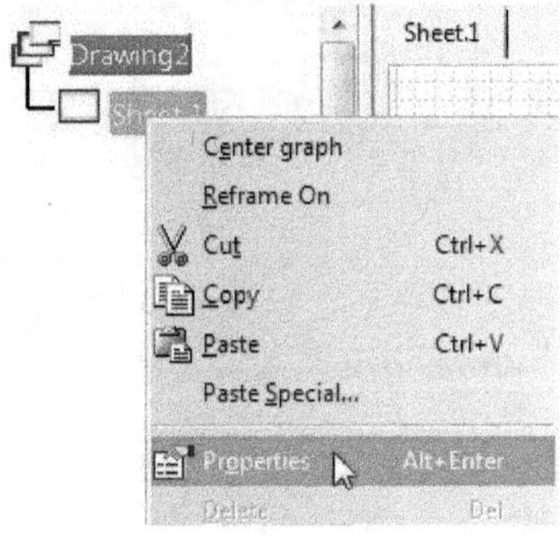

2. On the **Properties** dialog, set the **Scale, Format,** and **Orientation**.
3. Set the **Projection Method** to **Third angle standard**.
4. Click **OK**.

Frame and Title Block

After modifying the sheet properties, you have to add the frame and Title Block to the sheet.

1. On the Menu bar, click **Edit > Sheet Background**. The sheet turns grey.
2. On the **Drawing** toolbar, click the **Frame and Title Block** button.
3. On the **Manage Frame and Title Block** dialog, select the required style from the **Style of Title Block** drop-down.
4. Select **Create** from the **Action** section, and then click **OK**. This adds a frame and title block to the sheet.
5. To switch back the drawing sheet, click **Edit > Working Views** on the Menu bar.

View Creation Wizard

There are different standard views of a 3D part such as front, right, top, and isometric. In CATIA V5, you can create these views using the **View Creation Wizard** command.

1. Make sure that the Part or assembly of which you want to create the drawing is already opened.
2. Start a new drawing file.
3. On the **Views** toolbar, click **Wizard** drop-down > **View Creation Wizard** (or) click **Insert > Wizard > Wizard** on the Menu bar. This displays the **View Wizard** dialog.

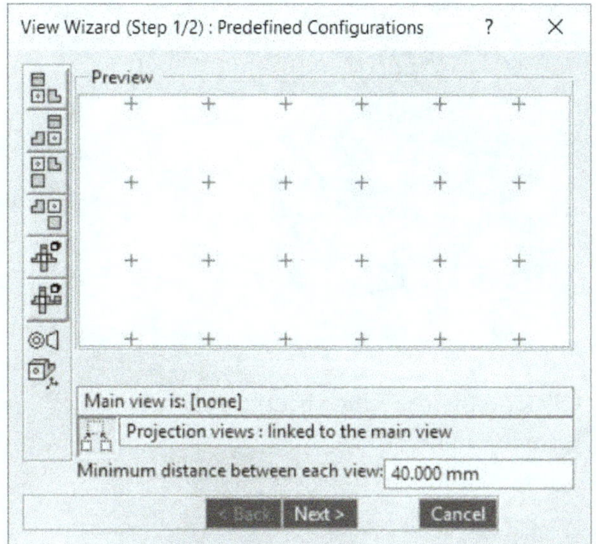

4. On the **View Wizard** dialog, click the **Configuration 1 using the 3rd angle projection method** button to create the Top, front and right views.

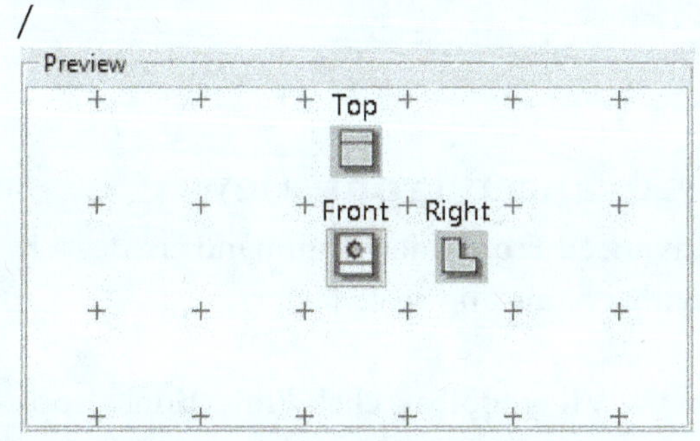

Likewise, use the other configuration buttons available at the left side on the **View Wizard** dialog to generate views as per your requirement.

5. Ensure that the **Views Link** button is pressed. This maintains a link between the front view and all other views. When you move the front view, the other views will also be moved.
6. Type-in the minimum distance between the views.
7. Click the **Next** button.
8. Click and drag the views in the **Preview** section to arrange them, if required.
9. Use the buttons available on the left side to add more views to the drawing, if required.

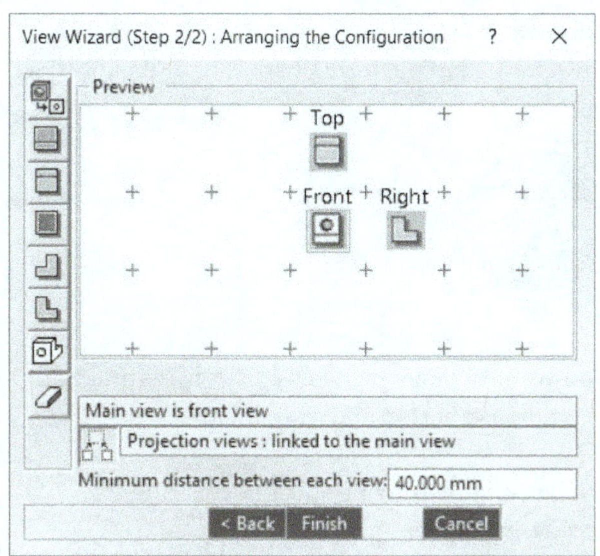

10. Click **Finish**. Now, you have to select a plane or face of the 3D model to define the front view.
11. On the Menu bar, click the **Window > Part/Product name**. The 3D model will be opened.
12. Click on a face or plane of the model.

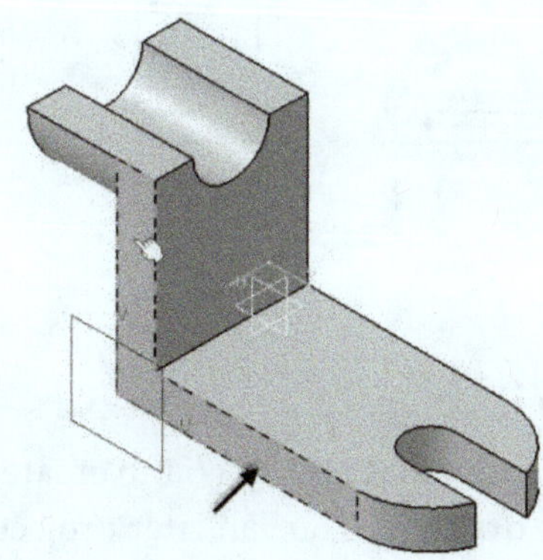

The previews of the views appear on the drawing sheet.

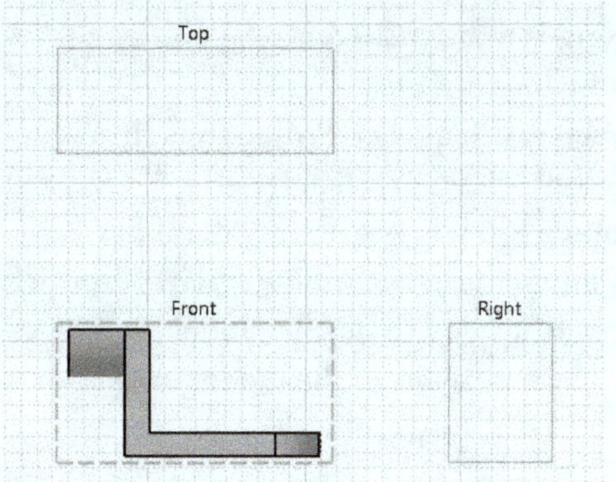

If you want to rotate the views, then click on the arrows located at the top right corner of the drawing sheet.

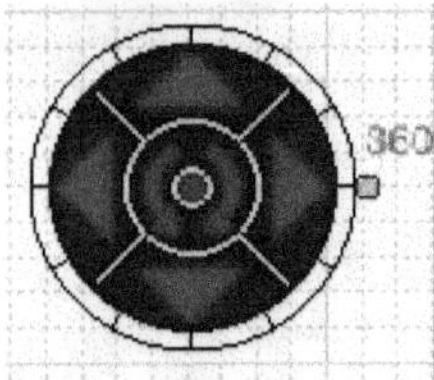

If you want to move the views, then press and hold the left mouse button and drag them.

13. Click on the drawing sheet to generate the drawing views.

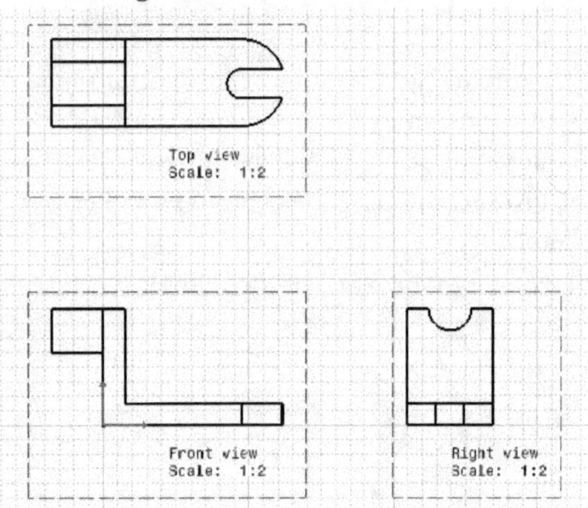

Front View

The **Front View** command allows you to create the front view of the drawing. You can later project this view to create other views.

1. Make sure that the part or assembly of which the drawing is to be created is opened.
2. Start a new drawing file.
3. On the **View** toolbar, click **Projections** drop-down > **Front View** (or) click **Insert > Views > Projections > Front View** on the Menu bar.
4. On the Menu bar, click **Window >** Part/Product name. This takes you to the 3D model.
5. Click on a face or plane of the model to define the orientation of the front view.

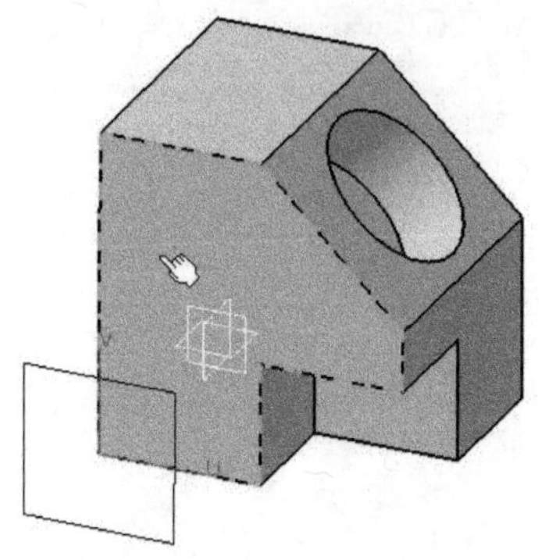

6. Click on the drawing sheet to generate the drawing view.

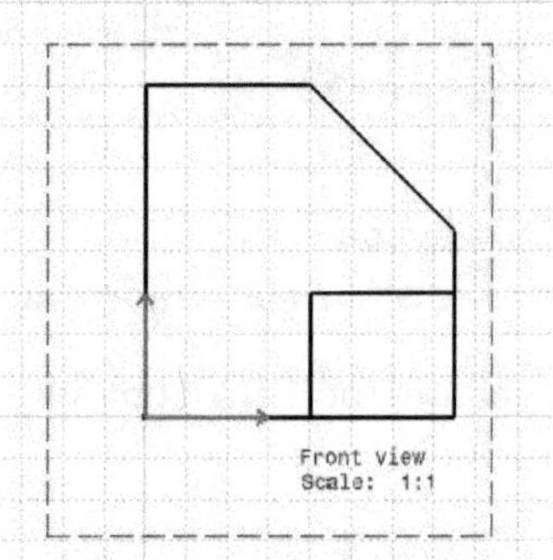

Advanced Front View

The **Advanced Front View** command creates a front view with a name and scale factor.

1. On the **View** toolbar, click **Projections** drop-down > **Advanced Front View** (or) click **Insert > Views > Projections > Advanced Front View** on the Menu bar.
2. On the **View Parameters** dialog, type-in values in the **View name** and **Scale** boxes.

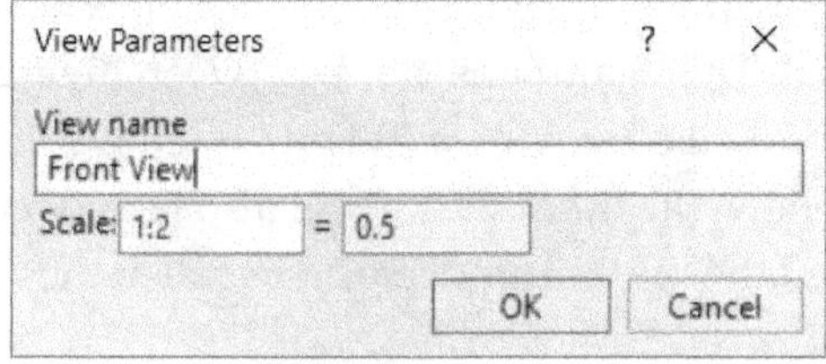

3. Click **OK** on the **View Parameters** dialog.
4. Switch to the 3D model and select a face or plane to define the orientation of the front view.
5. Click on the drawing sheet to generate the view.

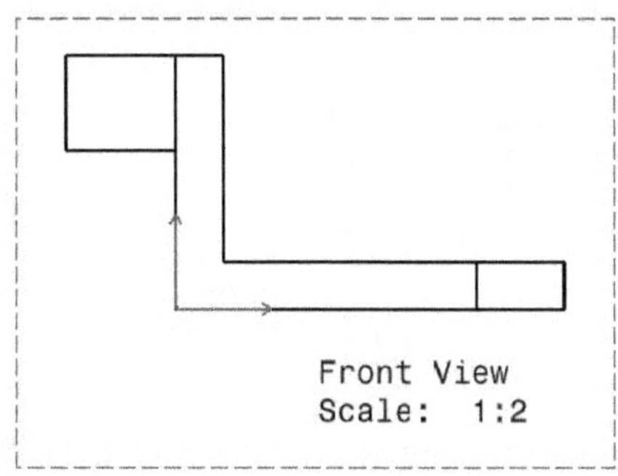

Projection View

After you have created the first view in your drawing, a projection view is one of the simplest views to create.

1. On the **Views** toolbar, click **Projections** drop-down > **Projection View** (or) click **Insert > Views > Projections > Projection** on the Menu bar.
2. After activating this command, move the pointer in the direction you wish to have the view projected.

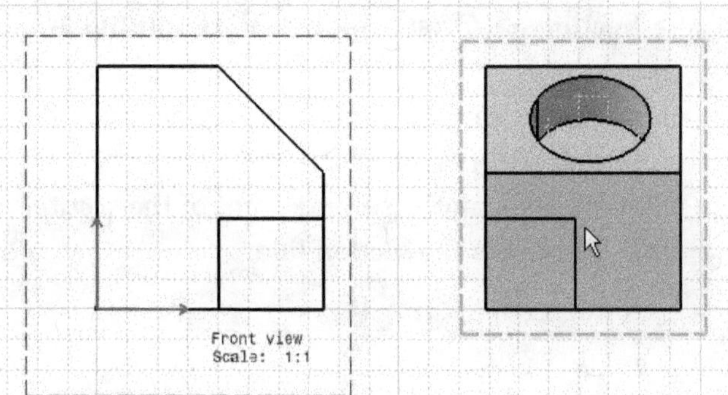

3. Next, click on the sheet to specify the location.

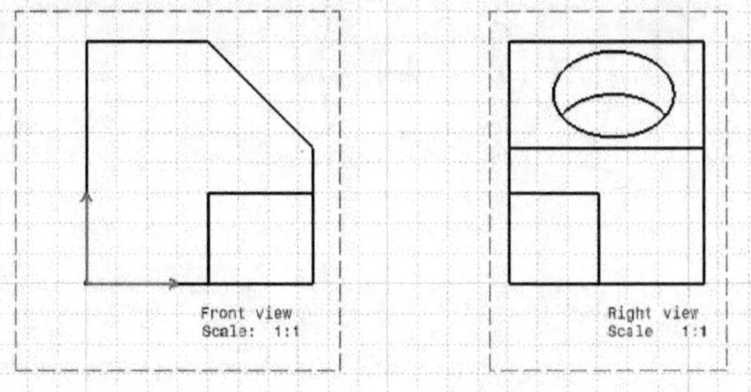

Auxiliary View

Most of the parts are represented by using orthographic views (front, top and/or side views). However, many parts have features located on inclined faces. You cannot get the true shape and size for these features by using the orthographic views. To see an accurate size and shape of the inclined features, you need to create an auxiliary view. You create an auxiliary view by projecting the part onto a plane other than horizontal, front or side planes.

1. On the **Views** toolbar, click **Projections** drop-down > **Auxiliary View** (or) click **Insert > Views > Projections > Auxiliary** on the Menu bar.
2. Now, click the angled edge of the model to establish the direction of the auxiliary view.
3. Move the pointer and click.

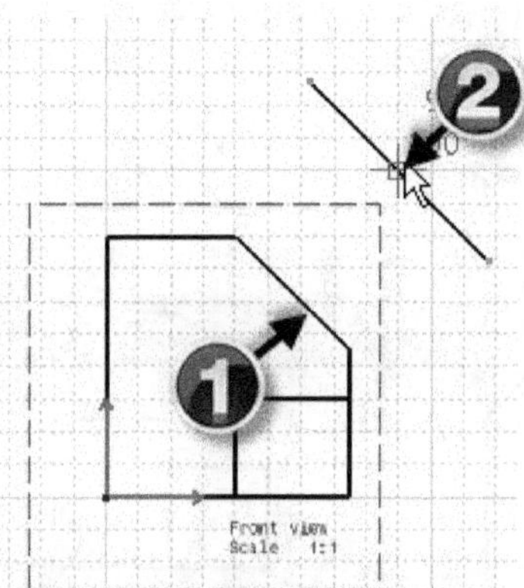

4. Drag the mouse to the desired location. Click to locate the view.

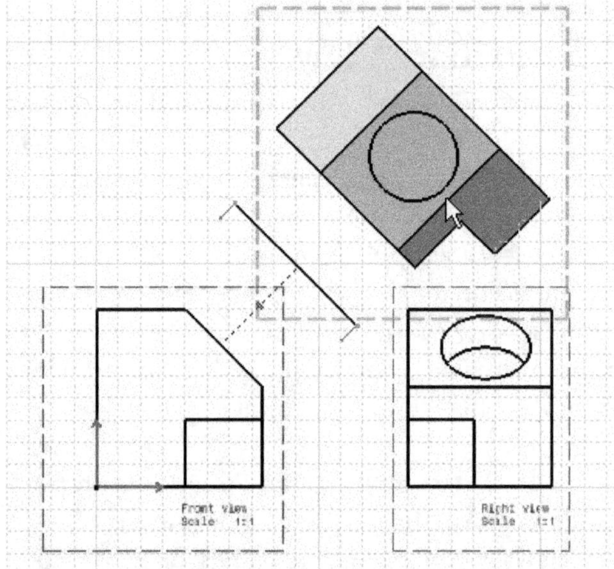

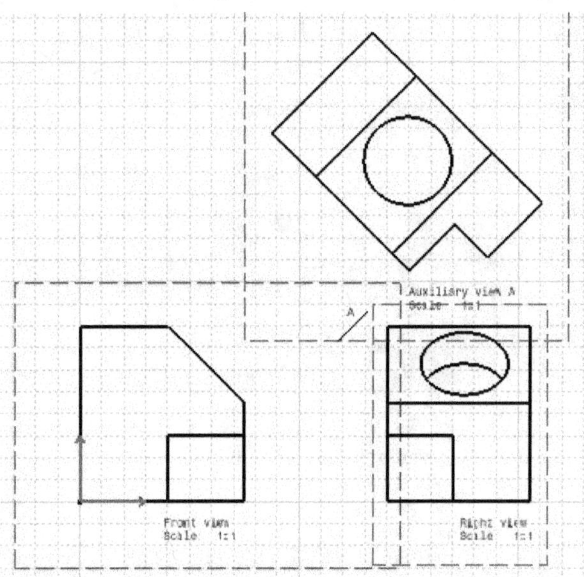

Isometric View

This command creates the Isometric View of the part/product.

1. On the **Views** toolbar, click **Projections** drop-down > **Isometric View** (or) click **Insert > Views > Projections > Isometric** on the Menu bar.
2. Switch to the 3D model and select a face or plane.
3. Click on the drawing sheet.

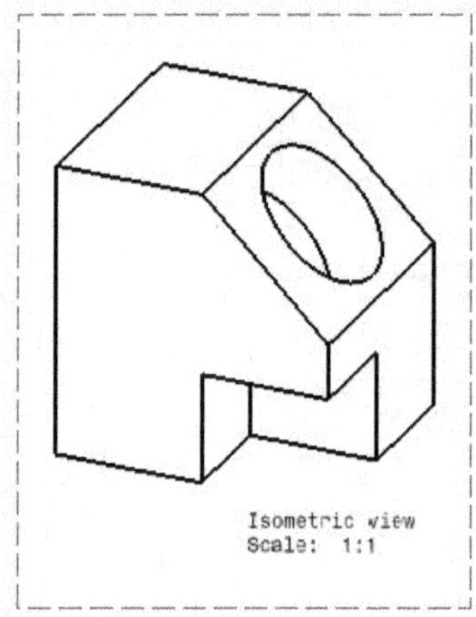

Section View

One of the common views used in 2D drawings is the section view. Creating a section view in CATIA V5 is very simple.

1. Activate the view to be sectioned. To do this, click the right mouse button on the view and select **Activate View**.
2. On the **Views** toolbar, click **Sections** drop-down > **Offset Section View** (or) click **Insert > Views > Sections > Offset Section View** on the Menu bar.
3. Draw a section line on the active view by selecting two points.
4. Double-click on the second point of the section line. This ends the section line.

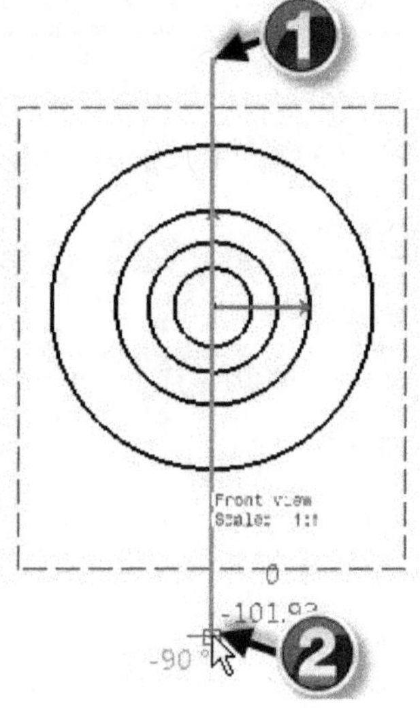

5. Move the pointer and click to locate the section view.

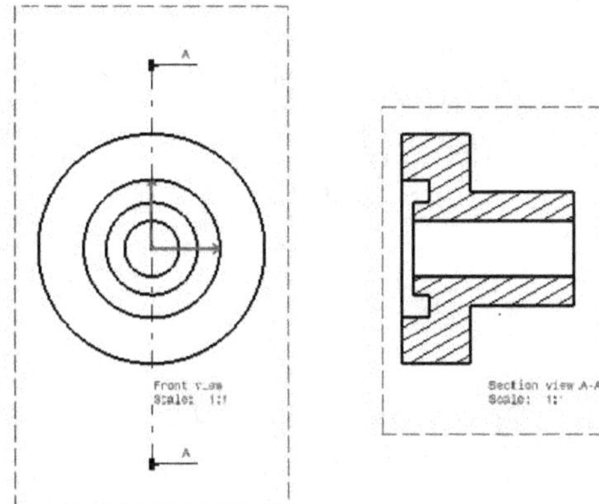

Offset Section View

If you want to create a section view by using a multi-segment section line, then activate the **Offset Section View** command.

1. Click to define the first point of the section line.
2. Move the pointer and click to define the second point.

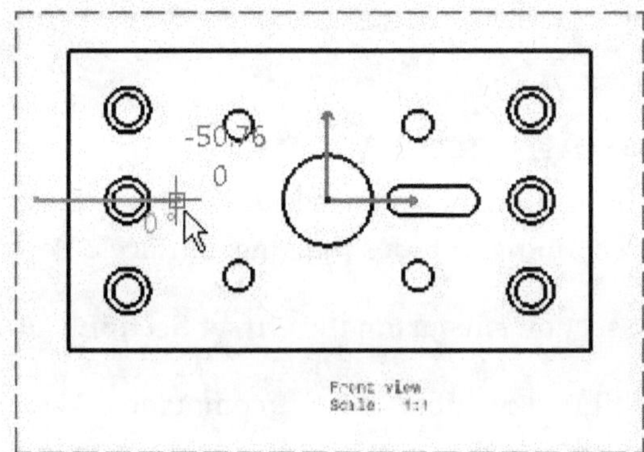

3. Move the pointer in the direction perpendicular to the section line and click. You will notice that a multi-segment line is created.

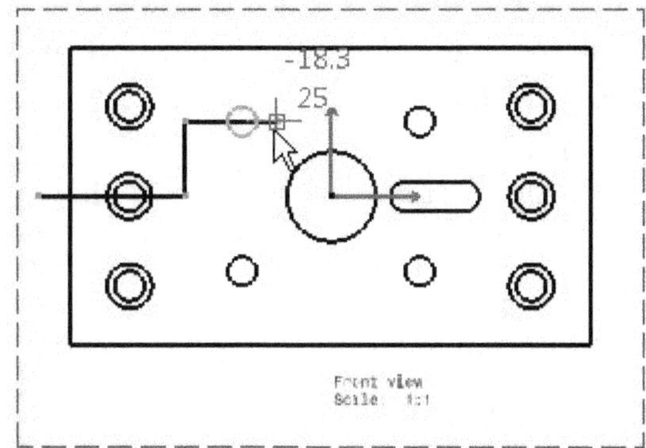

4. Likewise, create other multiple segments of the section line.
5. Double-click to end the section line.

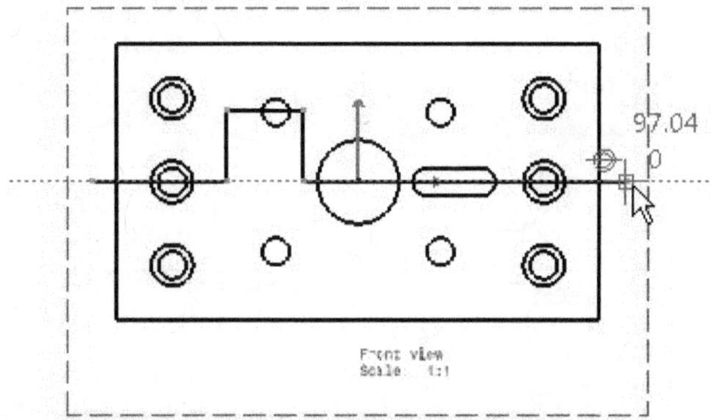

6. Move the pointer and click on either side of the section line.

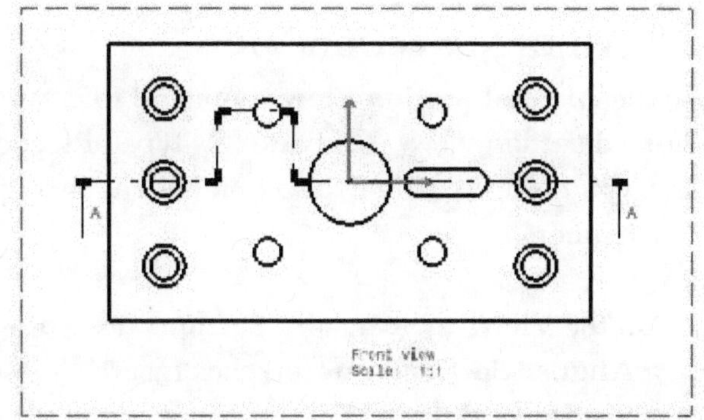

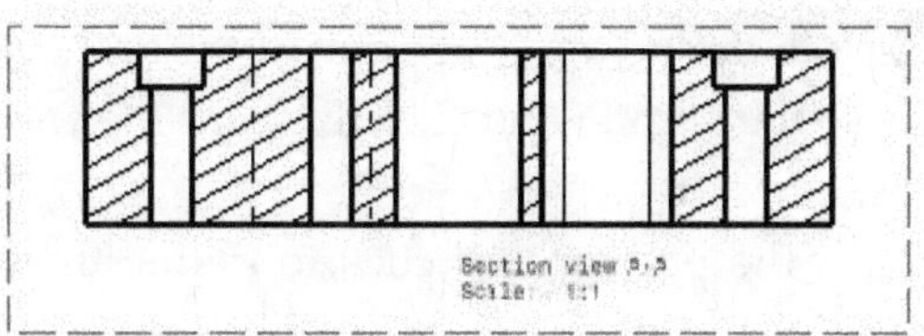

Half Section View

If you want to create a half section view, activate the **Offset Section View** command

1. Create a multi-segment section line, as shown below.

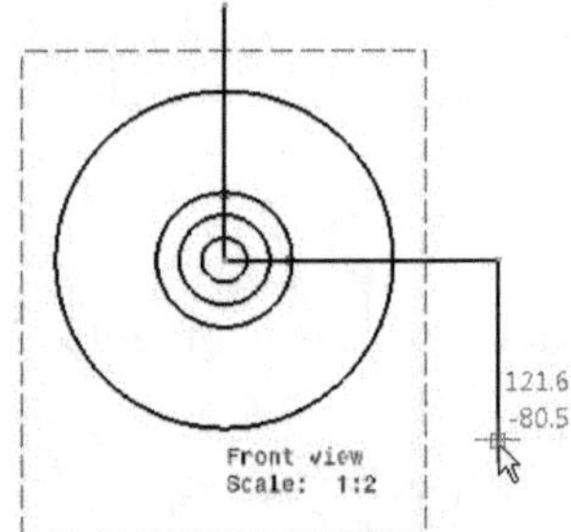

2. Double-click to end the section line.
3. Move the pointer and click to position the half section view.

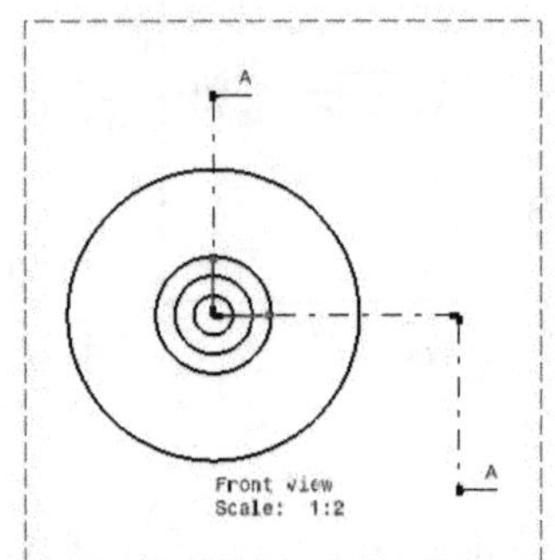

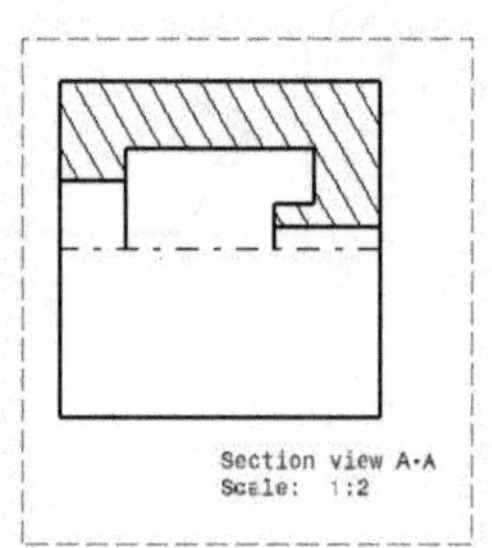

Aligned Section View

Use the **Aligned Section View** command to create a revolved section view. To create this type of section view, you need to create two section lines at an angle to each other.

1. On the **Views** toolbar, click **Sections** drop-down > **Aligned Section View** (or) click **Insert > Views > Sections > Aligned Section View** on the Menu bar.
2. Click to define the start point of the first line.
3. Move the pointer and click to define the end point of the first line.
4. Move the pointer and click to define the length and orientation of the second line.

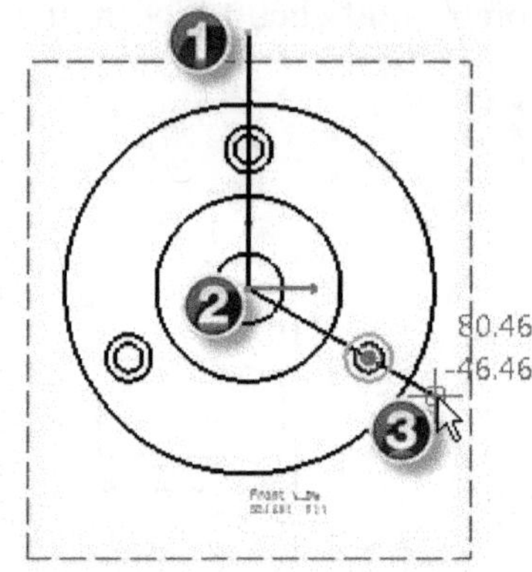

5. Double-click to end the section line.
6. Move the pointer and click to position the revolved section view.

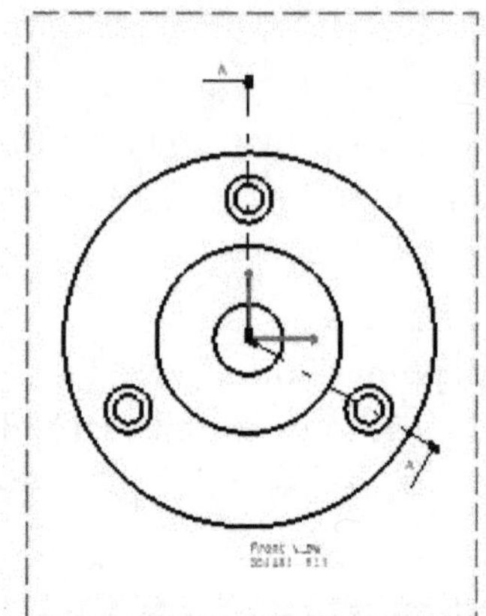

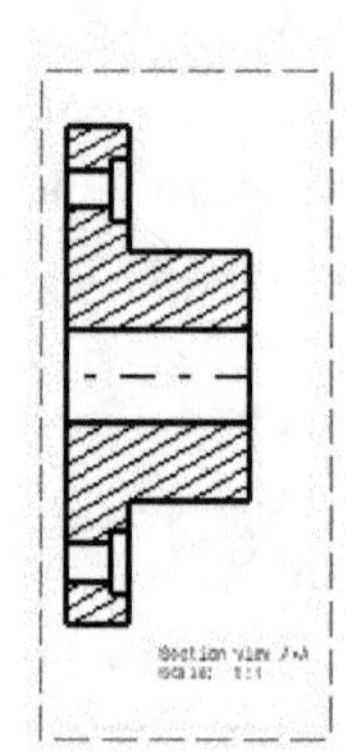

Creating Section Cuts

A section cut displays the surface that is exposed after sectioning. It hides the other surfaces. You can create section cuts using the **Offset Section Cut** and **Aligned Section Cut** commands. The procedure to create section cuts is similar to that of section views. The following image shows an offset section cut.

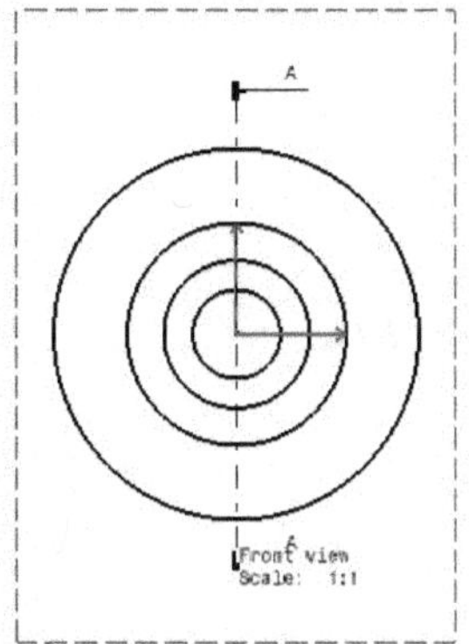

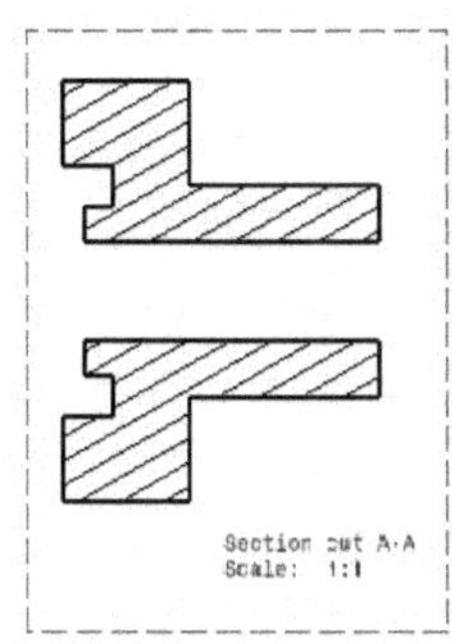

Detail View

If a drawing view contains small features that are difficult to see, a detailed view can be used to zoom in and make things clear. To create a detailed view, follow the steps given next.

1. On the **Views** toolbar, click **Details** drop-down > **Detail View** (or) click **Insert > Views > Details > Detail** on the Menu bar. This automatically activates the circle command.
2. Draw a circle to identify the area that you wish to zoom in.

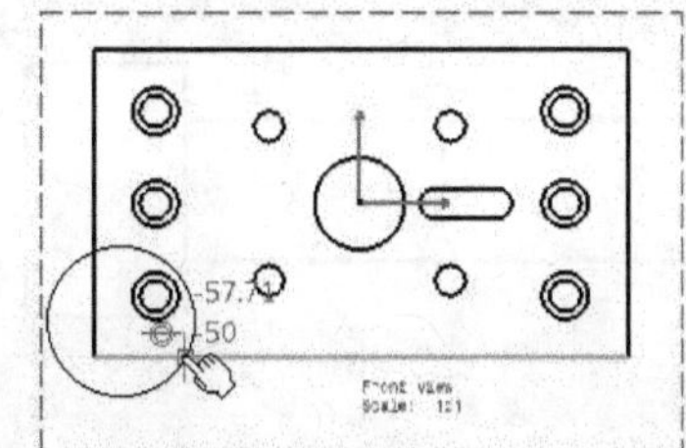

3. Once the circle is drawn, move the pointer and click to locate the view. The detail view will appear with a label.

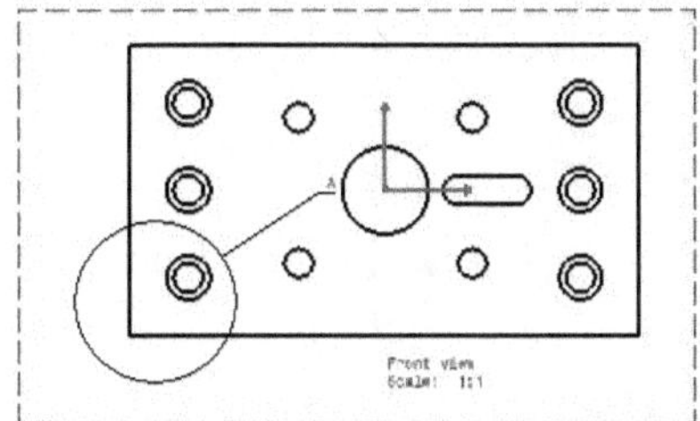

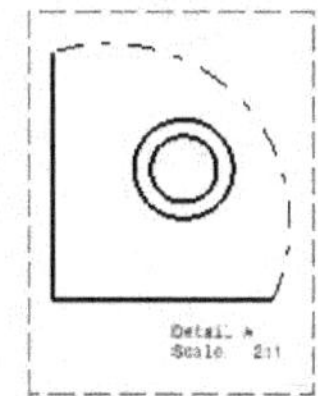

If you want to change the scale value, then click the right mouse button on the detail view and select **Properties**. On the **Properties** dialog, type-in a new value in the **Scale** box and click **OK**.

Detail View Profiles

This command creates a detail view using a user-defined profile.

1. On the **Views** toolbar, click **Details** drop-down > **Detail View Profile** (or) click **Insert > Views > Details > Detail View Profile** on the Menu bar. This activates the **Profile** command.
2. Draw a closed profile enclosing the area to be detailed.

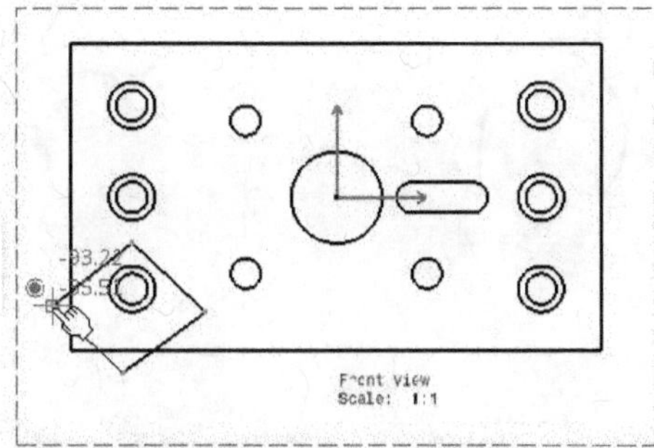

3. Move the pointer and click to locate the view.

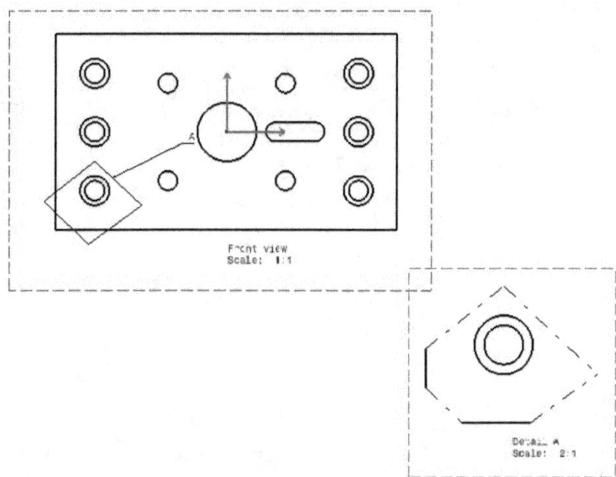

Clipping View

This command crops a view by the area defined by a circle.

1. On the **Views** toolbar, click **Clippings** drop-down > **Clipping View** (or) click **Insert > Views > Clippings > Clipping** on the Menu bar. This automatically activates the circle command.
2. Draw a circle on the view to be cropped.

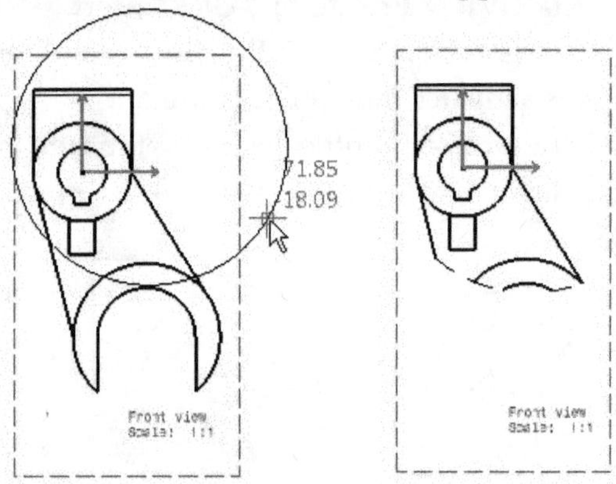

Clipping View Profile

This command crops a view by the area defined by a user-defined profile.

1. On the **Views** toolbar, click **Clippings** drop-down > **Clipping View Profile** (or) click **Insert > Views > Clippings > Sketched Clipping Profile** on the Menu bar.
2. Create a closed-profile on the view.

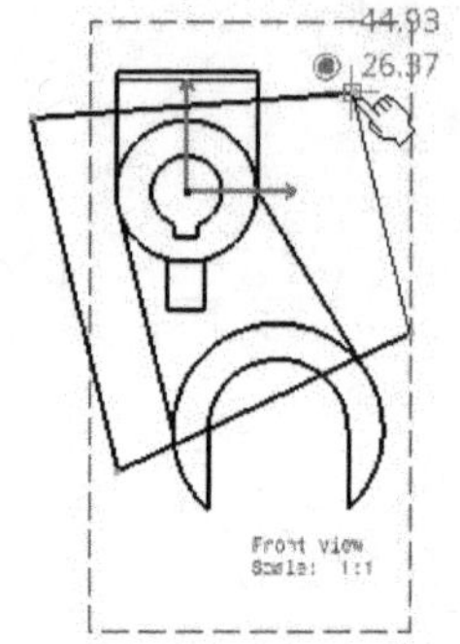

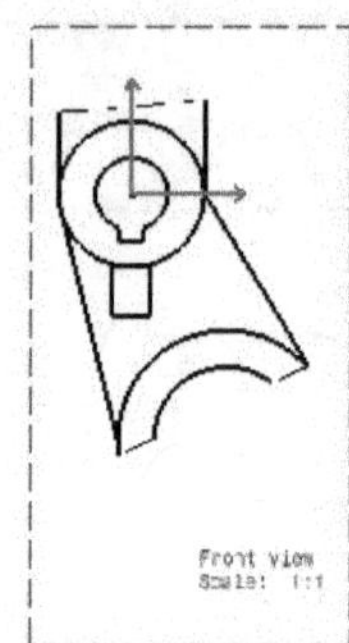

Broken View

You can add break lines to a drawing view, which is too large to fit on the drawing sheet. They break the view so that only important details are shown.

1. On the **Views** toolbar, click **Break view** drop-down > **Broken View** (or) click **Insert > Views > Break view > Broken View** on the Menu bar.
2. Click on the view to locate the beginning of the break. Next, you have to choose whether you want to create a vertical or horizontal break lines.
3. Select the vertical or horizontal dotted line to define the vertical or horizontal break lines.

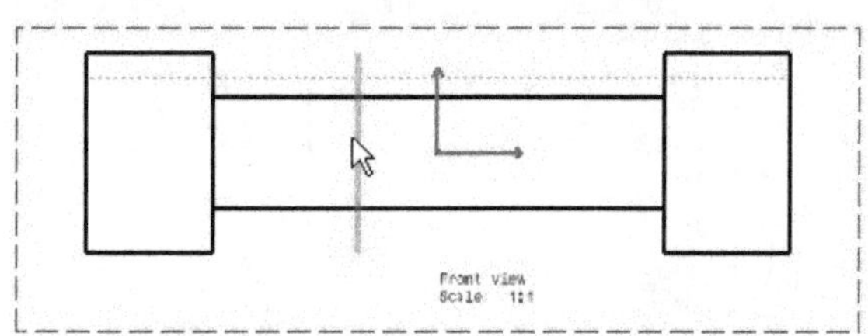

4. Move the pointer and click again to locate the end of the break.
5. Click on the sheet to generate break lines.

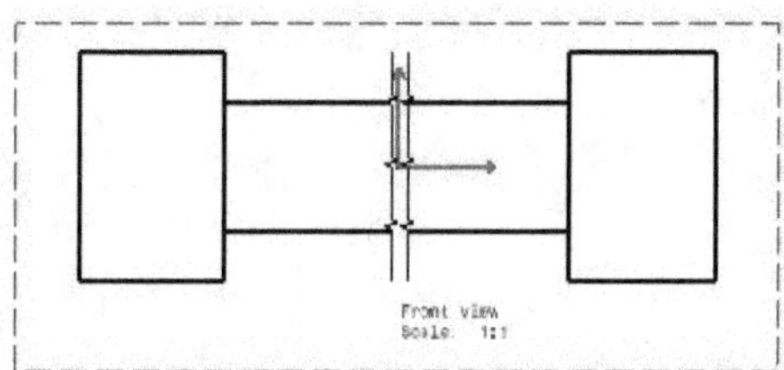

If you want to change the linetype of the break lines, then click the right mouse button on them and select **Properties**. On the **Properties** dialog, select a new linetype to be applied from the **Linetype** drop-down menu. Click **OK** to close the dialog.

 Breakout View

The **Breakout View** command alters an existing view to show the hidden portion of a part or assembly. This command is very useful to show the parts, which are hidden in an assembly view. You need to create a closed profile to breakout a view.

1. On the **Views** toolbar, click **Break view** drop-down > **Breakout View** (or) click **Insert > Views > Break view > Breakout View** on the Menu bar.
2. Draw a closed profile on the view to be broken.

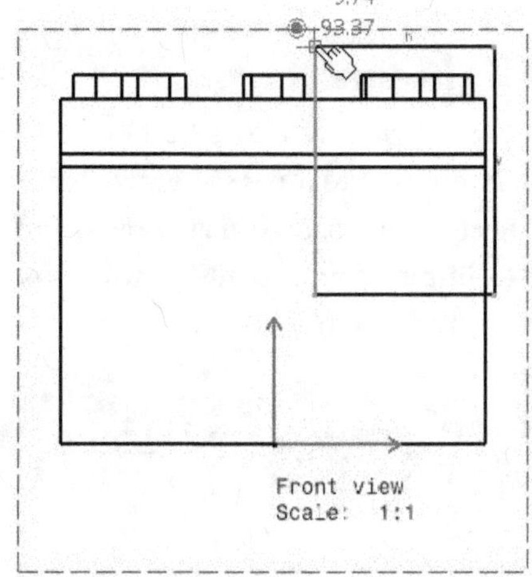

3. On the 3D Viewer window, click and drag the vertical line located at the center of the view. This defines the depth of the breakout.

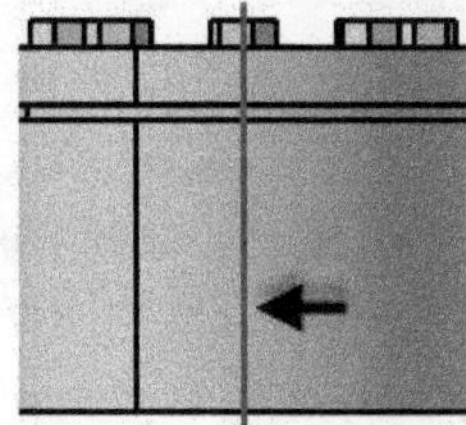

4. Click **OK** to close the **3D Viewer** window. This creates a breakout view.

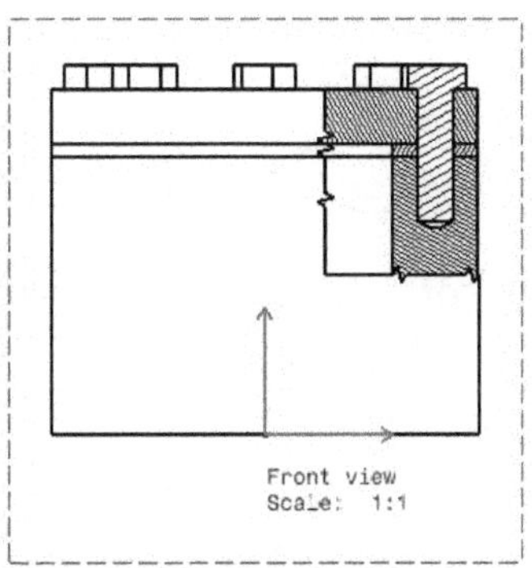

Exploded View

You can display an assembly in an exploded state as long as the assembly already has an exploded scene defined. Follow the steps given next to define the exploded scene in an assembly.

1. Open the assembly file.
2. On the **Scenes** toolbar, click the **Enhanced Scene** button (or) click **Insert > Create Enhanced Scene** on the Menu bar.
3. Click **OK** on the **Enhanced Scene** dialog. This activates the enhanced scene mode.
4. On the **Enhanced Scene** toolbar, click the **Explode** button, and then explode the assembly (refer to the **Explode** section of **Chapter 10: Assemblies**).
5. On the **Enhanced Scene** toolbar, click the **Exit Scene** button.
6. Save the assembly file

Follow the steps given next to insert the exploded scene in a drawing.

1. Open a drawing file.
2. On the **Views** toolbar, click **Projections** drop-down > **Isometric View** .
3. Switch to assembly file.
4. In the Specification Tree, go to **Application > Scene** and select the Exploded Scene.

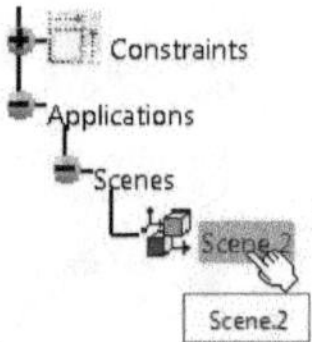

5. Click on a plane or face of the assembly model.
6. Click on the drawing sheet to generate the exploded view of the assembly.

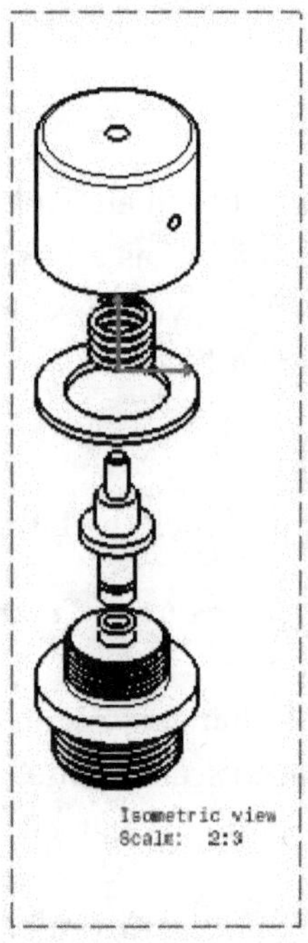

View Properties

When working with CATIA V5 drawings, you can control the way a model view appears by using the view properties. For example, if you want to show or hide the hidden lines, then follow the steps given next.

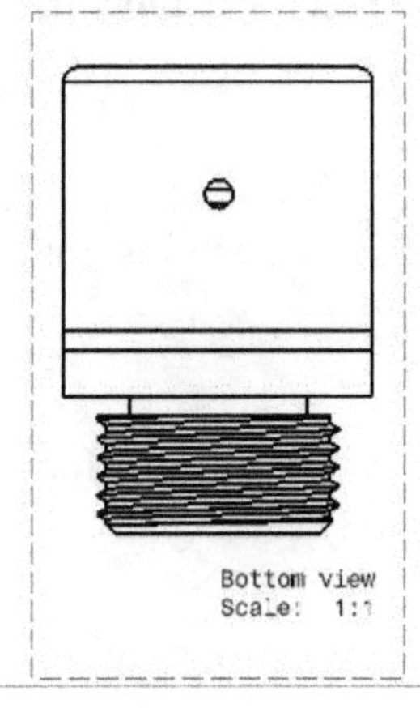

1. Click the right mouse button on the view and select **Properties**.
2. On the **Properties** dialog, under the **Dress-up** section, check the **Hidden Lines** option.
3. Click **OK** to apply the changes.

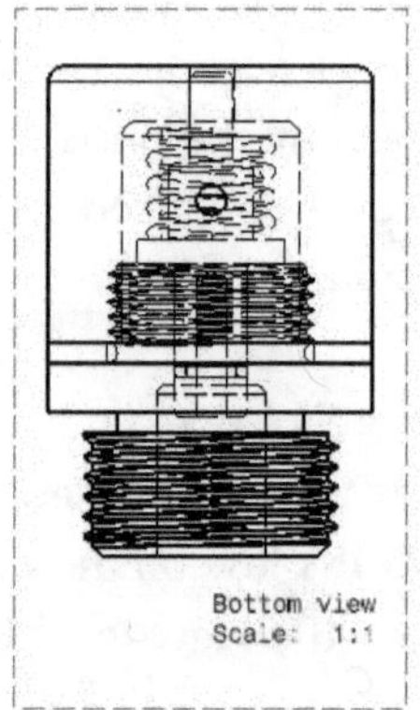

View Alignment

There are several types of views that are automatically aligned to a parent view. These include projected views, auxiliary views, and section views. For example, if you want to move any view, you need to move its parent view.

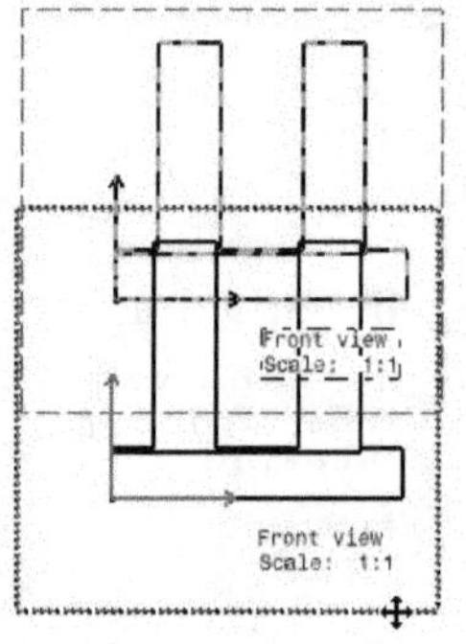

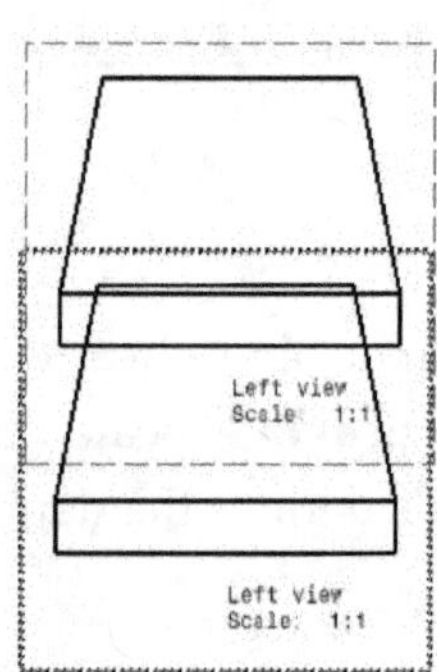

You can make the view independent of its parent view by breaking the link between them. To do this, click the right mouse button on the view. Select **View Positioning > Position Independently of Reference view**.

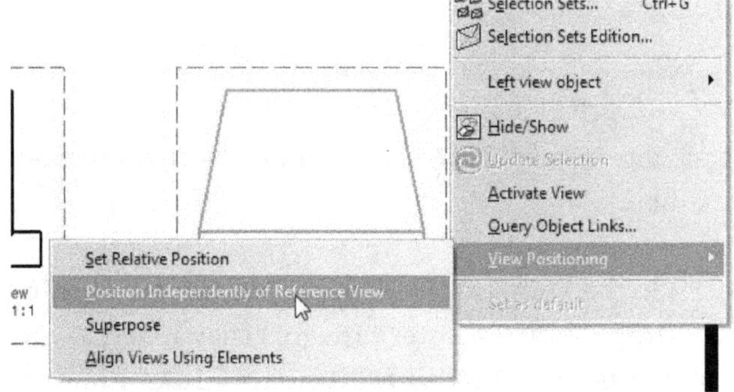

Now, you can move the view independently.

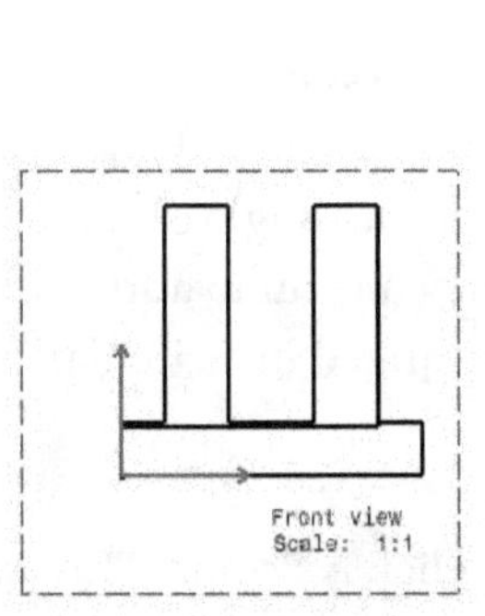

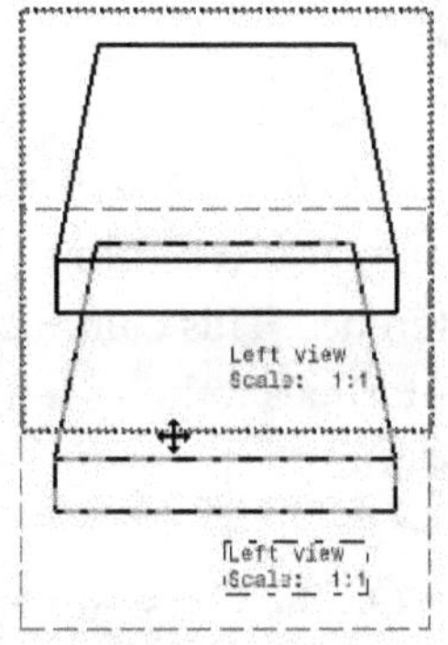

Bill of Material

Creating an assembly drawing is very similar to creating a part drawing. However, there are few things unique in an assembly drawing. One of them is creating parts list. A parts list identifies the different components in an assembly. Generating a parts list is very easy in CATIA V5. First, you need to have a view of the assembly.

1. On the Menu bar, click **Insert > Generation > Bill of Material > Bill of Material**.
2. Click on the drawing sheet to position the bill of materials.

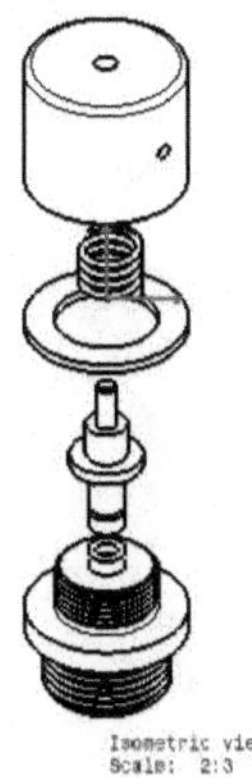

Bill of Material: Product1

Quantity	Part Number	Type	Nomenclature	Revision
1	Nipple	Part		
1	Gasket1	Part		
1	Pusher sub-assembly	Assembly		
1	Spring	Part		
1	Cover	Part		

Bill of Material: Pusher sub-assembly

Quantity	Part Number	Type	Nomenclature	Revision
1	Pusher	Part		
1	Gasket	Part		

Recapitulation of: Product1
Different parts: 6
Total parts: 6

Quantity	Part Number
1	Nipple
1	Gasket1
1	Pusher
1	Gasket
1	Spring
1	Cover

If you want only one set of bill of materials, then click **Insert > Generation > Bill of Material > Advanced Bill of Material** on the Menu bar. Click **OK** on the **Bill of Material Creation** dialog. Select the assembly view and click on the drawing sheet to position the bill of material.

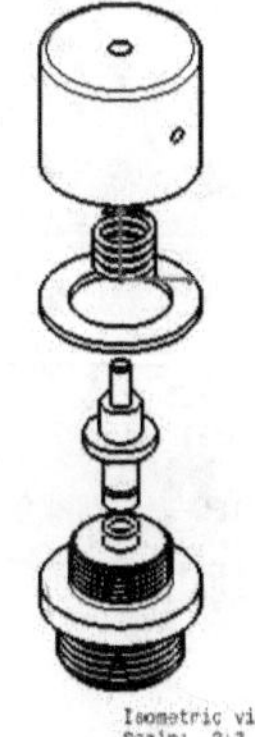

Quantity	Part Number	Type	Nomenclature	Revision
1	Nipple	CATPart	-	-
1	Gasket1	CATPart	-	-
1	Pusher	CATPart	-	-
1	Gasket	CATPart	-	-
1	Spring	CATPart	-	-
1	Cover	CATPart	-	-

If you want to modify the bill of material, then click the right mouse button on the bill of material. Select **Properties** to open the **Properties** dialog. On the **Properties** dialog, click on the tabs and modify the properties. Click **OK** to apply the changes.

Balloons

To add balloons to the assembly drawing, on the **Generation** toolbar, click **Dimension Generation** drop-down > **Generate Balloons** (or) click **Insert > Generation > Balloon Generation** on the Menu bar.

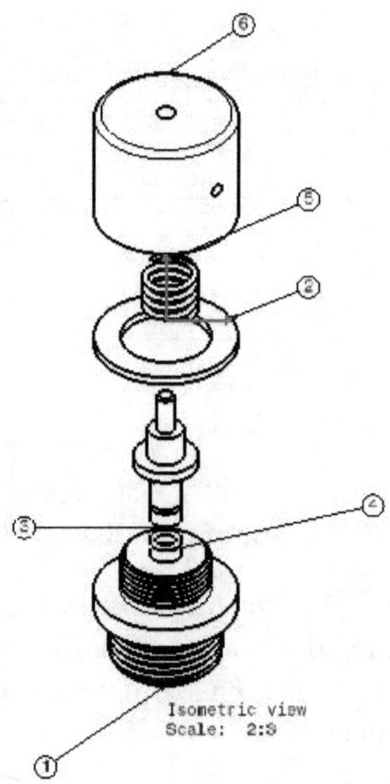

Centerlines

Centerlines are used in engineering drawings to denote hole centers and lines. If you want to display the centerlines of a drawing view, then open the **Properties** dialog of the view and check the **Centerline** option. Click **OK** to close the dialog.

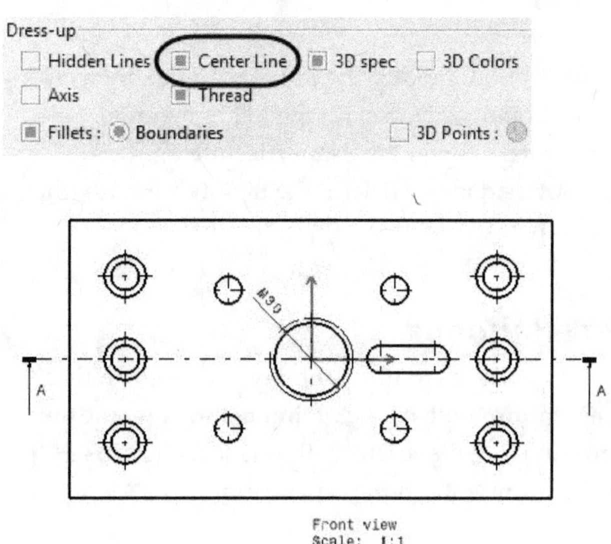

However, if you want to create centerlines manually, then use the commands available on the **Dress-up** toolbar.

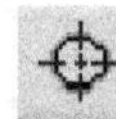

Center Line

Use the **Center Line** command to add centerlines manually.

1. On the **Dress-up** toolbar, click **Axis and Threads** drop-down > **Center Line** (or) click **Insert > Dress-up > Axis and Threads > Center Line** on the Menu bar.
2. Click on a circle or arc to add centerline to it.

Center Line with Reference

The **Center Line with Reference** command allows you to add centerlines that are at an angle to some reference. This command will be useful to add centerlines to holes that are arranged in a circular fashion.

1. On the **Dress-up** toolbar, click **Axis and Threads** drop-down > **Center Line with Reference** (or) click **Insert > Dress-up > Axis and Threads > Center Line with Reference** on the Menu bar.
2. Click on the hole to add a center line.
3. Click on a point or edge to define the reference. A centerline will be created on the hole.

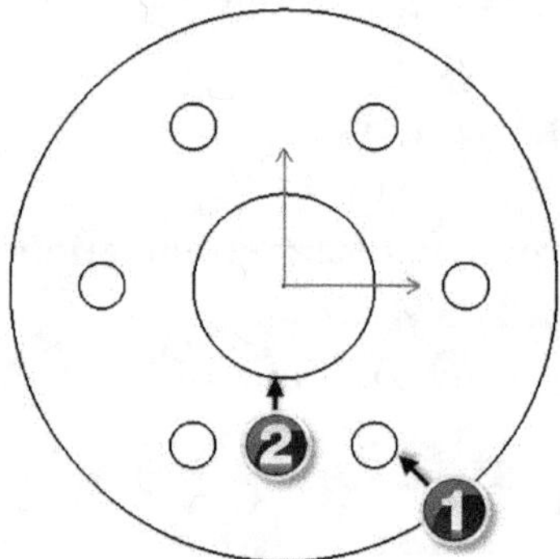

4. Likewise, create centerlines on other holes.

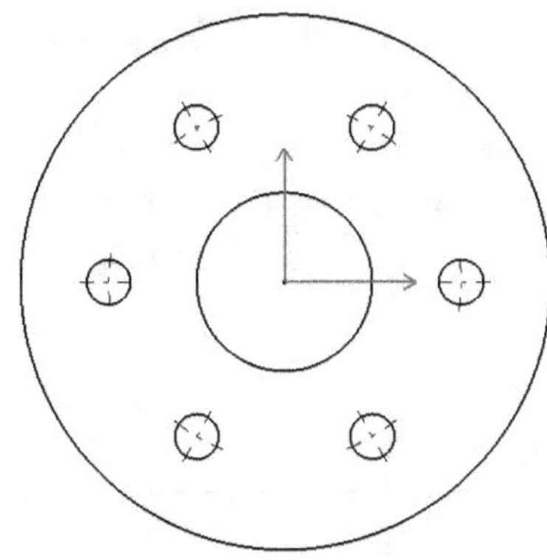

Dimensions

CATIA V5 provides you with different types of commands to add dimensions to the drawing.

Generate Dimensions

One of the methods to add dimensions to the drawing is to retrieve the dimensions that are already contained in the 3D part file. The **Generate Dimensions** command helps you to do this.

1. On the **Generation** toolbar, click **Dimension Generation** drop-down > **Generate Dimensions** (or) click **Insert > Generation > Generate Dimensions** on the Menu bar.
2. Select the type of constraints and dimensions to be retrieved from the 3D model.
3. Click **OK** on the **Generated Dimension Analysis** dialog. This generates dimensions of the model.

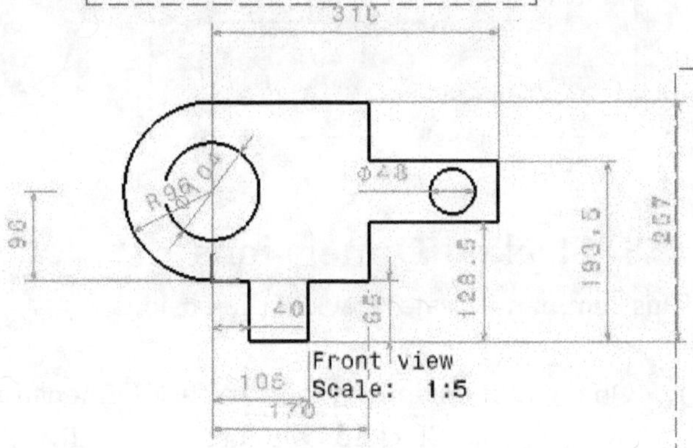

Generate Dimensions Step by Step

This command helps you to generate dimensions in a step-by-step manner.

1. On the **Generation** toolbar, click **Dimension Generation** drop-down > **Generate Dimensions Step by Step** (or) click **Insert > Generation > Generate Dimensions Step by Step** on the Menu bar.
2. On the **Step by Step Generation** dialog, type-in a value in the **Timeout** box. For example, if you type-in 1 in this box, the time taken to generate each dimension will be one second.
3. Click the **Next Dimension Generation** icon on the dialog. You will notice that the dimensions are generated one by one. Also, other options on the dialog become selectable. The functions of these options are given next.

Click this button to generate all the dimensions of the model.

Click this button to stop the dimension generation and close the dialog.

Click this button to pause the dimension generation.

Click this button to exclude a dimension.

Click this button to transfer a dimension to another view.

4. Click **OK** to complete the dimension generation.

Adding Dimensions

If you want to add some more dimensions, which are necessary to manufacture a part, use the **Dimensions** command (activate it from the **Dimensioning** toolbar) to create linear, radial or any type of dimension. As you activate this command, the **Tools Palette** toolbar appears.

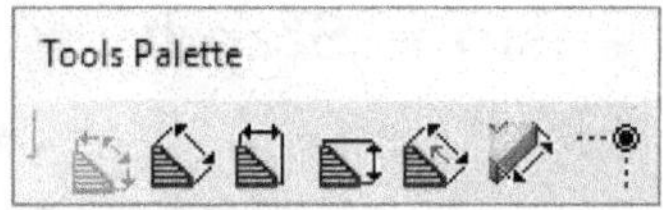

You can use the options on this toolbar to define the orientation of the dimension.

Chained Dimensions

This command creates chained dimensions.

1. On the **Dimensioning** toolbar, click **Dimensions** drop-down > **Chained Dimensions** (or) click **Insert > Dimensioning > Dimensions > Chained Dimensions** on the Menu bar.
2. Select two or more parallel edges from the drawing view.

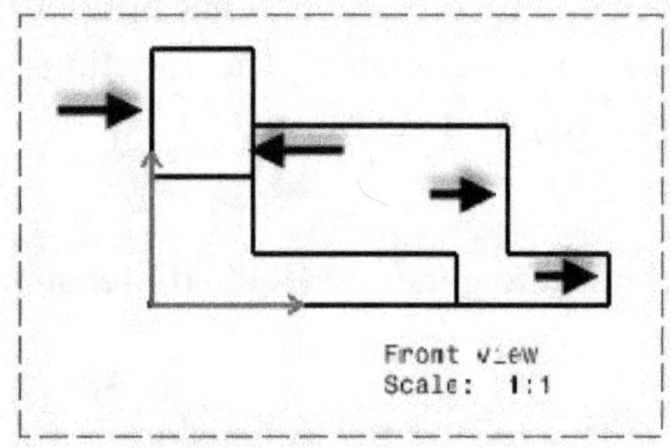

3. Move the pointer and click to position the chained dimension.

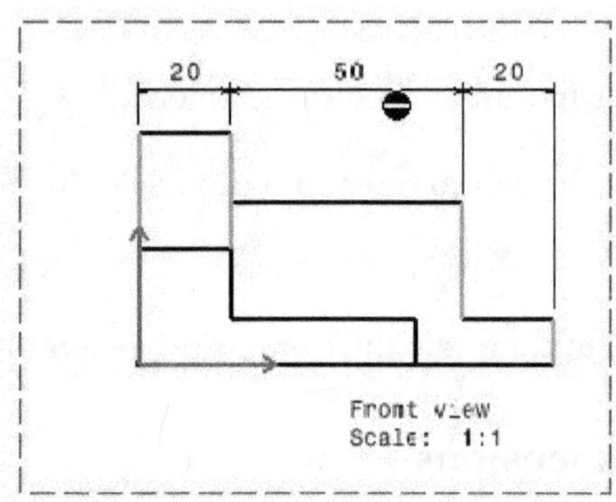

Cumulated Dimensions

Cumulated dimensions are another type of dimensions that you can add to a drawing.

1. On the **Dimensioning** toolbar, click **Dimensions** drop-down > **Cumulated Dimensions** (or) click **Insert > Dimensioning > Dimensions > Cumulated Dimensions** on the Menu bar.
2. Click on any edge of the drawing view to define the zero reference.

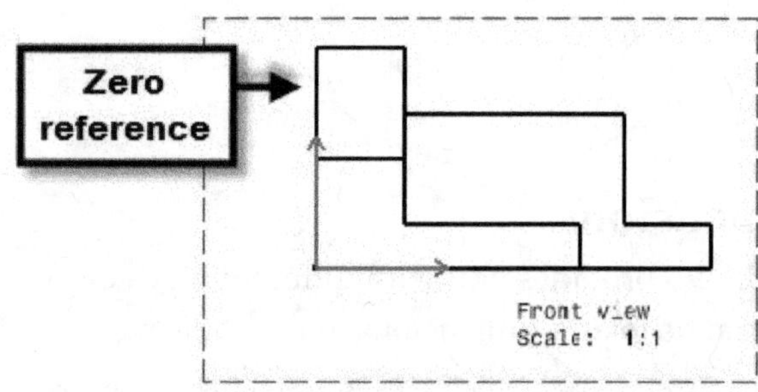

3. Now, click on an edge of the drawing view.
4. Likewise, click on other edges parallel to the zero reference.
5. Move the pointer and click to place the cumulated dimension.

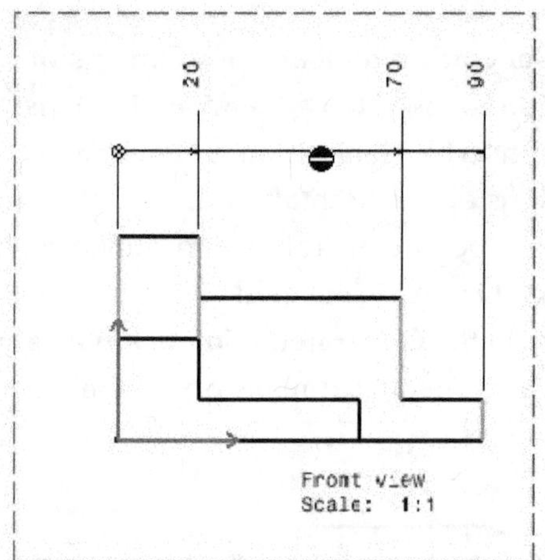

Stacked Dimensions

This command creates stacked dimensions.

1. On the **Dimensioning** toolbar, click **Dimensions** drop-down > **Stacked Dimensions** (or) click **Insert > Dimensioning > Dimensions > Stacked Dimensions** on the Menu bar.
2. Select two or more parallel edges from the drawing view.

3. Move the pointer and click to position the stacked dimension.

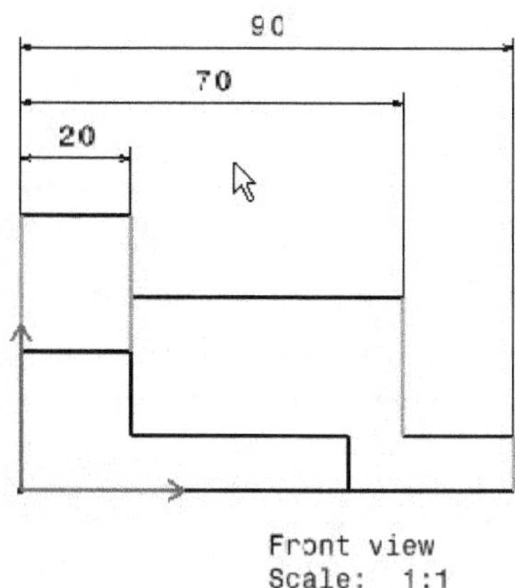

Angle Dimensions

This command creates angle dimensions.

1. On the **Dimensioning** toolbar, click **Dimensions** drop-down > **Angle Dimensions** (or) click **Insert > Dimensioning > Dimensions > Angle Dimensions** on the Menu bar.
2. Select two lines, which are positioned at angle to each other.

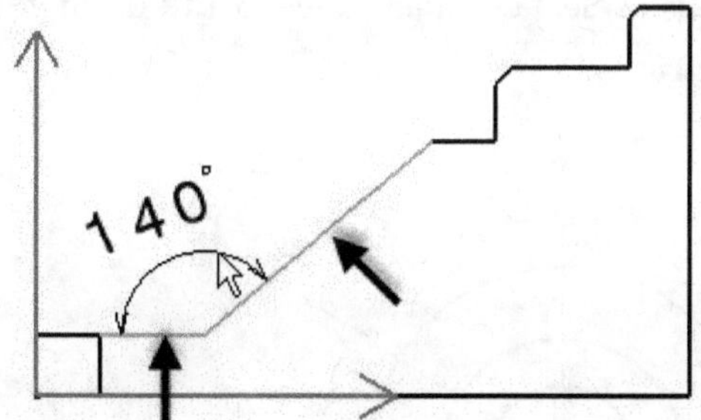

3. Click the right mouse and select any angle sector from the **Angle Sector** menu.

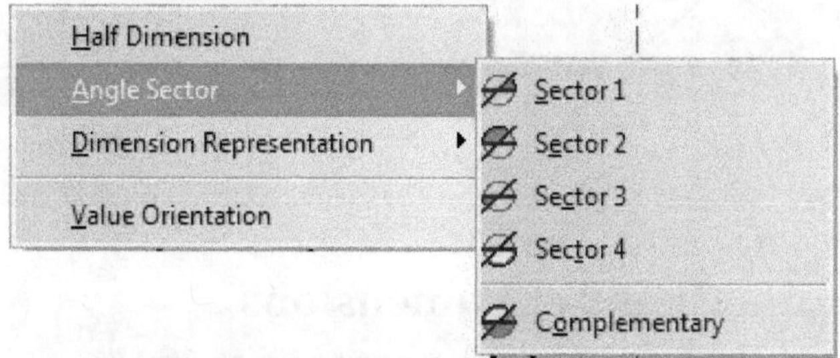

4. Click the right mouse button and select **Half Dimension**, if you want the half dimension of the angle.

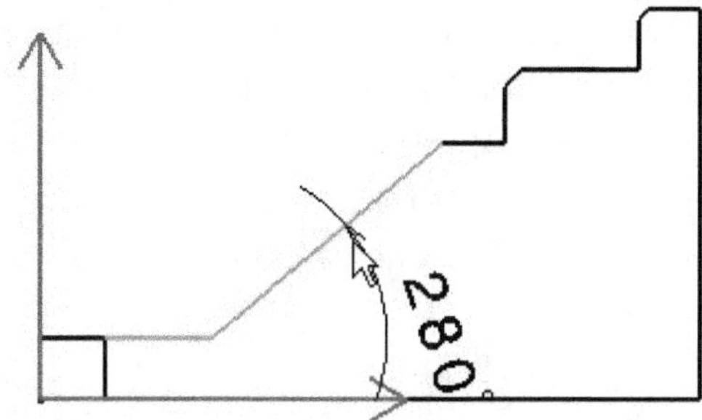

5. Click the right mouse button and select **Value Orientation**. This displays the **Value Orientation** dialog. On this dialog, you can define the orientation of the angle value. For example, if you set the **Reference** to **Screen** and **Orientation** to **Horizontal**, the value will be orientated horizontal to the screen.

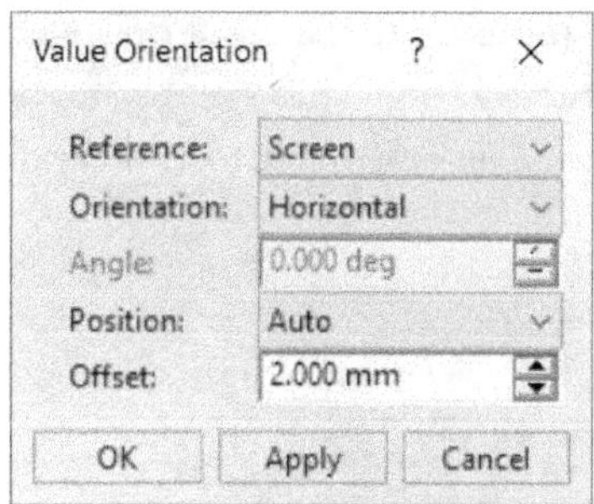

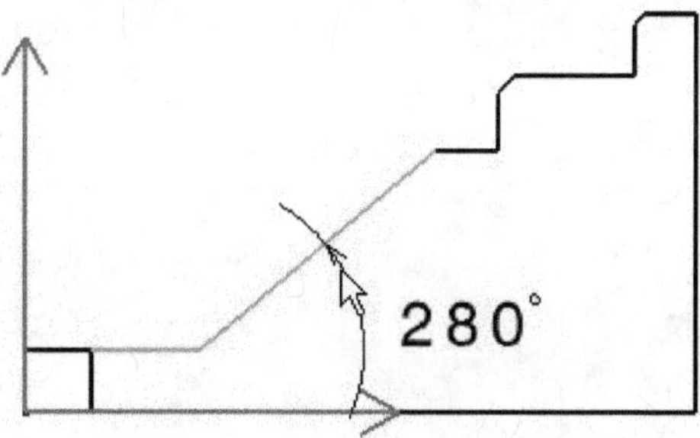

Also, you can use the **Position** drop-down to position the value outside or inside the dimension line. Type-in a value in the **Offset** box to define the gap between the value and the dimension line.

6. Click **OK** to close the dialog.
7. Click to position the dimension.

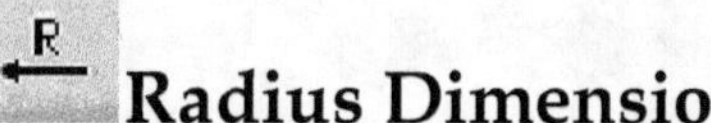

Radius Dimensions

This command creates radius dimensions.

1. On the **Dimensioning** toolbar, click **Dimensions** drop-down > **Radius Dimensions** (or) click **Insert > Dimensioning > Dimensions > Radius Dimensions** on the Menu bar.
2. Select an arc to be dimensioned.

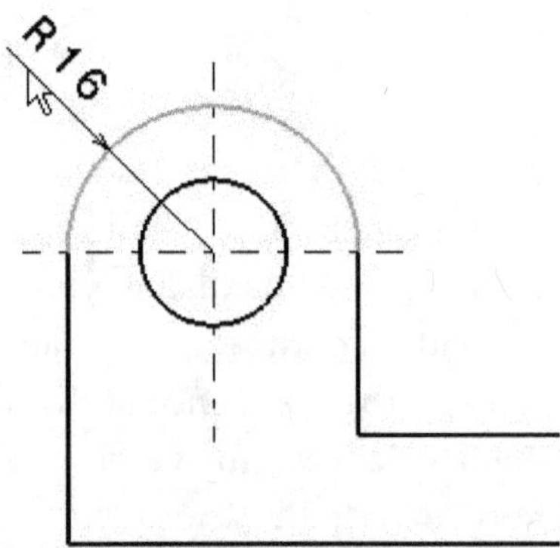

3. Click the right mouse button and deselect the **Extend to Center** option. This creates a radius dimension without extending it to the center of the arc.

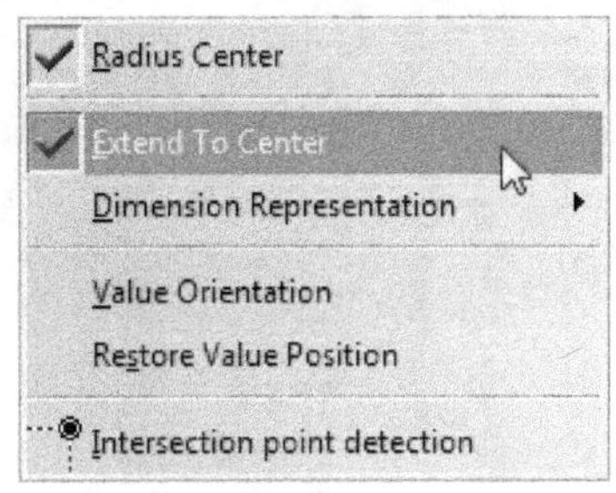

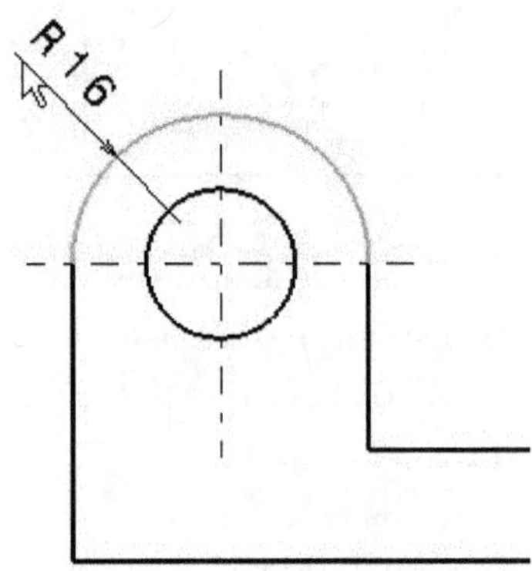

4. Click to place the dimension.

Diameter Dimensions

This command is used to create a diameter dimension for a shafted geometry.

1. On the **Dimensioning** toolbar, click **Dimensions** drop-down > **Diameter Dimensions** (or) click **Insert > Dimensioning > Dimensions > Diameter Dimensions** on the Menu bar.
2. Click on the silhouette edge of the shaft feature. You will notice that the diameter dimension of the shaft feature appears.
3. Move the pointer and click to position the dimension.

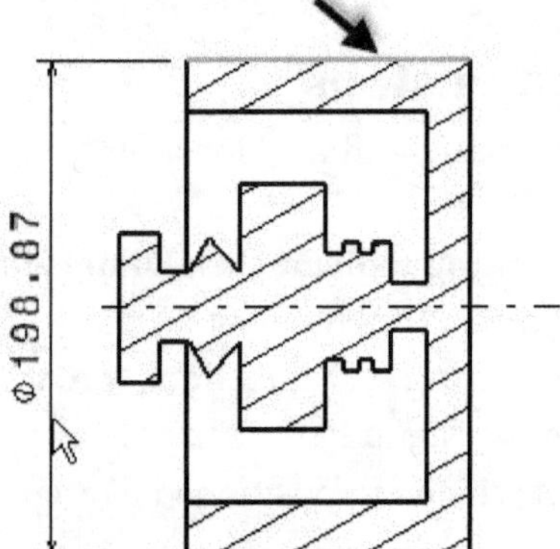

You can also select circular edges to add diameter dimensions.

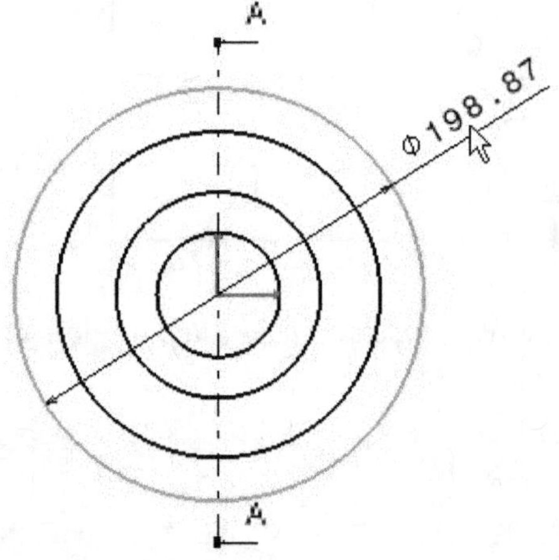

Chamfer Dimensions

This command creates a chamfer dimension.

1. On the **Dimensioning** toolbar, click **Dimensions** drop-down > **Chamfer Dimensions** (or) click **Insert > Dimensioning > Dimensions > Chamfer Dimensions** on the Menu bar.
2. Click on the top portion or bottom portion of the chamfer.

If you click on the top portion, the chamfer dimension will be created with reference to the top edge of the chamfer.

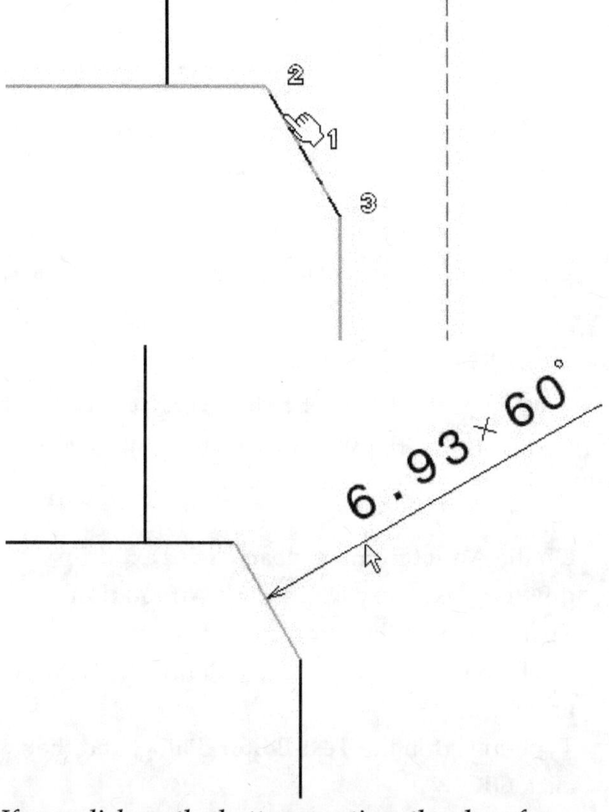

If you click on the bottom portion, the chamfer dimension will be created with reference to the bottom edge of the chamfer.

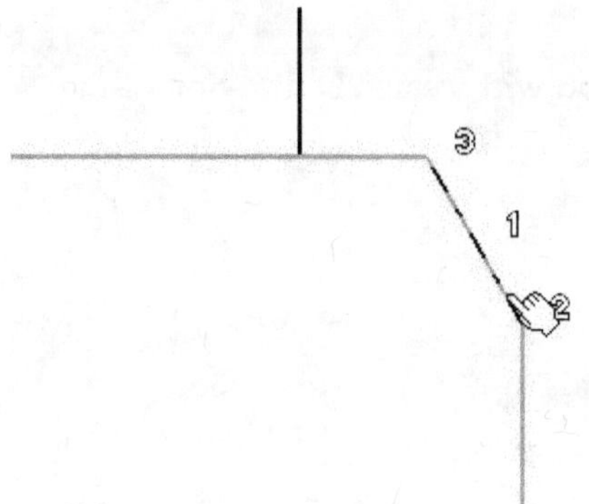

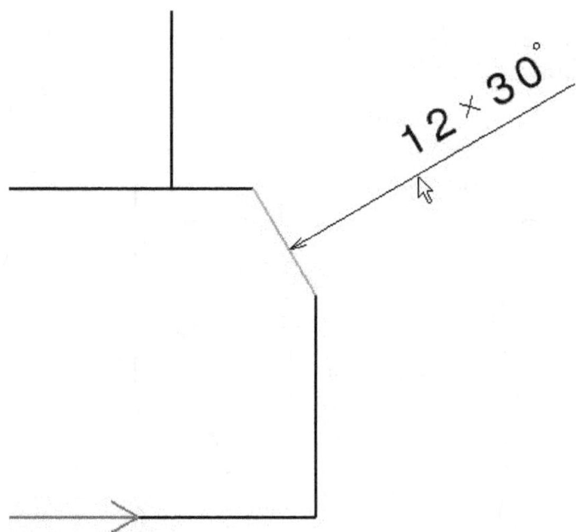

3. On the **Tools Palette** toolbar, select the format of the chamfer dimension. You can select **Length x Length**, **Length x Angle**, **Angle x Length**, or **Length**.

If you want a double-arrowed dimension, then select the **Two Symbols** icon on the **Tools Palette** toolbar.

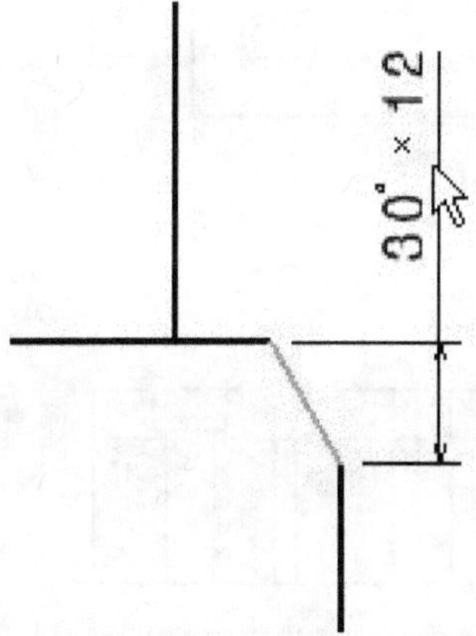

4. Move the pointer and click to position the dimension.

Thread Dimensions

This command generates the dimensions of a threaded feature.

1. Click the right mouse button on the drawing view with a thread feature.

2. Select **Properties**, and then check the **Thread** option under the **Dress up** section.
3. Click **OK** to close the dialog. The thread symbol appears in the drawing view.

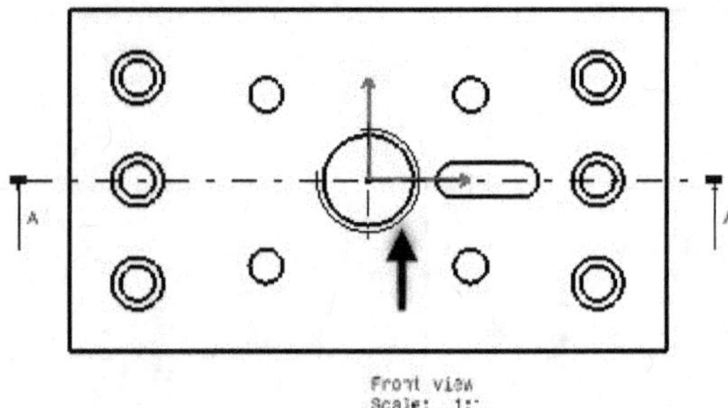

4. On the **Dimensioning** toolbar, click **Dimensions** drop-down > **Thread Dimensions** (or) click **Insert > Dimensioning > Dimensions > Thread Dimensions** on the Menu bar.
5. Select the thread symbol from the drawing view. This generates the dimension of the thread.

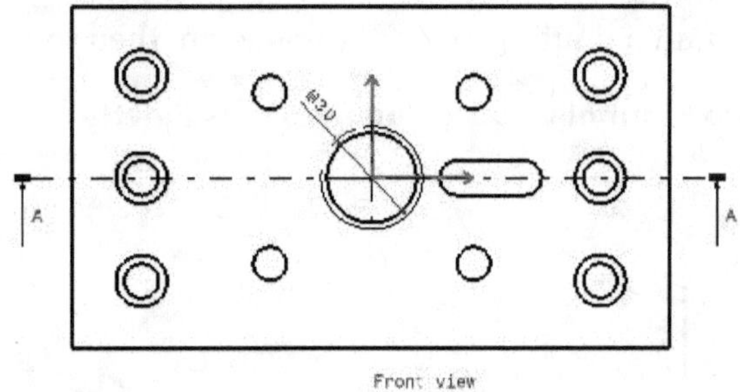

Likewise, you can select the thread symbol on the side or section views.

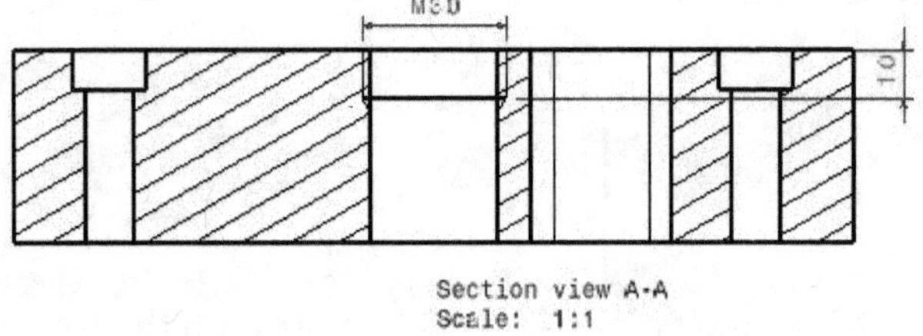

Coordinate Dimensions

This command generates the coordinate values of hole features. You need to ensure that the centerlines of the holes are created.

1. On the **Dimensioning** toolbar, click **Dimensions** drop-down > **Coordinate Dimensions** (or) click **Insert > Dimensioning > Dimensions > Coordinate Dimensions** on the Menu bar.
2. Select the centerlines of the hole.
3. Move the pointer and click to position the dimension.

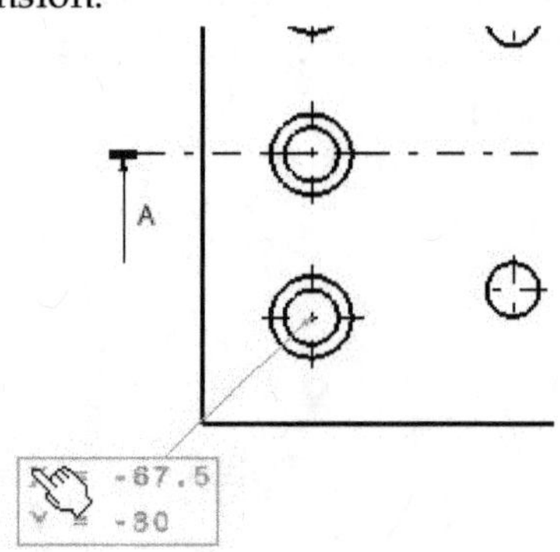

Text

Texts are important part of a drawing. You add text to provide additional details, which cannot be done using dimensions and annotations.

1. On the **Annotations** toolbar, click **Text** drop-down > **Text** (or) click **Insert > Annotations > Text > Text** on the Menu bar.
2. Click on the drawing sheet to define the location of the text.
3. Type-in text in the **Text Editor** dialog, and then click **OK**.

Examples

Example 1

In this example, you will create 2D drawing of the part shown below.

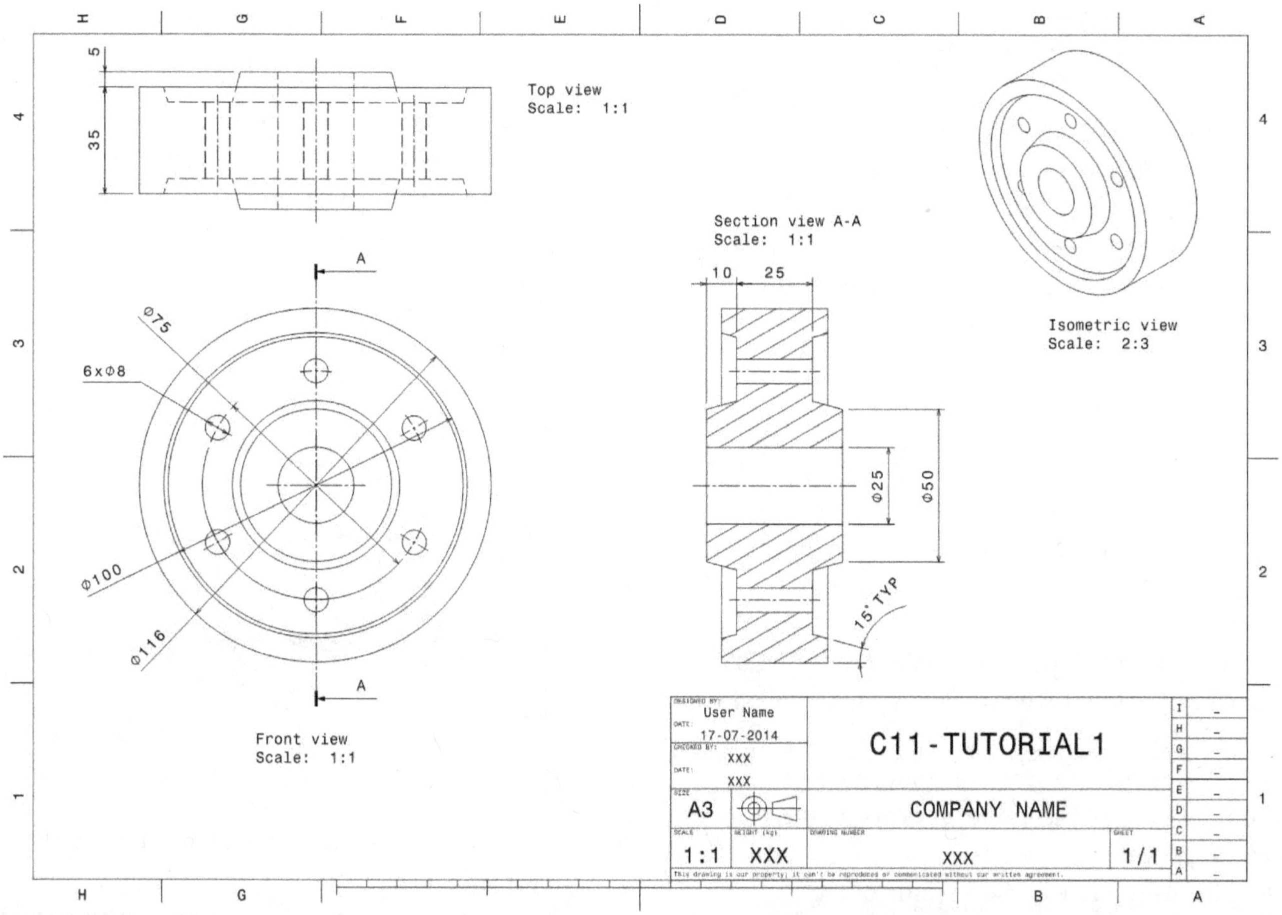

Starting a New Drawing

1. Start CATIA V5-6R2017.
2. Open the Exercise 1 file of Chapter 5.
3. On the **Standard** toolbar, click the **New** button.
4. On the **New** dialog, click **List of Types > Drawing**. Click **OK**.
5. On the **New Drawing** dialog, select **Standard > ISO**.
6. Set **Sheet Style** to **A3 ISO**.
7. Select **Landscape** option and click **OK**.
8. At the left side of the window, click the right mouse button on **Sheet.1** and select **Properties**.
9. On the **Properties** dialog, set **Projection Method** to **Third angle standard**.
10. Click **OK**.

Adding Borders and Title Block

1. On the Menu bar, click **Edit > Sheet Background**. This brings up the sheet background.
2. On the Menu bar, click **Insert > Drawing > Frame and Title Block** (or) click the **Frame and Title Block** button on the **Drawing** toolbar.
3. On the **Manage Frame and Title Block** dialog, select **Style of Title Block > Drawing Titleblock Sample 1**.
4. Select **Action > Create**, and then click **OK**.

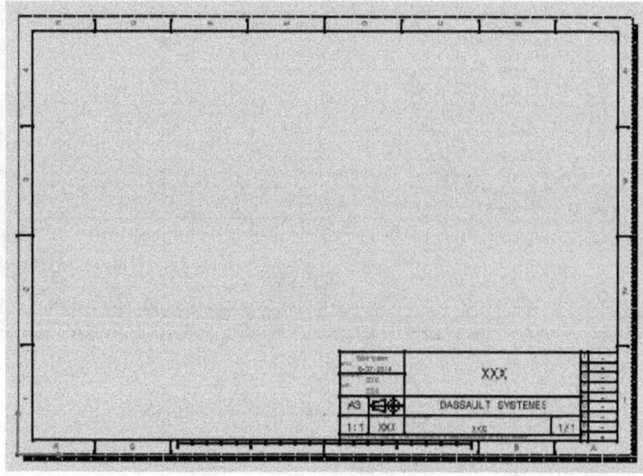

5. In the title block, double-click on DASSAULT

SYSTEMES and type-in your company name in the Text editor. Click **OK** to update the company name.

6. Double-click on the XXX located in the largest cell of the title block, and then type-in **C11-EXAMPLE1** in the Text editor. Click **OK** to update the drawing title.
7. On the Menu bar, click **Edit > Working Views**. This brings up the drawing sheet.

Generating Drawing Views

1. On the **View** toolbar, click the **Front View** button (or) click **Insert > Views > Projections > Front View** on the Menu bar. Now, you have to select a model face or reference plane to define the front view.
2. On the Menu bar, click **Window > C05-Exercise1.CATPart**. This switches you to the part file window.
3. Click on the front face of the model geometry. The front view of the model appears on the drawing sheet.
4. Drag the front view to the left side of the drawing sheet (click and drag the green dotted lines).
5. Click on the drawing sheet to generate the view.

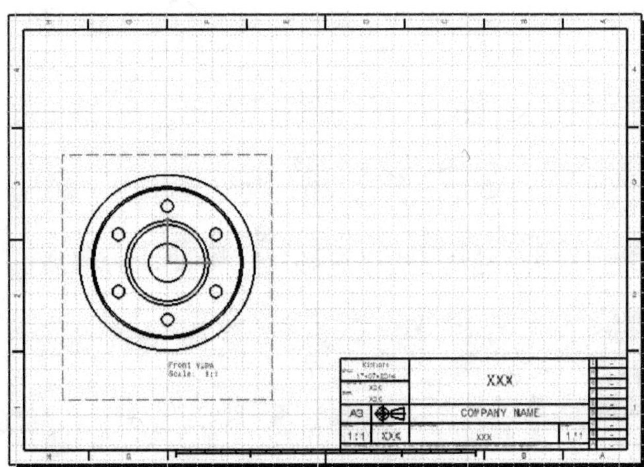

Now, you have to create the projected view.

6. On the **View** toolbar, click **Projections** drop-down > **Projection View** (or) click **Insert > Views > Projections > Projection**.
7. Move the pointer up and click to position the projected view.

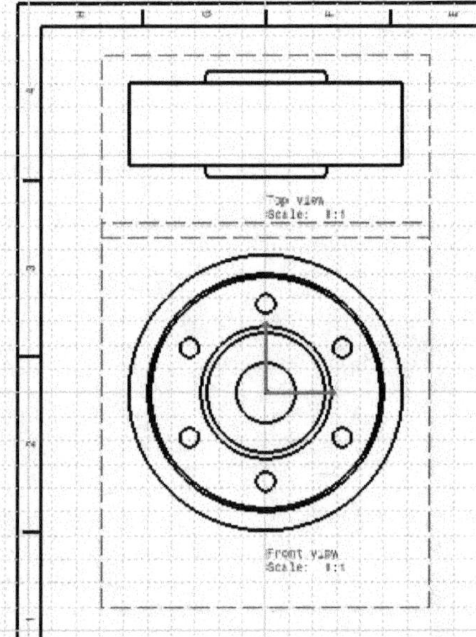

Now, you have to turn-on the hidden lines of the projected view.

8. Click the right mouse button on the projected view and select **Properties**.
9. On the **Properties** dialog, under the **Dress-Up** section, check the **Hidden Lines** option, and then click **OK**. The hidden lines appear on the projected view.

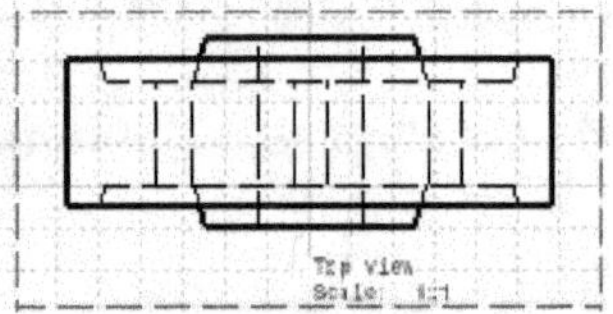

Now, you have to create the section view.

10. On the **View** toolbar, click the **Offset Section View** button (or) click **Insert > Views > Sections > Offset Section View**.
11. Draw a vertical line passing through the center of the front view.

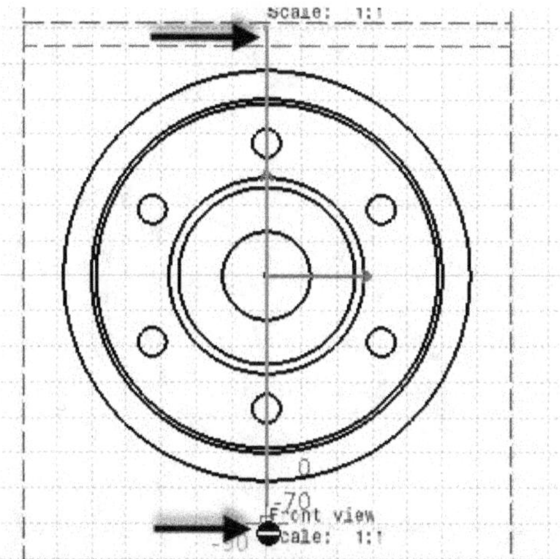

12. Double-click on the endpoint of line.
13. Move the pointer toward right and click to position the section view.

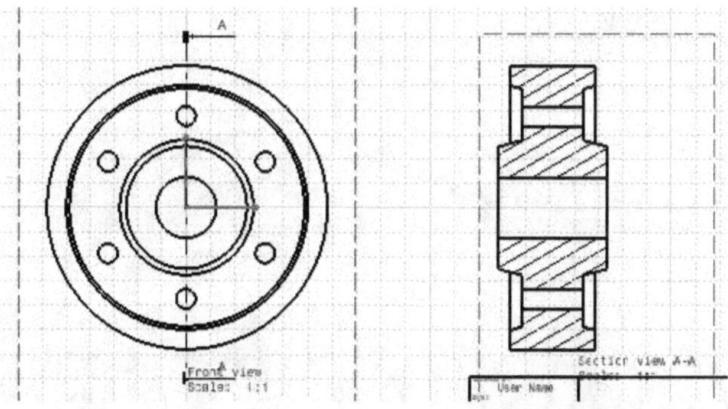

Now, you have to create the Isometric view.

14. On the **View** toolbar, click **Projections** drop-down > **Isometric View** (or) click **Insert > Views > Projections > Isometric** on the Menu bar.
15. On the Menu bar, click **Window > C05-Exercise1.CATPart**. This switches you to part file window.
16. Click on the front face of the model geometry. The Isometric view of the model appears on the drawing sheet.
17. Drag the view to the top-right corner of the drawing sheet.
18. Click on the drawing sheet to generate the Isometric View.

You can notice that the size of the Isometric View is large. You have to scale the Isometric View to have enough space for dimensions.

19. Click the right mouse button on the Isometric view and select **Properties**.
20. On the **Properties** dialog, under the **Scale and Orientation** section, type-in 2:3 in the **Scale** box. Click **OK** to update the view.
21. Drag the view to the top-right corner.

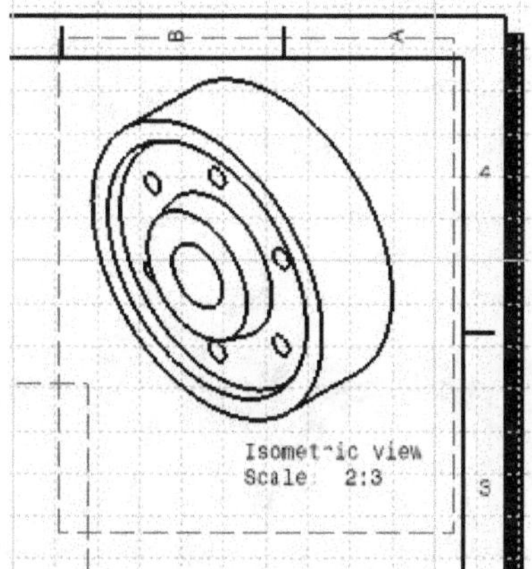

Add Axis lines

1. Click the right mouse button on the section view and select **Properties**.
2. On the **Properties** dialog, under the **Dress-up** section, check the **Axis** option.
3. Click **OK** to add axis lines to the section view.

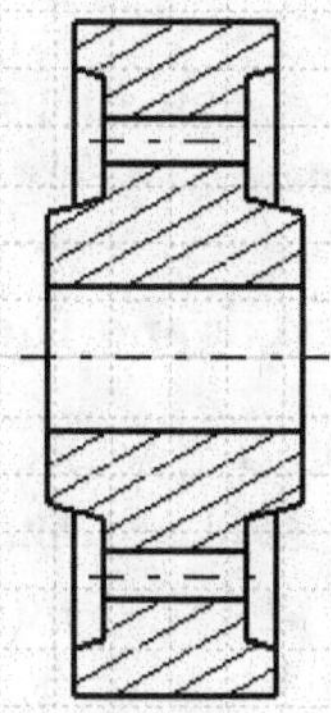

4. Likewise, add axis lines to the top view.

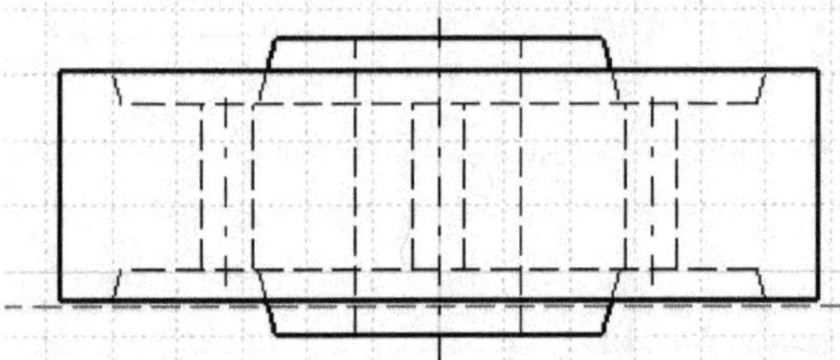

Add Center Lines to the Front View

1. On the **Dress-Up** toolbar, click **Axis and Threads** drop-down > **Center Line** (or) click **Insert > Dress-up > Axis and Threads > Center Line** on the Menu bar.
2. Click on the circle located at the center of the front view. This adds a centerline the front view.

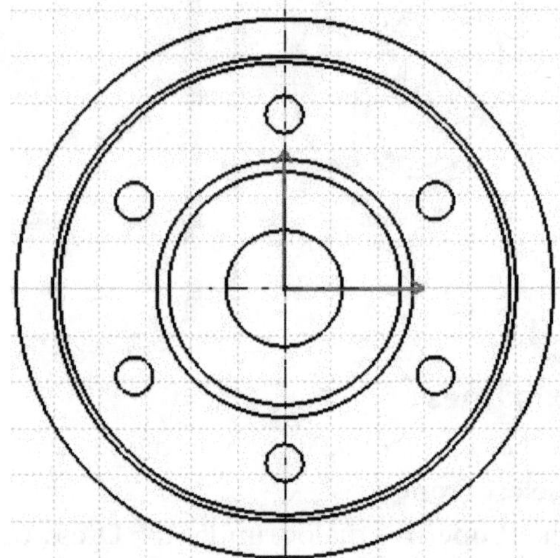

Now, you have to add centerlines to the other circles on the front view. Keep in mind that the orientation of the centerlines is different for each circle. To create centerlines with different orientation, you can use the **Center Line with Reference** command.

3. On the **Dress-Up** toolbar, click **Axis and Threads** drop-down > **Center Line with Reference** (or) click **Insert > Dress -up > Axis and Threads > Center Line with Reference** on the Menu bar.
4. Select anyone of the small circles, and then the large circle located at the center. This creates a centerline on small circle with reference to the center point of the large circle.

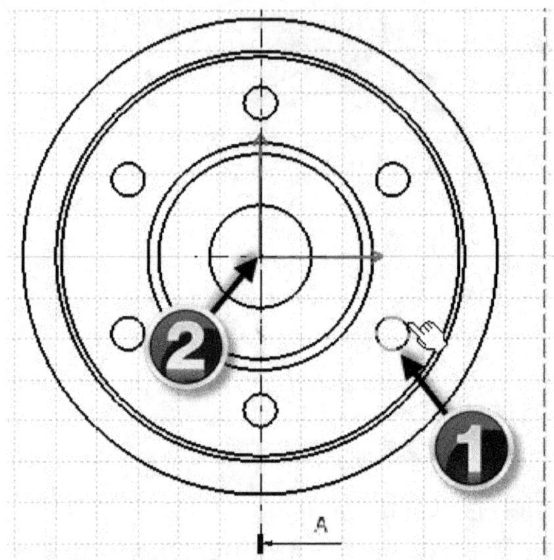

5. Likewise, create centerlines on the other small circles.

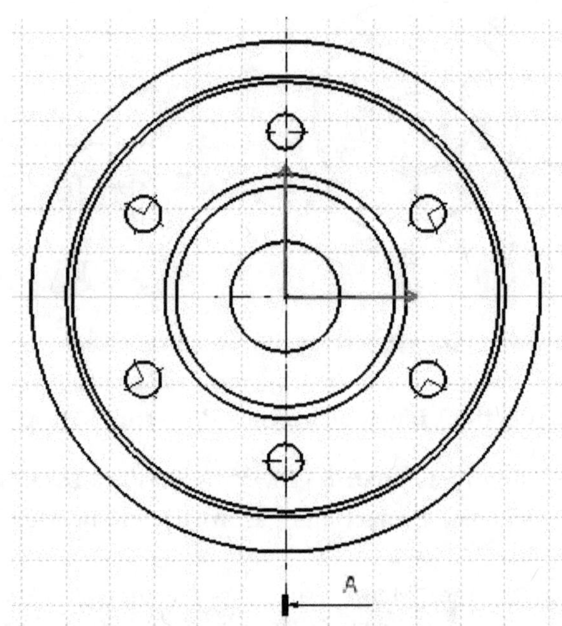

Add Dimensions to the drawing

1. On the **Dimensioning** toolbar, click **Dimensions** drop-down > **Dimensions** (or) click **Insert > Dimensioning > Dimensions > Dimensions** on the Menu bar.
2. Zoom into the front view and click on the outer most circle.
3. Move the pointer and click to position the dimension.

4. Likewise, dimension the second circle from outside.

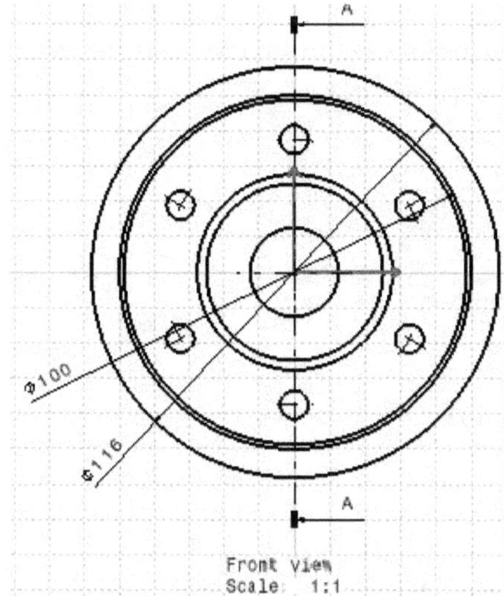

5. Activate the **Dimensions** command and click the small circle located at left side on the front view.
6. Move the pointer and click to position the dimension.

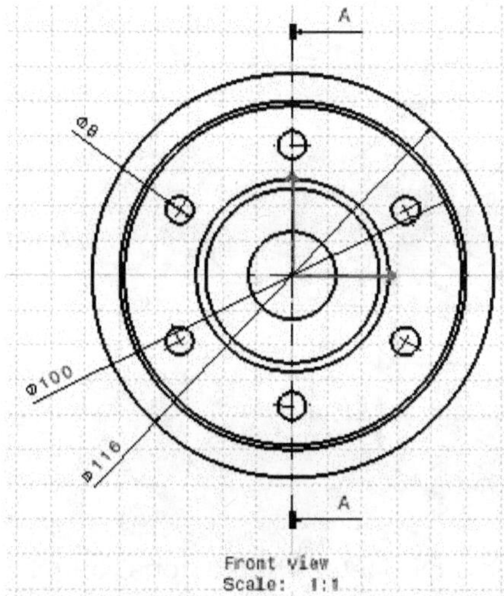

7. Click the right mouse button on the dimension and select **Properties**.
8. On the **Properties** dialog, click the **More** button located at the bottom right. This displays additional tabs on the dialog.
9. Click the **Dimension Line** tab and select **Representation > Two Parts**.

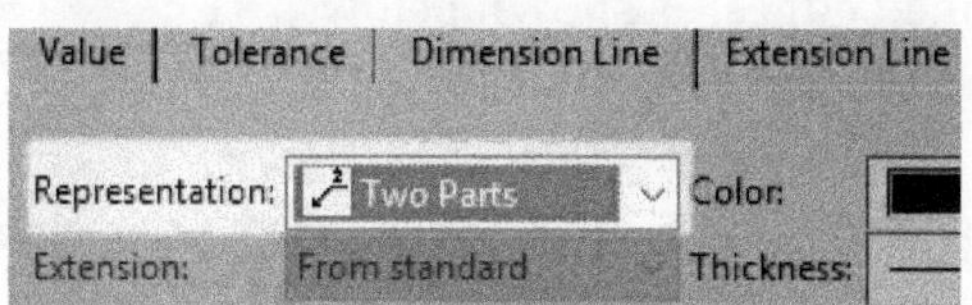

10. Click the **Dimension Texts** tab and type-in 6x in the box located on left-side of Main value.

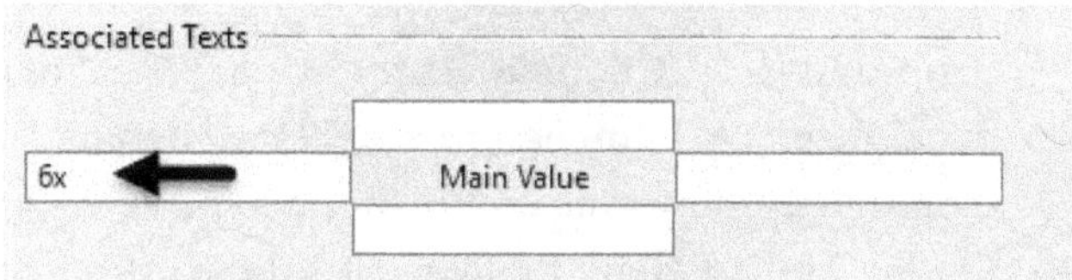

11. Click **OK**.

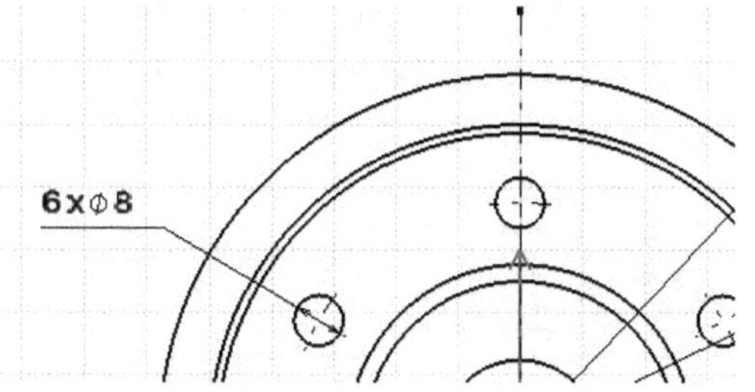

12. Activate the **Dimensions** command and click on the centerline of anyone of the small circles.

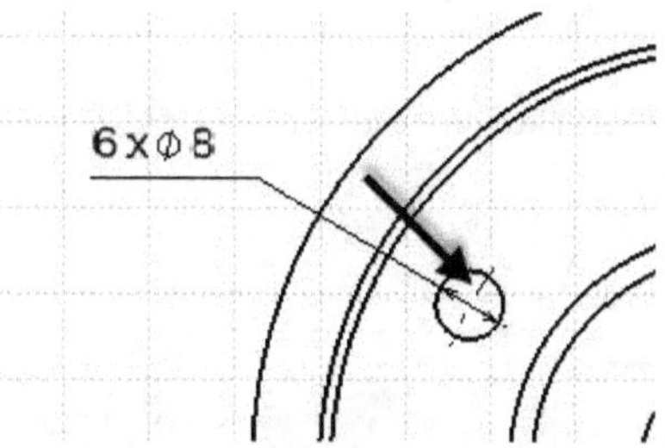

13. Move the pointer and click to position the dimension.

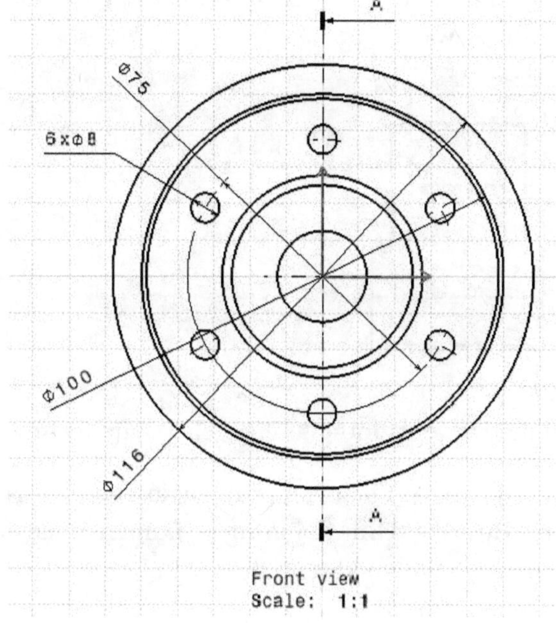

14. On the **Dimensioning** toolbar, click **Dimensions drop-down > Chained Dimensions** (or) click **Insert > Dimensioning > Dimensions > Chained Dimensions** on the Menu bar.
15. On the **Tools Palette** toolbar, click the **Intersection point detection** button.
16. Zoom into the top view and click on the end points, as shown below.

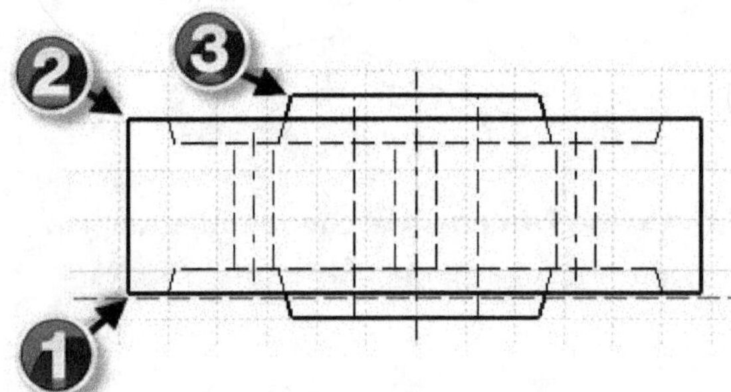

17. Move the pointer toward left and click to position the dimension.

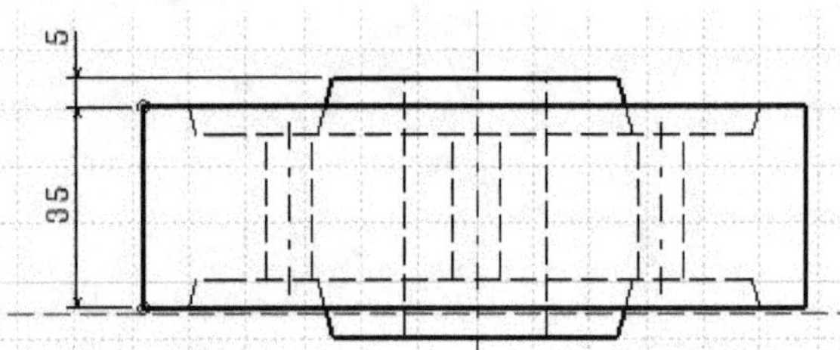

18. Likewise, create a chained dimension on the section view.

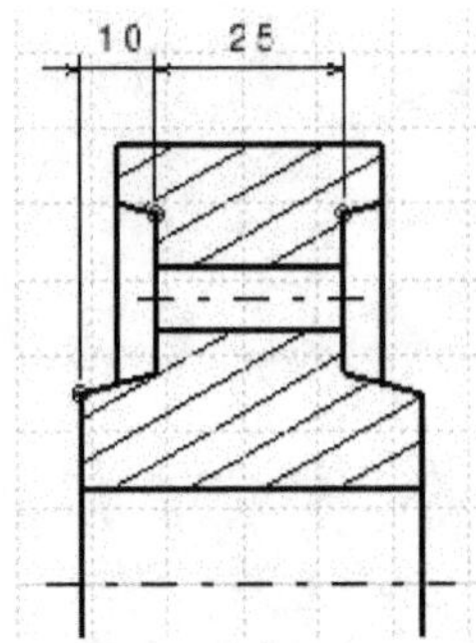

19. On the **Dimensioning** toolbar, click **Dimensions drop-down > Diameter Dimensions** (or) click **Insert > Dimensioning > Dimensions > Diameter Dimensions** on the Menu bar.
20. On the **Tools Palette** toolbar, deactivate the **Intersection point detection** button.
21. Zoom in to the section view and click on the innermost horizontal edge.

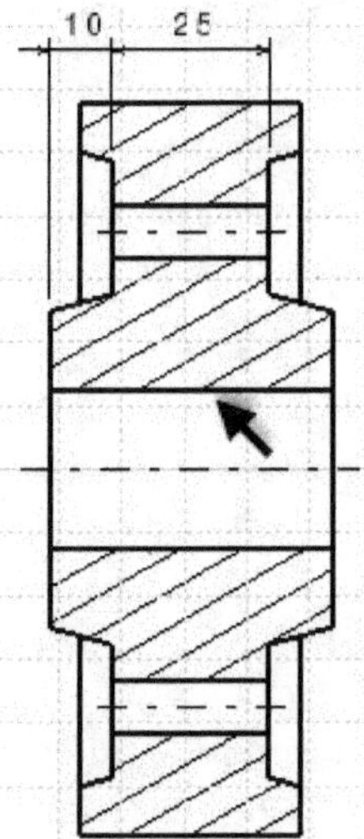

22. Move the pointer toward right and click to position the dimension.

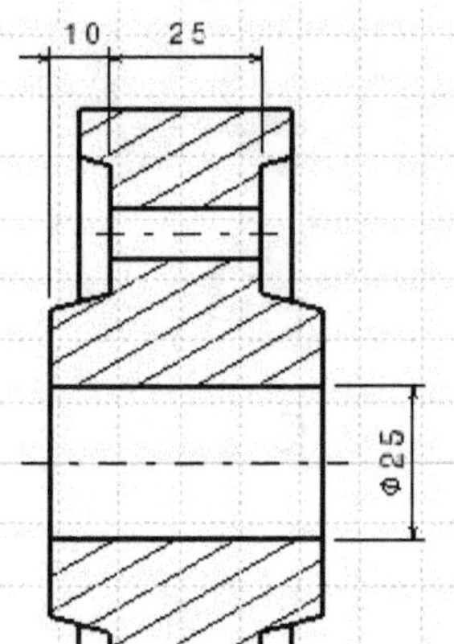

23. Activate the **Diameter Dimensions** command and select the **Intersection point detection** button on the **Tools Palette** toolbar.

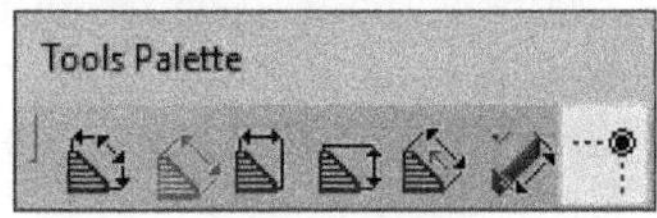

24. On the section view, select the vertices of the inclined edges, as shown below.

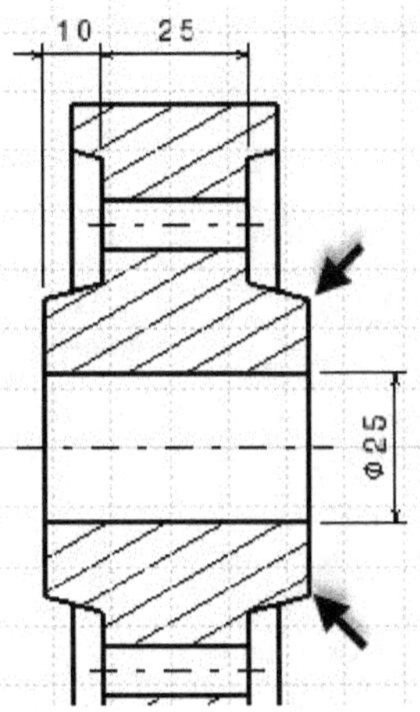

25. Move the pointer and click to position the dimension.

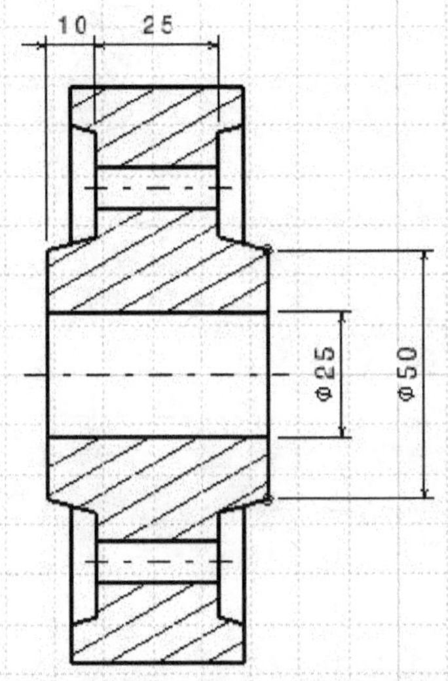

Now, you have to add an angular dimension to the inclined edge of the section view.

26. On the **Dimensioning** toolbar, click **Dimensions drop-down > Angle Dimensions** (or) click **Insert > Dimensioning > Dimensions > Angle Dimensions** on the Menu bar.
27. Zoom into the section view and select the inclined and horizontal edges at the bottom.
28. Move the pointer toward right and click to position the angle dimension.

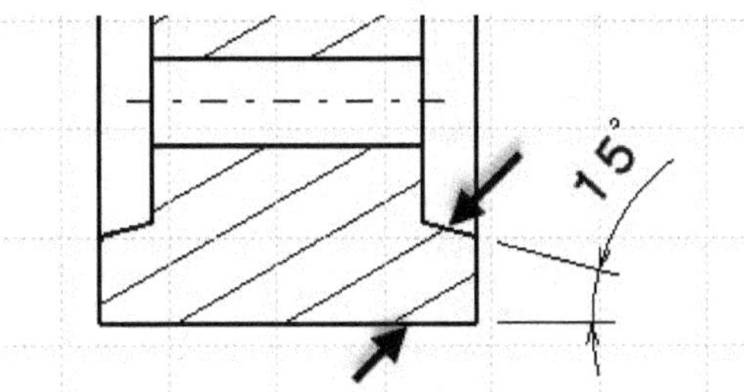

29. Click the right mouse button on the angle dimension and select **Properties**.
30. On the **Properties** dialog, click the **Dimension Text** tab, and then type-in TYP in the box located at right side of Main value.

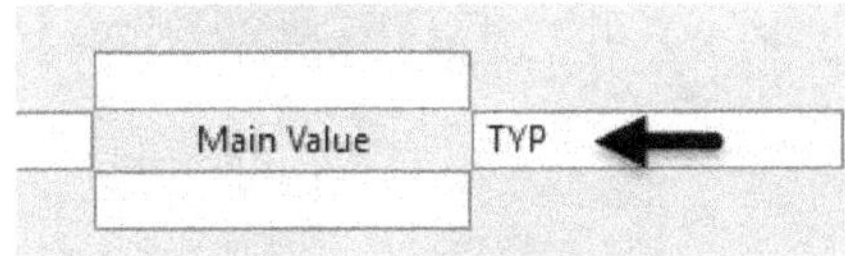

31. Click **OK** to update the dimension.

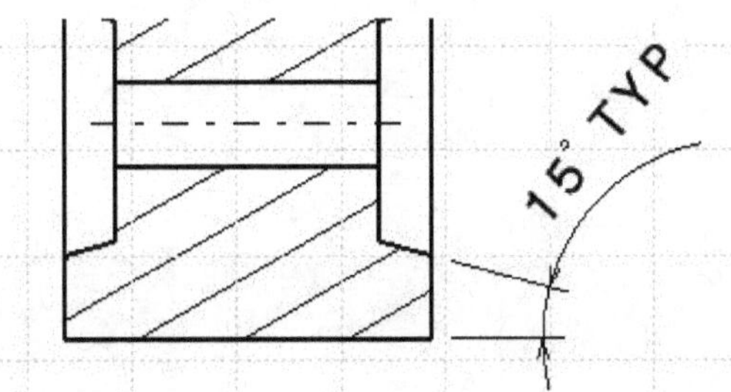

Printing the drawing

1. On the Menu bar, click **File > Print**.
2. On the **Print** dialog, click the **Page Setup** button to open the **Page Setup** dialog.
3. On the **Page Setup** dialog, check the **Use image format** option and click **OK**.
4. Select the printer from the **Printer Name** drop-down, and then click **OK**.
5. Specify the name and location of the file (in case of a PDF or image file).

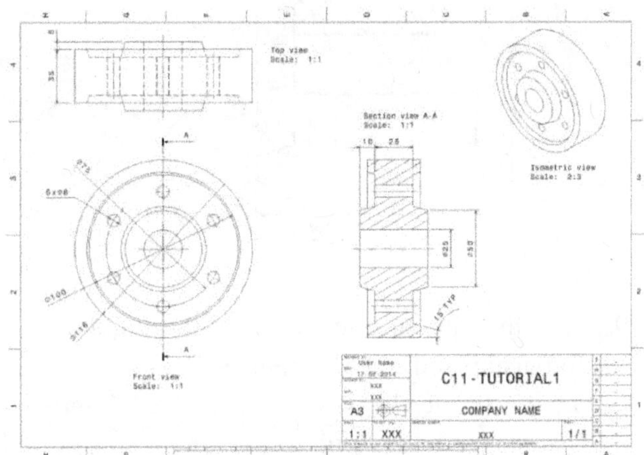

6. Save and close the drawing.

Example 2

In this example, you will create an assembly drawing shown below

.

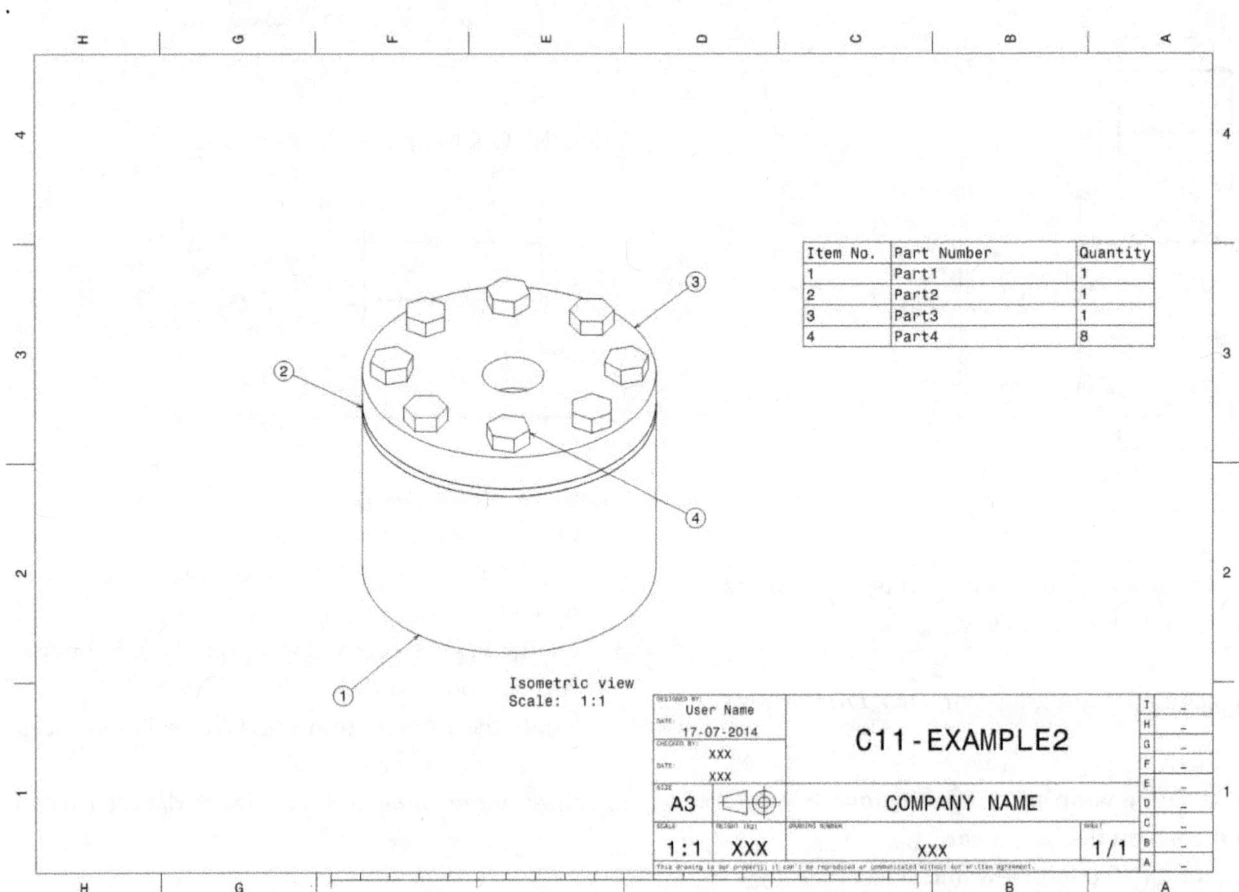

Item No.	Part Number	Quantity
1	Part1	1
2	Part2	1
3	Part3	1
4	Part4	8

1. Open the Example 2 file that you have created in Chapter 10.
2. Click **Start > Mechanical Design > Drafting**.
3. On the **New Drawing Creation** dialog, click the **Modify** button to open the **New Drawing** dialog.
4. On this dialog, set the **Sheet Style** to **A3 ISO**, and click **OK**.
5. On the **New Drawing Creation** dialog, click the **Empty sheet** option, and then click **OK**.
6. On the Menu bar, click **Edit > Sheet Background** and add title block to the background.

7. Update the company name and drawing title.
8. On the Menu bar, click **Edit > Working Views**.
9. On the **Views** toolbar, click **Projections** drop-down > **Isometric View** .
10. On the Menu bar, click **Window > C10-Example2** to switch to the assembly file.
11. In the Specification Tree, expand Part1 and select zx plane.

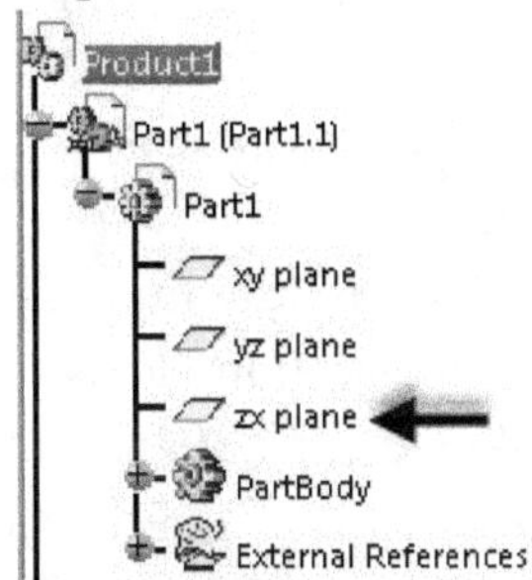

12. Click on the drawing sheet to generate the Isometric view of the assembly.

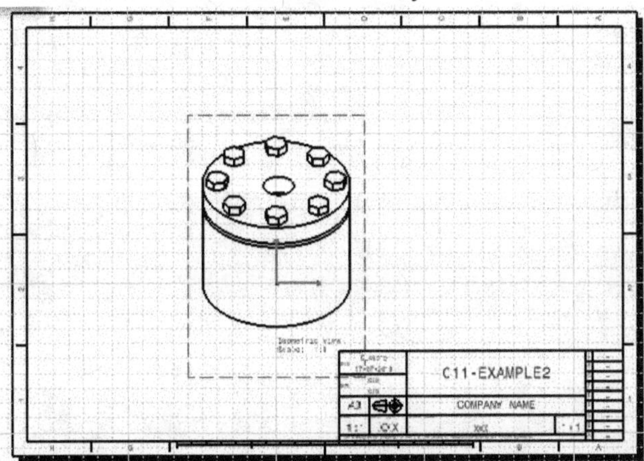

13. On the Menu bar, click **Insert > Generation > Bill of Material > Advanced Bill of Material**.
14. Click **OK**.
15. Click on the top-right corner to position the bill of material.
16. Click the right mouse button on the bill of material and select **Properties**.
17. On the **Properties** dialog, click the **Reported Properties** tab to view the properties of the BOM.
18. From the **List of Properties** section, select **Type**, **Nomenclature**, and **Revision** (press and hold the Ctrl key and click on them).

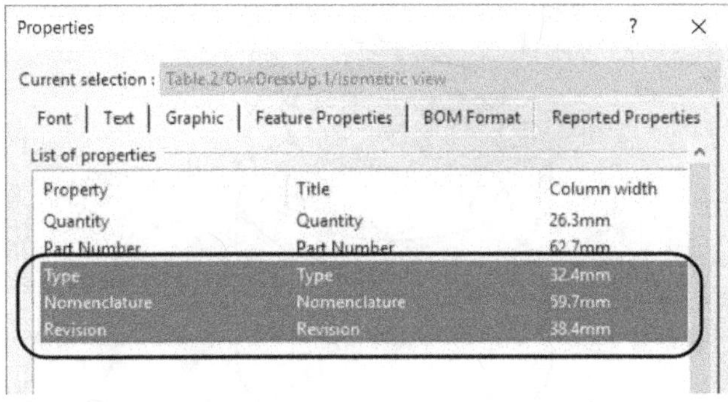

19. At the lower right corner of the dialog, click the **Delete** button.
20. Click the **New** button to add a new property to the table.
21. At the bottom of the table, set the values, as shown in figure.

22. Select the **Item No.** property from the table and click **Move Up** twice. This moves the **Item No.** property to the top of the table.
23. Likewise, move the **Quantity** property to the bottom of the table.

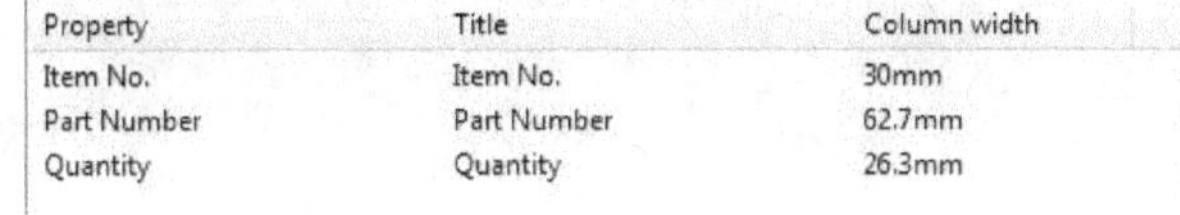

Property	Title	Column width
Item No.	Item No.	30mm
Part Number	Part Number	62.7mm
Quantity	Quantity	26.3mm

24. Click **OK** to update the BOM.

Item No.	Part Number	Quantity
1	Part1	1
2	Part2	1
3	Part3	1
4	Part4	8

25. On the Menu bar, click **Insert > Generation > Balloon Generation**. This automatically generates the balloons.
26. Drag the balloons to arrange them properly.

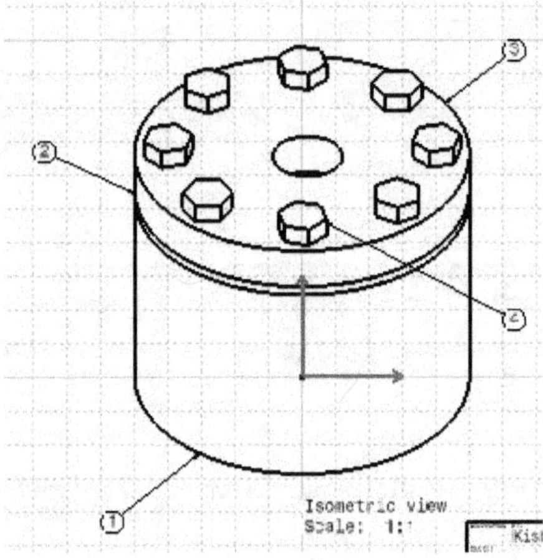

27. Save and close the drawing.

Questions

1. How to create drawing views using **View Creation Wizard** command?
2. How do you show or hide hidden edges of a drawing view?
3. How do you retrieve dimensions of the 3D part model?
4. How to update the drawing views when the part is edited?
5. How do you control the properties of dimensions and annotations?
6. List the commands used to create centerlines and center marks.
7. How do you add symbols and texts to a dimension?
8. How do you add break lines to drawing view?
9. How do you create revolved section views?
10. How do you create exploded view of an assembly?

Exercises

Exercise 1

Create orthographic views of the part model shown next. Add dimensions and annotations to the drawing.

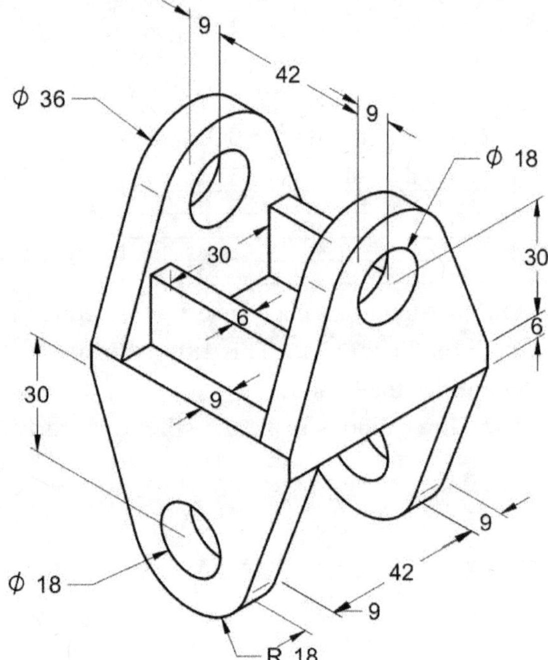

Exercise 2

Create orthographic views and an auxiliary view of the part model shown below. Add dimensions and annotations to the drawing.

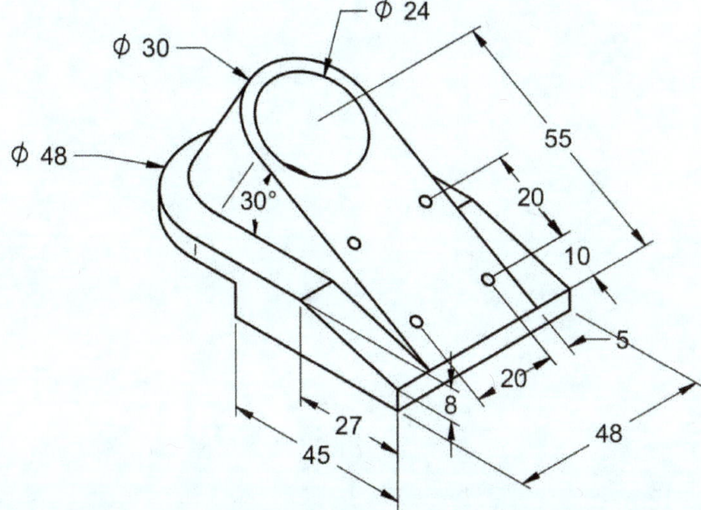

Chapter 12: Sheet Metal Design

You can make sheet metal parts by bending and forming flat sheets of metal. In CATIA V5, sheet-metal parts can be folded and unfolded enabling you to show them in the flat pattern as well as their bent-up state. There are two ways to design sheet-metal parts in CATIA V5. Either you can start the sheet-metal part from scratch using sheet-metal features throughout the design process or you can design it as a regular solid part and later convert it to a sheet-metal part. Most commonly, you design sheet-metal parts in **Generative Sheet metal Design** Workbench from the beginning. In this chapter, you will learn both the approaches.

The topics covered in this chapter are:

- *Walls*
- *Walls of edges*
- *Extrusion*
- *Flanges*
- *Bend Allowance*
- *Hems*
- *Tear Drops*
- *User Flanges*
- *Bends*
- *Conical bends*
- *Bend from flat*
- *Unfolding*
- *Folding*
- *Fold/Unfold*
- *Stamps*
- *Cut outs*
- *Convert to Sheet Metal*
- *Export to DXF*

Starting a Sheet Metal part

To start a new sheet metal part, follow the steps given next.

1. Select **Start > Mechanical Design > Generative Sheet Metal Design** on the Menu bar.
2. On the **New Part** dialog, type-in the name of the part, and then click **OK**.

 Sheet Metal Parameters

Sheet Metal Parameters define the material thickness, bend size, bend extremities, and bend allowances. You can define these parameters by using the **Sheet Metal Parameters** command.

1. On the **Walls** toolbar, click the **Sheet Metal Parameters** button (or) click **Insert > Sheet Metal Parameters** on the Menu bar.
2. On the **Sheet Metal Parameters** dialog, type-in **Thickness** and **Default Bend Radius** values. You can also use an excel sheet to define these values. Click the **Sheet Standard files** button and select the worksheet or text file containing the thickness and bend radius values.

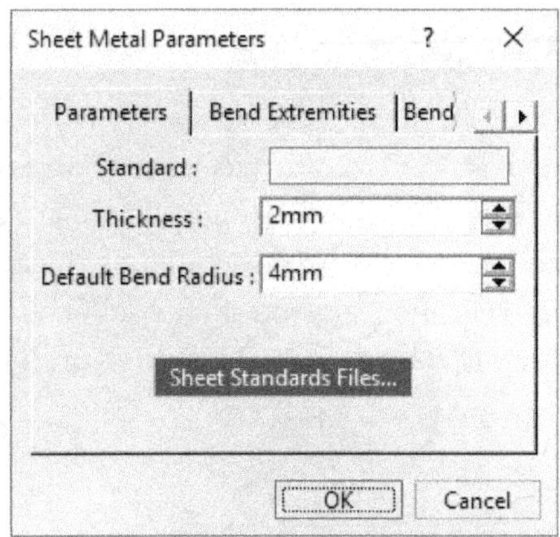

3. Click the **Bend Extremities** tab and select the type of relief to be provided to a bend. The options available in this tab are given next.

Minimum with no relief: This option provides no relief at the bend corners.

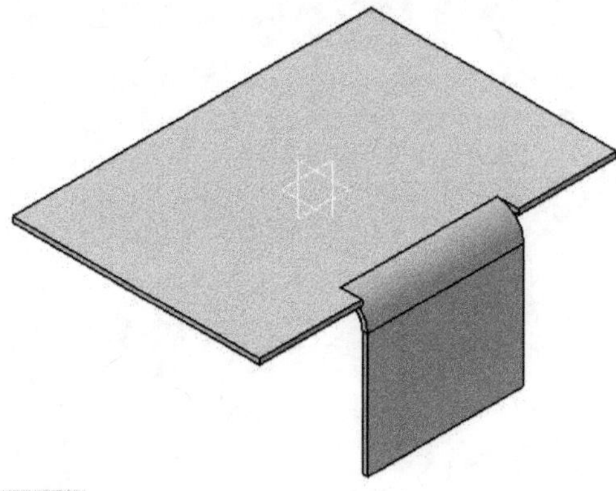

Square relief: A square relief is applied to bend extremes.

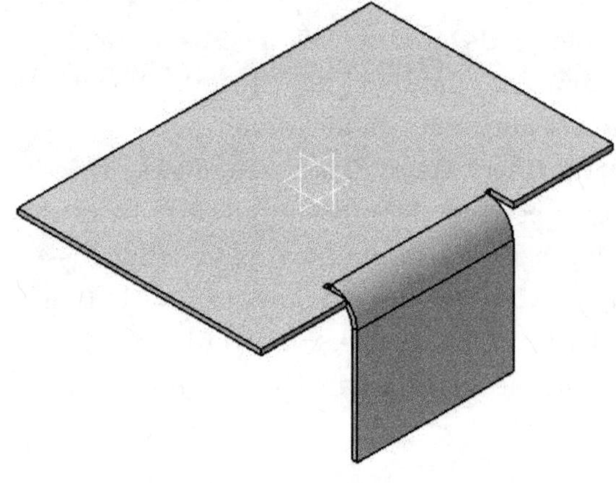

Round relief: A round relief is applied to bend extremes.

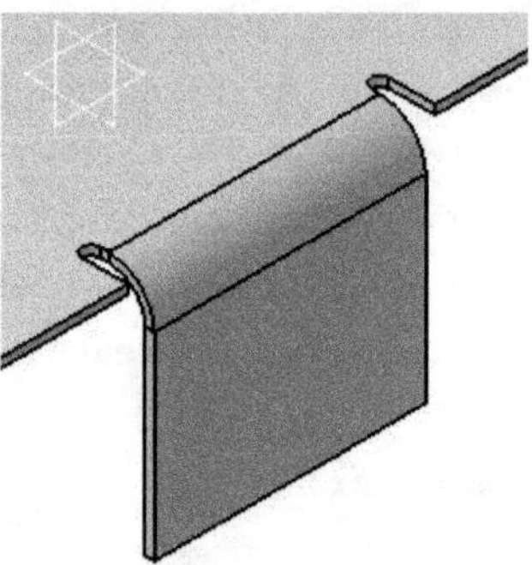

Linear: A linear relief is added between the end faces of the bend and supporting wall.

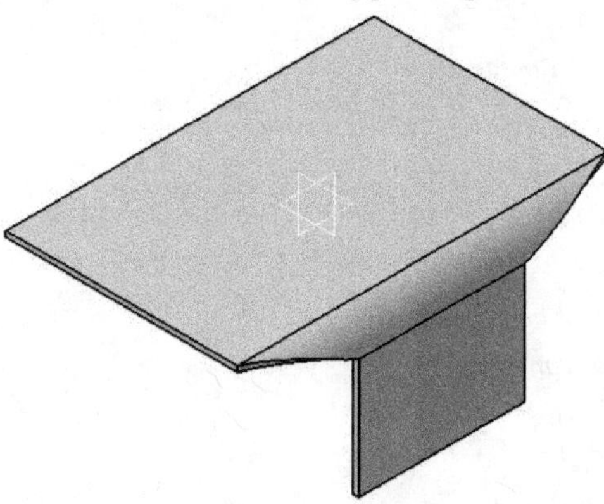

Tangent: The end faces of the bend will be tangent to the end faces of the supporting wall.

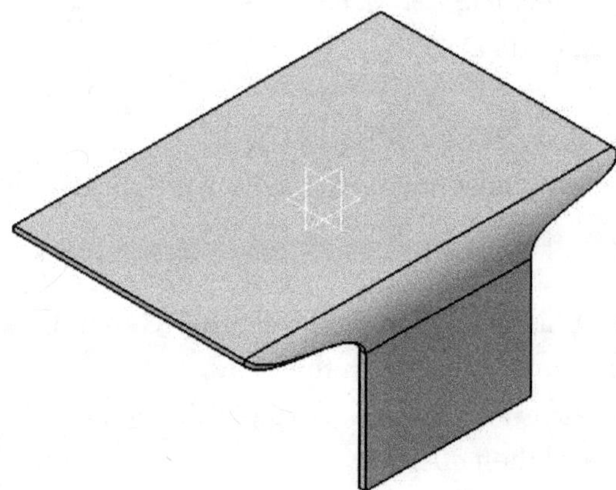

Maximum: This option provides maximum relief at the bend extremes.

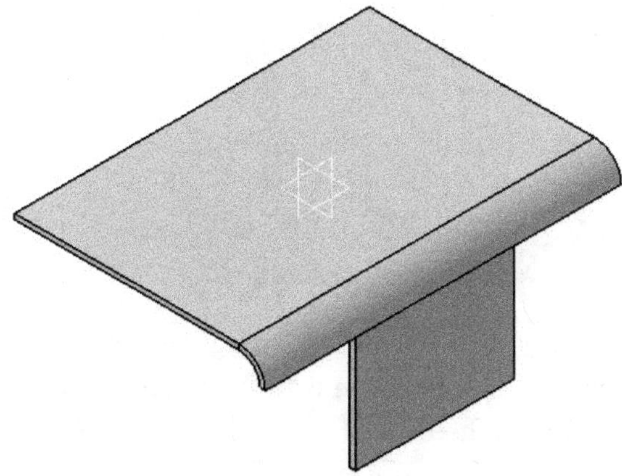

Closed: This option closes the corner formed by two intersecting bends.

Flat joint: This option applies no relief between two intersecting bends.

4. Click the **Bend Allowance** tab to view the K factor.

The **K Factor** is the ratio that represents the location of the neutral sheet measured from the inside face with respect to the thickness of the sheet metal part. The Neutral Factor defines the bend allowance of the sheet metal part. The standard formula that calculates the bend allowance is given below.

$$BA = \frac{\pi(R + KT)A}{180}$$

A = Bend Allowance

R = Bend Radius

K = Neutral Factor = t/T

T = Material Thickness

t= Distance from inside face to the neutral sheet

A = Bend Angle

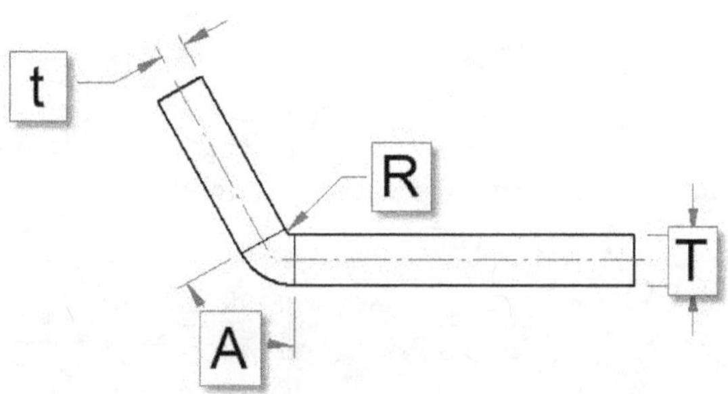

You can also define the bend allowance by using your own bend allowance formula. To enter a bend allowance formula, select the **formula editor** button located next to the **K factor** box. On the **Formula Editor** dialog, define a new formula using the available parameters.

5. Click **OK**.

Wall

The wall is a basic type of sheet metal feature.

1. To create a wall, create a closed sketch on a plane.

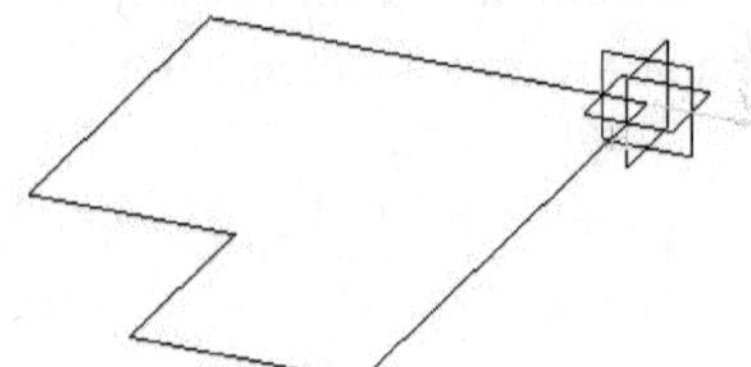

2. On the **Walls** toolbar, click the **Wall** button (or) click **Insert > Walls > Wall** on the Menu bar.
3. Click on the sketch.
4. On the **Wall Definition** dialog, click the **Sketch at middle position** button, if you want the sketch to be at the middle of the wall thickness.
5. Type-in a value in the **Offset** box, if you want to create the wall at an offset from the sketch.

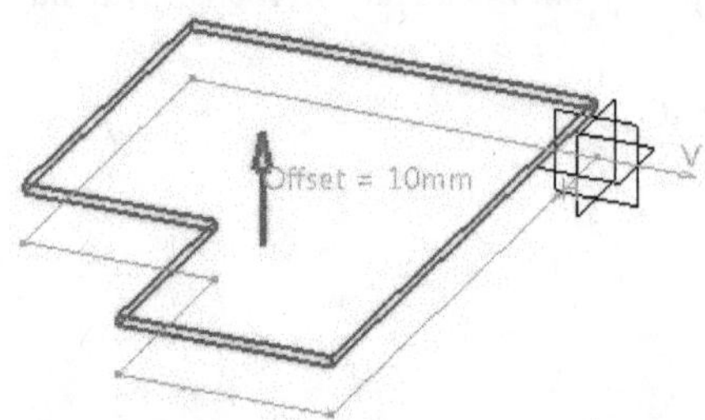

6. Click the **Invert Side** button to reverse the direction of the wall.
7. Click **OK**.

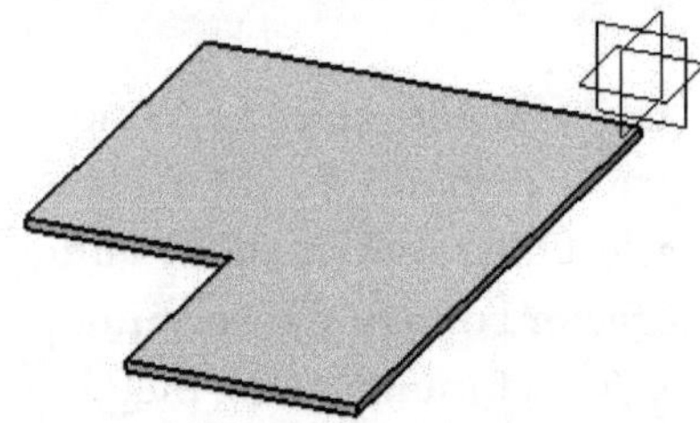

Wall on Edge

The second feature after creating a wall is wall on edge. You can create this feature along an edge or multiple edges of a sheet metal part.

1. On the **Walls** toolbar, click the **Wall on Edge** button (or) click **Insert > Walls > Wall on Edge** on the Menu bar.
2. Click an edge of the wall feature. The wall preview appears on the selected edge.

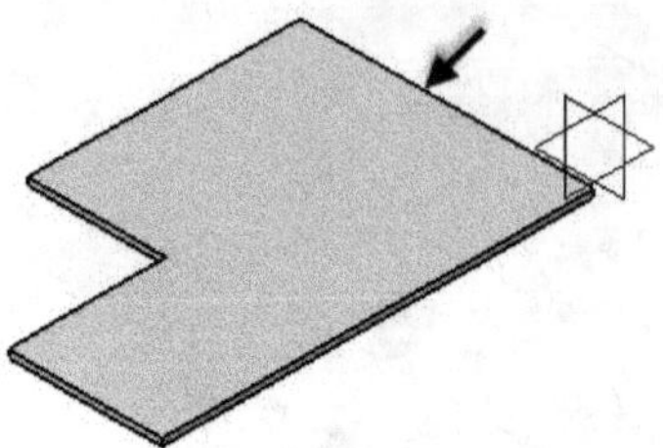

3. Click the green arrow and drag the pointer to change the height of the wall. You can also type-in a value in the **Height** box.

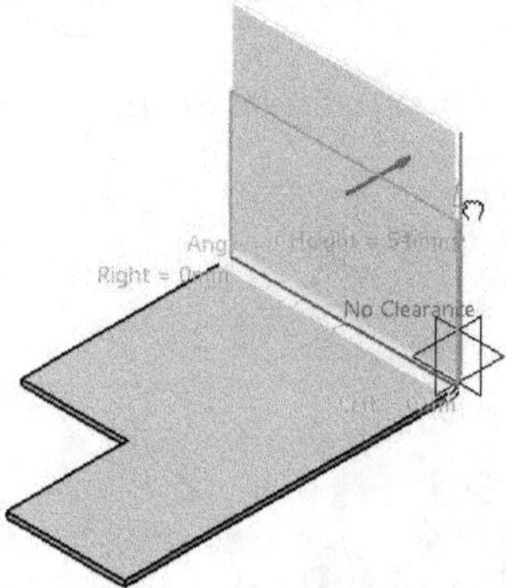

4. Set the **Length type**. The length type options are given next.

This option measures the length of the wall from the outer face of the base wall up to the outer edge of the new wall.

This option measures the length of wall from the inner face of the base wall up to the outer edge of the new wall.

This option measures the length of wall excluding the bend.

This option measures the length of wall from its outer edge up to the intersection point between the outer faces of new wall and base wall.

This option measures the length of the wall from its outer edge up to the intersection point between the inner faces of new wall and base wall.

5. Type-in a value in the **Angle** box.

If you want to match the outer face of the wall with a plane or face, then click **Angle > Orientation plane** and select a plane. The wall will be oriented according to the selected plane.

6. Select an option from the **Clearance mode** drop-down. These options are given next.

No clearance: This option creates a wall without any clearance.

Monodirectional: Applies clearance between the selected edge and bend portion of the wall.

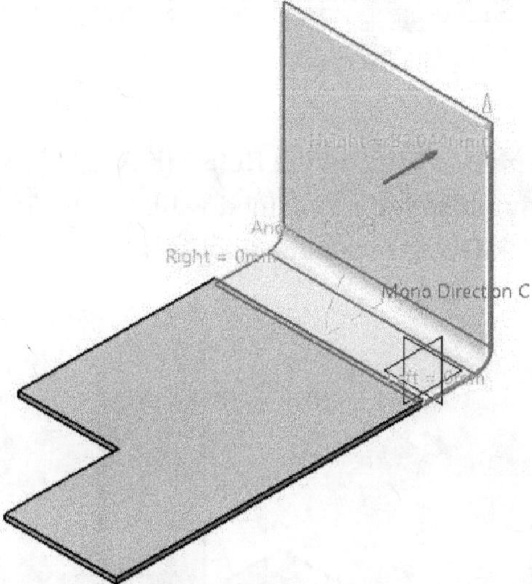

Bidirectional: Applies clearance on both sides of the bend. You can type-in a clearance value or use a formula to define the clearance.

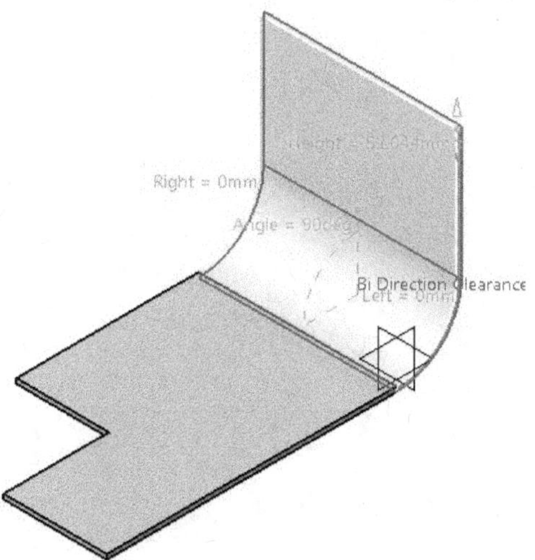

Click the **Reverse Direction** button, if you want to reverse the side of the wall. Use the **Invert Material Side** button to reverse the material side.

On the **Extremities** tab, click in the **Left limit** box and select a plane or face perpendicular to the selected edge to define the left limit of the wall. You can type-in a value in the **Left offset** box to offset the left limit.

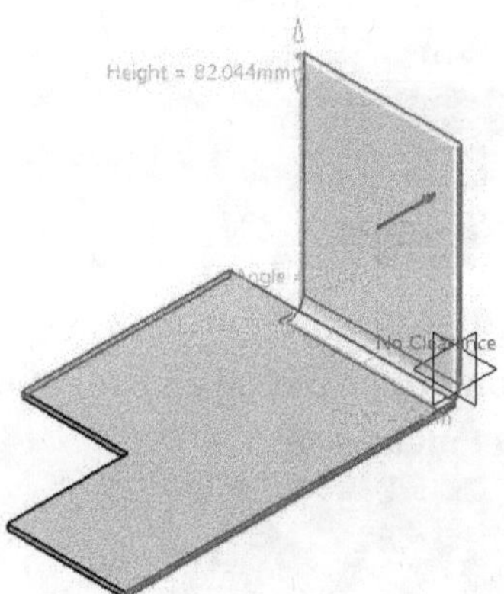

Likewise, define the right limit, offset using the **Right limit** and **Right offset** options.

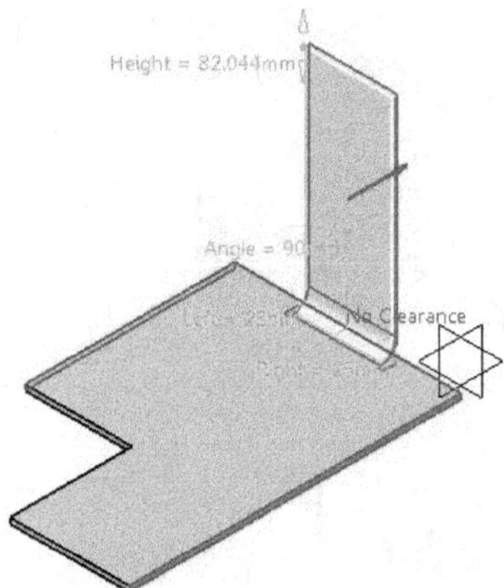

7. Click **OK**.

Sketch Based Wall on Edge

1. Activate the **Wall on Edge** command and select **Type > Sketch Based** on the **Wall On Edge Definition** dialog.

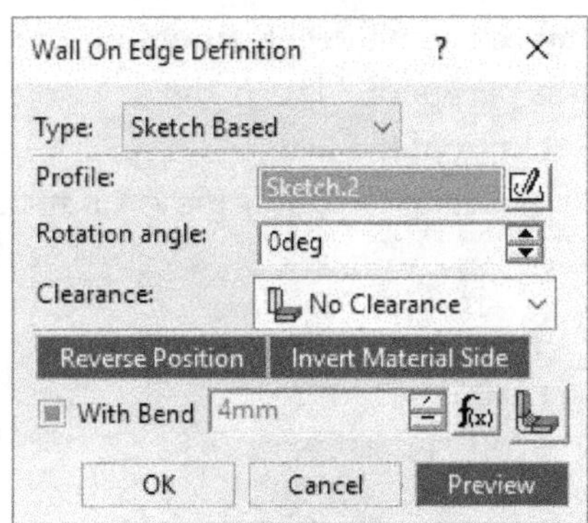

2. Click the sketch icon on the dialog and select the end face of the sheet metal wall.

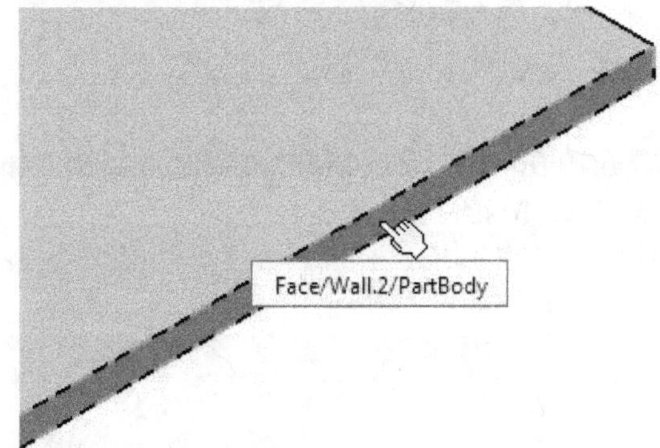

3. Draw the profile of the wall and exit the Sketecher workbench.

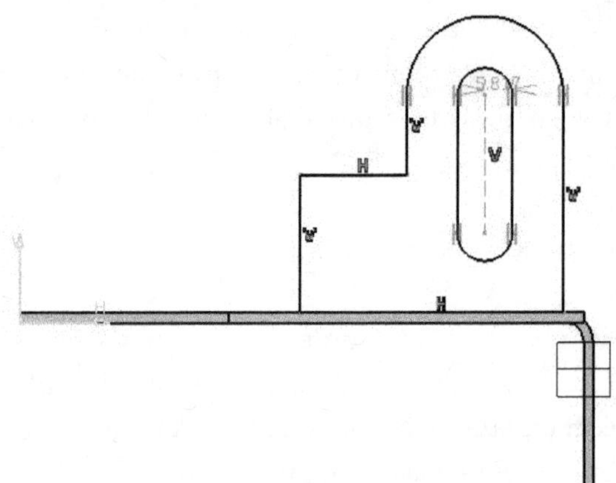

4. Select the edge coinciding with the sketch.

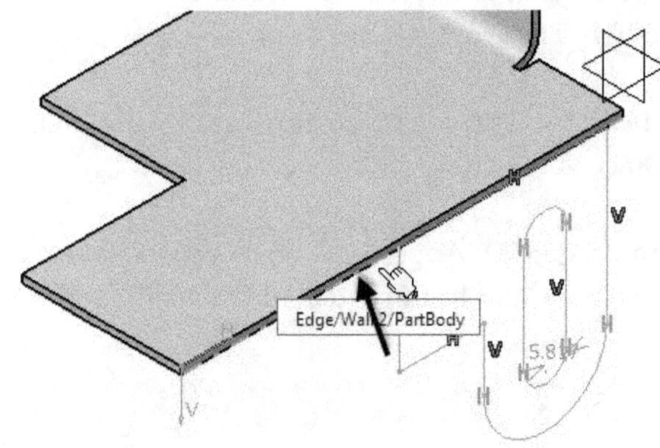

5. Type-in a value in the **Rotation Angle** box, if you want to create an inclined wall.
6. Click **OK** to create the wall.

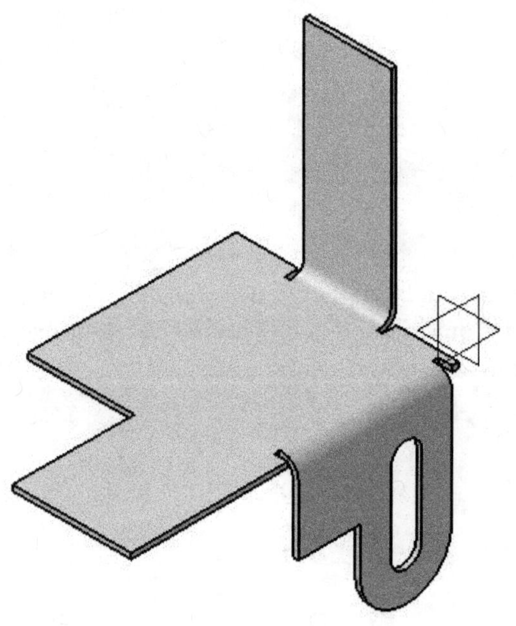

 Extrusion

The **Extrusion** command extrudes an open sketch.

1. On the **Walls** toolbar, click the **Extrusion** button (or) click **Insert > Walls > Extrusion** on the Menu bar.
2. On the **Extrusion Definition** dialog, click the sketch icon, and then select a face or plane.

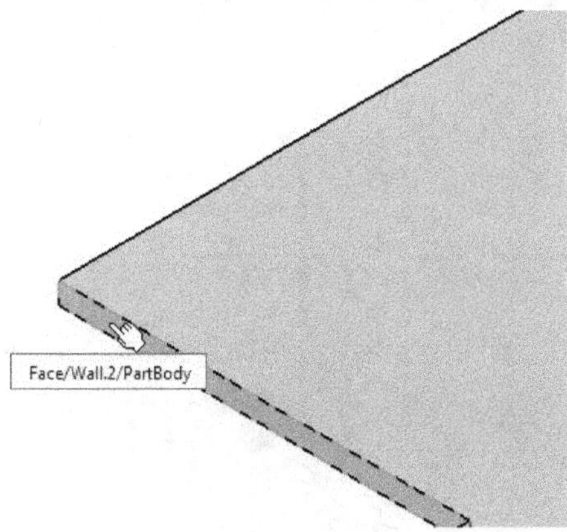

3. Draw open profile and exit the sketch.

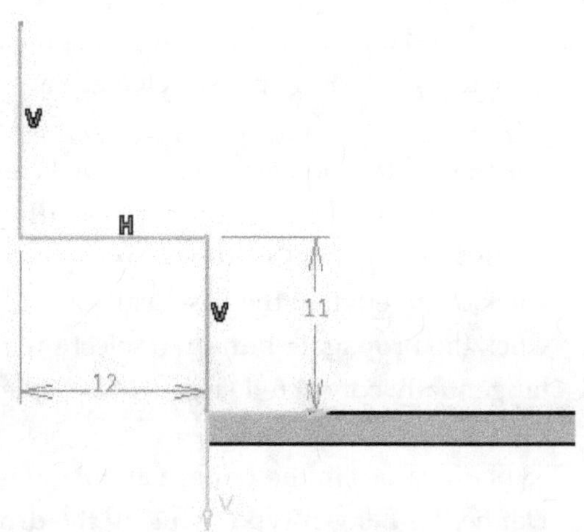

4. Select **Limit 1 dimension** from the **Limit 1** drop-down, and then type-in the extrusion distance.

You can select a **Limit 1 up to plane** or **Limit 1 up to surface** to define the first limit of the extrusion.

5. Likewise, define the extrusion distance along second direction using the **Limit 2** drop-down.
6. Check the **Mirrored extent** option, if you want to extrude the sketch in both the directions.

The **Automatic bend** option creates bends at the intersections between the sketch elements.

The **Exploded mode** creates individual features of each sketch elements.

Use the **Invert material side** and **Invert direction** button to reverse the material side and extrusion direction, respectively.

7. Click the **More** button to view additional options of the extrusion.
8. Click **OK** to complete the extrusion feature.

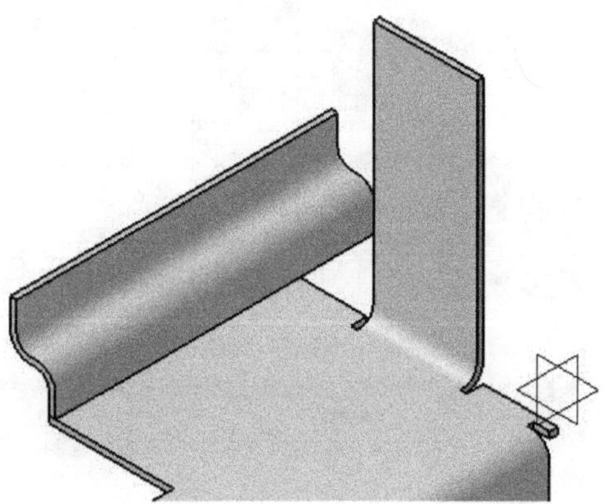

You will notice that there is no bend between the extrusion and the base wall. You can create a bend using the **Bend** command.

 Bend

This command creates a bend between two faces.

1. On the **Bending** toolbar, click **Bends** drop-down > **Bend** (or) click **Insert > Bending > Bend** on the Menu bar.
2. Select the support faces.

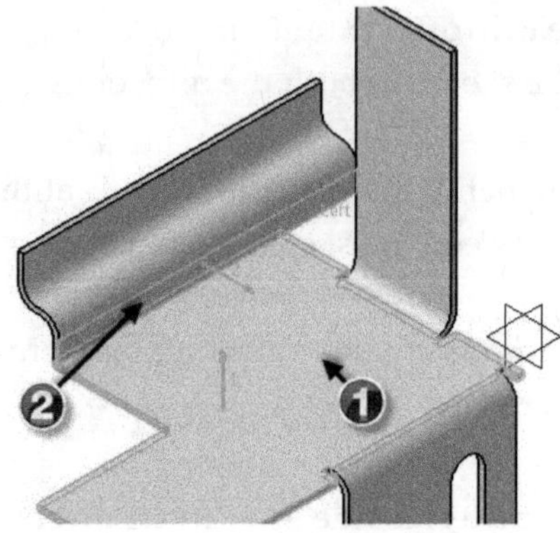

You will notice that all the bend parameters are greyed out on the dialog because the default sheet metal parameters will be used.

3. Click **OK.**

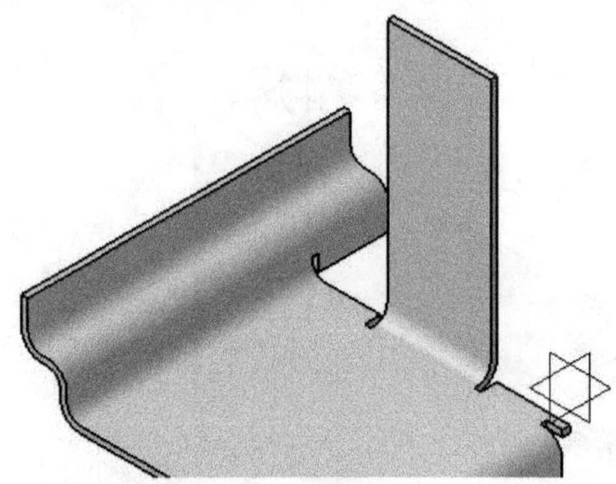

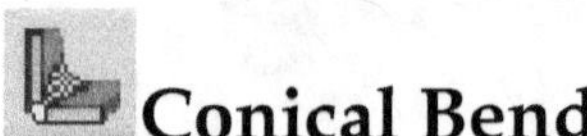

Conical Bend

This command creates a variable radius bend between two faces.

1. On the **Bending** toolbar, click **Bends** drop-down > **Conical Bend** (or) click **Insert > Bending > Conical Bend** on the Menu bar.
2. Select the support faces.
3. On the **Bend Definition** dialog, specify the **Left radius** and **Right radius** values.

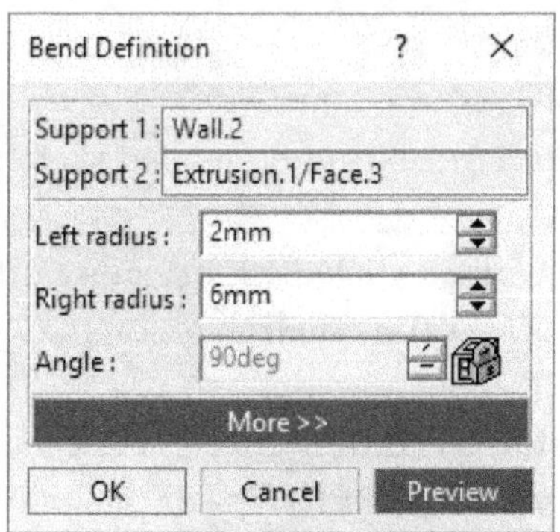

4. Click **OK**.

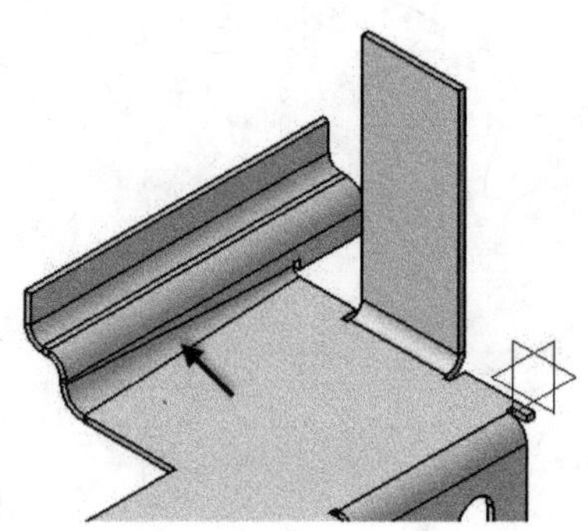

Flange

This command creates a flange by sweeping a parametric profile along the selected edge.

1. On the **Walls** toolbar, click **Swept Walls** drop-down > **Flange** (or) click **Insert > Walls > Swept Walls > Flange** on the Menu bar.
2. Click on an edge of the base wall.
3. Click the **Propagate** button to select the tangentially connected edges. The preview of the flange appears.
4. Type-in values in the **Length** and **Angles** boxes.
5. Define the **Length type** by using the drop-down next to the **Length** box.
6. Likewise, define the **Angle type** by using the drop-down next to the **Angle** box.
7. Check the **Trim Support** option, if you want trim the supporting wall.

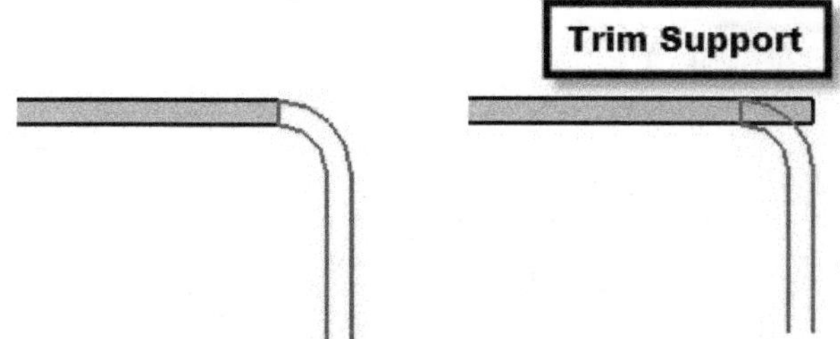

8. Check the **Flange Plane** option and click in the selection box next to it.
9. Select a plane. The flange will become coincident to that plane.

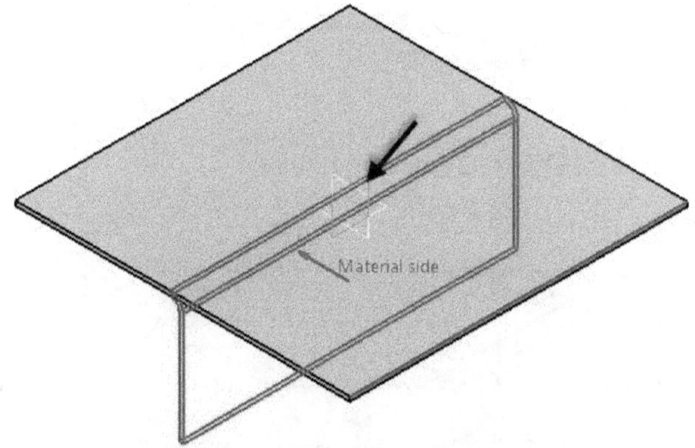

10. If you want to create the flange between two planes, then select the **Relimited** option from the drop-down located at the top on the dialog. Select the first and second limits by using the **Limit1** and **Limit2** options.

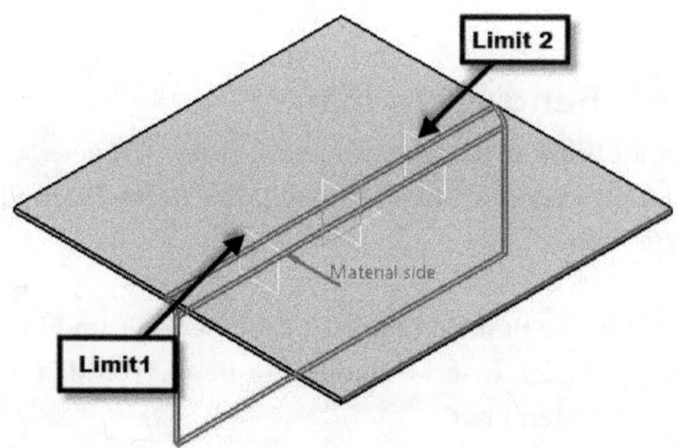

11. Click **OK**.

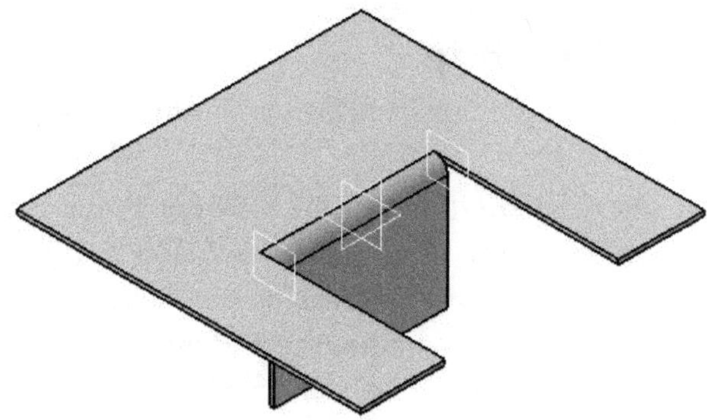

 Hem

The **Hem** command folds an edge of a sheet metal part.

1. On the **Walls** toolbar, click **Swept Walls** drop-down > **Hem** (or) click **Insert > Walls > Swept Walls > Hem** on the Menu bar.
2. Select the edge you need to fold.

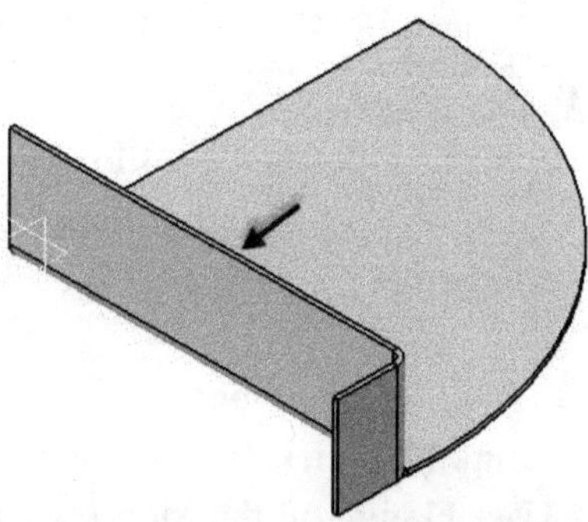

3. Type-in the length of the hem.
4. Click the **Propagate** button, if you want to fold the tangentially connected edges as well.
5. Click **OK**.

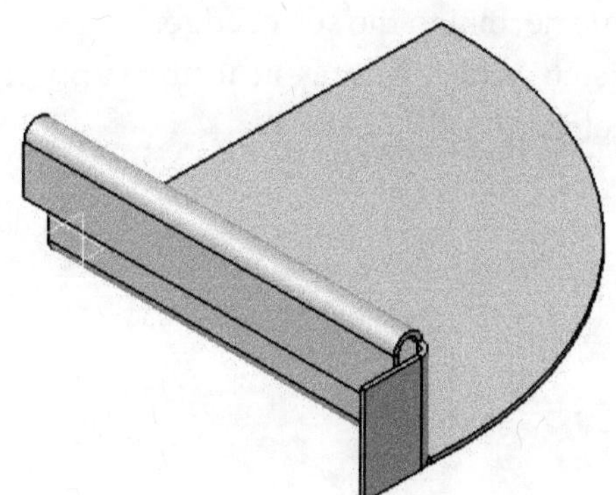

Tear Drop

This command folds and closes a sheet metal edge.

1. On the **Walls** toolbar, click **Swept Walls** drop-down > **Tear Drop** (or) click **Insert > Walls > Swept Walls > Tear Drop** on the Menu bar.
2. Select the edge you need to fold over.
3. Define the length of the inclined face.

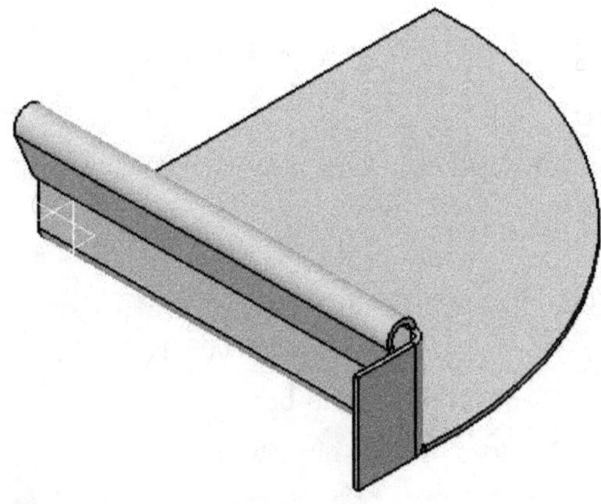

User Flange

This command sweeps a user defined profile along the selected edge. You have to ensure that the profile is tangent to the selected edge.

1. On the **Walls** toolbar, click **Swept Walls** drop-down > **User Flange** (or) click **Insert > Walls > Swept Walls > User Flange** on the Menu bar.
2. Click on an edge of the sheet metal.
3. Click the **Propagate** button to select the edges, which are connected tangentially.
4. On the dialog, click the sketch icon and select a face or plane normal to the select edge.
5. Draw a sketch, which is tangent to the support. Exit the sketch.

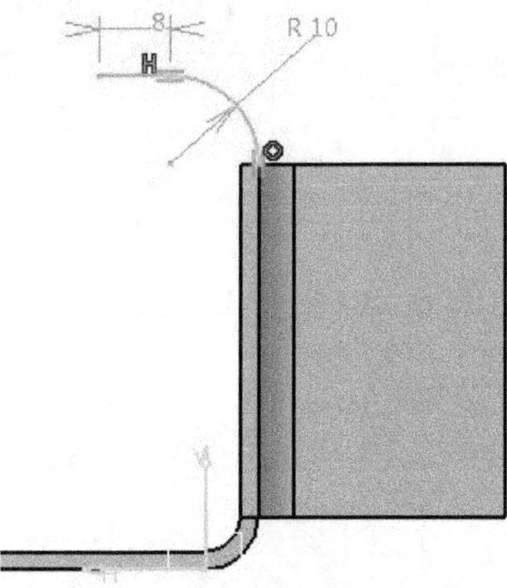

6. Click **OK** to create the flange.

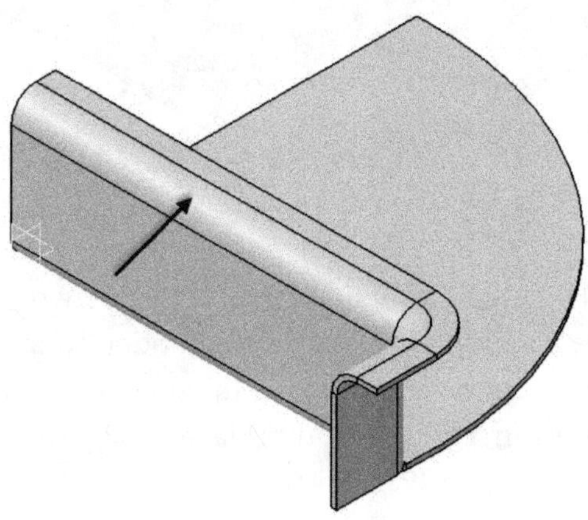

Bend From Flat

In addition to adding flanges and user flanges, you can also bend a flat sheet using the **Bend From Flat** command.

1. On the **Bending** toolbar, click **Bend From Flat** (or) click **Insert > Bending > Bend From Flat** on the Menu bar.
2. On the dialog, click the sketch icon, and then click on the face to bend.
3. Draw a sketch line on the flat sheet and click **Exit workbench**.

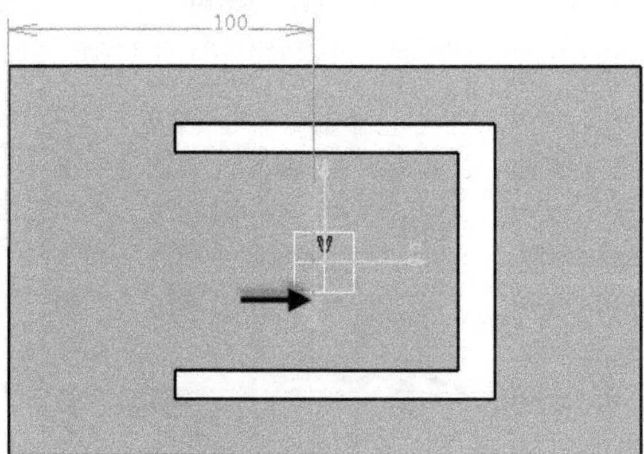

4. Click in the **Fixed Point** box and select a point to define the portion to be fixed.

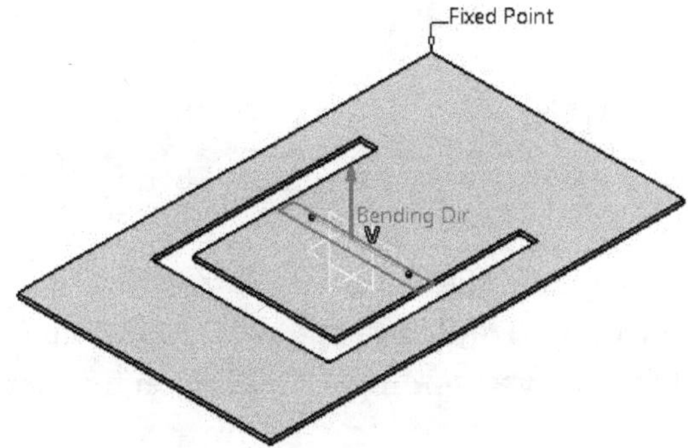

5. Click the blue arrow that appears on the bend, if you want to reverse the bend direction.
6. Type-in a value in the **Angle** box to change the folding angle.
7. Select the option to define the material side of the bend feature. These options are given next.

This creates the bend with the bend line at its center.

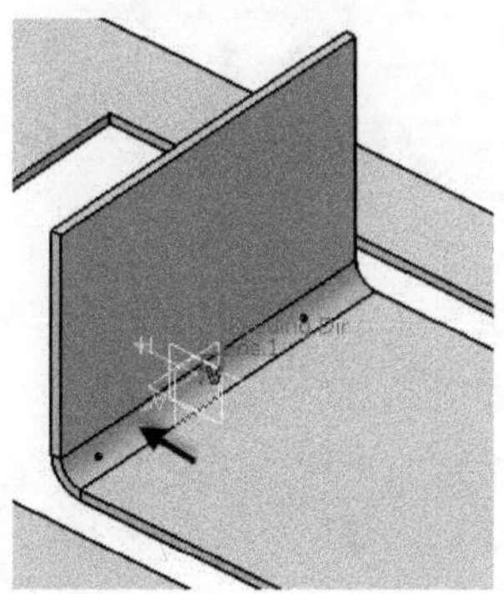

This creates the bend with the bend line at its starting edge.

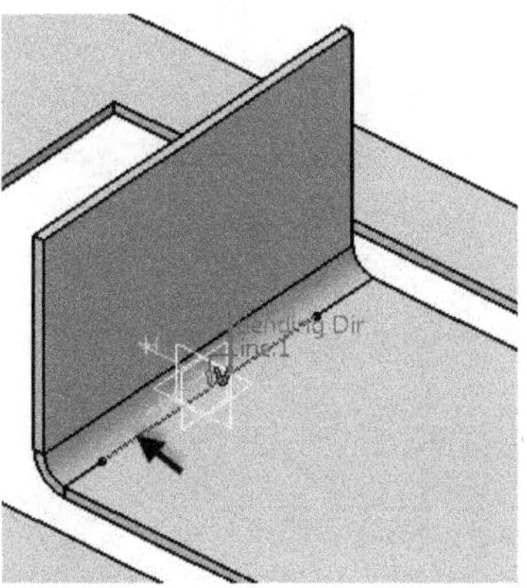

This creates the bend with the bend line at the intersection of the inner faces of the sheet metal part.

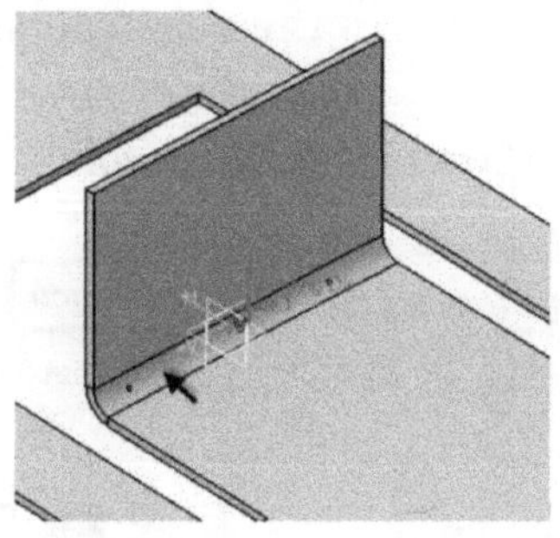

This creates the bend with the bend line at the intersection of outer faces.

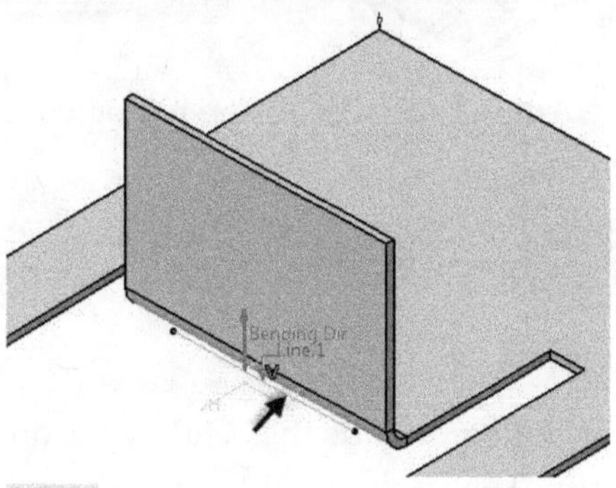

This creates the bend with the bendline at its ending edge.

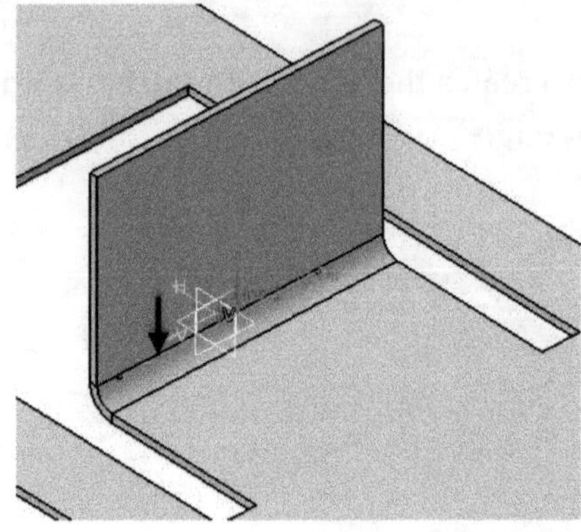

8. Click **OK** to complete the bend feature.

Unfolding

This command unfolds a bend to its original position.

1. On the **Bending** toolbar, click **Unfolding/Folding** drop-down > **Unfolding** (or) click **Insert > Bending > Unfolding** on the Menu bar.
2. Select the reference face and face to unfold.

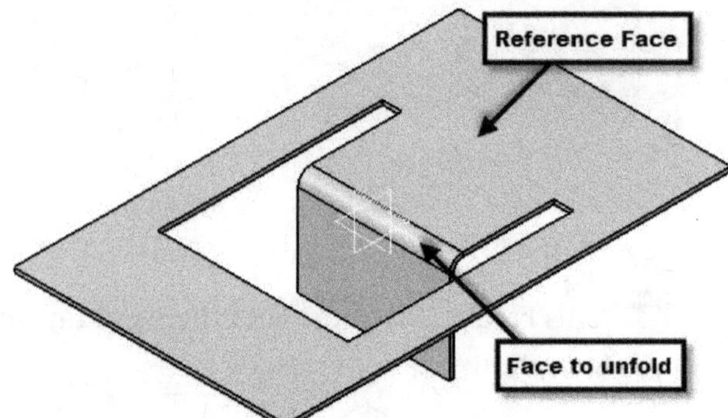

3. Select the **Angle** type. The different angle types are given next.

Natural: This option unfolds the bend to its original position.

Defined: This option unfolds the bend by the angle that you specify. The angle should not be that of the original position.

Spring back: This option unfolds the bend by using the angle that you specify. The angle is measured from its current position.

4. Click **OK** to unfold the bend.

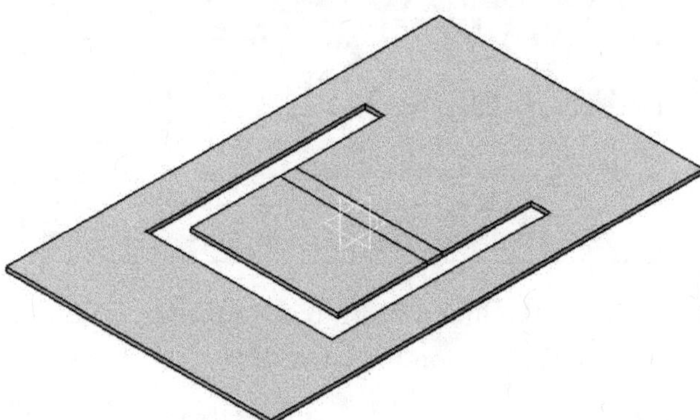

Folding

This command refolds the unfolded bend.

1. On the **Bending** toolbar, click **Unfolding/Folding** drop-down > **Folding** (or) click **Insert > Bending > Folding** on the Menu bar.
2. Select the reference face and face to refold.

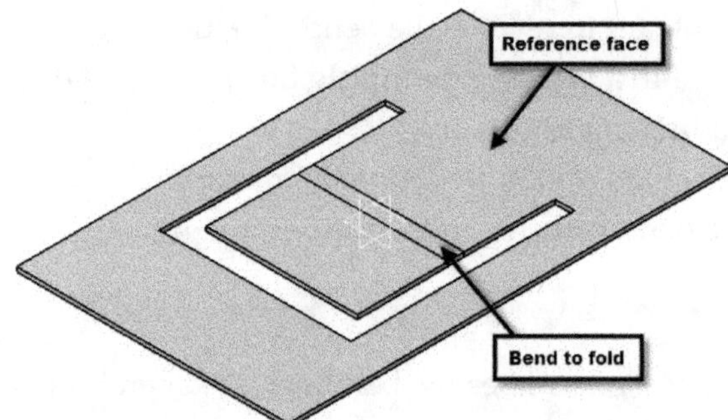

3. Select the **Angle type**, and then specify the bend angle.
4. Click **OK**.

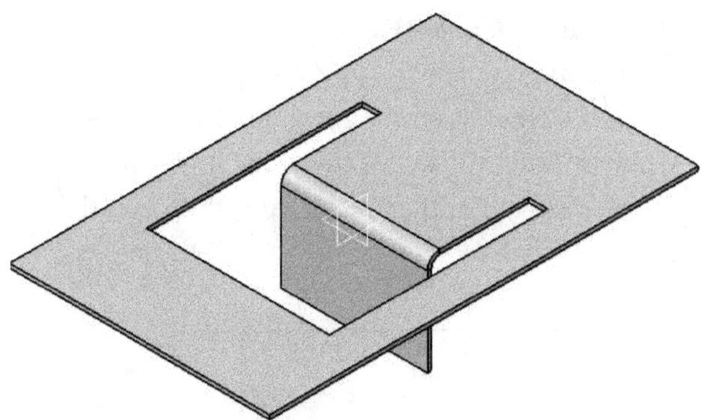

Fold/Unfold

The **Fold/Unfold** command flattens the part so that you can easily display the manufacturing information.

1. On the **Views** toolbar, click **Fold/Unfold** drop-down > **Fold/Unfold** (or) click **Insert > Views > Fold/Unfold** on the Menu bar. This flattens the entire sheet metal part.

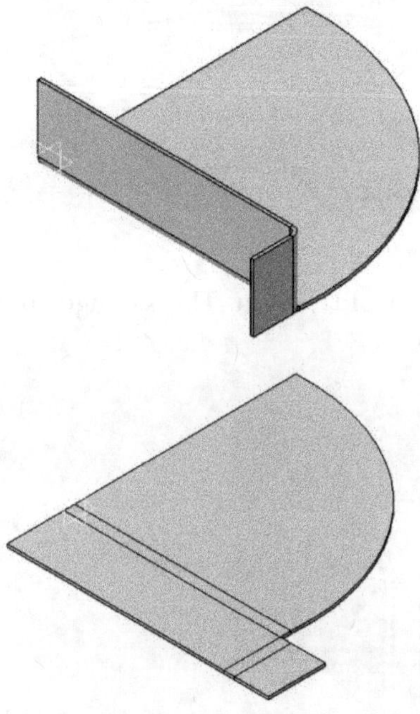

2. Again, click the **Fold/Unfold** button to refold the sheet metal part.

Multi Viewer

The **Multi Viewer** command lets you view the flattened view in a separate window.

1. On the **Views** toolbar, click **Fold/Unfold** drop-down > **Multi Viewer** (or) click **Insert > Views > Multi Viewer** on the Menu bar. A separate window will be displayed with the flattened view.
2. Select **Windows > Tile Horizontally** or **Tile Vertically** to view both the windows at a time.

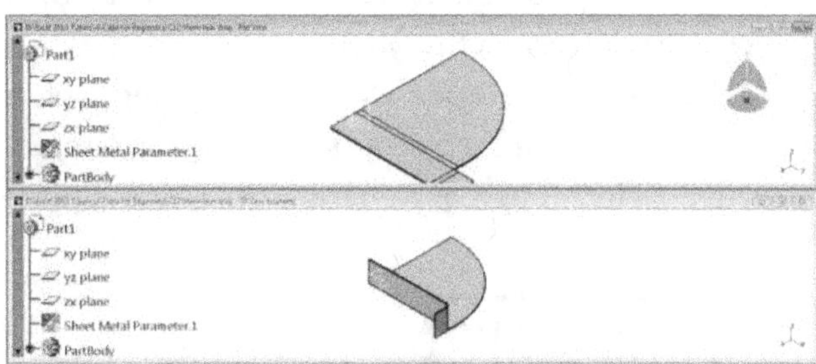

View Management

The **View Management** command lets you to switch between different views of the sheet metal part. You can also activate or deactivate views using this command.

1. On the **Views** toolbar, click the **View Management** button (or) click **Insert > Views > View Management** on the Menu bar.
2. On the **Views** dialog, select a view, and then click the **Current** button. This makes the selected view as current.

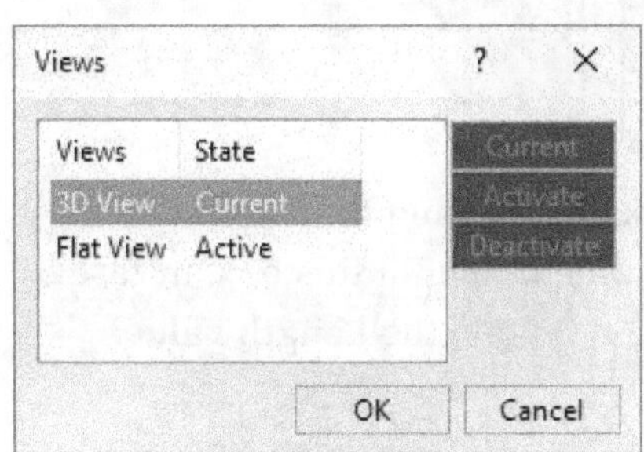

3. If you want to deactivate a view, then select it from the **Views** dialog, and then click the **Deactivate** button.

 CornerRelief

The **CornerRelief** command allows you to control the appearance of sheet metal seams. For example, when two flanges meet at a corner, this command applies a relief.

1. On the **Cutting/Stamping** toolbar, click **CornerRelief** button (or) click **Insert > Cutting > CornerRelief** on the Menu bar.
2. On the **Corner Relief Definition** dialog, select **Type > Circular**. This option creates a circular relief. Select **Type > Square** to create a square corner relief.

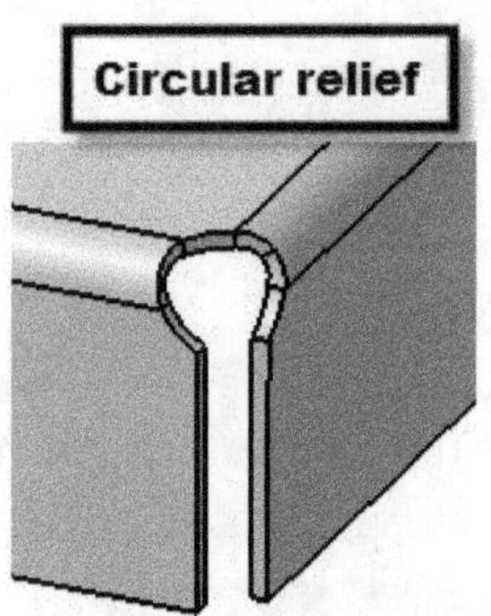

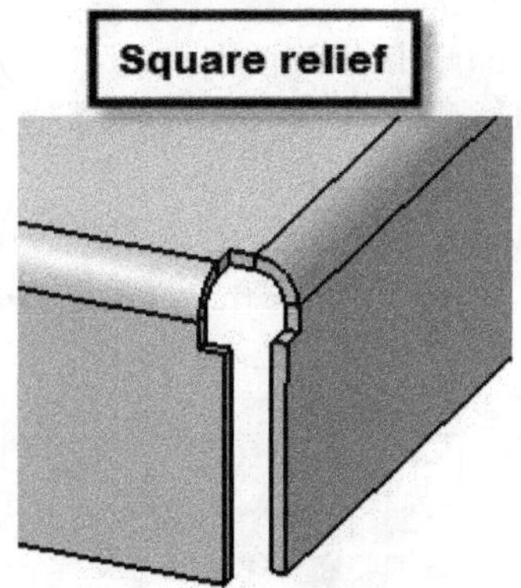

3. Select the bends forming the corner.
4. Type-in a value in the **Radius** box. In case of **Square** relief, type-in the **Length** value.
5. Click **OK**.

Corner Relief with User defined profile

You can apply a corner relief with the user-defined profile.

1. Click the **Fold/Unfold** button on the **Views** toolbar. This changes the view to Flat view.
2. Activate the **CornerRelief** command.
3. On the dialog, select **Type > User Profile**.
4. Click the **Sketch** icon next to the **Profile** box.
5. Click on the top face of the sheet metal part.
6. Draw a sketch at the corner, and then exit the workbench.

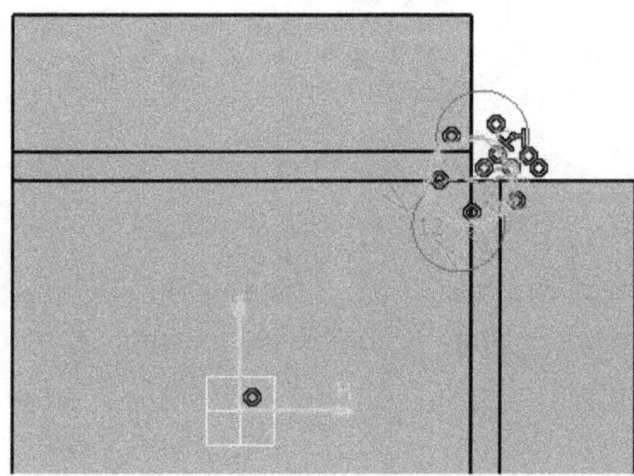

7. Select the bend faces forming a corner.

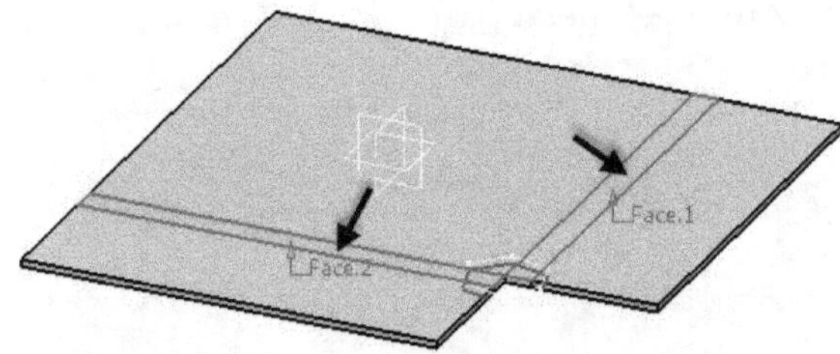

8. Click **OK** to create relief.
9. Click the **Fold/Unfold** button. This changes the view to 3D view.

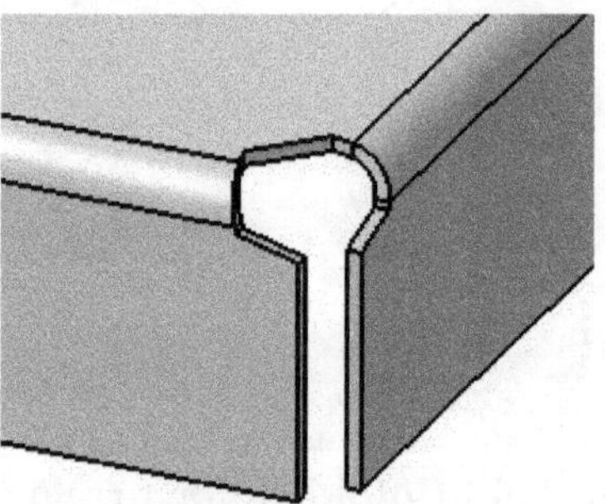

 Surface Stamp

The **Surface** command adds a stamp to a flat sheet by deforming it.

1. On the **Cutting/Stamping** toolbar, click **Stamping** drop-down > **Surface Stamp** (or) click **Insert > Stamping > Surface Stamp** on the Menu bar.
2. On the dialog, click the **Sketch** icon next to the **Profile** box.
3. Click on the sheet metal face to add a surface stamp.
4. Draw a sketch and exit the workbench.

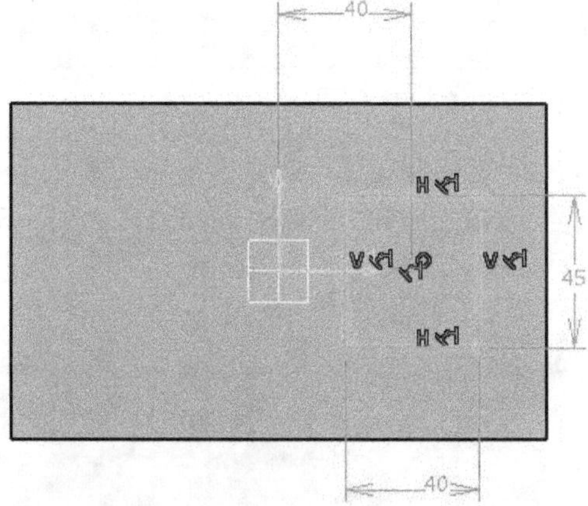

5. Select **Parameters choice > Angle**. This creates a stamp with a draft angle.

If you check the **Half pierce** option, the height of the stamp will be half of the sheet metal thickness. You can increase the height value up to the sheet metal thickness.

6. Specify the **Angle** and **Height** values. You can also define the height by using the **Limit** selection box. Click in this box and select a plane to define the length of the stamp.
7. Specify the **Radius R1** and **Radius R2** boxes. You can refer to the image available on the dialog to know **Radius R1** and **Radius R2**.

The **Rounded die** option rounds the edges of the sidewalls.

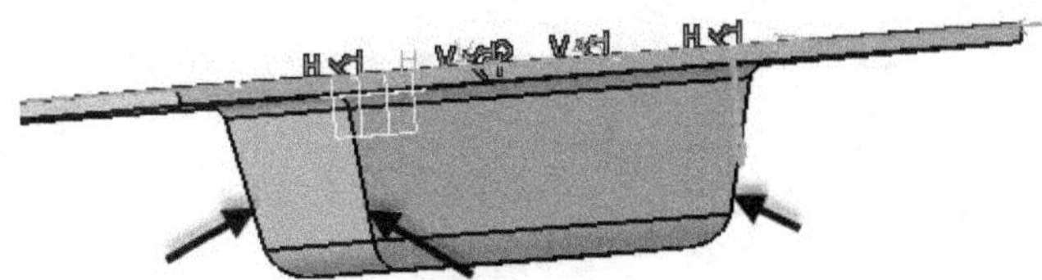

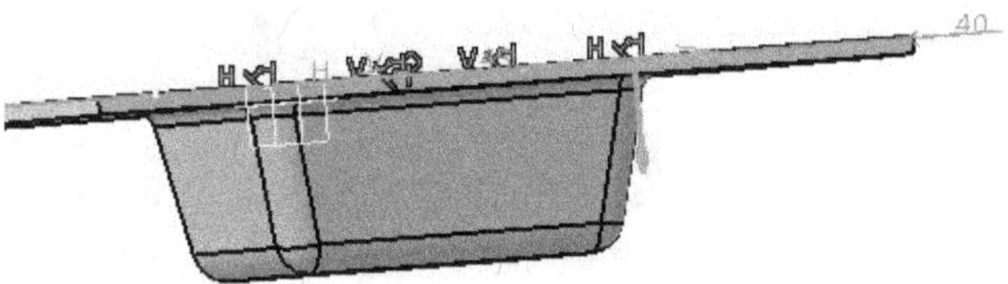

8. Click the **Upward sketch profile** button (or) **Downward sketch profile** button. The **Upward sketch profile** button uses the sketch to define the top face of the stamp.

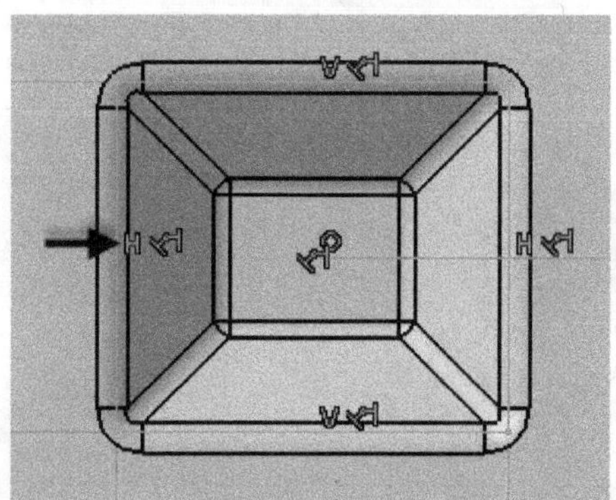

The **Downward sketch profile** button uses the sketch to define the bottom face of the stamp.

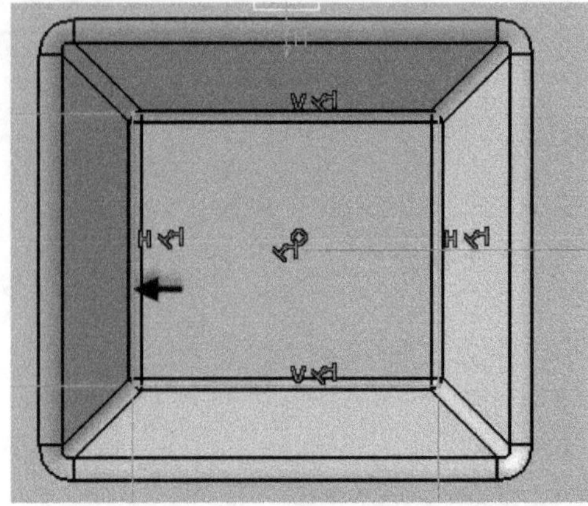

If you want to remove anyone of the sidewalls, then click in the **Opening Edges** box and select an edge from the sketch. The corresponding face will be removed.

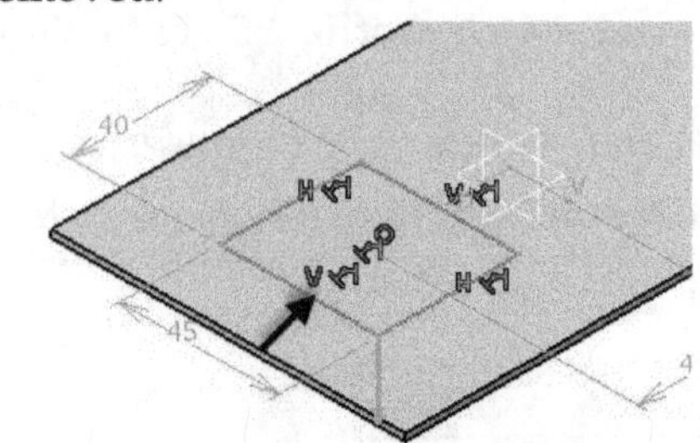

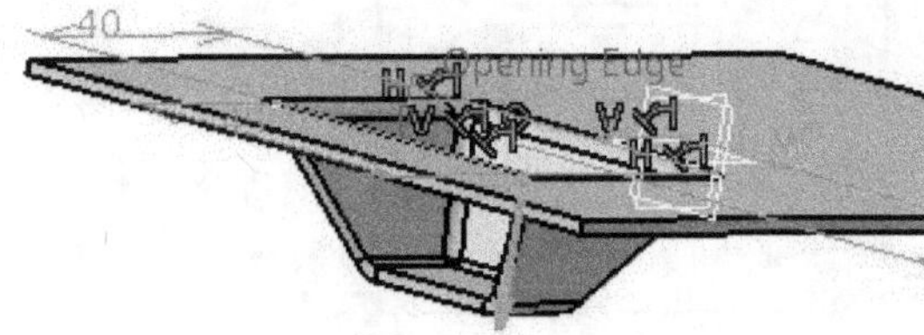

9. Click **OK** to complete the surface stamp.

Flanged Cut Out

The flanged cut out and surface stamp feature are almost alike, except that an opening is created in case of flanged cut out.

1. On the **Cutting/Stamping** toolbar, click **Stamping** drop-down > **Flanged Cut Out** (or) click **Insert > Stamping > Flanged Cut Out** on the Menu bar.
2. On the dialog, click the **Sketch** icon, and then click a face to add flanged cut out.
3. Draw a closed sketch and click **Exit workbench**.

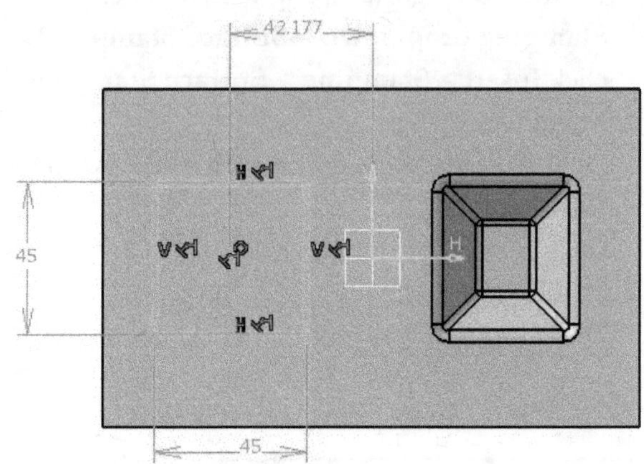

4. On the dialog, type-in a value in the **Height** box to define the height of the flanged cut out feature.
5. Type-in values of **Angle** and **Radius.**

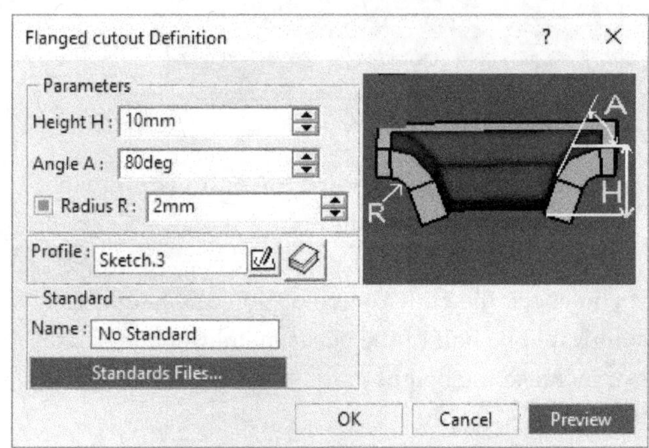

6. Click **OK** to create the flanged cut out.

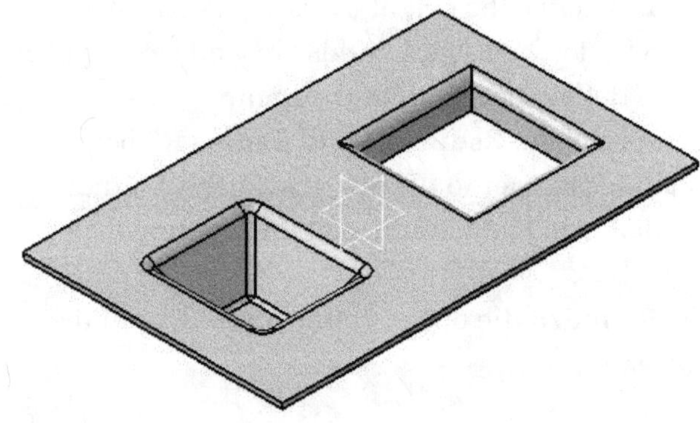

Bead

The **Bead** command creates a bead feature, which stiffens the sheet metal part. In order to create a bead feature, first you must have a sketch, which defines the bead size and shape. If the sketch is having curved edges, then ensure that they are tangent continuous.

1. On the **Cutting/Stamping** toolbar, click **Stamping** drop-down > **Bead** (or) click **Insert > Stamping > Bead** on the Menu bar.
2. Click on the open or closed sketch.

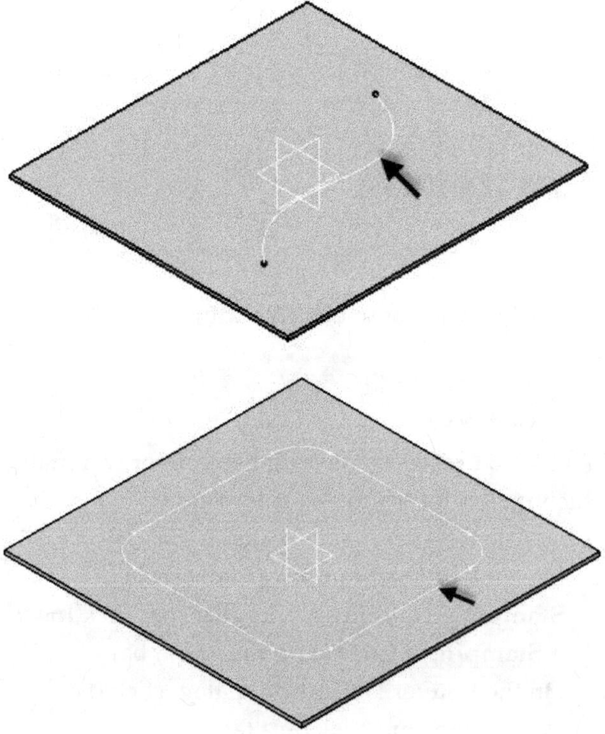

3. In case of an open profile, type-in the **Section radius, End radius, Height** and **Radius** values.

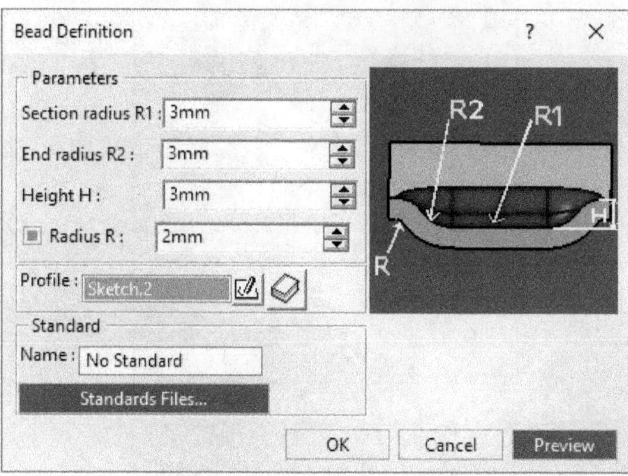

In case of a closed profile, type-in the **Section radius** and **Height** values.

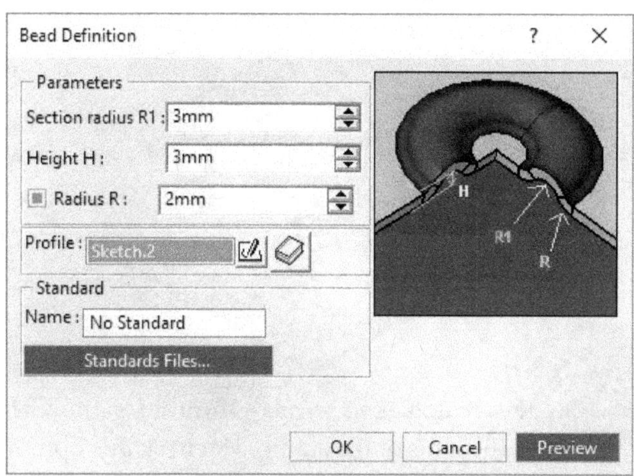

4. Click **OK** to complete the bead feature.

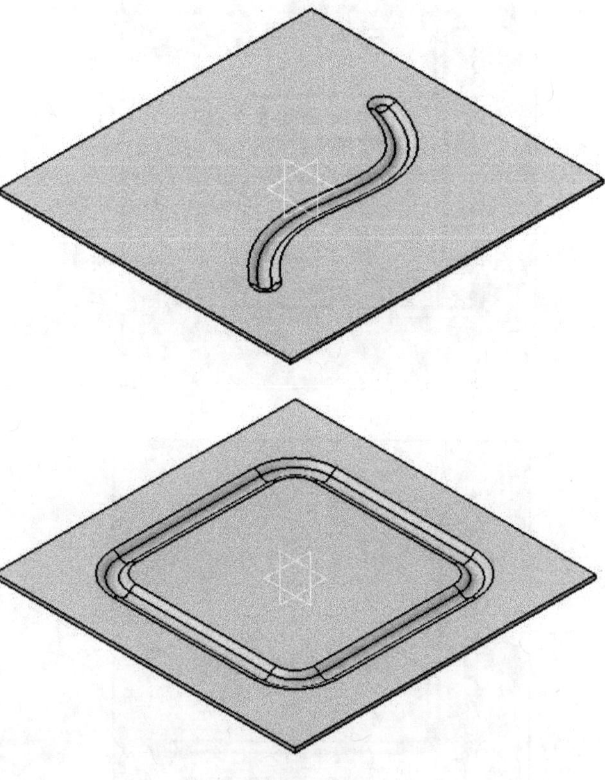

 Curved Stamp

The **Curved Stamp** command creates a stamp using the sketch, which has non-tangent elements.

1. On the **Cutting/Stamping** toolbar, click **Stamping** drop-down > **Curved Stamp** (or) click

Insert > Stamping > Curve Stamp on the Menu bar.

2. Click on the sketch, which has linear elements.

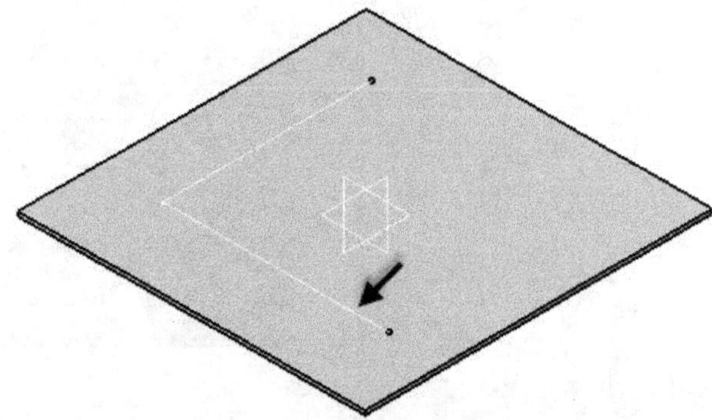

3. On the dialog, check the **Obround** option to round the ends of the stamp. Uncheck this option to create a stamp with straight ends.

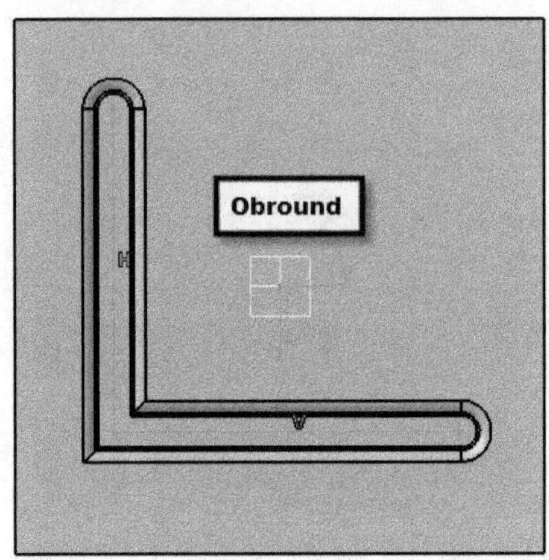

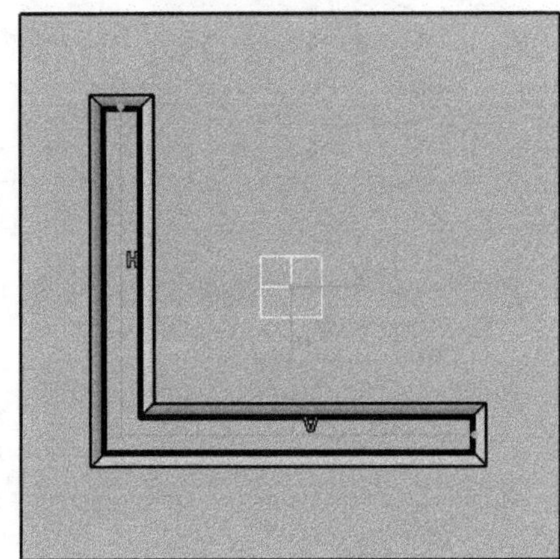

4. Type-in values in the **Parameters** section. The image on the dialog shows the parameters.

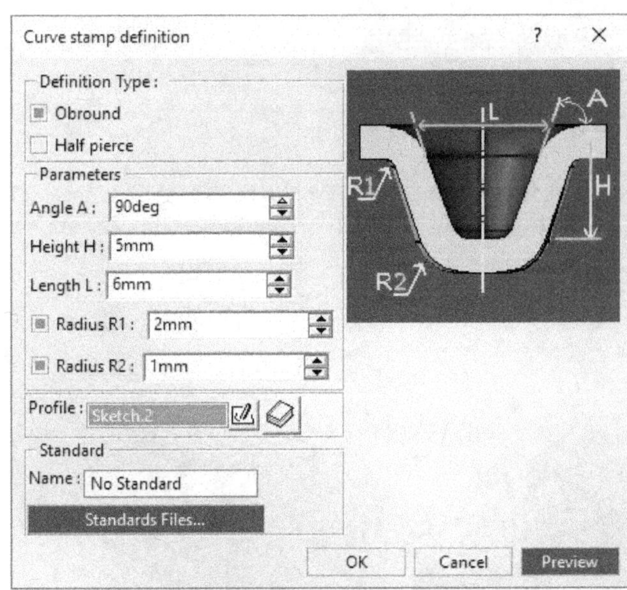

5. Click **OK** to complete the feature.

 Louver

CATIA V5 provides you with the **Louver** command, which makes it easy to create louvers.

1. On the **Cutting/Stamping** toolbar, click **Stamping** drop-down > **Louver** (or) click **Insert > Stamping > Louver** on the Menu bar.
2. On the **Louver Definition** dialog, click the sketch icon, and click on a face.
3. Draw a rectangle on the selected face and click **Exit workbench**.

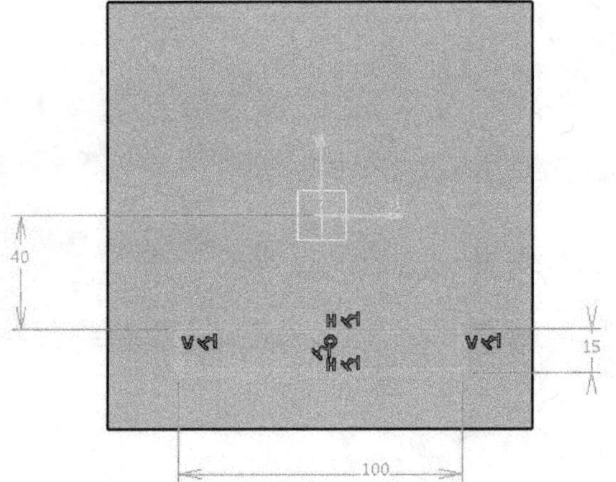

4. Click on a line of the sketch to define the opening edge.

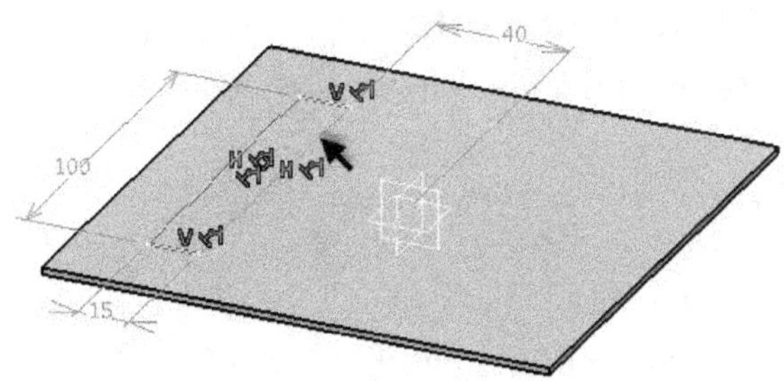

5. On the **Louver Definition** dialog, type-in a value in the **Height** box. This defines the height of the louver.
6. Click the arrow that appears on the louver to reverse the direction.
7. Type-in a value in the **Angle A1** box, if you want an inclined side face.
8. Type-in a value other than 90 in the **Angle A2** box, if you want an inclined bottom/top face.
9. Type-in the **R1** and **R2** values. This rounds the edges of the louver.

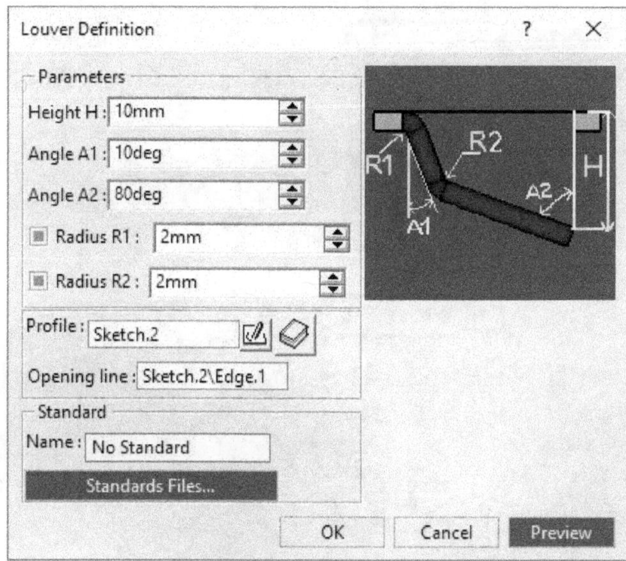

10. Click **OK**.

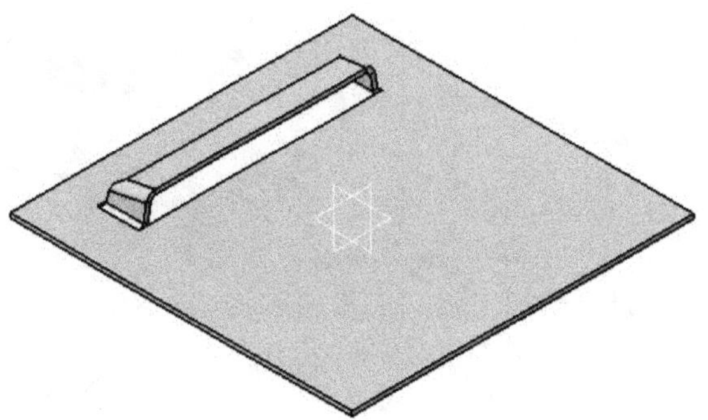

 Bridge

This command creates a bridge, which is similar to the louver.

1. Create a point on the sheet metal to define the location of the bridge.

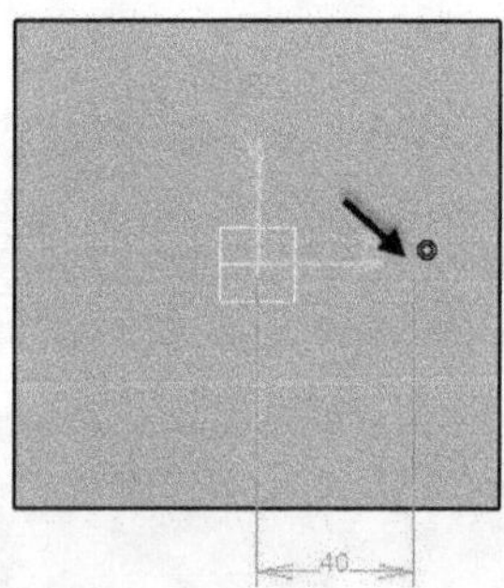

2. On the **Cutting/Stamping** toolbar, click **Stamping** drop-down > **Bridge** (or) click **Insert > Stamping > Bridge** on the Menu bar.
3. Select the point, and then click on the face to define the reference.
4. On the dialog, type-in values in the **Parameters** section. You can see the image displayed on the dialog to get a better understanding of these parameters.

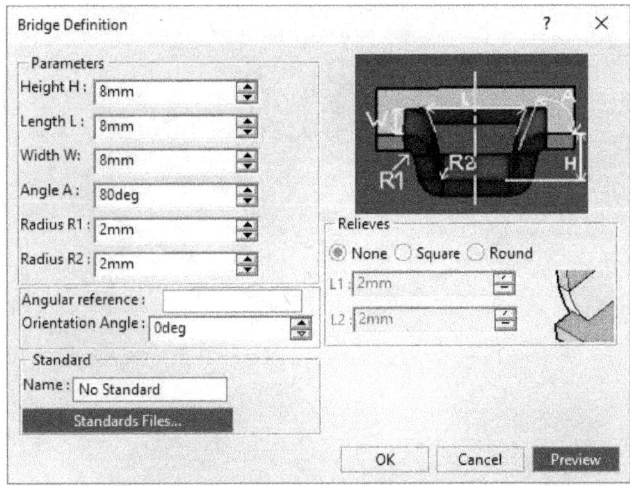

5. Click the vertical arrow that appears on the bridge. This reverses the direction of the bridge.
6. Click and drag the orientation handle attached to the bridge. This changes the orientation angle of the bridge.

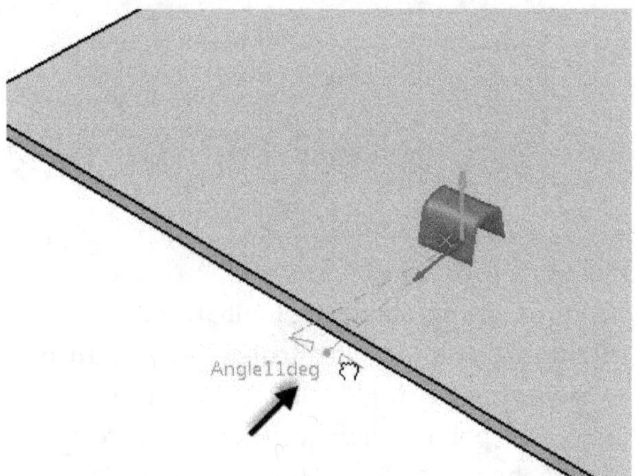

7. In the **Relieves** section, select the **Square** or **Round** option to apply relief at corners and sides.
8. Click **OK** to complete the feature.

Flanged Hole

This command adds a circular flanged opening to the sheet metal part.

1. Create a point on the sheet metal to define the location of the flanged hole.
2. On the **Cutting/Stamping** toolbar, click **Stamping** drop-down > **Flanged Hole** (or) click **Insert > Stamping > Flanged Hole** on the Menu bar.
3. Select the point, and then click on the sheet metal face to define the reference.
4. On the dialog, select the **Parameters choice**. There are four parameter choices: **Major Diameter**, **Minor Diameter**, **Two diameters**, **Punch & Die**.
5. Select the **Without cone** or **With cone** option. The **Without cone** option creates the hole without the conical protrusion.

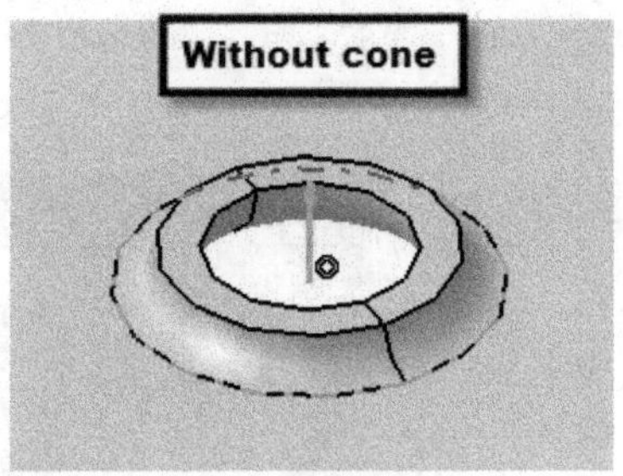

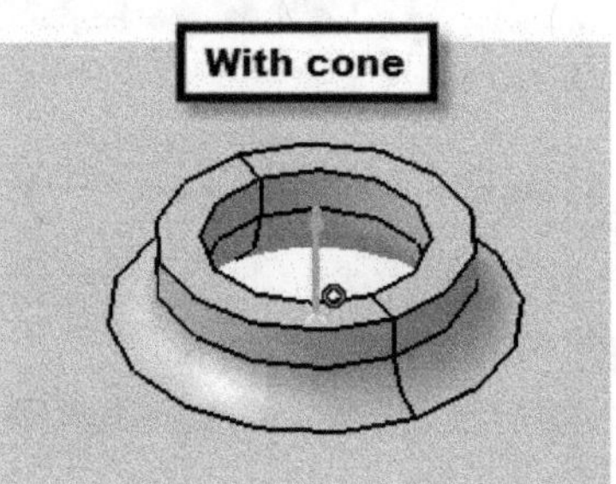

6. Type-in values in the **Parameters** section. Refer to the image located on the dialog to get a better understanding of the parameters.

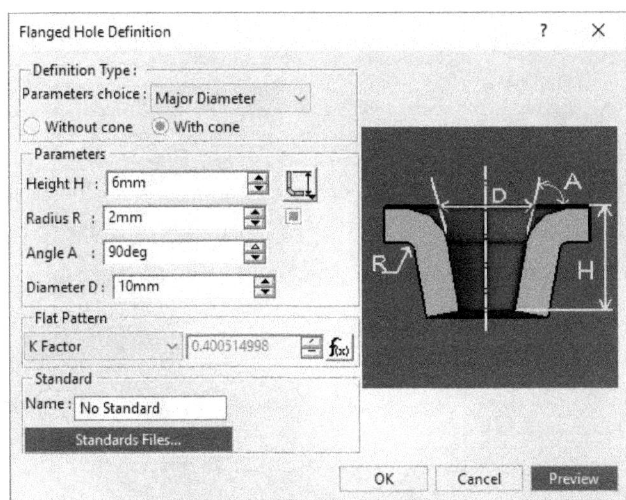

7. Click the arrow displayed on the flanged hole to reverse its direction.
8. Click **OK** to create the flanged hole

 Circular Stamp

This command adds a circular stamp to the sheet metal part. This command is similar to the **Flanged Hole** command except that it creates a closed circular stamp.

1. Create a point on the sheet metal to define the location of the flanged hole.
2. On the **Cutting/Stamping** toolbar, click **Stamping** drop-down > **Circular Stamp** (or) click **Insert > Stamping > Circular Stamp** on the Menu bar.
3. Select the point, and then click on the sheet metal face to define the reference.

The options on the **Circular Stamp Definition** dialog are similar to the **Flanged Hole Definition** dialog.

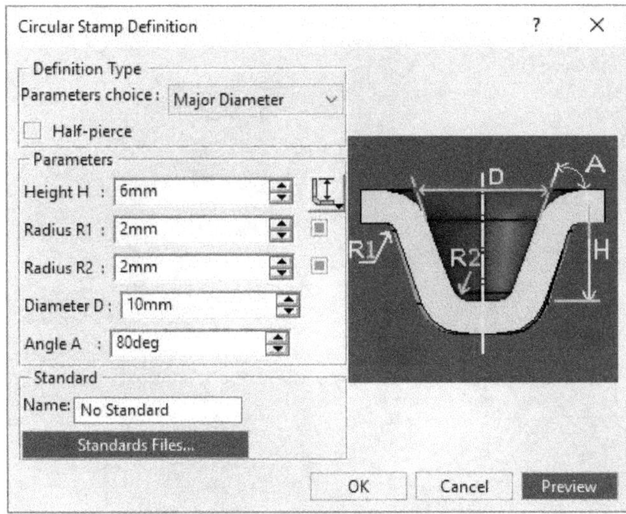

4. Click **OK**.

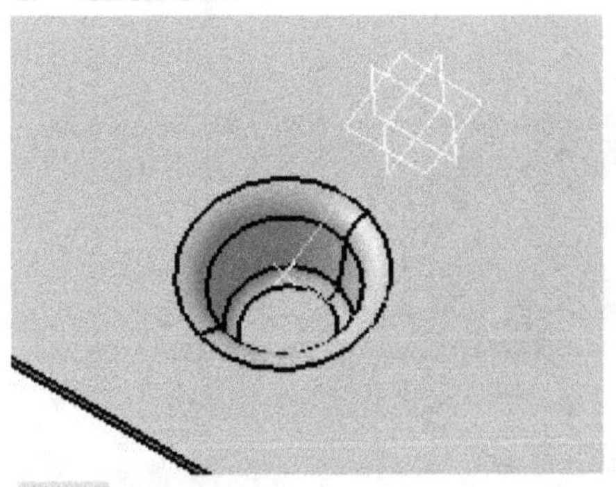

 Stiffening Rib

Stiffening ribs are features created across a bend to reinforce the sheet metal part.

1. On the **Cutting/Stamping** toolbar, click **Stamping** drop-down > **Stiffening Rib** (or) click **Insert > Stamping > Stiffening Rib** on the Menu bar.
2. Click on the external face of the bend. This defines the position of the bend.

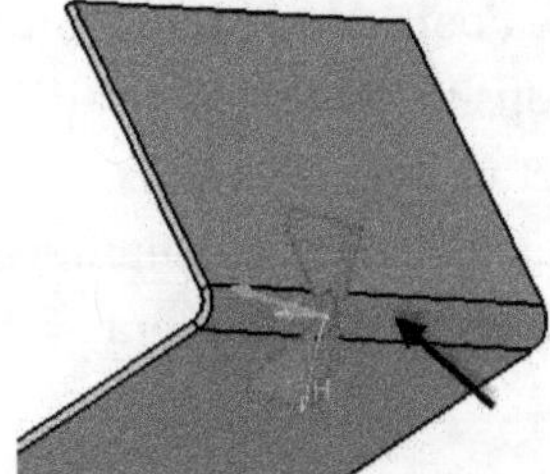

3. On the dialog, type-in values in the **Parameters** section.

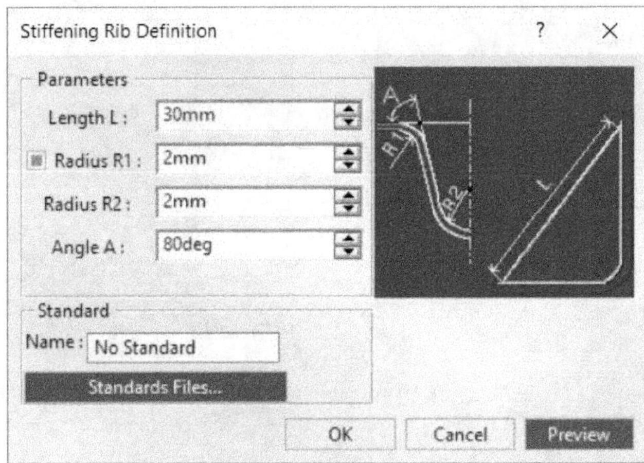

4. Click **OK**.

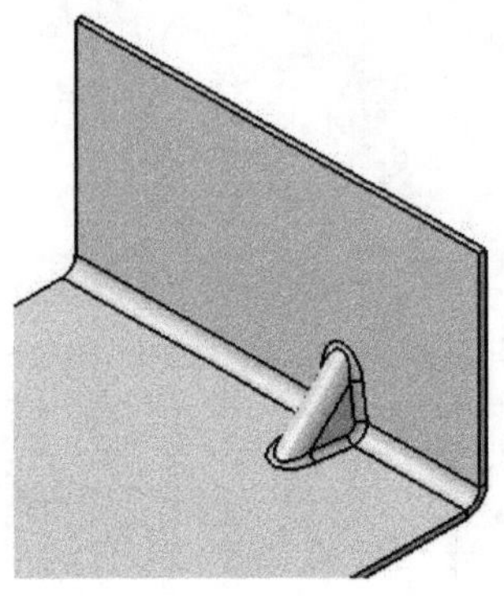

Dowel Stamp

This command creates a stamp resembling a dowel end.

1. On the **Cutting/Stamping** toolbar, click **Stamping** drop-down > **Dowel Stamp** (or) click **Insert > Stamping > Dowel Stamp** on the Menu bar.
2. Click on the face to add stamp.
3. On the dialog, click the **Positioned sketch** button, and then add dimensions to define the position of the stamp. Exit the sketch.
4. On the dialog, type-in a value in the **Diameter** box. This calculates the other parameters of the dowel, automatically.

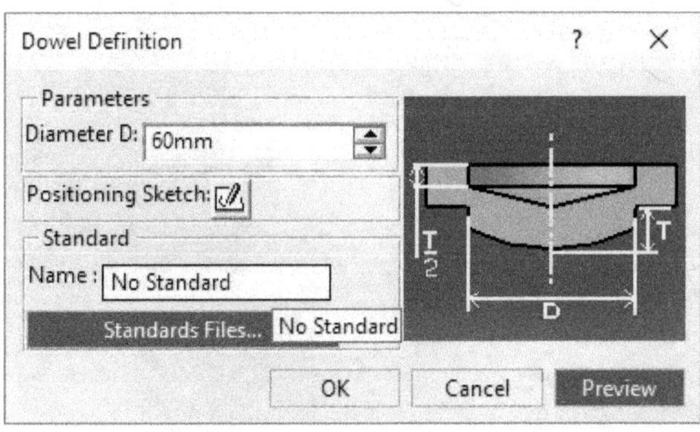

5. Click **OK**.

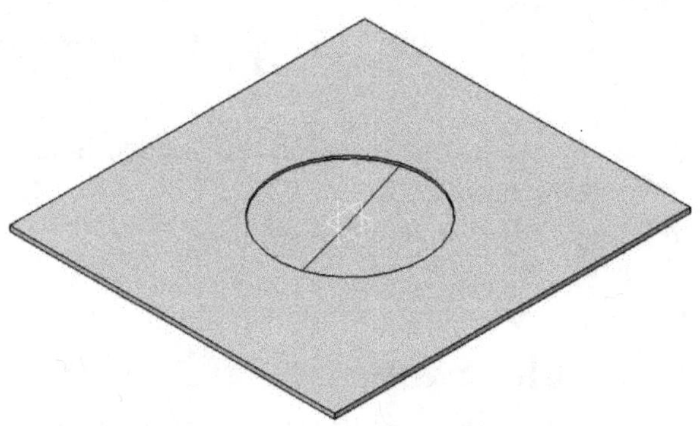

Cut out

When it is necessary to remove material from a sheet metal part, you must use the **Cut out** command.

1. Draw a sketch, and then click the **Cut out** button on the **Cutting/Stamping** toolbar (or) click **Insert > Cutting > Cut Out** on the Menu bar.
2. Select the sketch, if not selected.

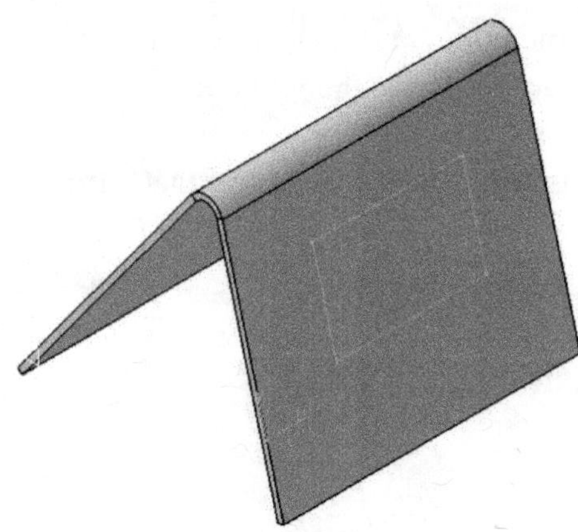

3. On the dialog, click **Cutout Type > Sheetmetal standard**. This allows you to cut the sheet metal up to its entire depth. If you select **Cutout Type**

> Sheetmetal pocket, cutout will be created only up to the thickness of the sheet.

4. Define the **End Limit**.

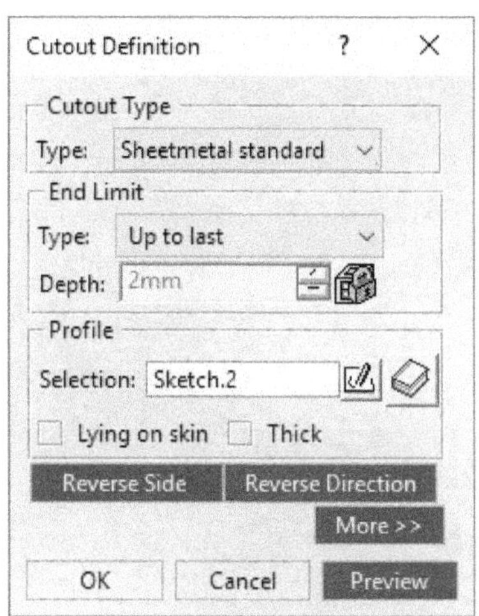

5. Click **OK**.

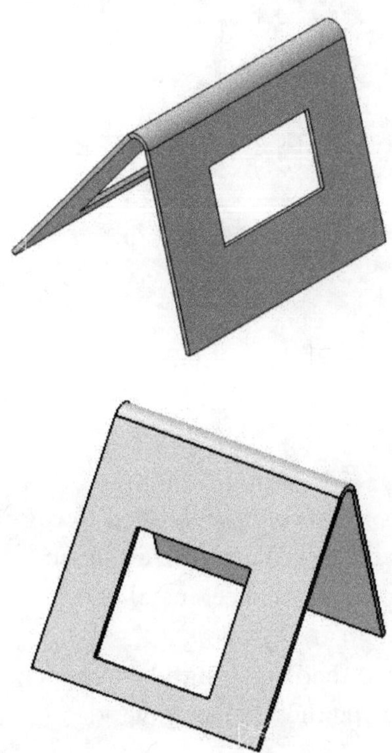

Circular Cutout

This command creates a circular cutout across a bend.

1. Create a point on the bend portion of the sheet metal part. To do this, you can unfold the sheet metal and create a sketch (or) use the reference **Point** command.

2. Refold the bend, if you have unfolded it.
3. On the **Cutting/Stamping** toolbar, click **Holes** drop-down > **Circular Cutout** (or) click **Insert > Cutting > Circular Cutout** on the Menu bar.
4. Select the point located on the bend.
5. On the dialog, type-in the **Diameter** value, and then click **OK**.

Hopper

The **Hopper** command creates a funnel that can be unfolded into flat pattern.

1. Create two sketches on planes parallel to each other. Ensure that the sketches do not have sharp edge and are open. In addition, the openings should be in the same direction.

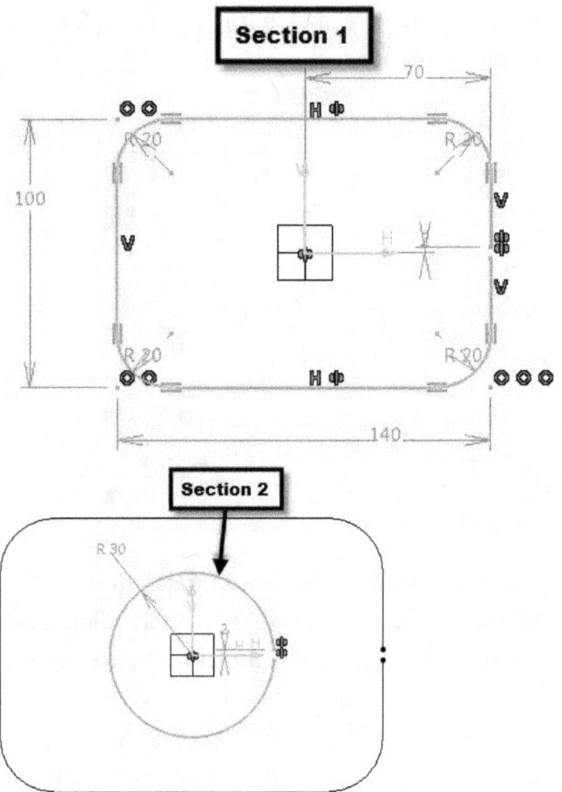

2. On the **Rolled Walls** toolbar, click the **Hopper** button (or) click **Insert > Rolled Walls > Hopper** on the Menu bar.
3. On the dialog, select the **Surfacic Hopper** option from the drop-down.
4. On the **Hopper** dialog, click the right mouse button in the **Selection** box, and then select **Create Multi-sections Surface**.
5. Select the first and second cross-sections.

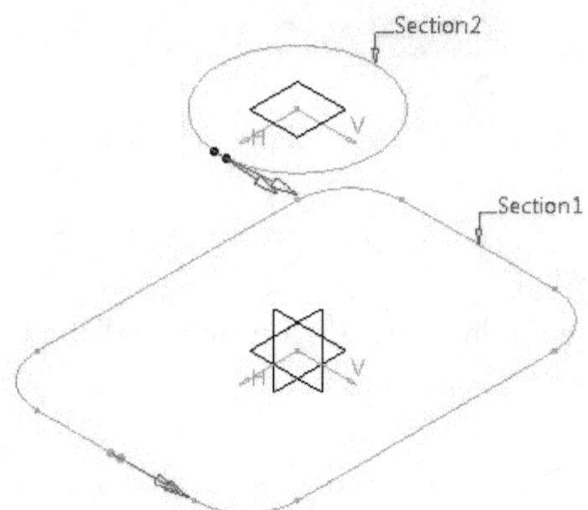

6. Click **OK**.

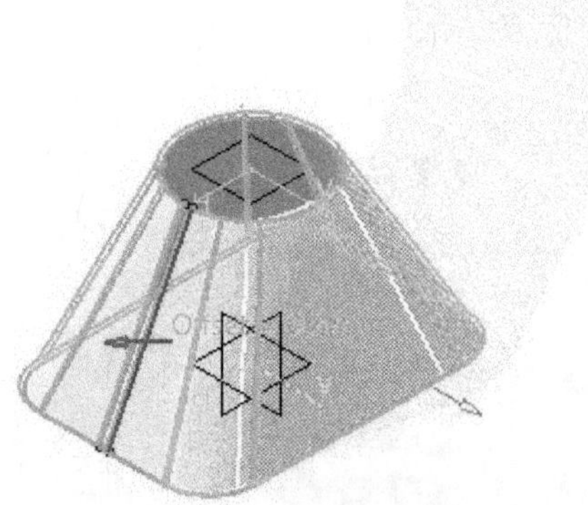

7. Click **OK** to complete the hopper.

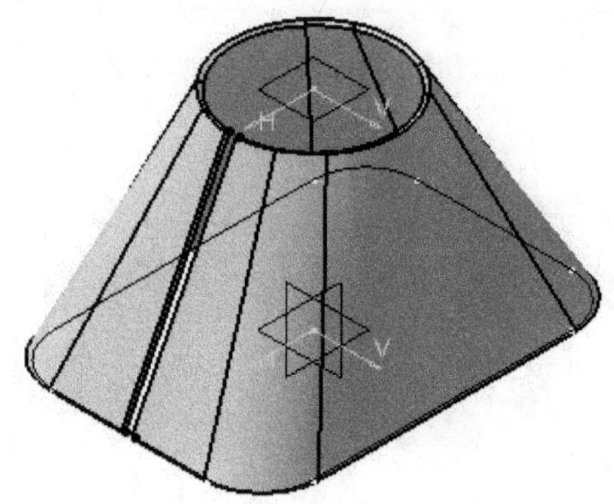

 Recognize

CATIA V5 has a special command called **Recognize**, which automates the process of converting an already existing part into a sheet metal part.

1. Create a part in the **Part design** Workbench, and then shell it using the **Shell** command.

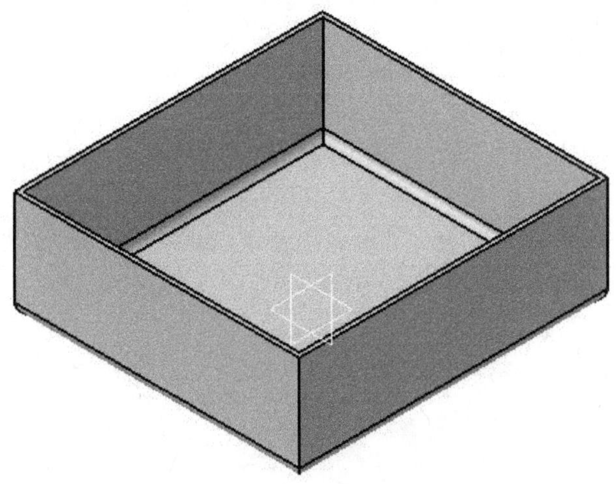

2. On the Menu bar, click **Start > Mechanical Design > Generative Sheetmetal Design**.
3. On the **Walls** toolbar, click the **Recognize** button (or) click **Insert > Recognize** on the Menu bar.
4. Click on the horizontal face to define the reference.
5. Click **OK** to convert the part into a sheet metal part. Now, you can perform other sheet metal operations.

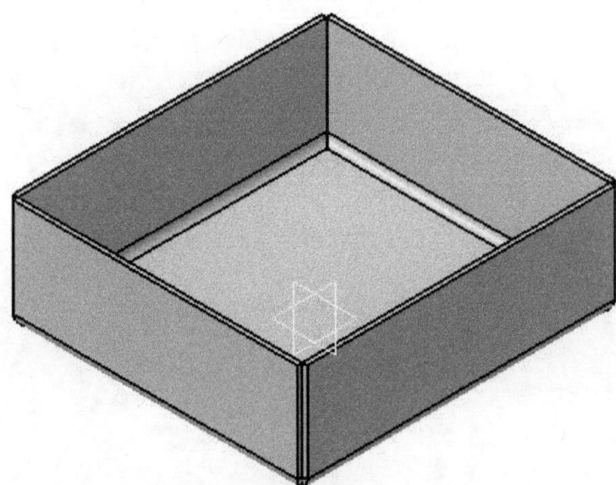

Sheet Metal Drawings

Creating drawing of a sheet metal part is same as creating any other drawing. However, you have to create the unfolded view of the sheet metal part. You can do this using the **Unfolded view** command.

1. Start a new drawing file.
2. On the **Views** toolbar, click **Projections** drop-down > **Unfolded view** (or) click **Insert >Views > Projections > Unfolded view** on the Menu bar.
3. Switch to the sheetmetal part window and select a face of the sheet metal part.

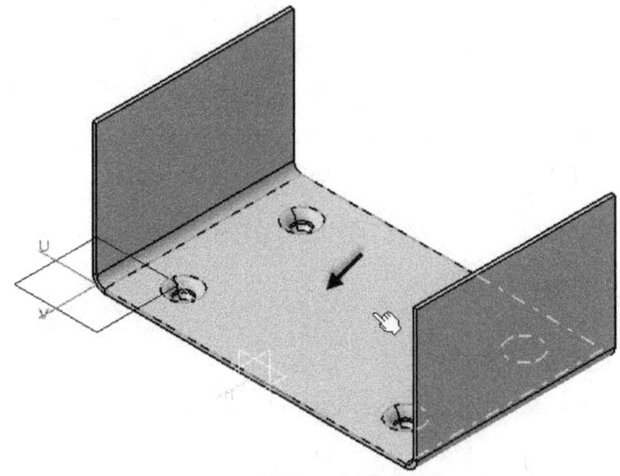

4. Click on the drawing sheet to place the unfolded view.

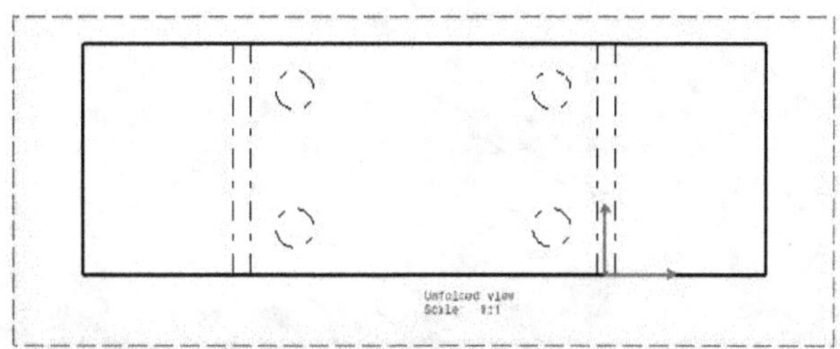

Save as DXF

In addition to creating drawings, you can directly export a sheet metal to DWF format.

1. On the **Manufacturing Preparation** toolbar, click the **Save as DXF** button (or) click **Insert > Manufacturing Preparation > Save As DXF** on the Menu bar.
2. On the **Save as DXF** dialog, type-in the tolerance value.
3. Set the **Reference skin** to **Top** or **Bottom**.
4. Select the data that you want to export from the **Technological data** drop-down.

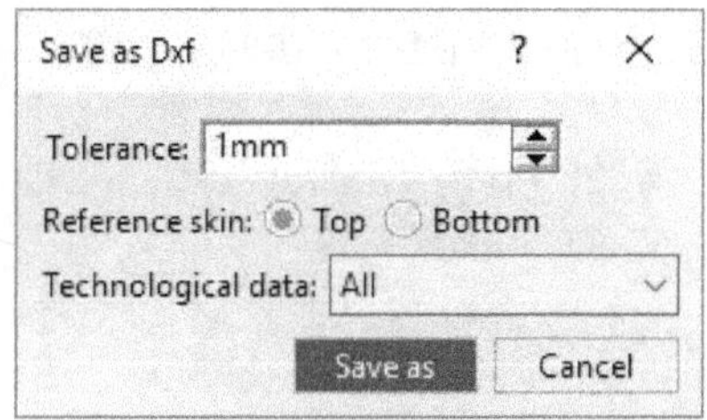

5. Click the **Save as** button, and specify the location of the file.
6. You can open the DXF file in AutoCAD or DXF viewer.

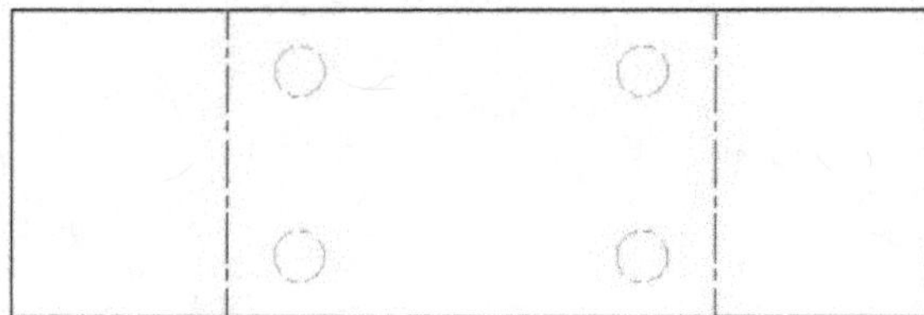

Examples

Example 1

In this example, you will construct the sheet metal part shown below.

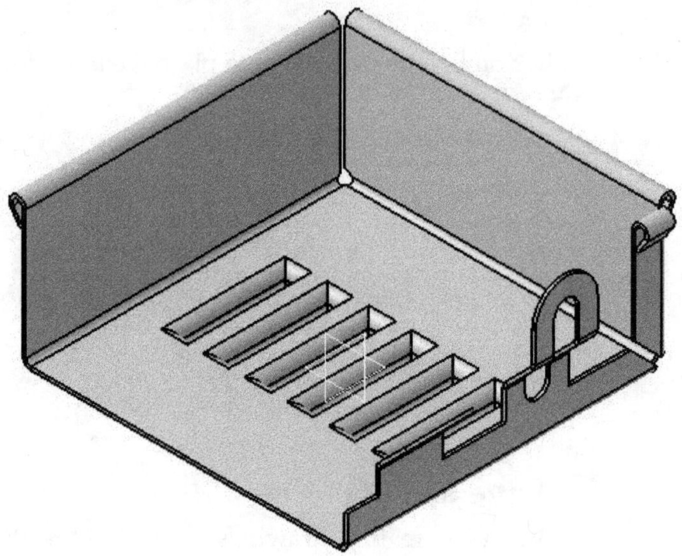

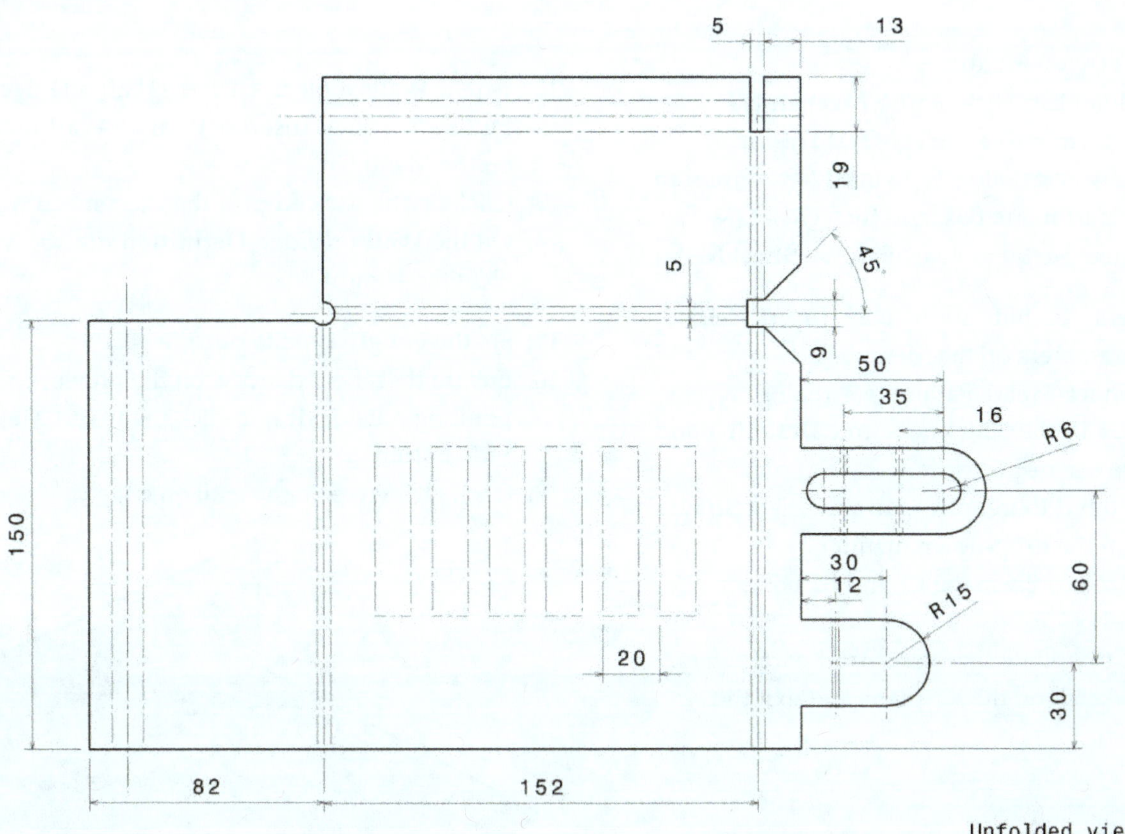

Unfolded view
Scale: 2:3

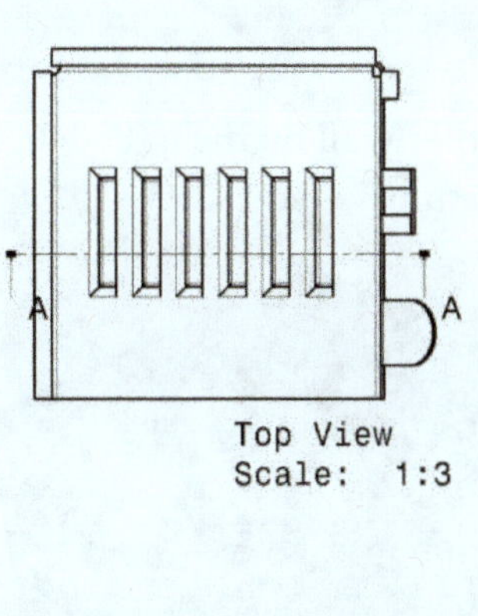

Top View
Scale: 1:3

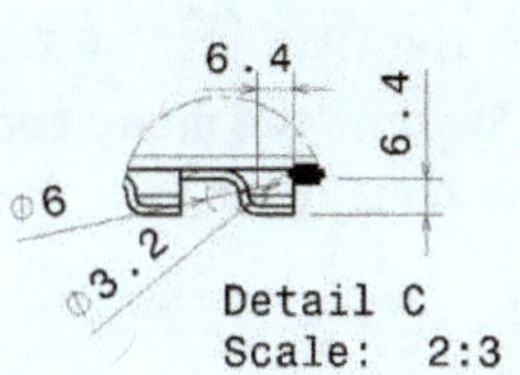

Detail C
Scale: 2:3

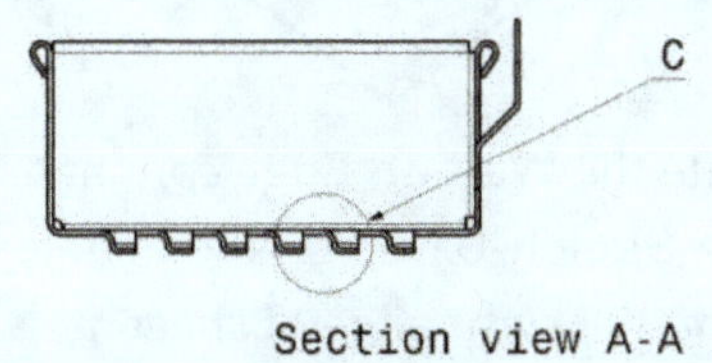

Section view A-A
Scale: 1:3

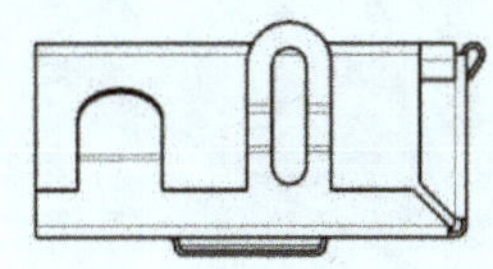

Auxiliary view B
Scale: 1:3

1. Start **CATIA V5-6R2017**.
2. On the Menu bar, click **Start > Mechanical Design > Generative Sheet Metal Design**.
3. On the **New Part** dialog, type-in C12-Example1 in the **Enter part name** box, and then click **OK**.
4. On the **Sheet Metal** toolbar, click the **Sheet Metal Parameters** button (or) click **Insert > Sheet Metal Parameters** on the Menu bar.
5. On the **Sheet Metal Parameters** dialog, type-in 1.6 and 2.4 in the **Thickness** and **Default Bend Radius** boxes, respectively.
6. Click the **Bend Extremities** tab and select **Square relief** from the drop-down menu.
7. Type-in **1.2** and **2.4** in the **L1** and **L2** boxes, respectively.
8. Click **OK** to update the sheet metal parameters.
9. Create a sketch on the XY plane and exit the workbench.

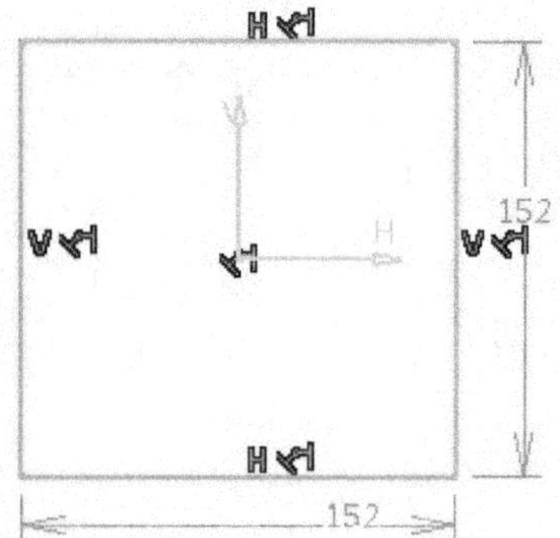

10. On the **Walls** toolbar, click the **Wall** button (or) click **Insert > Walls > Wall** on the menu bar.
11. Click **OK** to create the sheet metal wall.

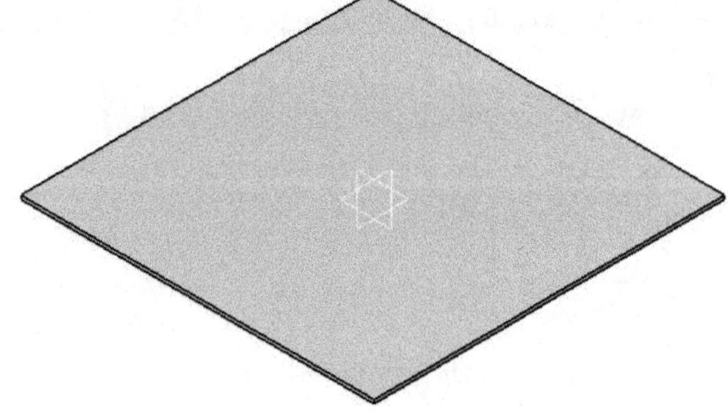

12. On the **Walls** toolbar, click the **Wall on Edge** button (or) click **Insert > Walls > Wall on Edge** on the Menu bar.
13. Click on the back edge of the sheet metal wall.
14. On the **Wall on Edge Definition** dialog, type-in **65** in the **Height** box.
15. Set the **Length type** to outside.
16. Ensure that the red arrow on the preview is pointing outside. If not, click the **Invert Material Side** button.
17. Click **OK** to create the wall on edge.

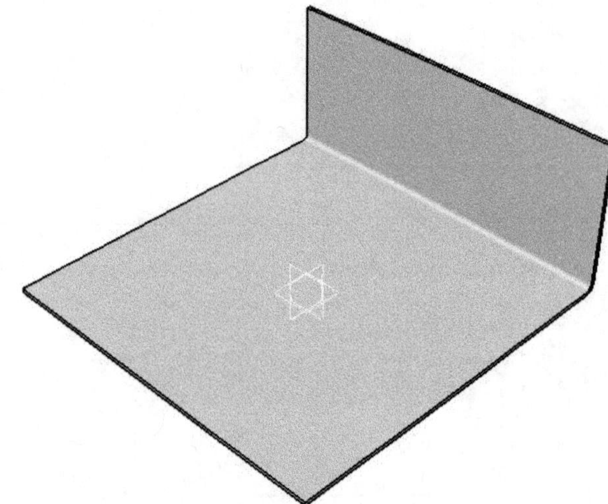

18. Create another wall on the left edge. The wall height is 65 mm.

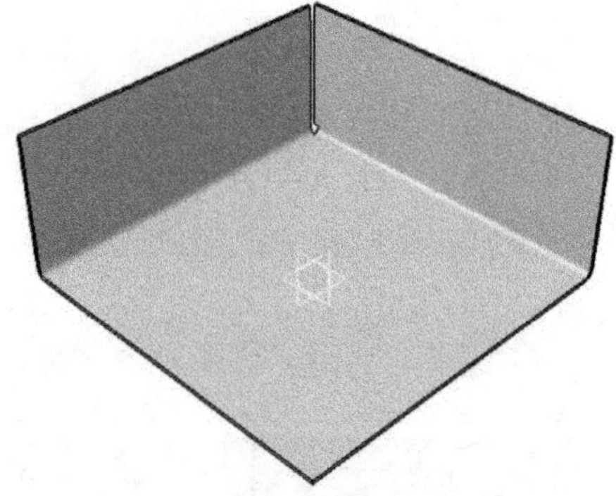

19. Activate the **Wall on Edge** command and select **Type > Sketch-Based** on the dialog.
20. Click on the right edge of sheet metal geometry to define the edge on which the wall will be created.

21. Click the sketch icon on the **Wall On Edge Definition** dialog and zoom into the model.
22. Click on the right end face of the model.

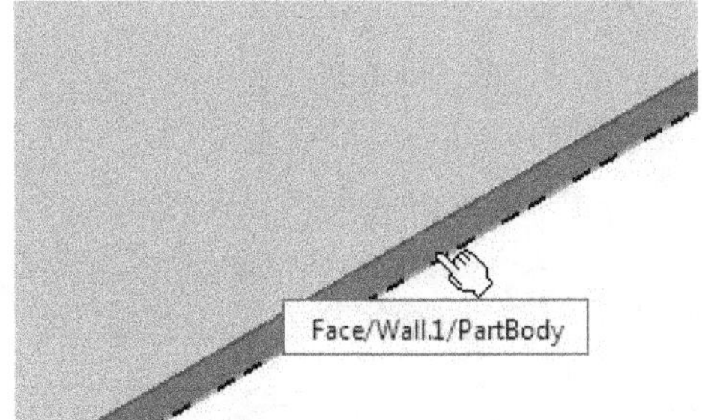

23. Draw the sketch of the wall and click **Exit workbench**.

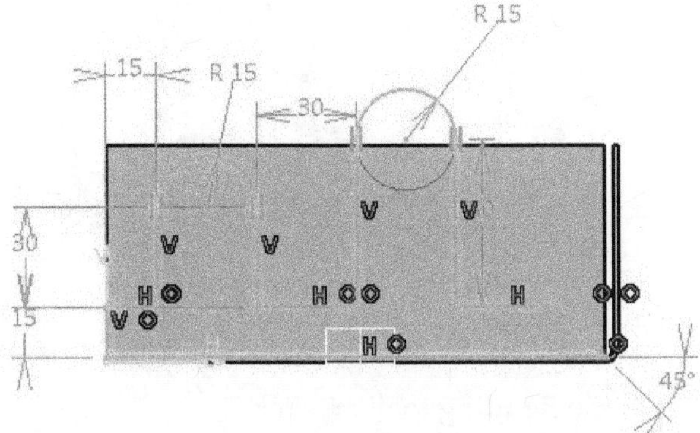

24. Click **OK** to create the sketch-based wall.

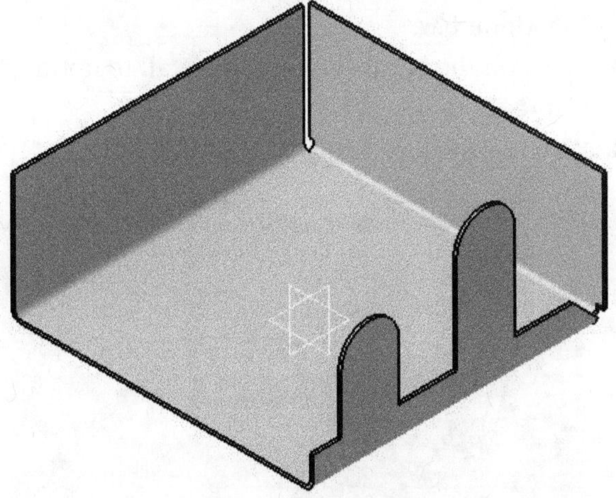

25. Likewise, create another wall on the vertical edge.

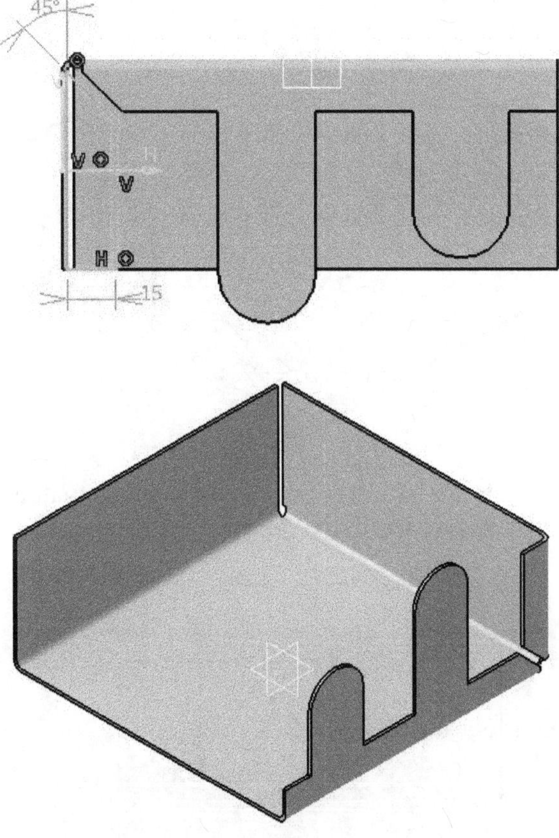

26. Draw a line on the outer face of the sketch-based wall and click **Exit workbench**.

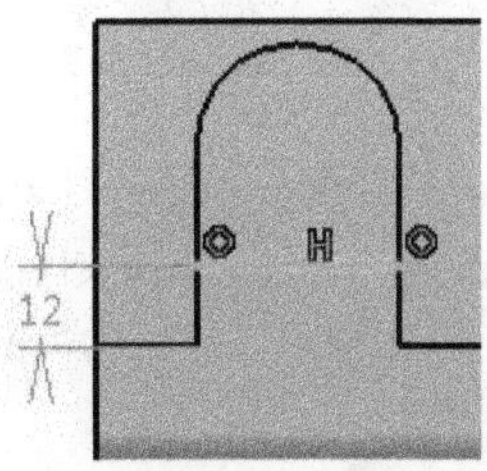

27. On the **Bending** toolbar, click the **Bend From Flat** button (or) click **Insert > Bending > Bend From Flat** on the Menu bar.
28. On the **Bend From Flat Definition** dialog, type-in 135 in the **Angle** box and click **OK**. This bends the wall by using the sketched line.

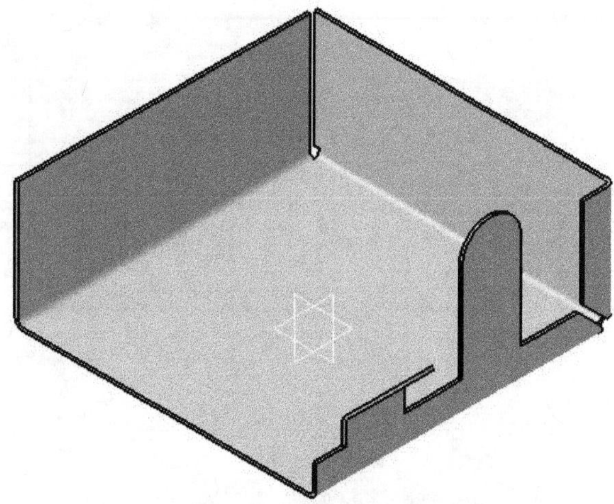

29. Sketch a horizontal line on the vertical wall and click **Exit workbench**.

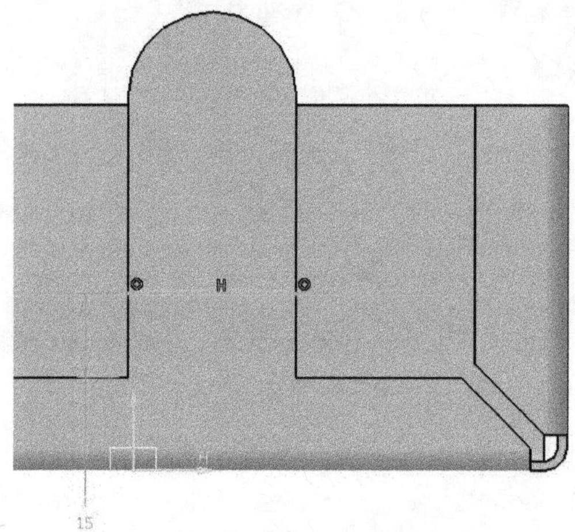

30. Activate the **Bend From Flat** command and bend the wall using the sketched line. The bend angle is 135 degrees.

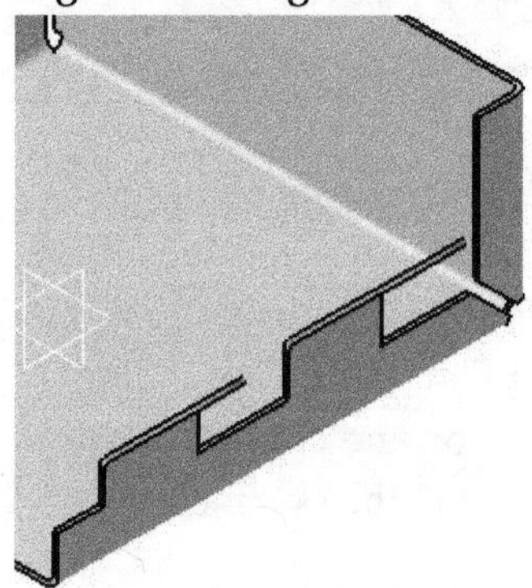

31. Sketch another horizontal line on the inclined face of the wall and bend it in the reverse direction. The bend angle is 135 degrees.

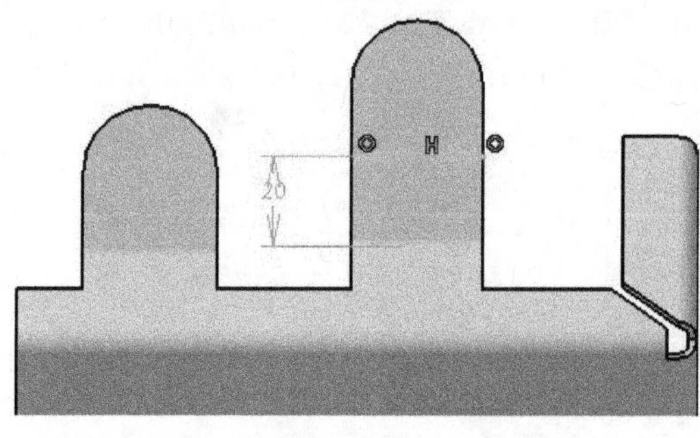

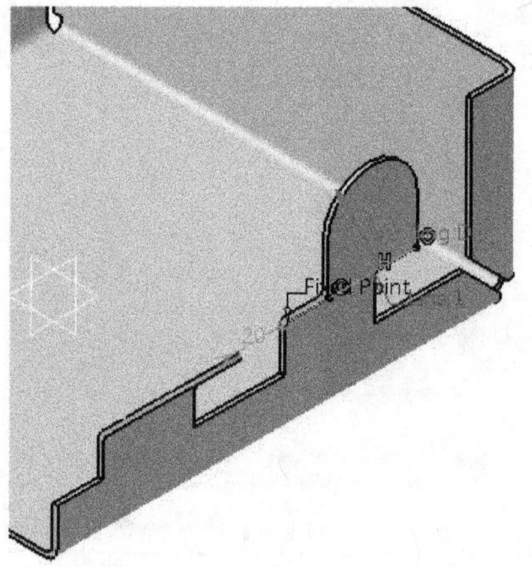

32. On the **Bending** toolbar, click **Folding/Unfolding** drop-down > **Unfolding** (or) click **Insert > Bending > Unfolding** on the Menu bar.
33. Click on the vertical face of the wall to define the reference face.
34. Click on the two bends to be unfolded.

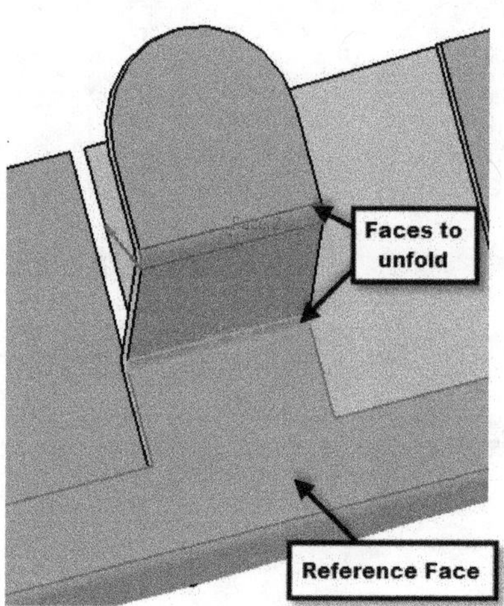

35. Click **OK** on the dialog.

36. Draw a sketch on the unfolded face and click **Exit workbench**.

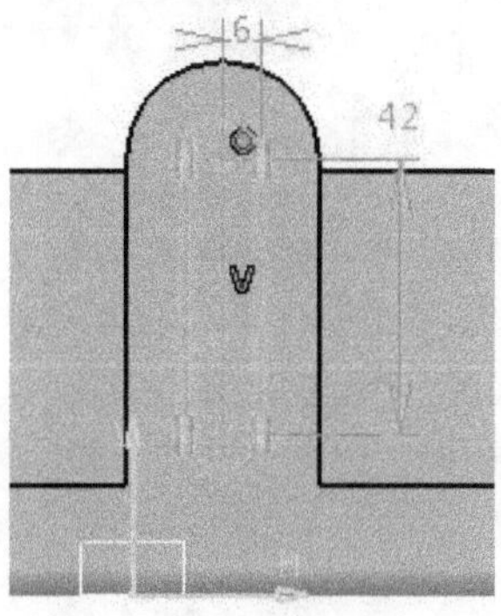

37. On the **Cutting/Stamping** toolbar, click **Cut Out** button (or) click **Insert > Cutting > Cut Out** on the Menu bar.
38. Leave the default settings on the **Cutout Definition** dialog and click **OK**.

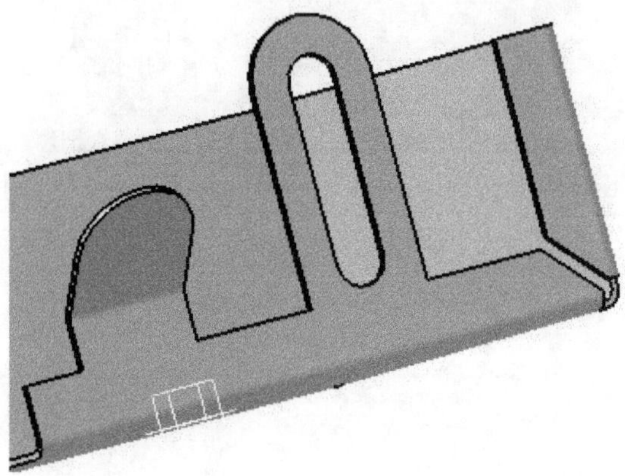

39. On the **Bending** toolbar, click **Folding/Unfolding** drop-down **> Folding** (or) click **Insert > Bending > Folding** on the Menu bar.
40. Click on the vertical face of the wall to define the reference face.
41. Click on the unfolded bend faces to be folded.

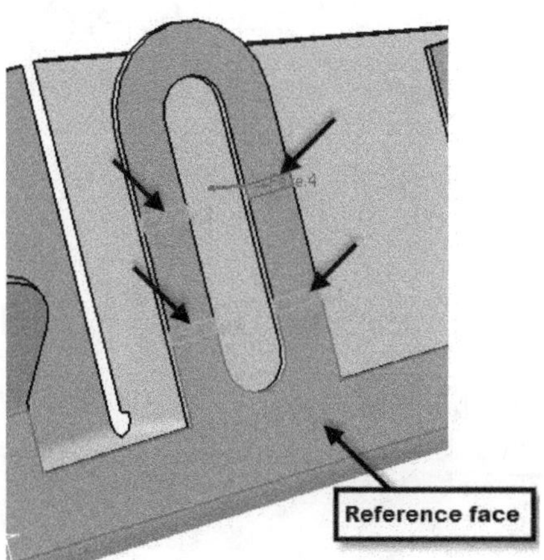

42. Click **OK**.

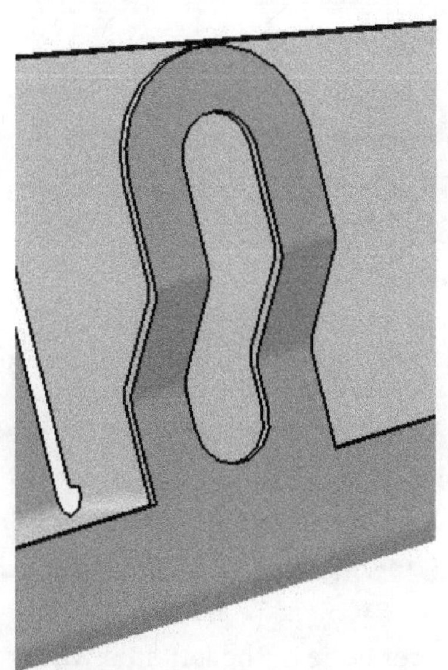

43. On the **Cutting/Stamping** toolbar, click **CornerRelief** button (or) click **Insert > Cutting > CornerRelief** on the Menu bar.
44. Zoom into the model and click on the bends, as shown below.

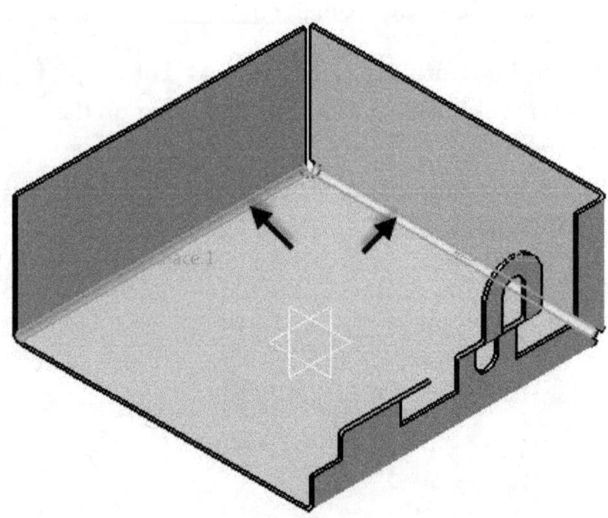

45. Select **Type > Circular** and type-in **4** in the **Radius** box.
46. Click **OK** to create the corner relief.

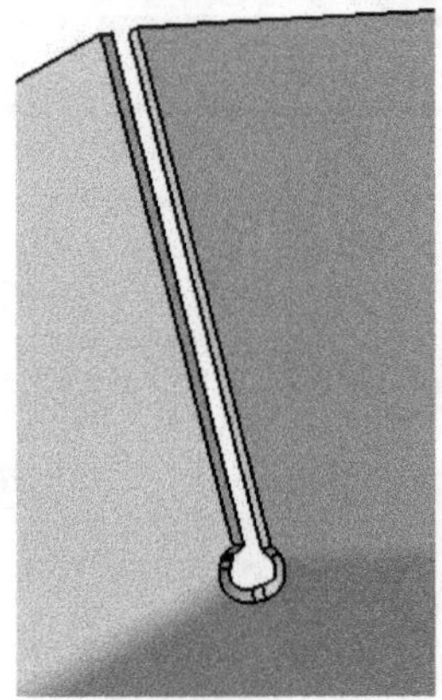

47. On the **Walls** toolbar, click **Swept Walls** drop-down > **Tear Drop** (or) click **Insert > Walls > Swept Walls > Tear Drop** on the Menu bar.
48. On the **Tear Drop Definition** dialog, select **Basic** from the drop-down menu, and then type-in **8** in the **Length** box.
49. Click on the outer edge of the left-side wall.

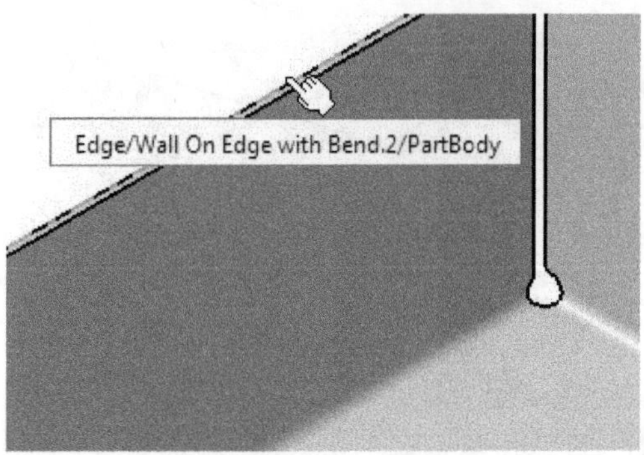

50. Click the **Reverse Direction** button on the dialog.
51. Click **OK** to create the teardrop.

52. Likewise, create teardrops on other vertical walls.

53. Draw a sketch on the top face of the base wall, and then click **Exit workbench**.

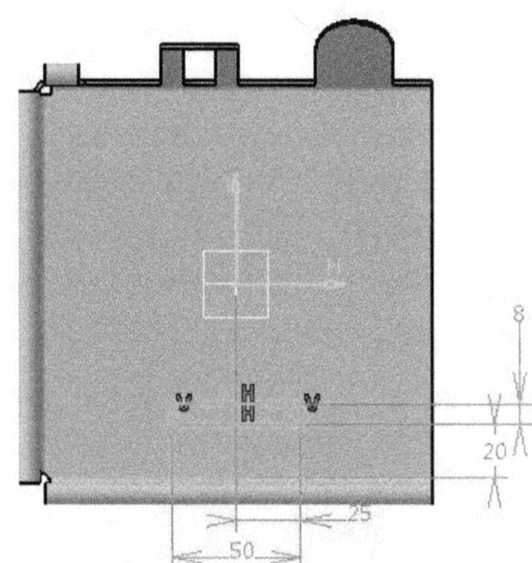

54. On the **Cutting/Stamping** toolbar, click **Stamping** drop-down **> Louver** (or) click **Insert > Stamping > Louver** on the Menu bar. You will notice that the sketch is selected, automatically. If not, you need to select the sketch.
55. On the **Louver Definition** dialog, type-in values, as shown below.

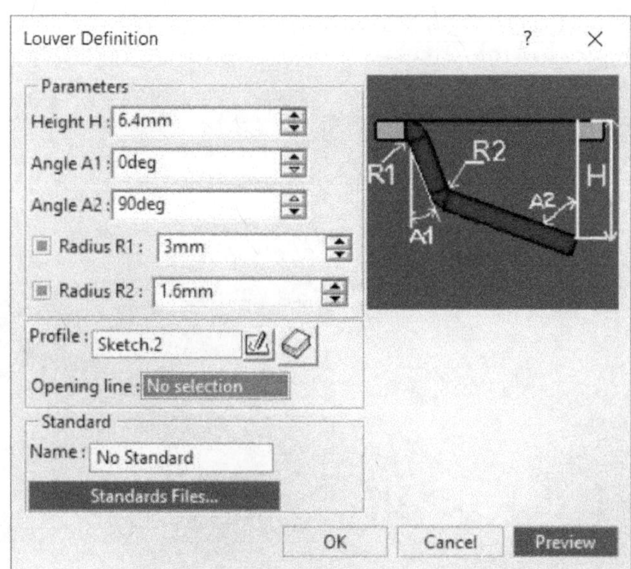

56. Select the inner horizontal line of the sketch to define the opening line.

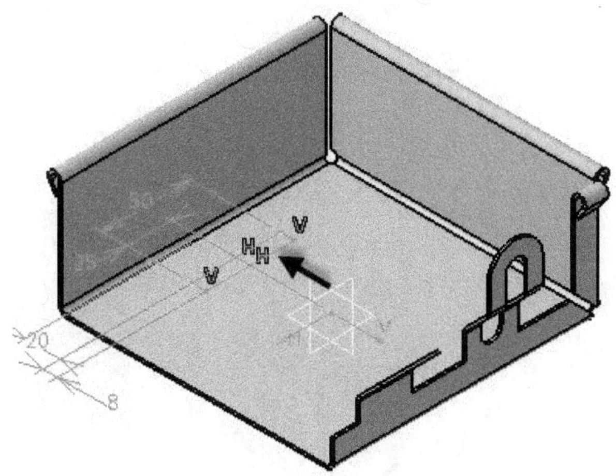

57. Click **OK** to create the louver.

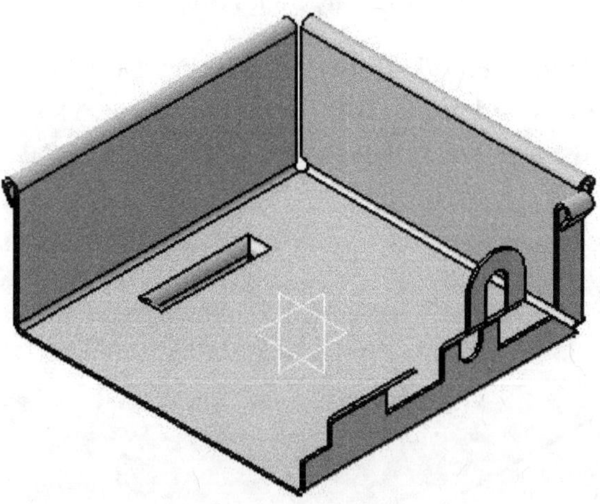

58. On the **Transformation** toolbar, click **Pattern** drop-down > **Rectangular Pattern** (or) click **Insert > Transformations > Rectangular Pattern** on the Menu bar.
59. On the **Rectangular Pattern** dialog, click in the **Object** selection box and select the louver from the geometry.
60. Click in the **Reference element** selection box and click on the front edge of the geometry. This defines the first direction of the rectangular pattern.
61. On the dialog, select **Parameters > Instance(s) & Length**.
62. Type-in **6** and **100** in the **Instance(s)** and **Length** boxes, respectively.
63. Click **OK** to create the pattern.

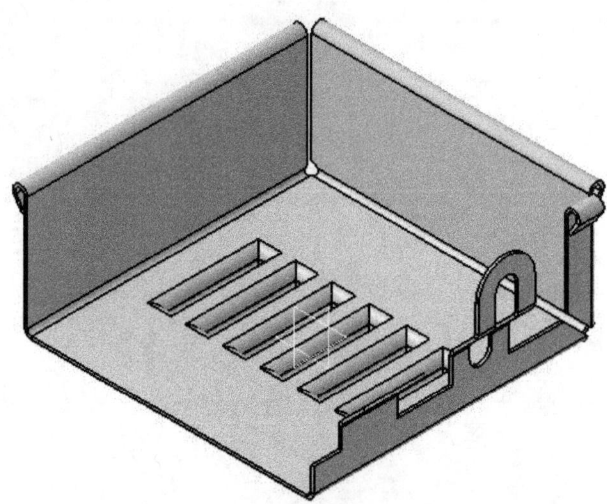

64. On the **Views** toolbar, click **Fold/Unfold** drop-down > **Fold/Unfold** (or) click **Insert > Views > Fold/Unfold** on the Menu bar. This displays the flattened view of the sheet metal part.

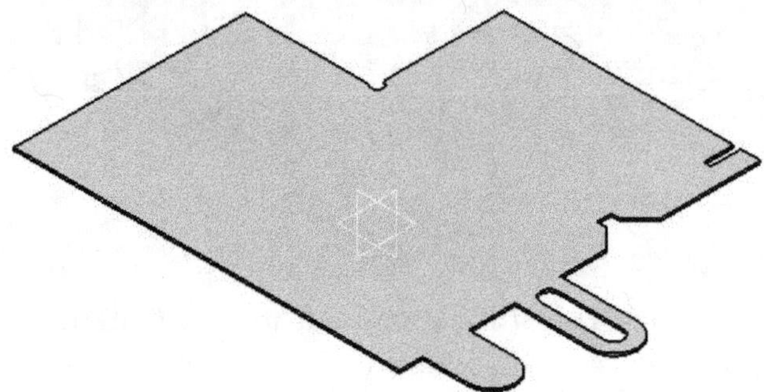

65. Again, click the **Fold/Unfold** button to switch back to the folded view
66. Save and close the sheet metal part.

Questions

1. How do you insert an unfolded view into a drawing?
2. Describe parameters that can be specified on the **Sheet Metal Parameters** dialog.
3. Define the term 'K Factor'.
4. List any two sheet metal part parameters that can be overridden when creating a feature.
5. What is the use of the **Circular Cutout** command?
6. List the types of swept walls that can be created in CATIA V5?
7. What does the **CornerRelief** command do?
8. What are the corner relief types available?
9. What is the difference between a surface stamp and flanged cut out?

Exercises

Exercise 1

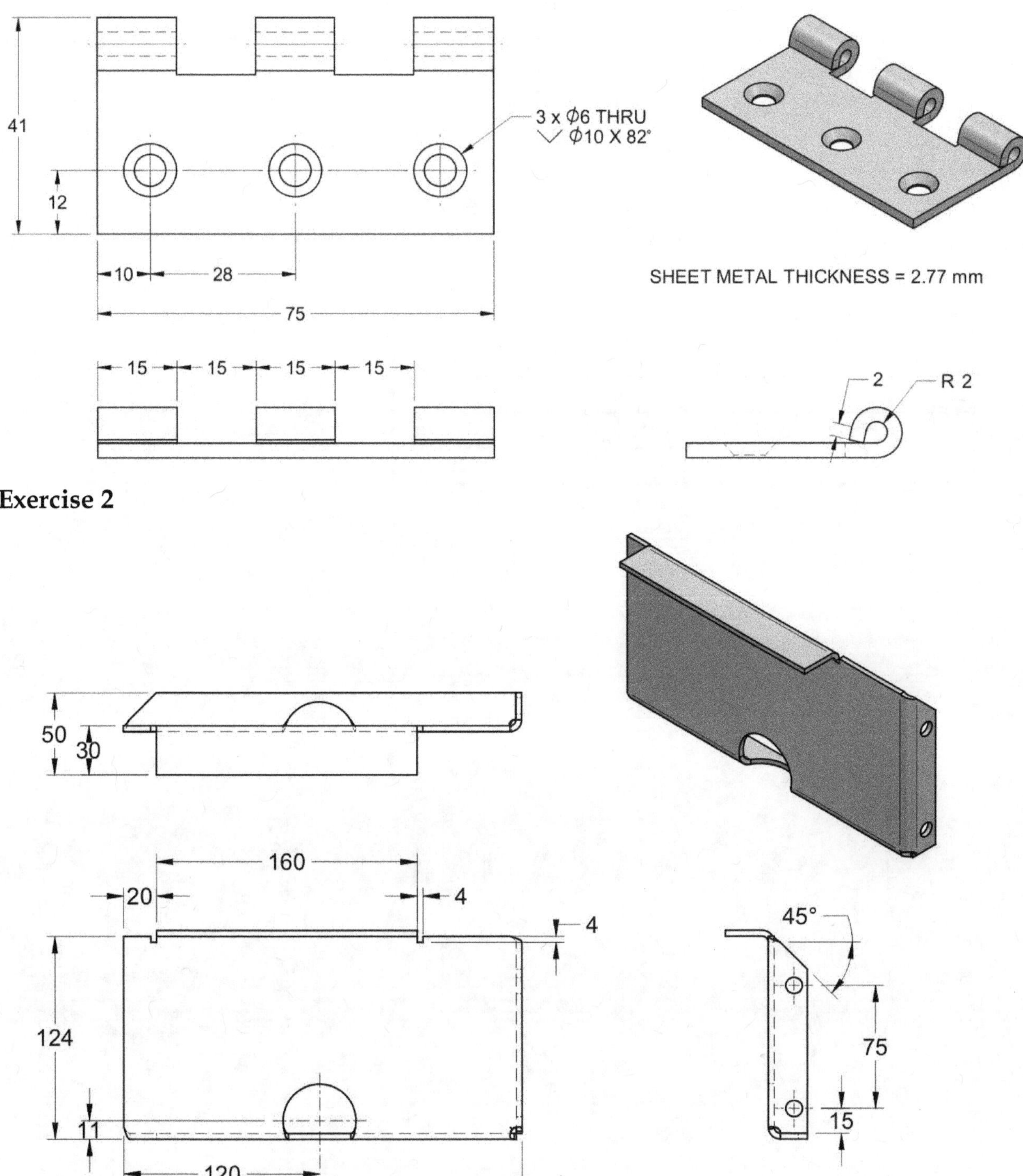

Exercise 2

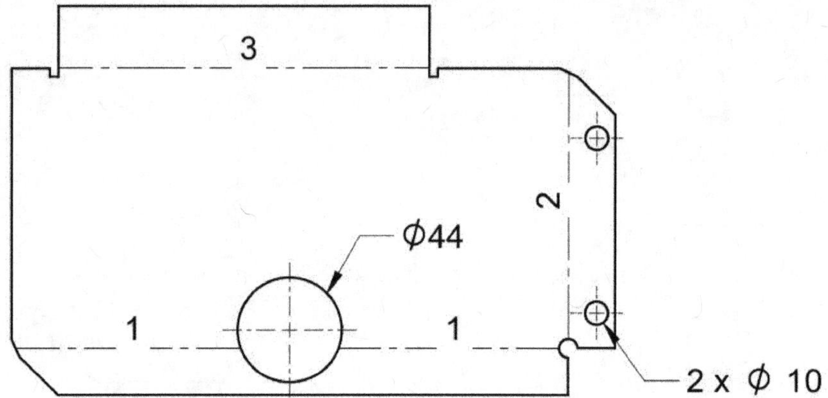

Sequence	Feature	Radius	Angle	Direction	Included Angle
1	Bend 1	3.58 mm	90.00 deg	Down	90.00 deg
2	Bend 2	3.58 mm	90.00 deg	Down	90.00 deg
3	Bend 3	3.58 mm	90.00 deg	Up	90.00 deg

Chapter 13: Surface Design

The topics covered in this chapter are:

- *Basic surfaces*
- *Sweep surfaces*
- *Multi-sections surfaces*
- *Blend surfaces*
- *Fill surfaces*
- *Offset Surfaces*
- *Healing*
- *Extract*
- *Trim*
- *Split*
- *Extrapolate*
- *Untrim*
- *Join*
- *Translate*
- *Rotate*
- *Symmetry*
- *Split (Body)*
- *Thick Surface*
- *Close Surface*
- *Wireframe Geometry*

CATIA V5 Surfacing commands can be used to create complex geometries that are very difficult to create using standard pads, revolve features, and so on. Surface modeling can also be used to edit and fix the broken imported parts. In this chapter, you learn the basics of surfacing commands that are mostly used. The surfacing commands are available in the **Generative Shape Design** workbench.

To activate this workbench, click **Start > Shape > Generative Shape Design** on the Menu bar.

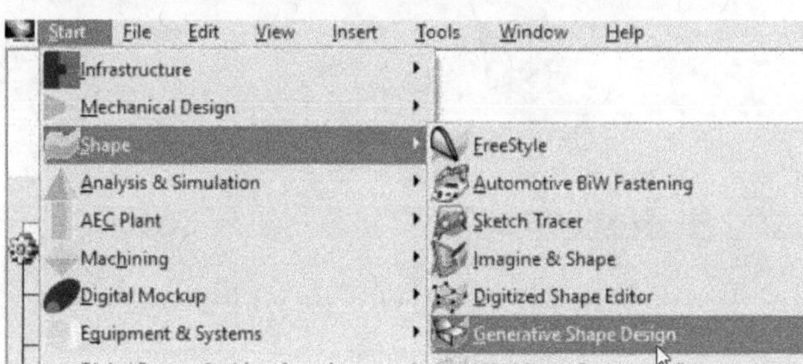

CATIA V5 offers a rich set of surface design commands. A surface is an infinitely thin piece of geometry. For example, consider a cube shown in figure. It has six faces. Each of these faces is a surface, an infinitely thin piece of geometry that acts as a boundary in the 3D space. Surfaces can be simple or complex shapes.

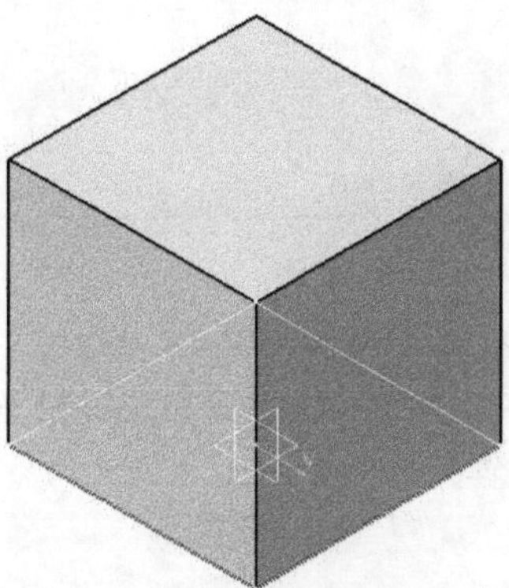

In solid modeling, when you have created solid

features such as a pad feature or a Revolved feature, CATIA V5 creates a set of features (surfaces) that enclose a volume. The airtight enclosure is considered as a solid body. The advantage of using the surfacing commands is that you can design a model with more flexibility.

 Extrude

1. To create an extruded surface, first create an open or closed sketch.

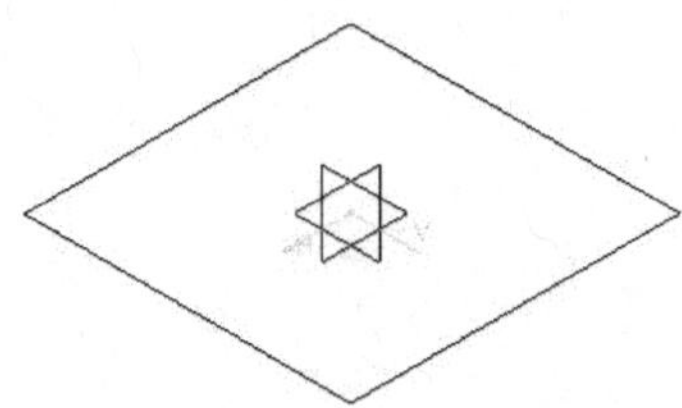

2. On the **Surfaces** toolbar, click the **Extrude** button (or) click **Insert > Surfaces > Extrude** on the Menu bar.
3. Select the sketch and type-in a value in the **Dimension** box available below the **Type** drop-down.

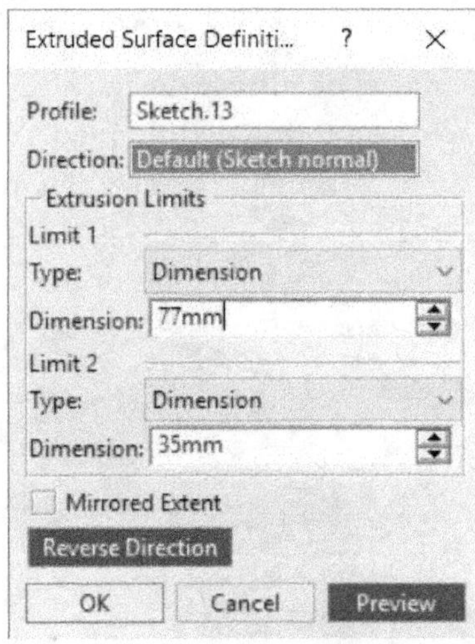

4. Click **OK** to create the extruded surface. You will notice that the extrusion is not capped at the ends.

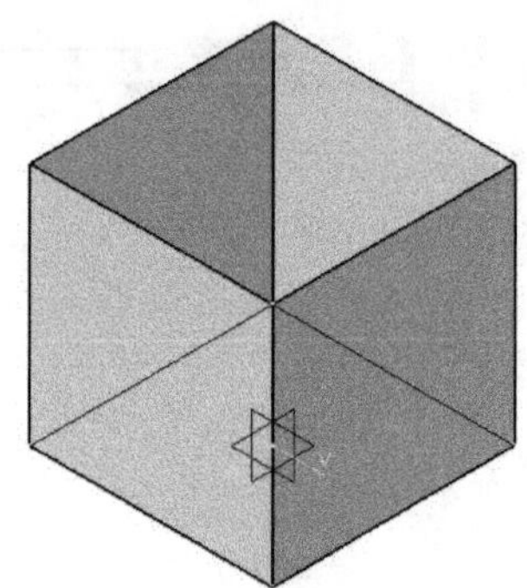

 Revolve

1. To create a revolved surface, first create an open or closed profile and the axis of revolution.

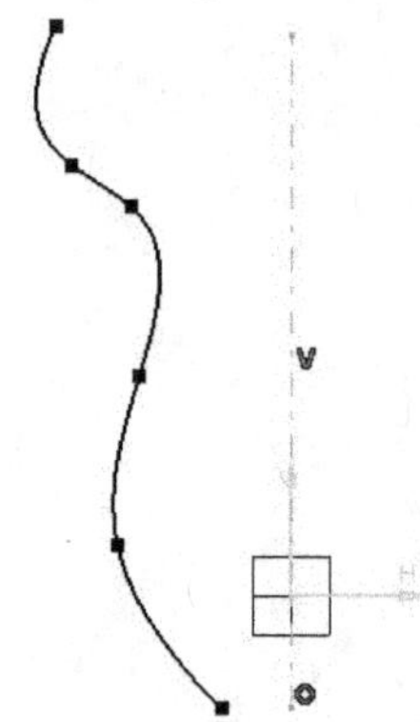

2. On the **Surfaces** toolbar, click **Extrude-Revolution** drop-down > **Revolve** (or) click **Insert > Surfaces > Revolve** on the Menu bar.
3. Select the sketch.
4. Type-in the angle of revolution in the **Angle 1** box and click **OK**.

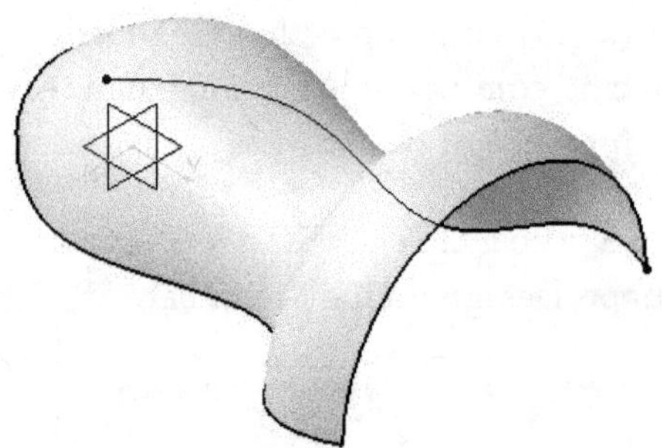

 Sphere

1. To create a sphere, first create a point to define its position.

2. On the **Surfaces** toolbar, click **Extrude-Revolution** drop-down > **Revolve** (or) click **Insert > Surfaces > Revolve** on the Menu bar.
3. Select the point. You can also create a point by right clicking in the **Center** selection box on the **Sphere Surface Definition** dialog, and selecting an option to create a point.
4. Type-in a value in the **Sphere radius** box (or) click and drag the radius handle that appears on the preview.

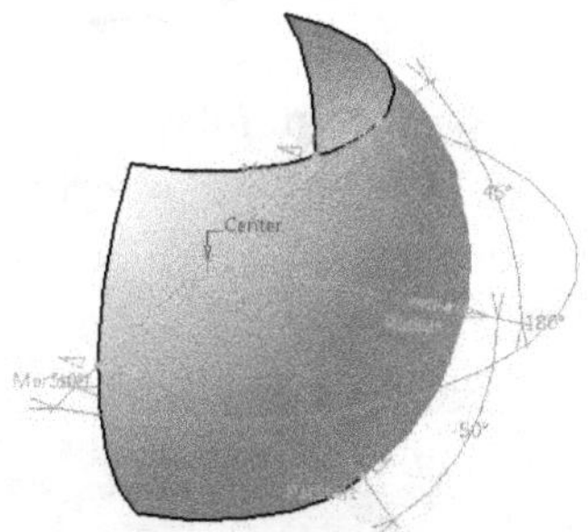

5. Type-in angle values on the dialog (or) click and drag the angle handles.

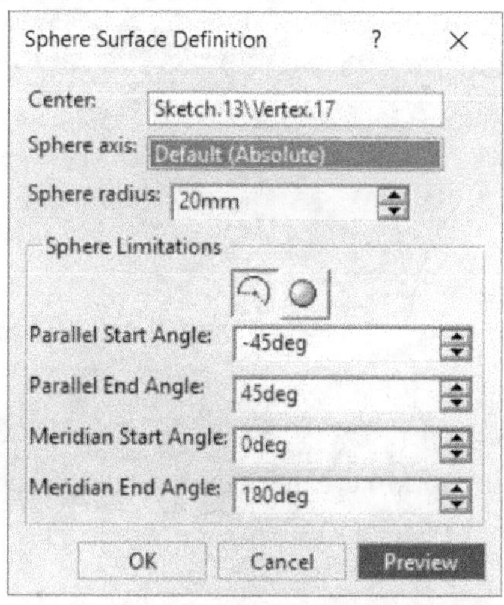

6. Click the whole sphere button on the dialog, if you want to create a whole sphere.
7. Click **OK** to create the sphere.

Cylinder

1. To create a cylinder, first create a point to define its position.
2. On the **Surfaces** toolbar, click **Extrude-Revolution** drop-down > **Cylinder** (or) click **Insert > Surfaces > Cylinder** on the Menu bar.
3. Select the point, and then click on a plane or axis. This defines the position and direction of the cylinder.

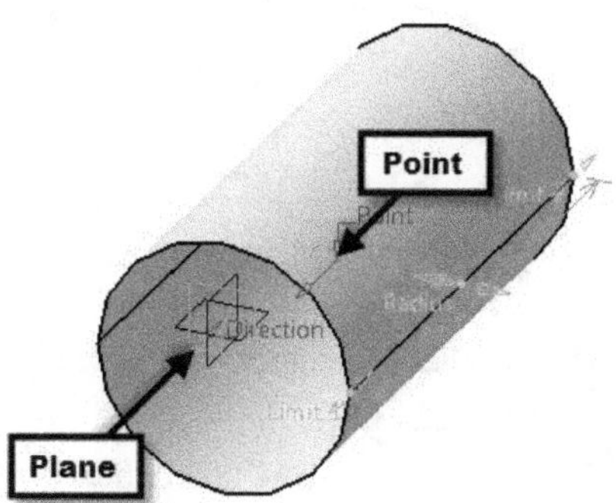

4. On the dialog, type-in values in the **Radius, Length 1, Length 2** boxes (or) using the handles to define the size of the cylinder.

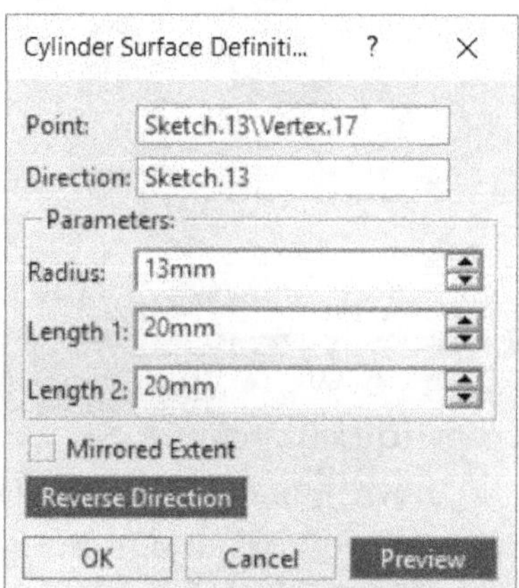

5. Click **OK** to complete the cylindrical surface.

Even if you create an enclosed surface, CATIA V5 will not recognize it as a solid body. You will learn to convert a surface body into a solid later in this chapter.

Sweep

This command creates a surface by sweeping a section along a guide curve.

1. Create a sweep profile and a guide curve.

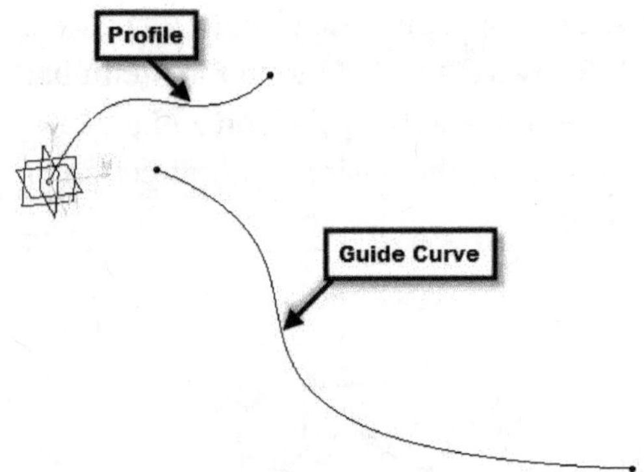

2. On the **Surfaces** toolbar, click **Sweeps** drop-down > **Sweep** (or) click **Insert > Surfaces > Sweep** on the Menu bar.
3. Click on the profile curve, and then click on the guide curve.
4. Click **OK**.

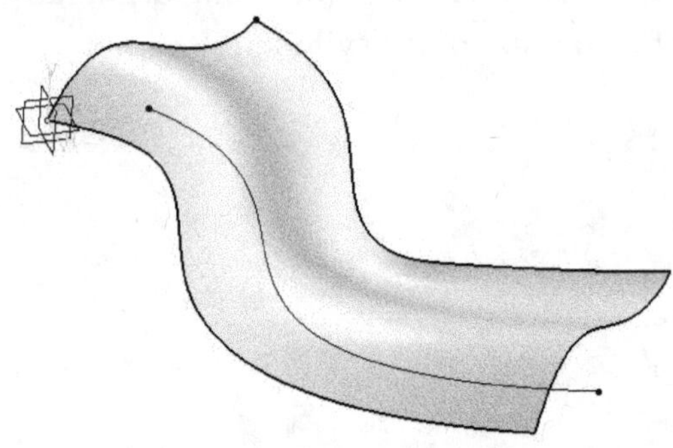

Sweep with two guide curves

The **With two guide curves** option creates a surface by sweeping a profile along two guide curves.

1. Create a profile and two guides. They should be separate sketches.
2. Activate the **Sweep** command.
3. On the dialog, select **Subtype > With two guide curves**.
4. Select the profile and two guide curves.

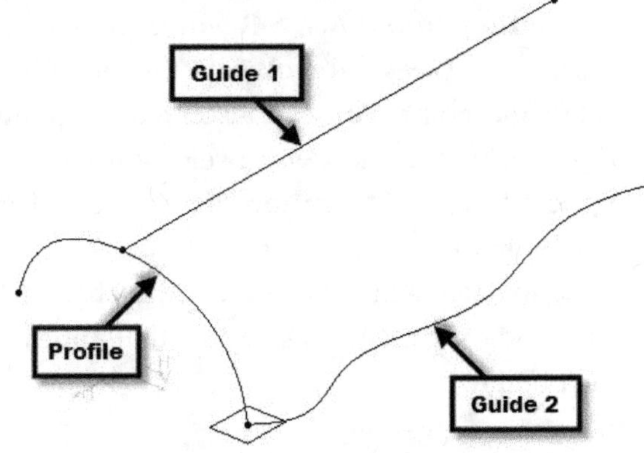

5. Select **Anchoring type > Two points**.
6. Click in the **Anchor point 1** box and select the intersection point between the first guide and profile.
7. Likewise, select the second anchor point.
8. Click **OK**.

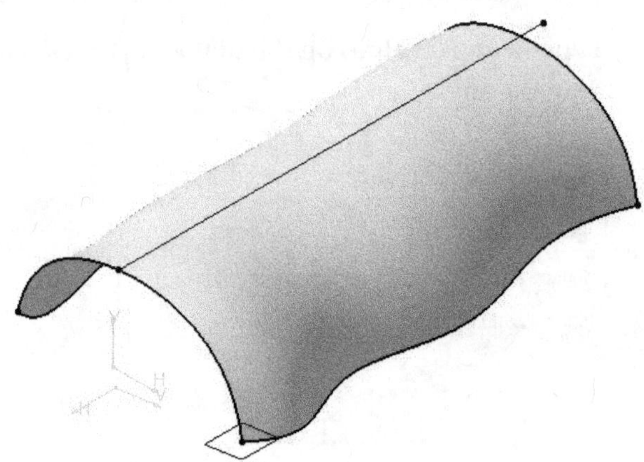

Two Limits

The **Two Limits** option creates a surface using two limiting guide curves.

1. Create two guide curves.
2. Activate the **Sweep** command.
3. On the dialog, select the **Line** button.
4. Select **Subtype > Two Limits**.
5. Select the two guide curves. The first guide curve will act as the spine.

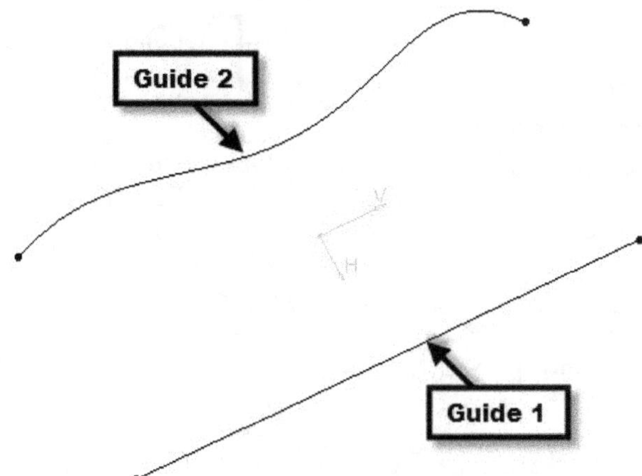

6. Type-in values in the **Length 1** and **Length 2** boxes. This defines the width of the swept surface beyond the two guide curves. You can also click the **Law** button to define the extension using various law types (Constant, Linear, S type, and Advance).
7. Click **OK**.

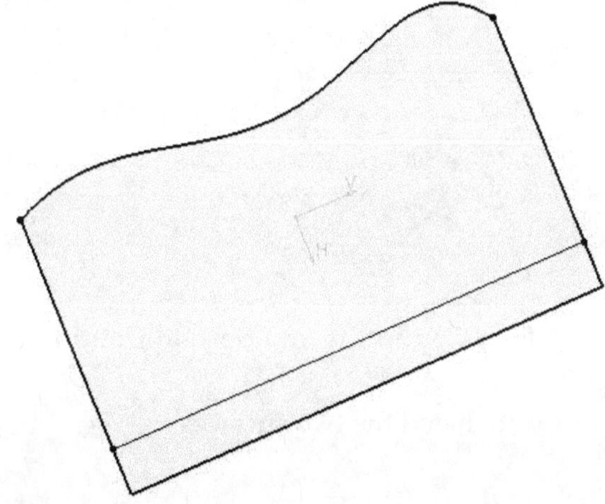

Three Guides

1. The **Three Guides** option creates a circular surface passing through three guide curves.
2. Create three guide curves.
3. Activate the **Sweep** command.
4. On the dialog, select the **Circle** button.
5. Select **Subtype > Three guides**.
6. Select three guide curves. The first guide curve will act as the spine.

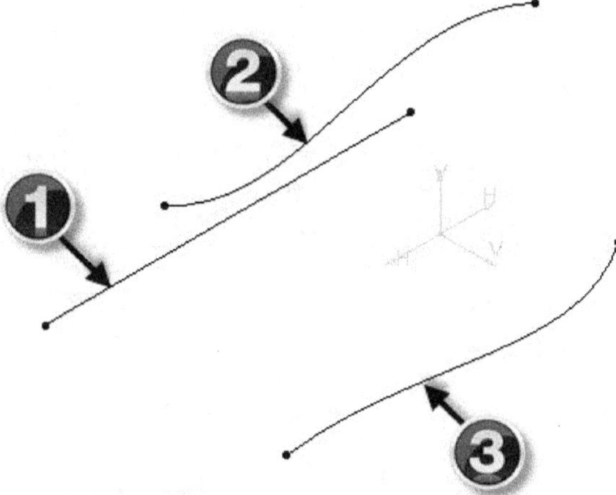

7. Click **OK**.

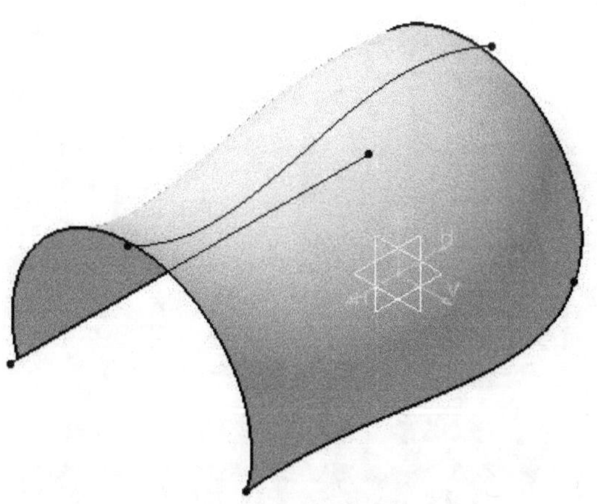

Multi-Sections Surface

This command creates a surface through multiple cross-sections. The shape of the geometry adjusts automatically to pass through the cross-sections.

1. Create cross-sections on different planes. The cross-sections can be closed or open curves, and they are not required to be on parallel planes. You can also add guide curves connecting the cross-sections.
2. On the **Surfaces** toolbar, click the **Multi-Sections Surface** button (or) click **Insert > Surfaces > Multi-Sections Surface** on the Menu bar.
3. Select two or more cross-sections. Ensure that arrows are pointing in the same direction.
4. Click in the **Guides** tab, and then select the guide curves.

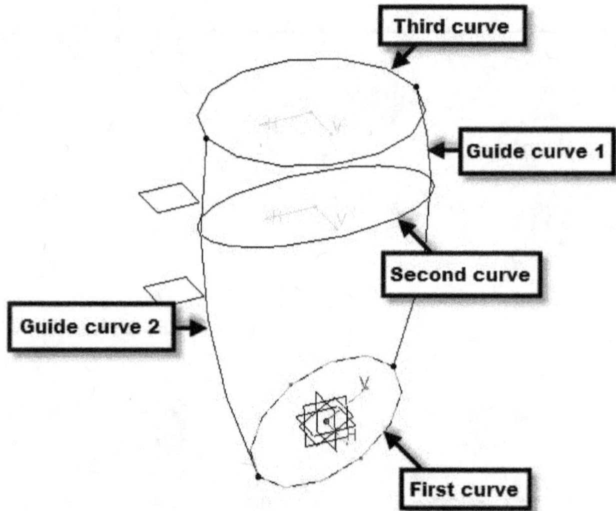

5. Click **OK**.

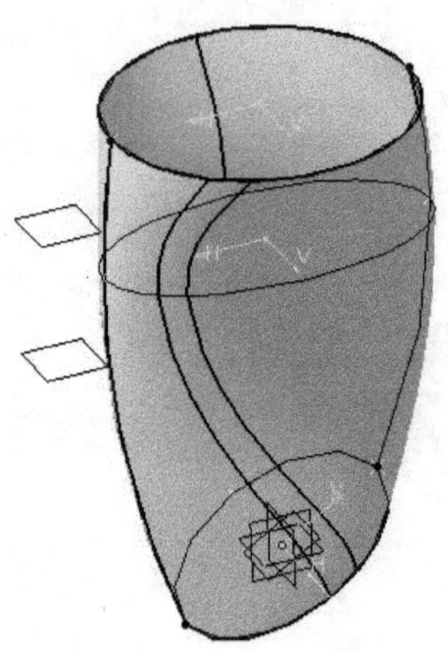

 Blend

The **Blend** command creates a surface blending two surfaces. This can be tangent, or curvature, continuous in both the directions.

1. On the **Surfaces** toolbar, click the **Blend** button (or) click **Insert > Surfaces > Blend** on the Menu bar.
2. Click on the first curve and first support.
3. Click on the second curve and second support.

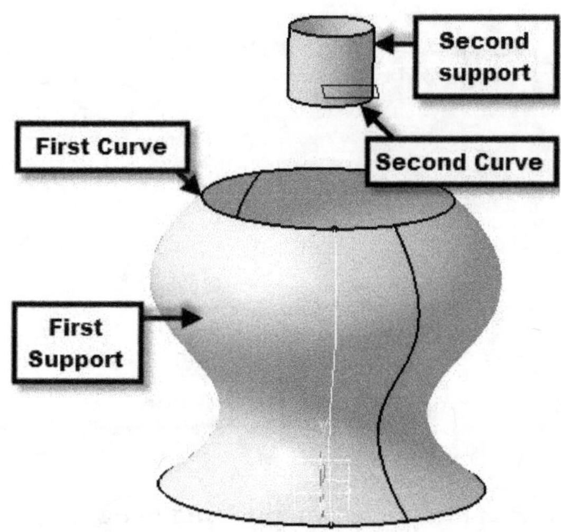

4. Click the **Preview** button on the dialog.

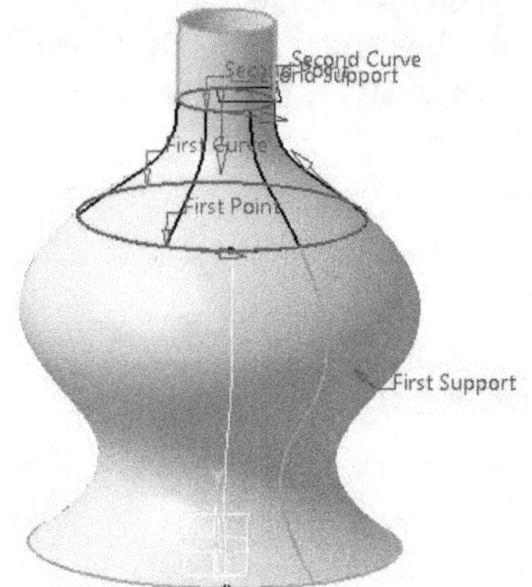

5. Set the **First Continuity** and **Second Continuity** type.
6. Click **OK** to blend the two surfaces.

 Fill

The **Fill** command can be used either to patch holes in models or to create complex surfaces. As a patching tool, the **Fill Surface** command is more robust than deleting holes or untrimming. It provides more discrete control over the definition of the resultant patch. However, you can also use this command to create complex surfaces.

1. On the **Surfaces** toolbar, click the **Fill** button (or) click **Insert > Surfaces > Fill** on the Menu bar.
2. Click on the outer boundary of the fill surface.
3. Click the **Inner Boundaries** tab and select the inner boundary.
4. Click in the **Passing element(s)** selection box, and then select the curve passing through the boundaries.

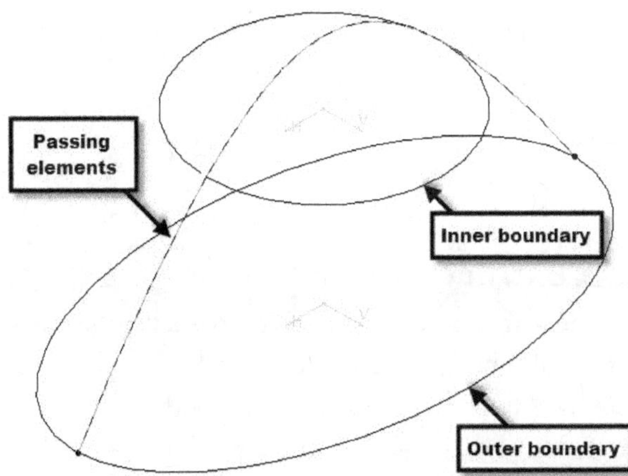

5. Click **OK**.

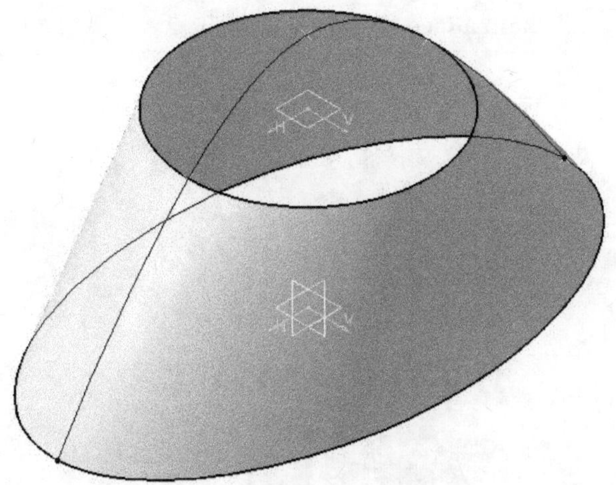

Offset Surface

To create an offset surface, follow the steps given next.

1. On the **Surfaces** toolbar, click **Offsets** drop-down > **Offset** (or) click **Insert > Surfaces > Offset** on the Menu bar.
2. Select the face to offset.
3. Type-in a value in the **Offset** box.
4. Click **Preview**.

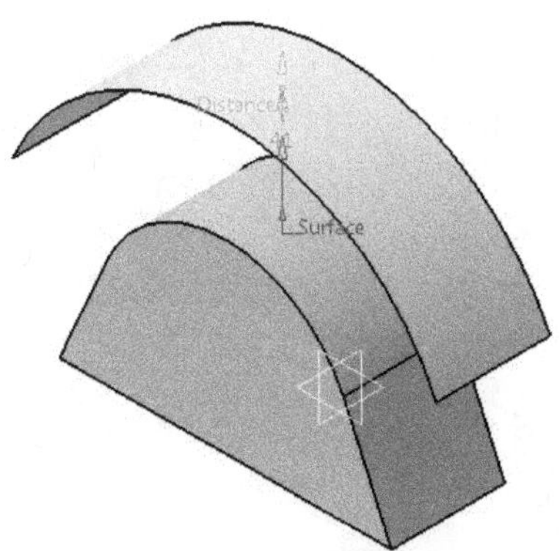

If you want to select multiple faces to offset, then click the right mouse button on a face and select **Create Join**. Now, select the faces that are connected to each other. Click **OK**.

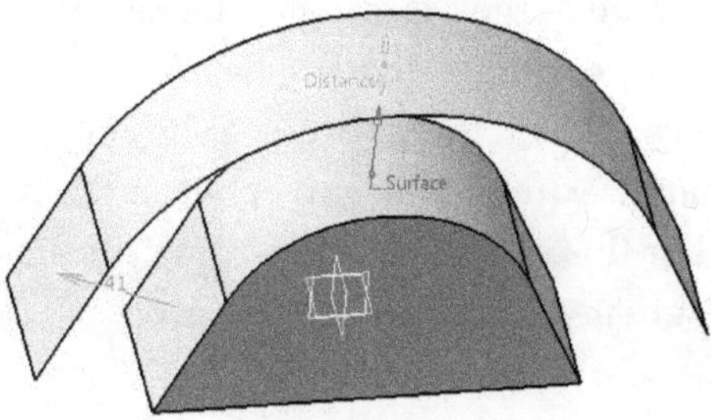

5. Click the **Reverse Direction** button, if you want to reverse the offset direction.
6. Check the **Both sides** option, if you want to create offset surface on the both sides.
7. Check the **Repeat object after OK** option, if you want to repeat the offset surfaces.

The **Smoothing** and **Regularization** options help you smooth complex geometries. Go to CATIA Help file to know more about these options.

 Healing

This command closes small gaps between surfaces.

1. On the **Operations** toolbar, click **Trim-Split** drop-down > **Healing** (or) click **Insert > Operations > Healing** on the Menu bar.
2. Select the surfaces to heal.

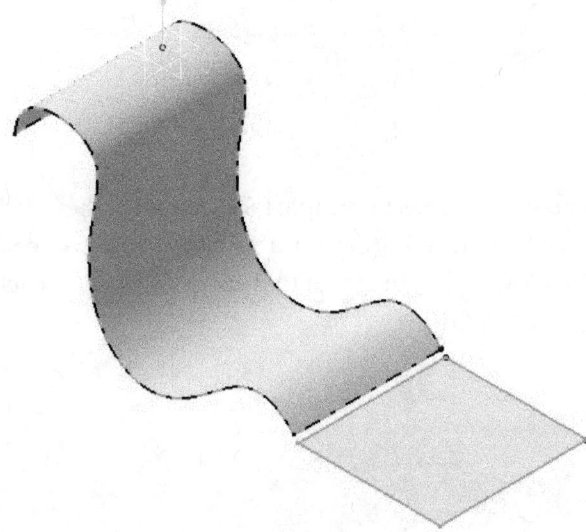

3. Select the **Continuity** type from the **Parameters** section.
4. Type-in a value in the **Merging distance** box. This is the approximate distance between the two surfaces. The merging distance should be greater than or equal to the gap between the two surfaces. For this example, the merging distance should be greater than or equal to 1 mm.
5. Click **OK**.

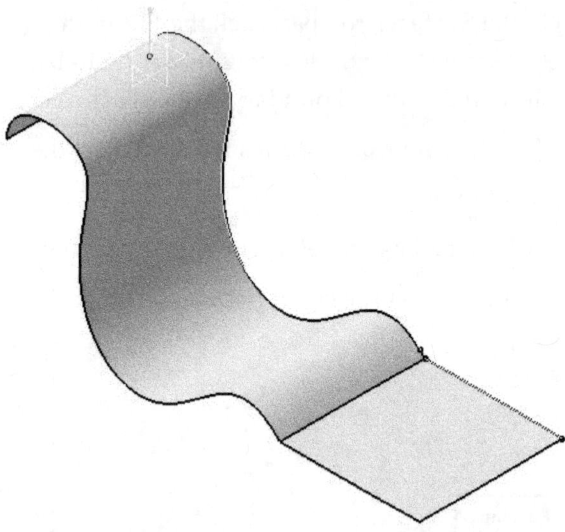

 Extract

In some cases, you may need to extract the surfaces of the solid body. You can use the **Extract** command to extract the surfaces of the solid body.

1. On the **Operations** toolbar, click **Extracts** drop-down > **Extract** (or) click **Insert > Operations > Extract** on the Menu bar.
2. Click on a face of the solid body.

3. If you select **Propagation type > Tangent Continuity**, the tangentially connected faces will be selected.
4. If you check the **Complimentary mode** option, the selection will be reversed.

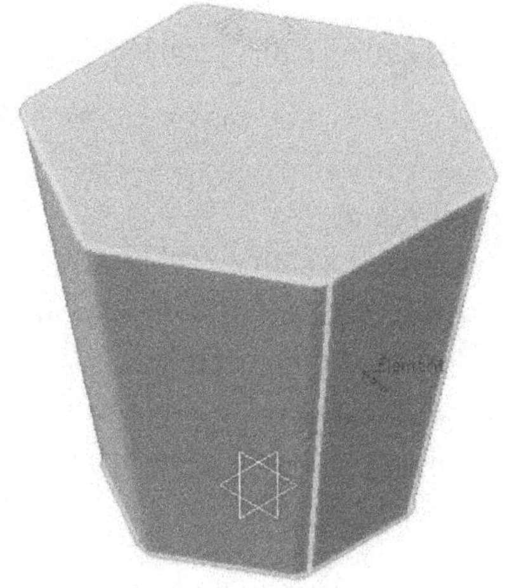

5. Click **OK** to extract the selected surfaces.

Trim

This command trims and assembles two intersecting surfaces.

1. On the **Operations** toolbar, click **Trim-Split** drop-down > **Trim** (or) click **Insert > Operations > Trim** on the Menu bar.
2. Click on the portions of the surfaces to keep.

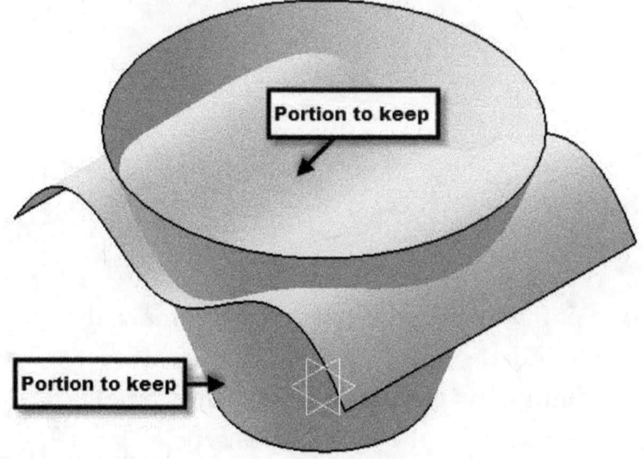

3. Click **OK**.

Split

This command splits and trims a surface using an intersecting surface.

1. On the **Operations** toolbar, click **Trim-Split** drop-down > **Split** (or) click **Insert > Operations > Split** on the Menu bar.
2. Select the element to cut and cutting element.

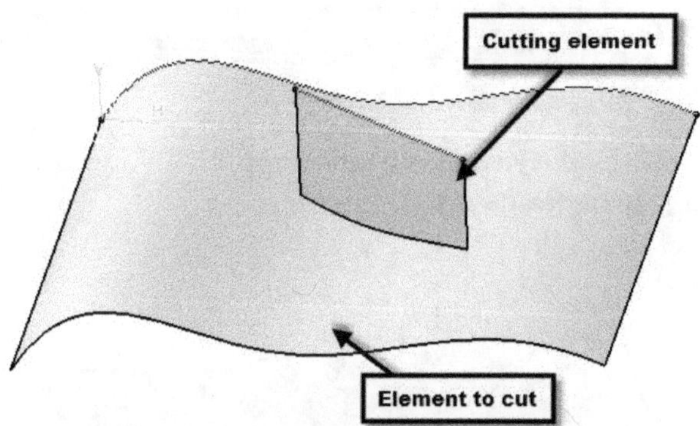

3. On the dialog, click the **Show Parameters** button to expand the dialog.
4. On the expanded dialog, select **Extrapolation type > Tangent**.
5. On the dialog, click the **Other side** button to change the side to be removed.

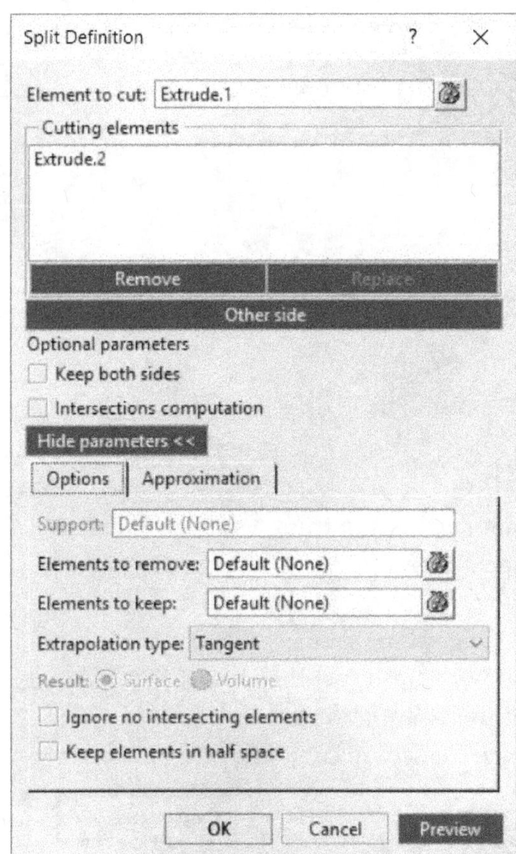

6. Check the **Keep both sides** option, if you want to keep both the sides of the surface.

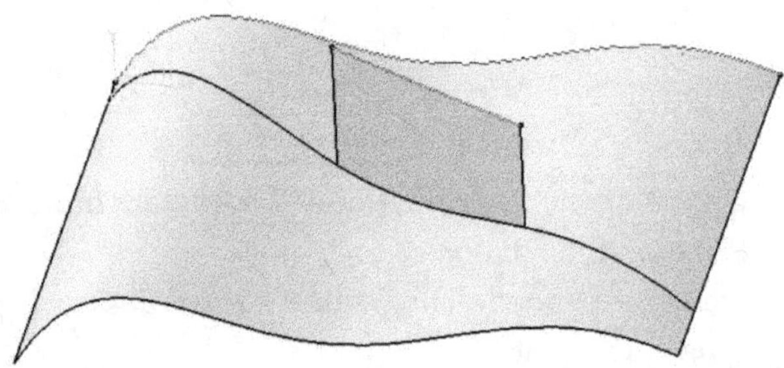

7. Click **OK**.

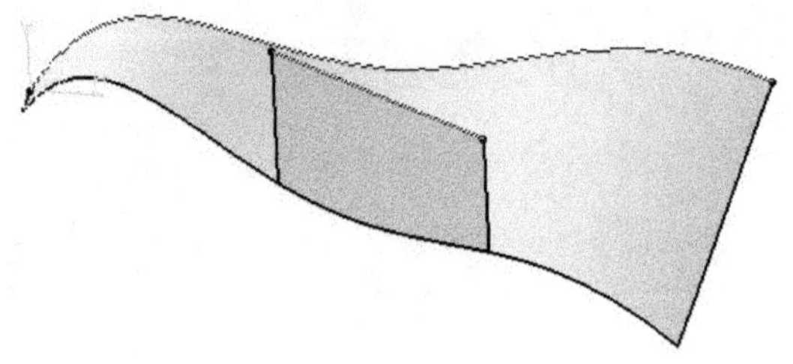

Extrapolate

During the design process, you may sometimes need to extend a surface. You can extend a surface using the **Extrapolate** command.

1. On the **Operations** toolbar, click **Extrapolate-Invert** drop-down > **Extrapolate** (or) click **Insert > Operations > Extrapolate** on the Menu bar.
2. Click on the edge of the surface to extend.

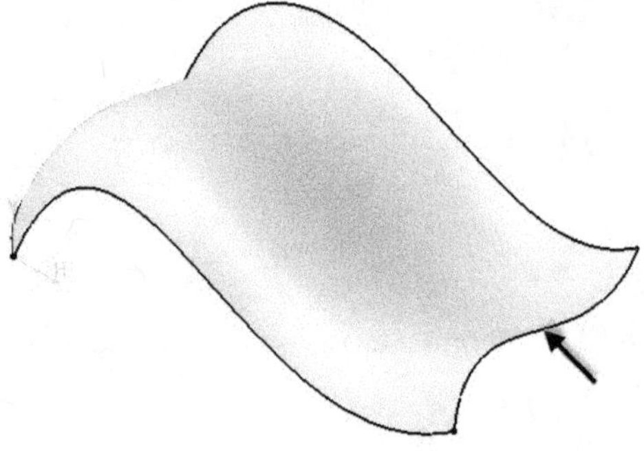

3. Type-in a value in the **Length** box or click and drag the limit handle to define the length of the extend surface.

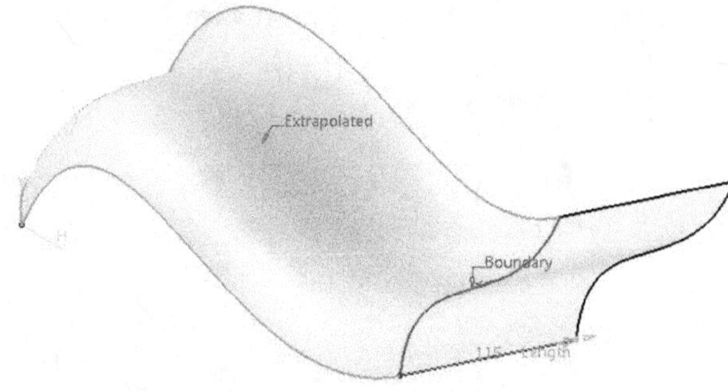

4. Set the **Continuity** type. You can make the extended surface **Tangent** or **Curvature** continuous with the original surface.
5. Likewise, set the **Extremities** type.
6. Check the **Assemble result** option, and then click **OK**.

Likewise, you can extend a curve by selecting its endpoint.

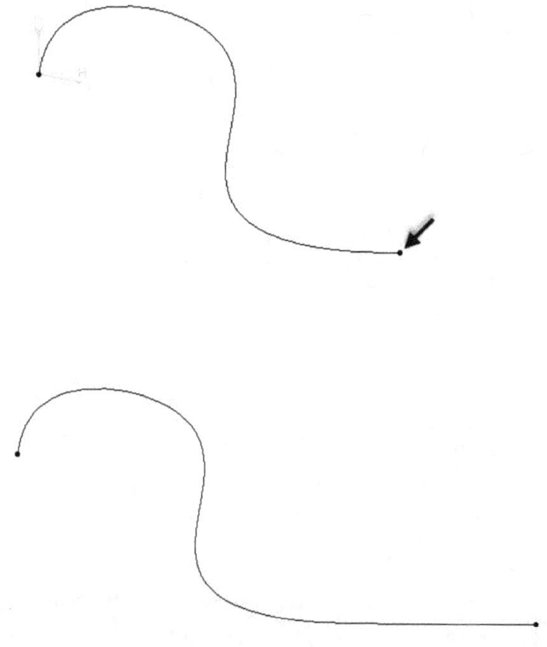

 Untrim

You can untrim a trimmed surface using the **Untrim** command.

1. On the **Operations** toolbar, click **Trim-Split** drop-down > **Untrim** (or) click **Insert > Operations > Untrim** on the Menu bar.
2. Click on the edge of the trimmed surface; the Warning message box appears showing, "The underlying geometry is infinite. Complete untrim could not be performed. Trimmed surface based on bounding box will be created".

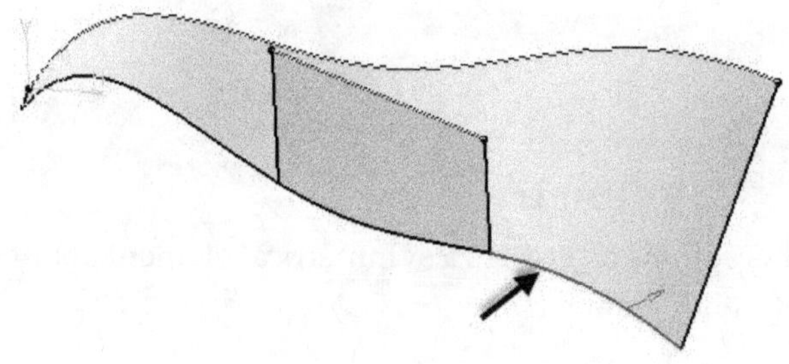

3. On the dialog, select the **Create Curves** button if you want to create a boundary curve on selected edge.
4. Click **OK**.

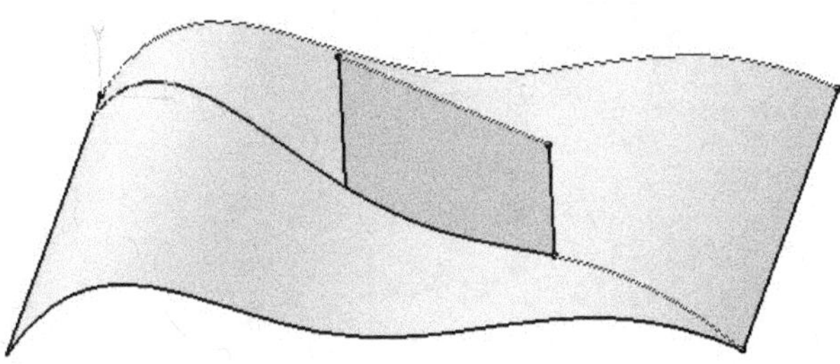

 Join

The surfaces created act as individual surfaces unless they are joined together. The **Join** command lets you combine two or more surfaces to form a single surface.

1. On the **Operations** toolbar, click **Join-Healing** drop-down > **Join** (or) click the **Insert > Operations > Join** on the Menu bar.
2. Select the surfaces to join.

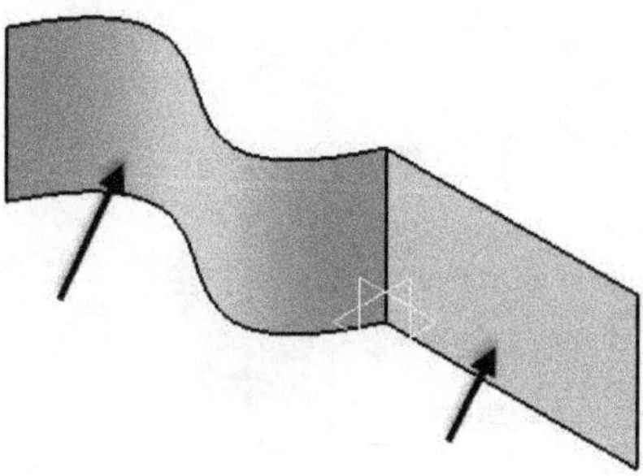

The value you type in the **Merging distance** box defines the maximum gap. All the surfaces within the gap will be joined. Note that the gap must be between the range of 0.001 and 0.1 mm.

3. Click the **OK** button to join the surfaces.

 Translate

The **Translate** command moves and copies a surface.

1. On the **Operations** toolbar, click **Transformations** drop-down > **Translate** (or) click **Insert > Operations > Translate** on the Menu bar.

2. Select the surface/element to translate.

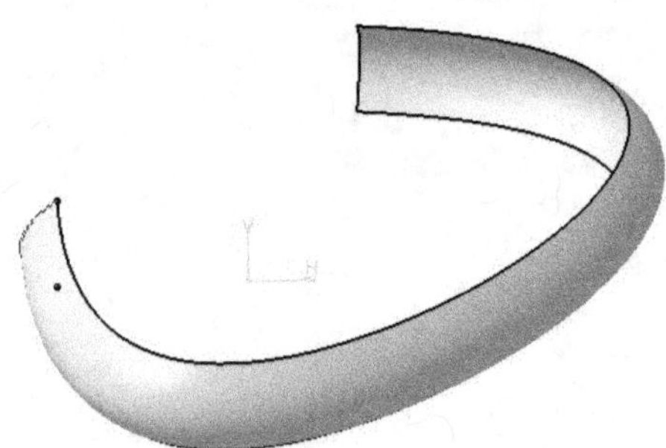

3. On the dialog, click **Vector Definition > Direction, distance**. You can also select **Point to Point** or **Coordinates** to define the direction and translation.
4. Select a line, axis, or plane to define the translation direction.
5. Type-in a value in the **Distance** box or drag the distance handle.
6. Click **OK**.

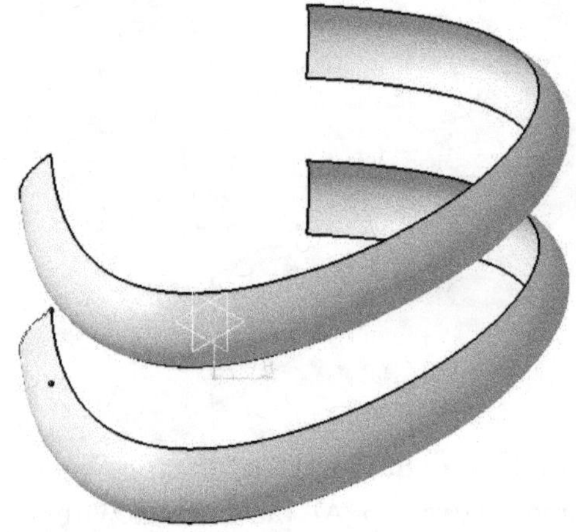

 Rotate

This command rotates an element about an axis.

1. On the **Operations** toolbar, click **Transformations** drop-down > **Rotate** (or) click **Insert > Operations > Rotate** on the Menu bar.
2. Select the surface/element to rotate.

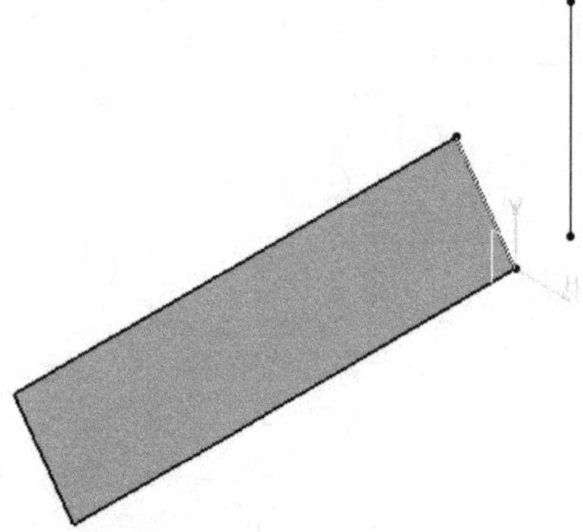

3. On the dialog, click **Definition mode > Axis-Angle**. You can also select **Axis-Two Elements** or **Three Points** to define the axis and rotation angle.
4. Select a line or axis to define the rotation axis.
5. Type-in a value in the **Angle** box.
6. Check the **Repeat object after OK** option, if you want to repeat the rotation after clicking **OK**.
7. Click **OK**.

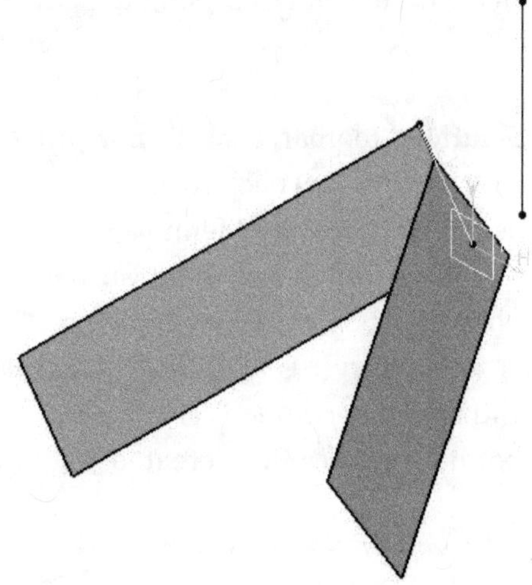

 Symmetry

This command creates a symmetrical element about a reference element.

1. On the **Operations** toolbar, click **Transformations** drop-down > **Symmetry** (or) click **Insert > Operations > Symmetry** on the Menu bar.

2. Select the element to transform.
3. Select a point, line or plane.

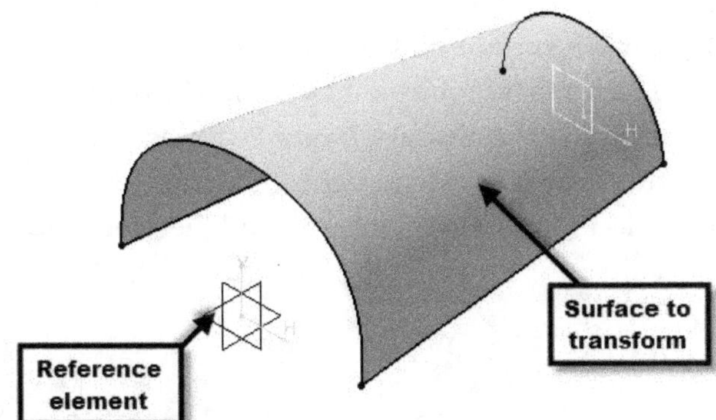

4. Click **OK**.

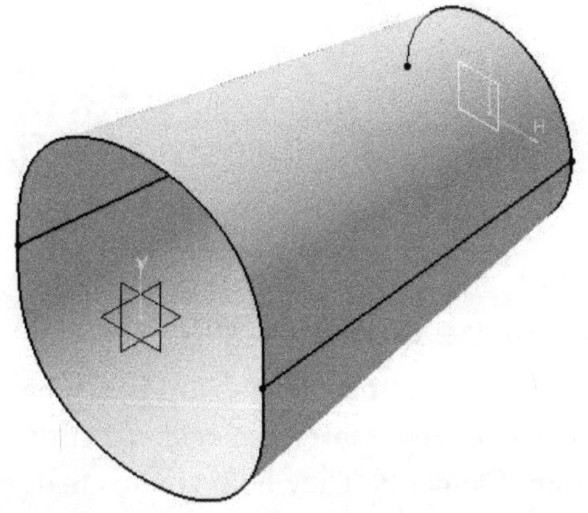

Split (Body)

This command splits a body using a plane, surface or face.

1. Create a body in the **Part Design** workbench.
2. Create a splitting surface.
3. Switch to the **Part Design** Workbench (click **Start > Mechanical Design > Part Design** on the Menu bar).
4. On the **Surface-Based Features** toolbar, click **Split** (or) click **Insert > Surface-Based Features > Split** on the Menu bar.
5. Click on the splitting surface or plane.

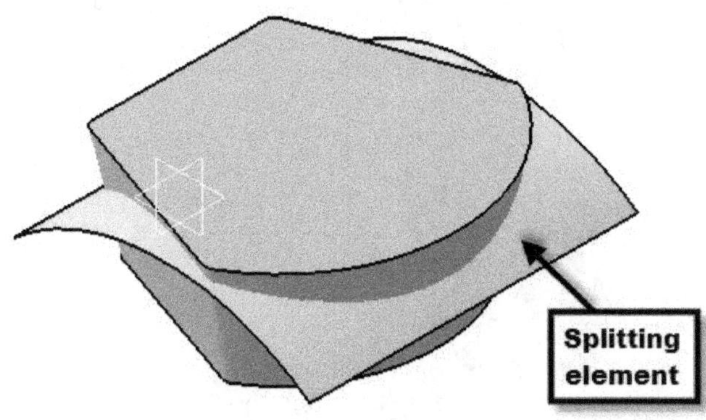

6. Click the arrow that appears on the geometry to reverse the side to be removed.
7. Click **OK**.

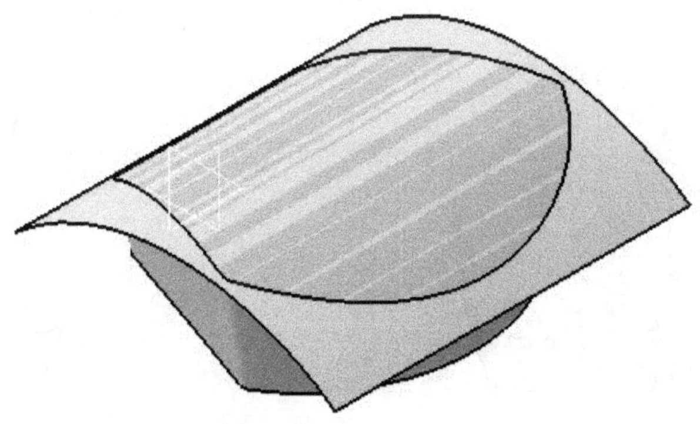

Thick Surface

Creating a solid from a surface can be accomplished by simply thickening a surface. To add thickness to a surface, follow the steps given next.

1. Switch to the **Part Design** Workbench (click **Start > Mechanical Design > Part Design** on the Menu bar).
2. On the **Surface-Based Features** toolbar, click **Thick Surface** (or) click **Insert > Surface-Based Features > Thick Surface** on the Menu bar.
3. Click on a face of the surface geometry.

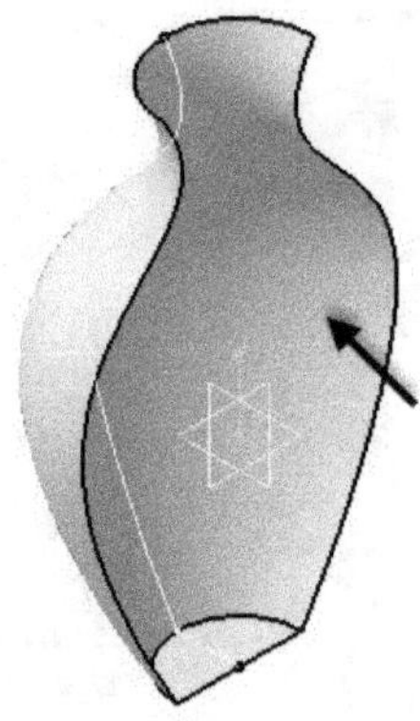

4. Enter the thickness value in the **First offset** box.
5. Click the arrows that appear on the geometry reverse the side to which the material added.
6. Click **OK**.

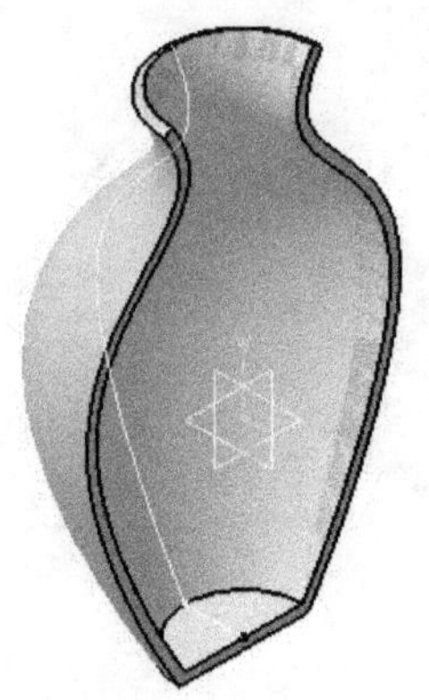

 Close Surface

This command creates are a solid body by filling the volume enclosed by a surface body.

1. Join the surfaces using the **Join** command.

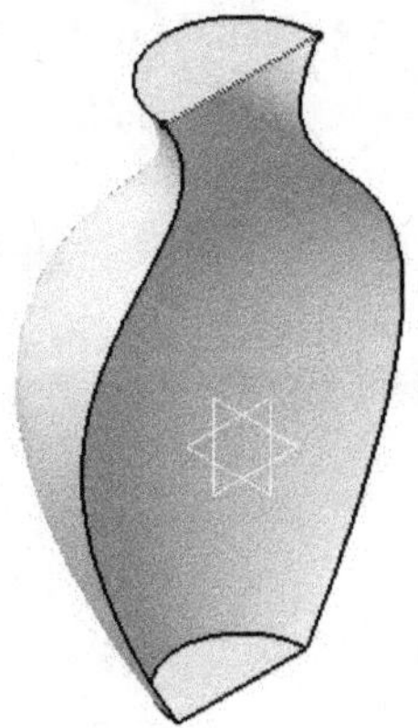

2. Switch to the **Part Design** Workbench (click **Start > Mechanical Design > Part Design** on the Menu bar).
3. On the **Surface-Based Features** toolbar, click **Thick Surface** drop-down > **Close Surface** (or) click **Insert > Surface-Based Features > Close Surface** on the Menu bar.
4. Select the surface geometry, and then click **OK**.

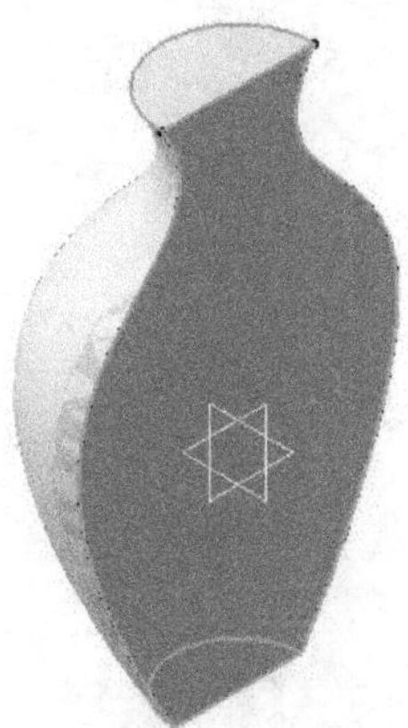

Wireframe Geometry

The Generative Shape Design workbench has commands to create three dimensional curves and wireframe elements. They help you to create complex surfaces.

 Circle

This command creates circles or arcs.

1. On the **Wireframe** toolbar, click **Circle-Conic** drop-down > **Circle** (or) **Insert > Wireframe > Circle** on the Menu bar.
2. Select a point to define the center point. You can also create a new point by clicking the right mouse button in the **Center** box, and then selecting an option to create a point.
3. Click on a plane or face to define the support surface.
4. Type-in a value in the **Radius** box or drag the Radius handle to define the radius.
5. Type-in values in the **Start** and **End** boxes to define the start and end limits of the arc.
6. Click the **Whole Circle** button on the dialog, if you want to create a complete circle.

7. Click **OK**.

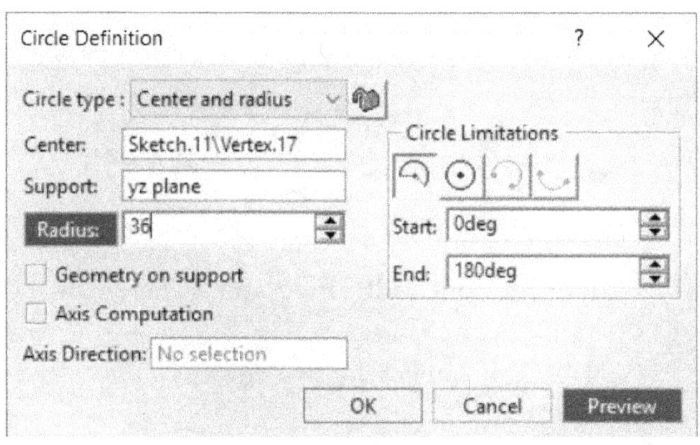

Spline

This command creates a three dimensional spline curve.

1. On the **Wireframe** toolbar, click **Curves** drop-down > **Spline** (or) **Insert > Wireframe > Spline** on the Menu bar.
2. Select a point or click the right mouse button and select an option to create a point.
3. Likewise, select or create points one-by-one.

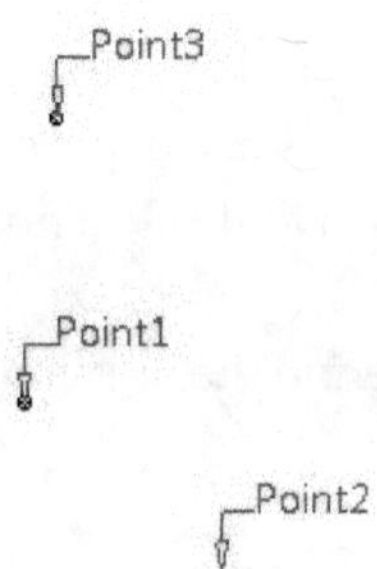

4. Check the **Geometry on support** option, if you want to create the spline on a particular plane or surface.
5. Check the **Close Spline** option, if you want to create a closed spline.

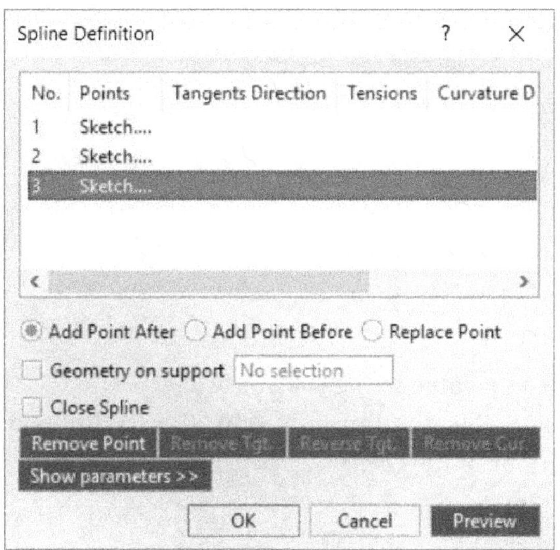

6. Click **OK**.

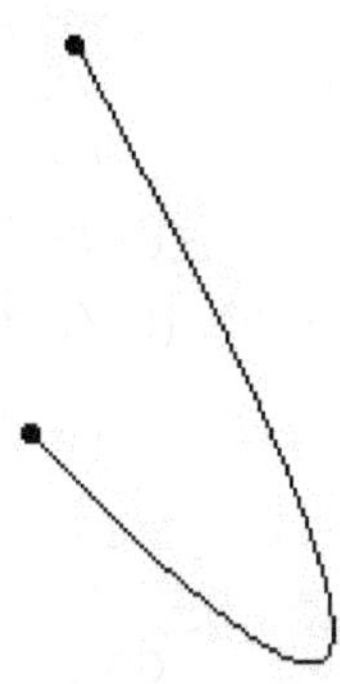

Corner

This command creates a corner curve between two curves.

1. On the **Wireframe** toolbar, click **Circle-Conic** drop-down > **Corner** (or) **Insert > Wireframe > Corner** on the Menu bar.
2. Click on a curve or point to define the first element.
3. Click on a curve or point to define the second element.

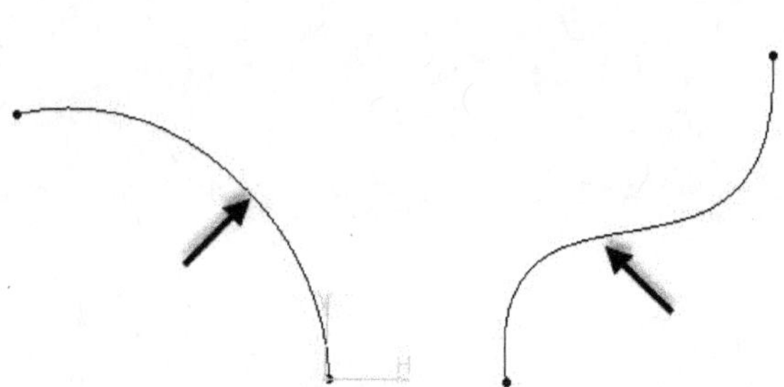

4. Type-in a value in the **Radius** box.
5. Click the **Next Solution** button to view different solutions of the corner.

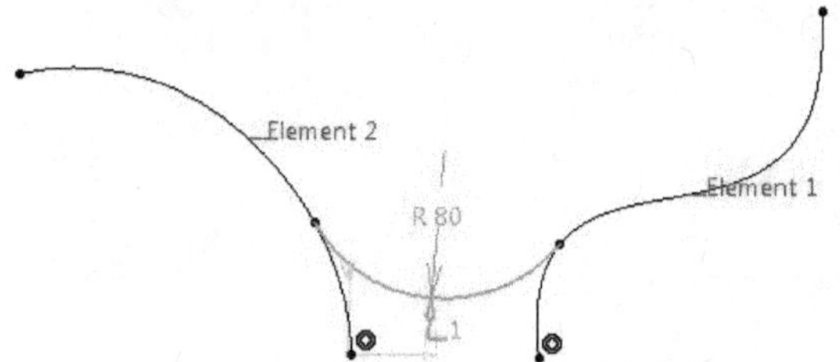

6. Check the **Trim element 1** and **Trim element 2** options, if you want to trim the first and second element.

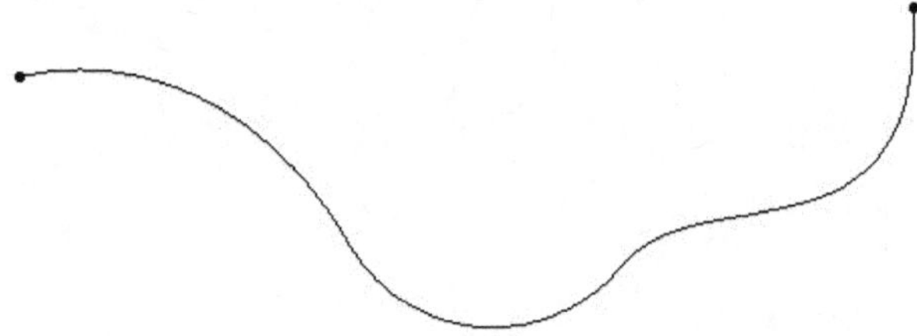

7. Click **OK**.

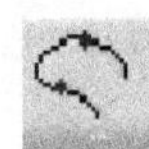

Connect Curve

This command creates a connecting curve between two elements.

1. On the **Wireframe** toolbar, click **Circle-Conic** drop-down > **Connect Curve** (or) **Insert > Wireframe > Connect Curve** on the Menu bar.
2. Click on the end point of the first curve.
3. Click on the end point of the second curve.

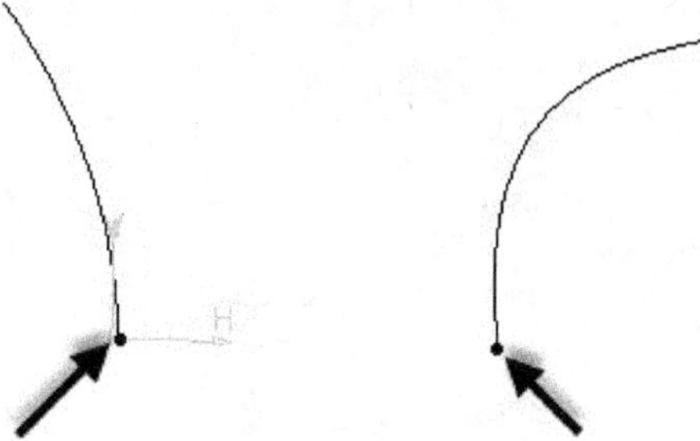

4. Define the **Continuity** type and **Tension** of the first and second curves.
5. Click **OK** to connect the two curves.

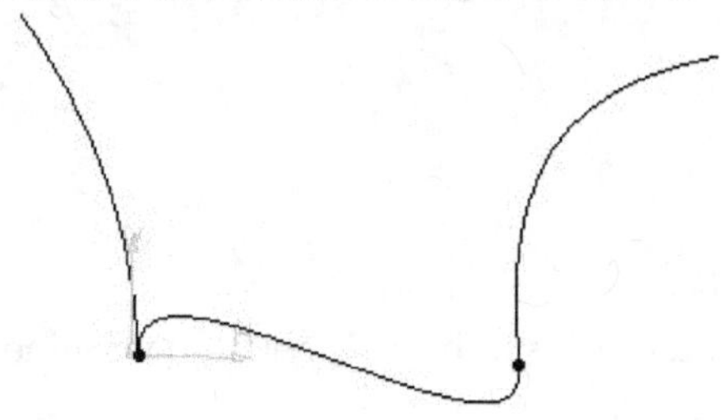

Helix

This command creates a helical curve.

1. On the **Wireframe** toolbar, click **Curves** drop-down > **Helix** (or) **Insert > Wireframe > Helix** on the Menu bar.
2. Select the starting point of the helix. You can also create a new point. To do this, click the right mouse button and select an option to create the point.
3. Select a line to define the axis or create a new line.

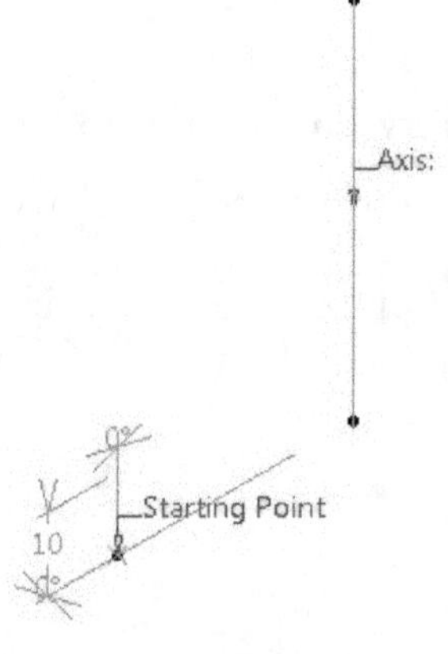

4. On the dialog, click **Helix type > Pitch and Revolution**. This defines the helix by using the pitch and revolutions that you specify. You can also select **Height and Pitch** or **Height and Revolution** options.
5. Select the **Constant Pitch** option. This creates a helix with a constant pitch. You can also select **Variable Pitch** option to create a helix with varying pitch. You have to define the start and end pitch of the variable pitch helix.
6. Type-in the **Pitch** and **Revolution** values.
7. Set the **Orientation** to **Counterclockwise** or **Clockwise**.
8. Type-in a value in the **Taper angle** box, if you want to create a tapered helix. You can apply an **Inward** or **Outward** taper to the helix.

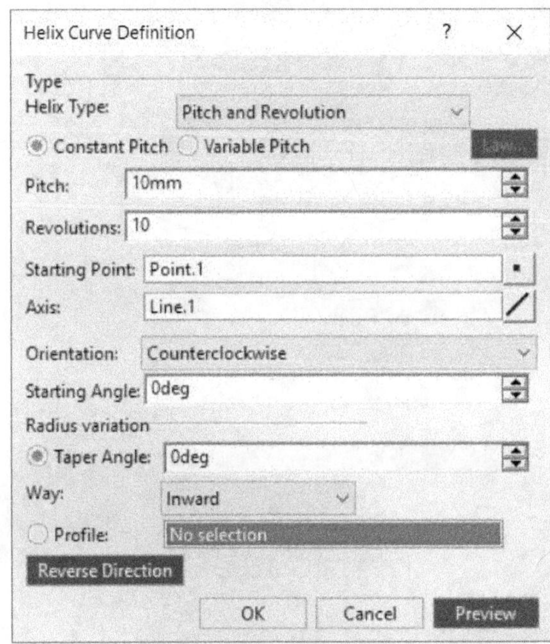

9. Click **OK** to create the helix.

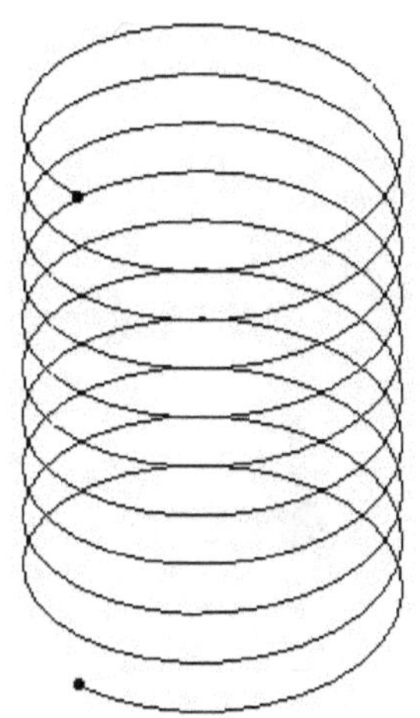

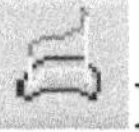 Projection

This command projects an element on to a supporting surface.

1. On the **Wireframe** toolbar, click **Project-Combine** drop-down > **Projection** (or) **Insert > Wireframe > Projection** on the Menu bar.
2. Select the element to project.
3. Select the supporting surface.

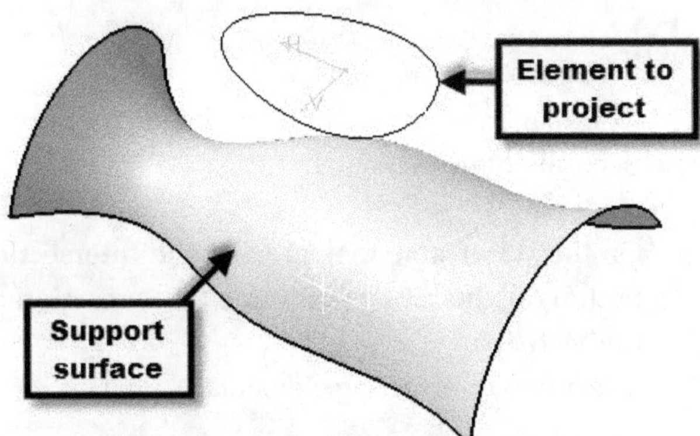

4. Select **Projection type > Normal**. This projects the element in the direction normal to the supporting surface. You can select the **Along a direction** option to define the direction of the projection. You can use a line or plane to define the direction.
5. If the curve is projected at multiple locations on the supporting surface, then check the **Nearest solution** option. This keeps the nearest projection.

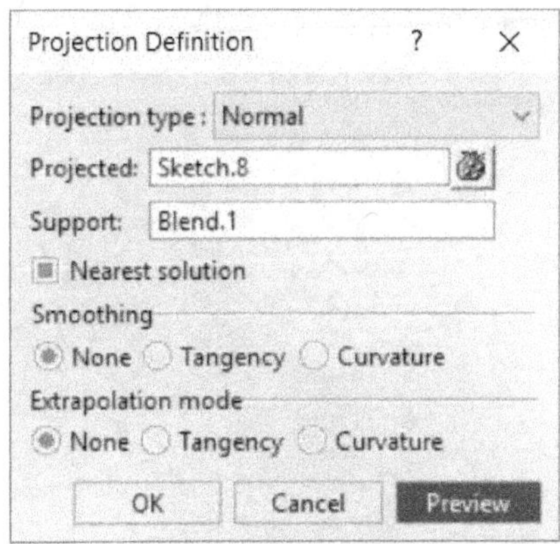

6. Click **OK**.

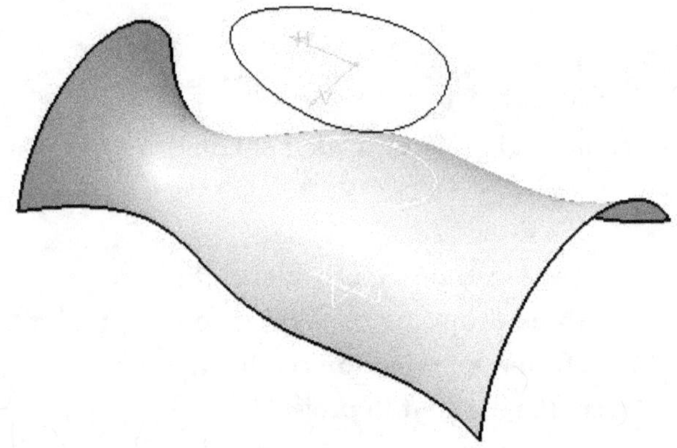

Intersection

This command creates a wireframe geometry at the intersection of two elements.

1. On the **Wireframe** toolbar, click the **Intersection** button (or) **Insert > Wireframe > Intersection** on the Menu bar.
2. Select two intersecting elements.

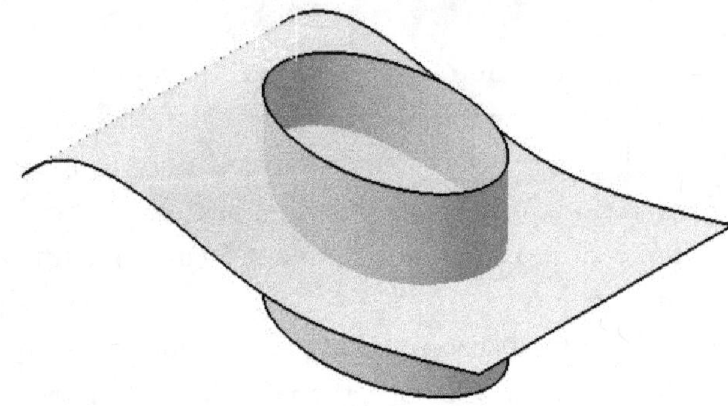

3. Click **OK**.

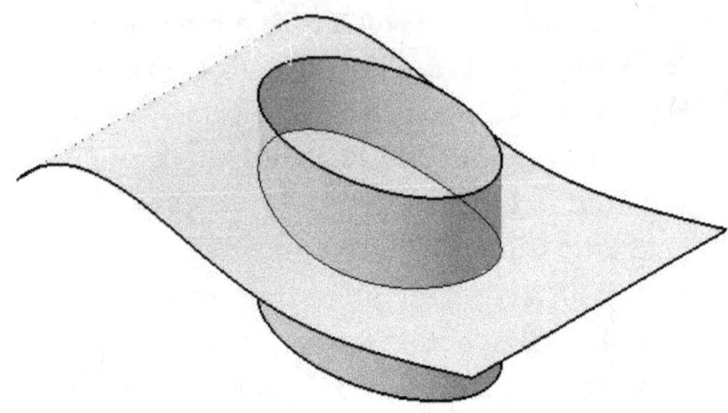

Other examples of the intersection curves are given next.

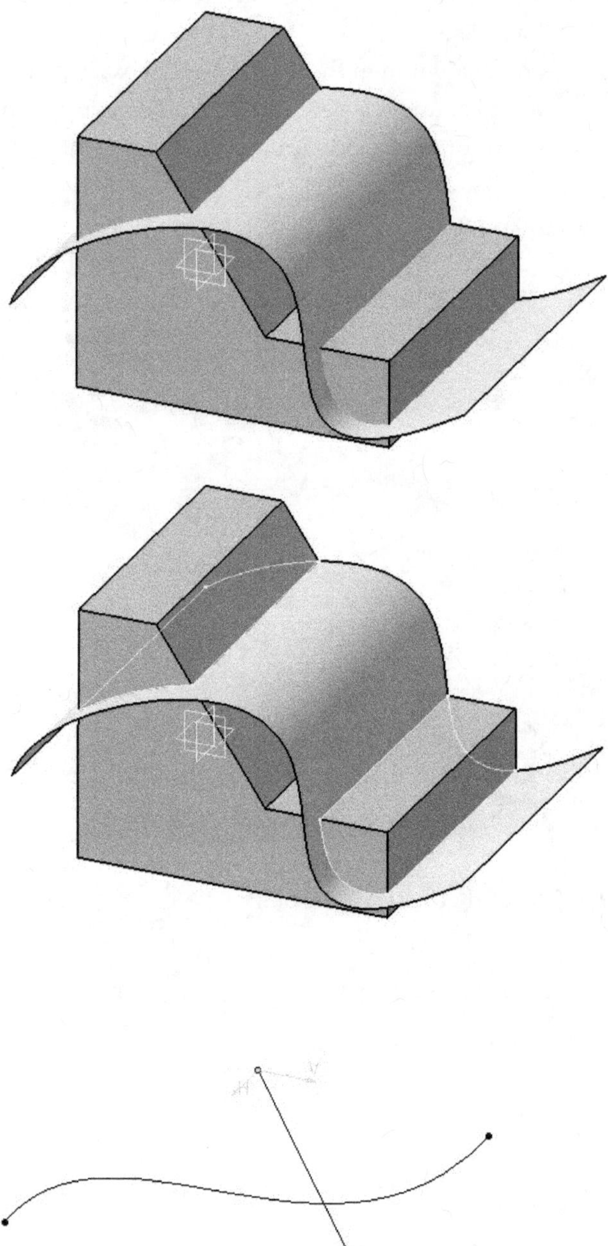

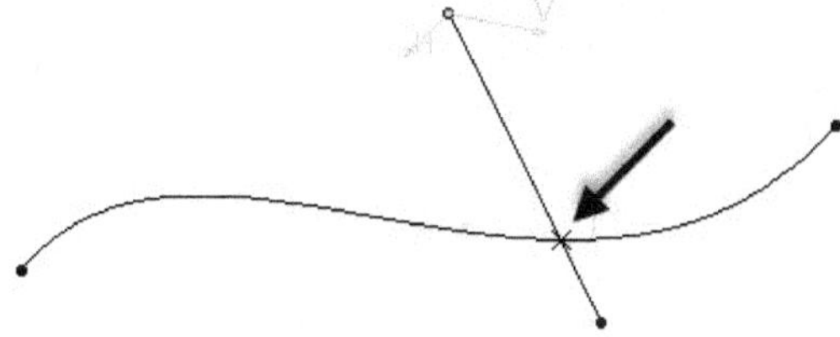

Example

In this example, you will construct the model shown below.

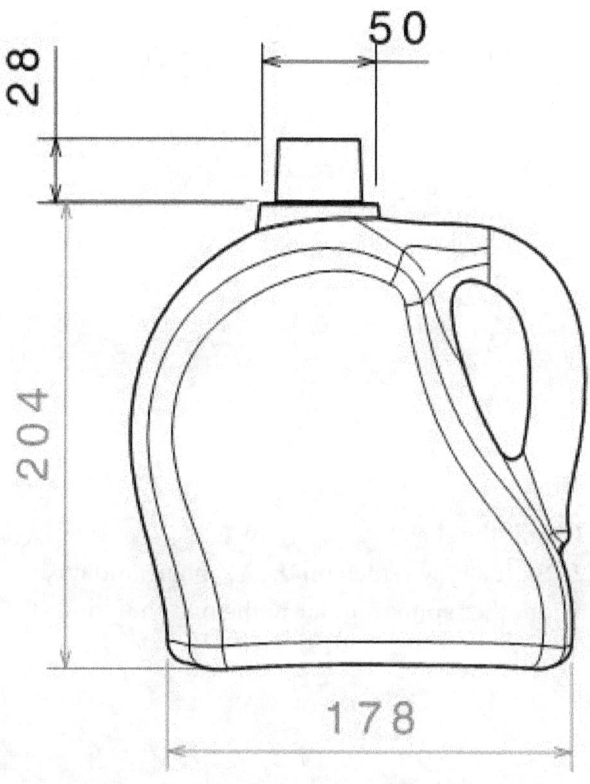

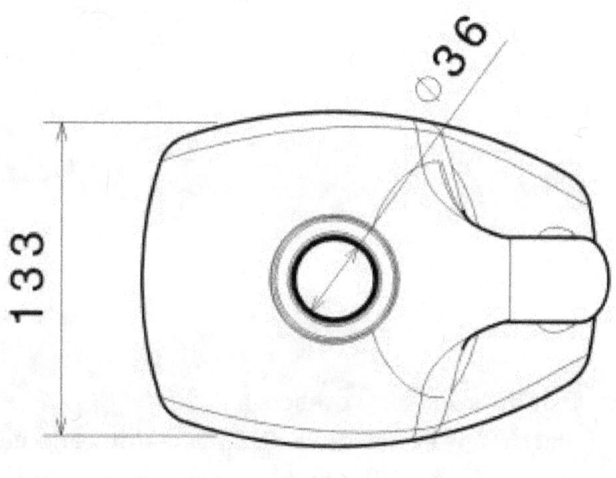

Drawing the Layout sketch

1. Start **CATIA V5-6R2017**.
2. On the Menu bar, click **Start > Shape > Generative Shape Design**.
3. Type in Example 1 in the **Enter part name** box, and then check the **Enable hybrid design** option.
4. Click **OK**.
5. Start a sketch on the YZ plane.
6. Draw a sketch similar to the one shown next. Use the **Axis** and **Spline** commands to draw this sketch.

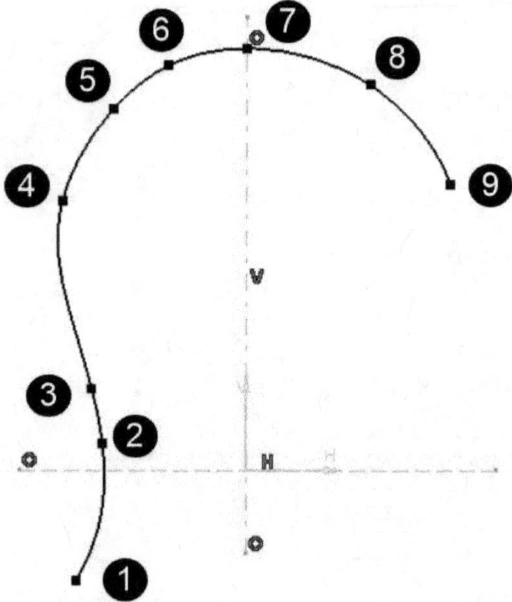

7. Activate the **Constraint** command and add dimensional constraints to the sketch.

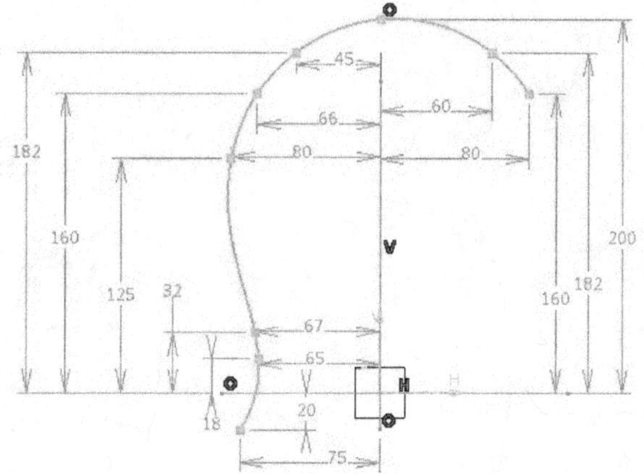

8. Exit the sketcher workbench.
9. Start a new sketch on the YZ plane draw another spline curve similar to the one shown in figure.

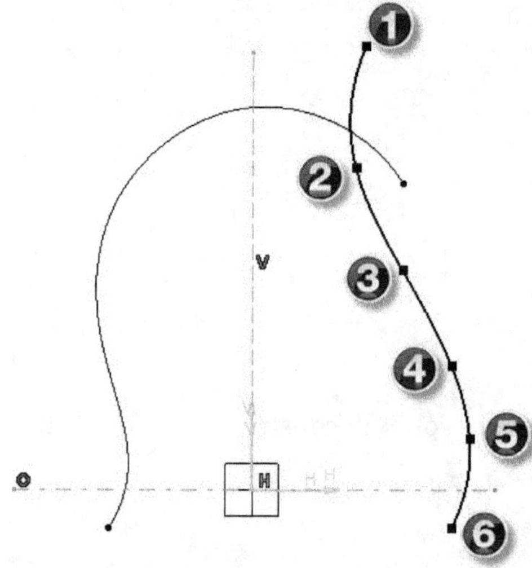

10. Add constraints to the spline.

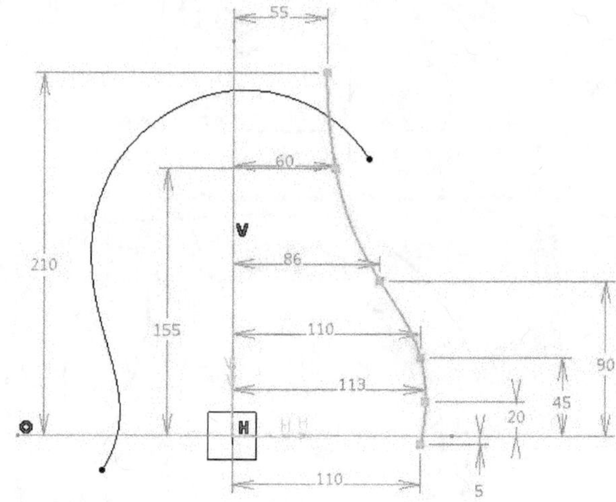

11. Exit the sketch.
12. Start a new sketch on the YZ plane and create another spline similar to the one shown next.

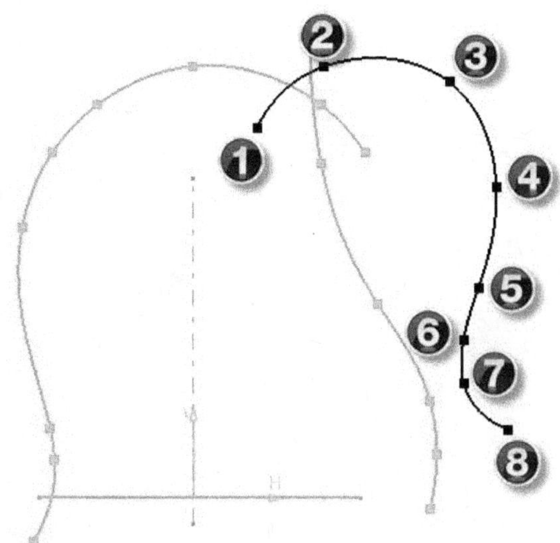

13. Add constraints to the spline.

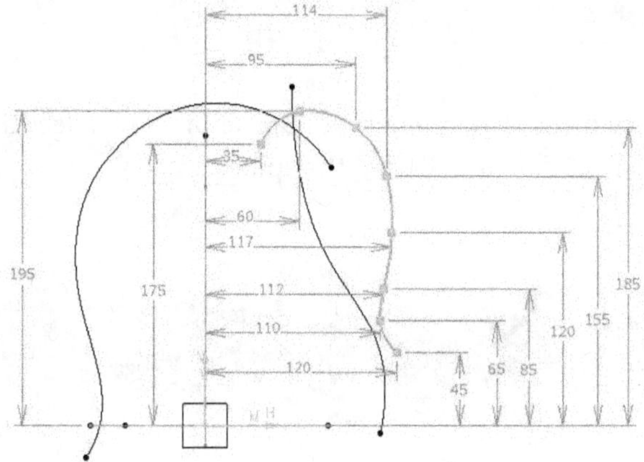

14. Exit the sketch.

If you find it difficult to create the layout sketch, then you can download it from our website.

Creating the Front Surface

1. Create an arc on the XY Plane and add dimensions to it. Exit the sketch.

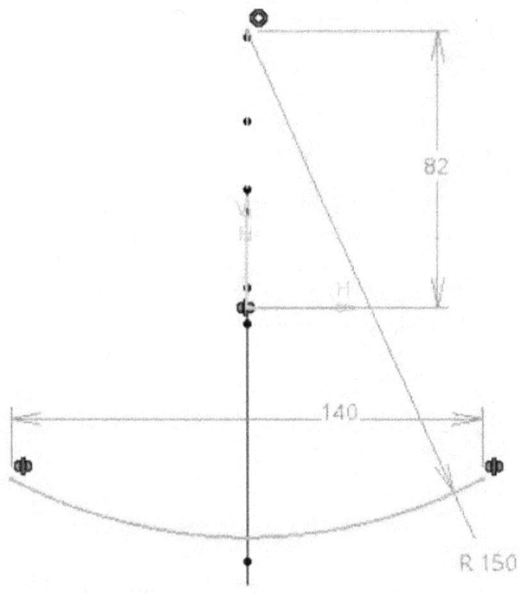

2. Create an arc on the ZX Plane and add dimensions to it. Finish the sketch.

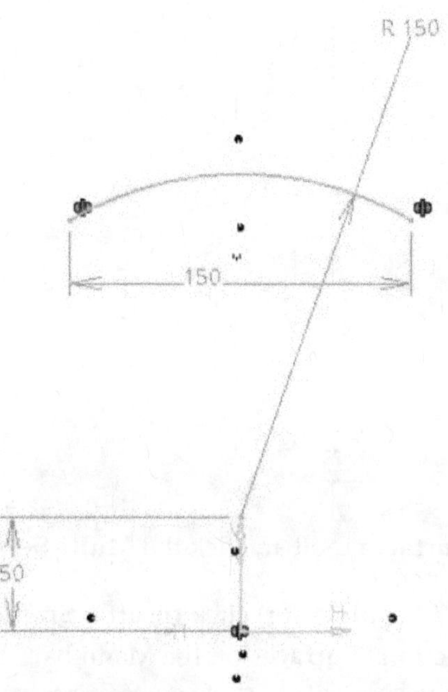

3. On the Menu bar, click **Insert > Wireframe > Plane**, and then create a reference plane normal to the front face spline.

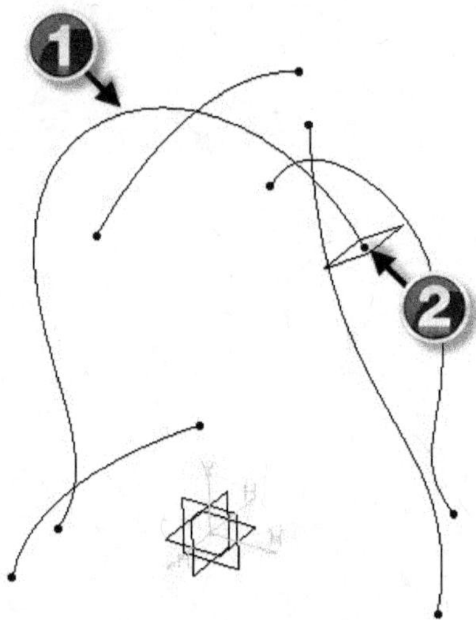

4. Create an arc on the plane normal to curve. Exit the sketch.

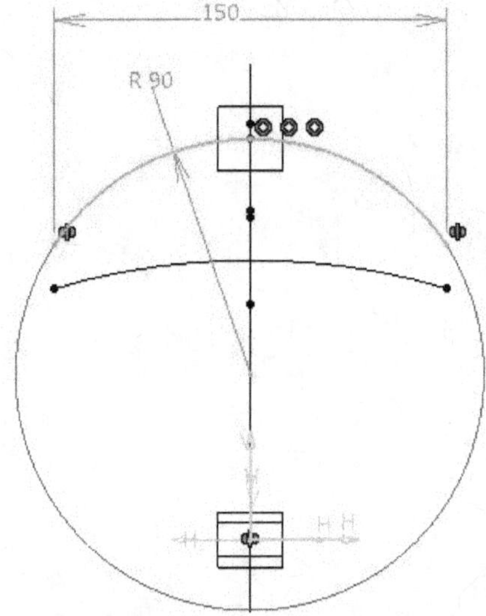

5. On the **Surfaces** toolbar, click the **Multi-Sections Surface** button (or) click **Insert > Surfaces > Multi-Sections Surfaces** on the Menu bar.
6. Select the three sections from the graphics window. You have to make sure that the arrows on the sections point in the same direction. You can double-click on the arrows to change the direction.

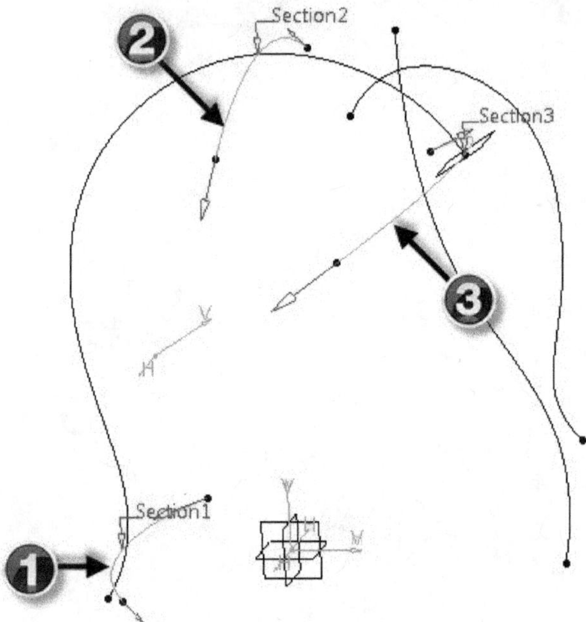

7. On the dialog, click the **Spine** tab and select the first sketch to define the spine.

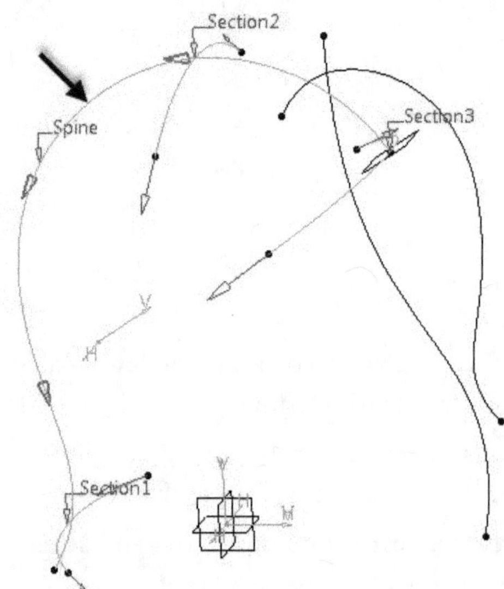

8. Click the **Preview** button to preview the surface. If you got the desired result, then click **OK** to create the surface.

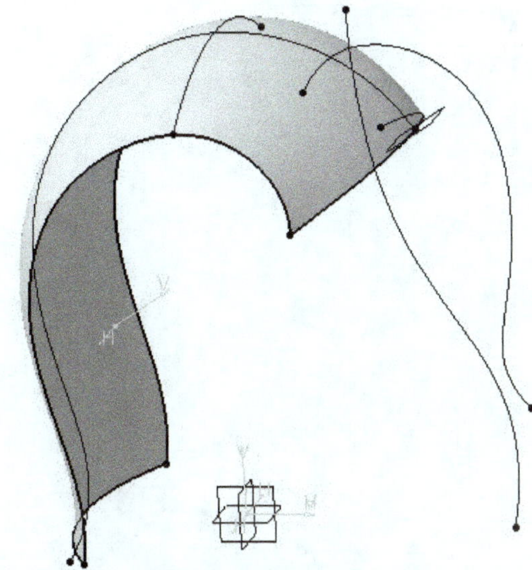

9. Save the file. As you are creating a complex geometry, it is advisable that you save the model after each operation.

Creating the Label surface

1. Create an arc on the XY plane. Exit the sketch.

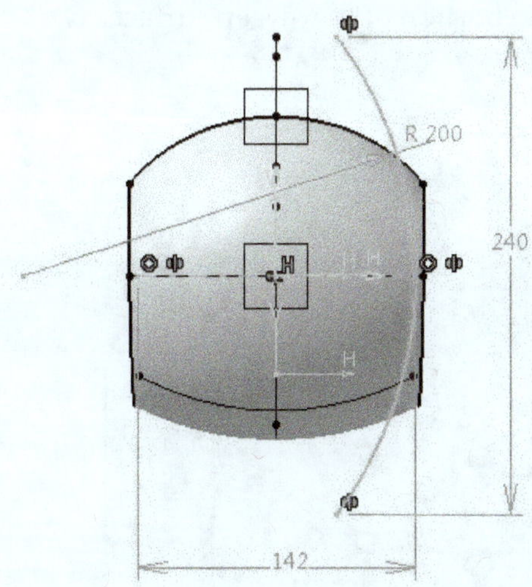

2. On the **Surfaces** toolbar, click the **Extrude** button (or) click **Insert > Surfaces > Extrude** on the Menu bar.
3. Select the newly created sketch, if not already selected.
4. On the dialog, under the **Limit 1** section, type-in **220** in the **Dimension** box. Click **OK**.

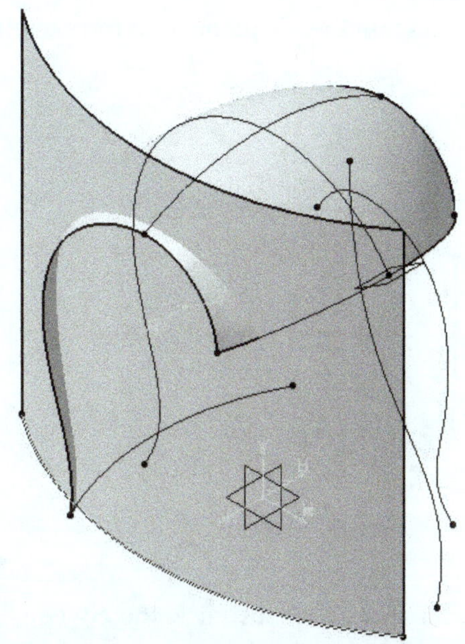

5. On the **Operations** toolbar, click **Transformations** drop-down > **Symmetry** (or) click **Insert > Operations > Symmetry** on the Menu bar.
6. Click on the Extrude surface, and then click the YZ plane.
7. Click **OK** to transform the extrude surface symmetrically.

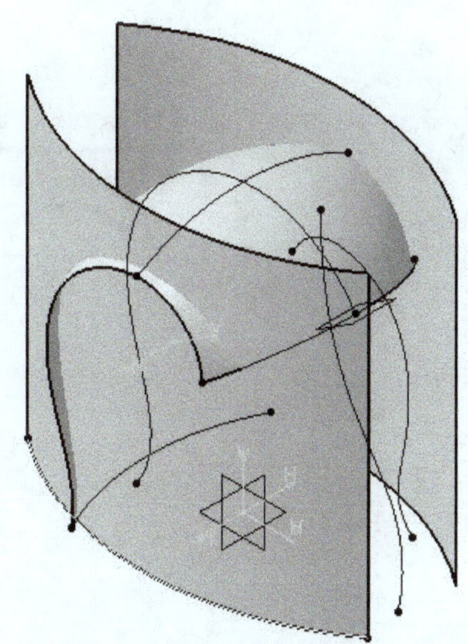

Creating the Back surface

1. Create an arc on the XY plane. Exit the sketch.

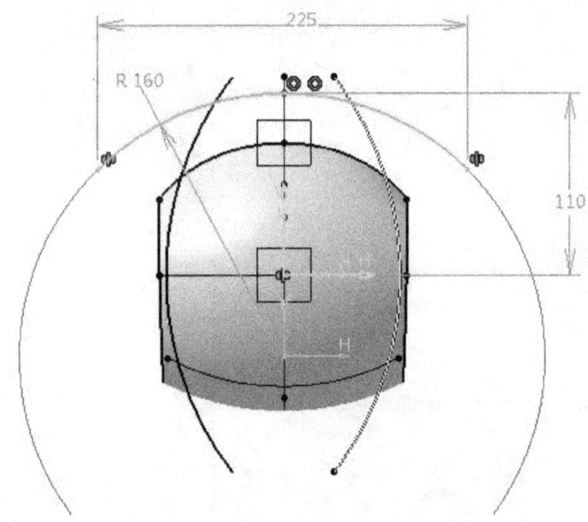

2. On the **Surfaces** toolbar, click the **Sweep** button (or) click **Insert > Surfaces > Sweep** on the Menu bar.
3. Select the profile and guide curve.

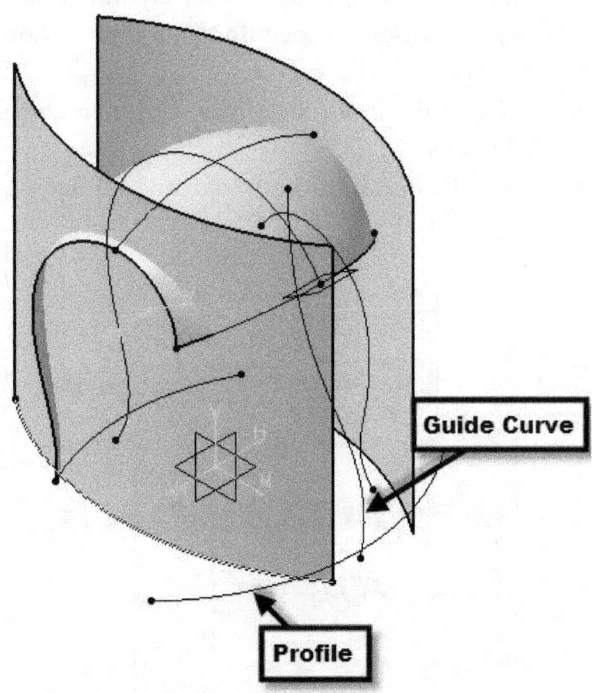

4. Click **OK** to create the surface.

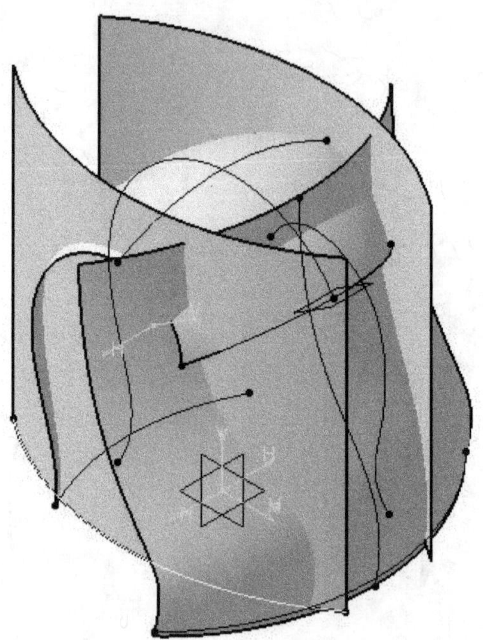

Trimming the Unwanted Portions

1. On the **Operations** toolbar, click **Split-Trim** drop-down > **Trim** (or) click **Insert > Operations > Trim** on the Menu bar.
2. On the dialog, select **Mode > Pieces**.
3. Click on the portion of the sweep surface, as shown below.

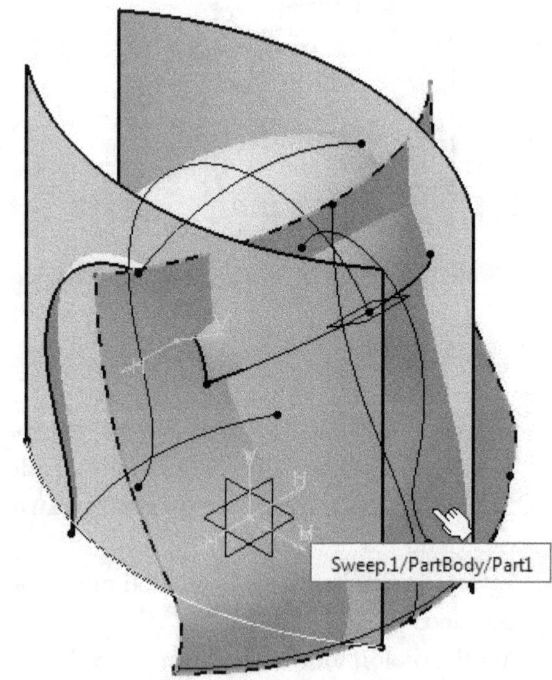

4. Click on the portion of the extrude surface, as shown next.

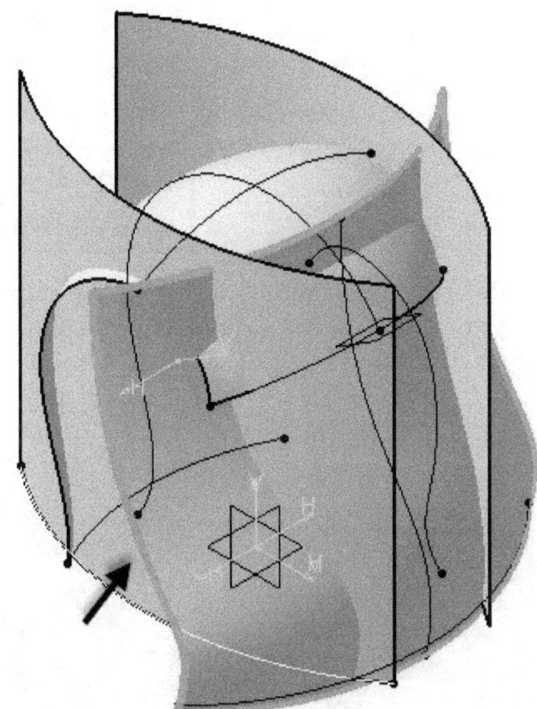

5. Click on the portion of the multi-section surface, as shown next.

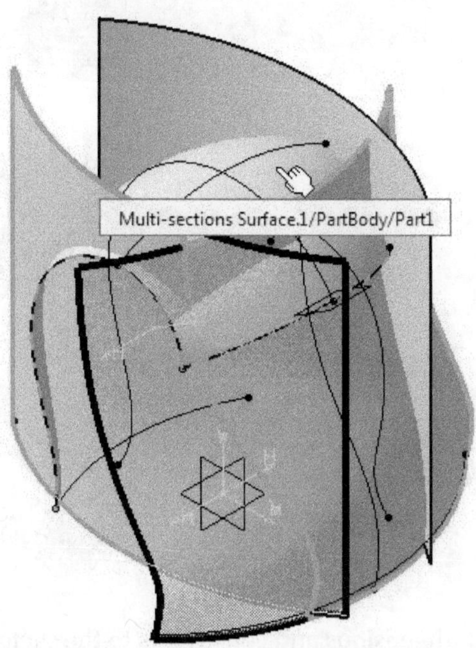

6. Rotate the model and click on the symmetry surface, as shown next.

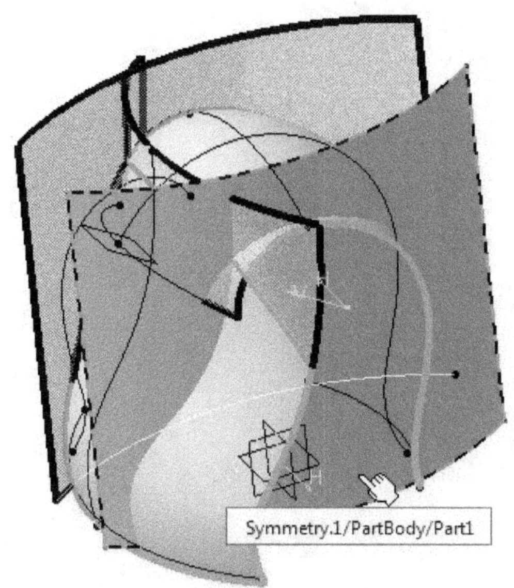

7. Click **OK** to trim the unwanted portions.

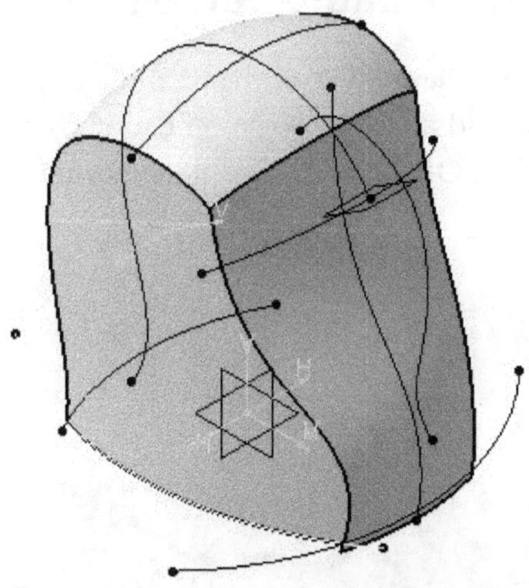

Trim the Sweep Surface using the Split command

1. On the **Operations** toolbar, click **Split-Trim** drop-down > **Split** (or) click **Insert > Operations > Split** on the Menu bar.
2. Click on the surface and the xy plane, as shown.

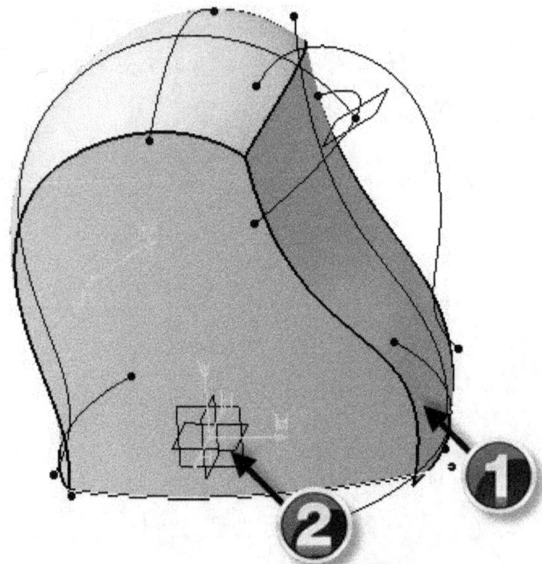

3. Click **OK** to trim the surface.

Creating the Handle Surface

1. Activate the **Plane** command and click on the spline and its lower end-point, as shown below. Click **OK** to create the plane normal to the spline.

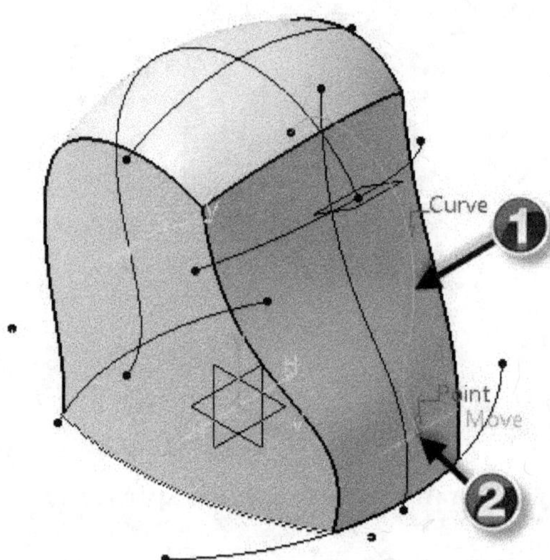

2. Start a sketch on the plane normal to the spline.
3. Activate the **Ellipse** command and create an ellipse on the sketch plane.
4. Use the **Axis** command and create major and minor axis, as shown.

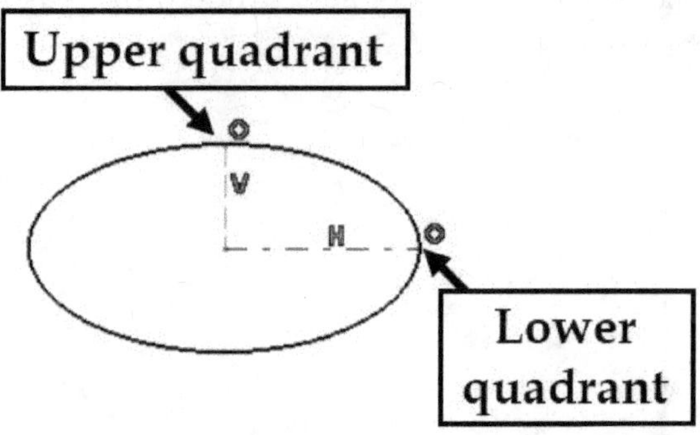

5. Make the upper quadrant point of the ellipse coincident with the end-point of the spline.

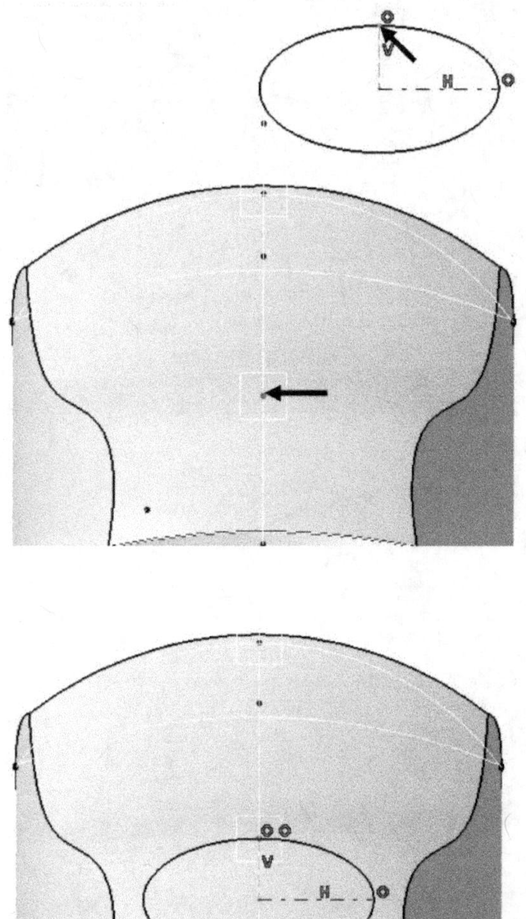

6. Add dimensions and constraints to the sketch.
7. Exit the sketch.

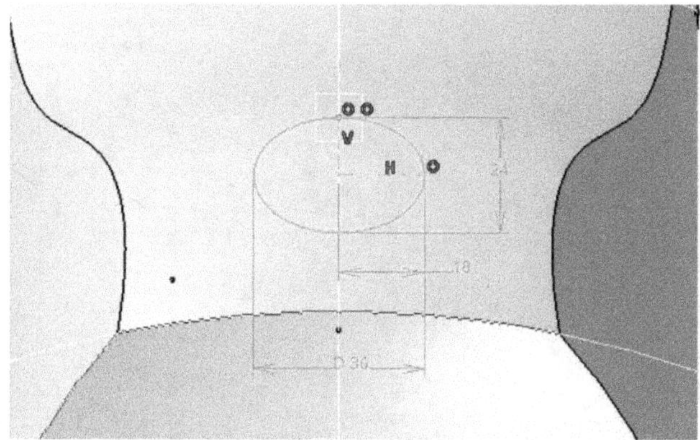

8. On the **Surfaces** toolbar, click **Sweeps** drop-down > **Sweep** (or) click **Insert > Surfaces > Sweep**. This selects the ellipses, automatically. If not, select the ellipse to define the profile.
9. Select the spline to define the guide curve.
10. Click **OK**.

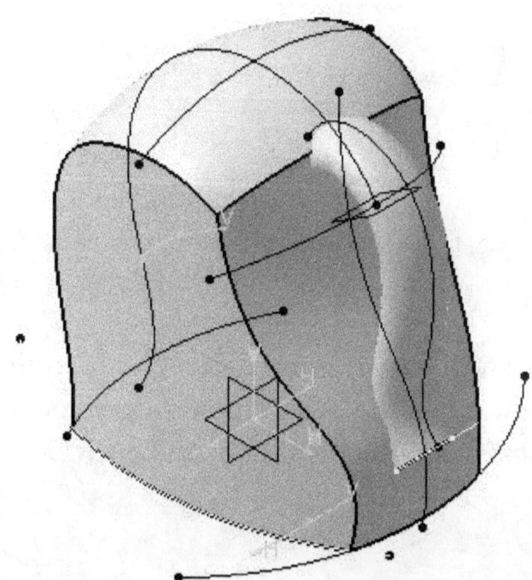

Blending the Front and back faces

1. On the **Operations** toolbar, click **Fillets** drop-down > **Edge Fillet** (or) click **Insert > Operations > Edge Fillet** on the Menu bar.
2. Click on the edge connecting the front and back faces.

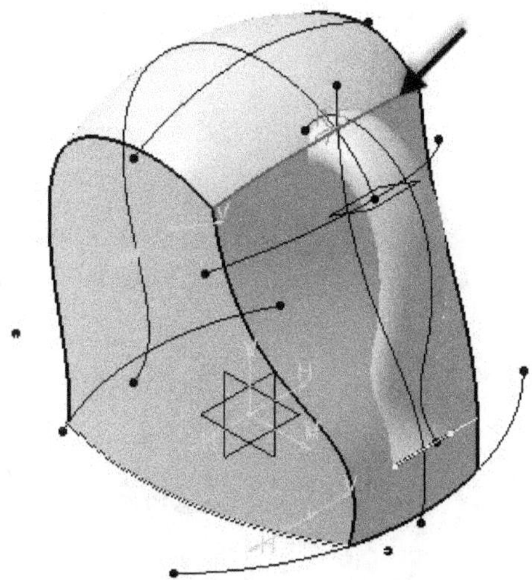

3. On the dialog, type-in 25 in the **Radius** box, and then click **OK**.

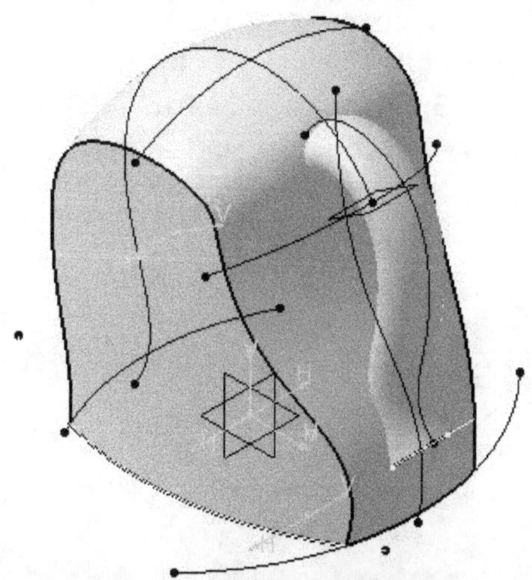

Trimming the Handle

1. Create a plane offset from the zx plane. The offset distance is 75 mm.

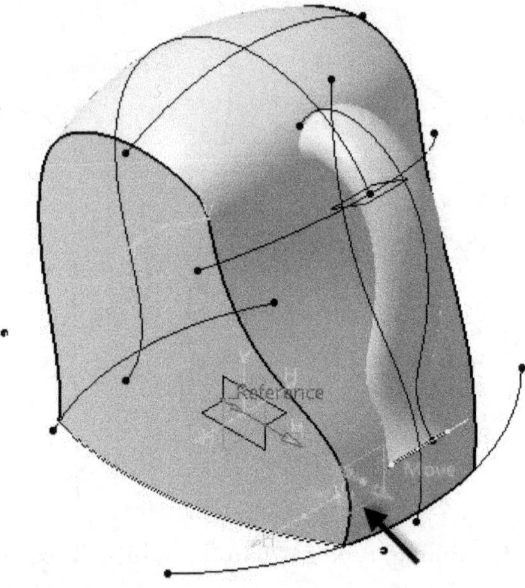

2. On the **Operations** toolbar, click **Split-Trim** drop-down > **Split** (or) click **Insert > Operations > Split** on the Menu bar.
3. Click on the sweep surface, and then the offset plane.

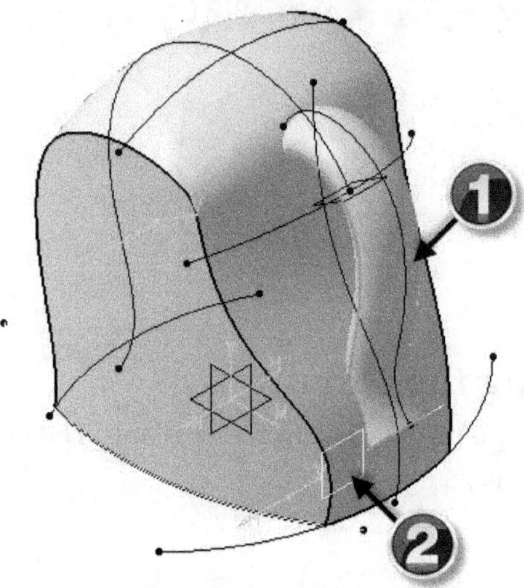

4. Click **OK** to trim the sweep surface.

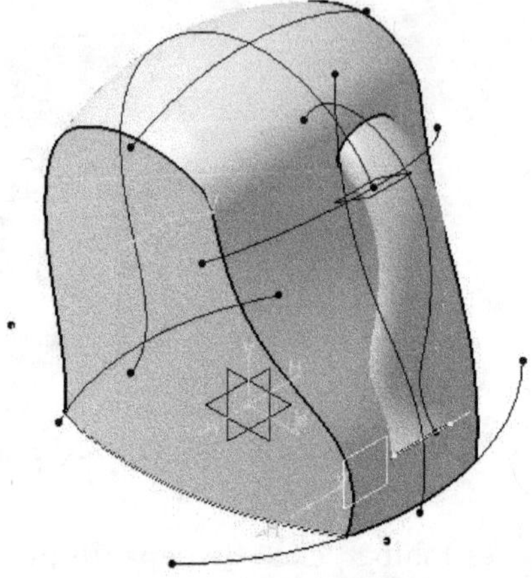

5. Create a reference plane, which is normal to the spline and located at the top end-point.

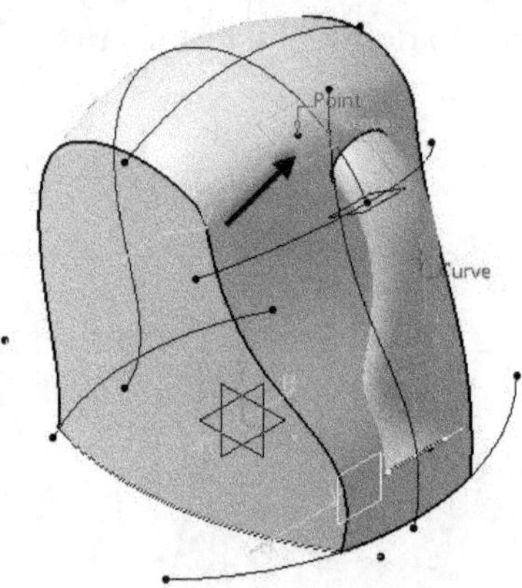

6. Start a sketch on the plane normal to the spline and draw an ellipse. Add dimensions to position the ellipse, and then Exit the workbench.

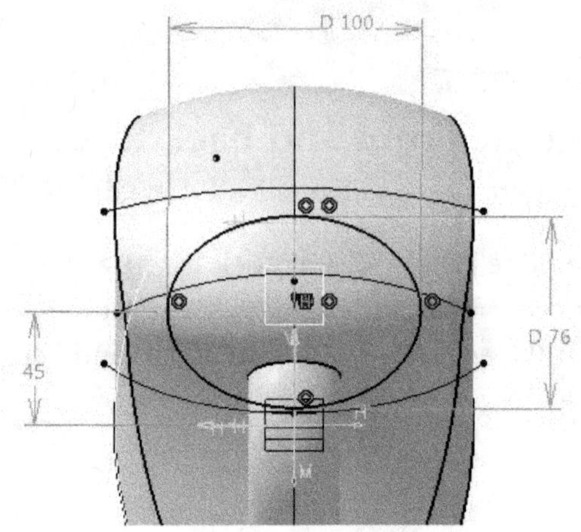

7. On the **Wireframe** toolbar, click **Project-Combine** drop-down > **Projection** (or) click **Insert > Wireframe > Projection** on the Menu bar.
8. On the **Projection Definition** dialog, click **Projection type > Along a direction**.
9. Click in the **Projected** selection box and select the ellipse.
10. Click on the main surface to define the support.
11. Click on the plane normal to the handle spline. This defines the projection direction.
12. Select **Tangency** under the **Smoothing** section.
13. Click **OK** to project the sketch on to the main surface.
14. Hide the sketched ellipse to avoid confusion.

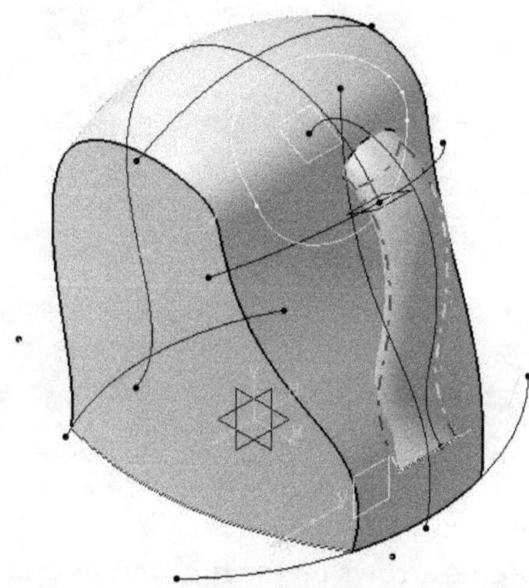

15. On the **Operations** toolbar, click **Split-Trim** drop-down > **Split** (or) click **Insert > Operations > Split** on the Menu bar.
16. Click on the main surface and projected curve.
17. Click **OK** to trim the main surface.
18. Click the right mouse button on the ellipse, and then select **Hide/Show**.

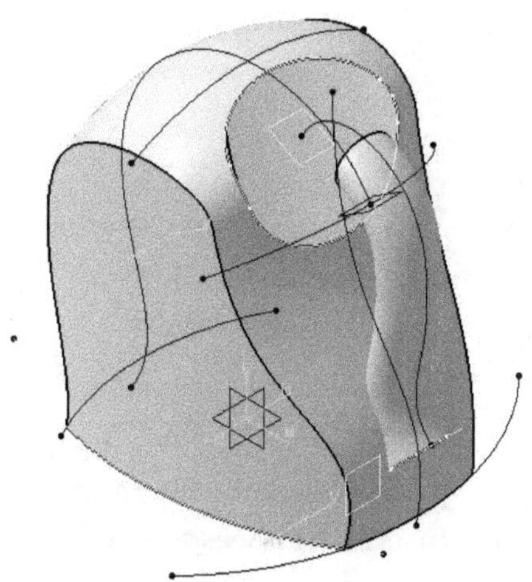

Blending the Top handle

1. On the **Wireframe** toolbar, click **Points** drop-down > **Point** (or) click **Insert > Wireframe > Point** on the Menu bar.
2. Click on the projected curve.
3. Click on the intersection point between the projected curve and sketch1.

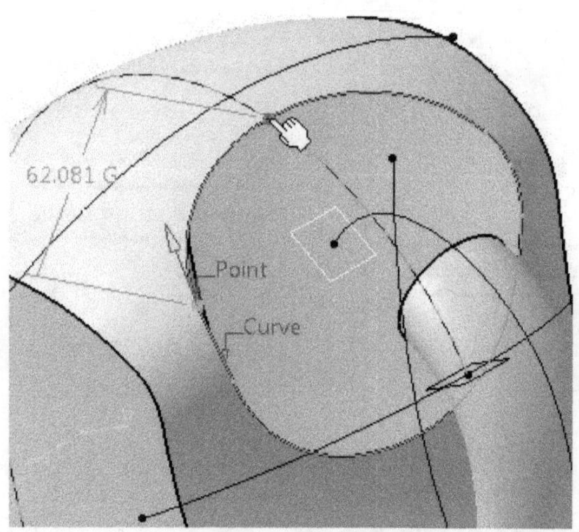

4. Click **OK** to create a point at the intersection.
5. Likewise, create a point on the handle edge, as shown below.

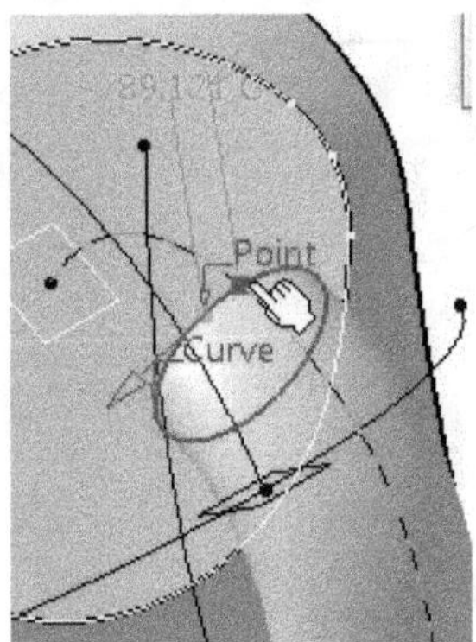

6. On the **Surfaces** toolbar, click the **Blend** button (or) click **Insert > Surfaces > Blend** on the Menu bar.
7. Click on the projected curve to define the first curve.
8. Click on the main surface to define the first support.
9. Click on the top edge of the handle to define the second curve.
10. Click on the handle to define the second support.

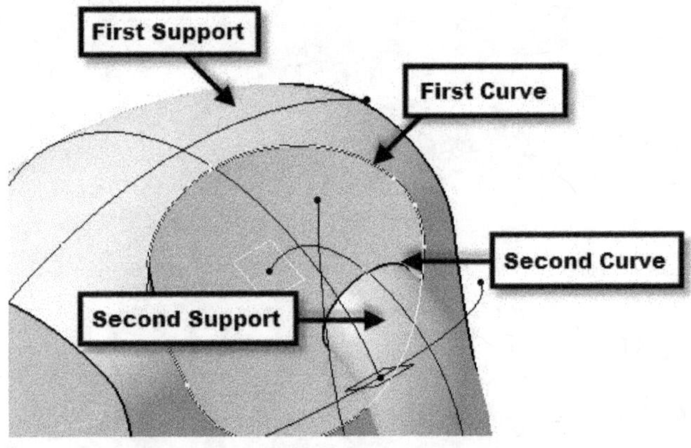

11. On the **Blend Definition** dialog, click the **Closing Points** tab, and then click in the **First closing point** selection box.
12. Click on the point intersection point on the first curve, as shown below.

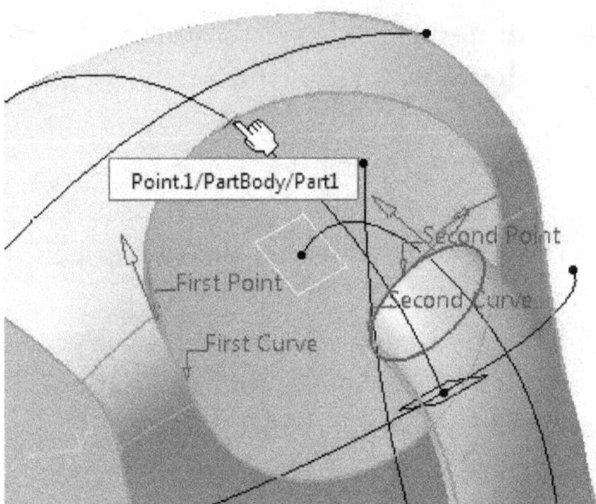

13. Click in the **Second closing point** selection box and select the intersection point on the second curve.

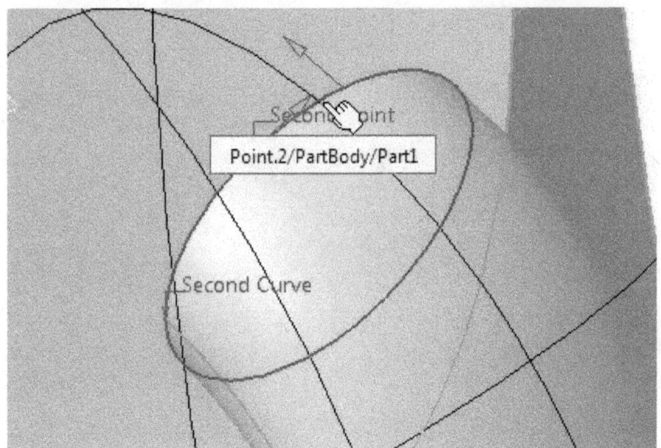

14. Ensure that the arrows on the first and second curves point in the same direction. If not, double-click on them to change the directions.
15. Click **OK** to blend the top portion of the handle with the main surface.

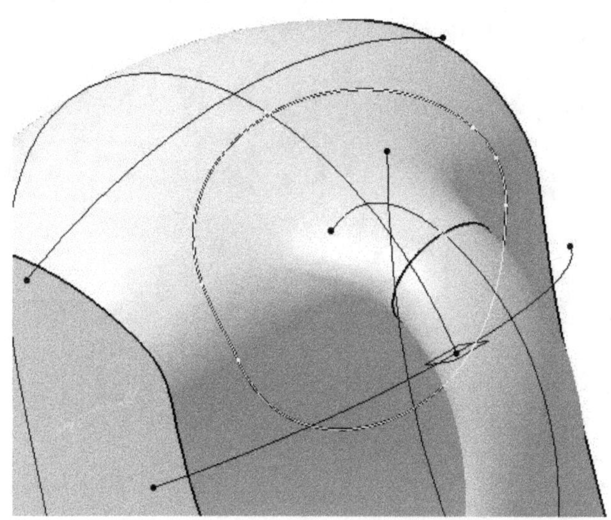

Blending the Bottom handle

1. Start a sketch on the YZ Plane and draw a tangent to the spline of the handle. Exit the sketch.

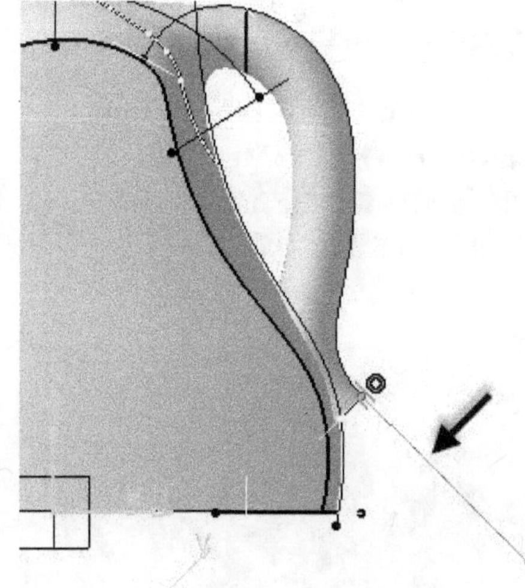

2. Activate the **Plane** command and select **Plane type > Angle/Normal to plane**.
3. Click on the tangent line and the YZ plane.

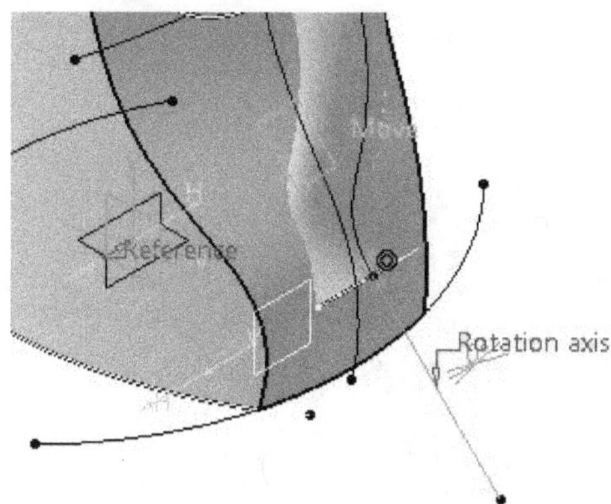

4. Click the **Normal to plane** button, and then click **OK** to create the plane.

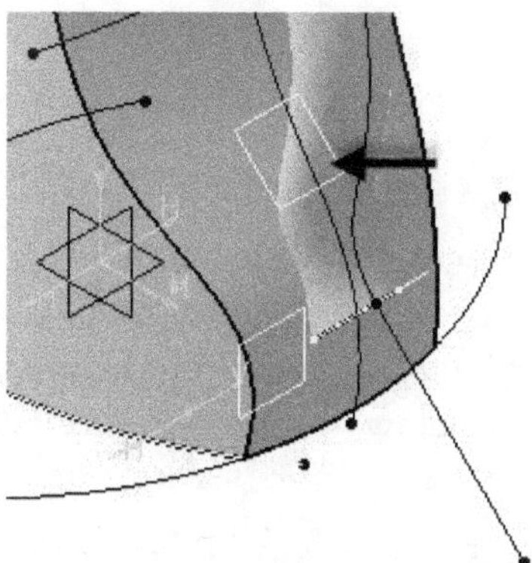

5. Create an ellipse on the new plane and trim it by half. Exit the sketch. Ensure that the sketch lies inside the handle surface.

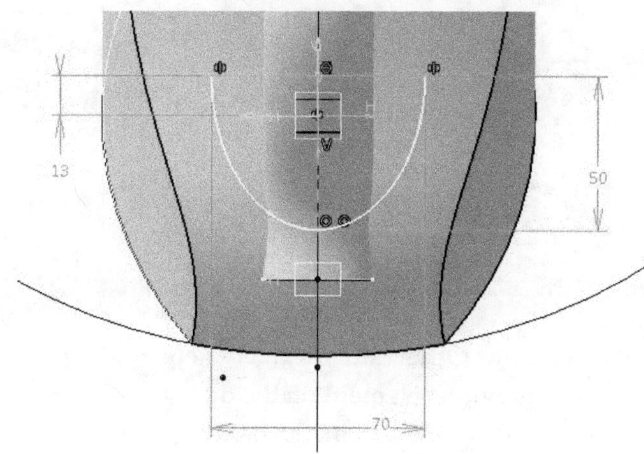

6. Extrude the sketch up to an arbitrary distance in both the directions.

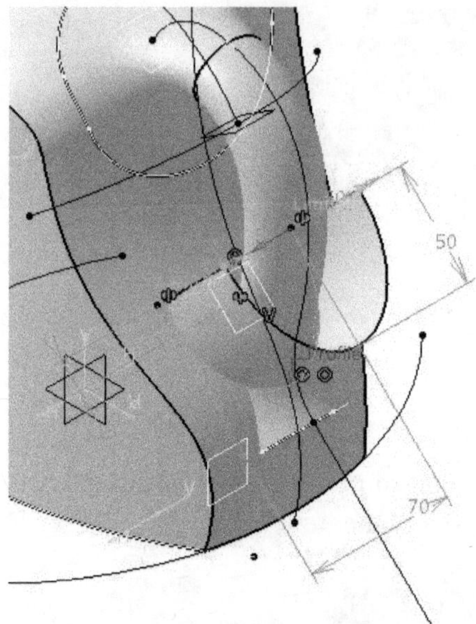

7. On the **Operations** toolbar, click **Split-Trim** drop-down **> Trim** (or) click **Insert > Operations > Trim** on the Menu bar.
8. Select **Mode > Standard** on the dialog.
9. Click on the portion of the handle and extrude surface, as shown below.

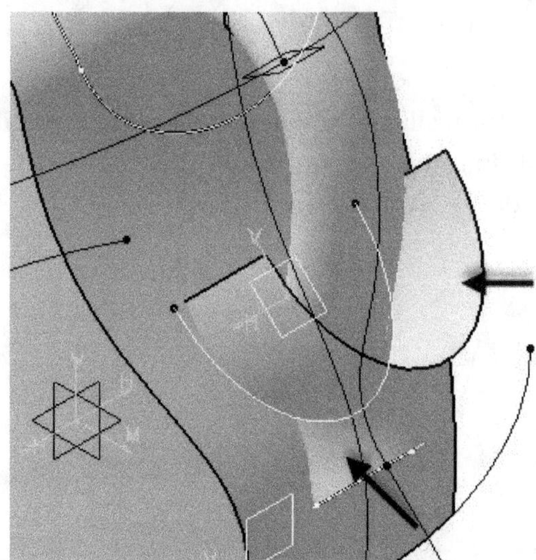

10. Click the **Other side/next element** and **Other side/previous element** on the dialog.
11. Click **OK** to create trim the handle.

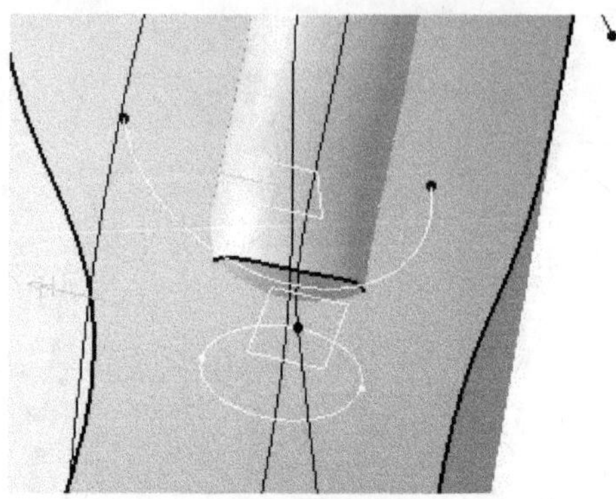

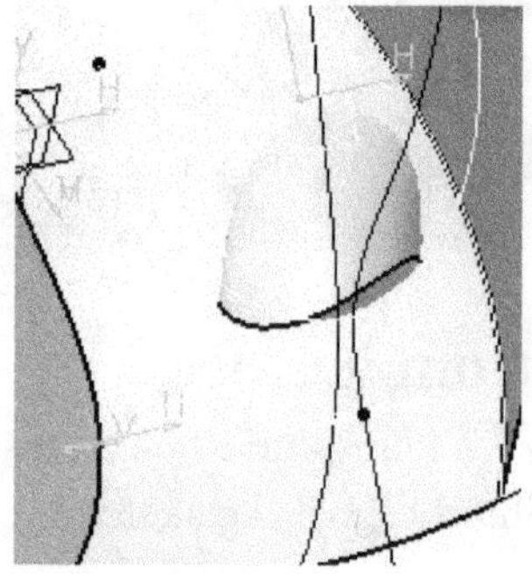

12. On the **Operations** toolbar, click **Split-Trim** drop-down **> Trim** (or) click **Insert > Operations > Trim** on the Menu bar.
13. Click on the portion of the handle and main surface, as shown below.

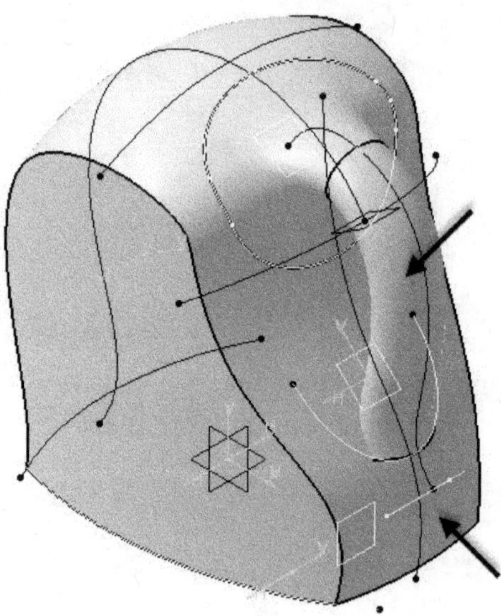

14. Click **OK** the trim the inside portion of the handle.

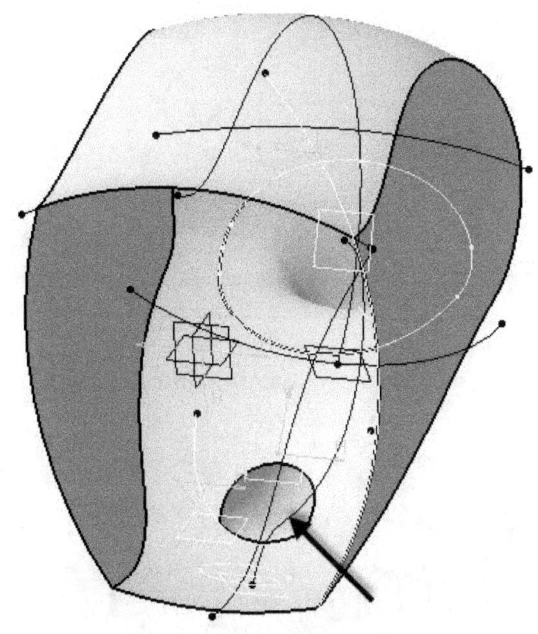

15. Activate the **Edge Fillet** command and fillet the edge of the handle. The fillet radius is 6 mm.

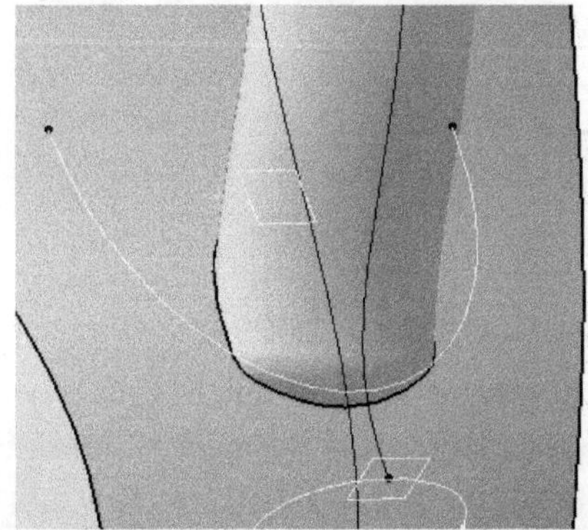

16. Fillet the intersection between the main surface and handle. The fillet radius is 5 mm.

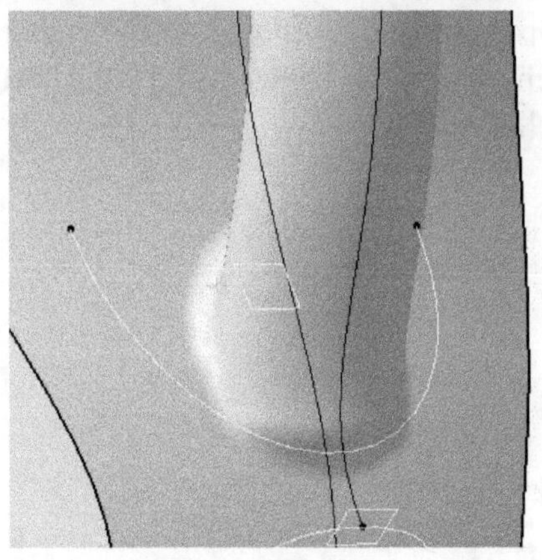

Joining the Surfaces

1. On the **Operations** toolbar, click **Join-Healing** drop-down **> Join** (or) click **Insert > Operations > Join** on the Menu bar.
2. Select the main surface and blend surface.

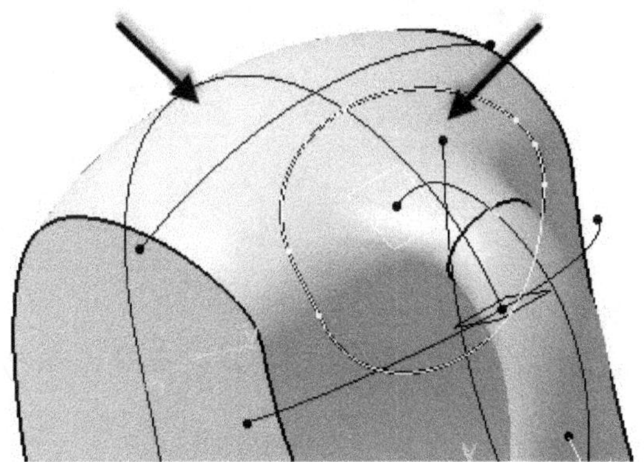

3. Click **OK** to join the surfaces.

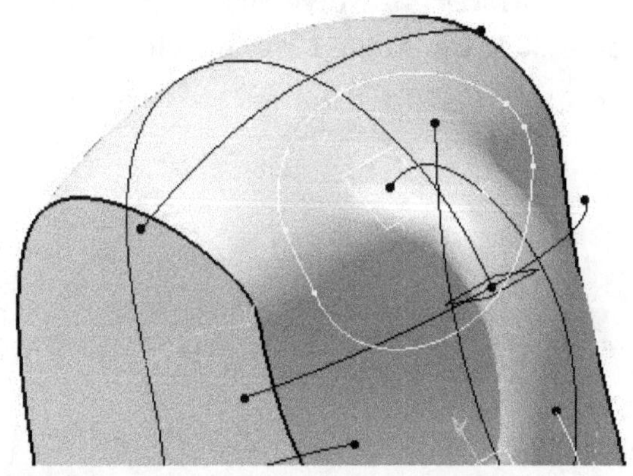

Creating the Neck and Spout

1. Start a sketch on the YZ Plane and draw the sketch for the revolved surface. Exit the workbench.

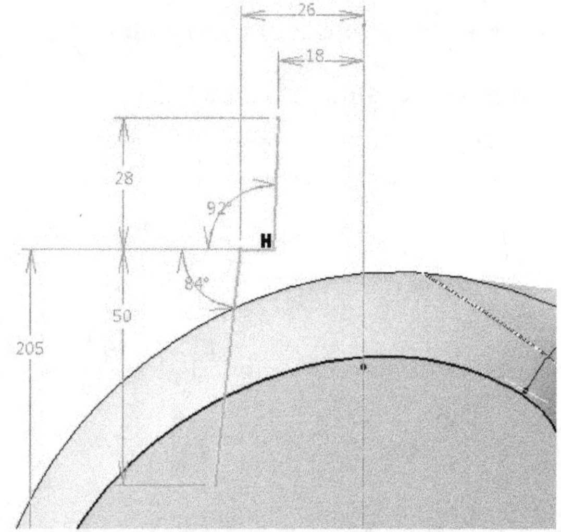

10. On the **Surfaces** toolbar, click **Extrude-Revolution** drop-down **> Revolve** (or) click **Insert > Surfaces > Revolve** on the Menu bar.
11. Type-in 360 in the **Angle 1** box and click **OK**.

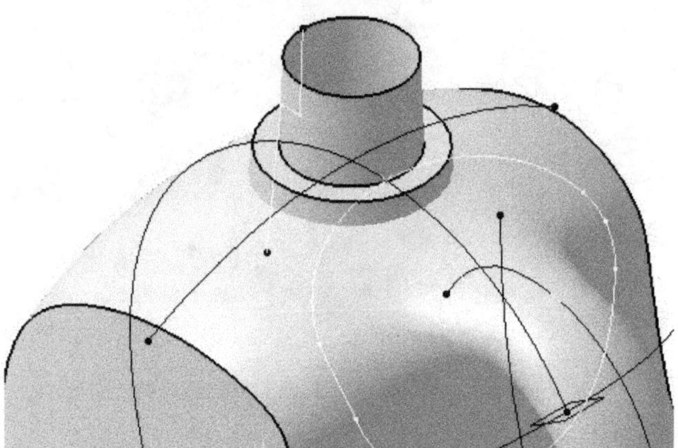

12. On the **Operations** toolbar, click **Split-Trim** drop-down **> Trim** (or) click **Insert > Operations > Trim** on the Menu bar.
13. Click on the portion of the neck and main surface, as shown below.

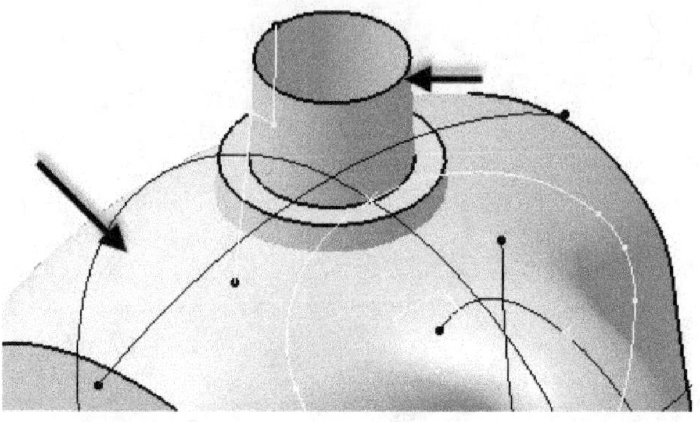

14. Click **OK** to trim the unwanted portion.

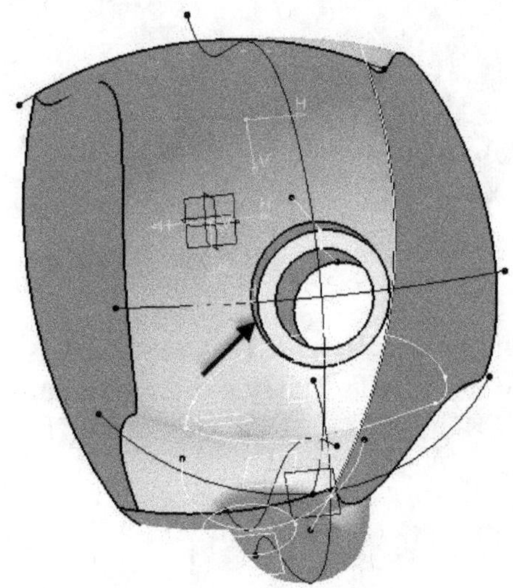

Creating the Edge Fillet

1. On the **Operations** toolbar, click **Fillets** drop-down **> Edge Fillet** (or) click **Insert > Operations > Edge Fillet** on the Menu bar.
2. On the **Edge Fillet Definition** dialog, click the **Constantq** con.
3. Select **Propagation > Tangency** on the dialog.
4. Click on anyone of the edges of the label surface, as shown below.

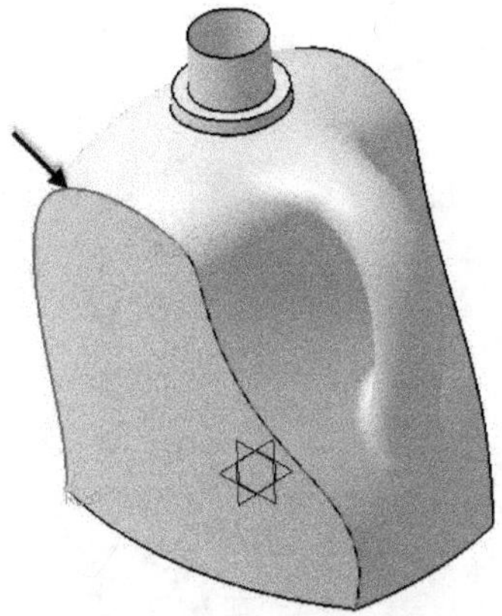

5. Click the icon next to the **Radius** box. The **Fillet values** dialog appears.
6. Click on the radius value located at the midpoint of the selected edge.

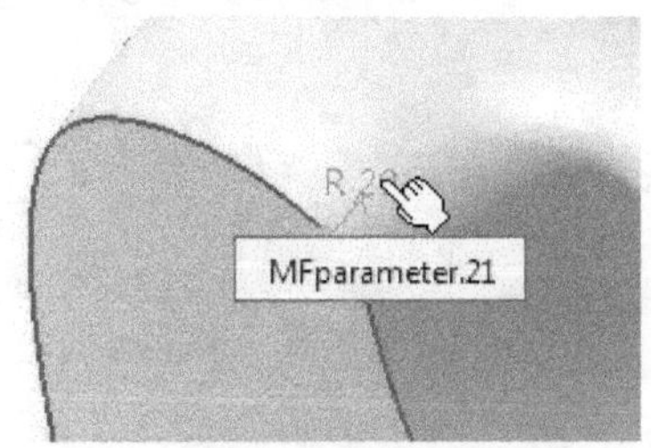

7. Type-in 10 in the **Current value** box, and then click **OK**.
8. Click **OK** to create the variable fillet.

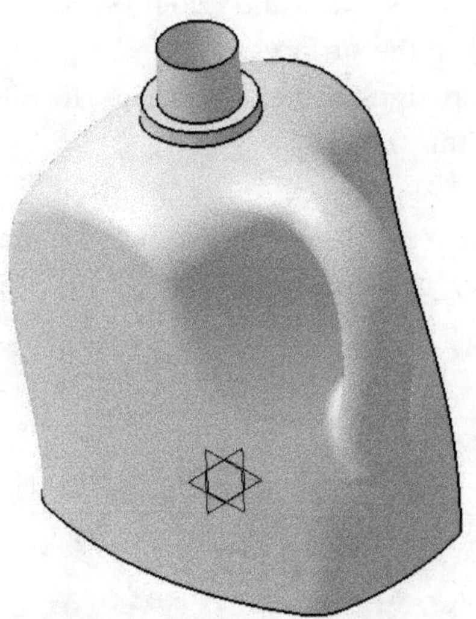

9. Likewise, create a variable fillet on the other label face.

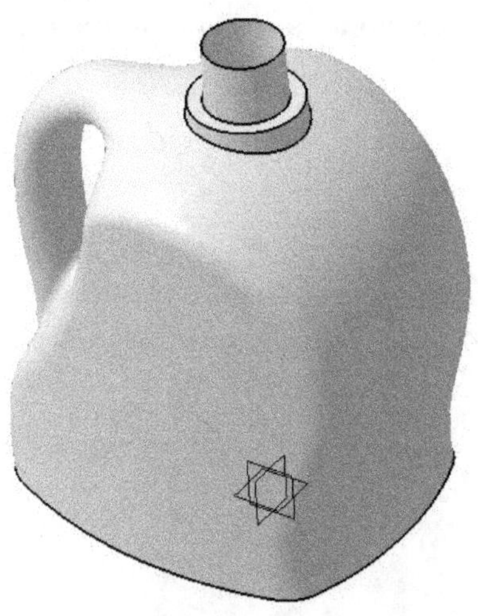

Creating a bump at the bottom

1. Create an offset plane from the XY Plane. The offset distance is 10 mm.

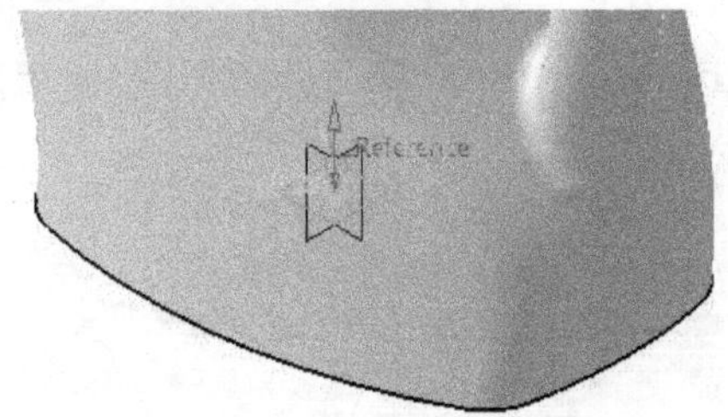

2. Start a sketch on the offset plane.
3. Create an ellipse, and then exit the workbench.

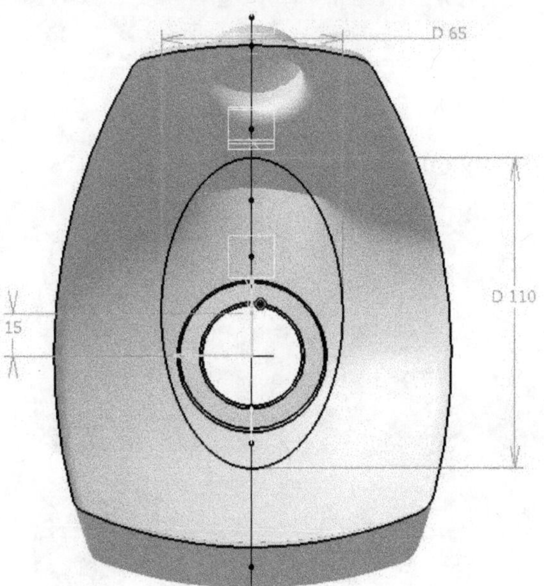

4. On the **Surfaces** toolbar, click the **Fill** button (or) click **Insert > Surfaces > Fill** on the Menu bar.

5. Rotate the surface model and click on the outer edges.

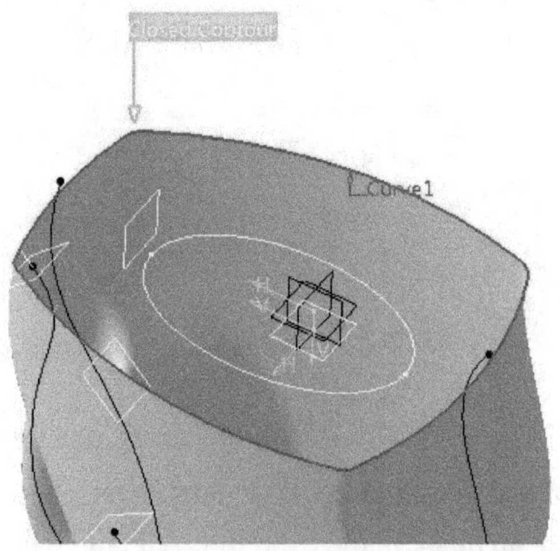

6. On the **Fill Surface Definition** dialog, click the **Inner Boundaries** tab and select the inner loop.

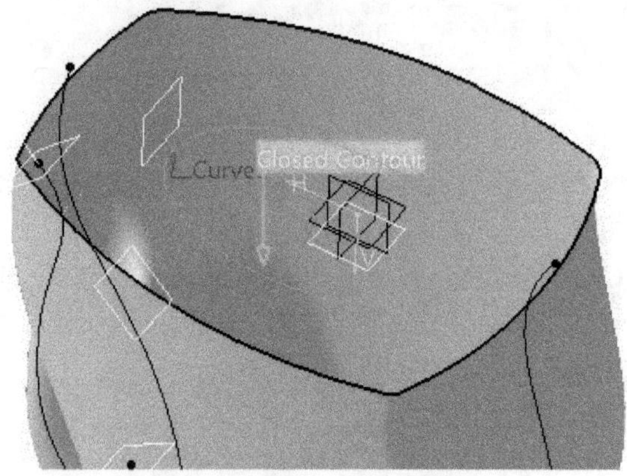

7. Click **OK** to create the fill surface.

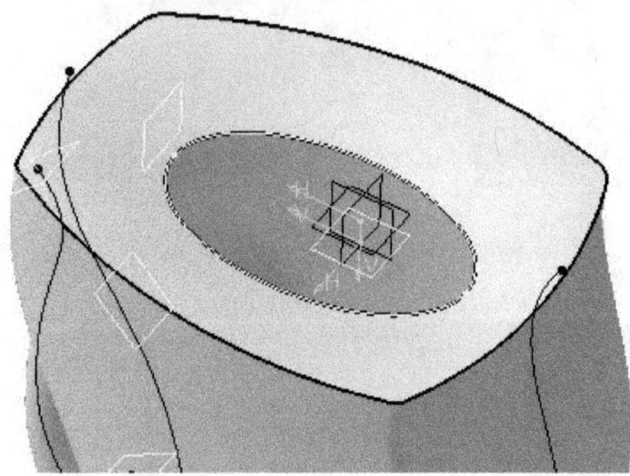

8. Activate the **Fill** command and select the inner loop.

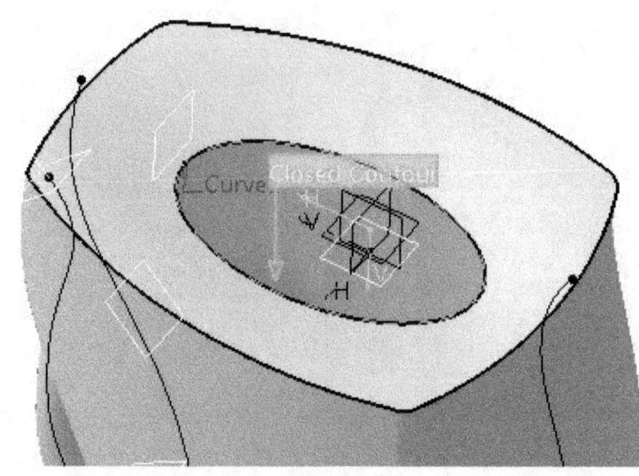

9. Click **OK** to create the fill.

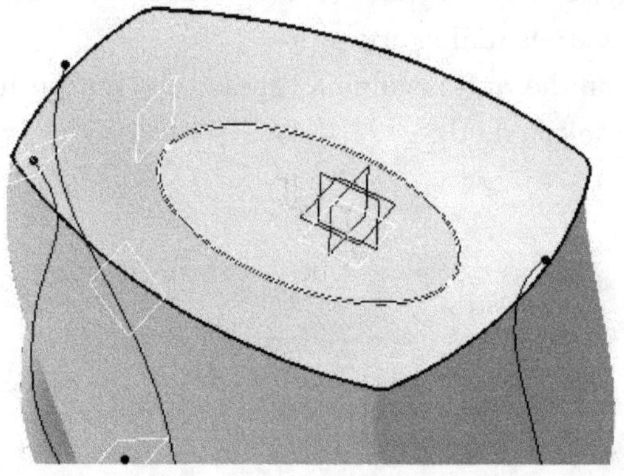

10. On the **Operations** toolbar, click **Join-Healing** drop-down > **Join** (or) click **Insert > Operations > Join** on the Menu bar.
11. Click on the main surface and two fill surfaces.
12. Click **OK** to join the surfaces.
13. Fillet the outer edges of the fill surface. The fillet radius is 10 mm.

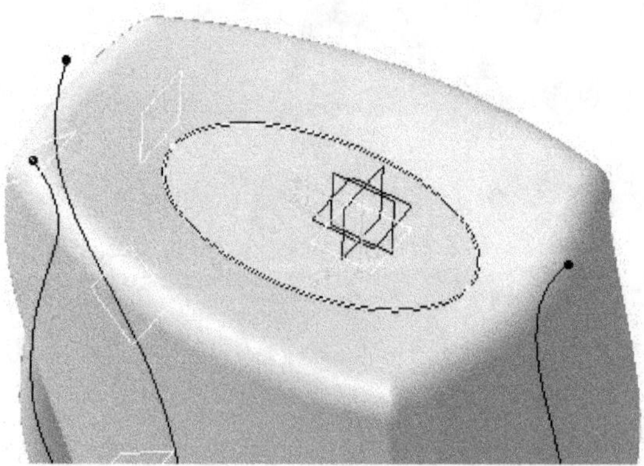

14. Fillet the inner edges of the fill surface. The fillet radius is 60 mm.

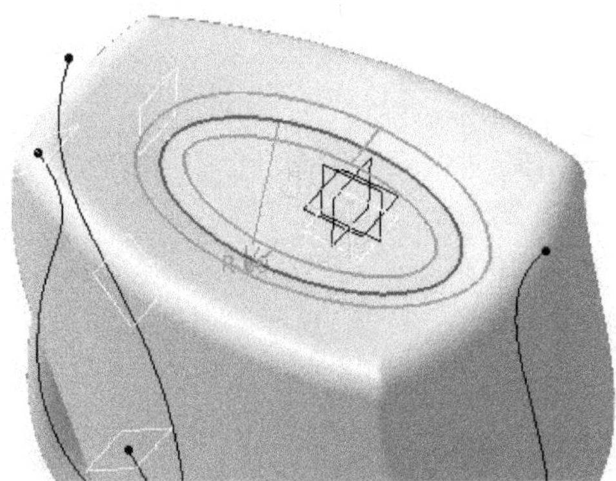

10. Fillet the sharp edges of the neck and spout. The fillet radius is 1 mm.

Adding thickness to the model

1. On the Menu bar, click **Start > Mechanical Design > Part Design**.
2. On the **Surface-Based Features** toolbar, click the **Thick Surface** button (or) click **Insert > Surface-Based Features > Thick Surface** on the Menu bar.
3. On the **Thick Surface Definition** dialog, type-in 1 in the **First Offset** box, and then click on the surface model.
4. Click **OK** to thicken the surface.
5. Hide the **Join** surface to view the solid model.

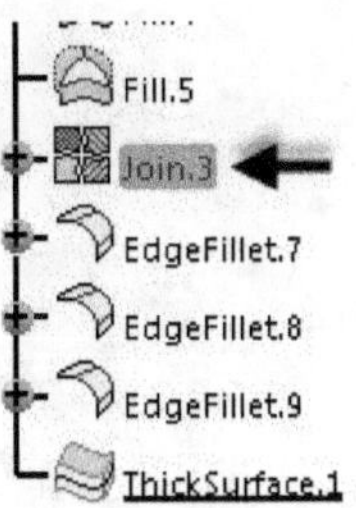

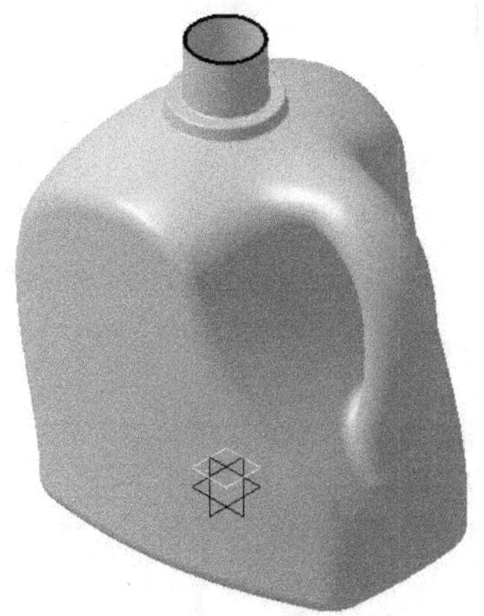

6. Save and close the file.

Questions

1. What is the use of the **Join** command?
2. Why do we use the **Fill** command?
3. What are the commands that can be used to delete the openings on a surface?
4. Which commands can be used to bridge gap between two surfaces?
5. Name the command that can be used to trim and join the surfaces.
6. How do you add thicknesses to a surface body?
7. What is the command used to extend surfaces from an edge?
8. How do you split a solid body?
9. What is the command used to offset face?

Index

www.ingramcontent.com/pod-product-compliance
Lightning Source LLC
LaVergne TN
LVHW060120070326
832902LV00019B/3057

* 9 7 8 1 9 7 6 1 8 1 5 3 5 *